Child Welfare and Child Well-Being

CHILD WELFARE AND CHILD WELL-BEING

New Perspectives From the National Survey of
Child and Adolescent Well-Being

Edited by

Mary Bruce Webb
Kathryn Dowd
Brenda Jones Harden
John Landsverk
Mark F. Testa

2010

OXFORD
UNIVERSITY PRESS

Oxford University Press, Inc., publishes works that further
Oxford University's objective of excellence
in research, scholarship, and education.

Oxford   New York
Auckland   Cape Town   Dar es Salaam   Hong Kong   Karachi
Kuala Lumpur   Madrid   Melbourne   Mexico City   Nairobi
New Delhi   Shanghai   Taipei   Toronto

With offices in
Argentina   Austria   Brazil   Chile   Czech Republic   France   Greece
Guatemala   Hungary   Italy   Japan   Poland   Portugal   Singapore
South Korea   Switzerland   Thailand   Turkey   Ukraine   Vietnam

Published by Oxford University Press, Inc.
198 Madison Avenue, New York, New York 10016

www.oup.com

Oxford is a registered trademark of Oxford University Press

Library of Congress Cataloging-in-Publication Data

Child welfare and child well-being : new perspectives from the national survey of child
and adolescent well-being / edited by Mary Bruce Webb . . . [et al.].
p.   cm.
Includes bibliographical references and index.
ISBN 978-0-19-539846-5
1. Child welfare–United States.   I. Webb, Mary Bruce.
HV741.C45 2009
362.70973—dc22
2009013845

9   8   7   6   5   4   3   2   1

Printed in the United States of America
on acid-free paper

ACKNOWLEDGMENTS

This book would not have been possible without the children, the caregivers, and the child welfare caseworkers and administrative staff who provided the data for the National Survey of Child and Adolescent Well-Being (NSCAW). It is remarkable to think that thousands of individuals who live and work under sometimes extreme stresses are willing to look beyond their own circumstances to contribute to a project that will result in no immediate or obvious benefit to themselves.

Of the hundreds of individuals who have contributed over the past decade to the planning and management of NSCAW, a few deserve special notice. Carol Wilson Spigner, as the Associate Commissioner of the Children?s Bureau when the work began, understood the opportunity to examine the interactions across the various dimensions of the child welfare system, and supported the planning of a survey with ambitious breadth and reach. Matt Stagner must be credited with the vision that NSCAW would become a resource for the child welfare research and policy community. Gaynel Abadie ensured that the complex mechanics of funding were balanced with the scientific needs of the survey. Janet Griffith, Jeannie Newman and their colleagues at Caliber Associates/ICF played a major role in persuading local agencies to participate. Richard Barth, one of the original principal investigators for the study, made immeasurable contributions through his thorough and practical knowledge of child welfare practice and policy. Another principal investigator in the early years, Desmond Runyan, guided much of the conceptual development around antecedents and sequelae of maltreatment. A dynamic workgroup of consultants was generous in sharing time and expertise, and their knowledge enabled a true multidisciplinary approach; members have included John Landsverk, Brenda Jones Harden, Mark Testa, Steve Barnett, Cheryl Boyce, Rob Clyman, Jill Duerr Berrick, Peter Digre, Greg Duncan, John Eckenrode, Byron Egeland, Diana English, John Fairbank, Michael Foster, Charles Glisson,

Robert Goerge, Kimberly Hoagwood, Sally Horwitz, Kelly Kelleher, Jess McDonald, Robert Ortega, and Karabelle Pizzigatti. Ron Haskins, who was instrumental in the authorizing legislation for NSCAW, has continued to work through the Brookings Institution and the Annie E. Casey Foundation to promote wide dissemination of results. Elliott Smith and others at the National Data Archive for Child Abuse and Neglect have provided many hours of advice to analysts using the NSCAW data.

Numerous individuals at Research Triangle International (RTI) were responsible for the successful implementation of the study, and a listing of all those who made contributions is not possible here. The fact that many of the RTI field staff and managers who are now conducting NSCAW II have been on the staff since the beginning of NSCAW I speaks to their commitment to this work and to the families who are represented here. Special mention must be made of Paul Biemer, who developed the survey design, and who has continued to be a creative leader and patient teacher. Mike Weeks, the first NSCAW Project Director at RTI and subsequent senior advisor, saw that the contract was carefully managed through many difficult times. Finally, Jenny Foerst?s sensitive editing of all the chapters in this book has greatly improved its readability.

The National Survey for Child and Adolescent Well-Being is funded through the Office of Planning, Research, and Evaluation at the Administration for Children and Families, U.S. Department of Health and Human Services. The information in this volume should not be construed as reflecting the official views of the Department of Health and Human Services, or of the Administration for Children and families.

CONTENTS

CONTRIBUTORS

Yu Bai, PhD
School of Public Health
University of North Carolina
Chapel Hill, North Carolina

Richard P. Barth, PhD
School of Social Work
University of Maryland
Baltimore, Maryland

Paul P. Biemer, PhD
RTI International and
University of North Carolina
Research Triangle Park, North Carolina

Christina M. Bruhn, PhD
Children and Family Research Center
School of Social Work
University of Illinois at Urbana-Champaign
Chicago, Illinois

Barbara J. Burns, PhD
Department of Psychiatry and Behavioral Sciences
Duke University School of Medicine
Durham, North Carolina

Sharon L. Christ, PhD
Odum Institute
University of North Carolina
Chapal Hill, North Carolina

Jenell Clarke, MSW
School of Social Work
University of Michigan
Ann Arbor, Michigan

KATHRYN DOWD, MPPA
RTI International
Research Triangle Park, North Carolina

JOHN J. ECKENRODE, PhD
Cornell University
Ithaca, New York

BYRON EGELAND, PhD
University of Minnesota
Minneapolis, Minnesota

ELIZABETH M. Z. FARMER, PhD
Department of Health Policy and Administration
Pennsylvania State University
University Park, Pennsylvania

E. MICHAEL FOSTER, PhD
School of Public Health
University of North Carolina
Chapel Hill, North Carolina

WILLIAM GARDNER, PhD
Center for Innovation in Pediatric Practice and
Center for Biobehavioral Health
Nationwide Children's Hospital
Departments of Pediatrics, Psychology, and Psychiatry
The Ohio State University
Columbus, Ohio

CHARLES GLISSON, PhD
Children's Mental Health Services Research Center
University of Tennessee
Knoxville, Tennessee

REBECCA L. GREEN, MSW
School of Social Work
University of North Carolina
Chapel Hill, North Carolina

ANDREW GROGAN-KAYLOR, PhD
School of Social Work
University of Michigan
Ann Arbor, Michigan

SHENYANG GUO, PhD
School of Social Work
University of North Carolina
Chapel Hill, North Carolina

GREGORY HANCOCK, PhD
University of Maryland
College Park, Maryland

BRENDA JONES HARDEN, PhD
University of Maryland
College Park, Maryland

JESSE HELTON, MA
Children and Family Research Center
School of Social Work
University of Illinois at Urbana-Champaign
Urbana, Illinois

SARAH MCCUE HORWITZ, PhD
Department of Pediatrics and the
Centers for Health Policy and Primary Care
    and Outcomes
Research
Stanford University
Stanford, California

MICHAEL S. HURLBURT, PhD
School of Social Work
University of Southern California
Los Angeles, California

CHARLES V. IZZO, PhD
Cornell University
Ithaca, New York

REBECCA KARB, MSW
School of Social Work
University of Michigan
Ann Arbor, Michigan

KELLY KELLEHER, MD, MPH
Center for Innovation in Pediatric Practice and
Center for Biobehavioral Health
Nationwide Children's Hospital
Departments of Pediatrics, Psychology, and Psychiatry
The Ohio State University
Columbus, Ohio

DAVID J. KOLKO, PhD
University of Pittsburgh School of Medicine
Western Psychiatric Institute and Clinic
Pittsburgh, Pensylvania

DANIEL KUEHN, BA
The Urban Institute
Washington, D.C.

JOHN LANDSVERK, PhD
Child and Adolescent Services Research Center
Rady Children's Hospital, San Diego
San Diego, California

LAUREL LESLIE, MD, MPH
Tufts Medicals Center, Floating Haspital for Children and
Child and Adolescent Services Research Center
Rady Children's Hospita, San Diegol
Boston, Massachusetts

ANNE M. LIBBY, PhD
School of Pharmacy
University of Colorado, Denver
Aurora, Colorado

JULIE McCRAE, PhD
University of Pittsburgh
Pittsburgh, Pennsylvania

SARAH A. MUSTILLO, PhD
Department of Sociology
Purdue University
West Lafayette, Indiana

ROBERT M. ORTEGA, PhD
School of Social Work
University of Michigan
Ann Arbor, Michigan

KATHLEEN PAJER, MD, MPH
Center for Innovation in Pediatric Practice and
Center for Biobehavioral Health
Nationwide Children's Hospital
Departments of Pediatrics, Psychology, and Psychiatry
The Ohio State University
Columbus, Ohio

JENNIFER ROLLS, MPH
Child and Adolescent Services Research Center
Rady Children's Hospital, San Diego
San Diego, California

MARY RUFFOLO, PhD
School of Social Work
University of Michigan
Ann Arbor, Michigan

ANNE SHAFFER, PhD
Separtment of Psychology
University of Georgia
Athens, Georgia

ELLIOT G. SMITH, PhD
Cornell University
Ithaca, New York

MATTHEW STAGNER, PhD
Chapin Hall
The University of Chicago
Chicago, Illinois

MARK TESTA, PhD
Children and Family Research Center
School of Social Work
University of Illinois at Urbana-Champaign
Chicago, Illinois

KEVIN WANG, PhD
RTI International
Research Triangle Park, North Carolina

MARY BRUCE WEBB, PhD
Administration for Children and Families
U.S. Department of Health and Human Services
Washington, D.C.

ELIZABETH C. WEIGENSBERG, PhD
Chapin Hall
University of Chicago
Chicago, Illinois

REBECCA WELLS, PhD, MHSA
School of Public Health
University of North Carolina
Chapel Hill, North Carolina

JESSICA VICK WHITTAKER, PhD
Center of Advanced Study of Teaching and Learning
University of Virginia
Charlottesville, Virginia

JINJIN ZHANG, MSC, MA
Child and Adolescent Services Research Center
Rady Children's Hospital, San Diego
San Diego, California

INTRODUCTION

The chapters in this book are based on a single data source, the National Survey of Child and Adolescent Well-Being (NSCAW). This landmark study marks the first effort to gather nationally representative data, based on firsthand reports, about the functioning and well-being of U.S. children and families who encounter the child welfare system through a child maltreatment investigation by child protective services (CPS). Before NSCAW, no nationwide source of data existed that could be used to describe the developmental status and functional characteristics of children who come to the attention of CPS; moreover, almost no information of any kind existed about the many children who remain at home after a CPS investigation.

Much of the large-scale child welfare research before NSCAW was limited to tracking service histories and service outcomes, such as number of placements or length of stay in foster care. Little knowledge was to be found of how these service pathways were associated with the needs of the children and families involved. By contrast, NSCAW is longitudinal; contains direct assessments as well as reports about each child from multiple sources; and is designed to address questions of relations among children's characteristics and experiences, their development, their pathways through the child welfare service system, their service needs, and their service receipt. Most of the chapters in this volume take full advantage of data collected during the first 3 years of the study, in order to capture a sense of how these children are faring over time.

The data collection instruments used in NSCAW were built around the central notion that children's needs should drive the actions taken on their behalf by child welfare caseworkers. Using an ecological framework (e.g., Bronfenbrenner & Morris, 1998), the design team began with a focus on the children, identifying measures of health, cognitive, social, and emotional functioning appropriate to each age group. With the children as the focal point, the team then moved outward in the framework to obtain measures of environmental factors likely to support or impinge on the children's growth, development, and well-being. These factors encompassed family, service system, and community influences.

In Chapter 1, Biemer, Dowd, and Webb present the NSCAW design features that inform the subsamples and measures used for analysis in all the chapters that follow. As will be seen, NSCAW has contributed to the body of child welfare knowledge by availing researchers of relatively objective data about children's characteristics and functioning, data that can serve as an assessment of service need, which in turn enables researchers to compare that need with services actually received. The advancement of research methods to accommodate the exploration of the complexities of child welfare research is another contribution of the NSCAW work and constitutes an underlying theme across all the chapters.

Academic disciplines tend to rely on and reinforce their own traditions and methodological preferences, while no single academic approach is likely to embrace the methods that would be useful for addressing the broad array of questions relevant to child welfare. The NSCAW project intentionally recruited researchers from across the disciplines to bring a diversity of theoretical and methodological perspectives to the work. The longitudinal nature of NSCAW, the possibilities for multiple levels of analysis, the use of age-specific variables and information from multiple respondents, the ambiguities in defining key constructs, and the complex sampling—all have been challenging to analysts, and the reader will find examples of these challenges (and the approaches used to address them) throughout the chapters. These chapters represent thoughtful, increasingly sophisticated approaches to the problems not only inherent in analyzing NSCAW data but also characteristic of child welfare research in general. The authors of chapters in this volume represent perspectives from the fields of developmental, educational, clinical, and organizational psychology, epidemiology, sociology, social work, economics, statistics, pediatrics, public policy, and public health.

After the description of NSCAW in Chapter 1, the book is organized around three substantive themes. Beginning with an emphasis on the children themselves, the authors examine how children's needs and characteristics interact first with the child welfare system and then with the larger system of services for children and families. Part 1 takes as its focus the characteristics, functioning, and developmental status of children in four separate age groups and employs methods and concepts that will be familiar to developmentalists who study attachment and early stimulation, resilience, and developmental psychopathology. Part 2 turns to topics of particular interest for child welfare policy and practice, taking into account the interactions between children's developmental status and system emphases and features. Part 3 provides a window into the interaction between the child welfare population and the broader child service system, using the children's mental health system as an exemplar. The use of children's and caregivers' characteristics to define service needs and service outcomes is a significant contribution of Part 3.

Conceptual Foundations of Child Well-Being

The lack of definitional clarity plagues many constructs in the social science and services literatures. Within the child welfare service sector, the construct *child well-being* suffers from particular ambiguity because of distinct conceptualizations among various disciplines; inclusion of multiple, far-reaching constructs; and the relatively recent appearance of well-being on the child welfare policy agenda. Seaberg (1990) asserts, in fact, that the challenge in defining *child well-being* within child welfare stems from the field's lack of a conceptual framework for this construct.

Early work provided a moral definition of *well-being* and proffered that the term could be defined from a variety of perspectives, including one arising in the context of an individual's needs and desires (see Gleeson, 1986). From the perspective of positive psychology, *well-being* is defined as life satisfaction or as individuals' positive evaluation of their lives (Diener & Seligman, 2005; Seligman, 2002). Another approach involves major social indicators to define *well-being* (Brown & Moore, 2005). Such an approach relies heavily on the contexts within which children live. Consequently, indicators associated with adverse child outcomes (e.g., child living in poverty, with single parent, with unemployed parent) are used in discussions of child well-being (McLanahan, 2000). Some indicators are more directly related to child functioning, such as rates of low-birth-weight infants, infant mortality, child death, teen deaths by homicide, teen births, school dropouts, and youth nonattendance at school or work (Annie E. Casey Foundation, 2009). Although these indicators of well-being are relatively easy to obtain and allow for population-based monitoring, in the child welfare arena they are less informative for policy development.

Attempts by child welfare scholars, policy makers, and practitioners to address well-being have focused largely on the contexts that promote or hinder it instead of on child functioning in itself. It is well documented, for example, that providing children safety and stability is linked to their well-being, or developmental functioning and mental health (Jones Harden, 2004; Newton, Litrownik, & Landsverk, 2000). Other contextual variables documented to be related to the well-being of children in the child welfare system include having fewer psychosocial problems among birth parents, living with relatives, experiencing minimal moves, experiencing a shorter duration of out-of-home care, and living in the least restrictive environment possible (Altshuler, 1998; Barth, 2005; Farrugia, Greenberger, Chen, & Heckhausen, 2006). In what is perhaps the most widely used measure of well-being in the child welfare field, Magura and Moses (1986) defined *child well-being* by way of specific dimensions of the child's caregiving environment, as well as in terms of the child's adjustment; in fact, only 4 of the 43 scales in this measure address children's functioning. One particular environmental construct increasingly used in developmental psychology and other fields is *social capital*, which emphasizes such features of social interaction as trust, obligations, expectations, and reciprocity in an individual's network of relationships (Coleman, 1990).

Testa's introduction to Part 3 and several of the Part 3 chapters employ this social capital framework.

A focus on the contextual correlates of child well-being can inform practitioners' decisions about the kinds of environments that best predict child well-being. Despite the apparent appeal of this approach, however, it should be used with caution because the link between child context and child outcome is imperfect. The literature on children's resilience, for example, documents the relatively high functioning of children who have experienced adversities commonly expected to result in poor child outcomes. Furthermore, Seaberg (1990) recommends that specific contextual factors, because of their relative importance for the child (e.g., survival needs versus life satisfaction), be weighted differentially and that the effects of crises and multiple risk factors be accounted for. Although a contextual approach is informative, a conceptualization of child well-being that focuses on child-specific factors would more accurately characterize implications of the child welfare context for children.

Using a developmental heuristic to define *child well-being* would represent a major step toward definitional clarity. Such an approach would entail a focus on the functioning of the child, instead of on contextual variables that predict child well-being. The rich empirical literature addressing the influences on and trajectories of child development offers such a definitional basis for *child well-being*. Expanding on the developmental knowledge base, Wulczyn, Barth, Yuan, Jones Harden, and Landsverk (2005) assert that *well-being* should be defined in terms of how children are functioning across time, relative to the children's biology and environmental situations. These authors highlight the interdependent trajectories of child development and systemic experiences of children in the child welfare system. Because of current child welfare data on the unique experiences of children who enter the child welfare system during specific developmental periods, these authors suggest a focus on children "starting out," those starting school, and those starting adolescence.

Most research on child development specifies "domains" of child functioning, which typically translate into children's physical/health, cognitive/academic, and socioemotional functioning. Some agreement exists among scholars and practitioners of various disciplines about what constitutes normative functioning for children in each domain. For example, the American Academy of Pediatrics (Hagan, Shaw, & Duncan, 2007) has outlined standards of physical health for American children, such as appropriate weight and gross motor capacities. The psychological and educational fields have conducted numerous studies and established multiple assessments that articulate normative ranges for the American child population's developmental, cognitive, and academic skills (e.g., Sattler, 2001). Although not as well established as in the cognitive arena, normative development in the socioemotional arena, as well as the clinical range for mental health problems, has been documented (e.g., Achenbach, Dumenci, & Rescorla, 2003; Denham, 1998).

It can be argued that child well-being entails normative functioning across developmental domains. Developmental theory and research has considered such normative functioning as representing children's competence. Notably, a segment of the developmental literature addresses the competent functioning of children who have experienced extreme environmental adversity (e.g., maltreatment). Children who achieve this level of functioning are referred to as "resilient" (Cicchetti, Rogosch, Lynch, & Holt, 1993; Masten & Coatsworth, 1998; Shaffer et al., Chapter 3, this volume). The constructs undergirding this work can inform the child welfare field as it struggles to establish a definition of *well-being*. For example, early conceptual work to define *competence* in children argues for a focus on the "whole" child (Zigler & Styfco, 2004; Zigler & Trickett, 1978). Emanating from this model, a focus on well-being would mean addressing children's functioning in the following areas: physical health, fine and gross motor skills, cognitive development, academic achievement, social relationships, mental health and behavioral functioning, and adaptive skills.

A developmentally based definition of *well-being* seems well suited for the child welfare system; it would emphasize the functioning of individual children in the context of the performance of other children exposed to similar risk factors. It would entail a focus on the "whole" child across developmental domains, including physical health and growth, cognitive and academic skills, and interpersonal relationships and mental health. Additionally, child well-being would be addressed over time, with attention to the developmental transitions that typically occur for children and the time-specific factors relevant to the child welfare system. Finally, it would require a consideration of the biological and environmental factors that affect children's development, particularly those emanating from their involvement with the child welfare system. This more focused and developmentally based definition could facilitate clearer child welfare policies and, in turn, inform services relevant to child well-being.

Child Development and The National Survey of Child and Adolescent Well-Being

The design of NSCAW was informed by a developmental framework and is operationalized through measures designed to capture the experiences, growth, and development of the children who come into contact with child welfare services. This emphasis on children's functioning is perhaps the single most important contribution of NSCAW. Part 1, edited by Brenda Jones Harden, is organized around child experiences and development unique to specific age groups. The availability in NSCAW of descriptive information about the characteristics and functioning of the children and families is in itself an important contribution, but the study design also allows researchers to examine how child and family characteristics interact with systems and service-level variables to influence pathways through the system and outcomes over time. The availability of information on children's functioning and outcomes from multiple informants enables the conceptualization of models of risk and resilience from a variety of theoretical and methodological perspectives. The diversity of perspectives that can be brought to bear in examining developmental outcomes for children is reflected across Part 1: Each chapter focuses on a specific developmental age, and each takes a unique approach in its treatment of risk and resilience factors likely to influence outcomes for children who are exposed to adverse circumstances.

The first chapter in Part 1 (Chapter 2), by Jones Harden, Vick, Hancock, and Wang, examines outcomes for infants and the youngest children in the NSCAW sample; in particular, it examines placement stability and the quality of the caregiving environment. Developmentalists have identified the early childhood period as particularly important for children's language development, social development, and readiness for formal schooling. Researchers who study the development of young children have been especially concerned about the effects of children's early attachment to caregivers, as well as the cognitive and emotional stimulation in the caregiving environment. Children who encounter child welfare services are thought to be at a particular disadvantage in both regards, because economic deprivation and unstable caregiving relationships are thought to be all too typical of their environments. The chapter illustrates that these two factors, attachment and quality of the caregiving environment, are complex: When both are considered, their respective influences are not straightforward.

The next chapter, Chapter 3, turns to the topic of children in their beginning school years. For children involved with child welfare, the transition to school brings new opportunities but also may present new obstacles to those who lack stability in their home or community environments. Shaffer, Egeland, and Wang scrutinize a major developmental construct—*resilience*—defined as adaptation in the face of adversity. The chapter identifies some factors that appear to promote more competent functioning in this high-risk group of school-aged children. Interestingly, potentially modifiable factors are found to be important, including school engagement and placement stability.

Adolescents are the focal group for Chapter 4. In it the authors turn to what may be considered the most significant risk factor in a child welfare population: the experience of maltreatment. Historically, the variation among definitions of *maltreatment* has proved to be a substantial methodological weakness in child welfare research (Feerick & Snow, 2006); any examination of sequalae of maltreatment necessarily hinges on how maltreatment is captured and described. Izzo and colleagues take advantage of the availability in NSCAW of multiple sources for determining children's maltreatment experiences, including adolescents' self-reports of their own experiences. This chapter advances the definitions and analysis of maltreatment and its consequences; in addition, it offers new information about the relationship between maltreatment and socioemotional outcomes in adolescents.

Closing Part 1, Chapter 5 by Gardner, Kelleher, and Pajer extends across age groups to describe the experiences of children who live in families affected by domestic violence. This chapter capitalizes on another unique contribution of NSCAW: information about the vast majority of children who remain in the parental home after a child maltreatment investigation. The high incidence of domestic violence among families involved in child welfare has been a topic of considerable policy interest, with many states beginning to include exposure to domestic violence as one of the circumstances that warrants the child welfare system's substantiation of maltreatment allegations. The chapter shows that recurring maltreatment is indeed of concern in this group, but it also highlights some of the challenges inherent in studying the interaction of domestic violence and child outcomes.

Child Well-Being and Child Welfare Services

The focus on children's well-being is, together with safety and permanency, one of three federal mandates for child welfare systems. Superficially, the role of the child welfare system in ensuring the well-being of the children it serves seems intuitive; however, not only does a lack of clarity persist about what constitutes achievement of child well-being, but a lack of consensus also persists about the extent to which the child welfare system should even be responsible for this achievement (Altshuler & Gleeson, 1999).

Child welfare is arguably the most complex of all child service systems; the very underpinnings of the system reflect two potentially conflicting views of the extent to which public child welfare agents are empowered to take protective state action on behalf of minor children (Wolfe, 1978). Under the narrow conception of government's role in protecting children, public intervention in private, autonomous family life is justified only if the bodily integrity, health, and sustenance needs (*human capital*) of the child are jeopardized (e.g., when bruises, burns, malnutrition, or other physical harms are evident). Responsibility for other child welfare outcomes, such as continuity of care (*social capital*), educational achievement (*cultural capital*), and economic maintenance (*financial capital*) is considered best left to the discretion of parents, extended kin, and other community members. Only if these primordial agents of child welfare violate the rules of minimally adequate care by abandoning, abusing, or grossly neglecting their protective responsibilities will state agencies and the courts, as a last resort, intervene and reassign selected child-caring responsibilities to bureaucratic agents, such as foster families, group homes, and institutions. By contrast, under the diffuse conception of government's role, public engagement with the family is justified whenever it enriches the entire portfolio of children's human, cultural, and social capital. It assumes that both child and public interests are best served by government programs that guarantee children the minimum developmental conditions of safety, permanence, and well-being that the state deems necessary for their growth into productive workers and responsible citizens.

The establishment accountability provisions under the Adoption and Safe Families Act of 1997 and, perhaps more important, the establishment in federal regulation of state Child and Family Service Reviews (CFSRs; Administration for

Children and Families, 2000) have given some impetus to states' pursuit of a more active, intensive service focus on child well-being. With the institution of CFSRs, states must examine the well-being of children in the child welfare system, including their physical, educational, and mental health needs. Rather than address children's functioning per se (e.g., achievement test scores, mental health diagnoses), the reviews assess whether the child welfare system has provided or brokered for services to meet children's needs. Specifically, the child well-being components of the CFSR are as follows:

- Families enjoy enhanced capacity to provide for their children's needs (indicators are assessment of needs and provision of services to families, child and family involvement in case planning, caseworker visits with children, caseworker visits with parents);
- Children receive appropriate services to meet their educational needs (indicators are assessment and provision for children's educational needs);
- Children receive adequate services to meet their physical and mental health needs (indicators are provision for physical health needs, including dental health, and provision for children's mental and behavioral health).

Data from the 2001–2004 CFSRs indicate that, of all the performance indicators assessed, child well-being tended to be the one on which states performed poorly (Administration for Children and Families, 2007). For example, the provision of services to address the mental health of children was listed as one of the three weakest performance indicators, with only four states receiving a *strength* rating for addressing the children's mental health. States were particularly challenged by the well-being outcome deriving from family capacity to facilitate the child's well-being. In contrast, higher performance was documented on the well-being outcome concerning children's educational needs. Early reports from the second round of CFSRs suggest that states continue to experience challenges in meeting the outcomes specified in the CFSRs.

The question therefore remains whether promoting child well-being is at the core of child welfare service delivery, or whether it is at cross-purposes with its other goals of ensuring safety and stability. Historically, the child welfare system has emphasized shaping children's experiences, not their functioning. Consequently, systemic priorities have been safety and permanency outcomes, not developmental outcomes. Accordingly, services are not designed specifically to promote child well-being. Positioning child well-being at the center of child welfare policy and practice would require significant conceptual and funding shifts.

Regardless of the specific influences on children's development, it is well established that in the child welfare system they manifest a variety of developmental deficits that cross domain and cross time. The growing body of evidence for these deficits argues compellingly that child well-being should be made a priority in the child welfare service arena; it follows that service delivery should be informed by an understanding of individual children's well-being, an understanding impossible to achieve without appropriate measurement of children's well-being, both individually and by group.

The mission of the child welfare system to serve the most vulnerable, high-risk members of society is complicated by the intense responsibility attending its capacity to intervene in the private lives of children and families, as well as by the high, life-and-health stakes attending its decisions. Child welfare services are constructed to serve the interests of both children and their families; caseworkers must sometimes balance conflicting interests between these two parties. At the same time, frontline staff's decisions about services are limited by laws and regulations attached to federal and other streams of funding, as well as by oversight from the courts. Child welfare agencies often must rely on other social service systems to implement needed services, even though incompatible philosophies or policies between child welfare and other systems make service provision difficult.

Adding children's individual characteristics and needs into this complex mix sets the agenda for Part 2, which is edited by Mark Testa. In this part of the book, four chapters present analyses on topics of special policy and practice concern in child welfare. These analyses are informed by an examination of the interaction between the system and the children's characteristics. The chapters raise an important policy question, previously asked by Barth (1999), of how much weight should be given to the traditional advantages of *bonding social capital,* which emphasizes strong relationships, when modern trends are placing a greater premium on *bridging social capital,* which can enrich the human and cultural capital children need in order to compete effectively in a postindustrial, global economy.

Testa, Bruhn, and Helton (Chapter 6) examine the growing use of kinship care as a placement option for children who must be removed from their homes of origin. As public policy increasingly favors children's kin instead of nonkin foster families for children's substitute care, research that more closely examines children's experiences and outcomes in these arrangements is of considerable interest. Chapter 6 highlights the tensions between the recruitment of blood relatives and the selection of trained, licensed foster parents as agents of children's well-being. Although in principle relatives can serve as licensed foster parents, the authors observe that in practice state licensing requirements may disqualify blood kin because of, for example, cramped housing quarters, lack of a telephone, or past arrests. The important question is whether kin should still be privileged under federal law for public assistance and foster care benefits if they are unable to meet state foster home licensing standards.

Testa, Bruhn, and Helton approach this issue by considering first whether any significant differences in placement stability and abuse re-reports emerge because of the relative continuity of "least-restrictive, most family-like" placement setting. Using NSCAW data, they construct a continuity-of-care scale that ranges from the most family-like (least restrictive), in-home setting (home of the birth parents) to the least family-like (most restrictive), out-of-home setting (group homes and institutions). Under this schema, kinship care in home settings (informal kinship care) is considered more continuous with care by birth parents than nonkinship care in out-of-home settings (formal foster family care). The authors draw on NSCAW data to estimate the mean differences in some key indicators of bonding and bridging social capital across placement settings. They go on to model the effects of these indicators and other demographic and economic characteristics on the outcomes of continuity, stability, and safety. Their findings suggest that, with respect to these traditional child welfare outcomes, both formal and informal kinship care offer some advantages while carrying no appreciably greater safety risks than foster family care.

In Chapter 7, Stagner and Kuehn offer a glimpse into the lives of adolescents in foster care, a population that has been of considerable interest to policy makers, as evidenced by legislation and regulation aimed at children "aging out" of foster care.[1] The prolonged dependence of youth is an acute problem for foster youth whose access to cultural, social, and financial capital is abruptly curtailed at age 18, when state custody is terminated, or by age 21 at the latest. Unless these youth have relatives' or adoptive parents' support—or support from the very households from which they were removed—a large proportion of emancipated foster youth run high risks of homelessness, single parenthood, welfare dependence, and criminal incarceration.

This chapter previews the challenges likely to be faced by older youth who have been in or have recently entered the foster care system. It draws on the concepts of social capital introduced in the previous chapter to explore variation in the sources of social support available to foster youth with different amounts of exposure to out-of-home care. They hypothesize that children remaining in the parental home will be higher in bonding social capital but lower in bridging social capital than children taken into foster care. They find partial support for their hypothesis in terms of the "closeness" in-home youth report feeling with their caregivers, but they find lower levels of child protection and monitoring there than for children in out-of-home care. For *bridging* social capital, they find the expected differences, with youth in out-of-home care having potential access to greater educational, occupational, and economic resources than youth who remained in the parental home. Interestingly, their analyses suggest that bridging social capital may decline over time for youth with increased amounts of time in the parental home. The authors conclude by reflecting on the respective tradeoffs that family preservation and child removal effect in the kinds of social support and capital that foster youth can access as they transition to independence.

Safety and permanence of living arrangements have traditionally been the chief outcomes for judging the effectiveness of child welfare systems. Accountability provisions in child welfare legislation have fostered even greater attention to the tracking and measurement of outcomes in these domains. In general, caseworkers prefer to direct their efforts at enhancing children's safety in their homes of origin so that the children can continue to live with their own families. In the third chapter of Part 2, Chapter 8, Barth, Guo, Weigensberg, Christ, Bruhn, and Green analyze the child and family characteristics that predict children's reunification with their families after out-of-home placement. For those children who are reunified, the authors analyze characteristics that foreshadow likely reentry to foster care.

Mindful of the possible relationships between children's developmental stage and the effects of family disruptions, child welfare researchers have begun to examine how the conditions of safety, permanence, and well-being vary according to human developmental periods (Wulczyn et al., 2005). Barth and colleagues adopt this perspective. Interestingly, in their regression models of reunification they find significant gender and ethnic main effects in only the group of children 11 years old or older, despite the extensive set of statistical controls for human capital, cultural capital, and social capital factors. As the authors note, the developmental period after age 10 is when children are transitioning beyond parental and school supervision to acquire the bridging social capital necessary for independent economic and social mobility in a post-traditional society.

The final chapter of Part 2, Chapter 9, turns to the issue of racial disparities, an issue that underlies almost all discussions of child welfare services, as well as children's services in general. Although much attention has been given to racial and ethnic differences in child welfare service receipt, Ortega, Grogan-Taylor, Ruffolo, Clarke, and Karb move beyond such hegemonic comparisons to consider each major racial and ethnic group separately. In delineating the special cultural characteristics policy makers and practitioners should keep in mind when planning programs or services for U.S. children, this chapter found an otherwise almost completely unexplored research possibility within the culture and race discourse: within-group comparisons. Although the attention to cross-race comparisons is warranted, it can obscure critical variation within groups.

Child Well-Being in the Context of the Broader Child Service System

The theme of Part 3 arises from the explicit recognition in NSCAW that services external to the child welfare system are an essential feature of services to the child welfare population. Substantial policy interest in integrating services, particularly mental health services, across service sectors arose from two papers published in the 1980s. In 1982 Jane Knitzer issued a clarion critique of the mental health service system in the United States, arguing that many children in need of such care were not even being identified because they were involved with other service systems, such as child welfare and juvenile justice, and these service systems were not integrated with the mental health service system. Knitzer's strongly titled monograph, "Unclaimed Children: The Failure of Public Responsibility to Children and Adolescents in Need of Mental Health Services" (Knitzer, 1982), led to the national Child and Adolescent Service System Program (CASSP; Day & Roberts, 1991), which was based on principles designed to better integrate child and youth services across service sectors. In 1987 Klee and Halfon published a study on "Mental Health Care for Foster Children in California" (1987), finding that only 1 among the 14 counties examined provided routine mental health evaluations for children in foster care settings, and in most counties less than a third of children ever received such evaluations. These findings from key stakeholder interviews were especially striking because the 154 program administrators, social workers, foster parents, and health care workers who were surveyed perceived that mental health problems were more severe than even medical problems for the foster child population. Given what is now known about the high rate of mental health, developmental, and other psychosocial problems present not only in children in foster care but, in general, for children investigated for child abuse and neglect (e.g., Burns et al., 2004), Klee and Halfon's findings were an early critical indicator of the need to examine the mental health care of children involved with the child welfare system.

In NSCAW extensive data were collected about services received outside the child welfare system, including health, educational, and mental and behavioral health services, as well as economic supports. Introduced by John Landsverk, Part 3 features service contexts for children and families who come to the attention of the child welfare system, with an emphasis on mental health services as an illustration of issues that must be considered in the interaction between child welfare and other services. The salience of mental health services for the child welfare population is marked by the high rates of behavioral and emotional problems found by NSCAW and other research. Behavioral issues, for both children and families, may in turn influence placement and permanency trajectories inside the child welfare system.

In Part 3 the first three chapters—by Horwitz and colleagues, Landsverk and colleagues, and Burns and colleagues—estimate the use of mental health services over the 36-month period of NSCAW: The Horwitz chapter is on children; the Burns chapter, on caregivers; and the Landsverk chapter, on the relationship between child welfare involvement at the individual level and mental health service involvement. The two final chapters, by Foster et al. and Glisson, offer analyses addressing the impact of contextual indicators at the child welfare agency level and addressing mental health outcomes at the child level.

Chapter 10, by Horwitz, Hurlburt, and Zhang, offers the best extant review of what is known from the studies of mental health service need and use in children involved in the child welfare system. Notably, this review includes several stand-alone articles generated by the NSCAW data set before this publication. This chapter yields two comprehensive views: one of the research literature leading up to the NSCAW study, and another that depicts mental health service use in this population over a full 36 months.

Horwitz and colleagues have been especially innovative in examining mental health service use for three distinct age groups of children: those aged 2 to 5 years, those 5 to 10 years, and those 11 years or older. As Garland, Hough, Landsverk, and Brown (2001) have argued, child welfare has the widest range of age for its child population and the largest proportion of very young children, outside of general pediatric populations. In addition to offering the most detailed examination of the use of mental health care by the younger children involved in child welfare, Chapter 10 is perhaps the first study that uses a measure of developmental functioning to examine need for care in the youngest group (2–5 year olds). The striking finding is the larger gap between need and use for this youngest segment of the NSCAW cohort. Meanwhile, the findings about the powerful role of race/ethnicity in use patterns confirms at the nationwide level major findings from all local studies that have examined this question (Garland, Landsverk, & Lau, 2003).

A longitudinal pattern of continuity of mental health care, detected by Horwitz and colleagues, is more precisely described in Chapter 11, by Landsverk, Hurlburt, Leslie, Rolls, and Zhang. Contrary to initial expectations, both studies found a high level of continuity in mental health care use over the 36-month NSCAW study period. Landsverk and colleagues adeptly extend prior analyses of NSCAW data by Leslie and her colleagues (Leslie et al., 2005), analyses that established a clear onset pattern—namely, that penetration into the child welfare system significantly increased the probability of receiving services from the mental health system. Chapter 11 approaches the question in various ways and finds that the pattern of continuity is robust across methods, which confers additional confidence in the finding. This hopeful finding suggests not only that the child welfare system serves as a gateway to the mental health system but also that the pathway through it to mental health service survives termination of child welfare system involvement. This chapter evinces the enormous value of the 36-month NSCAW timeframe.

The third chapter (Chapter 12) in Part 3 is authored by Burns, Mustillo, Farmer, Kolko, McCrae, Libby, and Webb. It reports with unprecedented depth their analyses of mental health care needs and service use for caregivers involved with the child welfare system who experience symptoms of depression warranting a psychiatric diagnosis. Noteworthy findings include the high rate of caregiver depression, a 40% rate that greatly exceeds both the rate of depression in the general population and the rate for female welfare recipients (Kessler, Chiu, Demler, & Walters, 2005; Rosen, Tolman, & Warner, 2004; Wang et al., 2005) and the large gap between need for mental health care and reported use of such care for serious depression. An unusual feature of this chapter is the highly innovative use of NSCAW longitudinal data to group depressed caregivers into the categories *early recovery, recovered and relapsed,* and *delayed recovery* in order that these caregivers' use of mental health services may be compared—a use of the data set not envisioned when the NSCAW study was designed. Another feature of this paper is its reporting a number of sobering consequences of caregivers' depressive illnesses for children and the role that mental health services may play in affecting those consequences. The chapter provides a model discussion of clinical and practice implications emerging from these empirical findings.

The final chapters of Part 3 are two of a very small set of publications that have used the nationwide sample characteristic of the NSCAW study to examine the impact of contextual variables on outcomes for children involved in the child welfare system. Glisson, in Chapter 13, reports on methods he has been developing since the mid-1990s to link experiences caseworkers report in their work groups to observable outcomes in the children whose care they manage. This study uses multiple-level and longitudinal techniques to demonstrate that children served by caseworkers in agencies with better work climates, where caseworkers are more engaged in work settings, show better psychosocial functioning over time than children served by agencies with worse work climates, where caseworkers report much lower engagement in their work settings. The message is that intervention at the agency level may well produce better outcomes for the individual child.

Chapter 14, authored by Foster, Wells, and Bai, is similar in logic to the chapter by Glisson, using a multiple-level contextual approach and testing the impact of contextual variables on child-level outcomes. While Glisson is interested primarily in using a social-psychological approach based in industrial and organizational psychology, Foster and colleagues use what may be termed an *administrative approach* derived from business and management sciences. They use a set of NSCAW data generated by key informant interviews with top management in the participating child welfare agencies, with a special focus on two separate types of management practices: systematic information processing and interagency collaboration.

The investigators in this final chapter hypothesize that child welfare agencies with high levels of both information processing and interagency collaboration will be associated with better child functioning outcomes. Foster and colleagues approach their analyses from an innovative conceptual framework positing that organizations must balance two competing emphases: *internal,* which is represented in this study by systematic information processing, and *environmental,* which is represented by interagency collaboration. Although the study does not find support for the hypotheses derived from their framework, the investigators show a remarkable ability to translate concepts from organizational theory to real-world, observable phenomena at the child welfare agency level. It should be noted that one other contextual-level analysis in the published literature (Hurlburt et al., 2004) has used NSCAW mental health services data at the child level and key informant data at the contextual community level to assess linkages between child welfare and mental health agencies on mental health service utilization. This article reports two significant outcomes that resulted from strong interagency linkages: Mental health service use by children in child welfare was more closely associated with need in communities with a higher degree of between-organization linkages, and disparities between white and black children in their mental health service use were significantly less in strongly linked communities.

Conclusion

The chapters composing this book showcase the value of NSCAW as a resource to the research community; they show how profitably the NSCAW data can be used to inform both policy and practice. The scope of the analyses made possible by the NSCAW data set is illustrated, moreover, by the breadth of this research. Each discipline tends to bring its own theoretical constructs and methodological preferences to the work, and researchers may with great variation in approach address issues that appear similar on the surface. Among users of NSCAW data, for example, it is not uncommon to find researchers using different variables to represent the same construct or to find them defining processes and outcomes differently. Some of these variations and their potential utility for future researchers will be evident in this volume.

Our view is that the field has reached a stage at which it can, as a whole, be enriched by these diverse perspectives because no one discipline can in isolation provide a "true" representation of an issue in child welfare. NSCAW is a broadly constructed survey. It is meant to provide data for initial topic explorations subject to follow-ups by interested investigators with more targeted, fine-grained data collections and analyses. The research presented in this book may best be characterized, therefore, as an introduction to the next generation of child welfare research.

NOTE

1. See the Foster Care Independence Act of 1999, 42 U.S.C. § 677 (2006), and the Fostering Connections to Success and Increasing Adoptions Act of 2008, Pub. L. No. 110-351, 122 Stat. 3949 (2008).

REFERENCES

Achenbach, T. M., Dumenci, L., & Rescorla, L. A. (2003). Are American children's problems still getting worse? A 23-year comparison. *Journal of Abnormal Psychology, 31*(1), 1–11.

Administration for Children and Families. (2000). *Children's Bureau child and family services reviews fact sheet*. Retrieved December 10, 2008, from http://www.acf.hhs.gov/programs/cb/cwmonitoring/recruit/cfsrfactsheet.htm

Administration for Children and Families. (2007). *Findings from the initial 2001-2004 child and family service reviews*. Retrieved July 10, 2007, from www.acf.hhs.gove/programs/cb/cwmonitoring/results/index.htm

Altshuler, S. (1998). Child well-being in kinship foster care: Similar to or different from non-related foster care? *Children and Youth Services Review, 20*(5), 369–388.

Altshuler, S., & Gleeson, J. (1999). Completing the evaluation triangle for the next century: Measuring child "well-being" in family foster care. *Child Welfare, 78*(1), 125–147.

Annie E. Casey Foundation. (2009). *Kids count data center*. Retrieved January 20, 2009, from http://www.kidscount.org

Barth, R. P. (1999). After safety, what is the goal of child welfare services: Permanency, family continuity, or social benefit? *International Journal of Social Welfare, 8*(4), 244–252.

Barth, R. P. (2005). Foster home care is more effective than shelter care. *Child Abuse & Neglect, 29*(6), 623–625.

Bronfenbrenner, U., & Morris, P. (1998). The ecology of development process. In W. Damon & R. Lerner (Eds.), *Handbook of child psychology: Vol. 1. Theoretical models of human development* (5th ed., pp. 993–1028). New York: Wiley.

Brown, B., & Moore, K. (2005). Child and youth well-being: The social indicators field. In R. Lerner, F. Jacobs & D. Wertlieb (Eds.), *Applied developmental science*. Thousand Oaks, CA: Sage Publications.

Burns, B. J., Phillips, S. D., Wagner, H. R., Barth, R. P., Kolko, D. J., Campbell, Y., et al. (2004). Mental health need and access to mental health services by youth involved with child welfare: A national survey. *Journal of the American Academy of Child and Adolescent Psychiatry, 43*(8), 960–970.

Cicchetti, D. V., Rogosch, F., Lynch, M., & Holt, K. (1993). Resilience in maltreated children: Processes leading to an adaptive outcome. *Development and Psychopathology, 5,* 629–647.

Coleman, J. S. (1990). *Foundations of social theory.* Cambridge, MA: Belknap Press of Harvard University Press.

Day, C., & Roberts, M. C. (1991). Activities of the child and adolescent service system program for improving mental health services for children and families. *Journal of Clinical Child Psychology, 20,* 340–350.

Denham, S. (1998). *Emotional development in young children.* New York: Guilford Press.

Diener, E., & Seligman, M. (2005). Beyond money: Toward an economy of well-being. *Psychological Science in the Public Interest, 5*(1), 1–31.

Farrugia, S., Greenberger, E., Chen, C., & Heckhausen, J. (2006). Perceived social environment and adolescents' well-being and adjustment: Comparing a foster care sample with a matched sample. *Journal of Youth and Adolescence, 35*(3), 349–358.

Feerick, M., & Snow, K. (2006). An examination of research in child abuse and neglect: Past practices and future directions. In M. Feerick, J. Knutson, P. Trickett & S. Flanzer (Eds.), *Child abuse and neglect: Definitions, classifications, and a framework for research.* Baltimore, MD: Brookes.

Garland, A. F., Hough, R. L., Landsverk, J. A., & Brown, S. A. (2001). Multi-sector complexity of systems of care for youth with mental health needs. *Children's Services: Social Policy, Research and Practice, 4,* 123–140.

Garland, A. F., Landsverk, J. A., & Lau, A. S. (2003). Racial/ethnic disparities in mental health service use among children in foster care. *Children and Youth Services Review, 25*(5-6), 491–507.

Gleeson, J. (1986). *Well-being, its meaning, measurement and moral importance.* Oxford, England: Oxford University Press.

Hagan, J., Shaw, J., & Duncan, P. E. (2007). *Bright futures: Guidelines for the health supervision of infants, children, and adolescents.* American Academy of Pediatrics.

Hurlburt, M. S., Leslie, L. K., Landsverk, J., Barth, R. P., Burns, B. J., Gibbons, R. D., et al. (2004). Contextual predictors of mental health service use among children open to child welfare. *Archives of General Psychiatry, 61*(12), 1217–1224.

Jones Harden, B. (2004). Safety and stability for foster children: A developmental perspective. *Future of Children, 14*(1), 39–47.

Kessler, R. C., Chiu, W. T., Demler, O., & Walters, E. E. (2005). Prevalence, severity, and comorbidity of 12-month *DSM-IV* disorders in the National Comorbidity Survey Replication. *Archives of General Psychiatry, 62*(6), 617–709.

Klee, L., & Halfon, N. (1987). Mental health care for foster children in California. *Child Abuse & Neglect, 11,* 63–74.

Knitzer, J. (1982). *Unclaimed children: The failure of public responsibility to children and adolescents in need of mental health services.* Washington, DC: Children's Defense Fund.

Leslie, L. K., Hurlburt, M. S., James, S., Landsverk, J., Slymen, D. J., & Zhang, J. J. (2005). Relationship between entry into child welfare and mental health service use. *Psychiatric Services, 56*(8), 981–987.

Magura, S., & Moses, B. (1986). *Outcome measures for child welfare services*. Washington, DC: Child Welfare League of America.

Masten, A. S., & Coatsworth, J. D. (1998). The development of competence in favorable and unfavorable environments. Lessons from research on successful children. *American Psychologist, 53*(2), 205–220.

McLanahan, S. (2000). Family, state, and child well-being. *Annual Review of Sociology, 26*, 703–706.

Newton, R. R., Litrownik, A. J., & Landsverk, J. A. (2000). Children and youth in foster care: Disentangling the relationship between problem behaviors and number of placements. *Child Abuse & Neglect, 24*, 1363–1374.

Rosen, D., Tolman, R. M., & Warner, L. A. (2004). Low-income women's use of substance abuse and mental health services. *Journal of Health Care for the Poor and Underserved, 15*(2), 206–219.

Sattler, J. M. (2001). *Assessment of children: Cognitive applications* (4th ed.). La Mesa, CA: Sattler.

Seaberg, J. (1990). Child well-being: A feasible concept? *Social Work, 35*(3), 267–272.

Seligman, M. E. P. (2002). Positive psychology, positive prevention, and positive therapy. In C. R. Snyder & S. J. Lopez (Eds.), *Handbook of positive psychology* (pp. 3–12). Oxford, England: Oxford University Press.

Wang, P. S., Lane, M., Olfson, M., Pincus, H. A., Wells, K. B., & Kessler, R. C. (2005). Twelve-month use of mental health services in the United States: Results from the National Comorbidity Survey Replication. *Archives of General Psychiatry, 62*(6), 629–640.

Wolfe, A. (1978). The child and the state: A second glance. *Contemporary Crises, 2*, 407–435.

Wulczyn, F., Barth, R. P., Yuan, Y. T., Jones Harden, B., & Landsverk, J. (2005). *Beyond common sense: Child welfare, child well-being, and the evidence for policy reform*. New Brunswick, NJ: Aldine Transaction.

Zigler, E., & Styfco, S. J. (2004). Moving Head Start to the states: One experiment too many. *Applied Developmental Science, 8*(1), 51–55.

Zigler, E., & Trickett, P. (1978). IQ, social competence, and evaluation of early childhood intervention programs. *American Psychologist, 33*, 789–798.

CHILD WELFARE AND CHILD WELL-BEING

1

Study Design and Methods

PAUL P. BIEMER, KATHRYN DOWD,
AND MARY BRUCE WEBB

Child maltreatment presents a major public health challenge in the United States. The number of reported child victims in 2005 was almost 900,000, which translates to 12.1 per thousand children in the population (Administration for Children and Families, 2007). Another 2.7 million cases were investigated by the authorities in the same year but did not meet the evidentiary threshold required to *substantiate* or *indicate* maltreatment.[1] This large group of investigated and victimized children comprises the sample for the National Survey of Child and Adolescent Well-Being (NSCAW).

The longitudinal data collected in NSCAW enable researchers to examine the risk factors and protective factors that best predict outcomes for children who encounter the child welfare system and to develop interventions that target the most salient and modifiable factors. The complexity of the challenges facing the children and families seen by the child welfare system, as well as the community and service system issues that influence the outcomes for this group, necessitated a multidisciplinary approach to NSCAW study design and data analysis. The survey was shaped by project staff and technical advisors from a wide range of disciplines, including statistics and methodology; developmental, clinical, and organizational psychology; pediatrics; social work; services research; epidemiology; economics; and sociology. The diverse perspectives in the chapters that follow reflect this initial engagement of researchers across disciplines.

Especially important to NSCAW has been a commitment to making the data available to the research community. The investment in a survey of this magnitude is unprecedented in child welfare; the survey has, moreover, emerged at a time of diminishing funding for research in child maltreatment and child welfare services. Even though numerous technical and logistical challenges, as well as multiple human subject reviews, had to be fulfilled to assure respondents of confidentiality, almost immediately the decision to archive the data yielded benefits. Researchers have obtained funding from governmental and private sources for analyses on many topics, including juvenile justice, domestic violence, substance abuse, mental health, and health disparities. Of particular note has been the Caring for Children in Child Welfare project funded by the National Institute of Mental Health, a project that has allowed for the collection of additional contextual data about the child service agencies located in the counties from which NSCAW children were sampled; many of the researchers from this multisite grant project have contributed to this book.

NSCAW's thoughtful approaches to the study design and analysis of data quality have resulted in a data set judged as valuable resource to the field. The information NSCAW has yielded is allowing the field of child welfare to broaden its conceptions of child well-being and to examine issues from multiple perspectives. The availability of the NSCAW data has stimulated interest in child welfare research across diverse disciplines, allowing researchers to bring to bear new theoretical perspectives and research methods for future child welfare research. Information that promotes a more careful consideration of child welfare clients' needs and of the potential consequences of agency decision making is critical to building a system that is truly responsive to children and their families.

Study Design

The NSCAW sample cohorts include 6,228 children, aged birth to 15 years at the time of sampling, who had contact with the child welfare system within the period October 1999 through December 2000.[2] These children were selected from two groups:

- 5,501 were interviewed from those who were subjects of child abuse or neglect investigations conducted by child protective services (CPS) during the reference period, and
- 727 were interviewed from among children who had been in out-of-home care for approximately 1 year at the time of sampling and whose placement had been preceded by an investigation of child abuse or neglect.

These children were selected from 92 primary sampling units (PSUs) in 97 counties nationwide. The sample of investigated or assessed cases included both cases that received ongoing services and those that received no services because allegations were unsubstantiated or because services were determined to be unnecessary. All analyses in this volume involve the CPS sample component and include data only through the 36-month follow-up.[3]

The study design required oversampling of groups of interest to policy makers, to ensure that the number of cases provided statistical power sufficient to analyze these groups separately. Included were infants, in order to ensure that a sufficient number of cases were processed to a stage of permanency planning; sexual abuse cases; and cases receiving ongoing services after investigation. The age of children at investigation was capped at 14 years to increase the likelihood that youth could be located over time—a task made more difficult when youth are emancipated. Both children who remained in the system and received services and those who left the system were followed for the full study period.

The longitudinal nature of the design was important for detecting changes over the years after the index investigation and included the following waves (Table 1.1):

1. Baseline in-person interviews or assessments with children, their primary caregivers (e.g., parents or other caregivers, such as foster parents and custodial kin caregivers), teachers (for school-aged children), and child welfare investigators;
2. Interim (12-month follow-up) interviews with current caregivers and with services caseworkers, focusing on services received since baseline and including a brief child well-being measure;
3. In-person (18-month follow-up) interviews and assessments with children, their primary caregivers, their teachers (for school-aged children), and caseworkers.
4. In-person (36-month follow-up) interviews and assessments with children, their primary caregivers, their teachers (for school-aged children), and caseworkers.[4]

Table 1.1 Child Protective Services Data Collection Timeline

	Wave 1	Wave 2	Wave 3	Wave 4	Wave 5
Start and end dates	11/15/99–04/30/01	10/01/00–03/31/02	04/01/01–09/30/02	08/01/02–02/28/04	09/05/05–12/30/07
Months after close of investigation	2–6	12	18	36	59–96
Respondent					
Child	X		X	X	X
Current caregiver	X	X	X	X	X
Investigator / services caseworker	X	X	X	X	X
Teacher	X		X	X	X

Note: Possible respondents for each case may be reduced from four to two or three, depending on service receipt and school status.

Sample Design

The sample was designed to allow for the generation of national estimates for the full population of children and families entering the system, with power to consider key subgroups of the child welfare population. The target population for the NSCAW CPS sample consisted of all children in the United States who were subjects of child abuse or neglect investigations (or assessments) conducted by CPS agencies, with one exception. Excluded from the study were four states where state law required that the first contact of a sampled child's caregiver be made by CPS agency staff rather than by an NSCAW data collector, which would have rendered acceptable response rates infeasible. The children in the NSCAW samples were not selected on the basis of their initial entry into CPS; therefore, these children and families may have experienced prior exposure to the system.

Variations in state and county laws regarding maltreatment investigation resulted in many definitional issues in amassing NSCAW sampling data. For example, some states consider the investigation or assessment to be a service provided by CPS. To address these differences to the extent possible, the definitions already in place for the National Child Abuse and Neglect Data System (NCANDS) were adopted.[5]

The NSCAW sample was selected according to a two-stage stratified sample design. At the first stage, the United States was divided into nine sampling strata. Eight of the strata corresponded to the eight states with the largest child welfare caseloads; the ninth stratum comprised the remaining 42 states and the District of Columbia. Within each of these nine strata, PSUs were formed and selected. The PSUs for the sample were defined, in general, as geographic areas that encompassed the population served by a single CPS agency. In most cases, these areas corresponded to a single county; however, some agencies serving a small number of children were combined with an adjacent county to form a PSU, and in larger metropolitan areas smaller geographic areas were defined within the county.

The sample PSUs were randomly selected using a probability-proportionate-to-size procedure that gave a higher chance of selection to PSUs having larger caseloads. To counterbalance this propensity to select areas having the largest caseloads, the sampling scheme prescribed selection of the same number of children within each PSU, regardless of caseload size. In this manner, a child who was investigated for child abuse or neglect during the NSCAW sampling period would be included in the sample with approximately equal probabilities within sampling strata, regardless of the relative size of the PSU caseload.

The NSCAW PSU frame was composed of all counties in the United States that were large enough to support at least one interviewer workload, or about 60 cases per year. Counties smaller than this caseload size were deleted from the frame; it was estimated that less than 3% of the target population resided in these 710 counties.

In order to achieve appropriate statistical precision in subareas of interest, eight mutually exclusive and exhaustive categories of children were identified for

Table 1.2   The Eight Within-PSU Sampling Domains for the NSCAW CPS Sample

Domain	Description	No. of Interviews
1	Infants (aged <1 year old) who were not receiving CPS agency– funded services.	360
2	Children aged 1 to 14 years old who were not receiving CPS agency–funded services.	1,061
3	Infants (aged <1 year old) who are receiving CPS agency–funded services and are not in out-of-home care.	769
4	Children aged 1 to 14 years old who were receiving CPS agency–funded services, were not in out-of-home care, and were investigated for allegations of sexual abuse.	375
5	Children aged 1 to 14 years old who were receiving CPS agency–funded services, were not in out-of-home care, and were investigated for allegations of other abuse or neglect.	1,659
6	Infants (aged < 1 year old) who were receiving CPS agency–funded services and were in out-of-home care.	368
7	Children aged 1 to 14 years old who were receiving CPS agency–funded services, were in out-of-home care, and were investigated for allegations of sexual abuse.	164
8	Children aged 1 to 14 years old who were receiving CPS agency–funded services, were in out-of-home care, and were investigated for allegations of other abuse or neglect.	745
Total	Children investigated for child abuse and neglect.	5,501

CPS, child protective services; NSCAW, National Survey of Child and Adolescent Well-Being; PSU, primary sampling unit.

the study. These categories form the eight within-PSU sampling strata, which are referred to as *sampling domains* to avoid confusion with the nine *sampling strata* formed for the primary-stage selection process (Table 1.2).

To select the sample of PSUs, each PSU in the population was assigned a size measure that was a function of the desired sampling rate for each of the eight domains within each stratum and the estimated target population size in each PSU. The actual PSU population counts came from the NCANDS database when they were available; otherwise, they came from data supplied by the state or county agencies. When neither was available, the population size for each domain was estimated by means of logistic and log-linear modeling methods. An independent sample was then drawn from each stratum, with probability proportional to size, by means of systematic sampling. Implicit stratification was achieved by sorting the county frame before the sample selection.

The first-stage sample consisted of 100 PSUs. After selection, 7 of the sampled PSUs were determined to be very small and were combined with adjacent counties. Of the original 100 sampled PSUs, 6 refused and were replaced with PSUs of approximately the same measure of size, and 8 were determined to be ineligible because they were in states requiring that first contact with the children be from CPS. The sample consisted of 92 responding, eligible PSUs.

The NSCAW sampling process was conducted over a 15-month period and included all children investigated between October 1999 and December 2000. The within-PSU sampling frame for selecting children into the CPS sample was constructed from lists of children who were investigated for child abuse or neglect within the sample PSUs during the reference period. Each month, the participating agencies provided files that contained all cases of children whose investigations were concluded in the previous month for child abuse or neglect.

Ineligible children were removed from the frame, including children 15 years old or older, children on file who were included in a file from a prior month, children who were members of the same family household as a previously selected child, and children who were investigated as perpetrators of the abuse rather than as victims. After applying the eligibility rules, a simple random sample of children was selected from within each domain. The number of interviews obtained in each of the eight domains is shown in the final column of Table 1.2; for detailed information about the achieved sample, by sampling domain and strata, see Appendix Table 1.A.

Measures

The measures for NSCAW were based on an ecological-developmental theory of risk and resiliency, to examine the antecedents and consequences of child maltreatment and the influence of contacts with the child welfare system. The challenge was to operationalize across a broad range of child ages and family situations the identified outcomes of child and family well-being and the mediating constructs comprising this theoretical model. Because NSCAW is a large, field-based study, the instrumentation had to include the methodological and logistical considerations relevant to collecting data cost-effectively and without unduly burdening respondents, protect respondents from the potential consequences of sharing "sensitive" information, and adequately address the requirements of a diverse, multicultural population. To provide continuity with other research, existing instruments for assessing children, families, services, and system or agency characteristics were chosen whenever possible.[6]

The study is not without limitations. Because the design is a prospective longitudinal study, for example, for infants it is likely that the index investigation, or the one that made the child eligible for selection into the study, was the child's first entry into the child welfare system. For older children, however, prior history is incomplete. Although the baseline interview included various reference periods, the data do not include all possible information about prior placements, services, episodes of maltreatment, or other child and caregiver experiences.

The collection of measures, although apparently thorough, cannot support every type of analytic investigation; many authors of the subsequent chapters point to the lack of data of one kind or another or to the particular characteristics of the measure included in NSCAW. Furthermore, the design did not include evaluation by clinicians but relied on reports from caregivers, caseworkers, teachers, and, for the older ones, children themselves. The multiple reports were intended to provide different perspectives on the same phenomena, but at times they varied enough in focus or definition to prohibit direct comparison or combination across informants. In addition, although these reporters know the sampled child in important ways, the measures may suffer from reporter bias. Finally, usable data from teachers was not sufficiently complete for many researchers. The possibility of acquiring data from a teacher was reduced at many points: where caregivers and legal guardians refused to authorize teacher contact; where erroneous school, name, and address information was provided by the caregiver; where authorization forms where lost and unusable; and where the district, school, or teacher refused to fulfill requests.

Investigations of Data Quality

The NSCAW study was conducted with high-risk, mobile participants who recently had been involved in an investigation and who therefore might have been especially suspicious of strangers asking for personal information. Moreover, the interview protocol contained highly "sensitive" questions, and the consent procedure warned respondents about the necessity of reporting to the authorities any evidence of potential danger to the child. For many reasons, data quality in NSCAW was assessed.

The NSCAW study design specified that quality control checks and other quality assurance procedures be conducted at every stage of the survey process. Despite these efforts, errors remain in the NSCAW data as they would in any large, complex data collection system. Outside of sampling error, these errors generally arise from four sources:

- Unit and item nonresponse;
- The frame (e.g., frame undercoverage, duplication, and misclassification);
- The measurement process, including the interviewer, the respondent, and the survey questionnaire; and
- Data processing, such as keying, editing, coding, and weighting.

Such errors are referred to as *nonsampling errors* in survey research literature. Each error source can adversely, unpredictably affect data analysis. For example, unit nonresponse can bias survey estimates, invalidating statistical inferences. Although the NSCAW weights contain adjustments meant to compensate for unit nonresponse, such adjustments can never completely eliminate nonresponse bias. Furthermore, the NSCAW survey instruments were long, detailed, and complex to administer and complete. Despite attempts to minimize errors occurring during the interview, the risk of residual measurement error in these data is substantial. Over the years, a number of investigations of survey error have been undertaken for

NSCAW. These include studies of unit nonresponse, item nonresponse, frame coverage error, and measurement error.

Unit Nonresponse Bias

Several investigations were conducted to learn the extent of bias arising from unit nonresponse, which is the failure to obtain an interview from an NSCAW sample member. *Nonresponse bias* may be defined as the expected difference between the sample estimate (based only on respondents) and an estimate of the same parameter as based on both respondents and nonrespondents. It can be shown that, for estimating means and proportions, nonresponse bias can be expressed as the product $(1-\rho)\,\delta$, where ρ is the expected response rate from the survey, and δ is the expected difference between the estimate as based on only respondents and the estimate as based on nonrespondents (Table 1.3). Because of the response rates obtained for NSCAW, the potential for nonresponse bias is high, particularly for follow-up waves.

Several distinct data sources were used to obtain information that would allow for the assessment of the δ component of nonresponse bias and, therefore, of the magnitude of that bias. Where the child or caregiver did not respond to the survey, other data sources were used, such as the sampling frame and baseline investigative caseworker data. In this way, nonrespondents and respondents were compared in order that potential nonresponse bias might be estimated. Although nonresponse bias was estimated for only a few characteristics, these estimates help indicate levels of nonresponse bias for other unavailable nonrespondent characteristics. The analysis showed that, when the final weight was used, the number of variables with practically significant relative bias was only 4%, or within the expected range for chance alone. Nonresponse biases in NSCAW are generally not of any practical importance.

Item Nonresponse Bias

Item nonresponse occurs when a response is missing for a questionnaire item that the respondent was eligible to answer and should have answered. This data may be missing for several reasons: The respondent may not have known the answer to a

Table 1.3 Overall Weighted Response Rates for Waves 1, 2, 3, and 4

Wave	Response Rate (%)
Wave 1	64.2
Wave 2 conditioned on Wave 1 response	86.7
Wave 3 conditioned on Wave 1 response	86.6
Wave 4 conditioned on Wave 1 response	85.3

Note: The estimate of ρ for wave $W > 1$ is obtained by multiplying the Wave 1 response rate by the Wave W conditional response rate shown in the table. Because of the response rates obtained for the National Survey of Child and Adolescent Well-Being, the potential for nonresponse bias is high, particularly for follow-up waves.

question and answered "don't know." For most analyses, a "don't know" response is considered missing data. Alternatively, the respondent may have refused to answer a question if the question was about a sensitive topic or if the respondent was worried about the confidentiality of the response. Data for an item may be missing also because the question was never asked of the respondent; this kind of missing data is called an *inadvertent skip*.

Several investigations have addressed item nonresponse bias in NSCAW. In one analysis, the NSCAW Wave 1 CPS data were analyzed to assess whether item missing rates suggested that respondents were concerned about the consequences of answering completely and honestly. The analysis found that "sensitive" items were subject to significantly greater item nonresponse than nonsensitive items (99.8%, as opposed to 98.2%); however, for sensitive items the nonresponse rate was still less than 2%, which is negligible for most analyses. The tendency for respondents to either actively or passively refuse to answer sensitive questions is quite small. This investigation concluded that, although respondents may be concerned about the privacy of their answers, no evidence exists to suggest a tendency for respondents to either falsify or withhold information.

A second study evaluated the amount of item nonresponse present in the three primary components of the CPS: the caseworker interviews, the caregiver interviews, and the child interviews.[7] This analysis concerned primarily item nonresponse at the level of a particular interview module in the three different types of interviews. The total item nonresponse rate was computed, as well as that due to each of the three types of item nonresponse ("don't know" responses, refusals, and inadvertent skips) for each module.[8] The investigation was confined to items in the CPS Wave 1 General Release file.

For the caseworker instrument, the overall level of item nonresponse was less than 4%; however, as seen from the column headed "Maximum Percent," some items had a much higher rate of item nonresponse (Table 1.4). Most of the item nonresponse was due to "don't know" responses. The module having the largest rates of item nonresponse was the Alleged Abuse section. Seven of the 48 items in this module had an item nonresponse rate significantly greater than 20%. This module also had the highest rates of item nonresponse due to inadvertent skips.

Table 1.4 Item Nonresponse by Type of Instrument and Type of Missing

	Caseworker	*Caregiver*	*Child*
No. of items	131	1,191	606
Overall average missing (%)	3.74	3.10	2.73
Responses were "don't know" (%)	3.18	0.89	1.18
Responses were "refused" (%)	0.18	0.25	1.51
Inadvertent skipped items (%)	0.38	1.96	0.04
Maximum missing (%)	74.33	96.88	100.00
No. of items with missing rate significantly greater than 20%	8	47	12

For the caregiver instrument, the overall level of item nonresponse was slightly less than the rate for caseworker instrument, averaging around 3%. Across modules, inadvertent skip was the major source of item nonresponse, followed by "don't know" responses. The Emotional Regulation–Temperament module, which was administered to caregivers of children 36 months old and younger, was the module most affected, with an overall item nonresponse rate of 28%. A total of 28 of 64 items had item missing rates significantly greater than 20%. The primary cause of this high rate was inadvertent skips, which occurred because new questions were added to the instrument after the data collection began.

The child instrument appeared to be the least affected by item nonresponse, with an overall rate of less than 3%. "Don't know" responses and refusals contributed equally to this rate. One module, Questions for Children in Out-of-Home Care, which asked children about their perceptions of their placement, was particularly problematic for children, however, with 12 items of 110 having nonresponse rates significantly in excess of 20%. This module and an adaptation of the Parent–Child Conflict Tactics Scale, Child Maltreatment, had the highest item nonresponse rates—the module rates being primarily because of "don't know" responses and the Conflict Tactics Scale rates being primarily because of refusals.

Frame Noncoverage Error

Ideally, the sampling frame used for a survey should allow a positive probability of selection for every member of the target population; however, obtaining a list of all children in the United States who have been investigated for child abuse or neglect at any particular point in time is both costly and logistically problematic. Although some child welfare agencies maintained accurate and current electronic lists of all children who had been investigated in 1999–2000, in other agencies the lists existed in hard copy form only or were computerized but incomplete because of key-entry delays. In addition, agencies had adopted different definitions of *investigation, open case,* and *closed case* and different criteria for whether family members not the subject of the investigation were listed as being investigated.

When units in the target population are missing from the frame, these units and the population members they represent have no chance of selection, resulting in a frame noncoverage error. As with nonresponse bias, it can be shown that bias in a estimate of the mean or proportion because of frame noncoverage error can be written as $(1 - \gamma)\epsilon$, where γ is the proportion of the target population covered by the sampling frame and where ϵ is the difference between the mean of the subpopulation covered by the sampling frame and the mean of the subpopulation not covered by the sampling frame. This formula suggests that a low frame coverage rate does not necessarily mean noncoverage bias will be a problem, because ϵ may be quite small. On the other hand, if ϵ is quite large (i.e., the mean characteristic for covered persons is different from that of noncovered persons), the noncoverage bias may be large even if the coverage rate is considered good.

Children in the target population were missing from the NSCAW frame for several reasons. First, in constructing the frame, counties or agencies with very few investigated children were purposely deleted from the frame to conserve resources and increase interviewer efficiency without appreciably biasing the estimates. The number of counties excluded was 710 from a total of 3,141 counties, or approximately 23%; however, less than 3% of the target population (investigated children) resided in these counties, which suggests that the noncoverage bias resulting from this exclusion is likely quite small because γ is at most 0.03. Unless the difference in characteristics in these counties, as opposed to those in in-frame counties, is quite large, excluding these counties should have little consequence for statistical inference. To assess to some extent the contribution to bias of this exclusion of small counties, data available on the 1999 NCANDS Detailed Case Data Component (DCDC) were used to estimate ϵ directly for the child characteristics available from that file: child age, gender, substantiation, race, and ethnicity. The relative biases were found to be quite small (less than 1%) for all of the variables.

Additional undercoverage of the target population occurred when four states were removed from the frame because these states required that the child welfare agency obtain approval before families could be contacted. These prior approvals could not be obtained, and the response rates were so low that the states had to be excluded. The NSCAW target population was then redefined to exclude all states requiring first contact of a family by the child welfare agency; consequently, the elimination of the so-called agency-first-contact states does not contribute to frame noncoverage bias. Nevertheless, because researchers may continue to make inferences to the entire U.S. child welfare population, disregarding that this small group of children was excluded, the exclusion was treated as a source of noncoverage bias and investigated, with 1999 NCANDS DCDC data being used for quantification. Using the same set of characteristics as in the small-county bias analysis, this study found that the bias was quite small for all of the variables (less than 1%) and, for most analysis, should have no important consequences for inferences to the entire target population.

For a variety of reasons, some of the agencies provided sampling frames that did not include all the children investigated for child abuse or neglect during the sampling period. This source of bias was also assessed to the extent possible. To evaluate this potential bias, the counts on the sampling frame were compared with those in the DCDC data for those counties with 1999 DCDC data. The analysis showed that, for the larger PSUs, frame counts were generally at least 70% of the corresponding DCDC values. One large PSU showed an exception, where the frame counts were considerably smaller than the DCDC. The problem in this PSU was the inadvertent exclusion of some cases by the agency when the sampling files were generated. The persons familiar with the data were quite confident, however, that the exclusion was not related to any characteristics of the children. Consequently, the cases were regarded as missing at random.

Even though cases appeared to be missing at random, distributions of demographic characteristics from several sources were examined. The distributions were all close, although some characteristics exhibited significant differences. To remedy this situation, the NSCAW weights were adjusted for the frame undercoverage in this PSU, using data obtained from the DCDC for age, gender, and substantiation and using data from the state for the race/ethnicity distribution. Although cases were missing at random and their omission is unlikely to cause bias in the estimates, the adjustment was made to help assure that any residual bias is minor in the NSCAW data as a result of this PSU's frame problem.

Measurement Error Variance

Measurement error arises from numerous sources, including the respondent, the interviewer, the questionnaire or the wording of a particular question, the interview setting (whether in private or in the presence of others), and the information system used to retrieve information, including the respondent's memory. Measurement error can be systematic—that is, when all respondents tend to make errors in the same direction—unsystematic, or variable. Systematic errors lead to biases in survey estimates, whereas variable errors lead to poor reliability. Studies of measurement error in the NSCAW have been confined primarily to the evaluation of variable error or reliability.

If appropriate precautions are not taken, the implications of poor reliability for most data analyses are severe. For descriptive statistics (such as means, totals, and proportions), poor reliability increases the standard errors of the estimates because the information content of the observations is substantially reduced. Fortunately, the extra-variation caused by random error is captured in the estimates of sampling variances, so the coverage properties of confidence intervals and the Type I errors of hypothesis tests are not affected by variable error.

For multivariate statistics and analysis, the consequences are more severe. Variable errors in covariates can bias the regression and correlation coefficients and render chi-square tests of independence or homogeneity invalid. For example, for simple linear regression analysis, it can be shown that the estimate of the regression coefficient, β, for independent variable x having reliability R is attenuated toward zero; rather than estimating β, the regression estimates $R\beta$ (Biemer & Trewin, 1997). It also follows that the coefficient of determination for the regression cannot exceed the reliability R. Poor reliability lessens the strength of relationships between dependent and independent variables, leading to fewer significant findings.

When two or more independent variables are measured with poor reliability in a multiple regression, the situation is much more complex. Regression coefficients can be biased in unpredictable ways, depending on the covariance among the errors of the regressors (Bollen, 1989). Consequently, analysts may not be able to trust that their significant results are valid when several variables in the analysis have poor reliability.

The study team assessed the reliability of a number of key NSCAW measures using two basic approaches: Cronbach's alpha and longitudinal modeling (Biemer,

Christ, & Wiesen, 2007). Cronbach's alpha is a well-known, widely used method for assessing reliability when multiple indicators of the same construct are available in one wave of data collection. The validity of Cronbach's alpha depends on assumptions about independent errors and construct unidimensionality that often do not hold in practice. Longitudinal models, most notably the simplex model, are not subject to these limitations. Instead, the estimation algorithm takes advantage of the panel survey design to estimate reliability. This approach models the change in the underlying construct over the waves of data collection and relies on assumptions about the constancy of variance components over time to distinguish between true score and error variance.

The results from applying these models were mixed. Sometimes the estimates from the longitudinal models were quite consistent with Cronbach's alpha, and in other cases they were quite different from alpha. In most cases, the longitudinal model estimates were considerably lower than Cronbach's alpha. Further analysis revealed that the longitudinal model estimates of reliability were more correct, because correlated errors among items in the Cronbach alpha estimates tended to bias the reliability estimates upward.

A large number of scale score measures were considered. For most of the scores, reliability was at least moderate to good, and a substantial number of measures exhibited good to excellent reliability. A few measures exhibited poor reliability, however. These results suggest that the following measures could be problematic for multivariate analysis:

- Conflict Tactics Scale, Parent–Child, Child Neglect Ever
- Home Observation for Measurement of the Environment–Short Form (0–2 years), Cognitive Stimulation
- Home Observation for Measurement of the Environment–Short Form (0–5 years), Emotional Support
- Rochester Assessment Package for Schools, Autonomy Support
- Rochester Assessment Package for Schools, Involvement
- School Engagement
- Teacher Report Form, Internalizing
- Violence Exposure–Revised, Mild Violence Witness Exposure
- Violence Exposure–Revised, Mild Violence Victimization Exposure
- Violence Exposure–Revised, Severe Violence Witness Exposure
- Violence Exposure–Revised, Severe Violence Victimization Exposure

Analysts were advised to exercise caution when including any of these variables in their analysis. Several approaches are available to analysts for reducing the effects of poor reliability on results and conclusions. Analysts should be aware of the potentially attenuating effects of measurement error on regression coefficients. The failure to find a significant effect where one was expected could be traced to poor reliability of the regressor variables. Furthermore, when several covariates have poor reliability, the risk of false inference is high because of the increased potential for biased model estimates. Analysts using NSCAW were advised to consider these risks and interpret their findings cautiously, fully considering the potential for bias as a result of poor reliability of the model covariates.

Another possible approach is to rescore a problematic scale in order to produce a new score having higher reliability. For example, Straus, Hamby, Finkelhor, Moore, and Runyan (1998) discuss four methods of scoring the Conflict Tactics Scale: *prevalence, chronicity, annual frequency,* and *ever prevalence.* The method used in NSCAW data was *ever prevalence.* It is possible that another method of scoring would produce an indicator having greater reliability. For some scale measures, it may be possible to use factor analysis to obtain a weighted score function having better reliability, as well as generally enhanced psychometric properties. This approach has already been taken for the 12-Item Short Form Health Survey (general physical health) score.

For yet another approach, a number of analytical techniques are available to take measurement error into account in data analysis. These techniques include instrumental variable methods (see, e.g., Fuller, 1987), errors-in-variables analysis (Carroll, Ruppert, & Stefanski, 1995), structural equation models (see, e.g., Bollen, 1989), and other latent variable methods (Heinen, 1996; Vermunt, 1996). These methods incorporate in the models terms that reflect the random and systematic effects of measurement error on the relationships between the dependent and independent variables.

The statistical methodology for applying these advance modeling techniques to data from complex surveys such as the NSCAW has only recently been developed. These methods have been incorporated into a few commercially available software packages such as Mplus and Latent Gold. For example, Chapter 4 explicitly takes into account the measurement error in the Conflict Tactics Scale, using latent class models; other examples appear throughout the book. Currently, SUDAAN and STATA (two of the primary packages for complex survey data analysis in the volume) do not provide procedures for explicitly representing measurement errors in general linear models. Because all the authors were well aware of the existence of measurement error in these data, they have appropriately considered the potential biasing effects of measurement error in interpreting their findings and reporting their conclusions.

The Accuracy of Re-Report Data

Special attention is warranted for the re-report data, because one of the explicit goals of NSCAW was to track children's progress through the child welfare system. Questions about who comes back into the system and why are of great interest to child welfare practitioners and policy makers. A *re-report* is defined here as any report to CPS involving the NSCAW sample child after the index investigation (the investigation that made the child eligible for inclusion in the sampling frame). Re-report data have been used extensively and in varying ways in data analysis. Because one of the fundamental goals of CPS is to ensure children's safety, the presence of a re-report may indicate that a previous investigation did not wholly achieve this goal, that the child's safety was still at risk at the time of the re-report. In addition, this indicator variable may be included in a model of child well-being to test whether the presence or absence of re-reports relates to lower functioning or developmental status, or to higher levels of risky behavior among older children. Another area of research explores whether children with one or more re-reports have higher levels of service receipt, including out-of-home placement, than children with no re-reports.

A limited investigation of the quality of the NSCAW re-report data was conducted (Biemer, Chiflikyan, Dowd, & Smith, 2007). This evaluation suggests that re-reports were substantially underrepresented in NSCAW data. On the basis of comparisons of caseworker data and agency administrative files of re-reports, it was estimated that approximately 60% of all re-reports were missing from case-worker interview data. The investigators estimated that approximately 45% of the missing re-reports were attributable to the NSCAW method for identifying the need for a caseworker interview. The other 55% is primarily because of errors during the caseworker interview. Caseworkers typically relied on information available in their case files during the interview; however, these files may have been incomplete, may have been outdated, or may have contained erroneous information leading to missed or false re-reports. In addition, information about the re-reports, such as dates and other circumstances, may have been in error.

For analysis meant to produce estimates of the proportion of children re-reported at least once, the missing data have severely biasing effects. Considerable negative biases emerged for virtually every subgroup examined, including estimates at the state level. This bias is due to the lack of symmetry in the errors (i.e., the number of false-negative errors in the data file far outweighs the number of false positive errors, which yields a net underestimation of the proportion of children who had at least one re-report). In addition, analysis that uses the number of re-reports as either a dependent or independent variable will be severely biased.

By contrast, for analysis meant to characterize children according to a dichotomization—regardless of whether the child has been re-reported—the results were more positive. For the child characteristics considered in the preliminary assessment, no significant differences were found between children who were cor-rectly classified by caseworker interview data as having been re-reported and those who were incorrectly classified. These findings suggest that using the caseworker-provided re-report data in current NSCAW releases as a basis for characterizing children who were re-reported will not lead to important biases or false inferences.

This investigation was limited for several reasons. The administrative data acquired from the agencies and considered the "gold standard" for much of the error analyses are themselves subject to error. If re-reports were also missing from the agency files, then the estimates of the caseworker false-negative error rates based on those data would be understated. This possibility has no bearing on the con-clusion, however, that the NSCAW data are not appropriate for estimating the proportion of children who were re-reported or the average number of re-reports per child. Another limitation to this investigation is that several important agencies did not respond to the request for administrative data and, consequently, were not included in the analysis. The data used represent only 60% of the NSCAW population.

Conclusion

The challenges inherent in designing and implementing a survey with the breadth of NSCAW are many; like any research, NSCAW has its strengths and its limitations. Incorporating multiple theoretical perspectives, multiple informants, multiple time points, and multiple environmental contexts has resulted in an incomparably rich data set for exploring the lives and experiences of children and families who come into contact with the child welfare system. By drawing on these different perspectives, the study provides data that can inform new understandings of the ways family, child, community, and service factors affect these children's well-being. This understanding in turn provides the foundation for policy, program, and practice improvements. At the same time, researchers must be fully aware of the analytic issues arising from data quality and incorporate such knowledge into their analytic strategies.

The information NSCAW makes available allows service providers to more thoroughly understand children's and families' service needs and to begin to target the best, most cost-effective services for those who enter the child welfare system. The level of detail NSCAW provides is equally critical to policy makers if they are to make wise decisions about changes in the child welfare system itself. Without knowing the answers to the questions central to practitioners, policy makers will, after all, face severe constraints in effecting positive systemic change. The results of this seminal study have contributed tremendously to the better service and policy understanding required for improving the entire field's responsiveness to child and family needs.

Appendix Table 1.A Comparison of CPS-Allocated Sample, No. Selected, and Wave 1 Responding Sample Size, for First- and Second-Stage Strata

| First-Stage Strata | Total | Not Receiving Services | | Receiving Services | | | | | |
| | | | | Not Placed in Out-of-Home Care | | | Placed in Out-of-Home Care | | |
		<1 yr old	1–14 yr Old	<1 yr old	1–4 yr old Sexual Abuse	1–14 yr old Other	<1 yr old	1–14 yr old Sexual Abuse	1–14 yr old Other
Allocated Sample Size (Targeted No. of Respondents)									
Key State #1	703	52	121	98	47	220	39	19	107
Key State #2	304	5	27	47	29	124	19	10	43
Key State #3	284	18	52	41	19	86	19	11	38
Key State #4	297	26	53	44	25	90	15	8	36
Key State #5	402	27	67	59	32	124	27	10	56
Key State #6	293	17	54	39	21	90	21	12	39
Key State #7	300	16	43	37	22	110	18	15	39
Key State #8	473	27	81	77	38	145	28	14	63
Remainder	2,381	151	397	341	179	760	148	78	327
Total	5,437	339	895	783	412	1,749	334	177	748
No. Selected									
Key State #1	1,359	89	241	179	102	449	70	38	191
Key State #2	503	17	54	75	39	209	33	14	62
Key State #3	445	19	72	67	31	147	32	22	55
Key State #4	435	43	96	60	35	132	18	1	50
Key State #5	686	63	160	73	29	213	45	9	94
Key State #6	433	27	85	60	32	128	30	19	52
Key State #7	439	27	75	51	32	150	28	22	54
Key State #8	683	48	133	97	54	202	41	23	85

(continued)

Appendix Table 1.A (continued)

| First-Stage Strata | Total | Not Receiving Services | | Receiving Services | | | | | |
| | | | | Not Placed in Out-of-Home Care | | | Placed in Out-of-Home Care | | |
		<1 yr old	1–14 yr Old	<1 yr old	1–4 yr old Sexual Abuse	1–14 yr old Other	<1 yr old	1–14 yr old Sexual Abuse	1–14 yr old Other
Remainder	3,978	262	999	472	264	1,187	204	104	486
Total	8,961	595	1,915	1,134	618	2,817	501	252	1,129
Responding Sample Size									
Key State #1	695	53	113	105	53	191	45	21	114
Key State #2	298	8	28	45	26	114	21	11	45
Key State #3	285	15	45	43	15	87	27	15	38
Key State #4	336	33	64	48	26	107	16	1	41
Key State #5	408	47	97	47	18	119	28	4	48
Key State #6	314	17	53	46	22	91	27	13	45
Key State #7	300	20	53	36	21	104	17	12	37
Key State #8	485	29	84	78	37	144	33	16	64
Remainder	2,380	138	524	321	157	702	154	71	313
Total	5,501	360	1,061	769	375	1,659	368	164	745

CPS, Child Protective Services.

Appendix Table 1.B Description of NSCAW Child, Family, and Caseworker Constructs, Source in NSCAW Data, and Rationale for Inclusion

Construct	Ages (of Child When Administered)	Data Source	Rationale
Child Areas			
1. Social Competence, Relationships			Critical for adaptation in a variety of domains and a frequent area of disruption for children with histories of maltreatment.
Relationships with parents and other significant adults	<11 ≥11	Observation Child	Warm and supportive relationships between children and adults can buffer children against stresses and help children heal from negative effects of maltreatment.
Peer relationships	≥5 ≥5	Child Teacher	Success in making and keeping friendships is linked to better school adjustment. Peer friendships provide children a support system and model for future relationships. Peer rejection is related to adolescent conduct disorder.
Global social competence	≥3 ≥5	Caregiver Teacher	Children with better developed social skills have greater success in forming social relationships and better long-term academic and occupational achievement.
2. Health, Cognitive Status			Health and intellectual functioning are among the most important indicators of well-being and have an influence on development in other domains.
Developmental/ cognitive status	All	Child	Cognitive functioning and neurodevelopmental status are important mediators of school success.
Communication skills	<6	Child	Language skills are the foundation for literacy skills taught in school.
Health and disabilities	All ages	Caregiver	Children with chronic health conditions and disabilities are more likely to experience maltreatment. Health status and injuries can be a direct consequence of maltreatment. Health and injuries influence the extent to which children can participate in activities.
3. Adaptive Behavior, Functional Status			Adaptive behavior reflects competence in achieving personal independence and meeting social demands such as academic adjustment and performance.

(continued)

Appendix Table 1.B (continued)

Construct	Ages (of Child When Administered)	Data Source	Rationale
Adaptive skills	≤10	Caregiver	The ability to function in daily life is an important marker of adjustment. For adolescents in out-of-home placements, living skills become an important focus of attention as they transition to independent living.
Academic achievement (including attendance, grade progression)	≥6 ≥5	Child Teacher	Academic achievement and completion of high school are critical for future economic viability.
Special education status and educational, developmental and support services received	All ages	Teacher Caregivers Caseworkers	Children's developmental and educational needs affect their participation in school and social activities. Documentation of services addressing these needs is an indicator of how the child welfare system operates.
School socialization	≥5	Teacher	Maltreated children often experience difficulties in social as well as academic aspects of school adjustment. The ability to function socially in the classroom is highly related to academic performance.
School engagement	≥5	Child Teacher	Motivations are affected by early experiences and in turn influence children's dispositions toward learning and school.
Future expectations	≥10	Child	Positive expectations for the future have been associated with positive socioemotional adjustment and self-perceptions of competency.
4. Behavior Regulation, Emotional and Mental Health			Behavioral and emotional processes are developed as part of the caregiver–child relationship and can be disrupted when this relationship is impaired. Successful development along with mental health are the hallmarks of adjustment and well-being.
Temperament	≤3	Caregiver	Temperament can either act as a risk or a resiliency factor by influencing how a child relates to others. It is also one of the antecedents of self-regulation.

Behavior problems	≥ 2 ≥ 5 ≥ 11	Caregiver Teacher Child	Behavior problems are one of the earliest signs of maltreatment, especially difficulty with impulse control and aggressive behavior. Behavior, especially externalizing, problems interfere with peer acceptance and academic performance and can be a precursor to later delinquency. Since they are often setting specific, this measurement requires multiple informants.
Mental health	≥ 2 ≥ 5 ≥ 8	Caregiver Teacher Child	Mental health is a broad construct that affects all aspects of well-being. In children it is highly associated with behavioral problems.
Criminality/ delinquency	≥ 11	Child	An elevated risk of delinquency and criminality exists among maltreated individuals. Avoidance of criminality is a marker of successful social adaptation.
Substance abuse and risky sexual behaviors	≥ 11	Child	Drug abuse and early sexual activities are associated with depression and maltreatment.
5. Life Experiences			Life experiences, such as maltreatment history and exposure to other types of violence, trauma, and loss all negatively influence child outcomes.
Child maltreatment	All ages ≥ 11 All ages	Caregiver Child Caseworker	It is critical to get more than the maltreatment information that forms the basis of the report.
Family/placement disruptions	All ages	Caregiver	Frequent placement changes and household disruptions are related to poorer child outcomes
Loss, violence, and other stressors in and out of the home	≥ 5	Child	All violence that is experienced (i.e., viewed as well as directly experienced) has a negative impact on mental health and on how children handle conflicts themselves.
6. Service Experiences	All ages ≥ 11 All ages	Caregiver Child Caseworker	Documentation of services received is critical to understanding the service provision process, the factors that affect the process, and the relationship among individual/family variables, services, and outcomes. Service experiences only asked of caseworkers for longer-term foster care (LTFC) cases at Wave 1.

(continued)

Construct	Ages (of Child When Administered)	Data Source	Rationale
Parent/Caregiver Areas			
1. Health Status			The health of the caregiver affects the functioning of the caregiver and thus how s/he relates to the child.
Mental health and substance abuse	All ages	Caregiver	Psychiatric disorders, especially parental depression, can be especially harmful to the quality of the parent–child relationship. It is one factor predisposing a parent to maltreatment as well as a result of maltreatment. Substance abuse is one of the reasons for reports to CPS. Substance abuse is also associated with parenting difficulties.
Physical health	All ages	Caregiver	Physical health affects how well a parent can provide caregiving and function in the larger world.
Services received by caregiver	All ages	Caregiver	Services received by parents may be critical to their ability to provide appropriate care for their children. If parents do not receive needed services, reunification may be unlikely.
2. Caregiver Attributes/Behaviors			Parenting attitudes and behaviors exist on a continuum, from positive and supportive to negative, with child maltreatment falling at the negative extreme.
Parent/caregiver behaviors Emotional nurturing and Cognitive/ verbal responsiveness and stimulation	<11	Caregiver Observation	Supportive parent–child relationships are the foundation upon which all developmental achievements are built. Parental sensitivity to the child's needs and interests, parental ability to structure an interaction, and acceptance of the child are highly related to the quality of the emotional bond between parent and child. Verbal and behavioral responsiveness are highly linked to children's communication and intellectual competence.
Behavioral monitoring and discipline	All ages <11 ≥10	Caregiver Observation Child	Use of appropriate discipline promotes socialization and behavioral self-regulation in children rather than short-term compliance. It is frequently under the guise of discipline that parents justify physical maltreatment. At the other extreme, lax supervision and the failure to provide any limits can cross the boundary from leniency to neglect.

3. Contextual Factors			These are influences on caregivers and children that affect perceived stress and well-being.
Neighborhood factors	All ages	Caregiver	The behavior of individuals and families has to be understood in terms of the environment of their community.
Family demographics	All ages	Caregiver	There is a need to provide background characteristics, roster of who lives in the home, employment, education, and other descriptive information.
Social support and other family resources, including assistance with child rearing	All ages	Caregiver	Perceived social support is believed to buffer the child and family against stress, thereby helping them better cope with their problems.
Domestic violence in the home	All ages	Female caregivers	Domestic violence is highly associated with child maltreatment, is a source of stress for the child, and may itself be considered a form of psychological maltreatment.
Criminal involvement of parents	All ages	Caregiver	This is another background factor that is associated with maltreatment.
Risk assessment	All ages	Caseworker	The relationship between caseworker perceived risk and strengths and long-term safety and well-being needs to be assessed.
Caseworker Areas			
Job role	All ages	Caseworker	Used to identify relevant questions for caseload
Work unit	All ages	Caseworker	Used to identify relevant questions for caseload
Caseload	All ages	Caseworker	Caseload level will determine amount of time worker is likely to be able to spend on services to sample child
Work environment and job satisfaction	All ages	Caseworker*	Work environment and job satisfaction are believed to influence workers' job performance and turnover
Demographics	All ages	Caseworker	Measures of caseworker demographics and professional background; also allows comparison of caseworker race/ethnicity with that of the sample child and family.

* These data were collected from services caseworkers only at the 12-month follow-up.
CPS, Child Protective Services; NSCAW, National Survey of Child and Adolescent Well-Being.

Appendix Table 1.C Description of Instruments Used to Measure Child and Family Well-Being

Social Competence/Relationships

Title, Author, Publisher, Date	General Description (Subtests, Score, Age, Time)	Standardization Sample	Psychometrics (Reliability and Validity)	Comments	References
Social Skills Rating System, Gresham and Elliott, 1990, American Guidance Service	3 Forms: Parent, Teacher, Student *Parent Form:* Social Skills Scale (Cooperation, Assertive, Responsibility, Self-Control subscales); Problem Behaviors Scale (Externalizing, Internalizing subscales); *Teacher Form:* same as Parent Form but includes an Academic Competence Scale; *Student Form:* Social Skills Scale (Cooperation, Assertive, Self-control, Empathy subscales) *Yields:* raw scores for Social Skills Scale and subscales; raw scores for Problem Behaviors Scale and subscales; standard scores for Social Skills Scale and Problem Behaviors Scale; *Age range:* ≥5	4,170 children/youth, gender-balanced, regular and special education students; slight overrepresentation of whites and blacks; 27% minority students; 1,027 parents and 259 teachers	*Internal Consistency:* α = .73–.95 (median α = .90) *Test-retest reliability:* Teacher rating: α = .84–.93; Parent rating α = .65–.87; Student rating: α = .68 *Criterion-Related Validity:* Teacher Form: Correlations between the Social Behavior Assessment (SBA) and the social skills scale ranged from −.15 to −.73. Total scale correlations were −.68. The social skills scale correlated .70 with the Harter Teacher Rating Scale (TRS). Parent Form: The Child Behavior Checklist- Parent Report Form (CBCL) correlates .58 with the social skills scale *Convergent Validity:* Teacher–parent ratings of social skills subscales at the preschool level range from r = .16 to .25 with a median of r = .18. All coefficients are significant at, at least the .02 level. *Internal Consistency for* NSCAW: α = .90 for	Multirater system Benes (1995) finds that Gresham & Elliot have provided a psychometrically sound means of measuring the perceived social skills of youth from preschool to secondary school with the SSRS.	Benes, 1995; Gresham & Elliott, 1990

(continued)

| | | | | Wellborn, Connell & Pierson, 1987; Connell, 1990 |

preschoolers and secondary-aged children and .87 for elementary-aged children

Reliability:
Construct: Parental Emotional Security r_{ii} = .49, α = .74 (all students) Construct: Peer Emotional Security r_{ii} = .40, α = .73 (all students)

Subdomain: Perceived Parental Support r_{ii} = .27, α = .86 (all students)

Validity: Parental Emotional Security: High Risk, Optimal, and High Risk vs. Optimal (extreme groups) — correlations and phi coefficients of .10–.50 (all significant at $p < .0001$) Peer Emotional Security: High Risk, Optimal, and High Risk vs. Optimal (extreme groups) — correlations and phi coefficients of .10–.50 (all significant at $p < .0001$) Parental Support: High Risk and Optimal—correlations and phi coefficients of .10–.50 (all significant at $p < .0001$) High Risk vs. Optimal (extreme groups)—correlations and phi coefficients of .51 and higher (all significant at $p < .0001$)

Internal Consistency for NSCAW: Cronbach's α for overall Relatedness score = .88

Rochester Assessment Package for Schools – Self-Report Instrument for Middle School Students (RAPS-SM); Wellborn, Connell & Pierson, 1987

Domains: Engagement, Beliefs about Self, and Experiences of Interpersonal Support

Subdomains: Ongoing Engagement, Reaction to Challenge, Perceived Competence, Perceived Autonomy, Perceived Relatedness, Experiences of Support from Parents, and Experiences of Support from Teachers

Age range: ≥11

2,429 male and female subjects from three middle schools in an urban school district and one from an adjacent suburban district; stratified by gender and ethnicity

Appendix Table 1.C (continued)

Social Competence/Relationships

Title, Author, Publisher, Date	General Description (Subtests, Score, Age, Time)	Standardization Sample	Psychometrics (Reliability and Validity)	Comments	References
			(the only score used). Subscales scores were not used because while Cronbach's alpha for the Parental Emotional Security and Involvement were fair (.65 to .76), alpha was very low for Autonomy Support and Structure (.28 to .66).		
Loneliness and Social Dissatisfaction Questionnaire for Young Children, Asher and Wheeler (rev.), 1985	16 principal items: yes/no/ sometimes questions focusing on feelings of loneliness, social adequacy vs. Inadequacy, subjective estimations of peer status, and appraisals of whether important relationship provisions are being met 8 "filler" items: e.g., re: hobbies to help children feel open and relaxed Score: created using all principal items Age range: as early as kindergarten and 1st grade		Item-to-Total Score correlation: ranged from .26 to .55 Internal reliability: α = .79 Validity: Low scores may be suspect due to the possibility of children providing socially desirable or defensive responses. The underreporting of feelings, thoughts, and behaviors that might reflect negatively on the self may result in scores that underestimate true feelings. Internal Consistency for NSCAW: Cronbach's α = .70 for 5–7 year olds and .89 for children aged 8 years and older.	Focus on school setting For research focused on connections between loneliness and related constructs, the use of only items that directly tap loneliness (i.e., vs. dissatisfaction) is recommended Note: in the study described in the reference article, one item was inadvertently omitted from the 16 principal items	Asher et al., 1984; Asher & Wheeler, 1985; Cassidy & Asher, 1992; & Parkhurst & Asher, 1992

Functional Status/Adaptive Behavior

Measure	Description	Sample	Reliability/Validity	Comments	References
Mini-Battery of Achievement (MBA); Woodcock, McGrew, & Werder, 1994, Riverside Publishing	*4 subtests:* Reading (includes letter-word identification, vocabulary, and comprehension), Writing, Mathematics, and General Knowledge); *Yields:* standardized scores, percentile ranks, age and grade equivalents, and 1-page narrative report via computer scoring program; *Age range:* ≥6	6,026 individuals 4 to 95 yr from 100 geographically diverse communities; Stratified by region, community size, gender, ethnicity, funding and type of college, distribution of adult education, and adult occupation in the community/ representative of the population at large	*Internal consistency reliability:* Reading *r* = .88–.98, Mdn *r* = .94 (across age groups); Mathematics *r* = .70–.98; Msn *r* = .93; Factual knowledge *r* = .80–.96; Mdn *r* = .87; *Test-retest reliability:* Reading *r* = .89; Mathematics *r* = .86; Factual knowledge *r* = .88; (6th graders); Concurrent validity: Reading *r* = .70–.75; Mathematics *r* = .57–.72; Factual Knowledge *r* = .64–.74 *Convergent and discriminant validity:* Correlations of specific areas higher with same areas than those of different areas.	Brief, broad battery of basic skills and knowledge; New measure/No reviews available; Items are a subset from WJ-R which had positive reviews	Woodcock et al., 1994
Vineland Adaptive Behavior Scale (VABS) Screener-Daily Living, Sparrow, Carter, & Cicchetti, 1993, Yale University Child Study Center Sparrow, Balla, & Cicchetti, 1984, American Guidance System (Full Vineland)	*3 domains:* communication (C), daily living skills (DL), socialization (S) *Yields:* standard scores, percentile scores, adaptive level, and age equivalence scores for each domain, Adaptive Behavior (AB) composite, and Maladaptive Behavior (MB) as well as age equivalent scores and adaptive levels for subdomains	536 children, representative in terms of gender, ethnicity, region of the country, community size, and parental education by 1980 U.S. Census Bureau data	*Internal consistency for* NSCAW: Cronbach's α for Reading = .74 and .61 for Math. *Reliability:* has been high. Results indicate excellent correspondence between the screeners and the full Vineland (correlations between .87 and .98) *Validity:* *Screener Standard Score Correlations w/ Vineland Full Scale:* Daily Living (ages 6–12) = .93 (ages 13–18) = .92		Sattler, 1992; Sparrow, Balla, & Cicchetti, 1984; Sparrow, Carter & Cicchetti, 1993

(continued)

Appendix Table 1.C (continued)

Social Competence/Relationships

Title, Author, Publisher, Date	General Description (Subtests, Score, Age, Time)	Standardization Sample	Psychometrics (Reliability and Validity)	Comments	References
	Age range: all ages		Correlations between Same-Day Administration of Vineland Screener and Survey Form: Standard Scores (DL) = .71 Age Equivalents (DL) = .90		
			For Full Vineland:		
			Internal consistency reliability: Mdn r = .90 (DL)		
			Test-retest reliability: r = .85 (DL)		
			Interrater reliability: r = .72 (DL)		
			Criterion-related validity: r = .55 (AB and Vineland Social Maturity Scale Social Quotient), r = .58 (AB and Adaptive Behavior Inventory for Children), r = .40–.70 (subdomains and AAMD Adaptive Behavior Scale); r = .13–.41 (VABS and K-ABC MPC), r = .12–.37 (VABS and PPVT-R)		
			Internal consistency for NSCAW: Cronbach's α = .91 for 0–2 year olds, .77 for 3–5 year olds, and .78 for 6–10 year olds		

Emotional Development, Behavior Regulation, and Mental Health

Child Behavior Checklist for Ages 2–3 (CBCL 2–3); Achenbach, 1991a, University of Vermont-Burlington 9 scales: 6 syndrome (Anxious/Depressed, Sleep Problems, Aggressive Behavior, Withdraw, Somatic Problems, and Destructive Behavior) and 3 compiled [Internalizing (I), Externalizing (E), and Total Problems (TP)]; *Yields:* raw scores for syndrome scales and standardized scores and percentiles for syndrome and compiled scales *Age range:* 2 to 3 yr	368 children ages 2 to 3 yr, gender-balanced, 3 SES levels equally represented, predominately white Northeasterners; Additional 640 mental health service recipients used to derive syndrome scales	*Test-retest reliability:* $r = .72$–93 (syndrome scales), $r = .87$ (I), $r = .84$ (E), $r = .91$ (TP); *Interrater agreement:* $r = .45$–.71 (syndrome scales), $r = .69$ (I), $r = .67$ (E), $r = .67$ (TP) (all 2 yr); $r = .39$–65 (syndrome scales), $r = .67$ (I), $r = .60$ (E), $r = .60$ (TP) (all 3 yr); *Stability:* $r = .50$–.69 (syndrome scales), $r = .65$ (I), $r = .67$ (E), $r = .78$ (TP); *Criterion validity:* differences between referred and nonreferred children on all syndrome scales; odds ratios for clinical range and referral status significant for all scores (3.7–10.9); *Construct validity:* significant relation with Richman Behavior Checklist ($r = .56$–.77); *Discriminant validity:* no significant associations with developmental test scores *Internal consistency in the NSCAW sample:* High for 2–3 year olds (Externalizing = .91, Internalizing = .80, and Total Problem Behavior = .95) and for 4–5 year olds (Externalizing = .92, Internalizing = .90, and	Based on empirical research/ reliable and valid; Comprehensive; Easy to administer and score; Used in IHDP	Achenbach, 1988; Achenbach, 1992; Freeman, 1985; Kelley, 1985

(continued)

Appendix Table 1.C (continued)

Social Competence/Relationships

Title, Author, Publisher, Date	General Description (Subtests, Score, Age, Time)	Standardization Sample	Psychometrics (Reliability and Validity)	Comments	References
			Total Problem Behavior = .96). Children classified as having clinical/borderline problem behaviors had scores above 60 for Externalizing, Internalizing, and Total Problem behaviors. These cutoffs were the same for the 2–3 year-olds and 4–15 year olds.		
Child Behavior Checklist (CBCL 4-18), Achenbach, 1991b University Associates in Psychiatry; Burlington, VT	*Behavior problem scales:* 2 broad problem scales — Externalizing and Internalizing; also, Withdrawn, Somatic Complaints, Anxious/ Depressed, Social Problems, Thought Problems, Attention Problems, Delinquent Behavior, Aggressive Behavior, and Sex Problems *Social competence scales:* Activities, Social, and School *Yields:* raw and standardized scores for each problem scale and compiled scores; *Age range:* 4–18 years	2,368 children; 73% white, 16% black, 7% Hispanic, 4% "other"; 81% from middle to upper class Separate norms were not developed for different ethnic groups or social classes because the differences between these groups were judged to be minimal	*Internal consistency:* very high for the Total, Internalizing, and Externalizing scores and reasonably good for most of the scale scores; noticeably lower for the social competence scores *Test-retest reliability:* high for both the problem and social competence scales in the short term *Interrater reliability:* reasonably high between parents *Construct validity:* the problem items cluster into meaningful scales, and the problem scales correlate highly with similar scales from other checklists and with corresponding DSM diagnoses	One component of a five-part assessment tool (rarely sufficient by itself as either a clinical or program evaluation tool); Computerized scoring available; Relatively easy to administer; May be used with a wide range of outpatient children; Supported by data on very large samples; May prove difficult for respondents with limited reading skills; May potentially misrepresent the capability of such groups as children with chronic illness;	Achenbach, 1991b

Measure	Description	Sample	Reliability/Validity	Comments	Source
			Criterion-related validity: in research studies, both the problem scales and social competence scales have discriminated between a number of different childhood problem groups and their respective comparison groups. *Internal consistency in the NSCAW sample*: High for 2–3 year olds (Externalizing = .91, Internalizing = .80, and Total Problem Behavior = .95) and for 4–15 year olds (Externalizing = .92, Internalizing = .90, and Total Problem Behavior = .96). Children classified as having clinical/borderline problem behaviors had scores above 60 for Externalizing, Internalizing, and Total Problem behaviors. These cutoffs were the same for the 2–3 year olds and 4–15 year olds.	Results may be distorted where parents have reason to exaggerate or minimize children's problems	
Youth Self-Report (YSR); Achenbach, 1991c; University Associates in Psychiatry; Burlington, VT	*Problem behavior scales*: 8 syndromes (Withdrawn, Somatic Complaints, Anxious/Depressed, Social Problems, Thought Disorder, Attention Problems, Delinquent Behavior, Aggressive Behavior); and 3 compiled (Internalizing, Externalizing, and Total Problems);	1,719 children out of a pool of 1,942 ages 11 to 18 who were considered to be healthy (i.e., not received mental health services or special remedial school in past 12 months). Sample representative in terms of gender, SES, ethnicity, and region.	*Test-retest reliability*: Whole sample $r = .80$ (Total Competence), $r = .79$[a] (Total Problems), $r = .80$[b] (Internalizing); $r = .81$[a,b] (Externalizing); Boys $r = .74$ (Total Competence), $r = .78$ (Total Problems), $r = .76$ (Internalizing); $r = .80$ (Externalizing); Girls $r = .84$	A number of translations of the instrument are available. Comparisons with appropriate age and sex group norms are possible. Psychometric properties of the Social Competence scales need additional research. Reading level of the adolescent may	Achenbach 1991c; Elliott & Busse, 1992

(continued)

Appendix Table 1.C (continued)

Social Competence/Relationships

Title, Author, Publisher, Date	General Description (Subtests, Score, Age, Time)	Standardization Sample	Psychometrics (Reliability and Validity)	Comments	References
	Social competence scales: Total Competence and Activities and Social; *Yields:* raw scores and standardized scores *Age range:* ≥11	Norms are provided for boys and girls separately divided into two age groups each.	(Total Competence), $r = .86$[a] (Total Problems), $r = .85$[a] (Internalizing); $r = .84$[ab] (Externalizing). [a]Time 1 > Time 2, $p < .05$, by t test. [b]When corrected for the number of comparisons, Time 1 vs. Time 2 difference was not significant. *Internal Consistency for NSCAW:* Total $\alpha = .96$, Externalizing $\alpha = .90$, and Internalizing $\alpha = .90$	affect time required to complete the instrument. Elliot & Busse (1992) recognize the satisfactory test-retest validity, adequate behavior reliabilities, and adequate discriminant validity for the problem scales, but not for the competence scales.	
Teachers Report Form; Achenbach, 1991d	*8 scales:* Withdrawn, Somatic Complaints, Anxious/ Depressed, Social Problems, Thought Problems, Attention Problems, Delinquent Behavior, and Aggressive Behavior; also Internalizing, Externalizing, and Mixed scales *Age range:* ≥5	1,391 children out of a pool of 1,613 ages 5 to 18 who were considered to be healthy (i.e., not received mental health services or special remedial school in past 12 months). Sample representative in terms of gender, SES, ethnicity, and region. Norms are provided for boys and girls separately divided into two age groups each.	*Test-retest reliability:* Whole sample $r = .93$ (Total Adaptive), $r = .95$ (Total Problems), $r = .92$ (Internalizing); $r = .95$ (Externalizing); Boys $r = .93$ (Total Adaptive), $r = .92$ (Total Problems), $r = .92$ (Internalizing); $r = .86$ (Externalizing); Girls $r = .94$ (Total Adaptive), $r = .99$ (Total Problems), $r = .87$ (Internalizing); $r = .97$ (Externalizing).		Achenbach, 1991d

Measure	Description	Standardization / Limitations	Reliability and Validity	Comments	References
			Internal Consistency for NSCAW: Cronbach's α = .96 for Total Problems, .90 for Externalizing, and .91 for Internalizing.		
Children's Depression Inventory; Kovacs, 1982; Multi-Health Rater Systems, Inc.	*Domains*: Single dimension of depression *Yield*: Total depression score with cutoff scores for determining depression *Age range*: ≥7	No large standardization sample and no norms for specific age groups or minority populations	*Internal consistency*: α = .71–.87; *Test-retest reliability*: r = .38–.87 (depending on interval and sample); *Concurrent validity*: correlated positively with Revised Children's Manifest Anxiety Scale scores and negatively with Coopersmith Self-Esteem Inventory; *Construct validity*: with non-clinically referred children, factor analysis found one factor; with clinically referred children, factor analysis has shown multiple factors. *Criterion-related validity*: correlates with global severity ratings of depression based on semi-structured interviews	Limited normative data Additional investigation of test-retest reliability is needed	Kovacs, 1982; Saylor, Finch, Spirito, & Bennett, 1984; Helsel & Matson, 1984; Hodges & Craighead, 1990
Composite International Diagnostic Interview Short Form (CIDI-SF) Kessler, et al., 1998	Screens for presence of 8 disorders: major depression, generalized anxiety, specific phobia, social phobia,	Pilot study involving nationally representative telephone survey	*Internal Consistency for NSCAW*: Cronbach's α = .81 for 7–12 year olds and .87 for 13–15 year olds. Internal consistency for alcohol and drug dependence: α = .70 to .94 (Cottler et al., 1991; Ustun et al., 1997)		Kessler et al. 1998

(continued)

Appendix Table 1.C (continued)

Social Competence/Relationships

Title, Author, Publisher, Date	General Description (Subtests, Score, Age, Time)	Standardization Sample	Psychometrics (Reliability and Validity)	Comments	References
	agoraphobia, panic attack, alcohol dependence, and drug dependence		*Inter-rater reliability* ranges from .67 to 1.0 (Andrews et al., 1995; Wittchen et al., 1991) Test-retest data show kappas of .62 to 78 for three disorders in NSCAW (Wittchen, 1994)		
Violence Exposure Scale for Children (VEX-R); Fox & Leavitt, 1995	*Domains:* Witness or Victim of violence at school, home, neighborhood, or on TV Age range: ≥6	134 Israeli children in the 2nd and 4th grades of two schools and their mothers 155 families with children ages 3 ½ to 4 ½ living in a low-income, moderately violent neighborhood near Washington, D.C., predominantly African American	Israeli children: *Reliability:* Cronbach's α = .822–.824 (mild violence), α = .484–.562 (severe violence) Home Subscale: α = .514 (mild violence), α = .040 (severe violence) *Validity:* There was no significant difference between child report as witness compared to victim regarding mild violence at home. There were no reports of child as victims of severe violence at home and very few reports of child as witness. Negative correlation between PRQ scores and child report of exposure to mild violence as a witness at home, r(134) = −.230, p < .05 and exposure to mild violence as a victim at home, r(134) = −.385, p < .01 D.C. children:		Fox & Leavitt, 1995; Raviv et al, 2001; Shahinfar et al., 2000.

Measure	Description	Sample	Psychometrics	References
			Reliability: Cronbach's α = .80 (mild violence), α = .86 (severe violence) *Validity:* Discordance between parent and child reports *Internal Consistency for NSCAW:* Cronbach's α = .96 for Total; Subscales range from .86 to 92	Briere, 1996; Briere & Lanktree, 1995
Trauma Symptom Checklist for Children (TSCC); Briere, 1996	*Domains:* Anxiety, Depression, Post-Traumatic Stress (PTS), Sexual Concerns, Dissociation, Anger *Yields:* Total and subscale raw scores *Age range:* ≥8	3,008 children combined from three nonclinical samples in Illinois, Colorado, and Minnesota sample representative of gender and ethnicity	*Internal consistency:* α = .82–89 *Concurrent validity:* with CBCL r = .72–80 *Reliability: Internal consistency* (Standardization sample for PTS scale) α = .87 *Convergent Validity:* CBCL Youth-report Internalization correlated most with PTS: r = .75 with p < .01	
Infant Behavior Questionnaire (IBQ); NLSY Adaptation: Baker et al., 1993; Rothbart, 1981, University of Oregon-Eugene; Worobey & Blajda, 1989, *Developmental Psychology*	*6 scales:* Activity Level, Smiling/Laughter, Fear, Distress to Limitations, Soothability, and Duration of Orienting; *Yields:* 6 scale scores; *Age range:* 1 yr	463 parents of children aged 3, 6, 9, and 12 mo; Heterogeneous social class	*Original Alpha reliability:* r = .79 (Activity Level, Smiling and Laughter, and Distress to Limitations), r = .81 (Fear), r = .71 (Duration of Orienting), r = .78 (Soothability); *Stability:* r = .11–86 (increased with age); *Discriminant validity:* interscale correlations less than intrascale correlations; *Concurrent validity:* few significant correlations between maternal ratings and observer report;	Baker et al. 1993; Hubert, et al., 1982; Rothbart, 1981; Rothbart & Mauro, 1990; Worobey & Blajda, 1989
			Recommended for studies with wide range of social class groups; Most specific of temperament measures in terms of behavior, context, and time frame; No norms available; Conflicting validity data between scales	

(continued)

Appendix Table 1.C (continued)

Social Competence/Relationships

Title, Author, Publisher, Date	General Description (Subtests, Score, Age, Time)	Standardization Sample	Psychometrics (Reliability and Validity)	Comments	References
			Adapted version *Split-half reliability:* r = .70 (2 wk), r = .79 (2 mo); *Test-retest reliability:* r = .33–.65, Mdn = .46 (2 wk and 2 mo), r = .20–.50, Mdn = .38 (2 and 12 mo)		

Child Health, Neurophysiological, and Cognitive and Academic Status

Title, Author, Publisher, Date	General Description (Subtests, Score, Age, Time)	Standardization Sample	Psychometrics (Reliability and Validity)	Comments	References
Bayley Infant Neurodevelopmental Screener (BINS); Aylward, 1995	*4 conceptual areas assessed:* Basic Neurological Functions/ Intactness, Receptive Functions, Expressive Functions, and Cognitive Processes *6 item sets* (for different developmental ages) The set contains 11 to 13 items. *Age range:* 2 yr	(For 9- and 18-month item sets): 608 infants at five sites representative in terms of gender, ethnicity, region, and parental education (For 3-, 6-, 12-, and 24-month item sets): 595 infants who participated in the St. John's Hospital/ Southern Illinois University School of Medicine Developmental Continuity Clinic	*Internal Consistency Reliability:* 3 mo α = .73; 6 mo α = .83; 9 mo α = .84; 12 mo α = .73; 18 mo α = .83; and 24 mo α = .85 *Test-Retest Reliability:* r = .71 (3 mo), r = .83 (9 mo), and r = .84 (18 mo) *Construct Validity:* The BINS correlates with the *Bayley Scales of Infant Development-Second Edition* (BSID-II; Bayley, 1993) (median r = .6275 for Mental Development Index and median r = .465 for Psychomotor Development Index), the *Battelle Developmental Inventory* (Battelle; Newborg et al., 1988) (for 12 mo Communication r = .50, Cognitive r = .51 and motor r = .50), and the *Denver*		Aylward 1995; Bayley 1993

Test	Description	Sample	Psychometric Properties	Comments	References
Battelle Developmental Inventory and Screening Test (BDI); Newborg, Stock, Wnek, Guidubaldi, & Svinicki, 1984, Riverside Publishing	5 *domains*: personal-social, adaptive behavior, motor, communication, and cognitive skills; *Yields*: developmental quotient age scores for domains, subdomains, and total; *Age range*: 4 yr	800 children in 10 age groups from 0 to 95 mo (49 to 108 children per age group); Roughly gender-balanced, predominantly white and urban, quotas set to match 1981 U.S. Census Bureau data	II (Frankenberg et al., 1990). They assess cognitive, language, and motor development. *Internal Consistency for NSCAW*: Cronbach's α ranges from .73 to .84 for various age groups. *Test-retest reliability*: $r = .76$–.99, most above .90 (domains and total); *Construct validity*: high intercorrelations of domain and subdomain scores that support prediction of common rate of development; supported by factor analysis; *Concurrent validity*: with SB $r = .43$, with Vineland $r = .94$	No significant differences in performance by race or gender; No formal requirements for training; Validity data use old tests as criterion measures; concurrent validity uses small sample sizes; Long-term stability studies needed; Domains more accurate for children over 2 yr	Jens, Huber, Coop, 1993; Newborg et al., 1984; Oehler-Stinnett, 1989; Paget, 1989
Kaufman Brief Intelligence Test (K-BIT); Kaufman & Kaufman, 1990, American Guidance Service, Inc.	2 *subtests*: Vocabulary (expressive vocabulary and definitions) and Matrices (ability to perceive relationships and complete analogies); *Yields*: standard scores, percentile ranks, normal curve equivalents, stanines, and qualitative descriptions for Vocabulary and Matrices subtests as well as IQ Composite; *Age range*: ≥4 yr	2,022 individuals ages 4 to 92 yr with 105 to 116 children at yearly age intervals through 10 yr, 148 to 207 individuals at biyearly age intervals through 19 yr, 213 adults ages 20 to 34 yr, 172 adults ages 35 to 54 yr, and 115 adults ages 55 to 90 yr; Stratified by gender, geographic region, SES, and ethnicity; from 60 different locations in 29 states; not randomly selected but matched U.S. population in terms of gender, race, and ethnicity	*Internal consistency*: $r = .89$–.98, Mdn = .92 (Vocabulary), $r = .74$–.95, Mdn = .88 (Matrices), $r = .88$–.98, Mdn = .93 (IQ); *Test-retest reliability*: $r = .96$ (Vocabulary), $r = .80$ (Matrices), $r = .93$ (IQ) (adolescents 13 to 19 yr); $r = .97$ (Vocabulary), $r = .86$ (Matrices), $r = .95$ (IQ) (adults 20 to 54 yr); *Content validity*: domains correspond to distinctions found in full-length measures of intelligence (i.e., Wechsler,	Well-constructed brief measure of intelligence; State of the art procedures used for norming; Internal consistency estimates may be inflated due to items included below/above basal/ceiling; Validity studies not performed to examine uses recommended by authors (i.e., screening); Interpretation of standard scores for subjects over 20 yr questionable given small sample size of normative group	Kaufman & Kaufman, 1990; Miller, 1995

(continued)

Appendix Table 1.C (continued)

Social Competence/Relationships

Title, Author, Publisher, Date	General Description (Subtests, Score, Age, Time)	Standardization Sample	Psychometrics (Reliability and Validity)	Comments	References
			K-ABC, Stanford-Binet, and Woodcock-Johnson-Revised); subtests both found to be good measures of general intelligence; *Construct validity:* subtest intercorrelations indicate overlap but distinction in domains ($r = .38–.75$, Mdn = .58); mean scores of standardization sample show expected pattern of increases and decreases across age range; *Concurrent validity:* with K-ABC MPC $r = .58–.69$, with K-ABC Achievement $r = .74–.76$; with WISC-R Full-Scale IQ $r = .75$ and .80 *Internal Consistency for* NSCAW: $\alpha = .84$ (Composite), $\alpha = .76$ (Verbal), $\alpha = .79$ (Matrices)		
Preschool Language Scale-3 (PLS-3); Zimmerman, Steiner, & Pond, 1992, The Psychological Corporation	*3 scales:* Expressive Communication (EC), Auditory Comprehension (AC), and Total Language which include pre-linguistic skills (attention, vocal development, and social communication) and language skills (syntax, morphology, vocabulary,	1,200 children 2 wk to 6–11 yr with 50 to 100 at each of 14 age levels; Gender-balanced and stratified by parent education, geographic region, and ethnicity by 1986 U.S. Census Bureau data update	*Internal consistency:* Mdn $r = .84$ (EC), Mdn $r = .79$ (AC), Mdn $r = .88$ (Total); *Test-retest reliability:* $r = .82–.92$ (EC), $r = .89–.90$ (AC), $r = .91–.94$ (Total); *Interrater reliability:* 89%, $r = .98$ (EC); *Construct validity:*	Relies on observed behavior/ eliminates problems of parental report; Age norms through age 6; offers a single measure throughout early childhood; Spanish version and data available but more information	Jens, Huber, & Coop, 1993; Wallace & Roberts, 1995; Stark, 1972; Wallace & Roberts, 1995; Zimmerman, Steiner, & Pond, 1992

(continued)

	concept development); *Yields*: standard and age equivalent scores for all 3 scales; *Age range:* <6 yr		discriminates language disordered children 66%–80% of the time; *Concurrent validity:* with PLS-R r = .86 (EC), r = .66 (AC), r = .88 (Total); with CELF-R r = .69 (AC), r = .82 (EC and Total)	is needed about its validity; No published reviews; most original deficiencies have been corrected	Ware, Kosinski, & Keller, 1998

Parental Health

Short-Form Health Survey (SF-12); Ware, Kosinski & Keller, 1998	8 *health concepts* (12 items): physical functioning, role limitations due to physical health problems, bodily pain, general health, vitality (energy/fatigue), social functioning, role limitations due to emotional problems, and mental health (psychological distress and psychological well being) *Age range: all ages*	12 items were selected and scored from the SF-36 Health Survey from the National Survey of Functional Health Status (NSFHS) database. Also, the Medical Outcomes Study (MOS), an observational study of adult patients with chronic conditions provided data to cross-validate.	Test-Retest correlations: α = .89 (Physical component summary) and α = .76 (Mental component summary) Validity: In 14 validity tests involving physical criteria, relative validity estimates ranged from 0.43 to 0.93 (median = 0.67). In 6 tests involving mental criteria, relative validity estimates ranged from 0.60 to 1.07 (median = 0.97). *Internal Consistency for NSCAW:* α = .79 (Mental Health), α = .59 (Physical Health)		

Parent/Caregiver Attitudes and Behaviors

The Home Observation for Measurement of the Environment (HOME); NLSY Adaptation: Baker et al., 1993; Caldwell & Bradley, 1984, University of Arkansas-Little Rock	6–7 *scales*: Emotional and Verbal Responsivity, Acceptance of Child's Behavior, Organization of the Environment, Provision of Play Materials, Parental Involvement with Child, and Opportunities for Variety (Infant/Toddler); Learning Stimulation, Language	174 infants, with 67 age 4 to 12 mo, 59 age 13 to 24 mo, and 48 age 25 to 36 mo; 51% male and 66% African American with 59 families receiving public assistance and most parents high school graduates (Infant/Toddler); 117 preschool age children (Preschool)	Infant/Toddler *Internal consistency:* r = .89 (total), r = .44–.89, Mdn = .74 (subscales); *Stability:* r = .62 (total), r = .29–.62, Mdn = .42 (subscales) (6 and 12 mo); r = .64 (total), r = .27–.64, Mdn = .34 (subscales) (6 and 24 mo); r = .77 (total),	Used in over 200 published studies including studies of intellectual and academic attainment, SES, language competence, low birthweight/disabled children, cognitive development, social and behavioral development, health-related outcomes, family ecology, program evaluation;	Bradley & Caldwell, 1981; Bradley et al., 1979; Bradley, Caldwell & Elardo, 2001; Bradley, Corwin, Burchinal, McAdoo & Garcia-Coll, 2001; and Bradley, Corwin, McAdoo & Garcia-Coll 2001

Appendix Table 1.C (continued)

Social Competence/Relationships

Title, Author, Publisher, Date	General Description (Subtests, Score, Age, Time)	Standardization Sample	Psychometrics (Reliability and Validity)	Comments	References
	Stimulation, Physical Environment, Warmth and Affection, Academic Stimulation, and Modeling (Preschool); *Yields:* total and subscale scores with separate means and standard deviations for 6, 12, 24, 36 to 42, and 48 to 57 mo; *Age range:* <11 yr		$r = .30–.77$, Mdn = .56 (subscales) (12 and 24 mo); Preschool *Internal consistency:* $r = .93$ (total), $r = .53–.88$, Mdn = .67 (subscales); *Stability:* $r = .70$ (total), $r = .05–.70$, Mdn = .33 (subscales) (36 and 54 mo); Both *Construct validity:* scores associated with race ($r = -.09–(-).54$), crowding in the home ($r = -.19–(-).51$), and SES ($r = -.02–.31$); mothers with higher HOME scores talked and read to infants more and turned on TV less; *Predictive validity:* higher than distal measures of environment (including SES); associated with measures of language development and success in school *Internal Consistency for NSCAW:* Cronbach's alphas for children aged 2 years and younger are less than .45.	Effective across race and various specialized groups; Sensitive to interventions designed to improve mother-child interaction; Can provide user with in-depth understanding of quality of environment and lead to identification of aspects of the home in need of intervention Newly devised supplement for families living in impoverished urban environments with excellent reliability and validity.	

Measure	Domains / Age range	Sample	Reliability	References
Conflict Tactics Scale (CTS1); Straus, Gelles & Smith, 1990	*Domains:* Physical Violence Scale (Note: This is only one subdomain of the CTS1) *Age range:* Adults	Nationally representative sample of adults	Cronbach's alphas for 3–5 year olds range from .41 for Emotional Support to .71 for Physical Environment. For 6- to 10 year olds, Cronbach's alphas range from .48 for Cognitive Stimulation and Emotional Support to .74 for Physical Environment. *Reliability:* α = .88 The violence items have face or content validity since they all describe acts of actual physical force being used by one family member on another. *Internal Consistency for NSCAW:* α = .90 (Any Domestic Violence), .77 (Minor Violence), and .86 (Severe Violence)	Straus, Hamby, Boney-McCoy, & Sugarman 1996; Straus, 1990; Straus, Gelles & Smith, 1990
Parent-Child Conflict Tactics Scales (CTSPC); Straus, Hamby, Finkelhor, Moore, and Runyan, 1998	*6 scales:* nonviolent discipline, psychological aggression, physical assault, supplemental questions on discipline in the previous week, neglect, and sexual abuse *Age range:* all ages	Nationally representative sample of 1,000 U.S. children	*Alpha reliability:* $r = .55$ (Overall Physical Assault), $r = .60$ (Psychological Aggression), $r = .70$ (Nonviolent Discipline), $r = .22$ (Neglect), $r = -.02$ (Severe Physical Assault) *Test-retest reliability:* data not yet available for the CTSPC, it is available from the three studies using the parent-to-child physical assault scale of the original CTS.	The low internal consistency reliability of the severe assault scale is because the items measure rare events. Straus, Hamby, Finkelhor, Moore, & Runyan, 1998

(continued)

Appendix Table 1.C (continued)

Social Competence/Relationships

Title, Author, Publisher, Date	General Description (Subtests, Score, Age, Time)	Standardization Sample	Psychometrics (Reliability and Validity)	Comments	References
Contextual Factors					
Social Support Questionnaire (SSQ3); Sarason, Levine, Basham & Sarason, 1983	Three-item measure of social support that can be administered in a few minutes and is psychometrically sound. (Derived from original SSQ of 27 items, 2 parts each)	182 male and female undergraduates (47 women and 29 men were only tested once and 61 women and 45 men were retested to provide test-retest data)	*Internal reliability:* $\alpha = .75$ (SSQ3 number), $\alpha = .79$ (SSQ3 satisfaction) $\alpha = .97$ (SSQ number and satisfaction) *Validity:* Correlations of number— $r(100) = .84$ ($p < .001$) and satisfaction— $r(97) = .85$ ($p < .001$) Correlations of SSQ3 with SSQ: Number— $r = .81$ ($p < .001$) and Satisfaction— $r = .85$ Correlations of SSQ3 with adjusted (short-form items removed) SSQ: Number — $r(179) = .80$ ($p < .001$) and Satisfaction — $r(172) = .84$ ($p < .001$) There were significant negative correlations for women between the SSQ(Number) and SSQ(Satisfaction) measures of social support and measures of emotional discomfort, such as the MAACL (Three Multiple Adjective Affect Check List Scales) Anxiety, Depression, and Hostility scales. A similar result obtained for the LP (Lack of Protection scale) that dealt with recollections of separation anxiety in childhood. The EPI		Sarason, Levine, Basham, & Sarason, 1983; Sarason, Sarason, Shearin, & Pierce, 1987

Instrument	Description	Psychometrics	Comments	References
Duke-UNC Functional Social Support Questionnaire (FSSQ); Broadhead, Gelhbach, deGruy, & Kaplan. 1998	*2 scales:* confidant support and affective support *Yield:* total score (sum of response values) *Age range:* adults *Time required:* 5 min	(Eysenck Personality Inventory) Extraversion measure was negatively correlated only with SSQ(Number) only and Neuroticism measure was negatively correlated with SSQ (Satisfaction) in women. The results for men were in the same direction, but not as strong. *Internal Consistency for NSCAW:* Cronbach's alpha for Total score on child report = .97, with subscales ranging from .71 for Nonviolent Discipline to .97 for Total Physical Assault. Cronbach's alpha for Total score on caregiver report = .92, with subscales ranging from .66 for Psychological Aggression to .95 for Very Severe Physical Assault. *Test-retest reliability:* r = .66 (2-week) *Construct validity:* demonstrated by significant correlations with health and demographic variables known to be significant correlates of social support *Concurrent validity:* shown by significant correlation with 3 out of 4 previously described social activities measures	Original scale weak on instrumental support—2 items on instrumental support added for LONGSCAN, increasing questionnaire to 3 scales Short, simple, used at age 4 in LONGSCAN, acceptable reliability and validity	Broadhead, et al., 1989; Broadhead, Gehlbach, DeGruy, & Kaplan, 1998

Note: Some instruments were modified for use in NSCAW. For some other instruments, only specific subscales were used during data collection. For information about adaptations and use of specific subscales, see the instrument tables in Chapter 3 of the *Data File Users Manual* (Dowd et al., 2006). Psychometrics provided here are those that have been published about the full, original instrument; where available, Cronbach's alphas have been provided for NSCAW (Administration for Children and Families, 2005).

NOTES

1. *Substantiation* is the child welfare system's official case decision that allegations of child maltreatment are valid. In some states, a case disposition of *indicated* can be made when evidence of maltreatment exists but is insufficient to substantiate allegations.

2. The information in this section draws heavily from the *NSCAW Data File User's Manual* (Dowd et al., 2006); full explanations of all elements of the study can be found there.

3. The study design information in the rest of this chapter applies only to the CPS component. A fifth and final wave of data collection was conducted for the CPS cohort at approximately 5 to 6 years after baseline. In 2008, baseline data collection began for a new cohort of NSCAW (NSCAW II).

4. A fourth follow-up assessment (Wave 5), 59 to 96 months after the close of the investigation, was fielded in age cohorts and was completed in December 2007.

5. Only 15 states contributed data to NCANDs in 1999; project staff worked with each site not contributing NCANDS data to map their administrative systems data to the NCANDS definitions.

6. For details about the child, family, and caseworker constructs; the age of the child when instruments were administered; the data source; and the rationale for use in NSCAW, see Appendix Table B. For descriptions of the instruments used to measure child and family well-being, including the standardization sample and psychometric properties, see Appendix Table C.

7. The detailed results of this study can be found in the *NSCAW Combined Waves 1–4 Data File User's Manual* (Dowd et al., 2006).

8. Nonresponse at one wave triggered the extension of the reference period to the most recently completed interview for the next respondent. In other words, if no caregiver interview had been completed at 18 months but one was completed at 36 months, the reference period in the interview at 36 months was extended to include the entire period back to the completed 12-month interview. Although this approach may have minimized some types of item nonresponse, it raises issues of respondent recall accuracy for some types of behavior or experience.

REFERENCES

Achenbach, T. (1991a). *Manual for the Child Behavior Checklist 2-3 and 1991 Profile.* Burlington, VT: University of Vermont, Department of Psychiatry.

Achenbach, T. (1991b). *Manual for the Child Behavior Checklist 4-18 and 1991 Profile.* Burlington, VT: University of Vermont, Department of Psychiatry.

Achenbach, T. (1991c) *Manual for the Youth Self-Report and 1991 Profile.* Burlington, VT: University of Vermont, Department of Psychiatry.

Achenbach, T. (1991d) *Manual for the Teacher's Report form and 1991 Profile.* Burlington, VT: University of Vermont, Department of Psychiatry.

Administration for Children and Families. (2005). *National Survey of Child and Adolescent Well-Being (NSCAW): CPS sample component, Wave 1 data analysis report.* Retrieved January 7, 2009, from http://www.acf.hhs.gov/programs/opre/abuse_neglect/nscaw/reports/cps_sample/cps_report_revised_090105.pdf

Administration for Children and Families. (2007). Child maltreatment 2005. Retrieved February 9, 2009, from http://www.acf.hhs.gov/programs/cb/pubs/cm05/cm05.pdf

Asher, S. R., Hymel, S., & Renshaw, P. D. (1984). Loneliness in children. *Child Development*, 55, 456–464.

Asher, S. R. & Wheeler, V. A. (1985). Children's loneliness: A comparison of rejected and neglected peer status. *Consulting Clinical Psychology*, 53, 500–05.

Ayleward, G. P. (1995) *The Bayley Infant Neurodevelopmental Screener Manual*. San Antonio, TX: The Psychological Corporation.

Baker, P. C., Keck, C. K., Mott, F. L. & Quinlan, S. V. (1993). *NLSY Child Handbook: A Guide to the 1986-1990 National Longitudinal Survey of Youth Child Data*, Revised Edition. Columbus, Ohio: Center for Human Resource Research.

Bayley, N. (1993). *Bayley Scales of Infant Development, Second Edition: Manual*. San Antonio, TX: The Psychological Corporation.

Benes, K. M. (1995). Review of the social skills rating system. In J. C. Conoley & J. C. Impara (Eds.), *The twelfth mental measurements yearbook* (pp. 964–967). Lincoln, NE: Buros Institute of Mental Measurement.

Biemer, P. P., Chiflikyan, R., Dowd, K., & Smith, K. (2007). Using administrative records to evaluate the accuracy of child abuse reports in a national survey of child abuse and neglect. *Proceedings of the Survey Research Methods Section, American Statistical Association* Retrieved February 3, 2009, from http://www.amstat.org/sections/SRMS/Proceedings/y2007f.html

Biemer, P. P., Christ, S., & Wiesen, C. (2007). Scale score reliability in the National Survey of Child and Adolescent Well-being. *Proceedings of the Survey Methods Research Section, American Statistical Association* Retrieved February 3, 2009, from http://www.amstat.org/sections/SRMS/Proceedings/y2007f.html

Biemer, P. P., & Trewin, D. (1997). A review of measurement error effects on the analysis of survey data. In L. E. Lyberg, P. Biemer, M. Collins, E. deLeeuw & C. Dippo (Eds.), *Survey measurement and process quality*. New York: Wiley.

Bollen, K. A. (1989). *Structural equations with latent variables*. New York: Wiley.

Bradley, R. H. and Caldwell, B. (1981). The HOME Inventory: A validation of the preschool scale for black children. *Child Development, 52*, 708–710.

Bradley, R. H., Caldwell, B., & Elardo, R. (1979). Home environment and cognition development in the first two years: A cross-lagged panel analysis. *Developmental Psychology, 15*, 246–250.

Bradley, R. H., Corwyn, R., Burchinal, M., McAdoo, H., & Garcia Coll, C. (2001).The home environments of children in the United States: Part II. Relations with behavioral development through age thirteen. *Child Development, 72*, 1868–1886.

Bradley, R. H., Corwyn, R., McAdoo, H., & Garcia Coll, C. (2001).The home environments of children in the United States: Part I. Variations by age, ethnicity, and poverty status. *Child Development, 72*, 1844–1867.

Briere, J. (1996). *Trauma Symptom Checklist for Children: Professional manual*. Florida: Psychological Assessment Resources Inc.

Briere J. & Lanktree, C. B. (1995). *The Trauma Symptom Checklist for Children (TSCC): Preliminary psychometric characteristics*. Unpublished manuscript. Los Angeles, California: University of Southern California School of Medicine, Department of Psychiatry.

Broadhead, W. E., Gehlbach, S. H., DeGruy, F. V., and Kaplan, B. H. (1988). Duke-UNC Functional Social Support Questionnaire: Measurement of social support in family medicine patients. *Medical Care, 26*, 709–723.

Broadhead, W. E., Gehlbach, S. H., DeGruy, F. V., and Kaplan, B. H. (1989). Functional versus structural social support and health care utilization in a family medicine outpatient practice. *Medical Care, 27,* 221–233.

Brock, D. M., *Sarason,* I. G., & Pierce, G. R. (1987). A brief measure of social support: Practical and theoretical implications. *Social and Personal Relationships, 4,* 497–510.

Caldwell, B. & Bradley, R. (1984). *Home observation for measurement of the environment (HOME)—revised edition.* Little Rock, AR: University of Arkansas.

Carroll, R. J., Ruppert, D., & Stefanski, L. A. (1995). *Measurement error in nonlinear models.* London: Chapman & Hall, CRC.

Cassidy, J. & Asher, S. R. (1992). Loneliness and peer relations in young children. *Child Development, 6,* 350–365.

Connell, J. P. (1990). Context, self, and action: A motivational analysis of self-system processes across the life span. In D. Cicchetti & M. Beeghly (Eds.), *The self in transition.* Chicago: University of Chicago Press

Dowd, K., Kinsey, S., Wheeless, S., Thissen, R., Richardson, J., Suresh, R., et al. (2006). *National Survey of Child and Adolescent Well-Being combined Waves 1-4 data file users' manual, restricted release version.* Ithaca, NY: National Data Archive on Child Abuse and Neglect, Cornell University.

Elliott, S. N. & Busse, R. T. (*1992*). Review of the Child Behavior Checklist. In J. Kramer & J. Conoley (Eds.), *The eleventh mental measurements* yearbook. Lincoln, NE: Buros Institute of Mental Measurement.

Fuller, W. A. (1987). *Measurement error models.* New York: Wiley.

Fox, N. A. & Leavitt, L. A. (1995). *The Violence Exposure Scale for Children (VEX).* College Park: University of Maryland.

Freeman, B. J. & Kelley, M. L. (*1985*). Review of Child Behavior Checklist. In J. V. Mitchell, Jr. (Ed.), *The ninth mental measurements yearbook.* Lincoln, NE: Buros Institute of Mental Measurement.

Gresham, F. M & Elliot, S. N. (1990). *Social Skills Rating System.* Circle Pines, MN: American Guidance Service.

Heinen, T. (1996). *Latent class and discrete latent trait models: Similarities and differences.* Thousand Oaks, CA: Sage Publications.

Helsel, W. J. and Matson, J. L., 1984. The assessment of depression in children: The internal structure of the Child Depression Inventory (CDI). *Behavior Research and Therapy, 22,* 289–298.

Hodges K. & Craighead W. E. (1990). Relationship of Children's. Depression Inventory factors to diagnosed depression. *Psychological Assessment, 2,* 489–492

Hubert, N., Wachs, T., Peters-Martin, P., & Gandour, M. J. (1982). The study of early temperament: Measurement and conceptual issues. *Child Development, 53,* 571–600.

Jens, K., Huber, C., & Coop, K. (1993). *Screening and assessment instruments for use with young children, 0–36 months of age.* Chapel Hill, NC: The Clinical Center for the Study of Development and Learning.

Kaufman, A. & Kaufman, N. (1990). *Kaufman Brief Intelligence Test (K-BIT): Expressive vocabulary, definitions, and matrices.* Circle Pines, Minn.: American Guidance Service.

Kessler, R. C., Andrews, G., Mroczek, D., Ustun, B., & Wittchen, H-U, (1998). The World Health Organization Composite International Diagnostic Interview Short-Form (CIDI-SF). *International Journal of Methods in Psychiatric Research, 7,* 171–185.

Kovacs, M. (1992). *Children's Depression Inventory.* North Tonawanda, NY: Multi-Health.

Miller, M. D. (1995). Kaufman Brief Intelligence Test. In J. J. Kramer & J. C. Conoley (Eds.), *The twelfth mental measurements yearbook.* Lincoln, NE: Buros Institute of Mental Measurement.

Newborg, J., Stock, J. R., Wnek, L., Guidibaldi, J. E., & Svinicki, J (1984). *Battelle Developmental Inventory, with recalibrated technical data and norms: Examiner's manual.* Rolling Meadows, IL: Riverside Publishing.

Oehler-Stinnett, J. (1989). Review of the Battelle Developmental Inventory. In J. C. Conoley and J. J. Kramer (Eds.), *The tenth mental measurements yearbook.* Lincoln, NE: Buros Institute of Mental Measurement.

Paget, K. D. (1989). Review of the Battelle Developmental Inventory. In J. C. Conoley and J. J. Kramer (Eds.), *The tenth mental measurements yearbook.* Lincoln, NE: Buros Institute of Mental Measurement.

Parkhurst, J. T., & Asher, S. R. (1992). Peer rejection in middle school: Subgroup differences in behavior, loneliness, and interpersonal concerns. *Developmental Psychology, 28,* 231–241.

Raviv, O. Erel, N. A. Fox, L. A. Leavitt, Alona Raviv, I. Dar, A. Shahinfar, C. W. Greenbaum (2001). Exposure to everyday violence among Israeli elementary school children: Effects of context and situation on child behavior. *Journal of Community Psychology, 29,* 117–140.

Rothbart, M. K. (1981). Measurement of temperament in infancy. *Child Development, 52,* 569–578.

Rothbart, M. K. & Mauro, J. A. (1990). Questionnaire approaches to the study of infant temperament. In J. W. Fagan & J. Colombo (Eds.), *Individual Differences in Infancy: Reliability, Stability, and Prediction.* Hillsdale, NJ: Erlbaum.

Sarason, I. G., Levine, H. M., Basham, R. B. & Sarason, B.R. (1983). Assessing social support: The Social Support Questionnaire. *Personality and Social Psychology, 44,* 127–139.

Sarason, I. G., Sarason, B. R., Shearin, E. N., & Pierce, G. R. (1987). A brief measure of social support: Practical and theoretical implications. *Journal of Social and Personal Relationships, 4,* 497–410.

Sattler, J. M. (1992). *Assessment of children (revised and updated third edition).* San Diego, CA: Jerome Sattler.

Saylor, C. F., Finch, A. J., Baskin, C. H., Furey, W. and Kelly, M. M. (1984). Construct validity for measures of childhood depression: Application of multitrait-multimethod methodology. *Journal of Consulting & Clinical Psychology, 52,* 977–985.

Shahinfar, A., Fox, N. A., & Leavitt, L. A. (2000). Preschool children's exposure to violence: Relation of behavior problems to parent and child reports. *American Journal of Orthopsychiatry, 70,* 115–125.

Sparrow, S. S., Balla, D. A., Cicchetti, D. V. (1984). *Vreeland Adaptive Behavior Scales.* Circle Pine, MN: American Guidance Services.

Sparrow, S., Carter, A. S., and Cicchetti, D.V. (1993). *Vineland Screener: Overview, reliability, validity, administration, and scoring.* New Haven, Conn.: Yale University Child Study Center.

Stark, J. (1972). *Preschool Language Scale.* In O. K. Buros (Ed.), *The seventh mental measurements yearbook. (Vol. 2).* Highland Park, NJ: Gryphon Press.

Straus, M., Gelles, R., & Smith, C. (1990). *Physical violence in American families: Risk factors and adaptations to violence in 8,145 families.* New Brunswick, NJ: Transaction Publishers.

Straus, M. A., Hamby, S. L., Boney-McCoy, S., Sugarman, D. B. (1996). The revised Conflict Tactics Scales (CTS2): Development and preliminary psychometric data. *Journal of Family Issues, 17,* 283–316.

Straus, M., Hamby, S. L., Finkelor, D., Moore, D., & Runyan, D. (1998). Identification of child maltreatment with the Parent-Child Conflict Tactics Scales: Development and psychometric data for a national sample of American parents. *Child Abuse & Neglect,* 22, 249–270.

Straus, M. A., Hamby, S. L., Finkelhor, D., Moore, D. W., & Runyan, D. (1998). Identification of child maltreatment with the Parent–Child Conflict Tactics Scales: Development and psychometric data for a national sample of American parents. *Child Abuse & Neglect, 22*(4), 249–270.

Vermunt, J. (1996). *Log-linear models for event histories.* Thousand Oaks, CA: Sage Publications.

Ware, J., Kosinski, M., & Keller, S. (1998). *How to score the SF-12 Physical and Mental Health Summary Scales,* 3rd ed. Lincoln, RI: Quality Metric Incorporated.

Wellborn, J., Connell, J., & Pierson, L. (1987). *The Rochester Assessment Package for School— Student, Teacher and Parent Report: Technical Report.* Rochester, NY: University of Rochester.

Woodcock, R. W., McGrew, K. S., & Werder, J. K. (1994). *Woodcock-McGrew-Werder Mini-Battery of Achievement.* Itasca, IL: Riverside Publishing.

Woroby, J. & Blajda, V. (1989). Temperament ratings at 2 weeks, 2 months, and 1 year: Differential stability of activity and emotionality. *Developmental Psychology, 25,* 257–263.

Zimmerman, I. L., Steiner, V. G., & Pond, R. P. (1992). *Preschool Language Scale-3.* San Antonio, TX: The Psychological Corporation.

PART I

Moving Toward a Developmental Framework in Child Welfare

Despite a lack of clarity as to what constitutes the well-being of children involved in the child welfare system and what service sector is responsible for its promotion, child well-being is explicitly addressed in current federal legislation, specifically the Adoption and Safe Families Act of 1997 (ASFA). Child welfare scholars have suggested that a developmental approach to measuring child well-being would benefit the child welfare field. For example, Wulczyn, Barth, Yuan, Jones Harden, and Landsverk (2005) assert that children should be assessed when child welfare services start and should persist so the impact of services on their development can be assessed. Seaberg (1990) has identified objective observation and developmental modification as essential characteristics of child well-being measurement. In their argument for the inclusion of child well-being measures in foster care administrative databases, Altshuler and Gleeson (1999) suggest that child well-being measures for the child welfare population should be developmentally focused, be repeatedly administered, have multiple sources of data, and be easy to use for caseworkers.

Such empirical and practice models for the assessment of child well-being have been described in the developmental literature, which has a long history of documenting the trajectories of children from high-risk backgrounds. From the end of the twentieth century through the beginning of the twenty-first century, developmentally oriented research has contributed substantially to the documentation of outcomes for children involved in the child welfare system. Specifically, this research has produced a solid evidentiary base on the developmental sequelae of child maltreatment. More recently, developmental researchers have begun to study the functioning of children in foster care. These studies, however, often rely on convenience samples from mental health or other specialty clinics, where high rates of impairments in children would be expected. In addition, the research is often cross-sectional rather than longitudinal, failing to profile children's long-term trajectories. Few studies have been based on populations of children involved in the child welfare system. Furthermore, these studies rarely address the linkages between children's developmental trajectory and their child welfare trajectory—linkages such as the influence of quality and stability of the home environment on their well-being.

Despite these caveats, the developmental literature offers a solid foundation on which to base empirical, practice-centered strategies for assessing child well-being. Specifically, the literature has identified salient constructs—across multiple domains of development—that predict long-term outcomes. The role of contextual variables in children's development, such as family risks and involvement with service systems, has been addressed also from conceptual and methodological perspectives (Bronfenbrenner & Morris, 1998). Additionally, developmental scientists have established a wide array of empirically validated tools to measure various arenas of child functioning. These tools are designed to garner data at multiple points during childhood and from multiple sources. Many allow child well-being to be assessed by an objective observer. Some have been adapted for use by professionals on the "front line"; typically these instruments are easy to administer, yet they retain psychometric rigor. In short, the measurement of child well-being has advanced significantly, in part because of the integration of various strands of the social science literature into child welfare research.

The National Survey of Child and Adolescent Well-Being (NSCAW) has benefitted from a developmental framework to provide rich evidence on the well-being of a nationally representative sample of children in the child welfare system. From the study's inception, a major goal of NSCAW has been to examine the linkage between children's developmental trajectories and their child welfare trajectories. To this end, data were collected from children's caregivers, from children's caseworkers, and from the children themselves. The well-being of children was measured in the domains of physical health, intellectual functioning, language functioning, academic skills, and mental health. Furthermore, the developmental impact of family risk, placement stability and duration, and other child welfare–specific variables was examined. The NSCAW study has yielded a massive corpus of evidence on the developmental and child welfare experiences of a national probability sample of children.

This study has confirmed findings from numerous smaller studies that children involved in the child welfare system are particularly vulnerable. No other study before it has addressed the methodological issues (e.g., convenience sampling) that decreased the credibility of previous findings in this regard. Additionally, the broad range of developmental outcomes examined in NSCAW has permitted an examination of the functioning of the *whole child* at multiple ages. The longitudinal nature of the study has permitted an assessment of well-being across time, providing one of the only data sets documenting developmental trajectories of children. Finally, the focus on child welfare variables, such as placement type and duration, has enabled documentation of the pernicious effect of these systemic variables on children's outcomes, which had not been previously achieved in child welfare research. The NSCAW study is a substantial contribution to the knowledge base about the well-being of children involved in the child welfare system and about the role of the child welfare system itself in promoting or inhibiting child well-being.

In order to produce the rich array of findings on child well-being, the NSCAW study had to attend to the definitional and measurement challenges related to this construct in the field of child welfare. A developmental heuristic allowed the study designers to view well-being through a perspective on child functioning that emphasized cross-domain, cross-time, and cross-environment developmental outcomes. This heuristic ensured that tools used to assess child well-being were well-established measures in the developmental field, including child and caregiver self-reports, direct child assessments, and researcher observations. Consequently, NSCAW has become a model for the field in adapting developmentally oriented methods and measurement tools for research on the impact of this particular service sector on children's functioning or well-being.

The chapters constituting Part 1 extend NSCAW's young legacy as the premier venue for obtaining and creating knowledge on the well-being of children in the child welfare system. Jones Harden, Vick, Hancock, and Wang (Chapter 2) focus on the development of young children by examining the influence of the early caregiving environment on children's developmental outcomes during the preschool period. Developmentalists have identified the early childhood period as particularly important for children's language and social development, as well as for their readiness for formal schooling. This chapter documents the contribution of the early caregiving environment to these outcomes, identifying in particular factors related to the children's child welfare experiences.

In Chapter 3, Shaffer, Egeland, and Wang consider a major developmental construct—*resilience*—defined as adaptation in the face of adversity. This chapter identifies the contribution of various child welfare and other ecological variables to cross-domain adaptation in a subsample of children who entered the NSCAW study during middle childhood. Although the multiple, profound adversities experienced by children in the child welfare system do render them vulnerable, this chapter documents that many of these children exhibit age-appropriate functioning.

Gardner, Kelleher, Pajer, and Wang (Chapter 5) examine the impact of an adverse family risk—intimate-partner violence (IPV)—on externalizing behavior problems in children across developmental stages (i.e., 4 to 16 years of age). Notably, their sample includes only children living with their birth parents, an underserved and less understood component of the child welfare population. This chapter emphasizes the importance of addressing IPV in child welfare services aimed at reducing rates of child maltreatment and levels of child psychopathology.

Similarly, Izzo, Smith, Eckenrode, Beimer, and Christ (Chapter 4) use children's externalizing behavior problems as an outcome variable, but only within an adolescent subsample. In contrast to the Gardner et al. chapter, this chapter examines the influence of physical abuse on behavior problems, combining reports from multiple sources to determine the existence of abuse. The finding that youth self-report of physical abuse was the reporting source most predictive of behavior problems informs a measurement perspective, as well as an understanding of the developmental trajectories of physically abused adolescents.

The trifecta of safety, permanency, and well-being has been the child welfare field's basis for policy, practice, and research; however, the efforts to understand and promote child well-being lag far behind child welfare initiatives regarding safety and permanency. Evidence from NSCAW, such as that reported in the studies composing this volume, can inform child welfare policy and practice debates so that a clearer definition of *child well-being* can be attained and the role of the child welfare service sector in promoting child well-being can be delineated. Given its prominence in current child welfare policy and practice, the construct *child well-being* represents a fertile frontier for research. Drawing from other empirical foundations, most notably developmental science, researchers have been able to amass a rich corpus of evidence about the well-being of children who have been maltreated and placed in foster care. The NSCAW study has addressed many of the methodological problems in these previous studies and has permitted researchers to disseminate solid evidence on the well-being of children sampled from the child welfare system.

As NSCAW matures it will provide data about a wider range of child functioning (e.g., biological data), data on well-being in early adulthood, and more precise data about the impact of child welfare experiences on children's well-being. Already NSCAW has verified that children enter the child welfare system with compromised developmental functioning and that specific child welfare experiences can negatively affect their well-being. Involvement with the child welfare system should be an opportunity to remedy the compromised developmental trajectories of this group of vulnerable children. It is hoped that child welfare policy makers, administrators, and practitioners will avail themselves of the lessons from NSCAW and other studies to help establish policy and practice effectively promoting child well-being.

REFERENCES

Altshuler, S., & Gleeson, J. (1999). Completing the evaluation triangle for the next century: Measuring child "well-being" in family foster care. *Child Welfare, 78*(1), 125–147.

Bronfenbrenner, U., & Morris, P. (1998). The ecology of development process. In W. Damon & R. Lerner (Eds.), *Handbook of child psychology: Vol. 1. Theoretical models of human development* (5th ed., pp. 993–1028). New York: Wiley.

Seaberg, J. (1990). Child well-being: A feasible concept? *Social Work, 35*(3), 267–272.

Wulczyn, F., Barth, R. P., Yuan, Y. T., Jones Harden, B., & Landdsverk, J. (2005). *Beyond common sense: Child welfare, child well-being, and the evidence for policy reform.* New Brunswick, NJ: Aldine Transaction.

2

Quality of the Early Caregiving Environment and Preschool Well-Being

An Examination of Children Entering the Child Welfare System During Infancy

BRENDA JONES HARDEN, JESSICA VICK WHITTAKER,
GREGORY HANCOCK, AND KEVIN WANG

The benefit of a high-quality caregiving environment to young children's later development is both intuitively compelling and empirically documented. Conversely, a low-quality home environment during the early years tends to hinder child well-being in cognitive and socioemotional domains (Bradley, Corwin, McAdoo, & Garcia Coll, 2001). Impaired parenting, in particular, in its extreme form manifested as child maltreatment, has pernicious effects on child outcomes (Azar, 2002).

Adopting an ecological range of perspectives, researchers have assessed the effects of the caregiving environment at both the micro level (e.g., parental characteristics) and the macro level (e.g., societal characteristics). Despite the resulting large body of evidence supporting the developmental importance of early environment for all children, few studies have been devoted specifically to the effects of the early environment on the functioning of children entering the child welfare system because of allegations of child maltreatment. This population is uniquely vulnerable, however, to a host of environmental risks, including poverty, parental psychopathology, and impaired parenting (Brown, Cohen, Johnson, & Salzinnger, 1998; Scannapieco & Connell-Carrick, 2005). Particularly vulnerable are children who enter the child welfare system as infants.

Infancy and the Child Welfare System

Infancy comprises the most rapid and complex development of the human organism (Bornstein & Lamb, 1992). Paradoxically, it is a time of extreme opportunity for children but is also a time of extreme vulnerability, particularly for those reared in high-risk environments (Shonkoff & Phillips, 2000). Within this developmental context, children entering the child welfare system as infants have caregiving and service experiences that are distinct (see Jones Harden, 2007). More extensive study of the epidemiologic and developmental trends for this population must be undertaken to inform child welfare policy and practice concerning very young children and their families.

From an epidemiologic perspective, infants in the child welfare system are distinguishable in various ways from their older counterparts (for a review, see Jones Harden, 2007). They are more likely to be maltreated, to experience a recurrence of maltreatment, and to die from maltreatment, particularly if they are under 1 year of age (Administration for Children and Families, 2007; National Clearinghouse on Child Abuse and Neglect Information, 2004). In the National Survey of Child and Adolescent Well-Being (NSCAW) sample, infants had a higher likelihood of all forms of maltreatment except sexual abuse (Administration for Children and Families, 2005). Neglect is particularly pernicious for infants, with consequences perhaps more deleterious for them than for older children (Erickson & Egeland, 2002). The foster care placement rate for infants is significantly higher than that for the older children as well: In the NSCAW study, approximately a quarter of the foster care population comprised children younger than 2 years old (Administration for Children and Families, 2005). These higher placement rates have been attributed to caseworkers' concerns about infants' vulnerability, specifically infants' inability to protect themselves in situations of maltreatment (e.g., disclose their maltreatment, seek help from another adult; Barth, 1997; Wulczyn, 2004). A final distinct trend for infants, although arguably more positive than those delineated previously, is that the rates of adoption are markedly higher for infants than they are for older children (Wulczyn, Kogan, & Dilts, 2001).

Emerging research is beginning to document the developmental vulnerability of infants in the child welfare system across a variety of outcomes, including physical health, cognitive and language skills, and socioemotional functioning (for a review, see Jones Harden, 2007). The NSCAW study, for example, found that more than half of children younger than age 2 were at risk for developmental delay (Administration for Children and Families, 2003, 2005). Smaller, cross-sectional studies have reported similarly high rates of developmental delay, speci-fically with regard to early cognition (e.g., Leslie, Gordon, Ganger, & Gist, 2002); however, few studies have traced the effects of early child welfare involvement on the cognitive abilities of these infants at older ages. A notable exception is the longitudinal research conducted on families with neglected children, in which early experiences of social deprivation were associated with later cognitive and academic difficulties (Erickson, Egeland, & Pianta, 1989).

As with cognitive abilities, for infants and young children in the child welfare system limited evidence exists regarding language functioning. In a unique study of maltreatment and language development, maltreated toddlers showed a shorter mean length of utterance, a more limited expressive vocabulary, and shorter bouts of contingent discourse during play sessions than lower socioeconomic-status-matched controls (Coster, Gersten, Beeghly, & Cicchetti, 1989). Data from NSCAW show that infants in child welfare have language skills less advanced than expected for children their age. Although no differences in language competence were associated with particular types of maltreatment or types of placement, language delays were found in 14% of young maltreated children (Administration for Children and Families, 2005), compared to prevalence rates ranging from 2.3% to 19% reported overall for preschoolers (Nelson, Nygrem, & Panoscha, 2006).

In the socioemotional domain, most studies of infants in the child welfare system have focused on their attachment to caregivers. A long line of research on maltreated infants has documented their insecure attachment patterns, more specifically "disorganized" attachment behaviors (Carlson, Cicchetti, Barnett, & Braunwald, 1989; Egeland & Sroufe, 1981). Similarly, infants in foster care have shown insecure attachments to their substitute caregivers (Dozier, Stovall, Albus, & Bates, 2001). Related evidence on parent–infant interaction in child welfare populations has suggested impaired relationships between maltreating parents and their children (Larrieu & Zeanah, 2004). Foster parents not evincing an emotional commitment to children have also been found to have problematic interactions with the infants in their care (Dozier et al., 2001).

Far more limited is the literature on other indicators of the socioemotional functioning of infants in the child welfare system. Although research suggests higher rates of behavioral problems in older maltreated children (e.g., Dodge, Pettit, & Bates, 1997), this construct rarely extends to infants and young children in the child welfare system. The limited evidence suggests higher rates of behavioral problems for young children in the child welfare system (Black et al., 2002); however, the literature tracing the effects of the early caregiving environment on other socioemotional outcomes (e.g., social skills) remains scarce.

Early Home Environments and Young Children in the Child Welfare System

Although few studies have focused on the global characteristics of the caregiving environments of young children in the child welfare system, a plethora of research has documented links between quality of care and the functioning of children beset by other risk factors. For example, the risk factor of family instability has been found to be particularly detrimental to young children also living in poverty (Jones Harden, 2004). Moreover, impaired parenting is both more likely to occur in impoverished households and more likely to produce negative developmental outcomes for the children (McLoyd, 1998). Studies based on cumulative risk models have documented that, as the number and intensity of the environmental risks increase, their impact on child outcomes is strengthened (e.g., Appleyard, Egeland, van Dulmen, & Sroufe, 2005).

Numerous studies have addressed the influence of home-environment quality as a whole on outcomes for children in the general population (Bradley, 1994). Recent research has documented that the home environments of children from families with notable risk factors are particularly compromised and particularly disadvantageous for child outcomes. For example, the quality of the home environments of young children tends to diminish if they are reared in poverty (Bradley et al., 2001); moreover, the link between the home environment and behavioral outcomes is stronger for children from impoverished families than for other groups (Bradley et al., 2001).

Because children and families in the child welfare system are subject to multiple risk factors affecting and affected by the caregiving environment, studies specifically addressing the caregiving environments these children face are urgently needed. Evidence from studies of maltreated children indicates that parental psychopathology and impaired parenting deleteriously affect child outcomes (Azar, 2002; Black et al., 2002; Lyons-Ruth, Alpern, & Repacholi, 1993). Unfortunately, these studies have relied primarily on convenience samples and have not typically drawn their samples from child welfare agencies. Similarly, the limited evidence on foster family environments has documented the contribution of parental psychological functioning and parenting behaviors to child outcomes (e.g., Orme & Beuhler, 2001), but they have not typically addressed other factors critical to a positive caregiving environment, factors such as number of children in the home and parents' provision of learning stimulation. New linkages must be forged between child welfare–specific factors and global factors related to caregiving environments as experienced by children in the child welfare system.

A small body of research has examined how children's developmental outcomes are influenced by some highly specific parenting and child welfare variables, such as maltreatment type, placement stability, and placement type. Although this evidence is somewhat ambiguous, it merits examination. Evidence from a major longitudinal study suggests that infants who are neglected may be more vulnerable to cognitive and language delays than infants who experience physical abuse or other maltreatment types (Erickson & Egeland, 2002; Erickson et al., 1989).

The data on placement stability suggest an overwhelmingly negative developmental impact of multiple placement transitions (Jones Harden, 2004; Ryan & Testa, 2005; Wulczyn, Kogan, & Jones Harden, 2003); however, these findings emanate primarily from studies of older children. A recent study of young children with and without prenatal drug exposure, who were not necessarily in the child welfare system, documented that instability of living arrangements was associated with higher rates of behaviorial problems and lower adaptive functioning (Bada et al., 2008).

Some research into placement type has found that young children make developmental gains when they are placed in foster care (e.g., Horwitz, Balestracci, & Simms, 2001). Others suggest that, because children who are placed tend to be the ones rescued from the harshest initial situations, they are more likely to have compromised developmental outcomes (Leslie et al., 2002; Rutter, 2000). Studies comparing nonkinship foster care to kinship foster care have found that children in kinship care have better developmental outcomes, though this finding may reflect kinship caregivers' tendency to select into their care children who are already higher functioning (Geen, 2004).

A few studies have looked beyond individual parenting variables to examine more global characteristics of the caregiving environments of young children in the child welfare system. For example, Linares, Motalto, Rosbruch, and Li (2006) found no differences between the home environments provided by biological parents and those provided by foster caregivers. Berger (2004) used home environment as a proxy for maltreatment risk and found that lower-income and single-parent mothers were more likely than others to provide poor-quality home environments. In their preliminary study of mothers at high risk for abusing their children, Weberling, Forgays, and Crain-Thoreson (2003) documented home environments that were concomitantly compromised. Finally, one study of foster families has linked compromised home environments to poorer child outcomes (Jones Harden, Clyman, & Vick, 2007).

Data Set Characteristics, Test Variables, and Goals

Lack of a nationally representative sample has limited the conclusions that can be drawn about infants in the child welfare system and their subsequent developmental outcomes. Because NSCAW is nationally representative, is longitudinal, and oversampled infants, its data set affords researchers a new opportunity to address specific gaps in the literature on infants and young children in the child welfare system. Using NSCAW data, we examined the associations between the early caregiving environments experienced by children who entered the child welfare system as infants and their outcomes as preschoolers. Factors specific to child welfare and the early caregiving environment (i.e., type of maltreatment, number of placements, type of placement) were investigated, as were other, more global characteristics of caregiving environments (i.e., number of children in the home, level of cognitive stimulation, emotional support). The influence of these factors on preschool outcomes was investigated across four developmental domains: cognition, language, social skills, and behavioral problems.

Four hypotheses were proposed: *(1)* Physical abuse and neglect experienced during infancy would negatively affect preschool children's well-being; *(2)* placement stability during infancy would positively affect preschool children's well-being; *(3)* foster care placement, overall, and nonkinship foster home environments, in particular, would be associated with compromised outcomes for preschool children; and *(4)* a high-quality early home environment (i.e., fewer children in the home, cognitive stimulation, emotional support) would positively affect preschool children's well-being.

Methods

Our analyses were on NSCAW data from baseline, Wave 2 (12-month follow-up), Wave 3 (18-month follow-up), and Wave 4 (36-month follow-up) child assessments and interviews with caregivers. Children who were 24 months old or younger at baseline were selected for these analyses, which yielded a sample of 1,720 infants. At the Wave 4 data collection, children's mean age was 44.46 months ($SD = 6.34$). Children in this sample were primarily white (52.8%) and black or African American (29.7%). Most of the children lived at home with their primary caregiver (78.2%); however, 12.2% lived with relatives, and 9.2% lived with nonkin foster families. In terms of gender, the sample was almost equally divided (49.2% female).[1]

Measures

CAREGIVER AND CHILD BACKGROUND CHARACTERISTICS Caregivers were asked to respond to a series of questionnaires about family composition (e.g., number of children in home) and caregiver demographic characteristics (e.g., age, race/ethnicity, marital status, education, and employment). Developed for the NSCAW study, a questionnaire was also administered to caregivers to elicit the characteristics of the children, including race/ethnicity, gender, height, weight, and, for children younger than age 4, head circumference. The NSCAW Case Initiation Database was designed to verify children's demographic information and whether they were in out-of-home care. Additionally, caregivers were asked to report on their children's health—specifically, to rate their child's overall health on a scale from *excellent* to *poor*.

CHILD PLACEMENT Throughout the study, child welfare system caseworkers provided information about the children's living situations. From these data several variables were derived, including the child's total number of placements and placement status at specific interview points. Placement data used in the current study are total number of placements at Time II based on caseworker interview.

QUALITY OF THE HOME ENVIRONMENT The quality and extent of stimulation and support in the home environment were measured with the Home Observation for Measurement of the Environment—Short Form (HOME-SF; Caldwell & Bradley, 1984). The HOME-SF was designed for the National Longitudinal Survey of Youth (NLSY) in consultation with the author of the original measure, Robert Bradley. The HOME-SF comprises both interview and observation items and yields two subscores, one measuring the cognitive stimulation of the child's environment and the other measuring the emotional relationship between the mother and the child. Good internal consistency has been reported for the HOME total score ($r = .80$), though coefficients for the subscales range from .30 to .80. Previous studies using the NLSY have demonstrated the reliability and construct validity of the HOME-SF.

MALTREATMENT TYPE   Children's experiences with maltreatment were assessed with a modification of the Maltreatment Classification System (MCS; Barnett, Manly, & Cicchetti, 1993). The Limited-MCS was used to collect data on five dimensions of maltreatment: the number of types, the combination of types, the severity of the most serious type, the child's age at onset of maltreatment, and the relationship to the child of the person responsible for the maltreatment. These data were collected in an interview with the caseworker who worked most closely with the child. The caseworker identified all the types of maltreatment recorded in the allegation preceding the child welfare system's maltreatment investigation. The most serious type of maltreatment was coded in greater detail.

COGNITIVE DEVELOPMENT   Depending on the child's age, one of two measures was used to assess cognitive development. The cognitive functioning of children younger than 4 years was measured with the Battelle Developmental Inventory and Screening Test (BDI; Newborg, Stock, & Wnek, 1988). Although this measure assesses children's functioning in five domains, for this study only the cognitive domain was administered. The test-retest reliability ranges from .90 to .99. Concurrent validity with the Vineland Adaptive Behavior Scales (Sparrow, Balla, & Cicchetti, 1984) has been established ($r = .94$; Newborg, Stock, Wnek, Guildubaldi, & Svinicki, 1984).

The Kaufman Brief Intelligence Test (K-BIT; Kaufman & Kaufman, 1990) was used to measure the cognitive functioning of children aged 4 years or older. It comprises a Vocabulary Subtest and a Matrices Subtest, as well as an IQ Composite; the composite measure was used for these analyses. The K-BIT yields standard scores for each child and was standardized on a sample that matched the U.S. population in terms of gender, race, and ethnicity. Vocabulary internal consistency ranges from .89 to .98; Matrices internal consistency, from .74 to .95; and IQ Composite internal consistency, from .88 to .98. Reported test-retest reliability is high; content validity and concurrent validity with other intelligence tests have been established (Kaufman & Kaufman, 1990).

LANGUAGE DEVELOPMENT   Analyses of communication skills were based on children's Total Language score from the Preschool Language Scale–3 (PLS-3; Zimmerman, Steiner, & Pond, 1992). The scale measures prelinguistic and language skills in children from birth to age 6 and is composed of three subscales: Expressive Communication, Auditory Comprehension, and Total Language. Internal consistency for the total scale is, on average, high ($M = .87$); reported reliability ranges from .91 to .94. Concurrent validity has been established with several other measures of children's language development.

BEHAVIORAL PROBLEMS   The Child Behavior Checklist (CBCL; Achenbach, 1991, 1992) was used to assess children's behavioral problems. One of two versions was used, CBCL 2–3 or CBCL 4–18, depending on the child's age. This measure includes two broad problem scales (Externalizing Behaviors and Internalizing Behaviors), as well as a Total Problems scale. A raw and standardized score are derived for each problem scale, and a total behavioral problem score is computed. Our analyses are on the Total Problems score, the test-retest reliability of which is high ($r = .91$ for CBCL 2–3), with the authors reporting good internal consistency and stability. The CBCL 2–3 and the CBCL 4–18 are significantly related to scores on scales from other checklists (Achenbach, 1991).

SOCIAL SKILLS The Parent Form of the Social Skills Rating System (Gresham & Elliott, 1990) was used to measure children's social skills. The Social Skills Scale comprises four subscales (Cooperation, Assertion, Responsibility, and Self-Control) and yields both a total score and scores for each subscale. The total score was used for these analyses. Internal consistency for the total scale ranges from .73 to .95; test-retest reliability, from .65 to .87. The total scale is moderately correlated with the Child Behavior Checklist—Parent Report Form ($r = .58$).

Analyses

All statistical analyses were conducted with SUDAAN software (RTI International, 2007). Analyses were based on a subset of $n = 1,720$ children aged 24 months or younger at baseline, and all employed the appropriate to NSCAW analysis weights. If data were missing for variables in a particular analysis, cases with missing data were excluded for that analysis. After computation of initial descriptive statistics for the covariates, predictors, and key outcomes (see Appendices A–C), focal analyses employed hierarchical general linear modeling techniques in which control variables were entered in earlier blocks and the key predictors were entered in subsequent blocks. For each analysis, the marginal contribution of the predictor variable, after controlling for the covariates, is documented as the Wald F value. The total model R^2 is presented for each analysis, as well, followed by the unstandardized slope (b).

Control variables (covariates) were the child's race/ethnicity (black or African American, white, Hispanic, "other"), gender (male, female), age in months, and health, as well as the mother's level of education. Predictors of specific interest were as follows:

- Type of maltreatment (i.e., most serious),
- Total number of placements,
- Placement status at each wave,
- Type of placement at each wave,
- Number of children in the home at each wave, and
- Measures of cognitive stimulation and emotional support in the home environment at all waves.[2]

Two interactions were also tested as predictors: *(1)* measures of cognitive stimulation and out-of-home placement, and *(2)* measures of emotional support and out-of-home placement. Key outcome variables were as follows:

- Measures of cognitive development for children under and at/above 4 years of age, language development for all children,
- Total behavioral problems for children younger than 4 and for children aged 4 years or older,
- Internalizing behavior problems for children younger than 4 and for children aged 4 years or older,
- Externalizing behavior problems for children younger than 4 and for children aged 4 years or older, and
- Social skills for all children.

Results

Maltreatment Type

The maltreatment type (i.e., most serious) measure was collapsed from its original 10 categories to 4: Physical maltreatment and sexual maltreatment remained unique categories; a broadened neglect category subsumed failure to provide for the child, failure to supervise, abandonment, and educational neglect. All remaining categories constituted "other." Results are summarized in Table 2.1.

Starting with younger children, lower-than-normal cognitive development was associated with physical abuse and neglect. Younger children who were physically abused had more behavioral problems than the neglect and "other"

Table 2.1 Impact of Maltreatment Type on Key Outcomes, with Adjusted Outcome Means

	Physical	*Sexual*	*Neglect*	*Other*
Cognitive Development (BD4_TDQ, <4 years) — $n = 819$, $R^2 = .125$, Wald $F = 3.559(.018)$				
	83.22	93.33	87.87	93.85
Cognitive Development (KB4_NORM, 4+ years) — $n = 144$, $R^2 = .345$, Wald $F = 1.334(.269)$				
	85.02	94.42	93.43	94.12
Language Development (CO4_TSTD) — $n = 968$, $R^2 = .129$, Wald $F = 5.165(.003)$				
	85.20	70.02	84.21	93.44
Behavior Problems (TC4_TPT, <4 years) — $n = 836$, $R^2 = .042$, Wald $F = 7.360(.000)$				
	55.86	56.22	51.42	48.69
Behavior Problems (BC4_TPT, 4+ years) — $n = 154$, $R^2 = .398$, Wald $F = 3.578(.017)$				
	55.37	47.68	53.66	54.15
Internalizing Behavior Problems (TC4_IPT, <4 years) — $n = 836$ $R^2 = .045$, Wald $F = 2.937(.038)$				
	55.82	56.22	52.75	49.78
Internalizing Behavior Problems (BC4_IPT, 4+ years) — $n = 154$, $R^2 = .300$, Wald $F = 0.701(.554)$				
	47.94	47.20	50.61	52.85
Externalizing Behavior Problems (TC4_EPT, <4 years) — $n = 836$, $R^2 = .070$, Wald $F = 7.115(.000)$				
	55.60	54.76	51.01	48.71
Externalizing Behavior Problems (BC4_EPT, 4+ years) — $n = 154$, $R^2 = .333$, Wald $F = 3.519(.019)$				
	55.27	47.46	53.61	53.27
Social Skills (PS4_SCR) — $n = 838$, $R^2 = .077$, Wald $F = .671(.572)$				
	91.48	86.07	88.41	87.29

Table 2.2 Impact of Total Number of Placements on Key Outcomes

n	(R^2)	$b_{1 \; Placement}$	$b_{2 + \; Placements}$	Wald F
Cognitive Development (BD4_TDQ, <4 years)				
745	0.134	1.836	**5.823**	2.575 (.082)
Cognitive Development (KB4_NORM, 4+ years)				
131	0.309	−1.226	−0.001	0.065 (.938)
Language Development (CO4_TSTD)				
881	0.085	2.985	**5.683**	2.583 (.082)
Behavior Problems (TC4_TPT, <4 years)				
763	0.024	1.993	0.570	0.629 (.536)
Behavior Problems (BC4_TPT, 4+ years)				
140	0.455	−1.055	5.122	0.971 (.383)
Social Skills (PS4_SCR)				
760	0.071	1.162	2.332	0.527 (.592)

maltreatment groups. Because of sample size concerns, significant results for the sexual abuse group are not presented.

Total Number of Placements

The numbers of out-of-home placements were collapsed into a three-category variable (0, 1, 2+). Results are summarized in Table 2.2. After controlling for the covariates, no significant differences were found between the number of placements and any outcome.

Placement Type at Each Wave

To assess the predictive value of the placement type at each wave, a variable was created for type of care at each wave. In Table 2.3 the effects of both nonkinship foster care and kinship foster care are presented. Table 2.4 documents differences between children who are in home and those who are in placement (nonkinship and kinship care groups collapsed). In Table 2.5 the functioning of children in nonkinship foster care is compared with the functioning of those in kinship care.

Table 2.3 shows that Wave 1 (baseline) foster care was significantly positively associated with younger children's cognitive development. Similarly, at Wave 1 younger children living at home had lower cognitive and language development than those placed out of home (both nonkinship foster care and kinship care). Additionally, fewer Wave 3 and Wave 4 behavioral problems were documented for the older children living at home than for those placed out of home, but children at home at Wave 3 showed lower levels of Wave 4 social skills. No differences were detected in cognitive development for older children or in behavioral problems for

Table 2.3 Impact of Type of Placement on Key Outcomes

Predictors	n	(R^2)	b_{fos1}	b_{kin1}	b_{fos3}	b_{kin3}	b_{fos4}	b_{kin4}	Wald F
Cognitive Development (BD4_TDQ, <4 years)									
Wave 1	897	0.154	**10.161**	1.606					7.062 (.001)
Wave 1, Wave 3	848	0.149	**7.750**	0.989	3.067	1.189			1.098 (.334)
Wave 1, Wave 3, Wave 4	845	0.140	**6.294**	0.491	4.807	1.729	−4.919	−0.892	0.798 (.472)
Cognitive Development (KB4_NORM, 4+ years)									
Wave 1	150	0.274	−3.193	2.361					0.754 (.474)
Wave 1, Wave 3	145	0.289	−6.526	2.190	5.982	1.518			1.194 (.308)
Wave 1, Wave 3, Wave 4	145	0.291	−6.881	1.661	6.145	11.665	2.965	−11.077	0.577 (.564)
Language Development (CO4_TSTD)									
Wave 1	1,052	0.081	5.527	6.412					2.271 (.110)
Wave 1, Wave 3	998	0.083	2.375	5.580	5.361	2.134			1.552 (.218)
Wave 1, Wave 3, Wave 4	995	0.071	0.110	4.732	6.992	3.645	−1.684	−1.974	0.138 (.871)
Behavior Problems (TC4_TPT, <4 years)									
Wave 1	915	0.025	1.169	0.276					0.598 (.552)
Wave 1, Wave 3	867	0.029	1.925	−0.235	−1.195	1.407			0.727 (.486)
Wave 1, Wave 3, Wave 4	864	0.030	2.288	−0.066	−2.232	1.475	3.358	−0.617	1.355 (.264)
Behavior Problems (BC4_TPT, 4+ years)									
Wave 1	161	0.361	4.300	4.265					1.066 (.349)
Wave 1, Wave 3	153	0.369	**9.573**	5.632	**−7.767**	−1.703			2.134 (.125)
Wave 1, Wave 3, Wave 4	153	0.387	**9.608**	5.341	−6.939	−3.735	−2.798	2.341	0.322 (.726)
Social Skills (PS4_SCR)									
Wave 1	910	0.060	−0.654	0.838					0.173 (.841)
Wave 1, Wave 3	853	0.078	−3.364	−1.924	3.543	6.360			1.783 (.174)
Wave 1, Wave 3, Wave 4	855	0.073	−3.363	−1.857	**6.784**	5.475	−6.095	0.577	1.221 (.300)

Note: In-home placement was the reference group.

Table 2.4 Influence of Type of Placement (Home vs. Nonkinship and Kinship Foster) on Key Outcomes

Predictors	n	(R^2)	Wald $F_{Wave\ 1}$	Wald $F_{Wave\ 3}$	Wald $F_{Wave\ 4}$
Cognitive Development (BD4_TDQ, <4 years)					
Wave 1	897	0.155	6.949 (.010)		
Wave 1, Wave 3	848	0.149	3.552 (.063)	1.905 (.171)	
Wave 1, Wave 3, Wave 4	845	0.140	2.114 (.150)	3.599 (.061)	0.998 (.321)
Cognitive Development (KB4_NORM, 4+ years)					
Wave 1	150	0.274	0.014 (.908)		
Wave 1, Wave 3	145	0.289	0.360 (.550)	2.377 (.127)	
Wave 1, Wave 3, Wave 4	145	0.291	0.424 (.517)	2.060 (.155)	0.351 (.555)
Language Development (CO4_TSTD)					
Wave 1	1,052	0.081	4.085 (.043)		
Wave 1, Wave 3	998	0.083	1.375 (.244)	2.509 (.117)	
Wave 1, Wave 3, Wave 4	995	0.071	0.562 (.456)	3.943 (.050)	0.276 (.601)
Behavior Problems (TC4_TPT, <4 years)					
Wave 1	915	0.025	0.449 (.504)		
Wave 1, Wave 3	867	0.029	0.433 (.512)	0.007 (.933)	
Wave 1, Wave 3, Wave 4	864	0.029	0.687 (.410)	0.076 (.784)	0.857 (.357)
Behavior Problems (BC4_TPT, 4+ years)					
Wave 1	161	0.361	2.124 (.149)		
Wave 1, Wave 3	153	0.369	4.576 (.035)	2.701 (.104)	
Wave 1, Wave 3, Wave 4	153	0.387	4.229 (.043)	3.666 (.059)	0.003 (.958)
Social Skills (PS4_SCR)					
Wave 1	910	0.060	0.002 (.967)		
Wave 1, Wave 3	858	0.078	0.799 (.374)	3.542 (.063)	
Wave 1, Wave 3, Wave 4	855	0.073	0.771 (.383)	8.025 (.006)	0.860 (.360)

Table 2.5 Impact of Type of Placement (Nonkinship Foster vs. Kinship Foster) on Key Outcomes

Predictors	n	(R^2)	Wald $F_{Wave\ 1}$	Wald $F_{Wave\ 3}$	Wald $F_{Wave\ 4}$
Cognitive Development (BD4_TDQ, <4 years)					
Wave 1	897	0.155	5.038 (.027)		
Wave 1, Wave 3	848	0.149	2.574 (.112)	0.415 (.521)	
Wave 1, Wave 3, Wave 4	845	0.140	2.340 (.130)	0.779 (.380)	0.489 (.486)
Cognitive Development (KB4_NORM, 4+ years)					
Wave 1	150	0.274	1.507 (.223)		
Wave 1, Wave 3	145	0.289	3.937 (.051)	0.906 (.344)	
Wave 1, Wave 3, Wave 4	145	0.291	2.646 (.108)	0.251 (.618)	1.108 (.296)
Language Development (CO4_TSTD)					
Wave 1	1,052	0.081	0.039 (.842)		
Wave 1, Wave 3	998	0.083	0.504 (.480)	0.554 (.459)	
Wave 1, Wave 3, Wave 4	995	0.071	0.922 (.340)	0.583 (.447)	0.002 (.962)
Behavior Problems (TC4_TPT, <4 years)					
Wave 1	915	0.025	0.282 (.597)		
Wave 1, Wave 3	867	0.029	1.646 (.203)	1.453 (.232)	
Wave 1, Wave 3, Wave 4	864	0.029	1.640 (.204)	1.880 (.174)	1.927 (.169)

Table 2.5 (Continued)

Behavior Problems (BC4_TPT, 4+ years)					
Wave 1	161	0.361	0.000 (.994)		
Wave 1, Wave 3	153	0.369	0.875 (.352)	1.952 (.166)	
Wave 1, Wave 3, Wave 4	153	0.387	1.125 (.292)	0.291 (.591)	0.461 (.499)
Social Skills (PS4_SCR)					
Wave 1	910	0.060	0.315 (.576)		
Wave 1, Wave 3	858	0.078	0.182 (.671)	0.330 (.567)	
Wave 1, Wave 3, Wave 4	855	0.073	0.173 (.678)	0.106 (.745)	1.488 (.266)

the younger children. Only one significant difference was detected between nonkinship foster and kinship foster placement: at Wave 1 younger nonkin foster children had higher cognitive development than those in kinship care.

Number of Children in the Household

To assess the predictive value of number of children in the home at each wave, a categorical measure of the number of children in the household (1, 2, 3, 4, 5+) was created. Results are summarized in Table 2.6.

All analyses yielded a statistically significant association between number of children (at differing waves) and key outcomes. Starting with younger children, number of children in the household at Wave 1 and Wave 4 appeared to affect cognitive development, although the direction of the association changes. For Wave 1 (baseline), having more children in the household was positively associated with younger children's cognitive development, whereas at Wave 4 (36-month follow-up) the association was negative. For older children at Wave 3 and Wave 4, having more children appeared to affect cognitive development negatively. Only at Wave 4 did number of children in the household affect language development, the association being negative. Having more children in the household at Wave 3 and at Wave 4 was significantly associated with behavioral problems for both younger and older children. At Wave 4 having more children in the household negatively affected children's social skills.

Cognitive Stimulation

Table 2.7 summarizes the predictive value of cognitive stimulation at three waves. No impact on cognitive development was detected for younger children; for the older children, however, Wave 1 stimulation levels appeared to positively affect cognitive development. Wave 4 cognitive stimulation positively affected language development. For younger and older children at Times 1 and 4, cognitive stimulation was significantly associated with increases in social skills and decreases in behavioral problems.

Table 2.6 Impact of Number of Children in the Household on Key Outcomes

Predictors	n	(R^2)	Wald F
Cognitive Development (BD4_TDQ, <4 years)			
Wave 1	906	0.150	3.216 (.017)
Wave 1, Wave 3	906	0.151	0.168 (.954)
Wave 1, Wave 3, Wave 4	861	0.192	5.434 (.000)
Cognitive Development (KB4_NORM, 4+ years)			
Wave 1	152	0.319	0.933 (.449)
Wave 1, Wave 3	152	0.380	3.872 (.006)
Wave 1, Wave 3, Wave 4	147	0.398	5.368 (.000)
Language Development (CO4_TSTD)			
Wave 1	1,063	0.091	1.463 (.221)
Wave 1, Wave 3	1,063	0.093	0.230 (.921)
Wave 1, Wave 3, Wave 4	1,013	0.118	2.538 (.007)
Behavior Problems (TC4_TPT, <4 years)			
Wave 1	925	0.030	0.333 (.855)
Wave 1, Wave 3	925	0.059	3.423 (.012)
Wave 1, Wave 3, Wave 4	881	0.068	2.209 (.031)
Behavior Problems (BC4_TPT, 4+ years)			
Wave 1	163	0.410	2.470 (.051)
Wave 1, Wave 3	163	0.470	3.213 (.017)
Wave 1, Wave 3, Wave 4	155	0.499	2.874 (.003)
Social Skills (PS4_SCR)			
Wave 1	918	0.083	1.532 (.201)
Wave 1, Wave 3	918	0.104	1.883 (.121)
Wave 1, Wave 3, Wave 4	867	0.136	2.962 (.002)

Table 2.7 Impact of Cognitive Stimulation on Key Outcomes

Predictors	n	(R^2)	$b_{Wave\ 1}$	$b_{Wave\ 3}$	$b_{Wave\ 4}$	Wald F
Cognitive Development (BD4_TDQ, <4 years)						
Wave 1	906	0.133	0.359			0.224 (.637)
Wave 1, Wave 3	845	0.127	0.310	0.956		2.050 (.135)
Wave 1, Wave 3, Wave 4	845	0.135	0.007	0.747	0.651	2.283 (.085)
Cognitive Development (KB4_NORM, 4+ years)						
Wave 1	152	0.322	**2.747**			7.283 (.008)
Wave 1, Wave 3	145	0.351	**2.653**	1.130		5.814 (.004)
Wave 1, Wave 3, Wave 4	145	0.351	**2.649**	1.105	0.185	4.077 (.009)
Language Development (CO4_TSTD)						
Wave 1	1,063	0.074	0.894			1.075 (.303)
Wave 1, Wave 3	995	0.062	0.918	0.107		0.458 (.643)
Wave 1, Wave 3, Wave 4	995	0.106	0.279	−0.115	**1.993**	5.740 (.001)
Behavior Problems (TC4_TPT, <4 years)						
Wave 1	925	0.038	−0.831			3.778 (.055)
Wave 1, Wave 3	864	0.052	−1.210	0.608		6.849 (.002)
Wave 1, Wave 3, Wave 4	864	0.078	**−0.880**	0.910	**−0.771**	5.922 (.001)

Table 2.7 (Continued)

Behavior Problems (BC4_TPT, 4+ years)							
Wave 1	163	0.368	−1.371				2.029 (.158)
Wave 1, Wave 3	154	0.382	−1.040	0.572			1.861 (.162)
Wave 1, Wave 3, Wave 4	154	0.431	−1.136	0.852	**−1.704**		2.686 (.052)
Social Skills (PS4_SCR)							
Wave 1	918	0.089	**1.919**				9.477 (.003)
Wave 1, Wave 3	851	0.085	**1.562**	0.473			4.745 (.011)
Wave 1, Wave 3, Wave 4	851	0.138	1.172	0.123	**1.784**		10.270 (.000)

Emotional Support

Table 2.8 summarizes the predictive value of emotional support at three waves. No significant associations emerged between emotional support and cognitive development for younger children. For the older children, emotional support at Wave 3 contributed to cognitive development; at Wave 4 it contributed significantly to

Table 2.8 Impact of Emotional Support on Key Outcomes

Predictors	n	(R^2)	$b_{Wave\ 1}$	$b_{Wave\ 3}$	$b_{Wave\ 4}$	Wald F
Cognitive Development (BD4_TDQ, <4 years)						
Wave 1	906	0.132	−0.134			0.050 (.823)
Wave 1, Wave 3	845	0.132	−0.157	1.128		1.912 (.154)
Wave 1, Wave 3, Wave 4	845	0.132	−0.150	**1.142**	−0.069	1.694 (.175)
Cognitive Development (KB4_NORM, 4+ years)						
Wave 1	152	0.281	1.000			0.522 (.460)
Wave 1, Wave 3	145	0.379	0.379	**3.223**		7.409 (.001)
Wave 1, Wave 3, Wave 4	145	0.390	0.595	**2.953**	1.244	6.683 (.000)
Language Development (CO4_TSTD)						
Wave 1	1,063	0.072	0.361			0.311 (.578)
Wave 1, Wave 3	995	0.077	−0.301	1.640		1.846 (.164)
Wave 1, Wave 3, Wave 4	995	0.100	−0.391	1.347	**1.776**	3.493 (.021)
Behavior Problems (TC4_TPT, <4 years)						
Wave 1	925	0.023	0.055			0.036 (.851)
Wave 1, Wave 3	864	0.038	−0.306	0.637		1.602 (.208)
Wave 1, Wave 3, Wave 4	864	0.047	−0.256	**0.774**	−0.553	1.848 (.145)
Behavior Problems (BC4_TPT, 4+ years)						
Wave 1	163	0.367	1.153			2.034 (.158)
Wave 1, Wave 3	154	0.394	1.409	−0.760		2.779 (.068)
Wave 1, Wave 3, Wave 4	154	0.430	1.155	−0.363	−1.722	4.233 (.008)
Social Skills (PS4_SCR)						
Wave 1	918	0.061	0.347			0.189 (.665)
Wave 1, Wave 3	851	0.094	−0.217	**1.642**		7.676 (.001)
Wave 1, Wave 3, Wave 4	851	0.177	−0.302	**1.041**	**2.463**	16.207 (.000)

Table 2.9   Impact of Interaction Between Cognitive Stimulation and No. of Out-of-Home Placements

n	(R^2)	$b_{1\ OOH}$	$b_{2+\ OOH}$	$b_{cog.}$	$b_{1\ OOH \times cog.}$	$b_{2+\ OOH \times cog}$	Wald F
Cognitive Development (BD4_TDQ, <4 years)							
745	0.139	−6.424	3.948	0.170	1.392	0.335	0.242 (.786)
Cognitive Development (KB4_NORM, 4+ years)							
131	0.356	17.060	**29.868**	3.192	−2.513	−4.672	1.868 (.161)
Language Development (CO4_TSTD)							
881	0.096	−12.585	5.232	0.602	2.436	0.026	1.117 (.332)
Behavior Problems (TC4_TPT, <4 years)							
763	0.035	3.230	−0.158	−0.726	−0.252	0.074	0.045 (.956)
Behavior Problems (BC4_TPT, 4+ years)							
140	0.469	3.022	−22.385	−0.433	−0.521	4.198	1.798 (.172)
Social Skills (PS4_SCR)							
760	0.094	6.809	−1.391	1.652	−0.842	0.697	0.629 (.536)

language development. Emotional support did not significantly affect younger children's behavioral problems. For older children's behavioral problems, the overall model with all three waves entered was significant; however, no one wave was a significant predictor. Wave 3 and 4 emotional support appeared to be associated with increases in social skills.

Interaction Between Cognitive Stimulation and Number of Out-of-Home Placements

To assess whether cognitive stimulation moderated the impact of number of out-of-home placements on key outcomes, interaction variables were created between the three cognitive stimulation variables and the number-of-placements variable through Wave 2 (Table 2.9). No significant effect of the interaction variable was found on any key outcome.

Interaction Between Emotional Support and Number of Out-of-Home Placements

To assess whether emotional support moderated the impact of number of out-of-home placement on key outcomes, interaction variables were created between the three emotional support variables and the number-of-placements variable through Wave 2 (Table 2.10).

The interaction of emotional support and number of out-of-home placements significantly affected younger children's behavioral problems, indicating that emotional support affords some protection against the impact of high numbers of out-of-home placements.

Table 2.10 Impact of Interaction Between Emotional Support and Number of Out-of-Home Placements

n	(R^2)	$b_{1\ OOH}$	$b_{2+\ OOH}$	$b_{emot.}$	$b_{1\ OOH\ \times\ emot.}$	$b_{2+\ OOH\ \times\ emot.}$	Wald F
Cognitive Development (BD4_TDQ, <4 years)							
745	0.163	−21.393	−11.015	−0.783	3.538	2.480	3.334 (.041)
Cognitive Development (KB4_NORM, 4+ years)							
131	0.328	17.844	36.890	1.600	−2.660	−4.917	1.724 (.185)
Language Development (CO4_TSTD)							
881	0.099	−17.230	−13.106	−0.199	2.950	2.624	1.990 (.143)
Behavior Problems (TC4_TPT, <4 years)							
763	0.056	**18.042**	9.185	0.486	−2.441	**−1.282**	7.072 (.002)
Behavior Problems (BC4_TPT, 4+ years)							
140	0.437	19.014	−21.604	0.526	−2.676	3.352	2.551 (.084)
Social Skills (PS4_SCR)							
760	0.870	1.545	3.137	0.942	−0.075	−0.201	0.009 (.991)

Discussion

Our analyses of the effects of the early caregiving environment on preschool children's developmental outcomes have produced a complex set of findings, underscoring the complexity of the experiences of children in the child welfare system. Children who experienced physical abuse and neglect scored lower than those who had not on tests of cognitive development; furthermore, younger children who had experienced physical abuse reportedly incurred more behavioral problems than those who had not. Contrary to our hypothesis, however, no significant associations emerged between the total number of placements during infancy and developmental outcomes at preschool age. In fact, children who remained in home during infancy had more compromised developmental outcomes in every domain except behavioral problems.

As anticipated, however, children in nonkinship foster care did have higher cognitive scores than children in kinship care. A high-quality early home environment, in general, promoted the well-being of preschool children who had entered the child welfare system as infants. Children who lived with greater numbers of children incurred more compromised outcomes in the cognitive, language, behavioral, and social domains. Conversely, both cognitive stimulation and emotional support in the home predicted higher cognitive and language scores, decreased behavioral problems, and increased social skills at preschool age; early out-of-home placement and lack of emotional support predicted children's behavioral problems. Interestingly, variables reflecting the direct daily care young children experience (e.g., emotional support) more consistently and robustly affected child outcomes than did structural variables associated with child welfare services (e.g., placement type).

Maltreatment Type

Although any maltreatment is hazardous to children's well-being (e.g., Cicchetti & Toth, 1995), ascertaining whether specific maltreatment types are associated with specific domains of functioning is important. We found that physical abuse during infancy was most detrimental to child outcomes. Physical abuse consistently has been associated with impaired cognitive ability (Eckenrode, Laird, & Doris, 1993; Kaplan, Pelcovitz, & Labruna, 1999), especially in infancy. Cognitive impairment found in infancy is often linked to the neurological effects of nonaccidental head trauma. For example, shaken infants are likely to present with developmental delay and mental retardation (Duhaime, Christian, Rorke, & Zimmerman, 1998). Multiple studies have documented the link between physical abuse and behavioral problems as well (Dodge et al., 1997; Lansford et al., 2006).

Consistent with the limited literature focusing on neglect in young children (Strathearn, Gray, O'Callaghan, & Wood, 2001), we found that neglected children incurred poor cognitive outcomes. Moreover, Egeland, Yates, Appleyard, and Van Dulmen (2002) suggest that physical abuse combined with parental psychological unavailability during the early years is strongly related to clinical levels of behavioral problems in later childhood and adolescence. It is important to note that the children in this study were exposed to multiple forms of maltreatment; our data reflect only the "most serious" type of maltreatment suffered by each child.

Placement Stability

Permanency is a central tenet of current child welfare policy and programmatic approaches. Emphasis on it emanated from a long line of research suggesting that multiple transitions were hazardous to children's well-being (Jones Harden, 2004). Analyses conducted on the entire NSCAW sample, too, revealed a strong relationship between numbers of moves and more compromised developmental outcomes (Administration for Children and Families, 2005). We therefore hypothesized that fewer placements would be associated with better developmental outcomes for preschool children.

That findings did not confirm this hypothesis calls for closer consideration of the children comprising this sample. Much of the research on placement stability in child welfare has involved older children (Newton, Litrownik, & Landsverk, 2000; Wulczyn et al., 2003). The negative effects of multiple transitions perhaps emerge when children encounter the developmental demands of later childhood. Additionally, the children in this sample moved a limited number of times (i.e., $M = 1.87$; $SD = 1.37$), and some evidence suggests that the threshold for the negative impact of placement change is high (children experiencing three to five placements; Newton et al., 2000; Ryan & Testa, 2005). Although the duration of the sampled children's placements is unknown, other research suggests that infants have a high initial movement rate (Wulczyn et al., 2003), with longer placements and permanency typically coming later.

Leaving the initial short-term placements characteristic of infancy may be less traumatic than leaving long-term care.

Placement Type

Young children enter foster care for various reasons, but mainly because of neglect. Some evidence suggests that caseworkers are more likely to place younger children into foster care because these children are completely unable to protect themselves (Barth, 1997; Wulczyn, 2004). The relation between placement and child outcomes is difficult to disentangle. Horwitz, Simms, and Farrington (1994) suggest, for example, that children's developmental delays not only lead to out-of-home placements but also arise from such placements. Despite the complexities involved, it is important to examine whether placement type influences young children's developmental functioning.

Contrary to our hypothesis, children in out-of-home care, overall, had better developmental outcomes than children who remained with their biological families. Some have argued that foster care may be protective for maltreated children (Horwitz et al., 2001), that the negative effects of maltreatment can be mitigated through a stable, nurturing relationship with another caregiver (Heller, Larrieus, D'Imperio, & Boris, 1999). The current data lend credence to such a proposition, at least with regard to nonkinship foster environments. That children who remained in home, despite having more problems overall, had fewer behavioral problems than those placed out of home suggests that placement may affect the behavioral domain uniquely. Early relationship disruption or loss perhaps overwhelms young children's capacity to regulate their behavior, with implications for their current and future mental health (Cicchetti & Toth, 1995; Waldinger, Toth, & Gerber, 2001).

A growing body of literature documents the more compromised functioning of kinship caregivers as compared with the functioning of nonkin foster parents (e.g., Jones Harden, Clyman, Kriebel, & Lyons, 2004). Nevertheless, evidence on developmental outcomes for the children reared in these distinct contexts is equivocal (e.g., Geen, 2004). Data from this study indicate that young children cared for by kin function socially and behaviorally as well as their counterparts in nonkinship foster care, but they perform worse in the areas of cognition and language. Because kinship caregivers may provide their children less stimulating environments (Clyman & Jones Harden, 2008), the children may be less advanced in the cognitive and language domains.

Home Environment

Our clearest and most robust findings related to the care that young children directly experience. We considered whether levels of cognitive stimulation and emotional support in the early caregiving environment may contribute to developmental outcomes. A plethora of evidence on non–child welfare samples documents the salience of these manifestations of care for cognitive, language, and socioemotional outcomes, especially for high-risk children (e.g., children reared in impoverished circumstances; Bradley et al., 2001).

Consistent with the literature, both cognitive stimulation and emotional support predicted better developmental outcomes in each domain. Interestingly, in studies addressing the quality of the home environment, cognitive stimulation has generally been associated with higher cognitive outcomes; emotional support, with higher socioemotional outcomes (Bradley et al., 2001). For this group of children, however, both cognitive stimulation and emotional support positively influenced both cognitive and socioemotional outcomes. The quality of the home environment—whether through the provision of development-enriching materials or through nurturing interactions—promoted the generalized development of these children. Quality of care may, therefore, better predict children's well-being than any prior event necessitating that care (e.g., maltreatment, placement).

Limitations

Although the comprehensiveness of the NSCAW data set is unprecedented, some limitations may qualify our findings. The goal of this study was to examine the child welfare experiences and associated developmental outcomes of children who entered the child welfare system as infants. Although evidence exists that the experiences of infants younger than 4 months of age are distinct from those of older infants, we could not answer this question because the infants in the NSCAW sample were older at baseline ($M = 13$ months). In addition, because the status of children in the child welfare system may change daily (e.g., child may move from birth family to transitional placement to relatives), we could not track children's whereabouts precisely; therefore, we made some assumptions and decisions about placement status that may incompletely reflect children's actual experiences.

Measurement challenges also merit special mention. Survey research typically precludes the use of relatively rich measures of infant and family functioning. Because all young children, regardless of where they resided, were included in the study, we could not capitalize on data on parental functioning. Questions about parental mental health and other parental characteristics were posed only to birth parents. In addition, this study would have benefited from data derived from assessments of parent–infant interaction and attachment, observational methods of infant socioemotional functioning (e.g., emotion regulation), and physiological techniques. The longitudinal nature of the study, moreover, required that we change the measure used to assess cognition, social skills, and behavioral problems. Because of a developmental shift that occurs around 4 years of age, two different measures were used in two of the three domains. Because the skills and behaviors informing each domain differed somewhat according to the age-specific version, we treated the two versions of each measure separately in the analyses.

Conclusion

Because our main objective was to examine the influence of the early caregiving environment on young children's developmental outcomes, we hoped to obtain empirical evidence that would inform future child welfare services targeted to young children and their families. Interventions found to benefit young children and families involved in the child welfare system have been documented elsewhere (see Jones Harden, 2007; Wulczyn, Barth, Yuan, Jones Harden, & Landsverk, 2006). Our current findings call for services that address specific child welfare domains, such as physical abuse, the transition to out-of-home placement, and the quality of the caregiving environment.

The negative effects of physical abuse for this sample were particularly salient. Although evidence on treatments aimed at preventing physical abuse is scant, some interventions have been found to reduce the abuse-related behaviors of parents of older children (e.g., Lutzker, Tymchuk, & Bigelow, 2001). Adapting these interventions to address the needs of young children and their families (e.g., focusing on shaken baby syndrome) not only may improve the cognitive and socioemotional well-being of young children but also may safeguard their physical health. The findings on neglect also argue for development of evidence-based interventions that address the specific etiology and developmental consequences of neglect.

Young children who remained in home or who were in kinship foster care tended to have more compromised functioning than children in nonkinship foster care. This finding underscores the pivotal role of child welfare agencies in promoting the well-being of children living with their biological families, including birth parents and familial caregivers. The priority in serving these children must be not only safety and permanency but also long-term well-being. Legislative mandates such as the referral of infants in the child welfare system for assessment under Part C of the Individuals with Disabilities Education Act should go far to ensure that the developmental needs of young children involved in child welfare are met. Caseworkers would benefit from training, monitoring, and support addressing the developmental needs of young children so as to fully implement evidence-based practices in their routine home visits and case management activities.

Although we found no association between number of placements and developmental outcomes, that young children experience a relatively low number of placements is a finding worth noting. Child welfare practitioners should be striving to maintain placement stability for young children; these data suggest that they are.

The current findings on the home environment are compelling. They underscore the importance to children's well-being—regardless of placement type—of cognitive stimulation and emotional support. Although the goal of most child welfare entities is to provide comprehensive services to families, often a focus on quality of care gives way to an emphasis on safety (e.g., is a responsible caregiver available for the child?) or on the structural elements of the caregiving environment (e.g., is there adequate space for the child?). If well-being is to be seriously addressed in child welfare practice, safety and structural monitoring must be accompanied by assessments of the home's ability to foster sound child development (e.g., does the home offer toys, objects, and experiences conducive to skill development, and do caregivers show emotional commitment to the child?). Interventions focusing on parent–child interactions (e.g., McDonough, 2000) are particularly well suited to addressing a lack of cognitive stimulation and emotional support, which may exist in both birth families and foster families.

Because children in the child welfare system generally are at high risk for poor outcomes, research must disentangle the factors that most render them vulnerable. This study suggests that specific factors in the early childhood environment do increase the vulnerability of young children, factors such as physical abuse and the lack of caregiver emotional support. These findings should inform policies and practices that aim to mitigate the deleterious outcomes these children face.

Scholars in many disciplines have asserted that long-term child well-being may be best effected with intervention during early childhood (e.g., Olds, Hill, Robinson, Song, & Little, 2000; Shonkoff & Meisels, 2000; Shonkoff & Phillips, 2000). Both the vulnerability and the potential inherent in infancy and early childhood demand that developmentally appropriate child welfare services be targeted for young children and their families (see Wulczyn, Barth, Yuan, Jones Harden, & Landsverk, 2005). This study calls for interventions that promote young children's well-being by specifically addressing physical abuse, the transition to out-of-home placement, and the quality of the caregiving environment. These specific, targeted interventions hold promise for the well-being of children throughout early childhood and beyond.

Appendix Table 2.A   Descriptive Statistics for Relevant Covariates

	n	*Mean*	*SD*
Maternal Education (GRADE1T)			
	1,088	11.17	5.51
Child Age in Months (CHAGE_B)			
	1,720	9.72	5.15
Child Health (CHRHELTH) %			
Excellent	1: 46.74%		
Very good	2: 26.25%		
Good	3: 17.46%		
Fair	4: 7.74%		
Poor	5: 1.80%		

Appendix Table 2.B   Descriptive Statistics for Predictors

	n	*Mean*	*SD*
Type of Abuse	%		
	Physical: 19.75%		
	Sexual: 4.66%		
	Neglect: 63.37%		
	Other: 12.23%		
	n = 1,380		
Total No. of Out-of-Home Placements Through Wave 2			
	1,419	0.77	1.10
Categorical No. of Placements Through Wave 2			
	0 placements: 57.15%		
	1 placement: 21.49%		
	2+ placements: 21.35%		
Placement Status			
Wave 1	Placed: 33.26%		
	Not placed: 66.74%		
Wave 3	Placed: 26.51%		
	Not placed: 73.49%		
Wave 4	Placed: 14.07%		
	Not placed: 73.49%		
Type of Placement			
Wave 1	In home: 64.45%		
	Foster home: 19.62%		
	Kin care setting: 12.93%		
Wave 3	In home: 74.16%		
	Foster home: 14.64%		
	Kin care setting: 11.20%		
Wave 4	In home: 87.13%		
	Foster home: 6.60%		
	Kin care setting: 6.27%		
No. of Children in the Home			
Wave 1	1 child: 34.30%		
	2 children: 26.86%		
	3 children: 17.62%		
	4 children: 9.77%		
	≥5 children 11.45%		
Wave 3	1 child: 40.52%%		
	2 children: 22.50%		
	3 children: 18.26%		
	4 children: 9.24%		
	≥5 children 9.48%		
Wave 4	1 child: 37.85%		
	2 children: 24.65%		
	3 children: 16.80%		
	4 children: 10.70%		
	≥5 children 10.00%		
Cognitive Stimulation			
Wave 1	1,720	6.31	1.59
Wave 3	1,493	7.45	1.75
Wave 4	1,478	10.60	2.49
Emotional Support			
Wave 1	1,720	7.05	1.80
Wave 3	1,493	7.24	1.84
Wave 4	1,478	8.79	2.03

Appendix Table 2.C   Descriptive Statistics for Key Outcome Variables

	n	*Mean*	*SD*
Cognitive Development (BD4_TDQ, <4 years)			
	1,236	87.61	17.39
Cognitive Development (KB4_NORM, 4+ years)			
	205	92.14	15.94
Language Development (CO4_TSTD)			
	1,447	86.49	19.19
Behavior Problems (TC4_TPT, <4 years)			
	1,259	52.59	10.66
Behavior Problems (BC4_TPT, 4+ years)			
	219	54.78	11.37
Social Skills (PS4_SCR)			
	1,247	87.02	15.64

Appendix 2.D: Statistical Methods

Control variables (covariates) were the child's race (black or African American, white, Hispanic, other), gender (male, female), age in months (CHDAGEM), and health (CHRHELTH), as well as the mother's level of education (HH416A). Predictors of specific interest included type of abuse (derived from CHRABUSE as described below), total number of placements (EDCOOHPL), placement status at each wave (CHDOOHSI, CH3OOHSI, and CH4OOHSI), type of placement at each wave (FOSTKIN1, FOSTKIN3, and FOSTKIN4), number of children at each wave (HHDNOCH, HH3NOCH, and HH4NOCH), and measures of cognitive stimulation and emotional support in the home environment at all waves derived from PHO, HO3, and HO4 measures of cognitive stimulation and emotional support in the following manner. The cognitive stimulation variables were derived as follows: Wave 1 labeled PHO_CS and PHO_CS1, for children <3 years; Wave 3 labeled HO3_CS and HO3_CS1, for children <3 years, merged with HO3_CS2, for children 3 to 6 years; and Wave 4 cognitive stimulation labeled HO4_CS and HO4_CS1, for children <3 years, merged with HO4_CS2, for children 3 to 6 years. The emotional support variables were derived as follows: Wave 1 labeled PHO_ES and PHO_ES1, for children <3 years; Wave 3 labeled HO3_ES and HO3_ES1, for children <3 years, merged with HO3_ES2, for children 3 to 6 years; and Wave 4 labeled HO4_ES and HO4_ES1, for children <3 years, merged with HO4_ES2, for children 3 to 6 years. Two interactions were also tested as predictors: measures of cognitive stimulation and out-of-home placement, and measures of emotional support and out-of-home placement.

Finally, key outcome variables included measures of cognitive development for children under and at/above 4 years of age (BD4_TDQ and KB4_NORM, respectively), language development for all children (CO4_TSTD), total behavior problems for children under and at/above 4 years of age (TC4_TPT and BC4_TPT, respectively), internalizing behavior problems for children under and at/above 4 (TC4_IPT and BC4_IPT, respectively), externalizing behavior problems for children under and at/above 4 (TC4_EPT and BC4_EPT, respectively), and social skills for all children (PS4_SCR). Missing data were managed in a listwise manner per each analysis.

NOTES

1. For further information on the study sample, see Appendix Table 2.A.
2. For a detailed description of how variables were derived, see Appendix 2.D.

REFERENCES

Achenbach, T. M. (1991). *Manual for the Child Behavior Checklist/4-18 and 1991 profile.* Burlington, VT: University of Vermont, Department of Psychiatry.

Achenbach, T. M. (1992). *Manual for the Child Behavior Checklist/2-3 and 1992 profile.* Burlington: University of Vermont, Department of Psychiatry.

Administration for Children and Families. (2003). *Report on the one-year-in-foster-care sample, National Survey of Child and Adolescent Well-Being.* Washington, DC: Author.

Administration for Children and Families. (2005). *Wave 1 report on the child welfare services sample, National Survey of Child and Adolescent Well-Being.* Washington, DC: Author.

Administration for Children and Families. (2007). *Child maltreatment 2005.* Washington, DC: Author.

Appleyard, K., Egeland, B., van Dulmen, M., & Sroufe, L. (2005). When more is not better: The role of cumulative risk in child behavior outcomes. *Journal of Child Psychology and Psychiatry, 46*(3), 235–245.

Azar, S. (2002). Parenting and child maltreatment. In M. Bornstein (Ed.), *Handbook of parenting: Vol. 4. Social and applied parenting* (pp. 361–378). Mahwah, NJ: Erlbaum.

Bada, H., Langer, J., Twomey, J., Bursi, C., Lagasse, L., Bauer, C., et al. (2008). Importance of stability of early living arrangements on behavior outcomes of children with and without prenatal drug exposure. *Journal of Developmental and Behavioral Pediatrics, 29*(3), 173–182.

Barnett, D., Manly, J. T., & Cicchetti, D. (1993). Defining child maltreatment: The interface between policy and child research. In D. Cicchetti & S. L. Toth (Eds.), *Defining child maltreatment: The interface between policy and child research* (Vol. 8, pp. 7–73). Norwood, NJ: Ablex.

Barth, R. P. (1997). Effects of age and race on the odds of adoption versus remaining in long-term out-of-home care. *Child Welfare, 76*(2), 285–308.

Berger, L. (2004). Income, family structure and child maltreatment. *Children and Youth Services Review, 26*(8), 725–748.

Black, M., Papas, M., Hussey, J., Hunter, W., Dubowitz, H., Kotch, J., et al. (2002). Behavior and development of preschool children born to adolescent mothers: Risk and 3-generation households. *Pediatrics, 109*, 573–580.

Bornstein, M., & Lamb, M. (1992). *Development in infancy.* New York: McGraw-Hill.

Bradley, R. H. (1994). The HOME Inventory: Review and reflections. In H. W. Reese (Ed.), *Advances in child development and behavior* (Vol. 25, pp. 241–288). San Diego, CA: Academic Press.

Bradley, R. H., Corwin, R., McAdoo, H., & Garcia Coll, C. (2001). The home environments of children in the United States: Part I. Variations by age, ethnicity, and poverty status. *Child Development, 72*(6), 1844–1867.

Brown, J., Cohen, P., Johnson, J., & Salzinnger, S. (1998). A longitudinal analysis of risk factors for child maltreatment: Findings of a 17-year prospective study of officially recorded and self-reported child abuse and neglect. *Child Abuse & Neglect, 22*, 1065–1078.

Caldwell, B. M., & Bradley, R. H. (1984). *Home observation for measurement of the environment*. Little Rock: University of Arkansas at Little Rock.

Carlson, V., Cicchetti, D., Barnett, D., & Braunwald, K. (1989). Disorganized/disoriented attachment relationships in maltreated infants. *Developmental Psychology, 25*, 525.

Cicchetti, D. V., & Toth, S. (1995). A developmental psychopathology perspective on child abuse and neglect. *Journal of the American Academy of Child and Adolescent Psychiatry, 34*, 541–565.

Clyman, R., & Jones Harden, B. (2008). *The family environments of kinship and foster caregivers*. Manuscript submitted for publication.

Coster, W., Gersten, M. S., Beeghly, M., & Cicchetti, D. (1989). Communicative functioning in maltreated toddlers. *Developmental Psychology, 25*, 1020–1029.

Dodge, K., Pettit, G., & Bates, J. (1997). How the experience of early physical abuse leads children to become chronically aggressive. In D. Cicchetti & S. Toth (Eds.), *Rochester Symposium on Developmental Psychopathology: Vol. 8. Developmental perspectives on trauma* (pp. 263–288). Rochester, NY: University of Rochester Press.

Dozier, M., Stovall, K. C., Albus, K., & Bates, B. (2001). Attachment for infants in foster care: The role of caregiver state of mind. *Child Development, 72*, 1467–1477.

Duhaime, A., Christian, C., Rorke, L., & Zimmerman, R. (1998). Nonaccidental head injury in children: The "shaken-baby syndrome." *New England Journal of Medicine, 338*, 1822–1829.

Eckenrode, J., Laird, M., & Doris, J. (1993). School performance and disciplinary problems among abused and neglected children. *Developmental Psychology, 29*, 53–62.

Egeland, B., & Sroufe, L. A. (1981). Attachment and early maltreatment. *Child Development, 52*, 44–52.

Egeland, B., Yates, T., Appleyard, K., & Van Dulmen, M. (2002). The long-term consequences of maltreatment in the early years: A developmental pathway model to antisocial behavior. *Children's Services: Social Policy, Research and Practice, 5*, 249–260.

Erickson, M., & Egeland, B. (2002). Child neglect. In J. Myers, L. Berliner, J. Briere, C. Hendrix, C. Jenny, & T. Reid (Eds.), *The APSAC handbook on child maltreatment* (pp. 3–20). Thousand Oaks, CA: Sage.

Erickson, M., Egeland, B., & Pianta, R. (1989). The effects of maltreatment on the development of young children. In D. Cicchetti & V. Carlson (Eds.), *Child maltreatment* (pp. 647–684). New York: Cambridge University Press.

Geen, R. (2004). Providing services to kinship foster families. In R. Geen (Ed.), *Kinship care: Making the most of a valuable resource*. Washington, DC: Urban Institute.

Gresham, F. M., & Elliott, S. N. (1990). *Social Skills Rating System manual*. Circle Pines, MN: American Guidance Service.

Heller, S. S., Larrieus, J. A., D'Imperio, R., & Boris, N. W. (1999). Research on resilience to child maltreatment: Empirical considerations. *Child Abuse & Neglect, 23*, 321–338.

Horwitz, S. M., Balestracci, K. M., & Simms, M. D. (2001). Foster care placement improves children's functioning. *Archives of Pediatrics & Adolescent Medicine, 155*(11), 1255–1260.

Horwitz, S. M., Simms, M. D., & Farrington, R. (1994). Impact of developmental problems on young children's exits from foster care. *Journal of Developmental & Behavioral Pediatrics, 15*(2), 105–110.

Jones Harden, B. (2004). Safety and stability for foster children: A developmental perspective. *Future of Children, 14*(1), 39–47.

Jones Harden, B. (2007). *Infants in the child welfare system: A development framework for policy and practice*. Washington, DC: Zero to Three.

Jones Harden, B., Clyman, R., Kriebel, D., & Lyons, M. (2004). Kith and kin care: Parental attitudes and resources of foster and relative caregivers. *Children and Youth Services Review, 26*, 657–671.

Jones Harden, B., Clyman, R., & Vick, J. (2007). *The contribution of the home environment to the cognitive and language functioning of preschool children in foster care*. Unpublished manuscript.

Kaplan, S., Pelcovitz, D., & Labruna, V. (1999). Child and adolescent abuse and neglect research: A review of the past 10 years: Part I. Physical and emotional abuse and neglect. *Journal of the American Academy of Child and Adolescent Psychiatry, 38*, 1214–1222.

Kaufman, A., & Kaufman, N. (1990). *Kaufman Brief Intelligence Test (K-BIT)*. Circle Pines, MN: American Guidance Service.

Lansford, J., Malone, P., Stevens, K., Dodge, K., Bates, J., & Pettit, G. (2006). Developmental trajectories of externalizing and internalizing behaviors: Factors underlying resilience in physically abused children. *Development and Psychopathology, 18*(1), 35–55.

Larrieu, J., & Zeanah, C. (2004). Treating parent-infant relationships in the conexts of maltreatment: An integrated systems approach. In A. Sameroff, S. McDonogh, & K. Rosenblum (Eds.), *Treating parent-infant relationship problems: Strategies for intervention* (pp. 243–266). New York: Guilford Press.

Leslie, L. K., Gordon, J. N., Ganger, W., & Gist, K. (2002). Developmental delay in young children in child welfare by initial placement type. *Infant Mental Health Journal, 23*(5), 496–516.

Linares, L. O., Montalto, D., Rosbruch, N., & Li, M. (2006). Discipline practices among biological and foster parents. *Child Maltreatment, 11*(2), 157–167.

Lutzker, J., Tymchuk, A., & Bigelow, K. (2001). Applied research in child maltreatment: Practicalities and pitfalls. *Children's Services: Social Policy, Research and Practice, 4*, 141–156.

Lyons-Ruth, K., Alpern, L., & Repacholi, B. (1993). Disorganized infant attachment classification and maternal psychosocial problems as predictors of hostile-aggressive behavior in the preschool classroom. *Child Development, 64*, 572–585.

McDonough, S. (2000). Interaction guidance: An approach for difficult-to-engage families. In C. Zeanah (Ed.), *Handbook of infant mental health* (pp. 485–493). New York: Guilford.

McLoyd, V. (1998). Socioeconomic disadvantage and child development. *American Psychologist, 53*(2), 185–204.

National Clearinghouse on Child Abuse and Neglect Information. (2004). *Child abuse and neglect fatalities: Statistics and interventions*. Retrieved January 1, 2008, from http://nccanch.acf.hhs.gov

Nelson, H., Nygrem, P., & Panoscha, R. (2006). Screening for speech and language delay in preschool children: Systematic evidence review for U.S. Preventive Services Task Force. *Pediatrics, 117*, 298–319.

Newborg, J., Stock, J. R., & Wnek, L. (1988). *Battelle Developmental Inventory (BDI)*. Allen, TX: Riverside.

Newborg, J., Stock, J. R., Wnek, L., Guildubaldi, J., & Svinicki, J. (1984). *Battelle Developmental Inventory: With recalibrated technical data and norms: Examiner's manual*. Itasca, IL: Riverside.

Newton, R. R., Litrownik, A. J., & Landsverk, J. A. (2000). Children and youth in foster care: Disentangling the relationship between problem behaviors and number of placements. *Child Abuse & Neglect, 24,* 1363–1374.

Olds, D., Hill, P., Robinson, J., Song, N., & Little, C. (2000). Update on home visiting for pregnant women and parents of young children. *Pediatrics, 30*(4), 105–148.

Orme, J., & Beuhler, C. (2001). Foster family characteristics and behavioral and emotional problems of foster children: A narrative review. *Family Relations, 50,* 3–15.

RTI International. (2007). *SUDAAN user's manual, release 9.0.1.* Research Triangle Park, NC: Author.

Rutter, M. (2000). Children in substitute care: Some conceptual considerations and research implications. *Children and Youth Services Review, 22,* 685–703.

Ryan, J., & Testa, M. (2005). Child maltreatment and juvenile delinquency: Investigating the role of placement and placement stability. *Children and Youth Services Review, 22*(9–10), 227–249.

Scannapieco, M., & Connell-Carrick, K. (2005). Focus on the first years: Correlates of substantiation of child maltreatment for families with children 0-4. *Children and Youth Services Review, 27*(12), 1307–1323.

Shonkoff, J., & Meisels, S. (Eds.). (2000). *Handbook of early intervention.* New York: Cambridge University Press.

Shonkoff, J., & Phillips, D. (Eds.). (2000). *From neurons to neighborhoods: The science of early childhood development.* Washington, DC: National Academy Press.

Sparrow, S. S., Balla, D. A., & Cicchetti, D. V. (1984). *Vineland Adaptive Behavior Scales (VABS).* Circle Pines, MN: American Guidance Service.

Strathearn, L., Gray, P., O'Callaghan, M., & Wood, D. (2001). Childhood neglect and cognitive development in extremely low birth weight infants: A prospective study. *Pediatrics, 108,* 142–151.

Waldinger, R., Toth, S., & Gerber, A. (2001). Maltreatment and internal representations of relationships: Core relationship themes in the narratives of abused and neglected preschoolers. *Social Development, 10,* 41–57.

Weberling, L., Forgays, D., & Crain-Thoreson, C. (2003). Prenatal child abuse risk assessment: A preliminary validation study. *Child Welfare, 82*(3), 319–334.

Wulczyn, F. (2004). Family reunification. *Future of Children, 14*(1), 95–113.

Wulczyn, F., Barth, R., Yuan, Y., Jones Harden, B., & Landsverk, J. (2006). *Beyond common sense: Child welfare, child well-being, and the evidence for policy reform.* Brunswick, NJ: Transaction/Aldine de Gruyter.

Wulczyn, F., Barth, R. P., Yuan, Y. T., Jones Harden, B., & Landsverk, J. (2005). *Beyond common sense: Child welfare, child well-being, and the evidence for policy reform.* New Brunswick, NJ: Aldine Transaction.

Wulczyn, F., Kogan, J., & Dilts, J. (2001). The effect of population dynamics on performance measurement. *Social Service Review, 75,* 292–317.

Wulczyn, F., Kogan, J., & Jones Harden, B. (2003). Placement stability and movement trajectories. *Social Service Review, 77,* 212–236.

Zimmerman, I. L., Steiner, V. G., & Pond, R. E. (1992). *PLS-3: Preschool Language Scale-3* San Antonio, TX: The Psychological Corporation.

3

Risk and Resilience Among Children Referred to the Child Welfare System

A Longitudinal Investigation of Child Well-Being in Multiple Domains

ANNE SHAFFER, BYRON EGELAND, AND KEVIN WANG

A driving goal of the child welfare system is to ensure the well-being of the youth it serves, yet defining *well-being*, both theoretically and practically, remains an elusive precondition to fulfilling this goal. To say that a child is "doing well" is a broad characterization begging a host of additional questions (doing well in terms of what aspects of functioning? for how long? despite what challenges?). Historically, the term *well-being* arose primarily as a reaction to the disease model and deficit-based approaches in mental health study and practice; therefore, operational definitions of *well-being* often emphasize measures of positive adaptation and self-appraisal (Seligman, 2002), as well as economic indicators (Diener & Seligman, 2005). Moreover, many definitions of *well-being* as applied to children and youth focus on the achievement of competent, developmentally appropriate functioning.

Most often, research on the well-being of children involved in the child welfare system has focused on circumscribed domains of functioning (i.e., behavioral problems, depressive symptoms) measured at single points in time and often without in-depth consideration of the child's daily-living context. These studies have tended to look for indicators or predictors of adaptation in these single areas. A broader conceptualization of well-being is far more likely, however, to afford a meaningful view into how a child, or group of children, is functioning. For example, well-being should not be conceptualized only as the absence of clinically significant psychopathology, because this approach does not require the competent achievement of salient developmental tasks. Conversely, an exclusive focus on overt indicators of competent functioning may overlook more internal processes of maladaptation and psychopathology (Luthar, 1991). To take a relatively simple but illustrative example, a child who is well behaved and doing well in school yet clinically depressed is not enjoying well-being, yet reliance on single indicators of well-being, without consideration of other areas of adaptation, may lead to such unwarranted conclusions.

Middle Childhood

In selecting, instead, the multiple domains of functioning with which to define child well-being, in this study we are guided by a developmental framework for middle childhood. During middle childhood, children face a specific set of developmental tasks founded on their history of past adaptation, the achievement of which founds future adaptation. For this reason, the identification of success or failure in salient developmental tasks provides a powerful predictor of future functioning, as well as an important marker of current functioning (Masten et al., 1999; Sroufe, Egeland, Carlson, & Collins, 2005).

By middle childhood, children have begun school and are gaining increasing independence, living in a world populated by peers, as well as caregivers. Behaviorally, positive adaptation includes good conduct, rule-abiding behavior, and an absence of aggression or other externalizing behaviors. Ideally, behavior should be assessed in multiple settings because children may show differences across settings, exhibiting good behavior at school, for example, but being overly aggressive or defiant at home. Likewise, emotional functioning is best assessed across multiple settings, and good emotional functioning can be defined as a lack of significant internalizing problems, such as symptoms of depression or anxiety.[1] Children in middle childhood who have not developed adequate self-control are likely to show signs of dysregulation, including symptoms of behavioral and emotional distress and difficulty responding functionally to developmentally appropriate demands. In terms of social functioning, middle childhood requires the successful negotiation of growing peer groups, the ability to interact positively with a variety of persons, and the development of stable friendships. Academically, positive functioning can be defined, at minimum, as average performance in relevant academic subjects.

Resilience and Child Maltreatment

Consideration of multiple domains of functioning, in terms of how a child is faring across several areas of well-being, brings our current research questions in line with contemporary theories of resilience. Resilience research identifies persons who do well despite their exposure to significant adversity; specifically, it identifies the *contextual* factors and processes that either protect a person from the negative effects of adversity, or increase his or her risk for maladaptive responses (Masten, 2001). Factors often associated with poorer functioning among children exposed to adversity include symptoms of psychopathology, family stress or poverty (Duncan & Brooks-Gunn, 1997; Luthar, 1999), and prior history of adaptation or maladaptation in salient developmental tasks (Egeland, Carlson, & Sroufe, 1993; Werner & Smith, 1992; Yates, Egeland, & Sroufe, 2003).

Yates et al. (2003) defined *resilience* as a developmental concept characterized by a dynamic process in which the child uses available resources to negotiate the salient issues of each developmental stage; it therefore refers to an ongoing process of adaptation, of building a foundation for overcoming subsequent challenges. Resilience does not *cause* children to do well in the face of adversity; instead, it reflects the developmental process by which children use both internal and external resources to adapt positively to past or current negative circumstances. Many children who face major adversity, for example, to some extent have resources such as social support, but not all children effectively use this support for coping and adapting. Children who can successfully garner resources in the context of adverse experiences are those whom Yates et al. (2003) would identify as resilient.

Common factors associated with positive functioning and adaptation include prior history of positive adaptation in salient developmental tasks (e.g., secure caregiver attachment in infancy), intellectual ability, effective coping strategies, positive home environment, and nurturing relationships with caregivers, as well as social support from other sources (Egeland et al., 1993; Masten et al., 1999; Yates et al., 2003). In the terminology of resilience research, such factors are *protective* when they are associated with positive adaptation for children who have experienced adversity; they are termed *promotive* when they are considered to be assets for development, regardless of the extent of adversity (Masten, 2001). In studies like our current one, in which contextual factors are considered only in terms of main effects, the term *protective factor* is not used: The data preclude analysis of interactions based on the extent of each child's exposure to adversity; instead, these variables are analyzed as promotive factors and are hypothesized to be positively correlated with competence in multiple domains.

Rather than focusing exclusively on adaptation in a single domain, many studies of resilience employ person-based methods to identify children who demonstrate positive adaptation across multiple developmentally salient domains. In the associated methodologies the goals are two-fold: *(1)* to identify those who have been exposed to significant adversity, and *(2)* to identify those in this group who are doing well despite that adversity. Traditionally, the emphasis is on children who are displaying adaptation that is average, not perfect: The research criteria do not require extremely positive functioning but only adequate functioning in most age-salient domains (e.g., Cicchetti & Rogosch, 1997; Masten et al., 1999). Past studies have varied in terms of how they identify cutoff criteria for positive adaptation: The criteria are based on the sample (i.e., using median or quartile splits), or they are based on normative data (i.e., using clinical cutoff scores).[2]

Not surprisingly, the study of resilience has more recently intersected with the study of child maltreatment (Heller, Larrieus, D'Imperio, & Boris, 1999; Kaufman, Cook, Arny, Jones, & Pittinsky, 1994; McGloin & Widom, 2001). Although plentiful evidence exists that childhood maltreatment is often associated with deleterious developmental outcomes for many children (Briere, Berliner, Bulkley, Jenny, & Reid, 1996; Cicchetti & Toth, 2000; Knutson, 1995), more recent research has shown that the variation in outcomes can begin to be explained by contextual factors that may influence development—findings consistent with an ecological model of development (Cicchetti & Toth, 2000; Wulczyn, Barth, Yuan, Jones Harden, & Landsverk, 2005; Zielinski & Bradshaw, 2006).

Among the individual characteristics of the child, for example, high self-esteem has been a protective factor for maltreated children studied in multiple samples (Cicchetti & Rogosch, 1997; Moran & Eckenrode, 1992). Higher intellectual functioning is another individual characteristic that has been longitudinally associated with positive adaptation among maltreated youth (Herrenkohl, Herrenkohl, & Egolf, 1994). Beyond individual characteristics, elements of the broader environmental context also have been shown to predict more positive outcomes for maltreated youth—elements such as engagement in school, relationships with caregivers and other adults, and caregiving environments that are safe, consistent, and stable. Higher levels of self-reported school engagement and more positive school experiences, for example, have been associated with better outcomes (i.e., lower rates of psychiatric disorders) among women who were sexually abused as children (Romans, Martin, Anderson, O'Shea, & Mullen, 1995). Nurturing relationships with caregivers, as well as other adults, are often associated with positive outcomes for maltreated children, as is a consistent caregiving environment (Heller et al., 1999; Zielinski & Bradshaw, 2006). Conversely, in a prospective, longitudinal study (Farber & Egeland, 1987), family vulnerability factors such as poverty and single parenting were found more commonly among nonresilient maltreated children. Additionally, residential instability, as measured by the number of moves or placements a child experiences, is inversely related to positive outcomes for maltreated children (Eckenrode, Rowe, Laird, & Brathwaite, 1995; Jones Harden, 2004).

As more researchers attempt to describe factors and processes that may lead to maltreated children's adaptation, questions about the best way to study these phenomena have emerged. In their review of research on resilience and maltreatment, Heller and colleagues (1999) identify several potential confounders in the extant literature and offer suggestions for more effective, rigorous future research. Many of their suggestions focus on identifying the potential effects of multiple variables that are often treated as one variable. For example, children who have experienced any kind of maltreatment are often considered as a homogeneous group, although some evidence exists for differential outcomes by type of maltreatment. Similarly, multiple potential risk factors often simultaneously beset a child. Although ample evidence exists that multiple risk factors combined into composite or index scores are more consistently associated with negative outcomes than the effects of any one specific risk factor, to understand the processes by which these factors operate, researchers should, according to Heller and colleagues, build analytic models in which the influence of single risk factors, in terms of the variance accounted for, can be observed. Accordingly, in our current study we examine the effects of several risk factors, both separately and together.

Several methodological suggestions for defining particular constructs also have been advanced (Heller et al., 1999). Definitions of *competent functioning* have certainly varied across studies. Heller and colleagues recommend a priori definitions derived from norm-referenced (as opposed to sample-based) cutoff scores from multiple (as opposed to single) measures. In addition, to obtain information on functioning across settings, they recommend use of multiple reporters whenever possible, although this recommendation brings with it difficulties concerning interreporter agreement (see Achenbach, McConaughy, & Howell, 1987). Heller et al. add that reports of current functioning are preferable to retrospective reports and that longitudinal data are the data most likely to accurately capture the nature of resilience as a dynamic process of adaptation over time.

Data Set Characteristics, Test Variables, and Goals

The data from the National Study of Child and Adolescent Well-Being (NSCAW) permit an investigation of child well-being that comprises multiple domains of functioning, multiple informants, and multiple waves of data collection; these data allow researchers to develop a fuller portrait of children's adaptation over the time elapsing after each child's initial referral to protective services. Such efforts to identify comprehensive measures of child functioning are prerequisites to developing effective strategies for identifying these children's mental health needs (Webb & Jones Harden, 2003; Wulczyn et al., 2005) and, in turn, for designing effective programs of prevention and intervention.

The primary goal of our research here is to explore well-being and resilience in multiple domains across middle childhood by focusing exclusively on children in the NSCAW sample who were aged 8 to 10 years at baseline and who were reported to have been exposed to significant adversity. The age range for our subsample permits an investigation of the developmental processes in an understudied age group. We devised our composite measures of well-being for these children in the domains of behavioral, emotional, social, and academic functioning, using information from multiple reporters, including caregivers, caseworkers, and the children themselves. Our secondary objective is to examine the relations of these domains of functioning to contextual factors possibly associated with adaptation in them. The NSCAW data permit an examination of contextual factors that may either exacerbate or ameliorate risks to child well-being; moreover, the longitudinal nature of NSCAW allows us to consider changes in these variables over considerable time as we follow these children to early adolescence.

Several studies of resilience and maltreatment have emphasized the importance of the assessment of functioning across multiple developmental domains (e.g., Kaufman et al., 1994; McGloin & Widom, 2001), but this topic remains understudied area in the child welfare literature. Our study represents an initial step toward studying multidimensional competence, as well as resilience, in the subsample of children who allegedly have been maltreated. To this end, our objectives include defining *competent functioning* across behavioral, emotional, social, and academic domains. In defining *competent functioning* in developmental domains, we benefit from the breadth of NSCAW, using information from multiple reporters and, when possible, standardized data. Related to this question of competency is our research objective of identifying children, at baseline and at the 36-month follow-up, at least adequately functional in behavioral, emotional, social, and academic domains, despite their adverse experiences. We also compare these children, in multiple domains and in terms of contextual (i.e., risk and promotive) factors assessed at the baseline interview, with their counterparts who are not doing well. Our next objective is to identify who among children referred to protective services for maltreatment allegations is doing well *across* (i.e., in at least three of four) developmentally salient domains, both at baseline and at the Wave 4 (36-month) follow-up.

In keeping with the goals of resilience research, in other words, we identify a subsample of children who have been exposed to significant adversity, and we explore a variety of contextual factors, as measured at baseline, likely to increase risk or enhance positive adaptation over time. We then assess the predictive ability of early contextual factors to identify children who are doing well at the time of the Wave 1 (baseline) and Wave 4 (36-month) follow-up interviews. Specific risk factors hypothesized to be negatively associated with functioning are early symptoms of psychopathology, a high number of out-of-home placements, and family-based risk factors, such as parental substance abuse, domestic violence history, and financial strain; hypothesized promotive factors are cognitive ability and school engagement, which are further hypothesized to be positively associated with functioning in multiple domains.

Methods

Our analyses focused on a subset of children who, being 8 to 10 years old, were in middle childhood at the time of the Wave 1 (baseline) assessment and who reportedly had been exposed to significant adversity. The study sample included 410 children (208 female). The relevant data on these children were collected at the NSCAW Wave 1 assessment and at the Wave 4 (36-month follow-up) assessment.

Data Sources and Exclusions

The data were derived from three sources: the children's self-reports, the caregivers' reports, and the child welfare system caseworkers' reports. Teachers' reports were also available but had relatively high rates of missing data for the participants in the current study (e.g., more than 33% of the participating children had missing teacher data at Wave 4). Moreover, although teachers' ratings of behavioral and emotional problems were somewhat higher and their ratings of social functioning were lower than ratings from the other sources, exploratory analyses indicated that results did not significantly change when teachers' reports were combined with caregivers' reports; therefore, teachers' reports were excluded from the current study. The respondent completing the caregiver's report was always the person fulfilling that role currently; therefore, some discontinuity in reporters exists for children who received new placements. Notably, however, 64% ($n = 262$) of the children in the study remained with their biological parents at the time of the baseline assessment.

Measures

SOCIODEMOGRAPHIC INFORMATION Children's age, gender, and race/ethnicity were noted during the initial case identification procedures and later verified during data collection interviews with all informants. Additional information about the children's families was provided by caseworkers.

MALTREATMENT HISTORY Caseworkers reported the types of alleged maltreatment, using a modified version of the Maltreatment Classification Scale (Manly, Cicchetty, & Barnett, 1994). Six types of maltreatment were reported: physical abuse, sexual abuse, emotional abuse, supervisory neglect (failure to supervise the child), physical neglect (failure to provide for the child), and abandonment. Subsequently, a variable was created based on the caseworkers' reports of the most serious type of abuse experienced by each child. For the purposes of the current study (i.e., to obtain appropriate sample sizes and to maintain consistency with the extant research literature), emotional abuse and abandonment were not considered, and supervisory and physical neglect were combined into one category; therefore, the children in the current sample are identified according to whether the most serious type of alleged maltreatment was categorized as physical abuse, sexual abuse, or neglect (for frequencies, see Table 3.1).

EXPOSURE TO ADVERSITY AND HARM At the baseline assessment, caseworkers rated the level of harm experienced by the child, using the Manly et al. (1994) coding scheme. Levels of adversity and harm ranged from *none to mild* to *moderate* or *severe*. For the current study these levels were dichotomized so that those children reported to have experienced moderate or severe harm were considered to have been exposed to significant adversity. This subsample of children exposed to significant adversity forms the analysis sample for the current study.

COMPETENT FUNCTIONING Child competence was assessed in four domains: behavioral functioning, emotional functioning, social functioning, and academic functioning. Whenever possible, and in keeping with the recommendations of Heller et al. (1999), the composite variables involved multiple reporters or sources of information. Potential informants included the child and current caregiver. Also in keeping with Heller et al. (1999), cutoff scores for each variable were established a priori and guided by either normative data (when available) or prior published research using NSCAW data.

Behavioral functioning was assessed from caregivers' report on externalizing behavior scores from the Child Behavior Checklist (CBCL; Achenbach, 1991), which reports them as T scores with established means of 50 and clinical cutoff scores of 65. T scores equal to or more than 65 are considered indicators of clinically significant levels of behavioral problems such as aggression, hyperactivity, or inattention. For the current study, scores less than 65 qualified as indicators of competent functioning. Although this range of scores includes some children who are in the borderline range of clinically significant behavioral problems, using 65 as a cutoff score is consistent with prior NSCAW research and with the assertion in resilience literature that a child may be functioning at levels somewhat worse than average and still be doing "okay" in the domain (Masten et al., 1999).

Emotional functioning was ascertained from caregivers' reporting of internalizing behavior scores from the CBCL (Achenbach, 1991), which, again, reports them as T scores with established means of 50 and clinical cutoff scores of 65. T scores equal to or more than 65 are considered indicators of clinically significant levels of emotional problems such as depression, anxiety, or somatic complaints. For the current study, scores less than 65 qualified as indicators of competent functioning.

Social functioning was assessed with ratings of social behavior and peer interaction as reported by caregivers. Scores from the Social Skills subscale of the Social Skills Rating System (Gresham & Elliott, 1990) are based on a norm-referenced standard scale with social functioning scores ranging from 40 (*poor*) to 130 (*excellent;* $M = 100$, $SD = 10$). Consistent with prior research on the NSCAW data set, a score of 85 or more was established as indicating social competence.

Academic functioning was assessed with the Reading and Math subtests of the Mini Battery of Achievement (Woodcock, McGrew, & Werder, 1994). The test is measured in standard scores ($M = 100$, $SD = 15$). For the current study, scores on the Reading and Math subtests were averaged; a score of 85 or more was established as indicating academic competence.

Finally, cross-domain functioning was determined by considering children's concurrent competence in multiple domains. A summary score was created for each to reflect the total number of domains in which competence was demonstrated. Multidimensional, or cross-domain, competence was defined as summary scores of 3 or greater, indicating competent functioning in at least three of the four developmental domains.

CONTEXTUAL FACTORS To assess associations with the outcome variables of interest, five contextual factors were considered, one type being family risk factors. According to knowledge gained during the child maltreatment investigation, caseworkers identified for each child the presence of family risk factors: parent's drug or alcohol abuse, parent's severe mental illness, parent's intellectual/cognitive impairment, parent's physical impairment, impaired parenting skills (e.g., inappropriate discipline), financial problems, and domestic violence. These risk factors were coded in terms of presence or absence and converted to an index score for each child (the number of risk factors coded as *present* divided by the total number of risk factors possible).

Another contextual factor, self-reported psychopathology at the initial assessment likely reflects compromised adaptational history; these measures help predict problems in later functioning. Two measures of psychopathology self-reported at baseline were included as indicators of the participants' history of psychological adaptation: Symptoms of depression, including feelings of sadness and low self-worth, were assessed with use of the Child Depression Inventory (Kovacs, 1992). Secondly, symptoms of trauma were assessed with use of an adapted version of the Trauma Symptoms Checklist for Children (section on posttraumatic stress disorder; Briere, 1996).

The other three contextual factors were number of out-of-home placements, cognitive ability, and school engagement. The number of out-of-home placements was derived from the caseworker report; in the regression analyses this measure was trichotomized into zero out-of-home placements, one out-of-home placement, and two or more out-of-home placements. The child's cognitive ability was assessed at baseline with the Kaufman Brief IntelligenceTest (K-BIT; Kaufman & Kaufman, 1990); the current study used a composite variable, the sum of standard scores from Vocabulary and Matrices subtests. School engagement was taken by a scale using self-report and adapted from the Drug-Free Schools Outcome Study Questions (U.S. Department of Education, 1995). Responses to items (e.g., *enjoys being in school, finds class interesting*) were summed for a total score.

Analyses

Descriptive, univariate, and multivariate analyses were completed with use of SUDAAN statistical version 9.0.1 (RTI International, 2007) to account for the complex stratified and weighted design of the study. Initial analyses compared competent and noncompetent groups in terms of demographic and contextual variables. Several demographic and contextual variables were coded categorically, and group comparisons were made using the Pearson χ^2 statistic. For variables that were coded continuously, group differences were analyzed with the use of weighted *t* tests.

A series of logistic regressions was run to test the roles of early contextual factors in predicting which children would do well at baseline and at Wave 4 (36-month follow-up) assessments. These regressions were planned to analyze the contribution of various contextual factors *after* controlling for demographic variables (i.e., gender and race/ethnicity). On each domain, regressions were run for which all contextual factors were entered simultaneously as predictors, allowing us to evaluate the unique variance accounted for by each predictor while controlling for all other predictors. In these regressions, stepwise models were built iteratively so that final models included only significant contextual predictors ($p < .05$ for Wald F statistics), as well as the demographic variables. The regression models began with all predictors; we used backward elimination to reduce the models to inclusion of only the significant predictor variables.

Results

Demographic Data and Outcome Scores

Children were identified as having experienced significant adversity and were therefore included in the current analyses if their caseworkers rated their harm or risk of harm greater than *moderate* (i.e., from *moderate* to *severe*). In terms of demographic data for the current subsample of 410, the subsample included 208 females, ages ranging from 8 to 10 (136 eight year olds, 147 nine year olds, 127 ten year olds), and was ethnically/racially diverse (121 black or African American, 194 white, 69 Hispanic, and 26 other races or ethnicities). Eighty-seven children were reported to child welfare services with physical abuse as their primary maltreatment type, 83 were identified with sexual abuse as their primary maltreatment type, and 160 were identified with neglect as their primary maltreatment type. Descriptive statistics for the outcome scores by domain (Table 3.1).

Competent Functioning in Individual and Multiple Domains

Our first goal in this study was to identify children evincing at least adequate functioning behaviorally, emotionally, socially, and academically at the Wave 1 and Wave 4 (36-month follow-up) assessments. For the behavioral (externalizing) and emotional (internalizing) domains, scores below the clinical range (i.e., T score < 65) indicated adequate functioning. For the social and academic domains, scores within 1.5 standard deviations below the normed means of the respective measures were used as cutoffs for adequate functioning. Based on these criteria, the frequencies and weighted percentages of children demonstrating competency in each domain are reported (Table 3.2). Wave 1 rates of competent functioning across the four domains ranged from 56.5% to 79.1%; Wave 4 rates of competent functioning ranged from 67.7% to 85.6%. At both assessments, the highest rates of competence were in the domain of emotional functioning.

Table 3.1 Descriptive Statistics for Continuous Measures of Competence Domains at Waves 1 and 4

	Wave 1 ($n = 410$)		Wave 4 ($n = 399$)	
	M	*SEM*	*M*	*SEM*
Behavioral	57.93	1.72	55.82	1.42
Emotional	56.29	0.92	52.54	1.21
Social	88.94	2.09	94.37	1.83
Academic	91.80	2.56	91.53	3.40

Table 3.2 Competence in Individual and Multiple Domains: Frequencies and Weighted Percentages

	Wave 1		Wave 4	
	Noncompetent	*Competent*	*Noncompetent*	*Competent*
Behavioral	146	264	115	284
	40.10%	59.90%	32.31%	67.69%
Emotional	128	282	79	320
	20.86%	79.14%	14.39%	85.61%
Social	178	232	115	284
	43.54%	56.46%	25.04%	74.96%
Academic	105	265	116	272
	29.57%	70.43%	29.38%	70.62%
Cross-domain	163	207	118	268
	42.12%	57.88%	32.87%	67.13%

Note: Subsample frequencies are unweighted and based on available data at each wave; percentages are weighted.

After identifying children functioning competently in at least single domains, our second goal was to identify at Wave 1 and Wave 4 the children doing well across at least three of the four developmentally salient domains (Table 3.3). At Wave 1, the rate of cross-domain competence was 57.9%; at Wave 4 the rate was 67.1%.

Competent and Noncompetent Cross-Domain Functioning: Contextual Factors

Our remaining goals for this study involved describing the differences between children who do well and those who do not, in multiple domains and in terms

Table 3.3 Functioning in Multiple Domains: Percentage Meeting Criteria for Competent Functioning at Waves 1 and 4

Wave 1 Variable	Behavioral	Emotional	Social	Academic	Cross-Domain
Gender					
Male	73.15%	70.78%	60.77%	68.18%	57.33%
Female	58.55%	86.41%	52.72%	72.80%	58.47%
χ^2 statistic	0.07	5.16*	0.60	0.15	0.01
Maltreatment Type					
Physical abuse	64.58%	78.92%	53.11%	76.84%	63.05%
Sexual abuse	40.90%	79.67%	30.70%	43.97%	23.98%
Neglect	62.76%	82.80%	71.34%	75.41%	69.77%
χ^2 statistic	1.79	0.28	6.05*	2.95	6.55*
Placement at Baseline					
Out of home	50.50%	57.63%	38.80%	67.89%	37.69%
In home	62.07%	84.10%	60.54%	71.04%	62.72%
χ^2 statistic	1.15	6.30*	4.37*	0.09	4.48*
					Continued

Table 3.3 (Continued)

Wave 1 Variable	Behavioral	Emotional	Social	Academic	Cross-Domain
Gender					
Male	64.70%	74.34%	73.80%	63.07%	60.91%
Female	70.29%	95.39%	75.96%	77.54%	72.87%
χ^2 statistic	0.37	15.18*	0.08	1.56	1.83
Maltreatment Type					
Physical abuse	75.30%	95.59%	78.44%	85.18%	73.20%
Sexual abuse	50.40%	86.27%	59.61%	51.49%	36.06%
Neglect	76.15%	79.69%	77.14%	64.39%	76.31%
χ^2 statistic	2.06	7.54*	1.60	3.94	4.68
Placement at Baseline					
Out of home	59.38%	80.57%	62.63%	68.91%	58.39%
In home	69.59%	86.76%	77.77%	71.01%	69.14%
χ^2 statistic	0.82	0.91	2.28	0.04	0.95

Note: Percentages are weighted and are computed according to data available for each outcome domain and wave.

of contextual factors. An initial step was to conduct a series of comparisons in terms of single domains of functioning and cross-domain functioning. We report the weighted percentage of children who met criteria for competent functioning at Wave 1 and Wave 4 in each domain, and across domains, based on gender, maltreatment type, and placement at baseline (see Table 3.3).

At Wave 1, fewer males demonstrated emotional competence. Significant differences by primary maltreatment type emerged: The sexually abused children showed lower rates of social and cross-domain competence. Children who were living out of home at baseline showed lower rates of emotional, social, and cross-domain competence. At Wave 4, fewer significant gender differences were detected, these being in emotional functioning. Fewer males than females demonstrated competent emotional functioning, with the pattern resembling that of the Wave 1 assessment. Also at Wave 4, rates of emotional competence were lowest for those children whose most serious type of maltreatment was neglect.

We report differences between the competent and noncompetent groups identified at Wave 1 and Wave 4, by the baseline contextual factors scored as continuous variables (Tables 3.4 and 3.5). At Wave 1, higher cognitive ability and higher school engagement were observed among those competent in the social and academic domains. Symptoms of depression were significantly higher for those identified as noncompetent in the social domain, while trauma symptoms were higher for those whose behavioral scores fell below the competence threshold. A higher number of out-of-home placements and increased level of family risks were observed among those children not meeting competence criteria in the emotional domain.

Table 3.4   Comparisons of Wave 1 Groups on Multiple Contextual Factors

	Cognitive Ability M (SE)	Depressive Symptoms M (SE)	Trauma Symptoms M (SE)	School Engagement M (SE)	No. Out-of-Home Placements M (SE)	Family Risks M (SE)
Behavioral						
Noncompetent	190.32	54.07	57.86	3.07	0.72	0.39
	(4.39)	(1.84)	(2.56)	(0.10)	(0.21)	(0.03)
Competent	191.78	51.17	51.85	3.23	0.56	0.40
	(4.53)	(1.60)	(1.32)	(0.06)	(0.11)	(0.02)
t test statistic	−0.23	1.19	2.61*	−1.22	0.69	−0.31
Emotional						
Noncompetent	188.42	55.34	54.63	3.04	1.31	0.48
	(5.22)	(1.65)	(1.77)	(0.10)	(0.29)	(0.03)
Competent	192.12	51.31	54.09	3.21	0.44	0.37
	(3.97)	(1.50)	(2.12)	(0.06)	(0.08)	(0.02)
t test statistic	−0.57	1.83	0.21	−1.48	3.03*	3.55*
Social						
Noncompetent	179.95	55.74	57.70	2.97	0.77	0.41
	(5.84)	(1.51)	(2.95)	(0.11)	(0.18)	(0.02)
Competent	199.24	49.95	51.83	3.30	0.51	0.38
	(2.43)	(1.74)	(1.16)	(0.04)	(0.11)	(0.02)
t test statistic	−3.06*	2.43*	1.92	−2.84*	1.23	0.73
Academic						
Noncompetent	163.52	55.21	56.28	2.89	0.74	0.42
	(6.44)	(1.91)	(4.52)	(0.12)	(0.24)	(0.04)
Competent	202.84	51.21	53.45	3.28	0.66	0.39
	(2.03)	(1.49)	(1.14)	(0.05)	(0.13)	(0.02)
t test statistic	−5.90*	1.57	0.64	−2.67*	0.29	0.66
Cross-Domain						
Noncompetent	177.52	55.64	57.62	2.98	0.90	0.42
	(5.69)	(1.46)	(2.80)	(0.10)	(0.22)	(0.03)
Competent	201.18	49.99	51.86	3.30	0.53	0.39
	(2.07)	(1.79)	(1.15)	(0.05)	(0.12)	(0.02)
t test statistic	−3.92*	2.38*	2.13*	−2.74*	1.50	0.86

*$p < .05$

At Wave 4, cognitive ability was significantly higher among those competent in the academic domain. In terms of early psychopathology, trauma symptoms at baseline were significantly higher among the individuals who were noncompetent in the behavioral domain at Wave 4. Baseline school engagement was significantly higher for children who were competent in the social and academic domains at Wave 4. Number of out-of-home placements and level of family risks as rated by the caseworkers did not differentiate the competent from the noncompetent in any domain of functioning at Wave 4.

Next we analyzed variables that distinguished children who had met criteria for cross-domain competence from those who had not. The children meeting criteria at baseline for competence in at least three of the four domains had higher cognitive

Table 3.5 Comparisons of Wave 4 Groups on Multiple Contextual Factors

	Cognitive Ability M (SE)	Depressive Symptoms M (SE)	Trauma Symptoms M (SE)	School Engagement M (SE)	No. of Out-of-Home Placements M (SE)	Family Risks M (SE)
Behavioral						
Noncompetent	189.71	55.28	59.69	3.05	0.83	0.38
	(4.01)	(1.67)	(3.16)	(0.11)	(0.26)	(0.02)
Competent	191.81	50.91	51.27	3.24	0.51	0.40
	(4.47)	(1.55)	(1.36)	(0.06)	(0.10)	(0.02)
t test statistic	−0.36	1.93	2.39*	−1.41	1.11	−0.72
Emotional						
Noncompetent	190.63	54.40	53.09	3.01	1.16	0.41
	(5.62)	(2.67)	(1.62)	(0.19)	(0.36)	(0.04)
Competent	191.18	52.05	54.53	3.20	0.53	0.39
	(3.80)	(1.32)	(2.08)	(0.06)	(0.09)	(0.02)
t test statistic	−0.08	0.80	−0.53	−0.92	1.76	0.40
Social						
Noncompetent	179.73	55.84	56.53	2.93	0.94	0.42
	(8.64)	(2.06)	(2.01)	(0.16)	(0.25)	(0.03)
Competent	195.61	51.21	53.43	3.26	0.51	0.39
	(3.05)	(1.54)	(1.99)	(0.04)	(0.09)	(0.02)
t test statistic	−1.66	1.70	1.33	−2.06*	1.62	0.78
Academic						
Noncompetent	179.13	54.51	55.98	2.96	0.66	0.36
	(7.05)	(2.25)	(4.55)	(0.12)	(0.21)	(0.03)
Competent	200.22	50.65	53.55	3.27	0.62	0.40
	(2.71)	(1.12)	(1.33)	(0.07)	(0.13)	(0.02)
t test statistic	−3.90*	1.56	0.54	−2.12*	0.16	−0.94
Cross-Domain						
Noncompetent	181.93	55.90	59.74	3.02	0.86	0.38
	(6.62)	(1.64)	(3.61)	(0.11)	(0.26)	(0.03)
Competent	195.74	49.47	50.95	3.26	0.52	0.39
	(2.88)	(1.14)	(1.31)	(0.07)	(0.10)	(0.02)
t test statistic	−1.90	3.32*	2.22*	−1.72	1.18	−0.43

*$p < .05$

ability and school engagement scores at Wave 4, as well as lower ratings of depression and trauma symptoms. Symptoms of trauma and of depression were both higher among those who had not met criteria for cross-domain competence.

Representing analyses of concurrent relations of contextual factors (i.e., predictors) to outcomes, results for the outcomes assessed at baseline are presented by domain (Table 3.6): Cognitive ability significantly predicted competent functioning in the social and academic domains and in cross-domain functioning. Symptoms of depression significantly predicted less competent functioning in the emotional domain, and symptoms of trauma significantly predicted less competence in behavioral and social functioning, as well as less in cross-domain functioning. Increased levels of school engagement were associated with a greater

Table 3.6   Stepwise (Backward Elimination) Logistic Regressions of Functioning on All Predictors: Final Reduced Models for Wave 1

	β	SE β	OR
A. Wave 1 Behavioral Functioning			
Intercept	2.49	0.59	12.08
Race/ethnicity			
Black or African American	−0.59	0.51	0.56
White	0.00	—	1.00
Hispanic	1.10	0.69	3.02
Other	1.15*	0.50	3.19
Trauma symptoms	−0.04*	0.01	0.96
B. Wave 1 Emotional Functioning			
Intercept	5.32	0.93	204.06
Gender			
Male	0.00	—	1.00
Female	1.06*	0.43	2.89
Symptoms of depression	−0.05*	0.02	0.95
Family risks	−3.08*	1.27	0.02
No. of OOH placements			
0	0.00	—	1.00
1	−0.00	0.53	0.99
2+	−1.33*	0.47	0.26
C. Wave 1 Social Functioning			
Intercept	−5.64	1.81	0.00
Cognitive ability	0.03*	0.01	1.03
Trauma symptoms	−0.03*	0.02	0.97
School engagement	0.98*	0.36	2.67
D. Wave 1 Academic Functioning			
Intercept	−17.05	2.42	0.00
Cognitive ability	0.08*	0.01	1.09
School engagement	0.80*	0.37	2.23
E. Wave 1 Cross-Domain Functioning			
Intercept	−7.20	1.80	0.00
Cognitive ability	0.04*	0.01	1.04
Trauma symptoms	−0.03*	0.02	0.97
School engagement	0.80*	0.32	2.22

* $p < .05$.
OOH, out-of-home.

likelihood of competence in the social and academic domains, as well as in cross-domain functioning. A higher number of out-of-home placements was negatively associated with emotional functioning, specifically for children who experienced two or more out-of-home placements as compared to those experiencing none or only one placement. Higher levels of family risks were negatively associated with competence in the emotional domain. Finally, the demographic variables of gender and race/ethnicity were retained in the final models for some outcome domains. Specifically, race/ethnicity was significant in the final model for emotional functioning, with those identified in the NSCAW sample as belonging to "other" ethnic groups (e.g., Asian, American Indian) more likely to show positive behavioral functioning outcomes. Similarly significant in the final models, females were more likely than males to show competent emotional functioning.

Results for the outcomes assessed at Wave 4 are presented by domain, representing analyses of longitudinal relations of contextual factors (i.e., predictors) to outcomes (Table 3.7). Again, results are presented by predictors: Cognitive ability significantly predicted more competent functioning in the academic domain. In terms of self-reported psychopathology, symptoms of depression significantly predicted less competent functioning in the emotional domain, while symptoms of trauma significantly predicted less competent behavioral and cross-domain functioning. Higher levels of school engagement at Wave 1 (baseline) were associated with a greater likelihood of competence in the social domain, as well as cross-domain functioning, at Wave 4. Number of out-of-home placements and

Table 3.7 Stepwise (Backward Elimination) Logistic Regressions of Functioning on All Predictors: Final Reduced Models for Wave 4

	β	SE β	OR
A. Wave 4 Behavioral Functioning			
Intercept	3.51	0.89	33.49
Trauma symptoms	−0.05*	0.02	0.95
B. Wave 4 Emotional Functioning			
Intercept	3.10	0.87	22.21
Gender			
Male	0.00	—	1.00
Female	2.04*	0.46	7.67
Race/ethnicity			
Black or African American	0.05	0.56	1.05
White	0.00	—	1.00
Hispanic	1.31*	0.60	3.69
Other	−1.58*	0.73	0.21
Symptoms of depression	−0.04*	0.02	0.96
C. Wave 4 Social Functioning			
Intercept	−1.91	1.04	0.15
School engagement	0.93*	0.37	2.53
D. Wave 4 Academic Functioning			
Intercept	−8.19	2.39	0.00
Cognitive ability	0.05*	0.01	1.05
E. Wave 4 Cross-Domain Functioning			
Intercept	1.11	1.67	3.02
Trauma symptoms	−0.05*	0.02	0.95
School engagement	0.71*	0.35	2.03

* $p < .05$.

level of family risks were not significant predictors of any Wave 4 outcome. Among the demographic variables, female children and Hispanic children were more likely to demonstrate competent emotional functioning, while those included in the "other" ethnic groups (e.g., Asian, American Indian) were less likely than other racial/ethnic groups to demonstrate competent emotional functioning.

Additional analyses were conducted for the Wave 4 outcomes in order to assess evidence of longitudinal change by controlling for outcomes at baseline. For all of the final models already discussed, an additional step was added to the regression model to include the corresponding outcome score at baseline; there-fore, any remaining significant predictors could be interpreted as predicting change in outcome scores beyond what was shown at baseline. For Wave 4 behavioral functioning, trauma symptoms remained a significant predictor after controlling for baseline behavioral functioning ($\beta = 1.85$, $SE = 0.43$). For emotional functioning at Wave 4, female gender ($\beta = 1.90$, $SE = 0.49$) and Hispanic ($\beta = 1.46$, $SE = 0.72$) and "other" ($\beta = -1.80$, $SE = 0.76$) ethnicity remained significant predictors of competent functioning after controlling for baseline measures. Symptoms of depression ($\beta = -0.03$, $SE = 0.02$) were margin-ally significant ($p = .06$). Predictors of Wave 4 social and academic functioning were not significant once baseline measures were included in the regression models. For cross-domain functioning at Wave 4, once baseline measures were controlled, school engagement was no longer statistically significant, but trauma symptoms ($\beta = -0.04$, $SE = 0.02$) remained significant.

Discussion

In this study the domains of competent adaptation were behavioral, emotional, social, and academic functioning. Each of these areas covers salient developmental tasks of middle childhood. In addition, cross-domain adaptation was defined as competent functioning in at least three of the four domains; it was included to account for how a child was doing in life, without relying on single outcome measures considered in isolation. In studying cross-domain functioning, we adopt a common research definition of *resilient functioning* and apply it to this sample of especially vulnerable children.

The contextual factors included in this study were examined in terms of their ability to differentiate functionally competent from noncompetent children and to predict the likelihood of competent functioning both concurrently (i.e., at the Wave 1 baseline assessment), and longitudinally (i.e., at the Wave 4 36-month follow-up assessment). Cognitive ability and school engagement, both assessed at baseline, were hypothesized to be positively associated with functioning in the outcome domains. Factors that were hypothesized to relate negatively to outcome domains were self-reported psychopathology at baseline (i.e., symptoms of depres-sion and symptoms of trauma, family risks as assessed at baseline, and number of out-of-home placements).

Levels of Functioning and Rates of Resilience

Overall, levels of functioning in the behavioral, emotional, social, and academic domains were below normative levels found in the general population; however, slight improvements in functioning from baseline to Wave 4 were observed in the current sample. These findings of slightly below-average functioning are expected for a group of children who have experienced significant adversity. Notably, the results of this study also show that slightly more than half of the participants met criteria for resilient functioning at baseline (i.e., competent functioning in multiple domains despite exposure to significant adversity); a full 67% of the sampled children were identified as resilient at Wave 4.

These rates of resilience are considerably higher than those that have been found in previous studies. A number of investigators (e.g., Cicchetti & Toth, 2000; Sternberg, Lamb, Guterman, & Abbott, 2006) have reported larger percentages of maltreated children with internalizing and externalizing problems in the clinical range on the CBCL, the same measure used in the current study. Furthermore, in a study of children who had substantiated reports of maltreatment and who remained with their biological parents, Kaufman et al. (1994) have reported that only 5% of children were classified as resilient according to functioning in academic, behavioral, and social domains, using cutoff criteria similar to ours.

Although the results of our current study may accurately reflect psychological functioning and adaptation in this sample, several caveats are warranted. Most notably, the composition of the current study's sample differs from those of the previous studies. While the previous studies generally recruited participants with significant and substantiated histories of maltreatment, the NSCAW sample was designed to capture all children referred to child protective services, regardless of case disposition.[3] Furthermore, that many family members involved in NSCAW were the subject of current child protective services investigation during the course of the study may have influenced reports of the child's functioning.

Additional issues regarding the nature of the data must be addressed in order to properly interpret our findings. First, the measures of adversity used here are based on caseworkers' ratings of the children's environments; compared with self-report or other means, they may be imprecise. Similarly, assessment of functioning in the behavioral, emotional, and social domains was based solely on the caregiver's report, which may have resulted in biased or incomplete data. Finally, no control group of children outside the child welfare system was available for comparison as a sample less likely to have suffered significant adversity.

Cognitive Ability, School Engagement, and Trauma as Contextual Predictors

Findings on associations of contextual factors with outcome domains were in the predicted directions, although not all relations were statistically significant. Several factors showed specificity in predicting functioning in particular domains as would be expected (i.e., cognitive ability predicted academic competence; depressive symptoms predicted emotional functioning). In other instances, predictors from the Wave 1 baseline assessment were significantly related to outcomes across a variety of domains (i.e., trauma symptoms predicted behavioral and social functioning). In the final logistic regression models, in which all predictors were ultimately reduced to models containing only those that retained statistical significance in predicting outcomes for each domain, cognitive ability, school engagement, and trauma symptoms were the most commonly retained variables across the Wave 1 and Wave 4 assessments. These three variables also significantly predicted cross-domain functioning, which is considered an indicator of resilient functioning, at baseline and (except for cognitive ability) at Wave 4.

Our results suggest that higher cognitive ability, better engagement in school, and lower trauma symptoms are each associated with a greater likelihood of competent functioning in several developmentally salient domains, as well as across domains, concurrently and 36 months later. Notably, number of out-of-home placements, a predictor related specifically to experiences with the child welfare system, was significantly associated with a decreased likelihood of competent functioning emotionally. However, out-of-home placements were associated with increased problems in the emotional domain only for those children who experienced two or more out-of-home placements; those who experienced only one out-of-home placement did not differ in terms of emotional functioning from those who were never placed outside the home.

Family Risks, Trauma, and Depression as Longitudinal Predictors

Number of family risks, whether separately or in combination with other predictors, was not a significant predictor of any outcome domain. This finding was surprising because many studies have shown that the cumulative effect of multiple stressors, including family risks, is associated with deleterious outcomes in childhood (Appleyard, Egeland, van Dulmen, & Sroufe, 2005; Deater-Deckard, Dodge, Bates, & Pettit, 1998; Sameroff, 2006). It may be that in the current study this variable, which is based on caseworker reports, is a somewhat inaccurate measure of family adversity, perhaps because of caseworkers' burden and difficulties experienced in obtaining complete information about families. Additionally, it may be that the nature of the current sample, with its broadly average levels of functioning, obscures the effects of family risk variables more than would be the case in a higher-adversity or lower-functioning subsample.

Notably, symptoms of trauma and, to a marginal extent, symptoms of depression, were two contextual factors that predicted longitudinal change. Controlling for baseline measures of outcomes of interest, trauma symptoms at Wave 1 still predicted a lower likelihood of competent behavioral functioning and cross-domain functioning at Wave 4. Similar results were found for symptoms of depression and emotional functioning at Wave 4, these findings barely missing statistical significance ($p = .06$).

Limitations

Several limitations may quality interpretation of our results. Limited information about maltreatment history was available for the current study; for example, it was not possible to compile and compare ratings of severity across maltreatment types. Moreover, this sample includes cases that were immediately closed, cases that were substantiated, and cases that were not substantiated for a variety of reasons; this heterogeneity may have affected results, especially with the lack of a comparison group outside the child welfare system.

Although our study attempts to include data from various sources and on salient developmental and contextual factors, availability of information for some domains is limited. This study included no measures of emotional and behavioral self-regulation, an important additional component to assessment of the emotional and behavioral domains of competence. Measures of the caregiving and social environment likely to affect the outcome domains of interest were not measured in the age group studied in the current subsample; examples of potentially important constructs for which measures were not available include children's reports of their relationships with their caregivers and other important adults, reports of social support available from familial and extrafamilial sources, and more refined measures of the home environment.

Our results, particularly in terms of the behavioral, emotional, and social outcome domains, also may have been influenced by reporter bias in that reports came from current caregivers, who may have been less likely than others to report problems experienced by their child. It may be that parents, particularly those referred to child protection services, rate their children more positively than teachers. In a previous study of resilience among maltreated children, one that used both parent and teacher data, teachers' ratings of the children's competence in academic, behavioral, and social domains were significantly lower than those of the parents (Kaufman et al., 1994). Because of the large amount of missing data in the teacher reports for this sample, however, teacher data was excluded from our analyses.

Another limitation qualifying interpretation of our results concerns the methods used to establish competent functioning in each outcome domain. The cutoff scores in each domain include scores that may be considered borderline noncompetent (e.g., CBCL T scores of 60 to 64). Consequently, the relatively high percentages meeting criteria for competent functioning in this sample of vulnerable children may be due in part to the operational definitions of competence. As noted already, however, precedence exists in NSCAW studies for using these cutoff scores; moreover, precedence exists in the resilience literature in general for using less stringent cutoffs to permit competence to be defined as "okay," not above-average, functioning.

Despite these limitations, our current results benefit greatly from key features of the NSCAW study design. In particular, the availability of data from multiple reporters, including the child, the caregiver, and the caseworker, and the longitudinal nature of the data are notable methodological assets. Moreover, the sample size and sampling procedures allow the weighted estimates to be generalized to the U.S. population of children referred to child welfare services—a rarity among studies of this kind.

Our use of multiple domains of competence as outcome measures is another asset to this study, serving to integrate child welfare research with the field of developmental psychopathology. As we noted at the outset, a child may vary in competence across areas of functioning or developmental tasks; therefore, studies of well-being are served by research methods that yield the "big picture" of functioning in and across multiple domains.

Conclusion

Grounded in the strengths of the NSCAW study design and resilience research, this study has implications for child welfare services and practice. That the children in this study showed average levels of overall functioning in comparison with normative groups may mitigate concerns that referral to the child welfare system alone is a significant or unique predictor of later problems in a group already at relatively high sociodemographic risk; however, this conclusion comes with the aforementioned caveats about the lack of a comparison group and possible reporter bias.

The results of this study do indicate that early problems, such as lower cognitive ability and elevated psychopathology, are vulnerability factors associated with later difficulties for children referred to the child welfare system because of alleged child maltreatment. From a developmental psychopathology perspective, early indicators such as these can be considered reflections of problems in the developmental history up to the time of assessment and therefore suggest the likelihood of compounding problems over time. In addition, that early factors such as trauma symptoms in 8–10 year olds predict later problems in other domains, beyond emotional functioning, illustrates the cascading effects that these risk factors can have across multiple domains.

These findings, in full context, emphasize the need for early comprehensive screening at the point of entry to child welfare services, in order that mental health services may be targeted to populations evincing early risk factors. Additionally, the positive associations of early school engagement with later functioning suggest that school engagement may be an effective avenue for preventive interventions targeting for these vulnerable children. Engagement in school can be a significant challenge for children who experience frequent residential moves, including foster children specifically and low-income children generally—an observation further warranting improved interventions that target academic success for these children.

Our findings also suggest directions for future research. One such direction would entail accounting for developmental change over time. Analytic strategies such as those that examine changes in slope or trajectory for the various outcome domains can provide useful follow-up to the results presented here. Because our findings show associations between certain contextual factors and outcomes in specific domains, longitudinal analyses can track more closely when and how these changes occur. In addition, mixed-level modeling can account for potential subgroup differences in changes over time; with this modeling, particular subgroups may show steady declines in functioning while others maintain competence.

Our goal here has been to bring research on child welfare outcomes into closer alignment with current perspectives in developmental psychopathology. We have emphasized the role of early contextual factors in exacerbating or ameliorating the likelihood of problematic developmental outcomes. Most important, we have examined outcomes simultaneously within and across multiple domains of functioning that are salient to middle childhood. In this age group many of the children who have participated in NSCAW are functioning competently by the Wave 4 assessment; we have identified several contextual factors that predict which children will not be doing so well at a comparable developmental stage. It is hoped that these findings will prompt future research involving more specific and sophisticated analyses of the roles of these contextual factors in developmental outcomes, both within the NSCAW data set and elsewhere. Future endeavors should also include the development of preventive interventions that can empirically test these theories and move the field toward more effective programming for children in the child welfare system.

NOTES

1. Good emotional (and behavioral) functioning fundamentally involves the development of self-regulatory and emotion-management skills, which prevent externalizing and internalizing problems; however, the measurement of such self-regulatory processes is complex and beyond the scope of our current investigation.
2. Normed data better facilitate comparisons across studies, however.
3. *Substantiation* is the child welfare system's official decision that investigated allegations of maltreatment of a child are valid.

REFERENCES

Achenbach, T. M. (1991). *Manual for the Child Behavior Checklist/4-18 and 1991 profile.* Burlington, VT: University of Vermont, Department of Psychiatry.

Achenbach, T. M., McConaughy, S. H., & Howell, C. T. (1987). Child/adolescent behavioral and emotional problems: Implications of cross-informant correlations for situational specificity. *Psychological Bulletin, 101*, 213–232.

Appleyard, K., Egeland, B., van Dulmen, M., & Sroufe, L. (2005). When more is not better: The role of cumulative risk in child behavior outcomes. *Journal of Child Psychology and Psychiatry, 46*(3), 235–245.

Briere, J. (1996). *Trauma Symptom Checklist for Children: Professional manual.* Lutz, FL: Psychological Assessment Resources.

Briere, J., Berliner, L., Bulkley, J. A., Jenny, C., & Reid, T. (Eds.). (1996). *The APSAC handbook on child maltreatment.* Thousand Oaks, CA: Sage Publications.

Cicchetti, D. V., & Rogosch, F. A. (1997). The role of self-organization in the promotion of resilience in maltreated children. *Development and Psychopathology, 9*, 797–815.

Cicchetti, D. V., & Toth, S. L. (2000). Developmental processes in maltreated children. In D. Hansen (Ed.), *Nebraska Symposium on Motivation: Child Maltreatment* (Vol. 46, pp. 85–160). Lincoln, NE: University of Nebraska Press.

Deater-Deckard, K., Dodge, K. A., Bates, J. E., & Pettit, G. S. (1998). Multiple risk factors in the development of externalizing behavior problems: Group and individual differences. *Development and Psychopathology, 10*, 469–493.

Diener, E., & Seligman, M. (2005). Beyond money: Toward an economy of well-being. *Psychological Science in the Public Interest, 5*(1), 1–31.

Duncan, G., & Brooks-Gunn, J. (Eds.). (1997). *Consequences of growing up poor.* New York: Russell Sage Foundation.

Eckenrode, J., Rowe, E., Laird, M., & Brathwaite, J. (1995). Mobility as a mediator of the effects of child maltreatment on academic performance. *Child Development, 66*, 1130–1142.

Egeland, B., Carlson, E., & Sroufe, L. A. (1993). Resilience as process. *Development and Psychopathology, 5*, 517–528.

Farber, E. A., & Egeland, B. (1987). Invulnerability among abused and neglected children. In E. J. Anthony & B. J. Cohler (Eds.), *The invulnerable child* (pp. 253–288). New York: Guilford Press.

Gresham, F. M., & Elliott, S. N. (1990). *Social Skills Rating System manual.* Circle Pines, MN: American Guidance Service.

Heller, S. S., Larrieus, J. A., D'Imperio, R., & Boris, N. W. (1999). Research on resilience to child maltreatment: Empirical considerations. *Child Abuse & Neglect, 23*, 321–338.

Herrenkohl, E. C., Herrenkohl, R. R., & Egolf, B. (1994). Resilient early school-age children from maltreating homes: Outcomes in late adolescence. *American Journal of Orthopsychiatry, 64*, 301–309.

Jones Harden, B. (2004). Safety and stability for foster children: A developmental perspective. *Future of Children, 14*(1), 39–47.

Kaufman, A., & Kaufman, N. (1990). *Kaufman Brief Intelligence Test (K-BIT).* Circle Pines, MN: American Guidance Service.

Kaufman, J., Cook, A., Arny, L., Jones, B., & Pittinsky, T. (1994). Problems defining resilience: Illustrations from the study of maltreated children. *Development and Psychopathology, 6*, 215–247.

Knutson, J. F. (1995). Psychological characteristics of maltreated children: Putative risk factors and consequences. *Annual Review of Psychology, 46*, 401–431.

Kovacs, M. (1992). *The Children's Depression Inventory (CDI) manual.* Toronto: Multi-Health Systems.

Luthar, S. S. (1991). Vulnerability and resilience: A study of high-risk adolescents. *Child Development, 62*, 600–616.

Luthar, S. S. (1999). *Developmental clinical psychology and psychiatry: Vol. 41. Poverty and children's adjustment.* Thousand Oaks, CA: Sage Publications.

Manly, J. T., Cicchetty, D., & Barnett, D. (1994). The impact of subtype, frequency, chronicity, and severity of child maltreatment on social competence and behavior problems *Development and Psychopathology, 6*, 121–143.

Masten, A. S. (2001). Ordinary magic: Resilience processes in development. *American Psychologist, 56*, 227–238.

Masten, A. S., Hubbard, J. J., Gest, S. D., Tellegen, A., Garmezy, N., & Ramirez, M. (1999). Competence in the context of adversity: Pathways to resilience and maladaptation from childhood to late adolescence. *Development and Psychopathology, 11,* 143–169.

McGloin, J. M., & Widom, C. S. (2001). Resilience among abused and neglected children grown up. *Development and Psychopathology, 13,* 1021–1038.

Moran, P. B., & Eckenrode, J. (1992). Protective personality characteristics among adolescent victims of maltreatment. *Child Abuse & Neglect, 16,* 743–754.

Romans, S. E., Martin, J. L., Anderson, J. C., O'Shea, M. L., & Mullen, P. E. (1995). Factors that mediate between child sexual abuse and adult psychological outcome. *Psychological Medicine, 25,* 127–142.

RTI International. (2007). *SUDAAN user's manual, release 9.0.1.* Research Triangle Park, NC: Author.

Sameroff, A. (2006). Identifying risk and protective factors for healthy child development. In A. Clarke-Stewart & J. Dunn (Eds.), *Families count: Effects on child and adolescent development* (pp. 53–76). New York: Cambridge University Press.

Seligman, M. E. P. (2002). Positive psychology, positive prevention, and positive therapy. In C. R. Snyder & S. J. Lopez (Eds.), *Handbook of positive psychology* (pp. 3–12). Oxford, England: Oxford University Press.

Sroufe, L. A., Egeland, B., Carlson, E. A., & Collins, W. A. (2005). *The development of the person: The Minnesota Study of Risk and Adaptation from Birth to Adulthood.* New York: Guilford.

Sternberg, K. J., Lamb, M. E., Guterman, E., & Abbott, C. B. (2006). Effects of early and later family violence on children's behavior problems and depression: A longitudinal, multi-informant perspective. *Child Abuse & Neglect, 30,* 283–306.

U.S. Department of Education. (1995). *Drug Free Schools (DFSCA) Outcome Study Questions.* Washington, DC: Author.

Webb, M. B., & Jones Harden, B. (2003). Beyond child protection: Promoting mental health for children and families in the child welfare system. *Journal of Emotional and Behavioral Disorders, 11,* 49–58.

Werner, E. E., & Smith, R. S. (1992). *Overcoming the odds: High risk children from birth to adulthood.* Ithaca, NY: Cornell University Press.

Woodcock, R. W., McGrew, K. S., & Werder, J. K. (1994). *Woodcock-McGrew-Werder Mini-Battery of Achievement.* Itasca, IL: Riverside.

Wulczyn, F., Barth, R. P., Yuan, Y. T., Jones Harden, B., & Landsverk, J. (2005). *Beyond common sense: Child welfare, child well-being, and the evidence for policy reform.* New Brunswick, NJ: Aldine Transaction.

Yates, T. M., Egeland, B., & Sroufe, L. A. (2003). Rethinking resilience: A developmental process perspective. In S. S. Luthar (Ed.), *Resilience and vulnerabilities: Adaptation in the context of childhood adversities* (pp. 243–266). New York: Cambridge University Press.

Zielinski, D. S., & Bradshaw, C. P. (2006). Ecological influences on the sequelae of child maltreatment: A review of the literature. *Child Maltreatment, 11,* 49–62.

4

Latent Classification of Physical Abuse as a Predictor of Adolescent Functioning

CHARLES V. IZZO, ELLIOT G. SMITH,
JOHN J. ECKENRODE, PAUL P. BIEMER,
AND SHARON L. CHRIST

Knowledge about the effect of child maltreatment on children's behavioral and psychosocial functioning has grown considerably as more sophisticated methodological approaches have been applied to this area of research.[1] The use of prospective longitudinal studies, broad-based assessment, and targeted sampling of the maltreated population have refined the kinds of questions that can be addressed, such as those about the importance of the timing of maltreatment and duration of effects (Ireland, Smith, & Thornberry, 2002), differences based on maltreatment characteristics (Rodgers et al., 2004; Trickett & McBride-Chang, 1995), and the domains of functioning affected (Malinosky-Rummell & Hansen, 1993; McGloin & Widom, 2001; Scannapieco & Connell-Carrick, 2005). Nonetheless, limitations in the measurement of maltreatment continue to hinder the development of the knowledge base (National Research Council, 1993). Obtaining a reliable indicator of actual maltreatment occurrence is difficult because all available sources of information have significant sources of bias. What is clear from the literature is that reliance on any single indicator is likely to misclassify a significant proportion of children, leading to inadequate estimates of maltreatment prevalence.

This problem is particularly salient in studies examining the influence of maltreatment on youth outcomes, because the high degree of measurement error associated with most available maltreatment indicators can distort the relationships that are observed (McGee, Wolfe, Yuen, Wilson, & Carnochan, 1995; Stockhammer, Salzinger, Feldman, Mojica, & Primavera, 2001; Theodore et al., 2005). To the extent that child welfare practice and federal and state policies are guided by this research, these methodological limitations may have significant practical consequences extending beyond basic research.

Measurement of Physical Abuse

Data from official child welfare system reports are commonly used as abuse indicators; they are readily available and are less susceptible than other sources to several biases associated with self-report. Child welfare system reports alone, however, often misclassify children as abused when no abuse occurred ("false-positives") and fail to detect a large proportion of true maltreatment cases ("false-negatives"). For example, results from the Third National Incidence Study of Child Abuse and Neglect (NIS-3) indicated that 66% to 78% of cases that met the NIS-3 criteria for maltreatment were never reported to the child welfare system (Sedlak, Hantman, & Schultz, 1997). Moreover, a previous study based on NIS-1 showed that the rates of reporting among NIS-1 cases varied substantially across different age groups and maltreatment types (Cicchetti & Barnett, 1991), suggesting that, among reported cases, some subpopulations may be biased in important ways. Additionally, Stockhammer et al. (2001) showed that child welfare system reports, when they were made, occurred an average of 2 years after the abuse first began, according to caregivers.

The use of substantiated reports is not much more reliable as a maltreatment indicator, partly because child welfare system investigators lack firsthand knowledge about the alleged incidents.[2] Furthermore, critical information about a case often comes from unreliable sources. Complicating matters even further, the decision to substantiate allegations of maltreatment often depends on several factors other than whether the maltreatment incident occurred. Drake and Johnson-Reid (2000) have suggested that substantiation hinges not only on evidence of past harm but also on such factors as risk for future harm and perceived need for services. Winefeld and Bradley (1992), in examining more than 3,000 cases, determined that the two strongest predictors of substantiation were severity of maltreatment and the age of the victim.

Using more rigorous classification methods, a recent study from the LONGSCAN study team compared definitions of *maltreatment* that are based on child welfare system records with two alternative definitions, in order to assess maltreatment among 8-year-old children reported to the child welfare system. One alternative definition was based on the Maltreatment Classification System (MCS), a theoretically grounded approach developed by Barnett, Manly, and Cicchetti (1993), and the other definition was based on the Second National Incidence Study (NIS-2). The MCS and NIS-2 both diverged substantially from the child welfare system definition and, in the case of physical and sexual abuse, predicted more developmental outcomes than did the child welfare system definition. These authors acknowledge the liabilities of using any single source of information about maltreatment.

The use of self-report methods may uncover maltreatment not detected by child welfare system sources alone; however, these methods have their own sources of bias and inaccuracy stemming from both cognitive factors (e.g., comprehension, recall, attributions) and situational factors (e.g., social desirability, fear of reprisal, interviewing conditions). Ideally, the self-report instrument should include several objective behavioral abuse indicators to avoid the influence of respondents' subjective appraisal and to increase reliability.

The literature is replete with self-report studies in which *abuse* is vaguely defined or abuse indicators are inadequate (see review in Knutson & Heckenberg, 2006). Moreover, many studies involving victim self-report rely only on adult retrospective reports (Kruttschnitt & Dornfeld, 1993; MacMillan et al., 2001; Thompson, Kingree, & Desai, 2004). Few studies have directly asked adolescents about their own experience of current or recent abuse. In a study of homeless youth, Tyler and Cauce (2002) interviewed 13–21 year olds, using a subset of items from the Conflict Tactics Scale (Straus & Gelles, 1988). Studies by McGee and colleagues asked adolescents whether and how severely they were physically abused, but these studies used only a single behavioral example ("hit or slapped") to facilitate reliable interpretation (McGee, Wolfe, & Olson, 2001; McGee et al., 1995).

The caregiver's report serves as a valuable addition to youth report measures because it may reveal abuse not detected by other sources. Common sense suggests that researchers should be concerned about parental underreporting of potentially incriminating acts, and limited evidence suggests that such underreporting occurs for some primary caregivers (Stockhammer et al., 2001). However, Knutson & Heckenberg (2006) suggest that these concerns may be overstated, because many parents adhere to parenting standards that differ radically from those of the investigator (Bower & Knutson, 1996). Consequently, acts that investigators (or child welfare system officials) consider abusive may be considered appropriate by the caregiver and may be freely disclosed.

Given the limitations of these and other physical abuse indicators, some have recommended using a multimethod or multisource approach to define *physical abuse* (Kaufman, Jones, Stieglitz, Vitulano, & Mannarino, 1994; Knutson & Heckenberg, 2006). Such an approach is rare in the child maltreatment literature, but useful examples do exist. Conceptual algorithms have been used that essentially assign cases abuse codes based on data from several, sometimes discrepant sources (e.g., Kaufman et al., 1994; Kraemer et al., 2003). These approaches have the advantage of employing transparent, easily understood decision rules that may extrapolate well into real-world settings. Other investigators (Knutson, DeGarmo, Koepll, & Reid, 2005; Weiss, Dodge, Bates, & Pettit, 1992) have used latent modeling approaches able to optimize estimation of the physical abuse score by incorporating both the score and the associated measurement error for each indicator.

Physical Abuse and Adolescent Outcomes

It is now well established that children who experience maltreatment are more likely to suffer a range of behavioral, psychosocial, and academic problems later in life (Lewis, Malloub, & Webb, 1989; Malinosky-Rummell & Hansen, 1993;

Scannapieco & Connell-Carrick, 2005; Widom, 1989). Physical abuse has been linked to both internalizing and externalizing problems, low self-esteem, and depression (Flisher et al., 1997; Kaplan et al., 1998; Kim & Cicchetti, 2006). Additionally, physically abused children have been shown to experience symptoms of posttraumatic stress for many years after the abuse incidents (Roth, Newman, Pelcovitz, van der Kolk, & Mandel, 1997).

Although the developmental effects are toxic, regardless of when abuse occurs, the impact is uniquely harmful when it occurs during adolescence. Findings by Ireland and colleagues underscored this point, suggesting that the greatest impact on adolescent and adult problem behavior comes from abuse occurring during the adolescent period (Ireland et al., 2002). An important mechanism through which abuse harms children is disruption of their ability to successfully negotiate norma-tive developmental tasks (e.g., self-agency, trust, emotion regulation, behavioral control), which later impairs their capacity to cope adaptively with challenges and hardships throughout youth and adulthood (Cicchetti & Lynch, 1995).

Peer associations take on central significance during this period (Hartup, 1983). A key task for adolescents is to establish healthy models of social relation-ships. The parent–child relationship serves as a powerful model in this regard, and youth are likely to replicate the unhealthy dynamics characteristic of abusive families in their interaction patterns with peers. In their study of adolescent peer relationships, Wolfe et al. (1998) found that maltreated youth reported a greater prevalence than nonmaltreated youth of both receiving and perpetrating abusive behavior in dating relationships. Maltreated youth were also more likely to be described as aggressive by their teachers. In addition to the immediate strain they may cause, these patterns of relationship conflict may ultimately lead to rejection by peers and impairments in self-esteem (Hymel, Bowker, & Woody, 1993). Similarly, findings from Salzinger et al. (2001) suggest that abused children develop maladaptive expectations about social relationships, expectations that contribute to internalizing behavior problems.

Adolescence is also a time when individuals must learn to cope with an increasing array of intense and stressful experiences. Physically abused adolescents' vulnerability to psychopathology may be elevated by their greater likelihood of experiencing additional stressors that compound their risk. A study by Larson and Ham (1993) indicated that, compared with their younger counterparts, older adolescents experience a greater number of stressful events related to peers, family, and school and that these accumulated stressors are more likely to produce negative effects. In addition to experiencing more numerous daily stressors, ado-lescents are more likely than younger counterparts to have a prior, substantiated maltreatment report; to have experienced a prior out-of-home placement; and to have suffered a combination of both physical and sexual abuse (Administration on Children and Families, 2005). This accumulation of stress and adversity can over-whelm their ability to cope effectively (Wadsworth & Compas, 2002), particularly when important resources are absent, such as trusted supportive relationships with peers or parents (Licitra & Waas, 1993).

Gender Differences in the Effects of Abuse

Because gender differences in the effects of child maltreatment can have implications for treatment and child welfare policy, understanding these differences has been identified as an important goal for child welfare research (National Research Council, 1993; Widom, 2001). Most studies addressing gender differences have focused on sexual abuse; among those that have addressed physical abuse, many have relied on adult retrospective reports or have been limited to younger age groups. Nevertheless, most studies comparing abuse effects by gender have found differences to be significant. In addition to studies based on clinical or other identified samples (McClelland, Farabee, & Crouch, 1997; Meyerson, Long, Miranda, & Marx, 2002), findings from nationally representative studies (Chandy, Blum, & Resnick, 1996; Thompson et al., 2004) have suggested that these gender differences may be found more universally and that they last well into adulthood.

Surprisingly few studies have examined gender differences in the effects of physical abuse on aggressive or externalizing behaviors; conclusions from existing studies have been equivocal. Some have suggested stronger associations for male youth than for female youth (Pakiz, Reinherz, & Giaconia, 1997; Wolfe et al., 1998), and others have reported no significant gender differences (Shields & Cicchetti, 2001; Weiss et al., 1992; Windle, Windle, Scheidt, & Miller, 1995). To the extent that differences do exist, one mediating factor may be a greater tendency for physically abused boys to receive poor parental supervision (Wall, Barth, & The NSCAW Research Group, 2005). Less is known about gender differences in the association of childhood aggression with physical abuse. Impairment in children's social information processing and problem-solving competence has been identified as a key mediator in that relationship (Dodge, Petit, Bates, & Valente, 1995; Wolfe et al., 1998), but no clear evidence of related gender differences has emerged (Weiss et al., 1992).

The literature has been more active with regard to depression and other internalizing disorders. With some exceptions (McGloin & Widom, 2001; Meyerson et al., 2002), studies investigating these disorders tend to find greater negative effects for girls (MacMillan et al., 2001; Widom & White, 1997). Eckenrode et al. (2007) reported similar findings in NSCAW, indicating that physical abuse is significantly related to more internalizing problems for girls but not for boys.

Although we expect to observe negative consequences of physical abuse for both boys and girls, several reasons lead us to expect some gender difference in these effects. First, gender difference in effects may be related to boys' and girls' generally different tendencies in expressing psychological and emotional distress, with boys displaying more externalizing and aggressive symptoms and girls displaying more depression and other internalizing symptoms (Casper, Belanoff, & Offer, 1996; Chandy et al., 1996). Girls also tend to experience greater overall exposure to negative life events (Davies & Windle, 1997), which adds to their psychological and emotional vulnerability. More specifically, girls are more likely than boys to experience combined physical and sexual abuse (Finkelhor, Hotaling, Lewis, & Smith, 1990), which likely influences the emotional and psychological effect of the maltreatment (Finkelhor & Brown, 1985). Finally, the differences may be related to a differential stress response between boys and girls (Hankin & Abramson, 2002). Findings by Cyranowski, Frank, Young, and Shear (2000) have suggested that girls, because of their greater interpersonal orientation, are especially vulnerable to depression after relationship conflict. Girls may also be more likely than boys to ruminate about stressors and to interpret them in ways that degrade their self-concept (Nolen-Hoeksema, 2001).

Measurement of Adolescent Outcomes

Some researchers have stressed that, to examine adequately the factors affecting disorder and competence, children must be assessed at several points along the developmental course and across multiple domains of functioning (Cicchetti & Rogosch, 1997; McGloin & Widom, 2001). For example, research has shown that the buffering function of protective factors is not always permanent. Herrenkohl, Herrenkohl, and Egolf (1994) identified a subset of maltreated children who were found to be functioning well during elementary school. By the time they reached high school, only a small proportion of them were still functioning well. Moreover, a child may function well in one or two domains but do poorly in several other domains (Luthar, 1993; Werner & Smith, 1992). With these considerations in mind, Cicchetti and Rogosch (1997) assessed child functioning across seven domains over 3 consecutive years. Similarly, McGloin and Widom (2001) incorporated eight domains of functioning in their definition of child competence.

Data Set Characteristics, Test Variables, and Goals

This study is important because it measures physical abuse that occurred during the early adolescent period and examines the psychological and behavioral consequences during the 3-year period after adolescents' entry into the National Survey of Child and Adolescent Well-Being (NSCAW). Few studies have examined physical abuse during adolescence, and most of these have relied on administrative data (see, e.g., Knutson & Heckenberg, 2006) or retrospective reports from adult victims (Kruttschnitt & Dornfeld, 1993; MacMillan et al., 2001; Smith, Ireland, & Thornberry, 2006; Thompson et al., 2004). The current investigation uses the strengths of the NSCAW data set (objective abuse indicators, multiple informants, temporal proximity to actual abuse incidents) to minimize error in the assessment of abuse and optimize the estimation of its association with adolescent outcomes. Specifically, we examine several components of adolescent functioning in the behavioral and psychosocial domains (i.e., internalizing and externalizing behaviors, depression, and trauma symptoms). We investigate *(1)* how functioning in these areas varies with abuse status and *(2)* how the relationships between abuse and outcomes vary according to children's gender. We examine these relationships with respect to outcomes at NSCAW Wave 1 (baseline), Wave 3 (18-month follow-up), and Wave 4 (36-month follow-up).

The NSCAW study is the first longitudinal, national probability study of children referred to the child welfare system because of alleged child maltreatment. It offers a particularly valuable opportunity to study physical abuse because it contains abuse-related information from multiple sources (caseworker, parent, and youth report) that, taken together, can provide a more reliable estimate of children's physical abuse histories than can be obtained by any one source alone. In our preliminary research (Eckenrode et al., 2007), we created a combined physical abuse score that classified youth as *abused* if they were reported as abused by any one source. We then compared this classification with each individual source of data. As expected, we found low correspondence among each of the three sources, with parent and youth report showing the highest agreement. We also found that both the combined score and the youth report predicted the greatest number of outcomes (11 of 15), and the caseworker report predicted the fewest (2 of 15). Although this classification approach had the value for maximizing the measure's sensitivity (i.e., minimizing false-negatives), many cases were likely incorrectly classified as positive for abuse. For example, cases with only one source indicating abuse were automatically classified as abuse cases, so information from the other two sources did not contribute to the probability of being classified into an abuse category. This approach results not only in less-accurate classification estimates but also in biased parameter estimates in models predicting adolescent outcomes.

Our current study addresses this problem by incorporating a physical abuse indicator that minimizes measurement error and therefore optimizes the estimation of the relationship between abuse and adolescent outcomes. Specifically, three independent sources of information on abuse are treated as indicators of true abuse status and are incorporated into a single, latent abuse variable. Rather than using a conceptually driven approach, we estimate a latent physical abuse variable by fitting a latent class model that incorporates all three abuse indicators. This approach has the advantage of yielding classifications that draw from all sources of information simultaneously, while allowing for the unknown misclassification (i.e., the false-positive and false-negative errors) associated with each measure (Biemer, 2004). An important feature of this approach is that it provides a new physical abuse variable that, theoretically, is free of measurement error. When used as an independent variable in the subsequent regression analyses, this variable achieves greater explanatory power than the observed variables of physical abuse.

Methods

We used data from the child protective services sample, focusing on the subset of youth aged 11 years or older at Wave 1 ($n = 1,179$), because NSCAW assessed many of the key variables of interest for this age group. The sample was 42.1% male, ranging in age from 11 to 16 years ($M = 12.7$ years), with 91.0% younger than age 15, and was predominantly low income, with 74.3% reporting less than $35,000 per year. The racial composition was 30.6% black or African American, 44.8% white, 15.5% Hispanic or Latino, and 9.1% other races. At the time of the Wave 1 (baseline) interview, 72.0% of youth lived in their home; of these, 89.6% lived with at least one biological parent. For youth placed outside the home, 33.0% had a relative as the primary caregiver, and 66.0% had a nonrelative as the primary caregiver. Caregivers in this sample reported an average of 4.5 people living in the home, and 100% indicated that at least one household member received financial support from the government. For 36.2%, the investigative caseworker indicated that the child had been the subject of a prior, substantiated report of maltreatment.

Measures

Caregiver and Youth Self-Reports   For both caregiver and youth self-report measures, we used the Conflict Tactics Scale (Straus, Hamby, Finkelhor, Moore, & Runyan, 1998), selecting a subset of Severe and Extreme Physical Abuse subscale items most easily interpreted as measuring intentional, serious harm to the child. If verified in a child welfare system investigation, these reported behaviors are sufficiently serious to substantiate a physical abuse report: hitting the child with a fist or kicking the child hard, hitting the child somewhere other than the bottom with a hard object, throwing or knocking the child down, grabbing the child around the neck or choking the child, beating the child as hard as possible, burning the child on purpose, and threatening the child with a knife or gun. Caregivers indicated how often they had engaged in each behavior toward the target child in the 12 months before assessment. Youth indicated how often they had received each kind of treatment by any adult who cared for them, not just their primary caregiver, in the 12 months before assessment. For both the caregiver and the youth measures, we computed a dichotomous prevalence score indicating whether any abusive act had occurred at least once in the 12 months preceding the assessment.

Caseworker Report   Usually caseworkers indicated the type of maltreatment alleged in the index report (i.e., the report that triggered each participant's entry into NSCAW) and whether this allegation was *substantiated, indicated,* or *unsubstantiated.*[3] When more than one allegation was made, caseworkers indicated which single allegation they judged to be the most serious type of maltreatment. We classified the child as *physically abused* only if the caseworker indicated *physical abuse* as the most serious allegation made and if the caseworker indicated that the allegation was either substantiated or indicated.

ASSESSMENT OF ADOLESCENT FUNCTIONING   We examined a range of variables in the behavioral and psychosocial domains; each variable was assessed at Waves 1, 3, and 4. In the behavioral domain, caregivers reported on the child's problem behaviors, using the Child Behavior Checklist (Achenbach, 1991), which was designed for youth aged 4 to 18 years and yields composite scores reflecting internalizing (ranging from zero to 58) and externalizing (ranging from zero to 60) behavior problems. Youth reported on their own behaviors, using the Youth Self-Report (Achenbach, 1991), which was also designed for youth aged 4 to 18 and yields composite scores for internalizing (ranging from zero to 51) and externalizing (ranging from zero to 56) behavior problems.

In the psychosocial domain, we included adolescents' reports of their own depressive symptoms during the 2 weeks preceding assessment, using the Children's Depression Inventory (for ages 7 to 18, scores ranging from zero to 52; Kovacs, 1992). Youth reported their trauma-related symptoms, using the posttraumatic stress subscale of the Trauma Symptom Checklist for Children (for ages 8 to 18, ranging from 0 to 29; Briere, 1996), and reported their expectations for the future, using a scale derived from the Adolescent Health Survey (for youth aged 11 or older, scores ranging from 5 to 40; Bearman, Jones & Udry, 1997).

Analyses

Because the prevalence estimates for physical abuse varied so greatly among the three sources (agreement among two or more sources occurred in only 13% of cases), we chose to incorporate all three indicators into a fourth, more accurate indicator. The method reported in Eckenrode et al. (2007; i.e., classify as *abused* if any of the three reports is positive), though preferable to using any single source, was limited because it failed to account for the likelihood of false-positive reporting from any one source or false-negative reporting from all three sources. Use of logistic regression to estimate abuse prevalence was also judged insufficient because of the degree of error associated with each indicator and the absence of a "true" abuse indicator against which to compare the estimated likelihood. We chose instead to classify youth into abuse categories, using latent class analysis (LCA).

Latent class analysis is a modeling method for predicting a person's true classification on the basis of his or her observed classifications, taking into account the potential classification errors in the observed data. For our application, it assigns a probability of being abused to each sample person in a specified subgroup defined by the independent variables in the model, assuming that all persons in the subgroup have an equal probability of being abused. In essence, LCA obtains estimates of the model parameters that maximize the likelihood of realizing the observed data. If the assumed model is correct, LCA provides estimates of latent class membership that are not biased by misreporting error. Consequently, by comparing the latent classifications with the observed classifications for each source, we can estimate the false-positive and false-negative error rates for each of the three sources.

We conducted analyses in two stages, first finding the best-fitting latent class model and then incorporating this model into a larger equation in which both the latent class and regression models were fitted simultaneously. To specify the best latent class model, we first tested several competing models, each including different model covariates and their interactions. The covariates, which included child gender, race, and whether a participant had a prior substantiated maltreatment report, were chosen on the basis of their potential to influence the classification error associated with one or more abuse indicators (e.g., likelihood of substantiation may vary by gender or race; parent self-report may vary, depending on prior substantiation history). We sequentially tested models within a range of complexity, from models involving only one covariate to the most complex model, which included all three covariates and their interactions. Our criteria for selecting the best model were as follows: L^2 and Cressie-Read statistics having p values greater than .05, minimum Bayesian information criteria, and plausible latent class probabilities. These factors having been considered, the best model included all three covariates and their interactions with the latent abuse variable, in addition to the three indicators of abuse. Notably, the class proportions, the error probabilities, and the overall study results were comparable across all models.

Second, we examined the association between physical abuse and adolescent outcomes by testing a series of regression models, each with the outcome regressed on several variables that were correlated with abuse indicators, outcomes, or both (child's age, gender, race, family income, report of prior maltreatment, and Wave 1 report of maltreatment type other than physical abuse), while simultaneously fitting the latent class model for physical abuse (Fig. 4.1). The latent class variable was incorporated as a covariate in the regression model. Only cases with all three abuse indicators present were included in the analysis. In addition, weights were not specified in the models reported here, because they appeared to cause spurious associations between abuse and outcomes. Because little research exists on probability weighting in LCA, we ran the model unweighted but included the key survey design variables as covariates (see, e.g., Korn & Graubard, 1991; Winship & Radbill, 1994). The path model in Figure 4.1 shows the relationships between the observed and latent variables for a typical model. The Wald chi-square test was used to compare the intercept values, which represent the outcome means for the latent abused and nonabused groups. Chi-square tests with $p < .05$ indicate significant effects of abuse on the outcome variable, after controlling for covariates.

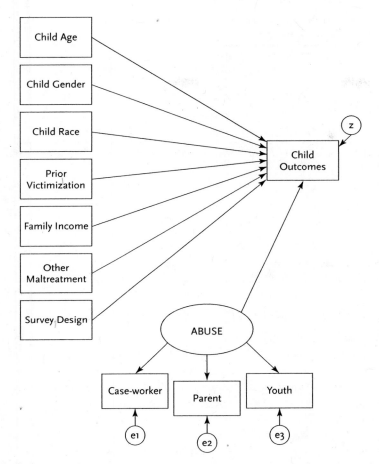

Figure 4.1 Typical path model for the regression on observed and latent explanatory variables.

Results

Class Proportions by Observed Abuse Indicators and by Latent Abuse Classification

As reported in Eckenrode et al. (2007), the prevalence rates varied considerably among the three abuse indicators. Youth self-report yielded the highest prevalence estimate (27.1%), followed by parent report (15.8%) and caseworker report (9.2%; Table 4.1). The prevalence rates for the latent abuse variable varied somewhat across models, but, on average, LCA classified about 20.0% of youth as having been physically abused. This result is substantially lower than the prevalence rate given by the youth report, and higher than that given by either the caseworker or the

Table 4.1   Prevalence of Physical Abuse Based on Observed Indicators and Latent Classification (Percent)

	Case Report (n = 1,072)	Parent Report (n = 818)	Youth Report (n = 1,104)	Latent Classification (n = 880)
Prevalence estimate				
Weighted	9.2	15.8	27.1	20.0[a]
Unweighted	16.2	16	27.4	

[a] Latent class analyses and regressions models were run simultaneously, so prevalence rates varied somewhat across dependent variables (16.3% to 23.8%). This statistic represents the mean prevalence rate across all Wave 1 models.

caregiver reports. Eckenrode et al.'s combined abuse estimate was considerably higher at 40.7%. That classification method, however, essentially guaranteed the highest estimate by treating a positive report from any one source as an indication of abuse.

Presence of Abuse as Indentified by Individual Sources and by Latent Classification

Part of the rationale for modeling a latent abuse variable is that sources often disagree about whether physical abuse has occurred; no one source can be relied on, because each is fallible. If agreement were high, the source of information used would matter less, because outcomes predicted would not differ greatly across each abuse measure. As reported in Eckenrode et al. (2007), we found substantial lack of correspondence among report sources. For example, only 12.2% had two sources indicating the presence of abuse, and only 0.8% had all three sources indicating abuse.[4]

These estimates indicate that the false-positive rate was highest for caregiver report: When caregivers reported that abuse had occurred, the latent classification indicated *no abuse* 31.5% of the time (Figs. 4.2 and 4.3). In contrast, the false-positive rate was about 17.8% for caseworker report and 18.0% for youth report. The false-negative rate was highest for caregiver report, indicating that when caregivers reported that no abuse had occurred, the latent classification indicated *abuse* 83.2% of the time. The false-negative rate for caseworker report was only slightly lower at 75.9% and was lowest for youth report at 19.6%. Overall, then, the rate of classification error was lowest for the youth report.

Physical Abuse and Adolescent Outcomes

The latent abuse measure was significantly related to every dependent variable we tested, at each wave (Table 4.2). In the problem behavior domain, the results from both measures indicated that physical abuse predicted externalizing behaviors and internalizing behaviors as measured by both caregivers' and adolescents' reports on

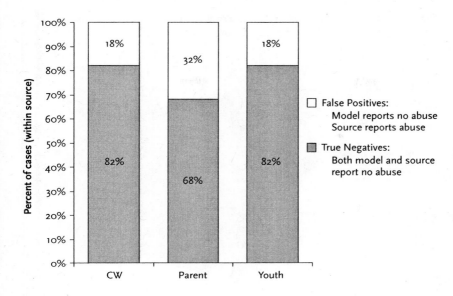

Figure 4.2 Correspondence of source with latent classification of "no abuse" (false-positive and true-negative rates).

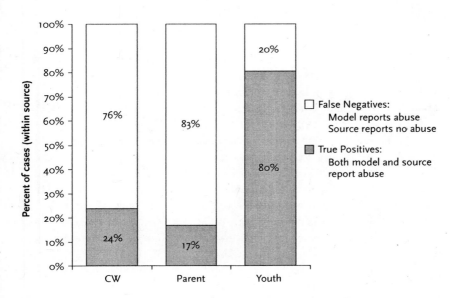

Figure 4.3 Correspondence of source with latent classification of "abuse" (false-negative and true-positive rates).

Table 4.2   Unstandardized Regression and Wald Chi-Square Coefficients Representing Comparisons Among Abuse Classes

	Wave 1		Wave 3		Wave 4	
Problem Behavior	χ^2	B	χ^2	B	χ^2	B
Externalizing—parent[a]	21.22		21.02		22.99	
	509.55**	(7.31)	484.56**	(5.67)	394.58**	(6.46)
Externalizing—youth[a]	17.46		14.43		16.78	
	485.62**	(4.66)	159.78**	(4.62)	178.48**	(5.09)
Internalizing—parent[a]	18.01		16.24		16.84	
	403.77**	(4.69)	258.01**	(3.87)	164.68**	(5.09)
Internalizing—youth[a]	14.30		24.00		16.65	
	175.31**	(4.96)	64.42**	(5.98)	114.85**	(3.97)
Psychosocial Functioning						
Depression[a]	15.40		14.96		14.67	
	250.37**	(4.45)	117.65**	(3.69)	199.34**	(3.82)
Trauma symptoms[a]	10.61		10.68		10.72	
	143.58**	(3.62)	453.08**	(2.59)	135.43**	(4.04)
Future expectations[b]	−1.46		−1.63		−1.84	
	364.44**	(.42)	36.95**	(.59)	396.91**	(.46)

Note: For all tests, analyses were conducted on unweighted data with $N = 880$. χ^2 values represent the significance test of the difference in intercept values between cases classified by the latent class analysis (LCA) as abused versus not abused. Each model contained the following covariates: child's age, race, and gender, family income, the child being a victim in a substantiated child welfare system report prior to the case report, and a dichotomous indicator of the presence of maltreatment other than physical abuse, assessed at Wave 1.
[a] Higher scores reflect worse functioning.
[b] Higher scores reflect better functioning.
$* p < .05$, $** p < .01$.

outcomes. In the psychosocial domain, results from both measures showed that abuse was related to increased rates of trauma symptoms and depression, as well as to less favorable expectations about the future.

Comparing the regression coefficients across waves, one can see that, for most dependent variables, no simple pattern was evident indicating steady increases or decreases in the strength of the abuse effect across waves. The effect for externalizing behavior appeared to decrease between Waves 1 and 3, and it then increased again by Wave 4. The effect for internalizing behavior appeared to increase dramatically from Waves 1 to 3 and then decrease somewhat by Wave 4. For other variables, the changes across waves were relatively small and less erratic.

Gender Differences in the Effects of Abuse

We conducted an additional set of tests examining whether the relationship between abuse and each outcome differed according to the child's gender. First,

Table 4.3   Significant Gender Differences in Association Between Latent Abuse and
Youth Outcomes

			Effects of Abuse on DV	
	Wave	Difference in Abuse Effects by Gender (χ^2)	Boys B	Girls B
Externalizing—youth[a]	4	4.23*	19.17**	14.03**
Internalizing—parent[a]	1	5.37*	15.67**	19.53**
Internalizing—youth[a]	3	4.14*	34.47**	21.26**
Future expectations[b]	1	3.51†	−1.58**	−1.36**
	4	7.04**	−2.11**	−1.65**

Note: For all tests, analyses were conducted on unweighted data with $N = 880$. χ^2 values represent the significance test of the difference between the abuse effect for boys, as opposed to girls. Each model contained the following covariates: child's age and race, family income, the child being a victim in a substantiated child welfare system report prior to the case report, and a dichotomous indicator of the presence of maltreatment other than physical abuse, assessed at Wave 1.
[a] Higher scores reflect worse functioning.
[b] Higher scores reflect better functioning.
† $< .10$, * $p < .05$, ** $p < .01$.
DV = dependent variable

we ran models identical to those already described, except that each Wald chi-square test indicated whether the difference between abuse classes for the dependent variable differed significantly between boys and girls. Then, when significant interactions were found, we examined the simple effects to describe the abuse effects for boys and girls separately.

Significant chi-square tests of the interaction between gender and abuse were found for youth-reported externalizing in Wave 4 and youth-reported internalizing in Wave 3 (Table 4.3). In both cases, analysis of simple effects indicated that the effect of abuse was significant for both boys and girls, but the magnitude of the effect was greater for boys than for girls. A significant interaction was also found for caregiver-reported internalizing problems in Wave 1, but in this case the simple effects analysis indicated that the effect of abuse was stronger for girls than for boys. Significant interactions were found for future expectations in Waves 1 and 4: the effect of abuse was greater for boys than for girls.

Discussion

We have examined the relationship between physical abuse and developmental outcomes in NSCAW's nationally representative sample of adolescents who were the subjects of child maltreatment reports. Though several studies have estimated these relationships, our current study uses advanced statistical techniques to reduce the impact of measurement error on such estimates. We have demonstrated here strong, durable relationships between physical abuse and a range of psychosocial and behavioral outcomes. These effects were significant for both boys and girls; however, in some cases the strength of the associations differed by gender. These findings enhance the body of knowledge on the consequences of physical abuse for adolescent functioning; they are particularly valuable for their broad generalizability to youth in the child welfare system.

We have introduced LCA as a statistical method for classifying youth as *abused nonabused,* using information from three independent sources. The prevalence estimated by LCA for physical abuse was higher than estimates based on reports from investigative caseworkers or parents alone, but it was slightly lower than estimates based only on youth reports. These results would be expected because of the strong incentives caregivers have for concealing abusive behavior and because of the barriers that prevent investigations from detecting abuse. The LCA prevalence rate was also lower than the estimate reported in Eckenrode et al. (2007; 20%, as opposed to 40%), which coded abuse on the basis of a positive report from any one source. We argue that LCA provides the most accurate estimate because it simultaneously factors in the class assignments from all three sources. Furthermore, unlike conceptually driven algorithms found in other studies (Eckenrode et al., 2007; Kraemer et al., 2003), LCA reduces overall classification error by statistically accounting for the error associated with each indicator, thereby increasing statistical power in the predictive models.

Substantial classification error was evident, in the current study, for each source. The highest error rates were associated with caregiver's reports: The latent classification was more likely to disagree with these reports than with caseworker reports or youth reports. The higher false-positive rate for caregivers seems counterintuitive because caregivers are unlikely to report maltreatment they did not commit. Many caregivers, however, may openly report hostile incidents if they perceive them as appropriate (i.e., nonabusive), whereas youth may refrain from reporting such incidents to avoid parental reprisal or further family disruption. The classification error was lowest when the youth was the reporting source. Considering that contemporary youth report of abuse rarely appears in the literature, these results underscore the limitations of existing literature on adolescent abuse and highlight the importance of including youth self-report in future studies.

Physical Abuse and Adolescent Outcomes

Our results illustrate several ways that physical abuse disrupts developmental processes critical to a child's healthy passage through adolescence. Youth classified as physically abused showed elevated levels of depression, internalizing behaviors, externalizing behaviors, and trauma symptoms. From a developmental psychopathology perspective, we would expect these effects to impede adolescents' achievement of later developmental tasks (Sroufe, 1992), such as establishing a stable, positive self-concept and developing close, satisfying relationships. To compound matters, that abused youth continue to report higher rates of trauma symptoms after 36 months suggests that the severe emotional response to abuse overwhelms some youths' resources for coping (Wadsworth & Compas, 2002) and perhaps their developing capacity for regulating emotions.

It is particularly noteworthy that these associations did not appear to diminish in Waves 3 or 4. For some youths, these sustained effects may reflect an ongoing response to repeated physical abuse. For many, however, these sustained effects may reflect early steps toward a longer-term trajectory of behavioral dysregulation and emotional-psychological distress. Moffitt's (1993) seminal research, which focused on patterns of delinquency and criminality, identified a history of harsh parenting as a key predictor of the persistence of emotional and behavioral problems into young adulthood. Similar results have been reported in other studies (for a review, see Malinosky-Rummell & Hanson, 1993).

Compared with our previous investigation using an alternative method for combining information on physical abuse from multiple sources (Eckenrode et al., 2007), results from the current study were stronger and more widespread. The differences reported here between *abused* and *nonabused* classes were highly significant for every Wave 1 outcome variable we tested. The Wave 1 findings reported in Eckenrode et al. (2007) were similar, except that the abuse effect on caregiver-reported internalizing problems was nonsignificant in that study. For later waves, the pattern of results between the two studies differed. The effect of the abuse variable on outcomes tested in Eckenrode et al. (2007) decreased or completely dropped out by Wave 4. In the current study, however, the abuse effect endured throughout Waves 1, 3, and 4.

Gender Differences in the Effects of Abuse

To the extent that gender differences existed in our results, they tended to suggest greater impairment for boys, with the exception of caregiver-rated internalizing problems. The gender interactions reported here for youth-reported externalizing behavior were not detected in Eckenrode et al. (2007). The current finding, however, is consistent with other research indicating that physically abused boys exhibit higher rates of externalized symptoms than abused girls (Pakiz et al., 1997).

As did our earlier investigation (Eckenrode et al., 2007), the current study reveals a gender interaction for caregiver-reported internalizing problems, indicating that the effect is stronger for girls than for boys. Although consistent with past research (McClelland et al., 1997), this finding was inconsistent with results for youth-reported internalizing, which indicated that the effect of abuse was stronger for *boys* than for girls. We have no definitive explanation for these discrepant findings, though they may reflect a known tendency associated with the instrument for caregiver and youth reports to differ substantially (Achenbach, McConaughy, & Howell, 1987). Youth tend to report more internalizing behaviors than caregivers (Herjanic & Reich, 1982), possibly because these behaviors are less readily observable by others. In some circumstances, such as those involving caregiver psycho-pathology, the caregiver's report may be distorted (Briggs-Gowan, Carter, & Schwab-Stone, 1996), whereas, in others, caregivers may accurately report problems that youth opt not to disclose. Although the reason that gender differences did not remain stable across waves remains unclear, it may be that the impact on internalizing behaviors for boys becomes more evident as they grow older.

The greater effects among boys for youth-reported internalizing are notable. The developmental psychopathology literature often highlights a tendency toward aggressive or externalizing behaviors for boys and depressive or internalizing problems for girls (Chandy et al., 1996), but our results demonstrate that this pattern is by no means universal (Chapman et al., 2004). In fact, Moffitt and colleagues, in their investigations of trajectories of problem behaviors, revealed a subset of boys whose early aggressive or delinquent behavior did not persist beyond adolescence, but these boys tended to experience elevated levels of anxiety or depressive symptoms when assessed in young adulthood (Moffit, Caspi, Harrington, & Milne, 2002). The NSCAW study may contain a similar subset of males, predisposed toward internalizing disorders, that partially accounts for this interaction. Regardless of the underlying reasons for them, these findings show that boys are vulnerable not only to aggression-related problems but also to depression and anxiety.

Our analyses do not reveal why these and the several other robust effects reported here were not found in the previous study. One likely explanation is that the abuse variable used in the Eckenrode et al. (2007) analysis was subject to much greater classification error (i.e., false-negative and false-positive classifications) that led to a loss of power in the analysis and greater potential for spurious effects caused by correlated errors. LCA attempts to eliminate such classification errors from the analysis by estimating the error parameters in the model, as well as the distribution of the true (latent) abuse variable, resulting in a (theoretically) error-free variable that can be used in the subsequent regression analysis. The contrast between the results of the two studies illustrates the danger in child maltreatment research of relying on single abuse indicators that contain a high degree of measurement error (Knutson & Heckenberg, 2006).

Limitations

Several limitations must be considered when the current findings are interpreted. Importantly, we must acknowledge the differences in how abuse is operationalized among the three indicators. Caregivers reported on violent acts they themselves perpetrated, whereas youth reported on violent acts committed against them by any adult who had taken care of them. Caseworkers reported on substantiation, which reflects not only the likelihood of abuse but also several legal and administrative processes unrelated to the accuracy of the abuse report (Drake & Johnson-Reid, 2000; Hussey et al., 2005). Consequently, in addition to coming from different sources, the three indicators differ somewhat in terms of the phenomena they represent.

Additionally, the relationships observed between abuse and adolescent outcomes may be somewhat influenced by reliance on the same source (caregiver or youth) for both abuse and the outcome variable. If this reliance were a significant problem, we would expect to observe a systematic change in the size of the regression coefficients across waves, but no such change was observed. Nevertheless, these relationships could be estimated even more accurately with latent modeling approaches that simultaneously incorporate outcome assessments from additional data sources, including youth, caregivers, teachers, and trained behavioral observers when possible (see Kaufman et al., 1994).

Another limitation is that this study does not account for adolescents' various abuse histories. For some, the associations between baseline abuse and later outcomes reflect the lasting impact of an initial set of abuse experiences. For many who continued to live in an abusive environment, however, or who experienced a long history of abuse before study entry, these associations reflect the added impact of sustained abuse and traumatization. In the NSCAW data, the history of official abuse reports, whether before or after the Wave 1 (baseline) assessment, cannot be determined for the entire sample; therefore, conclusions about the sustained effects of abuse on child outcomes must be made cautiously.

An advantage of the LCA approach in this application is that it removes the subjectivity associated with determining which of the three reports of abuse is the most credible and should be believed in an analysis; however, its limitation is that the validity of the LCA estimates depends, in large part, on the validity of the assumed latent class model. Nonetheless, this approach makes the best use of the available data by using the error estimates for each abuse indicator to estimate the best "true" indicator of physical abuse.

Conclusion

This study illustrates the value of drawing from multiple sources to assess adolescents' recent history of physical abuse. Although the search for corroborating reports is probably incorporated into the investigation protocols of most child welfare agencies, our findings highlight the danger inherent in making definitive conclusions when only one source can be obtained. Moreover, our findings indicate that the youth's report may be the best single source of information when multiple sources are not available.

The false-negative rate for caregivers was quite high, even though the confidentiality of their responses was ensured. One would expect caregivers' reports to be even less reliable during a child welfare system investigation, when disclosures have more serious legal and custodial implications. Although some information from caregivers can be useful, it should be used with caution and carefully weighed against other report sources whenever possible. Multiple reports offer no panacea for child welfare investigations, because in many instances sources will inevitably disagree (see Eckenrode et al., 2007). Child welfare researchers should develop clear, empirically validated guidelines to assist practitioners in making abuse determinations in the presence of conflicting reports. Such guidelines should reflect scientific evidence, such as that provided here, about the reliability of each data source.

Another key element of child welfare practice requires an understanding of the psychological effect of maltreatment on the child so that appropriate services may be arranged. Our results suggest that practitioners should not overrely on generalizations about gender differences in children's responses to maltreatment (e.g., boys develop externalizing problems, girls develop internalizing problems). Instead, evaluations should devote adequate effort to assessing both externalizing and internalizing problems for both boys and girls.

Although our current study demonstrates the value of estimating a categorical abuse variable (*abuse* vs. *no abuse*), methods for estimating abuse as a continuous variable are also needed. The categorical approach applies well in some legal, investigative, or research contexts in which the determination must be made about whether a caregiver committed abusive or otherwise deviant acts. Nevertheless, for predicting the psychological effect on abuse victims and their need for services, such categorical distinctions (e.g., *substantiation*) are of limited value (Drake, 1996; Knutson & Bower, 1994). Future studies should explore multi-source and multimethod approaches for optimizing continuous measures, such as duration.

Our results illustrate that, within a prospective longitudinal framework, physical abuse can have a lasting impact on several dimensions of adolescent functioning. Although the strength of the relationship differed by gender, much more important is the recognition that the effect was—for both boys and girls—significant and lasting. Recent research suggests that these effects can last into adulthood and be expressed in physical health, mental health, and other psychosocial problems (Felitti et al., 1998). Understanding these processes is essential in designing effective prevention programming and treatment protocols.

NOTES

1. Support for this research was provided by the Administration for Children and Families, U.S. Department of Health and Human Services, through RTI International. Additional support was provided by the Children's Bureau (Grant No. 90CA1750).
2. *Substantiation* is the child welfare system's official case decision that allegations of child maltreatment are valid.
3. In some states, a disposition of *indicted* exists to classify cases for which evidence of maltreatment existed but did not rise to the level of substantiation. In all states, *unsubstantiated* cases are all those that did not rise to the level of substantiation. Cases without a substantiation code from the caseworker numbered 109. We statistically estimated substantiation status for these 109 cases on the basis of (1) history of foster care placement, (2) the caseworker's rating of evidence to substantiate the abuse allegation, and (3) the caseworker's rating of harm to the child.

4. The correspondence among sources was somewhat attenuated because youth were asked about abuse inflicted by any adult in the household, whereas caregivers reported only their own treatment of the child. The correspondence likely would have been higher if youth had been asked only about abuse by the person responding to the caregiver instrument.

REFERENCES

Achenbach, T. M. (1991). *Manual for the Child Behavior Checklist/4-18 and 1991 profile.* Burlington, VT: University of Vermont, Department of Psychiatry.

Achenbach, T. M., McConaughy, S. H., & Howell, C. T. (1987). Child/adolescent behavioral and emotional problems: Implications of cross-informant correlations for situational specificity. *Psychological Bulletin, 101,* 213–232.

Administration on Children and Families. (2005). *National Survey of Child and Adolescent Well-Being: Characteristics of children and families at intake into child welfare services.* Washington, DC: Author.

Barnett, D., Manly, J. T., & Cicchetti, D. (1993). Defining child maltreatment: The interface between policy and child research. In D. Cicchetti & S. L. Toth (Eds.), *Defining child maltreatment: The interface between policy and child research* (Vol. 8, pp. 7–73). Norwood, NJ: Ablex.

Bearman, P. S., Jones, J., & Udry, R. J. (1997). *The National Longitudinal Study of Adolescent Health: Research design.* Chapel Hill: Carolina Population Center, University of North Carolina.

Biemer, P. P. (2004). Modeling measurement error to identify flawed questions. In S. Presser & et al. (Eds.), *Questionnaire development, evaluation, and testing methods.* New York: Wiley.

Bower, M. E., & Knutson, J. F. (1996). Attitudes toward physical discipline as a function of disciplinary history and self-labeling as physically abused. *Child Abuse & Neglect, 20,* 689–699.

Briere, J. (1996). *Trauma Symptom Checklist for Children: Professional manual.* Lutz, FL: Psychological Assessment Resources.

Briggs-Gowan, M. J., Carter, A. S., & Schwab-Stone, M. (1996). Discrepancies among mother, child, and teacher reports: Examining the contributions of maternal depression and anxiety. *Journal of Abnormal Child Psychology, 24*(6), 749–765.

Casper, R. C., Belanoff, J., & Offer, D. (1996). Gender differences, but no racial group differences, in self-reported psychiatric symptoms in adolescents. *Journal of the American Academy of Child and Adolescent Psychiatry, 35*(4), 500–508.

Chandy, J. M., Blum, R. W., & Resnick, M. D. (1996). Gender-specific outcomes for sexually abused adolescents. *Child Abuse & Neglect, 20*(12), 1219–1231.

Chapman, D. P., Whitfield, C. L., Felitti, V. J., Dube, S. R., Edwards, V. J., & Anda, R. F. (2004). Adverse childhood experiences and the risk of depressive disorders in childhood. *Journal of Affective Disorders, 82,* 217–225.

Cicchetti, D. V., & Barnett, D. (1991). Toward the development of a scientific nosology of child maltreatment. In D. V. Cicchetti & W. M. Grove (Eds.), *Thinking clearly about psychology: Essays in honor of Paul E. Meehl* (pp. 346–377). Minneapolis: University of Minnesota Press.

Cicchetti, D. V., & Lynch, M. (1995). Failures in the expectable environment and their impact on individual development: The case of child maltreatment. In D. V. Cicchetti & D. J. Cohen (Eds.), *Developmental psychopathology: Vol. 2. Risk, disorder, and adaptation* (pp. 32–71). New York: Wiley.

Cicchetti, D. V., & Rogosch, F. A. (1997). The role of self-organization in the promotion of resilience in maltreated children. *Development and Psychopathology, 9*, 797–815.

Cyranowski, J. M., Frank, E., Young, E., & Shear, M. K. (2000). Adolescent onset of gender difference in lifetime rates of major depression: A theoretical model. *Archives of General Psychiatry, 57*, 21–27.

Davies, P. T., & Windle, M. (1997). Gender-specific pathways between maternal depressive symptoms, family discord, and adolescent adjustment. *Developmental Psychology, 33*, 657–668.

Dodge, K. A., Petit, G. S., Bates, J. E., & Valente, E. (1995). Social information processing patterns partially mediate the effect of early physical abuse on later conduct problems. *Journal of Abnormal Psychology, 104*(4), 632–643.

Drake, B. (1996). Unraveling "unsubstantiated." *Child Maltreatment, 1*(3), 261–271.

Drake, B., & Johnson-Reid, M. (2000). Substantiation and early decision points in public child welfare: A conceptual reconsideration. *Child Maltreatment, 5*(3), 227–235.

Eckenrode, J., Izzo, C. V., & Smith, E. G. (2007). Physical abuse and adolescent development. In R. Haskins, F. Wulczyn & M. B. Webb (Eds.), *Child protection: Using research to improve policy and practice* (pp. 226–242). Washington, DC: Brookings Institution Press.

Felitti, V. J., Anda, R. F., Nordenberg, D., Williamson, D. F., Spitz, A. M., Edwards, V. E., et al. (1998). The relationship of adult health status to childhood abuse and household dysfunction. *American Journal of Preventive Medicine, 14*, 245–258.

Finkelhor, D., & Brown, A. (1985). The traumatic impact of child sexual abuse: A conceptualization. *American Journal of Orthopsychiatry, 55*, 530–540.

Finkelhor, D., Hotaling, G., Lewis, I. A., & Smith, C. (1990). Sexual abuse in a national survey of adult men and women prevalence, characteristics, and risk factors. *Child Abuse & Neglect, 14*, 19–28.

Flisher, A. J., Kramer, R. A., Hoven, C. W., Greenwald, S., Alegria, M., Bird, H. R., et al. (1997). Psychosocial characteristics of physically abused children and adolescents. *Journal of the American Academy of Child and Adolescent Psychiatry, 36*(1), 123–131.

Hankin, B. L., & Abramson, L. Y. (2002). Measuring cognitive vulnerability to depression in adolescence: Reliability, validity, and gender differences. *Journal of Clinical Child and Adolescent Psychology, 31*(4), 491–504.

Hartup, W. W. (1983). The peer system. In E. M. Hetherington (Ed.), *Handbook of child psychology: Vol. 4. Socialization, personality, and social development* (pp. 103–196). New York: Wiley.

Herjanic, B., & Reich, W. (1982). Development of a structured psychiatric interview for children: Agreement between children and parent on individual symptoms. *Journal of Abnormal Child Psychology, 10*, 307–324.

Herrenkohl, E. C., Herrenkohl, R. R., & Egolf, B. (1994). Resilient early school-age children from maltreating homes: Outcomes in late adolescence. *American Journal of Orthopsychiatry, 64*, 301–309.

Hussey, J. M., Marshall, J. M., English, D. J., Knight, E. D., Lau, A. S., Dubowitz, H., et al. (2005). Defining maltreatment according to substantiation: Distinction without a difference? *Child Abuse & Neglect, 29*(5), 479–492.

Hymel, S., Bowker, A., & Woody, E. (1993). Aggressive versus withdrawn unpopular children: Variations in peer and self-perceptions in multiple domains. *Child Development, 64*(3), 879–896.

maltreatment. Paper presented at the annual meeting of the Society for Research on Adolescence, San Francisco, CA.

Sroufe, L. A. (1992). Considering normal and abnormal together. The essence of developmental psychopathology. *Development and Psychopathology, 2,* 335–347.

Stockhammer, T. F., Salzinger, S., Feldman, R. S., Mojica, E., & Primavera, L. H. (2001). Assessment of the effect of physical child abuse within an ecological framework: Measurement issues. *Journal of Community Psychology, 29,* 319–344.

Straus, M. A., & Gelles, R. J. (1988). How violent are American families? Estimates from the National Family Violence Resurvey and other studies. In G. Hotaling, D. Finkelhor, J. T. Kirkpatrick, & M. A. Straus (Eds.), *Family abuse and its consequences: New directions in research.* Newbury Park, CA: Sage.

Straus, M. A., Hamby, S. L., Finkelhor, D., Moore, D. W., & Runyan, D. (1998). Identification of child maltreatment with the Parent-Child Conflict Tactics Scales: Development and psychometric data for a national sample of American parents. *Child Abuse & Neglect, 22*(4), 249–270.

Theodore, A. D., Chang, J. J., Runyan, D. K., Hunter, W. M., Bangdiwala, S. I., & Agans, R. (2005). Epidemiologic features of the physical and sexual maltreatment of children in the Carolinas. *Pediatrics, 115,* 331–337.

Thompson, M. P., Kingree, J. B., & Desai, S. (2004). Gender differences in long-term health consequences of physical abuse of children: Data from a nationally representative survey. *American Journal of Public Health, 94*(4), 599–604.

Trickett, P. K., & McBride-Chang, C. (1995). The developmental impact of different forms of child abuse and neglect. *Development and Psychopathology, 15,* 311–337.

Tyler, K. A., & Cauce, A. M. (2002). Perpetrators of early physical and sexual abuse among homeless and runaway adolescents. *Child Abuse & Neglect, 26,* 1261–1274.

Wadsworth, M. E., & Compas, B. E. (2002). Coping with family conflict and economic strain: The adolescent perspective. *Journal of Research and Adolescence, 12*(2), 243–274.

Wall, A. E., Barth, R. P., & The NSCAW Research Group. (2005). Maltreated adolescents: Risk factors and gender differences. *Stress, Trauma & Crisis, 8,* 1–24.

Weiss, B., Dodge, K. A., Bates, J. E., & Pettit, G. S. (1992). Some consequences of early harsh discipline: Child aggression and a maladaptive social information processing style. *Child Development, 63*(6), 1321–1335.

Werner, E. E., & Smith, R. S. (1992). *Overcoming the odds: High risk children from birth to adulthood.* Ithaca, NY: Cornell University Press.

Widom, C. S. (1989). Does violence beget violence - a critical-examination of the literature. *Psychological Bulletin, 106*(1), 3–28.

Widom, C. S. (2001). Child abuse and neglect. In S. O. White (Ed.), *Handbook of youth and justice.* New York: Kluwer Academic/Plenum Publishers.

Widom, C. S., & White, H. R. (1997). Problem behaviors in abused and neglected children grown-up: Prevalence and co-occurrence of substance abuse, crime and violence. *Criminal Behavior and Mental Health, 7,* 287–310.

Windle, M., Windle, R. C., Scheidt, D. M., & Miller, G. B. (1995). Physical and sexual abuse and associated mental-disorders among alcoholic inpatients. *American Journal of Psychiatry, 152*(9), 1322–1328.

Winefeld, H. R., & Bradley, P. W. (1992). Substantiation of reported child abuse or neglect: Predictors and implications. *Child Abuse & Neglect, 16,* 661–672.

Winship, C., & Radbill, L. (1994). Sampling weights and regression analysis. *Sociological Methods and Research, 3*(2), 230–257.

Wolfe, D. A., Wekerle, C., Reitzel-Jaffe, D., & Lefebvre, L. (1998). Factors associated with abusive relationships among maltreated and nonmaltreated youth. *Development and Psychopathology, 10*(1), 61–85.

5

Effects of Intimate-Partner Violence on Child Psychopathology

WILLIAM GARDNER, KELLY KELLEHER, AND
KATHLEEN PAJER

In the 1970s, shelter staff, social workers, and researchers began to report a high rate of emotional and behavioral problems in children and adolescents exposed to intimate-partner violence (Hilberman & Munson, 1977; Levine, 1975; Rounsaville & Weissman, 1977). These early reports described symptoms such as secondary enuresis; recurrent nightmares; withdrawal; fearfulness; physical problems such as ulcers, asthma, and headaches; temper tantrums; and aggressive interactions with peers, teachers, and caregivers. Although studies of this kind raised the alarm about a significant clinical problem, conclusions about the mechanisms underlying these associations were limited by small samples without comparison groups.

A large body of research has since described the effects on children's psychological functioning when they witness intimate-partner violence. These studies' results, however, have sometimes been conflicting. Most studies have reported that exposure to intimate-partner violence was associated with increased levels of symptoms of internalizing or externalizing disorders (Fantuzzo & Lindquist, 1989; Jaffe, Wolfe, Wilson, & Zak, 1986; McFarlane, Groff, O'Brien, & Watson, 2003; O'Keefe, 1994). Others were not able to replicate such findings (Barth et al., 2005; Jaffe, Wolfe, Wilson, & Zak, 1985; Jaffe et al., 1986), could only find an association between intimate-partner violence and internalizing disorders symptoms (Christopoulos et al., 1987; Cummings, Pepler, & Moore, 1999; Holden & Ritchie, 1991), or reported a link only between intimate-partner violence and externalizing symptoms (Sternberg et al., 1993).

Several conceptual reviews have confirmed an adverse effect (Edleson, 1999; Fantuzzo & Lindquist, 1989; Margolin & Gordis, 2000; Mohr, Noone, Fantuzzo, & Perry, 2000); two recent meta-analyses have examined the question more closely. Jaffe and colleagues reviewed 41 studies; the inclusion criteria for studies were *(1)* focus on exposure to domestic violence, *(2)* a sample comprising children and adolescents, and *(3)* use of a comparison group (Jaffe, Crooks, & Wolfe, 2003). All but one study reported a negative effect on children's mental health, with an average effect size of −.28. Kitzmann, Gaylord, Holt, and Kenny (2003) used similar criteria to compile studies, although they did not omit studies without control groups if correlational or multiple regression analyses were performed. The overall average effect size was −.29 from the 118 studies selected, nearly identical to the results from Jaffe's group.

Although these results support the hypothesis that exposure to intimate-partner violence is associated with poorer mental health in children, the relatively small average effect size (Cohen, 1977) is less than would be expected after a review of clinical or qualitative studies. Researchers have interpreted the relatively small average effect size to be the result of the complexity of the relationship between exposure to intimate-partner violence and child psychopathology. Confounding variables (e.g., low socioeconomic status of such families; Fantuzzo, Boruch, Beriama, Atkins, & Marcus, 1997; Straus, 1990) or moderating factors such as the child's gender (Baldry, 2003; Ballif-Spanvill, Clayton, & Hendrix, 2003; Herrera & McCloskey, 2001) or age at exposure (Wolfe, Crooks, Lee, McIntyre-Smith, & Jaffe, 2003) may have important effects. Moreover, parental aggression or other types of psychopathology may drive both intimate and parent–child interactions (Hazen, Connelly, Kelleher, Barth, & Landsverk, 2006; Katz & Low, 2004; Ross, 1996; Slep & O'Leary, 2001, 2005).

The methodological shortcomings of the literature and acknowledgment of the complex relationship between exposure to intimate-partner violence and child outcomes led to several position papers with guidelines for improving future research (Feerick & Prinz, 2003; Saunders, 2003). Design and protocol recommendations included the use of longitudinal studies with large samples and well-standardized instruments. In addition, researchers should use data-analysis methods sophisticated enough to detect developmental changes and assess the effects of other important variables, such as the child's gender, baseline child psychopathology, maternal psychopathology, and the child's ongoing exposure to violence. To the extent that the association between children's exposure to domestic violence and their psychological symptoms are mediated by their baseline psychopathology or victimization, child protection agencies may manage some cases more aggressively, with intensive case management or removal of the child from the offending environment, for example. Improving the science is critical, in other words, because it guides important social policy.

Gender, Age, and Maltreatment Interactions with Exposure to Intimate-Partner Violence

The child's gender, age at the time of exposure, and co-occurring maltreatment are particularly salient considerations. Children's psychological symptoms demonstrate clear gender-specific patterns, with boys much more likely than girls to have caregiver-reported behavioral symptoms in the early school years and girls more likely than boys to suffer anxiety and depression in later years. Previous studies have not involved participants in numbers sufficient to reveal both age and gender effects across diverse ethnic and racial groups. One study collected data from 1,265 18 year olds about their lifetime exposure to intimate-partner violence, as measured by the Conflict Tactics Scale (Straus, 1979), and then measured the correlation between these data and psychopathology that had been measured when the teens were 16 to 17 years old (Fergusson & Horwood, 1998). After adjusting for possibly confounding factors such as sociodemographic characteristics, exposure to father-initiated violence was found to be associated with conduct disorder, anxiety, and property crime; mother-initiated violence was associated with alcohol use disorders. No gender effect emerged. This study reveals the effects of the perceived aggressor's gender and gives extensive attention to possibly confounding or moderating factors in its analysis; however, its findings are limited because its exposure data were collected retrospectively.

A larger, prospective study of youths ($N = 11,484$) from the National Longitudinal Survey of Children and Youth reported similar findings. The participants were exposed to intimate-partner violence when they were 4 to 7 years of age and were assessed 2 and 4 years later (Moss, 2003). The rates of overt and indirect aggression were higher in boys than in girls, while girls had higher levels of anxiety than boys; however, the emotional-behavioral outcome differences between exposed and unexposed youths were, for all outcomes, statistically different for both genders. The way gender affects a child's response to intimate-partner violence is evidently complex and may not completely follow the gender patterns typical in psychopathology.

In addition to gender, the age at which a child is exposed to intimate-partner violence may affect the psychological functioning of the child, although many studies have not accounted for the effect of this variable. Jaffe, Wolfe, and Wilson (1990) propose that intimate-partner violence affects the child directly and indirectly. Direct effects result from the child's attempt to cope with environmental input that is negatively arousing, is frightening, or produces anger. The child's ability to cope is governed by developmental stage and previous experiences, which may translate into symptoms that differ by age. This energy focused on coping can also interfere with attainment of the next developmental stage or produce an abnormal developmental trajectory.

Studies that have examined the age of the child support the importance of developmental stage (Cummings, Zahn-Waxler, & Radke-Yarrow, 1984). For example, infants exposed to intimate-partner violence display higher rates of screaming and crying, poor sleeping habits, irritability, regressive behaviors, and easy arousal than infants not exposed to such violence (Bogat, DeJonghe, Levendosky, Davidson, & von Eye, 2006; Levendosky, Leahy, Bogat, Davidson, & von Eye, 2006). Despite such findings, McFarlane and colleagues (2003) could not find any difference in psychopathology in children aged 1 to 5 years and exposed to intimate-partner violence, but they found significant differences in children 6 to 18 years of age. Lemmey and colleagues (2001) reported no significant difference between exposed and unexposed 12- to 18-year-old youth on psychopathology, but found that exposed 4–11 year olds had significantly higher symptom levels.

The co-occurrence of child maltreatment has also been highlighted as a possible mediator or moderator of the effect of intimate-partner violence on offspring. Different forms of violence tend to cluster in families, with high rates of child abuse or neglect occurring with intimate-partner violence (Edleson, 1999; McCloskey, Figueredo, & Koss, 1995). Several studies have shown that, if the effects of child maltreatment are accounted for, the effect of intimate-partner violence on child psychopathology is reduced or no longer significant (McCabe, Lucchini, Hough, Yeh, & Hazen, 2005; Morrel, Dubowitz, Kerr, & Black, 2003). In a study of mothers victimized by intimate-partner violence, the children who had witnessed the violence and had been victims of child maltreatment had markedly worse outcomes on the Child Behavior Checklist (CBCL; Achenbach, 1991), which suggests an additive effect (Kernic et al., 2003). Researchers' understanding of co-occurring maltreatment is important for any study of the effects of intimate-partner violence on children.

Data Set Characteristics, Test Variables, and Goals

These findings from the literature have profound implications for policies and practices in both child welfare agencies and domestic violence service organizations. The effects of intimate-partner violence on child welfare agency practices cannot be overestimated. In a previous analysis of data from the National Survey of Child and Adolescent Well-Being (NSCAW), 45% of all female primary caregivers in a child welfare system sample reported that they were victims of intimate-partner violence at some time in their lives, and 29% had experienced such violence in the year preceding their interview (Hazen, Connelly, Kelleher, Landsverk, & Barth, 2004). The rates did not vary appreciably by sociodemographic characteristics such as race/ethnicity, education, urbanicity of residence, poverty status of household, and number of children in the household; however, a major correlate of domestic violence victimization in this population was caregiver depression, found in nearly 41% of women who experienced severe violence and in 30% of those who experienced less severe violence, as opposed to 19% of those who had not experienced any violence in the preceding year. For nearly one half of the women, violence had abated by the Wave 3 (18-month follow-up); however, a substantial minority was still enduring ongoing severe violence at follow-up. Unfortunately, child welfare agencies are often unaware of the extent to which caregivers and children in their caseloads are exposed to intimate-partner violence.

When the child welfare system does detect intimate-partner violence, it can affect the placement of the child (Kohl, Edleson, English, & Barth, 2005). Families with active domestic violence identified by the caseworker had their cases substantiated for child maltreatment at rates higher than those for families without identified domestic violence (52%, as opposed to 22%; $p < .001$).[1] Despite this relationship, domestic violence alone did not significantly predict placement of the child in out-of-home care. Placement appeared to be a function of multiple risks in a family. Families with active domestic violence were significantly more likely, however, to have these additional risks (e.g., prior maltreatment reports, substance abuse by the primary or secondary caregivers, maternal mental health problems, financial difficulties). Additionally, significantly ($p < .001$) more families with active domestic violence had higher cumulative risk scores (47%) than families without domestic violence (7.4%). The cumulative risk was the strongest predictor of out-of-home placement (odds ratio $= 9.8$, $p < .001$).

Some states' agencies consider an exposure to intimate-partner violence an additional risk factor in their assessment of future risk, whereas other states have gone so far as to make intimate-partner violence exposure cause for removal of the child from his or her home (Weithorn, 2000). In such considerations, the specific groups of children most at risk and the timing of the risk are critical. For domestic violence service organizations, any consistent relationship found between children's exposure to intimate-partner violence and children's emotional or behavioral problems would support implementation of appropriate screening and referral practices, as well as partnerships with child welfare organizations to manage such cases in ways that do not currently exist.

To address some of the current gaps in the literature, we conducted this prospective study of allegedly maltreated children's exposure to intimate-partner violence, using data from NSCAW. Because information on intimate-partner violence was not obtained from nonpermanent caregivers of children, for our analyses we used only children from NSCAW who had remained in their homes during and after the investigation. Among these 4,037 cases, 3,612 (89.5%) had baseline interviews with a female caregiver from whom data on domestic violence were obtained.[2] From these cases, we selected all cases for which complete data existed on the CBCL Internalizing Behaviors and Externalizing Behaviors scales for Waves 1, 3, and 4 (Achenbach, 1991). We further restricted analyses to those waves of observation during which children were older than 3 and younger than 17 years old. We made this choice to ensure substantial numbers of observations to tabulate for each age. These restrictions resulted in a final data set of 1,603 cases with complete data.

Our goals for this study were four-fold: to determine whether an association exists between children's exposure to intimate-partner violence and child maltreatment; to assess whether effects of exposure to intimate-partner violence persist; to determine whether boys and girls differ in the effects they incur from exposure to intimate-partner violence; and to determine whether the association between exposure to intimate-partner violence and child psychopathology is affected by race/ethnicity, age of the child, maternal psychopathology, or concurrent child maltreatment.

Methods

Measures

BACKGROUND CHARACTERISTICS   Information was gathered from caregivers on a wide range of caregiver and child demographic characteristics. Because our data set was finite, we restricted our focus to a few critical background variables: the child's gender, the child's race and ethnicity, the child's age at Wave 1 (baseline), and the caregiver's age.

CHILD EMOTIONAL AND BEHAVIORAL PROBLEMS   To track child outcomes, we used the CBCL (Achenbach, 1991), a 118-item caregiver-report questionnaire generating scaled scores. The CBCL is the most highly researched and arguably the most widely accepted measure of child psychopathology. An important advantage of the CBCL is that it generates age- and gender-normed T scores that have a mean of 50 and a standard deviation of 10. To simplify the presentation, in this study we report T scores for only the subscales on internalizing (e.g., anxiety and depression) and externalizing (e.g., oppositional and conduct problems).

INTIMATE-PARTNER VIOLENCE   The Conflict Tactics Scales (CTS; Straus, 1979) Physical Violence subscale was used to assess caregivers' experiences with domestic violence. This measure has "minor" and "severe" subscales based on the severity of the reported acts of violence. The minor items are about being pushed, grabbed, shoved, or slapped, whereas the severe violence items inquire about experiences of being choked, beaten up, and threatened with a knife or gun. Response categories range from zero (*never*) to 6 (*more than 20 times*), indicating the frequency of the violent acts in the 12 months preceding the assessment. For violent acts that did not occur during this 12-month period, the respondent was asked to indicate if such acts ever happened in an intimate relationship. As is common in CTS-based research, we used a summary score for any physical assault. This score equaled 1 if one or more of the acts in the scale occurred in the past year and equaled zero if none of the acts occurred during that time. We focused on intimate-partner violence in the year before assessment in order to minimize the effect of recall bias and maximize the possible effect that the violence would have on baseline child psychological function. When we say "exposed to intimate-partner violence," however, we mean that the child was in the care of a woman who reported herself to be a victim of intimate-partner violence. It does not mean that the child necessarily witnessed this violence.

CAREGIVER MENTAL HEALTH AND SUBSTANCE ABUSE SERVICES RECEIPT   We used the caseworker's first-wave judgments about whether the caregiver had a drug or alcohol problem (reported as *caregiver substance use*) and whether the caregiver had a mental health problem. We used caseworkers' reports of these problems because we lacked diagnoses from mental health or substance abuse professionals for most of the women.[3]

CHILD MALTREATMENT NSCAW asked caregivers about violence and abusive behavior toward children, using the parent-to-child version of the CTS (Straus, 1990). Specifically, we used the CTS summary scores that indicated whether in year preceding the assessment *(1)* the child had been *neglected*, *(2)* the child had suffered a *severe physical assault*, *(3)* the caregiver had behaved toward the child with *psychological aggression*, and *(4)* the child had suffered *sexual abuse*.

Analyses

Analyses were conducted with use of Wave 3 and Wave 4 sampling weights and the survey research programs in STATA 9.2 (StataCorp, 2006). We were not interested primarily in explaining interindividual differences in change over time, although these differences are important. Studies examining interindividual differences in change over time often estimate hierarchical models in which individual differences in linear trajectories are regressed on risk factors. Our question was simpler and motivated by a policy debate about the relevance of a child's exposure to intimate-partner violence to child custody determinations and other family interventions. We have two groups of children, one exposed to intimate-partner violence in the year preceding Wave 1 and another one not exposed. Considering them a few years later, our question is, How much worse off are the children who were exposed to intimate-partner violence? Notably, if the true model for an individual's developmental trajectory is nonlinear, then a linear growth-curve model will give an incorrect estimate of the harm associated with intimate-partner violence exposure: It will, more than likely, *underestimate* the harm. Simple mean comparisons are therefore better for answering our question about relative outcomes for the group of children exposed to intimate-partner violence.

Results

Wave 1 Intimate-Partner Violence and Its Covariates

We report the demographic background of the children in this data set, the rates of dysfunction among their female caregivers, and the caregivers' Wave 1 confirmations of intimate-partner violence (Table 5.1). The last row of Table 5.1 shows that 17.1% of caregivers reported in Wave 1 that a severe physical assault had occurred during the previous year (hereafter referred to as *Wave 1 intimate-partner violence*).

Intimate-partner violence did not vary as a function of the caregiver's gender, the child's demographic characteristics, or the current caregiver's mental health and substance use disorders, except that younger caregivers were more likely than older ones to report intimate-partner violence (Table 5.2). Perhaps as a

Table 5.1   Demographics, Caregiver Dysfunction, and Occurrence of Intimate-Partner Violence

		n	Percent (Weighted Estimates)
Child demographics	Male gender	743	49.3%
	African American or black	472	28.0%
	Hispanic	301	19.0%
Age at Wave 1	4–7	614	39.3%
	8–11	406	36.9%
	12–16	402	23.8%
Caregiver age	<35	911	56.6%
	35–44	525	33.9%
	45–54	136	8.0%
	>54	31	1.6%
Caregiver dysfunction	Alcohol or drug abuse	202	7.7%
	Mental health problem	273	11.3%
Intimate-partner violence report at Wave 1	Never	1,063	66.5%
	In the past, but not in past year	251	16.4%
	In the past year	289	17.1%
Total		1,603	100%

Note: The percentages are weighted for the sampling design and therefore differ slightly from percentages that may be deduced from the *n* column.

Table 5.2   Bivariate Relationships Between Wave 1 Past-Year Intimate-Partner Violence and Wave 1 Child and Caregiver Factors

	OR	95% LCI	95% UCI	*p*
Child male gender	0.84	0.46	1.51	0.55
Child African American	0.98	0.66	1.45	0.91
Child Hispanic	0.58	0.33	1.05	0.07
Child age	0.90	0.83	0.98	0.021
Caregiver age	0.72	0.53	0.98	0.039
Caregiver substance use	1.88	0.93	3.80	0.08
Caregiver mental health problem	1.76	0.71	4.37	0.22

consequence, younger children were also more likely than older children to have caregivers that reported intimate-partner violence.

Child Maltreatment and Intimate-Partner Violence at Wave 1

At each wave, we present the rates of child maltreatment, depending on whether the caregiver reported intimate-partner violence within the past year (Table 5.3). The associated *p* value indicates whether child maltreatment at the given wave was associated with Wave 1 intimate-partner violence. Rates of maltreatment usually declined, often sharply, across waves. Nevertheless, the rates remained high, even at

Table 5.3   Bivariate Associations of Wave 1 Intimate-Partner Violence and Child Maltreatment in Waves 1, 3, and 4

| Child Maltreatment Type | Wave 1 Intimate-Partner Violence | Wave 1 | | Wave 3 | | Wave 4 | |
		% Maltreatment	*p*	% Maltreatment	*p*	% Maltreatment	*p*
Neglect	Yes	59.3	0.051	46.8	0.032	42.5	0.30
	No	43.0		31.7		34.6	
Physical assault	Yes	11.4	0.43	6.9	0.029	7.9	0.88
	No	14.1		12.4		8.4	
Psychological aggression	Yes	97.5	0.001	96.7	0.001	92.2	0.06
	No	87.9		86.5		83.1	
Sexual abuse	Yes	15.3	0.14	2.6	0.51	2.9	0.62
	No	7.4		1.8		2.0	

Wave 4. Moreover, Wave 1 intimate-partner violence was associated with significantly higher rates of (severe) physical assault of the child (Wave 3), psychological aggression toward the child (Waves 1 and 3), and neglect of the child (Wave 3). Wave 1 intimate-partner violence was not associated with sexual abuse at any wave and was not associated with any of these forms of child maltreatment at Wave 4.

Child Emotional and Behavioral Problems

We report children's scores on the CBCL Internalizing and Externalizing measures by wave and by whether the child was exposed to intimate-partner violence at Wave 1 (Table 5.4; Figs. 5.1 and 5.2). On average, children in this sample had higher *T* scores on Externalizing than on Internalizing, meaning that their externalizing problems were more severe than their internalizing problems, where severity is calibrated in terms of deviance from the population as a whole. Both the internalizing and externalizing problems improved (that is, the scores declined) after Wave 1. The mean differences associated with exposure to intimate-partner violence were only modest in Waves 3 and 4, less than 4 points. The mean Internalizing scores for children exposed to intimate-partner violence were less than 56 points in

Table 5.4   Association of Wave 1 Intimate-Partner Violence with Child Psychopathology: Mean Differences

| Outcome | Wave 1 Intimate-Partner Violence | Wave 1 | | Wave 3 | | Wave 4 | |
		Mean	*p*	Mean	*p*	Mean	*p*
Internalizing	Yes	57.3	.016	54.4	.30	55.6	.029
	No	53.5		52.3		51.7	
Externalizing	Yes	60.7	.008	58.6	.06	57.2	.35
	No	56.9		55.8		55.5	

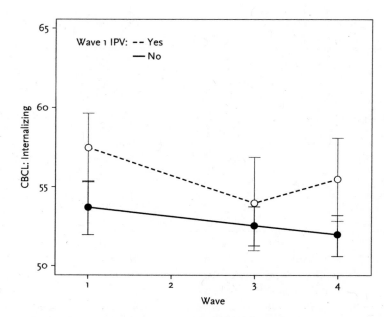

Figure 5.1 Child Behavior Checklist (CBCL) Internalizing Scale across waves, by Wave 1 exposure to intimate-partner violence (IPV).

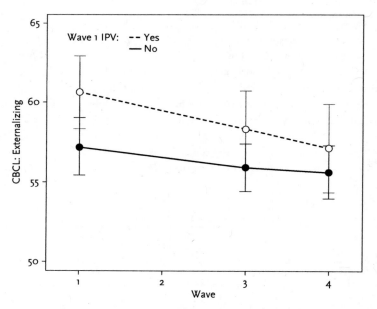

Figure 5.2 Child Behavior Checklist (CBCL) Externalizing Scale across waves, by Wave 1 exposure to intimate-partner violence (IPV).

Waves 3 and 4 (with 60 points being a borderline score for clinically referred children). The mean difference in Internalizing scores is not statistically significant at Wave 3 but is at Wave 4. Externalizing scores were higher (that is, the problems were more severe) at each successive wave. Nevertheless, differences between the children whose caregivers did report intimate-partner violence at Wave 1 and the children of caregivers who did not report such violence were again moderate and not statistically significant at Waves 3 and 4.

Child Emotional and Behavioral Problems as a Function of Gender and Age

Our second research goal concerned the effects of intimate-partner violence as differentiated by the child's gender. We present average CBCL Internalizing and Externalizing scores by child gender and Wave 1 intimate-partner violence exposure status (Figs, 5.3–5.6). We tested the means for the presence of a statistical interaction between child gender and intimate-partner violence exposure. The results of these tests were nonsignificant, meaning the intimate-partner violence had similar effects on boys and girls. The one exception was that exposure to intimate-partner violence increased boys' Externalizing scores at Wave 4 while having little effect on girls. This interaction, however, was only barely statistically significant ($p = .041$).

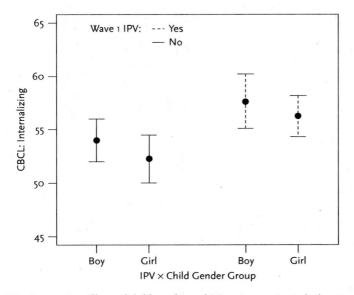

Figure 5.3 Interactive effects of child gender and Wave 1 exposure to intimate-partner violence (IPV): internalizing at Wave 1.

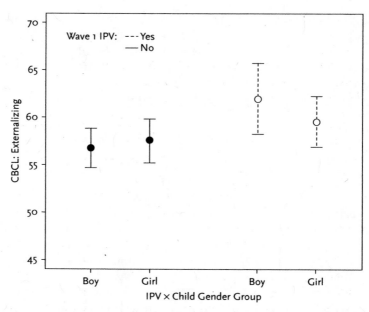

Figure 5.4 Interactive effects of child gender and Wave 1 exposure to intimate-partner violence (IPV): externalizing at Wave 1. CBCL, Child Behavior Checklist.

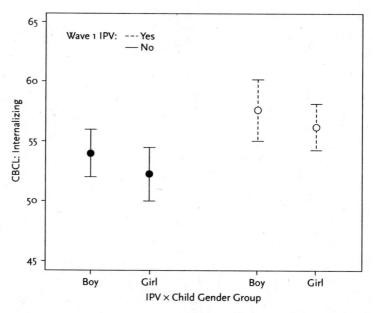

Figure 5.5 Interactive effects of child gender and Wave 1 exposure to intimate-partner violence (IPV): internalizing at Wave 4. CBCL, Child Behavior Checklist.

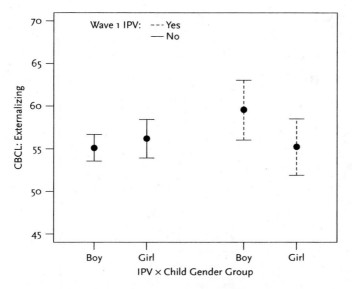

Figure 5.6   Interactive effects of child gender and Wave 1 exposure to intimate-partner violence (IPV): externalizing at Wave 4. CBCL, Child Behavior Checklist.

We also examined whether the effect of exposure to intimate-partner violence varied according to the age of the child at the time of exposure. This interactive effect was unlikely, because the effects of exposure to intimate-partner violence and of child age in themselves were small. Nevertheless, we tested whether there was a statistical interaction (i.e., a difference in the effect of intimate-partner violence on either the child's Internalizing or the child's Externalizing scores, depending on whether the intimate-partner violence occurred when the child was 5 years old or younger, or whether it occurred when the child was older than 5). No difference was found at any wave.

Children's Emotional and Behavioral Problems as a Function of Intimate-Partner Violence

We estimated the effects of caregiver-reported intimate-partner violence on child psychopathology at each Wave, controlling for the effects of concurrent child maltreatment and caregiver behavioral disorders. We report the results of three regression equations in which the dependent variables were CBCL Internalizing scores at Waves 1, 3, and 4 (Table 5.5). The independent variables in each equation were Wave 1 intimate-partner violence, the measures of child maltreatment, caregiver age and child age at Wave 1, and Wave 1 data on caregiver substance use and mental health problems. Because the variable for Wave 1 intimate-partner

Table 5.5 Adjusted Effects: CBCL Internalizing by Wave and Wave 1 Measures of Maltreatment, Neglect, and Caregiver Dysfunction

Wave 1 Risk Factor	Wave 1		Wave 3		Wave 4	
	Adjusted Difference	p	Adjusted Difference	p	Adjusted Difference	p
Intimate-partner violence	2.36	.09	1.05	.47	2.65	0.042
Psychological aggression	7.28	<.001	2.04	.34	4.00	0.12
Physical assault	3.53	.006	2.60	.10	3.38	0.011
Neglect	4.32	<.001	3.88	.001	2.08	0.013
Sexual abuse	3.44	.049	5.05	.07	5.66	<0.001
Male child	1.48	.043	2.31	.006	1.30	.07
Child age	0.28	.10	−.01	.97	0.02	0.89
Caregiver age	0.23	.73	0.72	.20	0.88	0.19
Caregiver substance abuse	0.11	.10	−0.05	.98	0.87	0.51
Caregiver mental health problem	4.94	.001	4.07	.012	6.76	<0.001

violence was coded 0|1, the regression coefficient for this variable represents an estimate of the effect of exposure to intimate-partner violence, adjusted for the other variables. Table 5.5 shows that, when adjusted for the other measures of child maltreatment and caregiver disorders, Wave 1 intimate-partner violence had a marginally significant effect on CBCL Internalizing scores in Wave 4. Notably, however, some forms of caregiver-reported child maltreatment and the caseworker's report of caregiver mental health problems had substantial, persistent effects on internalizing problems.

We present a similar analysis for the CBCL Externalizing measures (Table 5.6). In this case, however, the adjusted effect of Wave 1 intimate-partner violence is not

Table 5.6 Adjusted Effects: CBCL Externalizing by Wave and Wave 1 Measures of Maltreatment, Neglect, and Caregiver Dysfunction

Wave 1 Risk Factor	Wave 1		Wave 3		Wave 4	
	Adjusted Difference	p	Adjusted Difference	p	Adjusted Difference	p
Intimate-partner violence	2.03	.10	1.50	.28	0.53	.73
Psychological aggression	10.24	<.001	6.73	.012	7.11	.013
Physical assault	2.23	.14	1.31	.37	3.04	<.017
Neglect	3.85	<.001	2.35	.027	1.02	.20
Sexual abuse	4.69	<.001	6.58	<.001	5.89	<.001
Male child	−.25	.79	−.52	.53	0.21	.78
Child age	0.35	.008	0.41	.005	0.39	.013
Caregiver age	−.20	.75	−0.63	.30	−0.59	.35
Caregiver substance abuse	0.75	.56	1.36	.35	0.83	.57
Caregiver mental health problem	3.98	.002	1.74	.14	3.22	.006

significant for any wave. Again, other Wave 1 risk factors in Table 5.6 show strong, persistent effects at subsequent waves, including sexual abuse and caregiver mental health problems. It is not true, therefore, that the CBCL measures are insensitive to the effects of developmental insults.

Discussion

Child welfare agencies and domestic violence services organizations routinely encounter families with several kinds of violence. These families mean complex management challenges for agencies that have not traditionally worked together. For child welfare agencies, the primary question of child protection is raised in the context of poor outcomes for children exposed to intimate-partner violence. Similarly, for domestic violence service organizations the question of services and care for youth exposed to intimate-partner violence is a critical one.

In response to the experience of many family court judges, caseworkers, and domestic violence advocates, as well as growing research documenting the co-occurrence of child maltreatment and domestic violence, the National Council of Juvenile and Family Court Judges has published comprehensive recommendations in "Effective Interventions in Domestic Violence and Child Maltreatment: Guidelines for Policy and Practice" (National Council of Juvenile and Family Court Judges, 1998), otherwise known as the *Greenbook*. The Greenbook guides communities addressing co-occurring child maltreatment, domestic violence, and childhood exposure to domestic violence; specifically, it provides recommendations aimed at coordinating the work of the courts, child protective services, and community-based domestic violence organizations. These recommendations have been developed, however, in the absence of comprehensive literature on the effects of intimate-partner violence on child psychopathology.

Effects of Intimate-Partner Violence on Children's Emotional and Behavioral Problems

Our regression results in the current study indicate that exposure to intimate-partner violence, at least as measured by caregivers' self-reports, has few persistent effects on child psychopathology. We found that exposure to intimate-partner violence at Wave 1 was associated with modest increases in child internalizing and externalizing problems at Waves 3 and 4; however, only the association with the child's Wave 4 internalizing problems was statistically significant. Of greater consequence for child well-being is that exposure to intimate-partner violence at Wave 1 was associated with risk of the caregiver's neglect, physical assault, and psychological aggression toward the child at later waves.

We also have addressed gender and age as possibly interacting with the effects of Wave 1 intimate-partner violence on child psychopathology. We assessed whether boys and girls, because of their gender, were affected differently by exposure to Wave 1 intimate-partner violence. Although we found one significant interaction between exposure to intimate-partner violence at Wave 1 and children's later psychopathology, in general we found little evidence of consistent difference in the ways boys and girls were affected. Similarly, we found that the effects, or absence of effects, of intimate-partner violence exposure were similar for young children and for older children.

We have addressed whether Wave 1 intimate-partner violence is associated with child psychopathology when we adjust for Wave 1 child maltreatment and caregiver dysfunction. The answer is unambiguous: Only one statistically significant difference in child psychopathology emerges at later waves.

Limitations

One explanation for the relatively small effects of intimate-partner violence in our results may be the shortcomings of our methods for measuring intimate-partner violence (Fantuzzo & Lindquist, 1989; Margolin & Gordis, 2000; Mohr et al., 2000). Kitzmann and colleagues (2003) have shown that the effect sizes reported in studies of intimate-partner violence effects on child outcomes vary as a function of study sample composition (e.g., one group, or witnesses as compared with nonwitnesses, or witnesses as compared with children also physically abused), source population (e.g., shelters or the general community), domestic violence data collection instruments (e.g., Conflict Tactics Scale or police reports). Alternatively or additionally, use of exclusion criteria, matching, or statistical controls can affect production of effect sizes. Because of the complex nature and ambitious scope of NSCAW, one or more methodological variables may have affected our results.

Notably, the women in this study reported that they were the victims of a physical assault during the year before the interview, but they did not report on whether their child witnessed the violence. The intimate-partner violence in this study probably represents an unsorted mixture of witnessed and unwitnessed intimate-partner violence cases; if so, then the effect of witnessed intimate-partner violence likely has been diluted. Our conclusion that intimate-partner violence has little effect on child psychopathology may not apply, therefore, to children who actually witness intimate-partner violence, especially when the witnessed violence is severe.

Another limitation possibly tempering our conclusions stems from our exclusion of children in out-of-home care at Wave 1. In general, the age, gender, and types of maltreatment of children placed in out-of-home care were similar to those of the in-home children who composed our subsample. We cannot conclude, however, that the children in out-of-home care came from families with the same prevalence or intensity of intimate-partner violence as the children we analyzed. Moreover, the presence of intimate-partner violence in the original home may have even influenced placement of many of these children out of their homes. Consequently, caregivers who were victims of the most severe intimate-partner violence may have been excluded from our sample. Similarly, our results may have been affected by the exclusion of children who did not have complete data on the CBCL Internalizing and Externalizing subscales. For those who were included, important dimensions of psychological harm to children may be affected by caregiver intimate-partner violence but may have remained uncaptured by the CBCL Internalizing and Externalizing scales. No data on male caregivers or perpetrators were included in our analyses, either. This exclusion typifies studies of this kind; nonetheless, it must qualify our conclusions.

We were unable to determine whether the effect of intimate-partner violence on children varied according to the children's developmental stage at the time of exposure: Developmental stage was not evaluated in this study. Moreover, we know of no studies that have evaluated the developmental stages of the children instead of citing only their chronological ages. This topic requires research; however, we found no important effects of the child's age at the time of exposure, which means it is unlikely that effects of developmental stage could be large.

In this current study we examined the effect of exposure to intimate-partner violence in the year preceding Wave 1; however, effects of intimate-partner violence on development may be cumulative (Rossman, 2001). A child in an environment characterized by chronic intimate-partner violence is likely to be chronically at risk of being neglected, physically assaulted, treated in a psychologically aggressive manner, and perhaps even sexually abused. It is questionable whether the effects of chronic intimate-partner violence would even be distinguishable in such a thoroughly toxic environment.

Conclusion

These results convey several implications for clinical care and future research. The effect of caregiver intimate-partner violence on child psychopathology is less severe than the effect of child maltreatment on child psychopathology. This conclusion in no way implies, however, that caregiver intimate-partner violence should be ignored. Moreover, the relationship between intimate-partner violence and child or adolescent psychopathology may be complicated by several other environmental variables. Consequently, child welfare agencies with a mandate to protect children should understand that, although these results suggest less harm than some other studies, these children will still require evaluation and consideration of their individual conditions. No rule consistent across all youth can be formulated from these findings.

Because of the high rates of child behavior problems generally, children in the child welfare system should be receiving careful mental health assessments. From the standpoint of prevention, interventions focusing on only maternal victimization or on only child maltreatment may fail strategically to address behavior and emotional problems in children of families affected by violence. Moreover, others have reported an association between maternal exposure to intimate-partner violence and child maltreatment (Casanueva & Martin, 2007). Interventions that address maternal disciplinary practices and interaction with children are warranted because these factors may play crucial roles in these children's eventual mental health outcomes.

Until further research is conducted, the implications for social work practice in child welfare and domestic violence agencies remain less clear. Domestic violence services are a potential means by which child welfare–involved battered women may help their children avoid potentially harmful exposure to violence. Only 60% of women with caseworker-identified domestic violence are referred, however, for any domestic violence services. Of women who have a referral made on their behalf, 83% receive services (Kohl et al., 2005; Nuszkowski et al., 2007).

Improving these practices requires extensive training. Nationally, child welfare system agencies report that they do indeed cover the majority of regulatory, safety, and developmental issues for their caseworkers in routine training. In addition, training on co-occurring child maltreatment and intimate-partner violence is reportedly mandatory for at least some staff in 75% of the child welfare agencies and in 88% of the domestic violence agencies (Kohl et al., 2005; Nuszkowski et al., 2007). Nonetheless, only about one third of the agencies report actual co-training with their sister agencies. This figure suggests that child welfare and domestic violence agencies are operating independently and that additional policies are necessary to support collaborative training efforts.

Future research should further investigate the context in which intimate-partner violence occurs. Recent data suggest that much of intimate-partner violence is reciprocal, although when males strike out they are more likely to cause serious physical damage (Mills, Avegno, & Haydel, 2006; Whitaker, Haileyesus, Swahn, & Saltzman, 2007). The effects of intimate-partner violence on the psychological state of parents and on their parenting may be differentially affected by nonreciprocal as opposed to reciprocal violence. To close gaps in the body of knowledge informing child welfare practice, male caretakers' reports of violence should be examined, and reciprocity should be measured.

We also recommend that new methods of sampling and data analysis be explored. Most studies have used samples in which violence of some kind was already present. Because females are more likely to be physically injured, they are more likely to comprise these samples. This preponderance of female respondents may lead to biased data on the complex processes involved in intimate-partner violence. Slep, Heyman, Williams, Van Dyke, and O'Leary (2006) have successfully demonstrated a method for obtaining participants from the general population; more innovation in this area is warranted. Also important to future research will be the use of current data to develop testable theories about the mechanisms underlying development of intimate-partner violence and its effects on children. The addition of person-oriented analytic methods to the standard variable-oriented analyses as suggested by Bogat, Levendosky, and von Eye (2005) is a promising new direction.

NOTES

1. *Substantiation* is the child welfare system's official case decision that allegations of child maltreatment are valid.
2. Male caregivers gave interviews in 364 cases, and 61 interviews with female caregivers were missing data on domestic violence.
3. Caseworkers do not necessarily have the training to make these determinations, so the meaning of their judgments is open to question. As will be seen, however, caseworkers' reports of mental health problems in the women are important predictors of the child's mental health outcomes, so caseworker reports have at least *some* useful prognostic information.

REFERENCES

Achenbach, T. M. (1991). *Manual for the Child Behavior Checklist/4-18 and 1991 profile.* Burlington, VT: University of Vermont, Department of Psychiatry.

Baldry, A. C. (2003). Bullying in schools and exposure to domestic violence. *Child Abuse & Neglect, 27*(7), 713–732.

Ballif-Spanvill, B., Clayton, C. J., & Hendrix, S. B. (2003). Gender, types of conflict, and individual differences in the use of violent and peaceful strategies among children who have and have not witnessed interparental violence. *American Journal of Orthopsychiatry, 73*(2), 141–153.

Barth, R. P., Landsverk, J. A., Chamberlain, P., Reid, J., Rolls, J., Hurlburt, M., et al. (2005). Parent training programs in child welfare services: Planning for a more evidence-based approach to serving biological parents. *Research on Social Work Practice, 15*(5), 353–371.

Bogat, G. A., DeJonghe, E., Levendosky, A. A., Davidson, W. S., & von Eye, A. (2006). Trauma symptoms among infants exposed to intimate partner violence. *Child Abuse & Neglect, 30*(2), 109–125.

Bogat, G. A., Levendosky, A. A., & von Eye, A. (2005). The future of research on intimate partner violence: Person-oriented and variable-oriented perspectives. *American Journal of Community Psychology, 36*(1-2), 49–70.

Casanueva, C. E., & Martin, S. L. (2007). Intimate partner violence during pregnancy and mothers' child abuse potential. *Journal of Interpersonal Violence, 22*(5), 603–622.

Christopoulos, C., Cohn, D., Shaw, D., Joyce, S., Sullivan-Hansen, J., Kraft, S., et al. (1987). Children of abused women: I. Adjustment at time of shelter residence. *Journal of Marriage and the Family, 49*, 611–619.

Cohen, J. (1977). *Statistical power analysis for the behavioral sciences* (4th ed.). New York: Academic Press.

Cummings, E. M., Zahn-Waxler, C., & Radke-Yarrow, M. (1984). Developmental changes in children's reactions to anger in the home. *Journal of Child Psychology and Psychiatry, 25*(1), 63–74.

Cummings, J., Pepler, D., & Moore, T. (1999). Behavior problems in children exposed to wife abuse: Gender differences. *Journal of Family Violence, 14*, 133–156.

Edleson, J. L. (1999). The overlap between child maltreatment and women battering. *Violence Against Women, 5*, 134–154.

Fantuzzo, J., Boruch, R., Beriama, A., Atkins, M., & Marcus, S. (1997). Domestic violence and children: Prevalence and risk in five major U.S. cities. *Journal of the American Academy of Child and Adolescent Psychiatry, 36*(1), 116–122.

Fantuzzo, J., & Lindquist, T. J. (1989). The effects of observing conjugal violence on children: A review and analysis of research methodology. *Journal of Family Violence, 4,* 77–94.

Feerick, M. M., & Prinz, R. J. (2003). Next steps in research on children exposed to community violence or war/terrorism. *Clinical Child and Family Psychology Review, 6*(4), 303–305.

Fergusson, D. M., & Horwood, L. J. (1998). Exposure to interparental violence in childhood and psychosocial adjustment in young adulthood. *Child Abuse & Neglect, 22*(5), 339–357.

Hazen, A. L., Connelly, C. D., Kelleher, K. J., Barth, R. P., & Landsverk, J. A. (2006). Female caregivers' experiences with intimate partner violence and behavior problems in children investigated as victims of maltreatment. *Pediatrics, 117*(1), 99–109.

Hazen, A. L., Connelly, C. D., Kelleher, K., Landsverk, J., & Barth, R. (2004). Intimate partner violence among female caregivers of children reported for child maltreatment. *Child Abuse & Neglect, 28*(3), 301–319.

Herrera, V. M., & McCloskey, L. A. (2001). Gender differences in the risk for delinquency among youth exposed to family violence. *Child Abuse & Neglect, 25*(8), 1037–1051.

Hilberman, E., & Munson, K. (1977). Sixty battered women. *Victimology International Journal, 2,* 460–470.

Holden, G. W., & Ritchie, K. L. (1991). Linking extreme marital discord, child rearing, and child behavior problems: Evidence from battered women. *Child Development, 62*(2), 311–327.

Jaffe, P. G., Crooks, C. V., & Wolfe, D. A. (2003). Legal and policy responses to children exposed to domestic violence: The need to evaluate intended and unintended consequences. *Clinical Child and Family Psychology Review, 6*(3), 205–213.

Jaffe, P. G., Wolfe, D. A., Wilson, S., & Zak, L. (1985). Critical issues in the assessment of children's adjustment to witnessing family violence. *Canada's Mental Health, 33*(4), 15–19.

Jaffe, P. G., Wolfe, D. A., & Wilson, S. K. (1990). *Children of battered women.* Newbury Park, CA: Sage Publications.

Jaffe, P. G., Wolfe, D. A., Wilson, S. K., & Zak, L. (1986). Family violence and child adjustment—A comparative analysis of girls and boys behavioral symptoms. *American Journal of Psychiatry, 143*(1), 74–77.

Katz, L. F., & Low, S. M. (2004). Marital violence, co-parenting, and family-level processes in relation to children's adjustment. *Journal of Family Psychology, 18*(2), 372–382.

Kernic, M. A., Wolf, M. E., Holt, V. L., McKnight, B., Huebner, C. E., & Rivara, F. P. (2003). Behavioral problems among children whose mothers are abused by an intimate partner. *Child Abuse & Neglect, 27*(11), 1231–1246.

Kitzmann, K. M., Gaylord, N. K., Holt, A. R., & Kenny, E. D. (2003). Child witnesses to domestic violence: A meta-analytic review. *Journal of Consulting and Clinical Psychology, 71*(2), 339–352.

Kohl, P. L., Edleson, J. L., English, D. J., & Barth, R. P. (2005). Domestic violence and pathways in to child welfare services: Findings from the National Study of Child and Adolescent Well-Being. *Children and Youth Services Review, 27,* 1167–1182.

Lemmey, D., Malecha, A., McFarlane, J., Willson, P., Watson, K., Gist, J. H., et al. (2001). Severity of violence against women correlates with behavioral problems in their children. *Pediatric Nursing, 27*(3), 265–270.

Levendosky, A. A., Leahy, K. L., Bogat, G. A., Davidson, W. S., & von Eye, A. (2006). Domestic violence, maternal parenting, maternal mental health, and infant externalizing behavior. *Journal of Family Psychology, 20*(4), 544–552.

Levine, M. B. (1975). Interparental violence and its effect on the children: A study of 50 families in general practice. *Medicine, Science and the Law, 15*(3), 172–176.

Margolin, G., & Gordis, E. B. (2000). The effects of family and community violence on children. *Annual Review of Psychology, 51*, 445–479.

McCabe, K. M., Lucchini, S. E., Hough, R. L., Yeh, M., & Hazen, A. (2005). The relation between violence exposure and conduct problems among adolescents: A prospective study. *American Journal of Orthopsychiatry, 75*(4), 575–584.

McCloskey, L. A., Figueredo, A. J., & Koss, M. P. (1995). The effects of systemic family violence on children's mental health. *Child Development, 66*(5), 1239–1261.

McFarlane, J. M., Groff, J. Y., O'Brien, J. A., & Watson, K. (2003). Behaviors of children who are exposed and not exposed to intimate partner violence: An analysis of 330 black, white, and Hispanic children. *Pediatrics, 112*(3 Pt 1), e202–207.

Mills, T. J., Avegno, J. L., & Haydel, M. J. (2006). Male victims of partner violence: Prevalence and accuracy of screening tools. *Journal of Emergency Medicine, 31*(4), 447–452.

Mohr, W. K., Noone, L. M. J., Fantuzzo, J., & Perry, M. A. (2000). Children exposed to family violence: A review of empirical research from a developmental-ecological perspective. *Trauma Violence Abuse, 1*, 264–283.

Morrel, T. M., Dubowitz, H., Kerr, M. A., & Black, M. M. (2003). The effect of maternal victimization on children: A cross informant study. *Journal of Family Violence, 18*, 29–41.

Moss, K. (2003). Witnessing violence—aggression and anxiety in young children. *Statistics Canada: Supplement to Health Report, 14*(1), 53–66.

Nuszkowski, M. A., Cohen, J. H., Kelleher, K. J., Goldcamp, J. C., Hazen, A. L., & Connelly, C. D. (2007). Training, co-training, and cross-training of domestic violence and child welfare agencies. *Families in Society, 88*(1), 36–41.

O'Keefe, M. (1994). Adjustment of children from maritally violent homes. *Journal of Contemporary Human Services, 75*(7), 403–415.

Ross, S. M. (1996). Risk of physical abuse to children of spouse abusing parents. *Child Abuse & Neglect, 20*(7), 589–598.

Rossman, B. (2001). Longer term effects of children's exposure to domestic violence. In S. Graham-Bermann & J. Edelson (Eds.), *Domestic violence in the lives of children*. Washington, DC: American Psychological Association.

Rounsaville, B., & Weissman, M. M. (1977). Battered women: A medical problem requiring detection. *International Journal of Psychiatry in Medicine, 8*(2), 191–202.

Saunders, B. E. (2003). Understanding children exposed to violence: Toward an integration of overlapping fields. *Journal of Interpersonal Violence, 18*, 356–376.

Slep, A. M., Heyman, R. E., Williams, M. C., Van Dyke, C. E., & O'Leary, S. G. (2006). Using random telephone sampling to recruit generalizable samples for family violence studies. *Journal of Family Psychology, 20*(4), 680–689.

Slep, A. M., & O'Leary, S. G. (2001). Examining partner and child abuse: Are we ready for a more integrated approach to family violence? *Clinical Child and Family Psychology Review, 4*(2), 87–107.

Slep, A. M., & O'Leary, S. G. (2005). Parent and partner violence in families with young children: Rates, patterns, and connections. *Journal of Consulting and Clinical Psychology, 73*(3), 435–444.

StataCorp. (2006). *Stata statistical software: Release 9.2.* College Station, TX: Author.

Sternberg, K. J., Lamb, M., Greenbaum, C., Chichetti, D., Dawud, S., Cortes, R., et al. (1993). Effects of domestic violence on children's behavior problems and depression. *Developmental Psychology, 29*, 44–52.

Straus, M. A. (1979). Measuring intrafamily conflict and violence: The Conflict Tactics (CT) Scale. *Journal of Marriage and the Family, 41*, 75–88.

Straus, M. A. (1990). *Measuring physical and psychological maltreatment of children with the Conflict Tactics Scale.* Durham, NH: University of New Hampshire Family Research Laboratory.

Weithorn, J. D. (2000). Protecting children from exposure to domestic violence: The use and abuse of child maltreatment statutes. *Hastings Law Journal, 53*, 1–156.

Whitaker, D. J., Haileyesus, T., Swahn, M., & Saltzman, L. S. (2007). Differences in frequency of violence and reported injury between relationships with reciprocal and nonreciprocal intimate partner violence. *American Journal of Public Health, 97*(5), 941–947.

Wolfe, D. A., Crooks, C. V., Lee, V., McIntyre-Smith, A., & Jaffe, P. G. (2003). The effects of children's exposure to domestic violence: A meta-analysis and critique. *Clinical Child and Family Psychology Review, 6*(3), 171–187.

PART II

Child Welfare, Social Capital, and Child Well-Being

The three major child welfare outcomes of safety, permanence, and well-being can be translated into the concepts of human, cultural, and social capital as follows: *Human capital* refers to those basic conditions of bodily integrity, health, and stamina necessary for biological reproduction and physical labor. It can be distinguished from *cultural capital*, which encompasses the additional skills, expertise, education, and credentials that children acquire so that as adults they can independently pursue their own economic and social well-being. Because human capital is fully developed only after children biologically mature and because cultural capital is acquired after many years of informal socialization and formal education, children must be able during their dependency years to safely and reliably access the human, cultural, and financial capital of adults in order to grow and reach their own adult potential.

The third kind, *social capital*, makes accessible to children those adult resources necessary for their physical survival and healthy development. The concept refers to the more or less permanent relationships of care, commitment, and trust in which one or more adults (agents) assume, or are delegated, the discretion to act on behalf of the interests of the child (principal). In the language of agency theory, one can speak of the principal–agent relationships of child and parent, client and social worker, and ward and guardian, among others. Because of infants' complete dependence on adults, social capital must be made immediately available at birth in the form of gift relationships from parents, relatives, and other agents who closely identify with the child's well-being (*bonding social capital*). As children mature, they can be expected to participate in exchange relationships in their own family and later in the widening primary and secondary arenas of play, school, worship, work, and civic participation (*bridging social capital*). If all goes as intended, the cycle of social reciprocity is closed in adulthood as grown-ups grant

access to their human, cultural, and financial capital through restricted gift relationships with their own children, elderly parents, younger relatives, companions,
and friends, as well as through generalized gift relationships with more distant
acquaintances, anonymous citizens, and other human beings globally.

In Part 2 the contributors to this volume examine the challenges of modern
child welfare practice and policy by investigating various dimensions of what may
be termed the *principal–agent problem* in the protection and management
of children's human, cultural, social, and financial capital. The *problem* refers to
the risks that children incur from adult-agents' imperfectly fulfilling their best
interests. These risks can arise either from instrumental constraints on an agent's
exercise of meaningful choice, such as poverty, misinformation, and social
exclusion, or from dispositional deficiencies, such as lack of empathy, addictive
behaviors, and uninhibited egoism. At the hub of the problem is what may be called
the *dilemma of parental investment* (Trivers, 1985): On the one hand, it is in
everyone's interest for adults to invest altruistically in the fitness, care, and well-
being of children; on the other, a strong temptation exists for each adult to behave
egoistically and withhold his or her contribution at the expense of the common
good. At the parent–child level, such risks occasionally may play out in situations
that tragically degenerate into child abandonment, neglect, or abuse; at the social
organizational level, they may play out in the form of a "public good" problem that
can expose children to the secondary harms of bureaucratic neglect, physical and
sexual reabuse, and foster care drift.

Until now, child welfare researchers have lacked the child well-being data
required to subject the safety permanence–well-being hierarchy informing the
child welfare system standard operating procedure to serious scrutiny. The
National Survey of Child and Adolescent Well-Being (NSCAW) enables child
welfare researchers to give thoughtful consideration to the question previously
raised by Richard Barth (1999) of whether, after ensuring safety, it is always best to
emphasize family continuity and permanence over other well-being factors, such as
education and employment, that might require some discontinuity in children's
lives to achieve (Barth, 1999). A compelling case can be made on the basis of social
capital and agency theory for disadvantaged children's need to move beyond the
homogeneous social capital networks of family and local community in order to
compete effectively in a postindustrial, global economy. The significance of family
continuity, ascribed heritage, and legal permanence for assuring the health, longevity, and self-sufficiency for foster children is an unsettling question; nonetheless,
it is one that deserves careful consideration that draws from the best available data
on child well-being.

The welcome news from the chapters presented in Part 2 is that standard
operating procedure in child welfare stands up fairly well when measured against
the usual child welfare benchmarks of safety, continuity, stability, and permanence.
As described in the chapters authored by Testa, Bruhn, and Helms (Chapter 6) and
Barth, Guo, Caplick, and Green (Chapter 8), maintaining kinship continuity
appears to offer some advantages with respect to stability and legal permanence

while carrying no appreciably greater safety and perhaps lesser reentry risks than licensed family foster care. Three years after the child protective investigation was closed, almost 80% of children remained with or were restored to the custody of their birth families, with little evidence that that their safety or well-being was seriously compromised.

Of course, NSCAW is an observational study and presents formidable challenges to disproving the counterfactual that these children's lives would have been significantly improved if they had been retained under the fiduciary agency of the state or reassigned to the affine agency of families richer in access to financial and bridging social capital. The chapter by Stagner and Keuhn (Chapter 7) offers tentative evidence of this possible tradeoff. But even if future research were to indicate that such advantages are real, it would not automatically prove the superiority of out-of-home care. It may well be that similar improvements could be achieved by enriching the access of the children's own parents and relatives to the relevant financial and bridging social capital without uprooting the children from their families and communities. It is critical in this regard that child welfare researchers gain the firmer understanding of the racial and ethnic differences in child welfare outcomes that Ortega and his colleagues (chapter 9) describe—as well as the reasons these differences, as Barth and his colleagues find, persist after extensive controls are introduced for the human, cultural, and social capital of the children and families. Whether these residual disparities are the products of prejudice, paternalism agency risk, or model misspecification is important to know before deciding whether to reinforce the universalism and equality expected of fiduciary agency, or whether instead to restore responsibility to affine agents, who are more likely to safeguard the best interests of the children as if these interests were their own.

All of these issues refract on the original question of who is best able to exercise agency on behalf of children's acquisition of human and cultural capital and investment of social and financial capital. Standard operating procedure in child welfare is fairly clear that safety trumps permanence and permanence trumps well-being, meaning that, even if it could be proved that children's average lifetime earnings could be substantially boosted by nonkinship adoption, this fact would not be adequate grounds for removing a child from a safe but unstable birth home or from a stable but economically marginal kin home. If, in the future, policy makers are to reconsider the rank-ordering of child welfare values, then child welfare researchers will first have to ascertain that the right set of child well-being measures are in place for making such a determination. The field must be cautious not to marginalize the cultural preferences, outlooks, and voices of primordial solidarities to the point that only the maximization of material comfort effectively matters as an indicator of well-being.

To preserve the vitality of traditional social capital, it will be important to create new coordinating mechanisms that can mediate the reciprocal flow of influence between the older, primordial structures and the newer, bureaucratic structures. Absence of effective coordinating mechanisms engenders distrust and alienation of the populations who are the intended subjects of public child welfare policies; it undermines, as well, the capacity of bureaucratic structures to accomplish the broader social purposes for which they were constructed. As policy attention turns to considerations of child well-being, child welfare researchers will have an important role to play in parsing out the strengths and weaknesses of bonding social capital and legal permanence in enabling youth to acquire the human and cultural capital necessary for leading a productive and meaningful life. To fulfill this mission, it is incumbent on researchers to coordinate the values and morals of the society at large with the impulses, desires, and wishes of the children and families who are the intended subjects of public policy intervention.

REFERENCES

Barth, R. P. (1999). After safety, what is the goal of child welfare services: Permanency, family continuity, or social benefit? *International Journal of Social Welfare, 8*(4), 244–252.

Trivers, R. L. (1985). *Social evolution.* Menlo Park, CA: Benjamin-Cummings.

6

Comparative Safety, Stability, and Continuity of Children's Placements in Formal and Informal Substitute Care

MARK TESTA, CHRISTINA M. BRUHN, AND JESSE HELTON

Formal foster care is substitute care that is subsidized and supervised or licensed by government. It coexists with a much larger volume of substitute care that draws from the informal social networks of kin, friends, and neighbors. Of the estimated 2.9 million children living in households apart from their parents in 2001, approximately 2.1 million resided informally with extended kin, compared with 310,000 children who lived in formal foster care with relatives or nonkin foster parents.[1] Although originally structured as a residual placement resource for shoring up insufficiencies in the informal system, formal foster care now actively recruits and supports many of the same relatives, acquaintances, and neighboring families that it once excluded.[2] The blurring of the boundaries between formal and informal foster care in the late twentieth and early twenty-first centuries in the United States has greatly expanded the government's capacity for engaging families and local communities in the protection and care of abused and neglected children. At the same time, however, this blurring introduces fiscal uncertainties about the potential substitution of public dollars for voluntary private effort; moreover, it arouses anxieties about the safety and well-being of children left in kinship homes and other neighborhood-based sources of substitute care.

Attempts by federal policy makers, administrators, and legislators to develop a coherent policy framework that reconciles the tensions between these two systems of substitute care without unduly restricting the participation of kinship caregivers in the formal system or fully bureaucratizing the informal system have so far proved to be elusive. Across the United States, publicly funded substitute care remains an inconsistent patchwork of policies and programs. In some states, thousands of abused and neglected children are looked after in a hodgepodge of informal living situations. In other states, these same children are regularly taken into public custody and placed with extended family or into other neighborhood-based arrangements that are approved, subsidized, and supervised by local, county, or state government.

The different streams of federal financial assistance that governments can tap into to support children in these various informal and formal living situations also contribute to the state-by-state inconsistency. If children are diverted to the private custody (*in loco parentis*) of relatives, the children may qualify for federal Temporary Assistance for Needy Families (TANF), food stamps, and medical assistance but little else in the way of child placement services, permanency planning, or family counseling. If the children are taken into public protective custody, they may then qualify for these additional child welfare services but still may receive TANF or some other income subsidy, unless they and their family can also satisfy the foster-home licensing and federal eligibility requirements that would entitle them to full foster care reimbursement. In most states, foster care reimbursement ranges from two to four times the TANF grant amount, depending on the number of children in the home.

Primordial and Bureaucratic Agency

Federal financing policy and regulatory oversight appear to be torn: On the one hand, selected features of federal law and regulation favor the principle that kinship and community should matter when agencies are allocating rights for children and responsibilities for their substitute care. This principle is reflected, for example, in the Adoption Assistance and Child Welfare Act of 1980, 42 USC § 675(5)(A) (1980), which emphasizes placement in the "least restrictive (most family-like) and most appropriate setting available and in close proximity to the parents' home." It also appears in the preference for kinship placement that Congress attached to its 1996 welfare reform bill, which encourages states to place children with kin whenever such kin meet relevant child protection standards, 42 U.S.C. § 671(19) (1996), and again in the Adoption and Safe Families Act of 1997 exemption of children in kinship care from the requirement that states pursue termination of parental rights for children in foster care for 15 of the most recent 22 months, 42 U.S.C. § 675(5)(E) (1997).

On the other hand, other elements of federal law and regulation enforce the principle that rights and responsibilities should not be ascribed but instead assigned on the basis of an impartial assessment of a surrogate parent's background, qualifications, and financial means, without regard to kinship, race, sexual orientation, or ascribed heritage. This principle is reflected, for example, in the Howard M. Metzenbaum Multiethnic Placement Act of 1994, as amended by the Interethnic Adoption Provisions of 1996, 42 U.S.C. § 1996b (2006), which prohibit "the use of race, color, or national origin" to delay or deny children's placement in racially or ethnically different foster and adoptive homes. It appeared in the Supreme Court case *Miller v. Youakim,* 44 U.S. 125, 99 S. Ct. 957 (1979), which overruled state laws that had denied full foster care benefits to families for reasons of kinship alone. It surfaced in the U.S. Department of Health and Human Services regulations opposing different foster home licensing standards for familial caregivers (Administration for Children and Families, 2000).

The tension between these two opposing principles of child placement has been described in prior work as deriving from a chronic strain in modern societies between two contrasting perspectives on social organization: the *primordial* and the *bureaucratic* (Testa, 2001). Each perspective can be understood as an alternative solution to what lawyers and economists call the "principal–agent problem" (Buchanan, 1988): how best to ensure that substitute caregiver-agents routinely make parenting choices and investments embodying parental altruism and family mutualism, which create the home environment necessary for raising child-principals into healthy, productive adults.

The *primordial solution* to the principal–agent problem posits that the well-being of the child is best ensured by placing the child under the "affine agency" (Coleman, 1990) of extended kin and community members. It relies on the natural empathy of relatives, friends, and neighbors, who closely identify with the child's well-being by equating the satisfaction of the child's interests with their own; these caregivers, according to the solution, may be trusted to make parenting choices and investments that promote the best interests of the child.

The *bureaucratic solution* to the problem makes no such assumption about the identity of the agent's and principal's interests. Instead, it posits that the interests of the foster parent-agent and the child-principal will likely diverge. Bureaucratic rationality seeks to thwart agent opportunism by recruiting, licensing, and training special childcare agents who can be held accountable to performance standards and monitored under surveillance systems that discourage self-interested defections from responsible childcare. To lessen the risks of foster parents' diverting child maintenance stipends to their own consumption or otherwise defaulting in their other childcare responsibilities, for example, child welfare agencies screen the backgrounds of potential foster parents and enter into binding licensing agreements that specify caregiver routines (e.g., regular meal preparation), household amenities (e.g., bedroom size), and custodial responsibilities (e.g., prohibitions on corporal punishment). The bureaucracy and the courts monitor these agreements by means of regular home visitation, administrative case reviews, and judicial hearings.

In principle, relying on kinship empathy and enforcing foster-home licensing standards are not mutually exclusive solutions to the principal–agent problem. Uniting the primordial with the bureaucratic would appear to take advantage of the best of both worlds. But, in practice, state licensing standards (particularly household amenity requirements) can exceed the housing and income levels of available grandparents, aunts, uncles, and other relatives who otherwise could be relied on to act in the best interests of their family members. State governments have attempted in the past (in the 1980s) to address this primordial-bureaucratic mismatch by elaborating separate home-approval standards for relatives. The federal government rejected these developments, however, and in the late 1990s began rejecting Title IV-E claims for these kinship homes, on the grounds that federal law did not permit dual standards, Final Rule (65 FR 4020; January 25, 2000).[3] In its report to Congress, the U.S. Department of Health and Human Services dismissed implicitly the suggestion that the affine agency of kin was in itself sufficient to safeguard children's best interests (Administration for Children and Families, 2000). Instead it emphasized the possible risks of harm to children in nonlicensed settings (especially whenever the kinship placement left the child accessible to an abusive parent) and defended the importance of a unitary licensing system for both kin and nonkin caregivers.

Bonding and Bridging Social Capital

That many kinship caregivers are unable to meet state foster home licensing standards raises doubts in some minds about the adequacy of kinship care and other community-based sources of care for ensuring the well-being of maltreated children: Kinship and community networks tend to be homogeneous in lifestyle and socioeconomic characteristics (Lin, 2001). This homogeneity makes primordial groups rich, however, in what sociologists and economists call *bonding social capital* (Woolcock & Narayan, 2000), which can enhance children's expressive well-being (i.e., sense of belonging, emotional satisfaction, and self-esteem), though they may be less well-off in terms of *bridging social capital,* which links children to more heterogeneous opportunities, resources, and information for achieving instrumental outcomes (i.e., education, employment, and prestige). Deficits in bridging social capital may be less of a concern for children whose families already are financially well-off or enjoy higher social status, but this situation is rare among abused and neglected children, who come predominantly from poor families, low-status groups, and impoverished neighborhoods. Theoretically, in these circumstances, in exposing these children to richer home environments and more diverse schooling and employment opportunities, formal foster care offers a structural advantage over informal care from relatives. Whether, after safety, kinship and community continuity should be emphasized over advantages like material security, educational opportunities, and employment prospects is an issue increasingly commanding attention in both policy and practice fields (Barth, 1999).

Data Set Characteristics, Test Variables, and Goals

The goals of contemporary child protective intervention have privileged the preservation of the child's bonding social capital with his or her birth parents, except when maintaining such living arrangements jeopardizes the child's safety and health. If removal from parental custody is warranted, federal policy encourages the conservation of bonding social capital by placing the child in the "least restrictive (most family-like)" setting that maintains the continuity of sibling, kinship, and community ties. After removal, maintaining a safe, stable substitute care environment is most important until the child can be safely restored to parental custody. If family reunification proves infeasible, federal policy favors permanent placement of the child in the home of a relative, foster parent, or another family through the institutions of adoption or guardianship.

Several concerns may be raised about the benefits of conserving bonding social capital and the adequacy of affine agency in ensuring child well-being. Norms of familial duty and support create no legally binding obligations on the part of extended family caregivers, and methods of finding willing relatives often lack the individualized, careful assessment necessary to ascertain whether a kin home will be as good as a nonkin home (Bartholet, 1999). Many kinship caregivers are approaching old age, live on fixed incomes or on low wages, and reside in neighborhoods plagued by economic and social adversities that put children and families at risk. Child maltreatment frequently runs in families and co-occurs with drug abuse, domestic violence, and family poverty, which may make the extended family a risky agent for safeguarding the best interests of the child.

From these issues, specific research questions may be defined: how the safety, stability, and continuity of the substitute care of maltreated children in informal kinship care compare with the safety, stability, and continuity of formal foster care; whether the formal kinship care of these children differs significantly from the care of children placed in licensed, nonkinship foster family homes; whether the incorporation of informal caregivers into the formal system will likely improve the conditions of children in substitute care, as opposed to merely substituting public funds for voluntary family effort without substantially bettering the safety, permanence, and well-being of abused and neglected children.

With this study we consider these and related questions by drawing on National Survey of Child and Adolescent Well-Being (NSCAW) data to describe the safety, stability, and continuity of the living arrangements of children who come to the attention of child protective authorities. We examine many of these concerns by comparing survey measures of the safety, stability, and continuity of informal and formal caregiving arrangements for this child welfare system sample of children. Previous studies of kinship foster care have attempted to address the same issues with administrative data drawn from a single foster care system or group of states. This study, in contrast, benefits from the national representativeness of NSCAW.

In examining the comparative risks and protections of kinship and nonkinship care, informal and formal settings, we strive to advance thought surrounding alternative future scenarios: the elimination of federal funding for foster children in nonlicensed kinship settings, with a concomitant reduction of public reliance on extended families for formal foster care; or, alternatively, an adaptation of licensing standards by local, county, and state governments in order to incorporate larger numbers of kinship homes into the formal system. Conclusions from NSCAW-based findings can enrich the child welfare community's understanding of the range of possible public responses to the mission to protect and care for abused and neglected children in the United States.

Methods

Measures

CONTINUITY (RESTRICTIVENESS) OF CARE   Our measure of the continuity of substitute care was based on the Social Security Act provision for placement in the least restrictive, most family-like setting. Longstanding policy upholds the principle that children should not be deprived of the continuity of parental care except for urgent and compelling reasons. To measure how closely substitute care comported with this principle, we developed a measure of continuity (restrictiveness) of care that drew from responses to survey questions about the child's out-of-home placement type at the time of the survey and drew from an accompanying item that asked about the primary caregiver's relationship to the child.

From these two responses, we constructed a continuity-of-care scale that ranged from *most family-like (least restrictive), in-home setting* (home of the birth parents) to *least family-like (most restrictive), out-of-home setting* (group homes and institutions). In-between settings were differentiated by in-home and out-of-home status and then further subdivided into familial (adopted and biological) and nonfamilial categories.[4] We rank-ordered informal care by kin, followed by informal care by nonkin, as more family-like (less restrictive) than formal substitute care, because informal care is not subject to the same regulatory oversight and restrictions on family autonomy (e.g., permissions for out-of-state travel, medical care, and school pictures) as formal kinship and nonkinship foster care. We rank-ordered nonkinship foster care as less family-like (more restrictive) than kinship foster care because the nonkin foster caregiver is likely to be a stranger to the child. For this study, we assumed that children coded as residing in *out-of-home placement* were under the formal care and custody of child protective authorities. Children coded as having *in-home placement* were considered to be living in informal care arrangements.[5]

STABILITY OF PLACEMENT   The longitudinal NSCAW design permits insight into the dynamics of the expanding prevalence of formal kinship care. Our measure of placement stability was constructed with a set of derived variables: CGwSAME (where w = Wave 2, 3, or 4). If the caregiver at the current wave had the same name, birth date, and Social Security number as the caregiver who responded at baseline or the previous wave, the derived variable was set to 1 (*same*); otherwise, it was set to 0 (*different*).[6] Waves in which the interview was not completed and completed interviews that did not meet criteria for *same* or *different* were coded as missing. From these derived variables, a new variable was constructed, NEV_MOVED, that was initialized to 1 and changed to 0 if the child ever moved out of the Wave 1 (baseline) home.

MALTREATMENT RECURRENCE AFTER CHILD'S REMOVAL FROM PARENTAL HOME Despite the advantages of kinship care, children may be exposed to higher risk of abuse or neglect in the homes of extended kin than in the homes of licensed foster parents. A potentially mitigating factor, however, is that most children taken into protective custody enter because of parental drug addiction, which cuts across all families and alters somewhat the nature of the intergenerational link between childhood maltreatment and subsequent parental maltreatment of children in adulthood. Moreover, when placement with extended kin is considered, child welfare agencies increasingly look to the family of the parent who was not indicated in the allegations and findings.[7]

Previous analysis of safety risks for children in the NSCAW sample suggested that rates of subsequent reports of child maltreatment were no higher, possibly even lower, for children whose baseline placement was in kinship care than rates were for children in nonkinship foster care (Administration for Children and Families, in press). This rudimentary look at child safety did not adjust, however, for placement mobility or the identity of the perpetrator. We took a "counting process" approach to the analysis of maltreatment recurrence after a child has been removed from the parental home. This approach involved recording whether another report of abuse or neglect had been filed between the time a child entered a living arrangement and the time the child exited that arrangement. In order to implement this process, we linked maltreatment report dates to placement starting and stopping times. We identified starting and stopping dates for each living arrangement at Wave 1 (baseline), Wave 3 (18 months), and Wave 4 (36 months) and restricted the analysis to time reported within the study period.[8] This approach allowed us to use the longitudinal nature of the data set by setting child and caregiver predictors entered into statistical models equal to those relevant at the time the report was made.

The measure of time until re-report was calculated as the time between the start date and the report date (where present). For cases with no re-report, the date of placement change or of the next eligible caregiver interview defined the ending of the interval; however, where the last caseworker interview preceded the ending of the interval, the date of the last caseworker interview was substituted for the end date because no data on re-reporting were available for the period after the last caseworker interview. Intrasubject correlation was not taken into account in the analysis because SUDAAN software (RTI International, 2007) calculates variance at the level of the primary sampling unit and additional specification of stratification would not affect the model. The process was repeated with use of the dates that substantiated reports were made, where *substantiated report* was defined as a report for which the child welfare system's official decision was that evidence *indicated* or *substantiated* the allegations of child maltreatment or the child was at high or medium risk of harm.

BONDING SOCIAL CAPITAL NSCAW offers some insight into children's access to bonding social capital. Children aged 10 years or older were asked about their feelings of relatedness (affinity) and closeness to their primary caregiver. The first measure is a variant of the Relationships with Parents (Caregivers) Scale that was originally incorporated in the Rochester Assessment Package for Schools.[9] Some of the items used required reverse scoring; means rather than sums were calculated to accommodate the possibility of missing items.

One item asked children how true it was that they felt good, mad, or happy with their caregiver. A second asked them to assess their primary caregiver's interest in them, time spent with them, and actions taken to help them. A third item indicated whether their caregiver trusted them and had confidence in their ability to make independent decisions. Lastly, NSCAW asked children about the caregiver's fair treatment of the child, the caregiver's beliefs in the child's ability, and the child's understanding of the caregiver's wants and expectations. Children selected response options ranging from: 1 (not true at all) to 4 (very true). These items were then combined into a relatedness scale, with a higher score indicating a greater sense of affinity.

To capture children's sense of protection, another scale was computed for children aged 11 years old or older. Children were asked five yes/no questions: (1) "Is there an adult or adults you can turn to for help if you have a serious problem?" (2) "Do you feel you can go to a parent or someone who is like a parent with a serious problem?" (3) "Could you go to another relative with a serious problem?" (4) "Has there ever been an adult outside of your family who has encouraged you and believed in you?" and (5) "Would you say this person has made a difference in your life?" Finally, children were asked to rate a couple of items: "On a scale from 1 (not important at all) to 4 (very important), how important is religion or spirituality to you?" and "On a scale from 1 (never) to 4 (once a week or more) over the past year, how many times did you go to church [or synagogue, mosque, etc.], or attend religious or spiritual services or activities?"

Children aged 10 or older were also asked, "How close do you feel to your primary caregiver?" and "How much do you think he or she cares about you?" Children answered each question by selecting: 1 (not at all) to 5 (very close or much). The items were combined into a scale, with a higher score indicating a greater sense of closeness to the caregiver.

As part of the Home Observation for Measurement of the Environment (HOME; Caldwell & Bradley, 1984), caregivers of children aged 10 years old or younger were asked age-appropriate questions to evaluate the emotional support the child was receiving from various parental actions, materials, events, and conditions in their home environment. For example, HOME asked caregivers how important they believed teaching new skills to their child was, how many times a week they ate meals together, and how often they took their child out of the house with them to places like a grocery store? Scores for children aged 2 years or younger ranged from zero to 9, scores for children 3 to 5 ranged from zero to 12, and scores for children aged 6 to 11 ranged from zero to 13. A higher score indicated a greater sense of emotional support in the household.

BRIDGING SOCIAL CAPITAL   Although NSCAW does not directly capture information about a family's access to bridging social capital, such as diversity of social contacts, location in resource networks, or "reachability" in a status hierarchy (Lin, 2001), the survey does elicit information about family and caregiver resources such as educational attainment, employment status, and household poverty, which can serve as proxy indicators of access to social network resources. A socioeconomic scale was therefore created for the multivariate models (Table 6.1). This scale

Table 6.1   Family and Caregiver Socioeconomic Scale

	Obs.	*Wgt. (%)*
Caregiver Education		
Elementary and below	350	7%
Eighth grade	1,151	22%
General Education Degree or equivalent	891	16%
High school diploma	1,644	29%
Vocational degree	669	14%
Associate degree	388	6%
Registered nurse degree	21	0%
Bachelor's degree	245	5%
Master's degree	84	1%
PhD or MD	18	0%
Total	5,461	100%
Caregiver Occupational Prestige		
Unemployed*	2,753	46%
Farmer, office worker, laborer	558	11%
Service worker, protective services	488	9%
Operator	175	4%
Sales	150	3%
Tradesman, other	637	14%
Managerial, military	204	5%
Schoolteacher	79	1%
Computer programmer, medical tech.	134	2%
Accountant, engineer, politician	262	5%
Doctor, lawyer, college professor	25	0%
Total	5,465	100%
Yearly Family Income		
Less than $5,000	333	7%
$5,000 to $10,000	783	17%
$10,000 to $15,000	763	18%
$15,000 to $20,000	616	15%
$20,000 to $25,000	516	9%
$25,000 to $30,000	371	8%
$30,000 to $35,000	315	7%
$35,000 to $40,000	252	4%
$40,000 to $45,000	217	3%
$45,000 or more	825	12%
Total	4,991	100%

*Unemployed is coded at zero for occupational prestige.
Obs = number of observations; Wgt % = weighted percent

represented the primary caregiver's educational attainment, current occupational prestige, and family income level on a scale from zero to 30.[10] No information was obtained from the secondary caregiver or live-in partner of the current caregiver. On a scale of 1 to 10, caregiver education attainment ranged from less than 8th grade, 8th grade, and General Education Degree to doctoral degrees. We scored occupational prestige on a scale from 1 to 10 and rated it in accordance with the U.S. Bureau of Labor Statistics, (1999). An example of the range for this scale was farmer, office worker, and basic laborer at the lowest, to medical doctor, lawyer, and college professor at the highest.

Fifty-eight percent (58%) of the caregivers reported that they currently worked either full or part time outside the home. If a caregiver responded that she did not currently work full or part time, she did not receive a score for occupation prestige, though she still received a score for the educational attainment and family income portion of the scale. Consequently, those caregivers who did not work could not score more than 20 on the socioeconomic scale. Because our socioeconomic scale was intended to measure heterogeneous networking opportunities and resources, a caregiver not working in the paid labor force had a score deficit in this area.

Analyses

RESTRICTIVENESS OF BASELINE PLACEMENT   To parse the effects of formal and informal statuses of both kinship and nonkinship placements on the continuity of care, a series of ordinal logistic regressions was estimated for the restrictiveness of placement at Wave 4. Comparison of baseline placements was limited to informal kinship, informal nonkinship, formal kinship, and formal foster (nonkinship) care placements at Wave1, with formal foster care as the reference group. For the Wave 4 restrictiveness scale, these four placements were collapsed and assigned the same ordinal ranking, with biological and adopted placements coded as *least restrictive* and group care as *most restrictive*. The sociodemographic characteristics of baseline homes, as given in Table 6.1, were used in the two models as both controls and predictors, with indicators of bonding capital and bridging capital being added in Model 2.

STABILITY OF BASELINE PLACEMENT   This measure was constructed with the set of derived variables, CGwSAME, already described.[11] Those caregivers who stated that they were the same caregiver from baseline to Wave 4 (CGwSAME = 1) were coded as 1, with every other caregiver combination being coded as zero. Considered in a separate analysis were permanency destinations, excluding moves to permanent homes between the baseline and Wave 4. Two separate models again were evaluated for each set of results. Model 1 focused on sociodemographic variables, including caregiver age, marital status, number of dependents upon household income, child race, and child age.[12] Model 2 incorporated both bonding and bridging social capital. The bridging social capital scale (socioeconomic scale) combined the primary caregiver's educational attainment, current occupational prestige, and family income level on a scale from zero to 30.

MALTREATMENT RECURRENCE AFTER CHILD'S REMOVAL FROM PARENTAL HOME We calculated the regression estimates of the effects of predictor variables on the hazard rate of subsequent substantiated reports of maltreatment. *Substantiated report* was defined as a report for which the child welfare system's official decision was that evidence *indicated* or *substantiated* the allegations of child maltreatment or the child was at high or medium risk of harm. The substantiated re-reports that comprise the censor variable were based only on those reports that occurred while the child was in the placement that he or she was in at Wave 1 or Wave 3. Four separate models were specified to examine the impact of the theoretical constructs: Model 1 indicated the association of the number of dependents on household income and the placement type with time to re-report. Model 2 tests the association of bonding social capital with time to re-report. Model 3 incorporated the measure of bridging social capital. Model 4 incorporated all parameters from the first three models.

Results

Continuity (Restrictiveness) of Care

The data show that most children who came to the attention of child protective authorities either remained in or eventually returned to the custody of their birth parents (Table 6.2). At Wave 1, 83% of children were reportedly residing in the homes of their birth parents. This proportion dwindled to 80% as more children were removed than were returned to their home and more birth families than other families were lost from follow-up. Only a small percentage of children began in adoptive families, but the percentage rose to 3% at Wave 4 as children who could not be safely reunified with their birth families were adopted.

Table 6.2   Children in Informal and Formal Child Care Settings, Waves 1, 3, and 4

	Wave 1		*Wave 3*		*Wave 4*	
Living Arrangement	*N*	*Wgt %*	*N*	*Wgt. %*	*N*	*Wgt. %*
Birth family	3,305	83%	3,097	81%	3,004	80%
Adoptive family	43	1%	126	1%	322	3%
Informal kin care	202	3%	258	4%	79	1%
Informal nonkin care	83	2%	100	2%	68	2%
Formal kinship care	572	5%	440	5%	549	8%
Formal foster care	736	4%	519	5%	353	3%
Group/institutional care	104	1%	88	1%	105	2%

Note: An additional 1% of children reside in other out-of-home settings in all three waves.
Wgt %, weighted percent

A comparatively large fraction of children were found in or had been shifted to the informal custody of kin during the early phases of child maltreatment investigation. In many jurisdictions parents are encouraged to place their children informally during investigation or assessment as an alternative to the children's being taken into formal protective custody. A comparatively large fraction of these informal arrangements involved friends, neighbors, and other families biologically unrelated to the child, including primary caregivers who identified themselves as stepparents or other biologically unrelated parental surrogates. Although grouping stepparents with girlfriends and boyfriends (i.e., "paramours" in the older child welfare literature), family friends, and neighbors into the informal nonkinship care category may counter conventional understandings of relatedness by marriage, the burgeoning literature on the effects of nongenetic parenthood on child safety and parental investments in child well-being suggests some value in separating out nonbiologically related caregivers from biologically related caregivers (Case, Lin, & McLanahan, 2000; Daly & Wilson, 1985).

Placement with nonkin outside the formal system accounted for a constant 2% of sampled children's living arrangements. In contrast, the percentage of children in informal kinship care, after rising to 4% in Wave 3, dwindles to less than 1% of all living arrangements by Wave 4. Several explanations may account for this decline. One is that most informal kinship care is only temporary until unsafe home conditions can be remedied and the children can safely be restored to parental custody. Another is consistent with the "incorporation hypothesis" earlier advanced by Testa (1992) that suggests the growth in the formal kinship care arises in part from the incorporation of informal kinship arrangements into the formal system: Instead of actually declining over time, the population of informal kin caregivers gradually becomes absorbed into the formal foster care system. This explanation appears consistent with the corresponding expansion of formal kinship placements during this period to 8% of all living arrangements. At Wave 4, a much larger proportion of the NSCAW cohort is accommodated in formal out-of-home placements with kin than are placed in foster family homes, group homes, and institutions (combined). This result suggests that extended families may be taking a much larger role in the formal foster care system than official statistics and other survey data have previously suggested.

Stability of Placement

As expected, the less family-like (more restrictive) the placement setting, the lower the stability of care at Wave 1. Of all the children residing with their birth families at baseline, 90% were still with or back with their birth families at Wave 4. Most of this trend is attributable to the 84% who stayed with their families across all four waves (Table 6.3, final column). Diagonally, the percentages (shaded) show the proportion of children who remained in or returned to the same placement type: Stability declined as restrictiveness of placement increased. The off-diagonal percentages (above and below the shaded, diagonal percentages) identify the last observed destinations of children who left their baseline placement type by Wave 4.

Table 6.3   Mobility and Stability of Children by Placement Status.

Status at Baseline (Wave 1)	Status at Wave 4							
			Informal		*Formal*			
	Birth Family	*Adoptive Family*	*Kin*	*Nonkin*	*Kin*	*Foster Family*	*Group/ Institution*	*Never Moved*
Birth family	90%	1%	0%	2%	4%	2%	1%	84%
Adoptive family	14%	63%	0%	0%	1%	5%	12%	53%
Informal kin care	35%	3%	4%	1%	52%	2%	1%	65%
Informal nonkin care	16%	9%	5%	39%	12%	9%	6%	30%
Formal kinship care	26%	12%	5%	2%	45%	6%	1%	47%
Foster family care	28%	19%	3%	2%	9%	31%	5%	18%
Group and institutional care	29%	15%	2%	0%	19%	17%	13%	2%

Note: Row percentages for status at Wave 4 do not always total 100%, because placements classified as "other" are omitted from the mobility table.

Particularly noteworthy is the sharp drop-off in the percentage of children in informal kinship placements (4%). But as the percentages in the last column indicate, this dropoff was not because informal kinship placement was any less stable than other forms of substitute care: Two thirds (65%) of the children who were in informal kin care were still in the same home at Wave 4 that they were residing in at Wave 1. Instead, the major difference is the change in the "out-of-home" status of the baseline home. As illustrated in Figure 6.1, of the 65% of children in informal kinship care who never moved out of their baseline home, 86% were in formal kinship care at Wave 4. This change is consistent with the incorporation hypothesis that children informally placed with kin are gradually absorbed into the formal system (Testa, 2001), although it is not possible to determine from NSCAW what fraction of these arrangements were formally licensed as foster family homes and paid Title IV-E reimbursable stipends. By contrast, few (13%) of the 30% of children in informal nonkinship households who never moved out of their baseline homes were designated as living in formal foster care at Wave 4. Most maintained the same "in-home" status as from Wave 1.

Comparing children in formal kinship care with those in nonkinship foster care shows that children in kinship foster care are much more likely to remain in their baseline home (47%, as opposed to 18%). This result is consistent with past research showing that kinship foster placements are more stable than nonkinship foster placements (Koh & Testa, 2008). Moreover, NSCAW findings reveal that voluntary arrangements that begin as informal kinship placements are no less stable, and possibly more stable, than formal kinship placements. At Wave 4, 65% of children who were placed informally with kin at Wave 1 remained in the same home. Another noteworthy feature of these data is that few of the stable

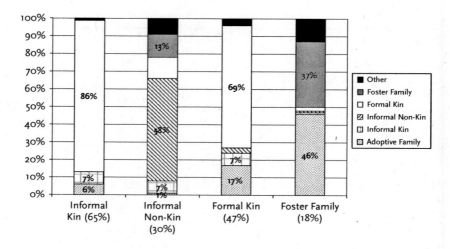

Figure 6.1   Legal designation of baseline homes at Wave 4 among children who never changed homes.

informal placements converted to formal adoptive homes (only 6%), compared with formal kinship homes (17%) and formal nonkinship homes (46%).[13]

Maltreatment Recurrence After Child's Removal From Parental Home

Placement mobility was adjusted for by isolating those reports of subsequent maltreatment that overlap with the dates that children were in a specific type of placement (Fig. 6.2). The height of the bars in Figure 6.2 measures the relative risk of re-reported maltreatment as adjusted for the length of time children spent in each specific form of care. The comparison yields the rate of re-reported maltreatment of children residing with their birth families (arbitrarily fixed at 1.0). The results indicate that rates of subsequent reports of child maltreatment were significantly lower while children were under the informal care of kin than rates were while children were in their biological parents' home. Children in nonkinship foster care experienced precisely the same relative risk of substantiated re-report as children in kinship foster care (.42 of the risk of children in biological parents' homes after covariates were controlled for), though the relative risk compared with that of children residing with their biological parents did not meet the .05 level of statistical significance. Similarly, children under the informal care of nonbiological caregivers (including stepparents) faced risks not statistically distinguishable from those for children residing with their biological parents.

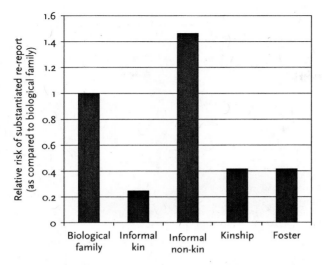

Figure 6.2   Relative risk of substantiated re-abuse, all waves (compared to birth families).

Bonding and Bridging Social Capital

Each of these scales—measuring affinity, closeness, protection, and emotional support—captures some dimension of *bonding* social capital. In the NSCAW sample, the availability of this form of social capital varied by placement type (Tables 6.4–6.7). Because of the varying age ranges of the scales, a dichotomous variable was developed to indicate whether the child scored in the lowest 12% of all social bonding scales.

Some relevant demographic characteristics affect the caregiver's capacity for *bridging* social capital, such as caregiver's age, caregiver's marital status, number of household dependents, child's race, child's age, and child's gender (Tables 6.8 and 6.9).

These various indicators of social capital and family resources provide descriptions consistent with the notion that kinship networks tend to be richer in bonding social capital while more bureaucratized forms of substitute care appear to provide better access to bridging social capital. Although subsample sizes are too small to exclude the possibility of chance differences, measures of relatedness, closeness, and protection register higher for relatives than for nonrelatives (see Table 6.4). Conversely, licensed foster family care appears to offer structural advantages, most notably in lower levels of household poverty, which is less the case for substitute care settings drawn from kinship and informal helping networks.

The differences in bonding social capital visibly narrow by Wave 4; scores converge for all placement types. In a prior study, Testa (2001) reported a similar convergence in placement stability rates between kinship and nonkinship foster homes as time in care elapsed. It was unclear, however, whether this convergence

Table 6.4   Indicators of Bonding Social Capital by Placement Type.

| | Informal Care | | | | Formal Care | | | | | |
| | Kin | | Nonkin | | Kinship | | Foster Family | | Birth Parents | |
Scales	Mean	SE	Mean	SE	Mean	SE	Mean	SE	Mean	SE
Relatedness	3.5	0.1	3.1	0.3	3.4	0.1	3.2	0.1	3.2	0.1
Protection	4.5	0.2	4.1	0.6	4.4	0.1	4.4	0.2	4.2	0.1
Closeness	4.4	0.2	3.7	0.6	4.2	0.1	4.0	0.2	4.4	0.1
Emotional support (home)										
Age 0–2	6.8	.4	7.7	.4	7.0	.2	7.5	.1	6.8	.1
Age 3–5	6.7	.8	9.7	1.2	8.7	.5	9.7	.3	8.5	.2
Age 6–11	9.6	.7	10.5	.2	9.4	.3	9.2	.4	9.2	.2
Composite bonding										
Lowest 12% of all scores	11%	.05	14%	.1	6%	.01	4%	.01	9%	.01
Wave 1	N = 202	3%	N = 83	2%	N = 572	5%	N = 736	4%	N = 3705	83%
Relatedness	3.5	0.1	3.0	0.2	3.3	0.1	3.4	0.1	3.3	0.1
Protection	4.7	0.1	3.0	0.8	4.6	0.1	4.0	0.3	4.3	0.1
Closeness	4.6	0.1	3.5	0.5	4.4	0.1	4.2	0.2	4.5	0.1
Emotional support (home)										
Age 0–2	7.4	.2	8.5	.3	7.4	.2	7.7	.1	6.9	.1
Age 3–5	8.7	.8	8.8	.7	9.6	.2	9.4	.3	8.4	.2
Age 6–11	9.6	.8	10.2	.8	9.8	.2	9.3	.6	9.6	.2
Composite bonding										
Lowest 12% of all scores	11%	.05	14%	.1	5%	.01	7%	.02	12%	.01
Wave 3	N = 258	4%	N = 100	2%	N = 440	5%	N = 519	5%	N = 3097	81%
Relatedness	3.5	0.1	3.5	0.2	3.3	0.1	3.3	0.1	3.4	0.0
Protection	4.5	0.2	4.3	0.5	4.2	0.3	4.3	0.2	4.4	0.1
Closeness	4.7	0.1	4.3	0.4	4.4	0.1	4.3	0.1	4.6	0.0
Emotional support (home)										
Age 0–2	7.6	.4	N/A	N/A	8.3	.3	7.1	.5	6.9	.3
Age 3–5	9.4	.3	9.4	.3	9.5	.2	9.7	.4	8.9	.1
Age 6–11	9.4	.5	11.1	.2	9.8	.5	10.7	.3	9.6	.1
Composite bonding										
Lowest 12% of all scores	1%	.01	9%	.09	4%	.01	6%	.02	6%	.01
Wave 4	N = 79	1%	N = 68	2%	N = 549	8%	N = 353	3%	N = 3004	80%

arose from families becoming more attached over time or from less committed families relinquishing their caregiving responsibilities. Restricting the comparison to the subset of children who never left their baseline homes suggests that families and children over time select out of less committed family relationships. Already, at

Table 6.5 Indicators of Bonding Social Capital by Placement Type for Children Who Never Moved From Baseline Home.

| | Informal Care | | | | Formal Care | | | | | |
| | Kin | | Nonkin | | Kinship | | Foster Family | | Birth Parents | |
Scales	M	SE	M	SE	Mean	SE	Mean	SE	Mean	SE
Relatedness	3.3	.1	3.1	.4	3.5	.1	3.6	.1	3.2	.1
Protection	4.4	.4	3.7	.9	4.4	.2	4.0	.4	4.2	.1
Closeness	4.5	.3	3.5	.8	4.3	.2	4.4	.2	4.4	.1
Emotional support (home)										
Age 0–2	7.5	.3	4.7	1.5	7.4	.2	7.5	.2	6.8	.2
Age 3–5	6.8	.5	9.7	1.3	9.5	1.0	9.6	.8	8.7	.2
Age 6–11	10.1	.8	10.7	.3	9.7	.3	9.0	1.0	9.2	.2
Composite bonding										
Lowest 12% of all scores	4%	.02	20%	.2	2%	.01	5%	.02	8%	.01
Wave 1	N = 93	3%	N = 30	2%	N = 237	4%	N = 188	1%	N = 2,226	90%
Relatedness	3.4	.1	3.0	.3	3.4	.1	3.3	.2	3.4	.04
Protection	4.5	.2	2.9	.8	4.7	.2	3.6	.7	4.3	.1
Closeness	4.4	.2	3.4	.5	5.6	.2	4.5	.2	4.5	.1
Emotional support (home)										
Age 0–2	7.6	.2	7.4	.6	7.5	.3	7.6	.2	6.9	.1
Age 3–5	9.1	.5	10.9	.2	9.4	.2	9.6	.4	8.5	.2
Age 6–11	7.8	.7	10.4	1.2	9.7	.2	9.6	.4	9.4	.2
Composite bonding										
Lowest 12% of all scores	17%	.1	20%	.2	3%	.01	10%	.03	12%	.01
Wave 3	N = 133	3%	N = 40	2%	N = 173	4%	N = 142	1%	N = 2,128	90%
Relatedness	3.6	.1	3.1	.4	3.4	.1	3.6	.1	3.4	.03
Protection	4.9	.1	3.5	1.0	4.5	.2	4.5	.2	4.4	.1
Closeness	4.7	.2	3.6	.7	4.3	.1	4.7	.1	4.6	.1
Emotional support (home)										
Age 0–2	8.0	.2	N/A	N/A	8.0	.5	6.1	1.2	6.9	.4
Age 3–5	9.2	.5	N/A	N/A	9.5	.4	9.7	.4	8.9	.2
Age 6–11	8.9	.5	10.8	.4	9.9	.7	12.1	.6	9.7	.1
Composite bonding										
Lowest 12% of all scores	1%	.01	30%	.2	4%	.01	2%	.01	5%	.01
Wave 4	N = 40	1%	N = 18	1%	N = 241	5%	N = 75	1%	N = 2,170	90%

Wave 1, children who remained with their foster families had bonding scores equal to or higher than those for children who remained in formal kinship care. Moreover, some indication exists that children's sense of protection and closeness increased in foster family care but generally remained at original levels in kinship foster care (see Table 6.5).

Table 6.6 Indicators of Bridging Social Capital by Placement Type.

| | Informal Care | | | | Formal Care | | | | | |
| | Kin | | Nonkin | | Kinship | | Foster Family | | Birth Parents | |
Indicators	Percent	SE	Percent	SE	Percent	SE	Percent	SE	Percent	SE
Caregiver education (>HS)	38%	.1	31%	.1	25%	.1	36%	.04	25%	.02
Caregiver employed	54%	.1	67%	.1	45%	.1	61%	.03	61%	.01
HH below poverty line	42%	.1	41%	.1	41%	.1	12%	.03	61%	.02
SES scale (mean)	11.1	.9	12.7	1.3	11.5	.8	14.8	.4	10.4	.2
Wave 1	N = 202	3%	N = 83	2%	N = 572	5%	N = 736	4%	N = 3,705	83%
Caregiver education (>HS)	22%	.1	16%	.1	21%	.04	39%	.1	26%	.02
HH below poverty line	43%	.1	56%	.1	26%	.05	10%	.03	56%	.02
SES scale* (mean)	8.7	.7	7.9	.8	9.1	.4	12.3	.8	7.7	.2
Wave 3	N = 258	4%	N = 100	2%	N = 440	5%	N = 519	5%	N = 3,097	81%
Caregiver education (>HS)	20%	.1	28%	.1	32%	.1	42%	.1	29%	.01
Caregiver employed	36%	.1	37%	.1	58%	.04	57%	.1	59%	.02
HH below poverty line	47%	.1	38%	.1	29%	.04	11%	.04	52%	.02
SES scale (mean)	13.1	1.2	18.2	1.0	15.5	.7	17.5	.9	13.2	.3
Wave 4	N = 79	1%	N = 68	2%	N = 549	8%	N = 353	3%	N = 3,004	80%

* A complete socioeconomic scale could not be created for Wave 3 because most data on caregiver occupation were missing. Therefore, the Wave 3 scale ranged from zero to 20.

Table 6.7 Indicators of Bridging Social Capital by Placement Type for Children Who Never Moved From Baseline Home.

	Informal Care				Formal Care				Birth Parents	
	Kin		Nonkin		Kinship		Foster Family			
Indicators	Percent	SE	Percent	SE	Percent	SE	Percent	SE	Percent	SE
Caregiver education (>HS)	43%	.1	29%	.2	17%	.1	40%	.1	26%	.02
Caregiver employed	66%	.1	75%	.1	43%	.1	47%	.1	61%	.6
HH below poverty line	33%	.1	45%	.2	43%	.1	8%	.03	60%	.03
SES scale (mean)	12.5	1.3	13.0	1.8	10.7	.9	14.2	.5	10.6	.2
Wave 1	N = 93	3%	N = 30	2%	N = 237	4%	N = 188	1%	N = 2226	90%
Caregiver education (>HS)	15%	.04	19%	.1	15%	.1	34%	.1	27%	.02
HH below poverty line	61%	.1	57%	.1	29%	.1	7%	.03	55%	.02
SES scale (mean)	7.4	.5	7.7	1.0	8.8	.6	12.0	.4	7.8	.2
Wave 3	N = 133	3%	N = 40	2%	N = 173	4%	N = 142	1%	N = 2128	90%
Caregiver education (>HS)	9%	.04	34%	.2	22%	.1	21%	.1	30%	.02
Caregiver employed	27%	.1	54%	.2	53%	.1	42%	.1	58%	.02
HH below poverty line	68%	.1	39%	.2	41%	.1	24%	.2	53%	.02
SES scale (mean)	11.4	.8	19.4	1.3	14.1	1.1	18.4	1.2	13.2	.4
Wave 4	N = 40	1%	N = 18	1%	N = 241	5%	N = 75	1%	N = 2170	90%

Table 6.8 Demographic Characteristics of Caregiver and Household.

	Informal Care				Formal Care					
	Kin		Nonkin		Kinship		Foster Family		Birth Parents	
Characteristics	Mean	SE	Mean	SE	Mean	SE	Mean	SE	Mean	SE
Caregiver age	46.8	1.6	37.5	2.0	50.9	2.1	44.6	0.9	31.4	0.3
Caregiver married	41%	.1	69%	.1	49%	.1	68%	.04	28%	.02
HH size	4.5	0.4	5.4	0.4	4.3	0.2	5.5	0.4	4.2	0.1
Child race										
White	33%	.1	80%	.1	46%	.1	40%	.1	47%	.03
Black or African American	47%	.1	4%	.02	33%	.04	37%	.1	27%	.03
Hispanic	16%	.1	11%	.1	14%	.03	15%	.1	19%	.03
Other	4%	.02	5%	.04	7%	.02	8%	.02	7%	.01
Child age	6.7	.6	9.7	.9	6.3	.5	5.9	.4	6.9	
Child gender: Male	43%	.1	44%	.1	39%	.05	56%	.05	50%	.02
Wave 1	N =202	3%	N =83	2%	N =572	5%	N =736	4%	N = 3,705	83%
Caregiver age	48.7	1.5	33.6	2.0	48.3	0.9	43.6	1.3	33.0	0.3
Caregiver married	46%	.1	72%	.1	51%	.1	67%	.1	32%	.02
HH size	4.2	0.2	5.3	0.4	4.6	0.3	4.9	0.3	4.2	0.1
Child race										
White	43%	.1	62%	.1	35%	.1	38%	.1	46%	.03
Black or African American	30%	.1	22%	.1	39%	.1	40%	.1	27%	.03
Hispanic	17%	.1	10%	.1	21%	.1	15%	.04	20%	.03
Other	10%	.04	6%	.03	5%	.02	7%	.02	7%	.01
Child age	7.7	.6	9.1	.9	7.1	.5	7.6	.3	8.2	.1
Child gender: Male	37%	.07	44%	.1	53%	.06	47%	.07	50%	.02
Wave 3	N = 258	4%	N = 100	2%	N = 440	5%	N = 519	5%	N = 3,097	81%
Caregiver age	45.6	3.7	36.8	4.7	45.7	1.0	42.1	1.1	33.1	0.4
Caregiver married	55%	.1	82%	.1	49%	.04	68%	.1	32%	.02
HH size	4.5	0.4	5.1	0.2	4.3	0.2	5.2	0.3	4.3	0.1
Child race										
White	50%	.5	84%	.1	35%	.1	47%	.1	48%	.03
Black or African American	21%	.2	2%	.01	40%	.1	29%	.1	27%	.03
Hispanic	16%	.2	7%	.1	17%	.1	19%	.1	18%	.02
Other	13%	.1	7%	.04	8%	.02	5%	.01	7%	.01
Child age	8.1	1.2	10.9	.7	9.1	.5	10.0	.4	9.6	.2
Child gender: Male	58%	.1	49%	.1	43%	.04	50%	.07	51%	.02
Wave 4	N = 79	1%	N = 68	2%	N = 549	8%	N = 353	3%	N = 3,004	80%

At all waves children under the informal care of nonbiologically related adults reported the lowest bonding levels of all living arrangements. This result suggests that informal arrangements with friends and neighbors, as well as care by stepparents, emotionally functions differently from care by extended kin. By Wave 4, the bonding

Table 6.9   Demographic Characteristics of Caregiver and Household for Children Who Never Moved From Baseline Home.

| | Informal Care | | | | Formal Care | | | | | |
| | Kin | | Nonkin | | Kinship | | Foster Family | | Birth Parents | |
Characteristics	M	SE	M	SE	M	SE	M	SE	M	SE
Caregiver age	48.1	1.6	37.3	2.4	49.0	1.5	42.8	1.1	31.3	.3
Caregiver married	61%	.1	80%	.1	54%	.1	68%	.1	28%	.02
HH size	4.9	.7	5.9	.4	4.3	.2	5.5	.7	4.2	.1
Child race										
White	30%	.1	75%	.1	44%	.1	45%	.1	47%	.04
Black or African American	45%	.1	3%	.02	34%	.1	40%	.1	27%	.03
Hispanic	21%	.1	15%	.1	14%	.1	9%	.03	19%	.02
Other	4%	.03	7%	.06	8%	.04	6%	.03	7%	.01
Child age	6.1	.8	9.9	1.1	6.0	.7	4.4	.6	6.9	.2
Child gender: Male	51%	.1	50%	.2	40%	.07	43%	.08	51%	.02
Wave 1	N = 93	3%	N = 30	2%	N = 237	4%	N = 188	1%	N = 2,226	90%
Caregiver age	51.7	2.1	37.5	2.4	50.7	1.0	46.5	1.2	32.7	.3
Caregiver married	37%	.1	68%	.1	46%	.1	75%	.1	34%	.02
HH size	4.4	.2	5.6	.5	4.8	.5	6.2	.9	4.2	.1
Child race										
White	47%	.1	61%	.1	32%	.1	40%	.1	46%	.03
Black or African American	38%	.1	18%	.1	36%	.1	38%	.1	27%	.02
Hispanic	7%	.03	13%	.1	26%	.1	13%	.1	20%	.02
Other	8%	.1	8%	.1	6%	.03	9%	.03	7%	.01
Child age	7.0	.7	11.5	1.0	7.1	.7	5.8	.6	8.2	.2
Child gender: Male	42%	.09	36%	.1	49%	.1	61%	.07	51%	.02
Wave 3	N = 133	3%	N = 40	2%	N = 173	4%	N = 142	1%	N = 2,128	90%
Caregiver age	46.2	5.5	31.7	2.1	50.8	1.1	49.8	2.0	32.6	.4
Caregiver married	46%	.2	95%	.04	40%	.1	80%	.1	34%	.02
HH size	4.5	.6	5.5	.3	4.1	.1	5.4	.8	4.3	.1
Child race										
White	50%	.2	81%	.1	38%	.1	55%	.1	48%	.04
Black or African American	26%	.1	0%	0	38%	.1	28%	.1	27%	.03
Hispanic	23%	.1	1%	.01	18%	.1	13%	.1	18%	.02
Other	1%	.01	18%	.2	6%	.03	4%	.02	7%	.01
Child age	9.1	1.7	12.9	1.5	8.7	.5	9.7	.8	9.6	.2
Child gender: Male	70%	.1	31%	.2	45%	.08	78%	.08	52%	.02
Wave 4	N = 40	1%	N = 18	1%	N = 241	5%	N = 75	1%	N = 2,170	90%

scores for informal and formal care clustered more closely together, but this pattern apparently arose from the more committed families entering formal status. The scores for children in informal nonkin care who remained in the same home for all waves showed little change in bonding social capital (see Table 6.5).

Differences in access to bridging social capital by placement type, as measured indirectly by poverty status, household size, and caregiver characteristics, did not compress much over time within informal care arrangements. Some compression did arise, however, within formal care. Although approximately 40% of kinship foster care and both types of informal arrangements had Wave 1 household incomes below the federal poverty level, at Wave 4 the poverty rates were lower for formal kinship care than for informal arrangements. Although this pattern may reflect the higher foster care maintenance payments provided to most kin caregivers once they become incorporated into the formal system, the absence of difference in poverty status among children who never move suggests that selectivity biases operate to screen in more affluent kinship homes by means of the foster home licensing process. This finding is also reflected in the bifurcation of the substitute care population into an informal segment characterized by higher poverty, lower employment, and lower educational attainment of caregivers, on the one hand, and a formal segment characterized by lower poverty, higher employment, and higher educational attainment of caregivers, on the other hand. Even though the informal segment accounts for only 3% of children's living arrangements, in contrast to the formal segment's 11%, the obvious discrepancies in the social and economic conditions of these dual populations do raise questions of fairness and adequacy.

Baseline Placement Type and Restrictiveness of Placement at Wave 4

In general, the regression analysis model did not predict strong and significant relationships between type of placement at Wave 1 and restrictiveness of care at Wave 4 (Table 6.10). In terms of placement at Wave 1, children in informal nonkin placements (including stepparents' homes) had a tendency to move into more restrictive placements than children in formal foster care ($p < .10$). The marginal significance of the difference reinforces earlier results suggesting that informal arrangements with nonkin perform differently than other arrangements.

Both older children and males tended to move into more restrictive placements at Wave 4 ($p < .10$), consistent with higher rates of institutionalization for boys and older youth. Unexpectedly, children who lived in a formal kinship placement at Wave 1, when we controlled for different types of social capital, displayed a moderately strong trend of moving into a more restrictive placement at Wave 4 than a child in formal nonkinship foster care. Similarly, children in baseline placements with low social bonding tended to move, although not significantly, into less restrictive, more family-like placements at Wave 4. This anomalous result is consistent with previous research finding that children in less affectionate kinship arrangements are more likely to return to parental custody than children in more affectionate relationships (Testa & Slack, 2001).

Stability of Baseline Placement

We report the odds ratio estimates of the effects of predictors on the log-odds of exiting from the baseline placement (Tables 6.11 and 6.12). Table 6.11 restricts

Table 6.10 Odds-Ratios Estimates of Effects on Continuity (Restrictiveness) of Care.

Characteristics	Model 1		Model 2	
	OR	CI	OR	CI
Demographic				
Caregiver age				
<35 yr	1.12	.44–2.80	1.45	.58–3.6
36–54 yr	1.58	.87–2.86	1.58	.80–3.09
>55 yr				
Caregiver married	1.14	.68–1.92	1.22	.70–2.16
HH # of dependents	1.01	.90–1.12	.98	.89–1.08
Gender: Male	1.52†	.94–2.48	1.57†	.96–2.58
Race				
Black or African American	1.14	.64–2.03	1.17	.65–2.09
Hispanic	1.97	.73–5.36	1.97	.77–5.0
Other	1.03	.39–2.71	.98	.36–2.69
White				
Child age	1.0*	1.01–1.11	1.05†	.99–1.11
Informal kin	1.02	.46–2.24	1.23	.57–2.64
Informal nonkin	2.6*	1.0–6.83	2.97†	.96–9.12
Formal kin	1.38	.89–2.18	1.52†	.93–2.51
Foster care				
Bonding Capital				
Lowest 12% of scales			.49	.16–1.54
Bridging Capital				
SES			.99	.94–1.05

$^\dagger p < .10$, $^* p < .05$, $^{**} p < .01$.
CI, 95% confidence interval; HH, household; OR, odds ratio.

placement stability to only those caregivers who stated that they were the same caregiver from baseline to Wave 4. Table 6.12 takes into consideration permanency destinations, distinguishing those moves into permanent homes from other placement changes that occurred between the baseline and Wave 4.

Again, two separate models were evaluated for each table. Model 1 focused on sociodemographic variables, including caregiver age, marital status, number of dependents upon household income, child's race, and child's age.[14] Model 2 incorporated both bonding and bridging social capital. The bridging social capital scale (socioeconomic scale) combines the primary caregiver's educational attainment, current occupational prestige, and family income level, yielding scores ranging from zero to 30. The subpopulation used in this analysis excluded baseline placements in group homes or residential care because nearly all children in these types of placements experienced a change in caregiver.

Both Tables 6.11 and 6.12 show that formal (nonkinship) foster care was associated with the greatest likelihood of instability, with the odds ratios ranging from 8.77 to more than 17.21 times as large as that for a child in the home of a birth

Table 6.11   Odds-Ratio Estimates of Effects on the Odds of Movement of Children out of Baseline Home to Both Permanent and Nonpermanent Destinations.

Characteristics	Model 1		Model 2	
	OR	CI	OR	CI
Caregiver age				
<35 yr	.68	.27–1.71	.62	.24–1.57
35–54 yr	.58	.25–1.36	.59	.25–1.42
>55 yr				
Caregiver married	.83	.61–1.14	.83	.58–1.18
HH # of dependents	.98	.90–1.06	.99	.91–1.08
Child race				
Black or African American	.77	.54–1.09	.78	.55–1.09
Hispanic	.82	.39–1.72	.96	.45–2.08
Other	.88	.48–1.62	.79	.42–1.47
White				
Child age	.99	.97–1.02	.99	.96–1.02
Child gender: Male	.77	.51–1.16	.80	.51–1.25
Bonding Capital				
Lowest 12%			1.55	.91–2.63
Bridging Capital				
SES			.96**	.93–.99
Continuity of Care				
Birth family				
Adoptive family	3.78*	1.19–11.9	2.41	.68–8.54
Informal kin	3.56**	1.61–7.8	3.23**	1.52–6.9
Informal nonkin	1.99	.78–5.1	2.10	.80–5.54
Formal kin	2.57**	1.52–4.3	2.45**	1.44–4.2
Foster family	14.02**	7.6–25.9	17.21**	9.23–32.1

CI, 95% confidence interval; HH, household; OR, odds ratio.

parent at baseline. When permanency moves were ignored (Table 6.12), formal foster care remained highly unstable, whereas children under the care of kin and other informal nonkin caregivers were statistically indistinguishable from children residing in the homes of birth parents. Controlling for bonding social capital in Table 6.11 tempered the effect of adoptive placements on stability, meaning that, when emotional closeness between a child and an adopted parent was considered, the effect size fell below statistical significance. Two other findings of note were that children in baseline placements with high socioeconomic scale scores were less likely to move and children living with married parents were less likely to move to nonpermanent destinations (see Table 6.12).

Maltreatment Recurrence After Child's Removal From Parental Home

We report the regression estimates of the effects of predictor variables on the hazard rate of subsequent substantiated reports of maltreatment (Table 6.13).

Table 6.12   Odds-Ratio Estimates of Effects on the Odds of Movement of Children out of Baseline Home to Nonpermanent Destinations Only

	Model 1		Model 2	
Characteristics	*OR*	*CI*	*OR*	*CI*
Caregiver age				
<35 yr	.68	.19–2.49	.68	.19–2.48
35–54 yr	.50	.14–1.81	.55	.15–1.99
>55 yr				
Caregiver married	.52**	.32–.83	.58*	.34–.95
HH # of dependents	1.02	.90–1.15	.99	.87–1.14
Child race				
Black or African American	1.13	.73–1.77	1.01	.62–1.66
Hispanic	1.03	.58–1.84	1.09	.58–2.05
Other	1.23	.59–2.58	.84	.40–1.77
White				
Child age	1.01	.97–1.06	1.03	.98–1.08
Child gender: Male	.77	.47–1.25	.82	.51–1.33
Bonding Capital				
Lowest 12%			1.24	.61–2.53
Bridging Capital				
SES			.96*	.92–.99
Continuity of Care				
Birth family				
Adoptive family	2.04	.58–7.14	1.70	.31–9.20
Informal kin	.93	.39–2.18	.81	.34–1.97
Informal nonkin	1.93	.69–5.36	1.59	.51–4.96
Formal kin	1.74	.72–4.27	1.68	.66–4.29
Foster family	8.77**	4.5–17.3	10.29**	5.02–21.1

CI, 95% confidence interval; HH, household; OR, odds ratio.

Coefficients and hazards ratios representing Model 1 indicate that the number of dependents upon household income and placement type had a significant association with time until re-report. Number of dependents upon household income was associated with substantiated reporting: For each additional dependent upon household income, likelihood of reporting increased by 6%. Placement type was also associated with time until re-report: Children living with formal kinship care providers or with nonkin foster parents experienced lower rates of and longer times until re-report than biological families established as a reference category.

Model 2 showed that the indicator of bonding social capital had a significant association with time until re-report such that children whose scores were among the lowest 12% of scores, were 1.88 times more likely to be the subjects of substantiated re-reporting of maltreatment than children whose scores were not among the lowest 12%. This result suggests that children who either self-report higher scores on the relatedness-to-caregiver scale or on items related to feelings of being protected, or whose emotional support subscale scores on the HOME inventory were higher, were less likely to be the subjects of repeat maltreatment.

Table 6.13   Hazard-Ratio Estimates of Effects on the Risk of Recurrence of Substantiated Maltreatment.

	Model 1		Model 2		Model 3		Model 4	
	HR	CI	HR	CI	HR	CI	HR	CI
Demographic								
Caregiver age								
<35 yr	.77	.23–2.54	1.81	.79–4.13	.80	.22–2.88	1.90	.76–4.72
35–54 yr	.51	.15–1.79	1.21	.53–2.81	.55	.14–2.17	1.35	.50–3.65
>54 yr								
Caregiver married	.95	.55–1.64	.82	.46–1.47	1.06	.59–1.90	.93	.49–1.76
HH # of dependents	1.15*	1.02–2.29	1.13*	1.00–1.28	1.15*	1.02–1.31	1.13	1.00–1.29
Child race or ethnicity								
Black or African American	.91	.51–1.65	.82	.46–1.44	.89	.47–1.66	.79	.43–1.43
Hispanic	1.31	.65–2.64	1.39	.66–2.92	1.33	.66–.69	1.40	.67–2.94
Other	1.29	.53–3.12	1.37	.52–3.63	1.31	.52–3.32	1.35	.48–3.81
White								
Child age	.99	.95–1.03	.99	.95–1.03	.99	.95–1.03	.99	.95–1.03
Child gender male	.96	.54–1.71	1.00	.55–1.80	.96	.53–1.75	1.01	.56–1.85
Bonding Social Capital								
Lowest 12% of all scales			1.88*	1.06–3.32			1.95*	1.09–3.46
Bridging Social Capital								
SES scale					.94*	.89–1.00	.93*	.87–1.00
Placement Type								
Birth family								
Informal kin	.65	.24–1.76	.21**	.10–.49	.73	.27–1.99	.25**	.11–.58
Informal nonkin	1.17	.25–5.37	1.30	.26–6.45	1.26	.26–5.99	1.46	.29–7.40
Formal kin	.28**	.13–.59	.40**	.23–.69	.30**	.13–.67	.42**	.23–.75
Foster family	.29**	.12–.67	.40*	.18–.89	.29*	.90–.89	.42	.14–1.24

CI, 95% confidence interval; HH, household; HR, hazard ratio.

With regard to placement type, placement with informal kinship care providers, formal kinship care providers, or nonkin foster parents demonstrated a statistically significant relationship with substantiated re-reports: Children in these types of placement were less likely to experience a substantiated report than children living with biological parents.

Model 3 incorporated the measure of bridging social capital. The results indicated that, in families in which caregivers scored one point higher on the socioeconomic status scale, children were 6% less likely to be the subjects of substantiated re-reports. The association between number of dependents upon household income and reporting remained significant. The association between placement type and risk of re-report also remained, but the higher risk associated with informal kinship care providers did not meet the test of statistical significance.

Model 4, which incorporated all parameters from the first three models, yielded results strongly resembling those produced by the first three models, suggesting that, to the extent that substantiated reporting is a valid measure of safety, children living with informal kinship care providers and formal kinship care providers were safer than counterparts still living with biological parents. The identified risk of substantiated re-reporting for children living in nonkinship foster care placements was also lower than that for children living with biological parents, but the estimate did not meet the test of statistical significance in the final model. Those children living with caregivers with whom they acknowledged having a closer relationship, as measured by the variables selected for this analysis, and children living with caregivers having more resources, again as measured by variables selected for this analysis, were safer.

Table 6.14 reflects patterns of re-report, whether substantiated or unsubstantiated, in the periods in which children were in the homes of the caregivers interviewed at Waves 1 and 3. The patterns recall the results for the analysis of

Table 6.14 Hazards Estimates of Effects on the Risk of Recurrence of Reported Maltreatment.

	Model 1		Model 2		Model 3		Model 4	
	HR	CI	HR	CI	HR	CI	HR	CI
Demographic								
Caregiver age								
<35 yr	.48	.19–1.21	.48	.14–1.62	.51	.20–1.32	.48	.14–1.71
35–54 yr	.47	.22–1.02	.46	.16–1.32	.51	.23–1.14	.46	.16–1.39
>54 yr								
Caregiver married	.68*	.49–.94	.62*	.42–.90	.76	.55–1.06	.70	.48–1.02
HH # of dependents	1.06	.98–1.15	1.06	.98–1.16	1.06	.97–1.16	1.06	.97–1.17
Child race or ethnicity								
Black or African American	.99	.65–1.50	.93	.59–1.46	.94	.60–1.46	.88	.55–1.41
Hispanic	1.57**	1.14–2.17	1.56**	1.12–2.18	1.52*	1.07–2.17	1.51*	1.05–2.17
Other	1.63	.92–2.88	1.52	.81–2.85	1.62	.89–2.97	1.50	.77–2.95
White								
Child age	.98	.95–1.02	.98	.95–1.01	.99	.96–1.02	.99	.95–1.02
Child gender male	.91	.67–1.22	.92	.67–1.25	.94	.69–1.28	.96	.70–1.32
Bonding Social Capital								
Lowest 12% of all scales			1.49†	.98–2.27			1.55*	
Bridging Social Capital								
SES scale					.94*	.89–.99	.94*	
Placement type								
Birth family								
Informal kin	.28**	.12–.66	.16**	.06–.38	.30**	.13–.71	.16**	.06–.42
Informal nonkin	1.13	.40–3.22	1.23	.42–3.54	1.07	.34–3.36	1.15	.36–3.69
Formal kin	.53†	.26–1.10	.61	.27–1.35	.60	.28–1.28	.65	.28–1.55
Foster family	.41**	.24–.68	.46**	.26–.81	.57†	.31–1.03	.62	.33–1.16

†*p* < .10, **p* < .05, ***p* < .01.
CI, 95% confidence interval; HH, household; HR, hazard ratio.

substantiated reporting in some regards and differ in others. Number of dependents upon household income did not attain statistical significance; however, the variable representing socioeconomic status showed the same pattern of significance for all reporting as for substantiated reporting. This pattern is replicated for the variable representing bonding capital: Those children who reported closer relationships, or were observed to have closer relationships, with caregivers were less likely both to be the subjects of re-reports and to be the subjects of substantiated re-reports. With regard to placement, patterns remained similar, although only informal kinship care yielded a statistically significant difference from homes of biological parents for time until re-report. This finding may be due to a lower degree of surveillance in informal kinship homes, or it may be due to a lower incidence of either retrospective disclosure of past abuse by children or reporting by formal caregivers of past maltreatment, often sexual abuse (Title, Poertner, & Garnier, 2001).

Discussion

The reported differences in placement stability and in safety by placement type accrue special significance when considered in the context of social capital. Abused and neglected children's access to bridging social capital is scarcer in existing kinship and informal networks because of fragile marital ties, family poverty, and limited employment opportunities. Their access to bonding social capital in these networks seems more favorable, however, especially in the early stages of child protective intervention. The obvious question such differences raise is, after safety, how much more importance should be placed on preserving children's bonding social capital than on extending their access to bridging social capital? After all, attaining bridging social capital for them by, for example, placing them in more affluent foster homes or uprooting them from their communities and relocating them to neighborhoods with better schooling and more job opportunities may introduce further disruption into their lives.

With respect to the traditional child welfare outcomes of continuity and stability, both formal and informal kinship care appear to offer greater advantages while carrying no appreciably greater safety risks than foster family care. Nonetheless, a compelling case can be made for foster children's development of capacity to cross the conventional boundaries of family and local community to compete effectively in a postindustrial, global society (Barth, 1999). How should the advantages of kinship for continuity, stability, and safety be weighed against the diminishing importance of extended family and local neighborhood for ensuring the long-term health, longevity, and economic self-sufficiency of foster youth?

Answers to this question depend on the priority assigned to the principle of *equal opportunity*—namely, that all children should be guaranteed the developmental conditions necessary to lead economically productive, rewarding lives. Traditionalists who consider kinship care a form of family permanence in its own right accept some social and economic inequalities as the price to be paid in return for retaining family autonomy, religious freedom, and community identity in matters of childrearing. For example, homeschooling, license-exempt childcare by extended kin, and faith-based healing customs create childrearing conditions different from the more uniform life chances obtainable in public schools, licensed childcare centers, and medical hospitals.

Some of the economic disadvantages experienced by children reared and educated in diverse primordial settings may be alleviated by extending to their families and local communities the public dollars that would have been spent on them in more bureaucratized care settings. This measure is already being taken, for example, through school transportation and book allowances for private education, public payments to kinship caregivers, and government grants to faith-based, social service organizations. Proponents of so-called big-government conservatism argue that drawing on the cultural and social capital of the primordial group may be more effective in addressing dependent, neglected, and delinquent youth than bureaucratic agents, which by law must remain culturally neutral (Glazer, 1988).

The advantages associated with decentralized and debureaucratized forms of substitute care argue for extending the richer benefits available to formal foster caregivers and adoptive parents not only to formal kinship caregivers through boarding payments and subsidized guardianship but also to informal kinship caregivers. Findings from NSCAW suggest that this extension may already be occurring indirectly through the incorporation of informal kinship caregivers into the formal system as paid kin and licensed foster parents. Some jurisdictions have enacted or are considering legislation that would extend these same benefits to informal kin caregivers who assume private guardianship of dependent children outside the formal child protection system.

Equalizing the subsidies paid to relatives, regardless of their sources of support from TANF or Title IV-E foster care, seems only fair, but it does raise the long-standing concern over whether the infusion of public subsidies and bureaucratic standards into primordial-based patterns of loyalty and mutual aid strengthen or weaken the voluntary capacity of traditional agents to safeguard the well-being of children. Nathan Glazer (1988) argued that every piece of social policy substitutes for some primordial arrangement a costly new bureaucratic arrangement in which public agents take over some part of the traditional role of the extended family, community group, or ethnic group. Careful consideration should be given to whether a social program enlarges the capacity of traditional agents to fulfill their caregiving responsibilities or merely strengthens their dependence on governmental assistance (Testa, 2008).

In the Deficit Reduction Act of 2005, Congress eliminated federal reimbursement for child placement services and administrative costs for children under the care and custody of child protective authorities and placed in nonlicensed, kinship homes. Although the immediate effect of the change is reduction of federal expenditures, states can recoup federal dollars by licensing relatives' homes, which in the long term will increase federal spending because states must pay licensed relatives the same amount currently paid to nonkin foster families. States can already choose to license kinship homes so long as they apply the same minimum safety standards that are imposed on foster homes. States faced with the prospect of losing IV-E reimbursements for kinship foster care may instead revise their licensing safety standards downward to the "lowest common denominator."

Although this action would likely qualify additional kin for higher federal foster care payments, the consequences for the improved safety and stability of children's substitute care are not immediately obvious. The NSCAW data show that children in informal and formal kinship care already profile as safe as and more stable than children in fully licensed foster family homes. The unintended consequences of revising home licensing standards, as Glaser forewarns, may simply be to incorporate additional kinship capacity into the formal foster care system at greater cost without necessarily improving child welfare outcomes. Likewise, revising home licensing standards downward inadvertently risks attracting additional "stranger" foster care capacity into the system, which is currently screened out under the more stringent requirements that states traditionally impose on foster homes with respect to separate bedrooms, sufficient family income, and medical checkups. Whether this enlarged capacity improves or compromises child welfare outcomes warrants careful monitoring.

With respect to worries about formal kinship care's substituting for voluntary family effort, the best available evidence from national welfare reform and the subsidized guardianship waiver experiments suggests that any such substitution effects are minimal. As TANF caseloads have fallen and states have extended guardianship subsidies to relatives, kinship foster care caseloads have also declined. This pattern suggests that the fears about the "woodwork effects" of extending foster care benefits to relatives may be overstated. Still, the diminished importance of the extended family and local neighborhood in structuring future social and economic opportunities weakens arguments in favor of retaining existing kinship preference laws, opening them to attack as antiquated and irrelevant biases (Bartholet, 1999; Giddens, 1990). For skeptics of the value of deferring bureaucratic principles to primordial solidarities, the only rational justification for privileging kinship and neighborhood-based care is to demonstrate empirically that these preferences advance the desired expressive outcomes of safety, stability, and permanence better than other placement options—without unduly compromising the instrumental outcomes of education, employability, and other inputs to social mobility.

Conclusion

The evidence we have presented here suggests that kinship care delivers on its promise with respect to continuity, safety, and stability outcomes but that grounds may exist for concern that the advantages of kinship could diminish as public policy attention turns to the instrumental inputs to child well-being. The NSCAW study can fulfill an important role in comparing the strengths and weaknesses of bonding and bridging social capital, and of informal and formal care arrangements, in order to equip young people with the cultural and human capital necessary for leading healthy, self-sufficient, and economically rewarding lives in a postindustrial, global society.

Perhaps the tradeoffs are not as stark as is sometimes supposed. Some research hints at a positive linkage between a foster child's educational achievement and having an affectionate bonding relationship with a permanent substitute caregiver, although undoubtedly the causality is bidirectional (Kang, 2004). Investment in early education programs may help abused and neglected children realize gains in future academic achievement (Reynolds, Ou, & Topitzes, 2004). Additional research is needed to better inform the child welfare community and policy makers whether alternatives exist for extending bridging social capital to foster youth—for example, mentoring programs, educational liaisons, educational vouchers, college scholarships, and individual development accounts. Such alternatives may confer advantages resembling those of more disruptive measures, such as removal of children to wealthier homes, better schools, and more affluent neighborhoods. Whatever the empirical evidence reveals, it will always be important to respect and to coordinate permanency planning decisions in accordance with the preferences of the children and families directly affected and to balance these preferences against the morals and values of the society at large.

NOTES

1. Estimates are based on 2001 statistics from the Adoption and Foster Care Analysis and Reporting System (AFCARS) and the 2001 Survey of Income and Program Participation reported in Kreider and Fields (2005).
2. Before the Supreme Court ruling in *Miller v. Youakim*, 44 U.S. 125, 99 S. Ct. 957 (1979), foster children placed in the homes of relatives were routinely denied full foster care benefits.
3. Title IV-E is a subpart of Title IV of the federal Social Security Act, which deals with federal payments for foster care, adoption, and guardianship assistance payments, 42 U.S.C. §§ 671–679b (2006).
4. The two derived variables used to construct this scale were the type of out-of-home placement the child was currently living in (CHDOOHPL) and the primary caregiver's self-identified relationship to the child (CHDRELCG). The first variable was constructed by combining and reconciling discrepancies in reported placement type and situation information from the child, caregiver, and caseworker. If discrepancies were found between the three reports, the first nonmissing response from the caregiver was given priority, followed next by the child's response, and followed lastly by the caseworker's. The same sequence was used for resolving discrepancies in caregiver's relationship to the child.
5. We recognize that this coding is only an approximation of the child's actual legal status, but no more exact indicators of formal and informal custody are available in NSCAW.
6. Data collection interviews for NSCW were conducted at Wave 1 (baseline), Wave 2 (12 months), Wave 3 (18 months), and Wave 4 (36 months).

7. Although imperfect as a measure of the extent of placement with the nonabusing parent's family, it is instructive that one third of kinship care homes come from the child's paternal family.

8. Wave 2 was excluded because several of the measures of interest were not available for it.

9. The overall scale score was not incorporated in the NSCAW data set. Although subscale scores are incorporated in the data set, these scores have been shown to exhibit lower internal consistency than desired; they were not used in the current analyses.

10. This variable was missing in 510 cases because of missing data from the family income variable.

11. The subpopulation used in this analysis excluded baseline placements in group home or residential care because nearly all children in these types of placements experienced a change in caregiver.

12. The measure of dependents was truncated to exclude questionable data (a maximum of 76 dependents were reported based on the original measure).

13. For more detailed analysis of the association of kinship care with permanence through adoption and guardianship, see Chapter 8.

14. The measure of dependents was truncated to exclude questionable data (a maximum of 76 dependents were reported, according to the original measure).

REFERENCES

Administration for Children and Families. (2000). *Report to the Congress on kinship foster care*. Washington, DC: U.S. Department of Health and Human Services.

Administration for Children and Families. (in press). *National Survey of Child and Adolescent Well-Being: Children involved with the child welfare system (Wave 1)*. Washington, DC: Author.

Barth, R. P. (1999). After safety, what is the goal of child welfare services: Permanency, family continuity, or social benefit? *International Journal of Social Welfare, 8*(4), 244–252.

Bartholet, E. (1999). *Nobody's children: Abuse and neglect, foster drift, and the adoption alternative*. Boston: Beacon Press.

Buchanan, A. (1988). Principal/agent theory and decision making in health care. *Bioethics, 2*(4), 317–333.

Caldwell, B. M., & Bradley, R. H. (1984). *Home observation for measurement of the environment*. Little Rock: University of Arkansas at Little Rock.

Case, A., Lin, I., & McLanahan, S. (2000). How hungry is the selfish gene? *Economic Journal, 110*(10), 781–804.

Coleman, J. S. (1990). *Foundations of social theory*. Cambridge, MA: Belknap Press of Harvard University Press.

Daly, M., & Wilson, M. (1985). Child abuse and other risks of not living with both parents. *Ethology and Sociobiology, 6*(4), 197–210.

Giddens, A. (1990). *The consequences of modernity*. Stanford, CA: Stanford University Press.

Glazer, N. (1988). *The limits of social policy*. Cambridge, MA: Harvard University Press.

Kang, H. (2004). *Coping with the educational disadvantages of children in public care: Substitute caregivers' educational expectations and involvement*. Unpublished doctoral dissertation, University of Illinois at Urbana-Champaign.

Koh, E., & Testa, M. F. (2008). Propensity score matching of children in kinship and non-kinship foster care: Do permanency outcomes still differ? *Social Work Research, 32*, 105–116.

Kreider, R. M., & Fields, J. (2005). *Living arrangements of children: 2001.* Current Population Reports. Washington, DC: U.S. Census Bureau.

Lin, N. (2001). *Social capital: A theory of social structure and action.* Cambridge, England: Cambridge University Press.

Reynolds, A. J., Ou, S. R., & Topitzes, J. W. (2004). Paths of effects of early childhood intervention on educational attainment and delinquency: A confirmatory analysis of the Chicago child-parent centers. *Child Development, 75*(5), 1299–1328.

RTI International. (2007). *SUDAAN user's manual, release 9.0.1.* Research Triangle Park, NC: Author.

Testa, M. F. (1992). Conditions of risk for substitute care. *Children and Youth Services Review, 14*(1/2), 27–36.

Testa, M. F. (2001). Kinship care and permanency. *Journal of Social Service Research, 28*(1), 25–43.

Testa, M. F. (2008). New permanency strategies for children in foster care. In D. Lindsey & A. Shlonsky (Eds.), *Child welfare research: Advances for policy and practice.* Oxford, England: Oxford University Press.

Testa, M. F., & Slack, K. S. (2001). The gift of kinship foster care. *Children and Youth Services Review, 24*(1), 79–108.

Title, G., Poertner, J., & Garnier, P. (2001). *Child maltreatment in out-of-home care: What do we know now?* Urbana, IL: Children and Family Research Center.

U.S. Bureau of Labor Statistics. (1999). *Revising the standard occupational classification system.* Washington, DC: Author.

Woolcock, M., & Narayan, D. (2000). Social capital: Implications for development theory, research and policy. *World Bank Research Observer, 15*(2), 225–249.

7

The Social Capital of Youth in Foster Care

An Assessment and Policy Implications

MATTHEW STAGNER AND DANIEL KUEHN

Increasingly, adoption and reunification have dominated policy discussions in child welfare. Also increasing has been the attention on youth who age out of the foster care system. Comparatively little attention has been paid to the earlier experiences of youth who remain in out-of-home care for long periods, even though major policy developments in child welfare relate directly to this population. The increasing use of kinship foster care (hereafter *kinship care*) and familial guardianship can profoundly affect these children in adolescence and beyond. Although it seems intuitive that both legal familial guardianship and child welfare system kinship care would favor connections to extended family over connections to the "strangers" in traditional foster care, placements with extended family affect these children's retention of ties to immediate family. These connections between the child and his or her immediate family are important for the fulfillment of all three key components of the child welfare mission: safety, permanence, and well-being.

Placement Policy History

On September 30, 2006, about 510,000 children and youth in the United States were in foster care. Of these, about half were aged 11 years or older (Administration for Children and Families, 2008). The movement toward kinship care within the foster care system, as well as familial guardianship outside the system, profoundly affects these youth. Although variability in state practice persists (Berrick, 1998), kinship care is increasingly important in all states, with state and local child welfare agencies increasingly placing youth with kin. Between 1986 and 1990 the number of children placed in formal kinship care rose to 31% of all placements (Testa, 2004). As of September 2006, 24% of all children in foster care were in kinship placements, a total of 124,571 children nationwide (Administration for Children and Families, 2008).

This rise in kinship care has been driven not only by a diminishing supply of foster homes and by changes in funding but also by changes in philosophy (Berrick, 1998). Although concern about youth's social capital is not directly cited as driving the increasing reliance on kinship care, it is at least indirectly related because kinship care is thought generally to protect the child while maintaining his or her established ties to the extended family (Berrick, 1998). In this way, though placements with kin lead to longer stays in foster care, they are thought to benefit youth by retaining some connection to the biological parents.

"Informal" kin guardianship policies have also garnered support. These policies move youth out of formal care and into the care of relatives. Support for guardianship grew in the 1990s as the Children's Bureau invited demonstrations of innovative services, which allowed the use of Title IV-E dollars, 42 U.S.C. §§ 671–679b (2006), normally restricted to costs associated with foster care maintenance. These new allocations included payments to families assuming guardianship. Guardianship arose as a response to permanency-planning tensions between the benefits of established, enduring relationships and the benefits of legally binding relationships (Testa, 2004). It benefits from an established connection with family but does not impose one that is legally binding; it is characterized by few disruptions in comparison with adoption (Testa, 2004). Children in this type of care are more likely to belong to a minority race and tend to be older than other children in care.

A key age of interest is between 11 and 15 years. In the child welfare community, focus is increasing on the transition of youth out of care at age 18 (or older in some states); many of these exiting youth entered care in their early teens. Each year, about 25,000 youth exit care in this way (Administration for Children and Families, 2008). In 1999 the passage of the John H. Chafee Foster Care Independence Program renewed policy interest in those aging out of the foster care system. The law provided the possibility of extended Medicaid coverage, increased assets that young people in foster care can maintain, and increased funding to support programs for this group (Allen & Nixon, 2000). In addition, the law encourages states to serve youth who are likely to remain in foster care until age 18, to prepare them for the transition to adulthood. States may set their own age eligibility guidelines, and some serve individuals as young as age 12. Many youth in the NSCAW sample who entered care between 11 and 15 can be expected to remain in care until age 18. The social capital they have as they enter care, as well as the enhancement or deterioration of social capital over their time in care, is important to policies surrounding parental visitation, mentoring, and the roles and training of foster parents.

The Importance of Social Capital and Social Support

Many researchers have documented the importance of *social capital,* or the related concept of *social support.*[1] Runyan et al. (1998) found that social capital matters for young children in "unfavorable environments." The supportive role fulfilled by the family, the peer group, the school, and the community predicts positive outcomes for children (Rosenfeld, Richman, & Bowen, 2000). Social capital for foster youth is important both because of the connections they may lack because they were removed from their homes and because of the special challenges they face in out-of-home care. Adolescents who have received child welfare services exhibit more delinquency, for example, and fewer social skills than youth in the general population (Wall, Barth, & The NSCAW Research Group, 2005). In particular, the "key junctures" of a person's life require special attention to risk and protective mechanisms because a potential risk trajectory may be diverted to a more constructive path at these junctures (Rutter, 1987). If families of origin are not available to provide needed guidance at these key junctures, extended family, foster families, social service systems, and youth-serving agencies may fill this role.

Social capital from family may be particularly important for well-being and avoidance of behavioral problems. Using an ecological model, Bowen and Chapman (1996) investigated the impact of poverty, neighborhood danger, and social capital on the well-being of at-risk youths. They found that social capital, particularly parental support, had a greater impact on youth's well-being than their reports and perceptions of danger from their neighborhoods. Research has focused on the relative importance of parental monitoring, knowledge, and warmth in preventing youth from undertaking delinquent and undesirable behaviors, finding that youth's relatedness to caregivers and caregivers' monitoring of youth may serve as protective factors against substance abuse and delinquent behaviors (Anderson, Holmes, & Ostresh, 1999; Borowsky, Ireland, & Resnick, 2001; Huizinga, Catalano, & Miller, 1994). Caregivers' lower monitoring of youth's activities increases the opportunity for youth to engage in sexual activity and delinquent acts, as well as substance abuse (Newman, Fox, Flynn, & Christeson, 2000; Patterson & Dishion, 1985).

Social capital may also lessen youth's stress. Numerous studies have linked stress with emotional and behavioral problems in both children and adolescents (e.g., Compas, 1987). Stressful events in childhood and adolescence can negatively affect the developmental process itself. Educational performance provides a tangible example of the disruption of social capital. Eighty percent of children change schools when they change out-of-home placements (Berrick, Courtney, & Barth, 1993), which strains their ability to perform at the same level as other students. Foster youth who change schools face additional disruptions in peer and teacher relationships, which further complicates their ability to develop and maintain meaningful peer and mentor connections that could provide a protective social network. Resiliency frameworks emphasize the critical role of social capital as a key coping mechanism against stressors. Roberts, Kaplan, Shema, and Strawbride

(2000) found that increased rates of family support contribute to higher self-esteem in children. Ohannessian, Lerner, Lerner, and Eye (1994) found increased levels of peer support may help counteract the damaging effects of living in an unhealthy family environment. Moreover, familial and other social capital can mitigate the effects of early maltreatment (Folkman, Chesney, Pollack, & Phillips, 1992; Hazan & Shaver, 1994; Hines, Merdinger, & Wyatt, 2005).

Data Set Characteristics, Test Variables, and Goals

This study explores social capital, one crucial dimension of a youth's condition while he or she remains in out-of-home care. Youth who come into out-of-home care may be removed from key sources of social capital, although they may also find new sources. Removal of a youth from his or her home of origin may create substantial risk of disruption in that youth's network of supports in family, school, and neighborhood, which are considered *bonding social capital,* according to Testa, Bruhn, and Helton's (Chapter 6) social capital framework. On the other hand, foster placement may provide material and social advantages that are absent in the home of origin. These advantages are *bridging social capital,* which may be measured by the caregiver's educational attainment, employment status, poverty level, and income. These characteristics determine access to networks and experiences likely to be useful to youth. The positive presence of these factors in caregivers generally "bridges" youth to important resources.

Compared with youth *not* in long-term foster care, those who remain in care for long periods may experience significant changes in access to social capital. This exploratory study addresses, specifically, three questions about the conditions and roles of social capital in the lives of youth in out-of-home care: *(1)* at the point of child welfare intervention, whether social capital for youth placed out of home differs from that for youth remaining in the parental home; *(2)* whether social capital for those out of home for 3 years or longer differs from social capital for those who return home sooner; and *(3)* whether social capital changes over time for those placed out of home for 3 years or longer and how this experience compares with that of those who remain at home.

The first question, whether social capital for those in out-of-home care differs from that of those remaining at home, relates to policies that may encourage or discourage placement in out-of-home care at the point of initial child welfare system intervention. An enhanced understanding of the differences in social capital can help policy makers better assess what is gained, as well as what is lost, by placing youth in substitute care. This assessment, in turn, can guide the implementation of structures able to reinforce existing support or compensate for lost support.

The second question, whether the social capital for youth in long-term substitute care differs from the support of those who return home sooner, engages policies surrounding reunification with biological parents. An enhanced under-standing can help policy makers assess whether those who remain in care long term .are particularly advantaged or disadvantaged in terms of social capital.

The third question, whether the social capital of those in substitute care for longer than 3 years changes over time, speaks to the youth's eventual transition to adulthood; comparing these changes over time with changes over time for those who never entered care helps trace the effects of placement on social capital. Though a youth still in care after 3 years may yet return home, an understanding of how social capital may increase or decrease over time helps found an under-standing of a youth's social capital when he or she is approaching adulthood, whether this developmental transition occurs after a return home in the late teens or while aging out of substitute care.[2]

The National Survey of Child and Adolescent Well-Being (NSCAW) affords a unique opportunity to examine social capital for youth in long-term out-of-home care, making possible for the first time nationally representative compar-isons of social capital among those who remain in care, those who never enter care, and those who enter care but return home quickly. Moreover, NSCAW permits observation of changes in social capital from the time of entry into out-of-home care until 36 month later (the Wave 4 follow-up interviews). Using NSCAW's child protective services sample of 5,501 children recruited into the study between October 1999 and December 2000, after they were reported to child welfare on allegations of being maltreated, this study focuses on those who entered out-of-home care between the sentinel investigation date for NSCAW and the Wave 1 baseline data collection.[3] At baseline, 260 youth aged 11 to 15 years were in out-of-home care. We compare the 137 youth who were in out-of-home care at baseline *but returned home* between the Wave 1 and Wave 4 inter-views ("movers") with the 123 youth who *remained in out-of-home care* for the duration of the study ("stayers"). Additional data from the NSCAW Wave 5 follow-up of adolescents will eventually allow analysts to understand in greater depth the connection between social capital in the early years of care and later well-being.

Methods

Measures

In addition to the basic demographic, income, and case history variables used in this study, several scales of behavior, social capital, and social capital were used. Many of these scales required a recombination of measures in NSCAW.

MOVERS AND STAYERS   Youth were considered "movers" if they were in out-of-home care at Wave 1 of the survey but returned home by Wave 4 of the survey, about 36 months later. Youth who did not return home by Wave 4 were considered "stayers."

CHILD BEHAVIOR Child behavior problems were measured with the Child Behavior Checklist score (CBCL; Achenbach, 1991), including both the Internalizing and Externalizing subscales.

ENFORCEABLE TRUST *Enforceable trust,* the first component of bonding social capital, is composed of a caregiver monitoring measure and a child protection measure. For assessment of monitoring, youth were asked six questions (Dishion, Patterson, Stoolmiller, & Skinner, 1991). Youth were asked about leaving home without telling their parents, their parents' knowledge of where they were, who they were with, curfews, communication between the youth and their parents about when they expected to return home, and frequency of being left home alone. These questions were combined to form a 30-point scale of parental monitoring at Wave 1 and Wave 4. A scale constructed from the protective factors measures, which was provided in NSCAW, was used to measure child protection.

BONDED SOLIDARITY *Bonded solidarity* includes relatedness, which was measured with a shortened version of the Relatedness scale from the Rochester Assessment Package for Schools (Connell, 1991; Lynch & Cicchetti, 1991). The total relatedness scale was composed of four subscales on autonomy, involvement, emotional security, and structure. Also included in bonded solidarity were questions on closeness to caregiver. Closeness with biological parents was defined by four sets of questions asked of youth. The first set of questions asked youth how much contact they had with each biological parent. The second set of questions established the quality of this contact by asking how often the children talked about important issues with their biological parents. More weight was given to the first set of questions when establishing the measure. The closeness scale was produced separately for biological parents and caregivers.

SCHOOL CONNECTIONS Youth were asked 16 questions about their relationships with their peers. Seven of these questions, which deal primarily with the youth's experiences and difficulties establishing relationships with peers at school, are combined to form the "peer rejection" measure, a 35-point scale. The other nine questions, which address the amount of support the youth receives from peers at school, are combined with an additional question on participation in peer support groups to form a measure of "social capital," a 46-point scale.

Analyses

Stata was used to construct the variables and perform the hypothesis tests (StataCorp, 2005). The analysis consisted of hypothesis testing of differences between youth who were and those were not in out-of-home care at Wave 1, between movers and stayers, between mover characteristics at Wave 4 and those at Wave 1, and between stayer characteristics at Wave 4 and those at Wave 1.

Results

Social Capital Differences Between Out-of-Home Youth and In-Home Youth

The placement of youth into foster care may create a tradeoff between bonding and bridging social capital. Those remaining at home would be expected to maintain stronger bonding social capital because of closer ties with family. Those placed into out-of-home care, by contrast, may gain bridging social capital by being placed with higher-income, better-connected foster parents.

In the NSCAW sample, those who entered out-of-home care at baseline were older than those who remained in the parental home, were significantly more likely to be of black or African American race than they were to be of another race, were less likely to be Hispanic than to be non-Hispanic, and were less likely to have experienced physical abuse.

The youth placed into out-of-home care at baseline had higher bonding social capital in some ways but not in others. Their caregivers provided more monitoring and were more protective than the biological parents of those youth remaining in home (Fig. 7.1). The lower monitoring and protection provided to in-home youth may relate to the deficits of parents whose children eventually enter the child welfare system. Nonetheless, the out-of-home youth felt less close to their caregivers. No significant differences emerged in terms of relatedness, autonomy, involvement, emotional security conferred by the caregiver, structure, and closeness to biological parents (not shown).

Table 7.1   Characteristics of Youth Aged 11 to 15 Years at Baseline, by Placement Status

	Not in Out-of-Home Care at Wave 1	In Out-of-Home Care at Wave 1	T Value
Gender			
Boys	0.43	0.48	−1.48
Girls	0.57	0.52	1.48
Race			
Black	0.26	0.38	−3.61[***]
White	0.49	0.47	0.77
Hispanic	0.17	0.08	4.60[***]
Other	0.08	0.08	−0.18
Type of abuse			
Physical abuse	0.30	0.24	1.87[*]
Sexual abuse	0.13	0.15	−0.81
Emotional abuse	0.06	0.07	−0.71
Physical neglect	0.11	0.10	0.93
Neglect	0.26	0.22	1.18
Other neglect	0.07	0.08	−1.00

***$p < .01$, **$p < .05$, *$p < .10$.

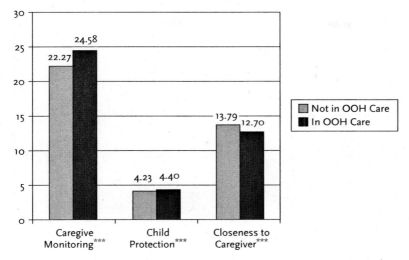

Figure 7.1   Bonding social capital by out-of-home status at baseline. The *y* axis represents a scale of responses to multiple questions about social capital. Additional information on the creation of the scales is available from the author. ***p < .01. OOH, out of home.

Youth in out-of-home care at baseline also have less of a connection to peers at school (Fig. 7.2). They are significantly less likely to feel connected to a peer group, though they are also less likely to report peers with deviant behavior.

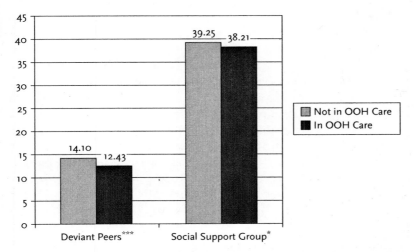

Figure 7.2   School connections by out-of-home (OOH) status at baseline. The *y* axis represents a scale of responses to multiple questions about social capital. Additional information on the creation of the scales is available from the author. ***p < .01, *p < .10.

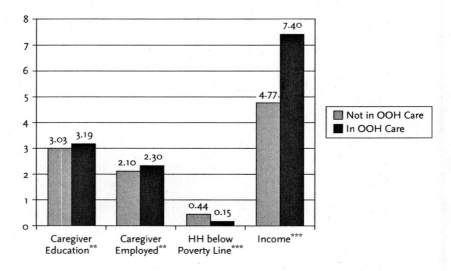

Figure 7.3   Bridging social capital by out-of-home (OOH) status at baseline. The y axis represents a scale of responses to multiple questions about social capital. Additional information on the creation of the scales is available from the author. $***p < .01$, $**p < .05$.

Youth who entered out-of-home care had significantly more bridging capital, with caregivers having higher education, more employment, higher incomes, and less poverty (Fig. 7.3).

Overall, those placed in out-of-home care gained bridging social capital and caregiver monitoring while they lost bonding social capital. This tradeoff is what one would expect where placement is being driven primarily by concerns for the child's safety. Youth who entered care differed in other ways from the population of youth who remained at home; therefore, placement into care might not have been the cause of these differences in social capital.[4] Youth who entered out-of-home care had higher Child Behavior Checklist Internalizing scale scores (Achenbach, 1991) and lower reading achievement. In terms of risk behaviors, those who entered out-of-home care reported higher sexual behavior ratings, more delinquent behavior, and more drug abuse. The relationship of these differences to the documented differences in social capital should be explored more conclusively in a study with a larger number of youth.

Social Capital Differences Between Long-Term and Shorter-Term Out-of-Home Youth

Youth who were in care in both Wave 1 and Wave 4 ("stayers" in out-of-home care) were next compared with those who were in care in Wave 1 but left care by Wave 4

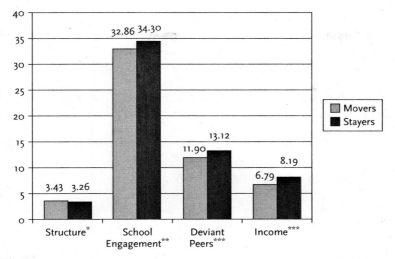

Figure 7.4 Social capital at baseline by mover/stayer status at Wave 4. The *y* axis represents a scale of responses to multiple questions about social capital. Additional information on the creation of the scales is available from the author. *$p < .01$, **$p < .05$, ***$p < .01$.

("movers"). While bridging social capital would be expected to remain higher for those in out-of-home placement, bonding social capital would be expected to be stronger for those who returned home.

At Wave 1 few significant differences existed in bonding capital, with only a difference in structure being provided by the caregiver and favoring those who moved back home. No difference existed for households with higher incomes. At Wave 1, eventual movers out of care showed significantly more structure in their relationships with caregivers than stayers. Stayers also had *higher* school engagement, though they also still had peers with more deviant behavior. As expected, those who remained in care had greater bridging social capital, but only as measured by income. No significant differences were found in caregiver education, employment, or poverty.

Again, the compositions of these two populations differ, and some of the differences in social capital may be related to these differences. Stayers were more likely to be black and less likely to be white. They were less likely to have suffered physical or sexual abuse, but they were more likely to have been victims of neglect. Stayers were more likely to be in foster homes at Wave 1 and less likely to be in kinship placements. This finding is interesting because kinship placements are generally expected to result in slower movement to permanency when all age groups are considered.

Change in Social Capital for Long-Term Out-of-Home Youth

Stayers began foster care with some advantages in social capital (more school engagement and higher income). It is possible that bonding social capital increases for those who remain in care, but it is also possible that bonding social capital decreases. Our analysis revealed deterioration in the closeness of attachments to birth parents between Wave 1 and Wave 4 (Fig. 7.5) for youth who remain in care. Because these youth remained in care for 3 years, the decline in closeness to biological parents may be expected. Caregivers' monitoring also decreased over time for this group, but other elements of social capital remained steady for this group, including protectiveness, relatedness, autonomy, involvement, emotional security conferred by parents, structure, and closeness to caregiver.

Changes in bridging social capital emerged for stayers by Wave 4, but the changes appear contradictory (Fig. 7.6). Fewer caregivers were employed, but fewer were living in poverty. Further analysis would be required to explain whether the economic situations of the households of youth in out-of-home care deteriorated.

To better understand changes in social capital over time for youth who remain in care, one can consider what happens to social capital over time for youth *never* placed into care. For this group, many indicators of bonding social capital increased between Wave 1 and Wave 4, including the caregiver's monitoring and the child's sense of protection (Fig. 7.7). Closeness to biological parents declined, as it did for youth staying in care.

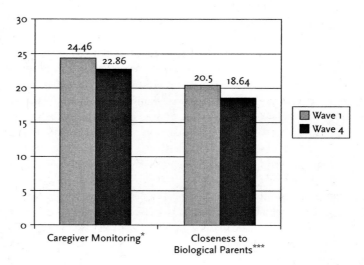

Figure 7.5 Social capital for out-of-home stayers at Wave 1 and Wave 4. The *y* axis represents a scale of responses to multiple questions about social capital. Additional information on the creation of the scales is available from the author. *$p < .01$, ***$p < .01$.

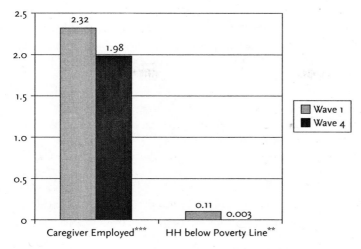

Figure 7.6 Bridging social capital for out-of-home stayers. The *y* axis represents a scale of responses to multiple questions about social capital. Additional information on the creation of the scales is available from the author. $^{**}p < .05$, $^{***}p < .01$.

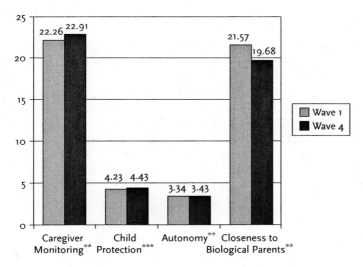

Figure 7.7 Social capital for youth not in out-of-home care at baseline. The *y* axis represents a scale of responses to multiple questions about social capital. Additional information on the creation of the scales is available from the author. $^{**}p < .05$, $^{***}p < .01$.

Discussion

This study was undertaken to explore the characteristics of youth in foster care (aged 11 to 15 years at baseline) and to assess their access to social capital. Youth in out-of-home care at the beginning of the survey were found to have some indicators of greater bonding social capital than those remaining in home (e.g., more monitoring and more protective caregivers). They gained significant bridging social capital, however, particularly in terms of foster parents' higher incomes and rates of employment. They were lower in some other forms of bonding social capital, feeling less close to their caregivers, as one would expect for those recently placed into care. These findings support the known tensions surrounding the placement of youth into out-of-home care. Even with the small sample size in this study, we can confirm that out-of-home placement provides greater safety at the expense of closeness to primary caregivers.

Over time, experiences in care may erode some social capital resources. Stayers, who remained in out-of-home care for both Waves 1 and 4, saw closeness to biological parents decline; however, this decline happens for those *not* placed in out-of-home care as well. It may be a function of the youth's advancing age rather than placement in care. Nevertheless, the consequences for this decline in closeness to biological parents may have greater consequences for those placed in out-of-home care, affecting the probability of return home or successful support during the transition to adulthood. It must, therefore, be taken into account by policy makers.

Results of this study are necessarily limited in several ways. First, the youth in this study represent only youth who entered care between the ages of 11 and 15 years; results cannot be generalized to all youth in foster care, because some youth enter care at older, as well younger, ages. Second, the number of youth in out-of-home care in NSCAW is small; therefore, analyses are limited in this study to simple bivariate comparisons that indicate issues future research may explore in more detail. Finally, the time for following youth is limited to 3 years. As future waves of NSCAW data become available for this cohort, the child welfare community will be able to learn more about social capital changes in the later teen years and the ways these changes influence the transition to adulthood.

Conclusion

Assessing social capital for youth in foster care matters because policy makers must understand how those who are placed in out-of-home care differ in terms of support from those who remain in the parental home. This knowledge can affect policies about placement decisions, as well as the ongoing responses to families once a placement decision is made. Equally important to policy is an understanding of the ways social capital evolves for youth in care: Although many youth who enter care between 11 and 15 years of age return home before aging out of care, for those who do not quickly return to their homes connections to family may change, and the availability of different kinds of support may change.

The NSCAW study provides several measures of social capital and offers a unique opportunity to examine this issue preliminarily, even though the number of youth in placement is small. This exploratory study supports the view of out-of-home care placement as a tradeoff between bridging and bonding social capital. Bridging social capital is clearly improved for those who enter and remain in care; the outcome for bonding social capital is less clear. Although this tradeoff is unlikely to drive placement decisions (which are generally driven by immediate safety concerns or other factors), recognizing this tradeoff may lead policy makers to think about ways to overcome the lower level of bonding social capital for youth in care while extending these youth's access to bridging social capital. The policy movement toward kinship care and kin guardianship, as well as increased funding for the preparation of youth for the transition to adulthood through the Chafee Program, should involve more explicitly measuring and addressing the social capital of youth in care.

Whether youth who have been subjects of maltreatment investigations return home as teens or remain in care until the age for exiting, the lessened connections to biological parents raises challenges for the child welfare system. Although parents may be expected to reduce or change monitoring as their children age, the situation of foster youth may be different. For those not in out-of-home care in this sample, monitoring actually increased during the follow-up period. The contrasting reduction in caregivers' monitoring for youth who remained in out-of-home care raises concerns about youth risk behaviors that may further impede a successful transition home or out of care into adulthood. Because the foster care system holds a special interest in reducing children's risks and preparing them for independence, youth must be provided with continual oversight. Future analysis of the Wave 5 NSCAW youth sample will allow researchers to understand more fully how social capital relates to late teen outcomes.

NOTES

1. We use the term *social capital* throughout this chapter, though several of the authors cited here use related terms.
2. This comparison is significantly limited because of the many unmeasured differences between those who never enter care and those who remain in care for more than 3 years.
3. Restricting the population to this time period of entry into out-of-home care maximized the likelihood that the placement was related to the sentinel investigation that placed the child into NSCAW. It also provided an equal starting point for children's entry into care in order to track the experiences of these youth over the ensuing 3 years of the study (to Wave 4).
4. Because of the small sample size and exploratory nature of this analysis, we did not conduct multivariate analyses.

REFERENCES

Achenbach, T. M. (1991). *Manual for the Child Behavior Checklist/4-18 and 1991 profile.* Burlington, VT: University of Vermont, Department of Psychiatry.

Administration for Children and Families. (2008). Preliminary estimates for FY 2006 as of January 2008. *The AFCARS Report* (14). Retrieved November 26, 2008, from http://www.acf.hhs.gov/programs/cb

Allen, M. L., & Nixon, R. (2000). The Foster Care Independence Act and John H. Chafee Foster Care Independence Program: New catalysts for reform for young people aging out of foster care. *Journal of Poverty Law and Policy, July-August*, 197–216.

Anderson, B. J., Holmes, M. D., & Ostresh, E. (1999). Male and female delinquents' attachments and effects of attachments on severity of self-reported delinquency. *Criminal Justice and Behavior, 26*(4), 435–452.

Berrick, J. D. (1998). When children cannot remain home: Foster family care and kinship care. *Future of Children, 8*(1), 72–87.

Berrick, J. D., Courtney, M. E., & Barth, R. P. (1993). Specialized foster care and group home care: Similarities and differences in the characteristics of children in care. *Children and Youth Services Review, 15*(6), 453–469.

Borowsky, I. W., Ireland, M., & Resnick, M. D. (2001). Adolescent suicide attempts: Risks and protectors. *Pediatrics, 107*(3), 485–493.

Bowen, G. L., & Chapman, M. V. (1996). Poverty, neighborhood danger, social support, and the individual adaptation among at-risk youth in urban areas. *Journal of Family Issues, 17*(5), 641–666.

Compas, B. E. (1987). Stress and life events during childhood and adolescence. *Clinical Psychology Review, 7*, 275–302.

Connell, J. (1991). Competency, autonomy, and relatedness: A motivational analysis of self-system processes. In M. Gunnar & L. Sroufe (Eds.), *Self-processes and development* (Vol. 23, pp. 43–77). Hillsdale, NJ: Erlbaum.

Dishion, T. J., Patterson, G. R., Stoolmiller, M., & Skinner, M. L. (1991). Family, school, and behavioral antecedents to early adolescent involvement with antisocial peers. *Developmental Psychology, 27*(1), 172–180.

Folkman, S., Chesney, M. A., Pollack, L., & Phillips, C. (1992). Stress, coping, and high-risk sexual behavior. *Health Psychology, 11*(4), 218–222.

Hazan, C., & Shaver, P. R. (1994). Attachment as an organizational framework for research on close relationships. *Psychological Inquiry, 5*(1), 1–22.

Hines, A. M., Merdinger, J., & Wyatt, P. (2005). Former foster youth attending college: Resilience and the transition to young adulthood. *American Journal of Orthopsychiatry, 75*(3), 381–394.

Huizinga, J. D., Catalano, R. F., & Miller, J. Y. (1994). Urban delinquency and substance abuse: Initial findings. Research summary (N. NCJ 143454). Retrieved February 2008, from http://www.ncjrs.gov/pdffiles/urdel.pdf

Lynch, M., & Cicchetti, D. (1991). Patterns of relatedness in maltreated and nonmaltreated children: Connections among multiple representational models. *Development and Psychopathology, 3*, 207–226.

Newman, S. A., Fox, J. A., Flynn, E. A., & Christeson, W. (2000). *America's after-school choice: The prime time for juvenile crime, or youth enrichment and achievement*. Retrieved January 16, 2009, from http://www.fightcrime.org/reports/as2000.pdf

Ohannessian, C. M., Lerner, R. M., Lerner, J. V., & Eye, A. (1994). A longitudinal study of family adjustment and emotional adjustment in early adolescence. *Journal of Early Adolescence, 14*(3), 371–390.

Patterson, G. R., & Dishion, T. J. (1985). Contributions of families and peers to delinquency. *Criminology, 23*(1), 63–79.

Roberts, R. E., Kaplan, G. A., Shema, S. J., & Strawbridge, W. J. (2000). Are the obese at greater risk for depression? *American Journal of Epidemiology, 152*(2), 163–170.

Rosenfeld, L. B., Richman, J. M., & Bowen, G. L. (2000). Social support networks and school outcomes: The centrality of the teacher. *Child and Adolescent Social Work Journal*, *17*(3), 205–226.

Runyan, D. K., Hunter, W. M., Socolar, R. R., Amaya-Jackson, L., English, D., Landsverk, J., et al. (1998). Children who prosper in unfavorable environments: The relationship to social capital. *Pediatrics*, *101*(1 Pt 1), 12–18.

Rutter, M. (1987). Psychosocial resilience and protective mechanisms. *American Journal of Orthopsychiatry*, *57*(3), 316–331.

StataCorp. (2005). *Stata statistical software, release 9*. College Station, TX: Author.

Testa, M. F. (2004). When children cannot return home: Adoption and guardianship. *Future of Children*, *14*(1), 114–129.

Wall, A. E., Barth, R. P., & The NSCAW Research Group. (2005). Maltreated adolescents: Risk factors and gender differences. *Stress, Trauma & Crisis*, *8*, 1–24.

8

Explaining Reunification and Reentry 3 Years After Placement in Out-of-Home Care

RICHARD P. BARTH, SHENYANG GUO, ELIZABETH
C. WEIGENSBERG, SHARON L. CHRIST, CHRISTINA
M. BRUHN, AND REBECCA L. GREEN

When a child who has been the subject of a child maltreatment investigation is placed into out-of-home care, the foundational assumption of child welfare services is that such placement effects a level of safety justifying such services and moves the child toward familial support characterized by permanency.[1] Among options for achieving permanency, the default preference is to return the child to his or her home. These reunifications with the original family are not, however, failsafe: A substantial proportion will necessitate the child's reentry into foster care. Reducing the likelihood of these reentries is one of child welfare's explicit policy goals. Therefore, other means of exiting foster care often become the focal options—especially adoption and guardianship.

The number of factors that can plausibly explain each reunification outcome is large, but most studies on reunification have been limited to a small number of predictors gleaned from child welfare workers' case-administration data. Reliance on administrative data often means that models are incompletely specified and that some findings may be explained in terms of odd administrative rules (CTS-PC; Terling, 1999). Furthermore, many studies either ignore differences in children's stages of development or fail to consider how age-related differences in developmental needs, physical vulnerability, cognitive ability, and maturational demands mediate permanency-related processes.

Factors Predicting Reunification and Time to Reunification

The focus on the child's developmental status as a stratification variable is a relatively new development in the study of reunification. Historically, age has been considered as one of many covariates that may affect reunification; however, age and reunification findings have shown that different factors influence the likelihood of reunification at different ages. Other covariates routinely addressed are those readily available in administrative databases: race, gender, reason for entry into out-of-home care, living arrangements, and geographic location. Less commonly examined are family and child characteristics, such as poverty, substance abuse, housing, and child behavior. Least examined are systems factors and service factors.

The demographic features most often cited as probable influences on reunification are race and age. (Gender is not consistently or strongly associated with reunification.) The finding that black or African American children are less likely to return home than white children appears durable (e.g., Goerge & Lee, 1998; Lu et al., 2004; Wulczyn, 2004). Studies have indicated that, as factors correlated with race are controlled for in analyses, the effect of race is attenuated but may remain important (Needell, Brookhart, & Lee, 2003).

The effects of age have been studied to some extent, with findings that age not only has an independent association with likelihood of return home but also interacts with other relevant factors in predicting reunification. Reunification rates fluctuate with age, with infants and adolescents being less likely to return home than children of other ages (Wulczyn, 2004). Goerge and Lee (1998) found mixed effects of age, whereas Courtney (1994) found interaction effects between age and placement type. Wells and Guo (1999) found that neither age nor gender predicted reunification independently but that age interacted with race. Wildfire, Barth, & Green (2007) found several effects that differed by age group: Factors associated, by age, with an increased time till reunification included female gender (for children 7 months to 11 years old); black or African American race (for newborns and adolescents); behavioral problems (for children 6 to 10 years old); higher family cumulative risk (for children 3 to 10 years old); noncompliance with case plan goals (for children younger than 6 years); and kinship care (for children 6 to 12 years old).

Family structure also has been examined in relation to reunification. Single-parent family status was found to decrease likelihood of reunification (Davis, Landsverk, Newton, & Ganger, 1996; Wells & Guo, 1999), although one study found that this factor affected only children placed in kinship care (Courtney, 1994). For single-parent families, being black as opposed to white or Hispanic was associated with a decreased likelihood of reunification (Harris & Courtney, 2003). Sibship has been studied to some extent, with findings suggesting that placement of siblings together in care positively affects reunification outcomes, while number of siblings has no effect (Webster, Shlonsky, Shaw, & Brookhart, 2005).

The child's and family's problems are often assumed to have brought the family to the attention of child protective services, and reunification is often thought to be conditioned on remediation of these problems. Parental problems found to decrease likelihood of reunification include substance abuse (Eamon, 2002) and poverty (Courtney, 1994). Although the findings concerning poverty are in dispute (Eamon, 2002), likelihood of reunification was found to be positively affected by parents' employment (Kortenkamp, Green, & Stagner, 2004) and negatively affected by housing problems (Courtney, McMurtry, & Zinn, 2004). Incarceration of a parent may also negatively influence likelihood of reunification or may at least necessitate specialized policy and practice approaches (Hayward & DePanfilis, 2007). Although domestic violence may be considered a factor affecting likelihood of reunification, this construct has not been studied explicitly as a predictor. Moreover, policy and practice considerations for parents with severe mental illness have been analyzed (Risley-Curtiss, Stromwall, Truett Hunt, & Teska, 2004), but the degree to which presence of mental illness, as well as its variations and severity, affects likelihood of reunification is unknown.

Several studies have indicated that the child's problems influence likelihood of reunification. Reason for the child's entry into care, for example, has been associated with reunification. Courtney (1994) found that alleged sexual abuse increased likelihood of return home more than alleged neglect, whereas other allegations of abuse did not. Wells and Guo (1999) found that neglect and dependency were associated with less likelihood of return home than physical abuse. Landsverk, Davis, Ganger, Newton, and Johnson (1996) found that children with externalizing behaviors, or emotional-behavioral problems, were less likely to be reunified than children without such problems. The findings of Barth, Courtney, Berrick, and Albert (1994), consistent with Wells and Guo (1999) and Connell, Katz, Saunders, and Tebes (2006), indicate that children with easily identifiable physical, mental, and emotional problems are less likely to return home than their less-troubled counterparts. Interestingly, Landsverk et al. (1996), Barth et al. (1994), and Courtney (1994) all found that, for children placed with kin, special needs were not associated with likelihood of return home.

Factors related to placement have been found in several instances to have a strong predictive effect with regard to reunification. Goerge and Lee (1998) found that children in kinship care were reunified one-fourth to one-half as fast as children in other placement types. Courtney (1994) also found placement effects; however, he found that the effect of kinship care in reducing rates of reunification was eliminated after 5 months. The relationship between kinship care and increased time to reunification has been disputed (Wells & Guo, 1999), and findings may differ according to which additional factors are controlled for in analyses. Region of placement has also been found in more than one study to influence reunification dynamics. Goerge and Lee (1998) found that placement in a large urban setting predicted less likelihood of reunification than other settings. Courtney (1994) found this same pattern, but only for children in kinship care. Placement dynamics may warrant further examination.

Parental visiting has long been credited as a pivotal factor in reunification decisions (Fanshel & Shinn, 1978). Visitation continues to be one of the strongest predictors of reunification. Davis, Landsverk, Newton, and Ganger (1996) determined that maternal visiting was the strongest predictor of reunification, with children whose mothers visited as recommended being 10 times more likely to be reunified than children whose mothers did not visit as recommended. A study by Leathers (2002) demonstrated that rates of parental visiting can be increased by such interventions as holding visits in the foster home and that involvement of birth mothers in administrative case reviews and other planning activities, such as school conferences, were predictive of number of maternal visits. Visiting and other forms of involvement may be markers for degree of parental ambivalence, which may be one of several pivotal forces in the determination of reunification outcomes (Hess & Folaron, 1991).

That involvement of parents in planning for the futures of their children and that establishment of focused objectives intended to facilitate return home can positively impact likelihood of reunification and other permanency outcomes was shown in the mid-1970s (Stein, Gambrill, & Wiltse, 1978). Since that time, several studies have indicated that brief, intensive, family-centered services can increase the likelihood of reunification. Fraser, Walton, Lewis, Pecora, and Walton (1996) found that brief, intensive, family-focused services can be more effective than routine models in promoting reunification. Furthermore, integrating services to address not only the child's problems but also parental problems such as substance abuse, domestic violence, housing, and mental health can increase likelihood of reunification (Marsh, Ryan, Choi, & Testa, 2006). Development of applications for these findings, as well as empirical examination of other promising practices, is critical to future progress.

Factors Predicting Reentry to Out-of-Home Care

As with reunification, rates of reentry to foster care also vary widely across studies, but, on the whole, evidence suggests that it is quite common. One third of children in Illinois who were returned home in the 1980s reentered foster care (Goerge, 1990), 37% who were reunified in Texas reentered foster care within 3.5 years, and among children from 10 different states, about 30% who were reunified in the early 1990s reentered care during subsequent decade (Wulczyn, 2004).

Explanations for these reentries vary considerably, although some findings arise with notable consistency. Courtney (1994), who studied reunified foster children in California, found that several groups of children had faster rates of reentry than their comparison groups, including those who had health problems, were black or African American, were from families receiving Aid to Dependent Children, spent 3 months or less in care, were placed in nonkinship care, or had a greater number of placements during their first stint in care. He also found that children aged 7 to 12 years old had slower rates of reentry than age groups younger or older. Festinger (1996) studied 210 children and families returning home from foster homes and group facilities in 20 agencies in New York City. Almost one fifth (19.5%) of the children reentered within 2 years. Multivariate analyses showed that lower ratings of caregivers' parenting skills and less social support were the strongest predictors of reentry within 12 months of leaving care. Reentry during the second year was linked to the number and severity of the caregiver's problems. Terling (1999) found that 37% of the children reunited with their families in Texas reentered out-of-home care within 3.5 years. Correlates of higher reentry were identified as child maltreatment other than physical abuse, prior child welfare services history, parental incompetence, being non-Hispanic, criminal history, substance abuse, and lack of social support. Notably, child welfare workers' risk assessments were found to be unrelated to reentry. For 33 Oklahoma counties, McDonald, Bryson, and Poertner (2006) studied the relationship between reunification and reentry rates. Consistent with prior research (e.g., Wulczyn, Brunner, & Goerge, 1999), they found a relationship between early reunification (before 6 months) and higher reentry rates, although those counties where a majority of children were reunified very early—within the first 30 days—had lower reentry rates.

Only a few studies have examined reentry in greater depth, using more detailed case readings or collecting observational or interview data, and using a developmental perspective. Frame, Berrick, and Brodowski (2000) examined reunification and reentry among 98 infants in Alameda County, California, and found that maternal criminal history was a key predictor of reentry but found no clear relationship to many other expected predictors, including type of maltreatment, parental visiting, gender, or time in out-of-home care. Miller, Fisher, Fetrow, and Jordan (2006) studied 4- to 7-year-old children who had returned home and then had returned to care after at least 3 months of in-home assessment. The authors found that parental receipt of substance abuse treatment, children's receipt of special education, children's receipt of therapy, overall parent skill, parental use of harsh discipline, and the quality of neighborhood were related to reentry. Festinger's (1996) New York study of 210 children younger than age 15 showed that the situations that resulted in reentry were generally more problematic than others, and that these situations were often characterized by limited parenting skills, poor social support, and a history of mental health and homelessness. Nevertheless, none of these factors could be isolated as significantly different for reentry cases than for nonreentry cases. Miller et al. (2006) studied reentry for young children, aged 4 to 7 years old, reunified from foster care; the authors concluded that key factors—neighborhood characteristics and parenting skills, for example—that are not measurable from administrative data records were associated with failed reunifications.

This next generation of research on reentry does not yet sufficiently approximate consensus to closely guide our current analyses, but the findings do at least suggest possible predictors. Moreover, the contradictory, tentative nature of existing findings may be owing to different dynamics within age groups that were not distinguished, as well as to unmeasured factors that, if included in all the models, would have provided more consistent results. Insufficient power also likely reduced chances of identifying significant factors.

Data Set Characteristics, Test Variables, and Goals

The current study offers many advantages over previous studies that rely mainly on administrative data. The analyses, in addition to relying on the rich set of survey data on family and child characteristics, are stratified by the age group of the child. Because children enter foster care for different reasons that depend largely on age, with different types of permanency outcomes, we conceptualize age group as a proxy for the child's stage of development and, to some extent, as a proxy for the developmental challenges confronted by the parents, substitute caregivers, and child welfare workers. Although other chapters in Part 3 of this volume focus on outcome differences by child and case characteristics, such as the child's race/ ethnicity or the placement type, many prior analyses have shown that differences among age groups go far in explaining child welfare service outcomes (e.g., Berrick, Needell, Barth, & Jonson-Reid, 1998; Kohl & Barth, 2007; Wulczyn, Barth, Yuan, Jones Harden, & Landsverk, 2005), and more recent literature suggests the necessity of age groups as an organizing framework for permanency analyses (Wildfire et al., 2007).

The rationale for the use of age as a predictor is informed by many factors— especially the child's changing vulnerability to harm from maltreatment, with younger children risking more morbidity and mortality from maltreatment than older children. The reasons for involvement with child welfare services also change, with more reports for physical abuse and failure to supervise (supervisory neglect) and a higher preponderance of clinical levels of behavior problems emerging for older children. These changes mean a likely change in the makeup of families involved with child welfare. In Testa and colleagues' conceptual map (Chapter 6), these age differences link to changes in the child's world and to society's expectations for children of different ages. For younger children the expectation is primarily that the child will be safe and have a family to provide for him or her, whereas for older children society also expects that the child will not do harm to himself or herself or others and will develop habits that increase the ultimate likelihood of his or her growing into a self-sufficient adult.

For these analyses we have identified zero to 6 months as infancy, because these very young children tend to have unique circumstances when they enter care and leave care (Wulczyn et al., 2005). In addition, these infants are the most vulnerable to homicide and to childhood death; require the closest, most continual care from their parents; and are least likely to be involved with daycare or other services. At this age they are almost completely dependent on the *bonding social capital* of their families, because they have not yet entered the world in which *bridging social capital*—in the form of community services—becomes more salient.

Children 7 months to 2 years old are becoming toddlers. This is still a period of substantial dependency and vulnerability for children and the period when verbal behavior and physical mobility emerge. This period typically ends at the time that children are walking and expressing their independence. Depending on the policy and service framework, children may be engaged, by this time, in daycare, early intervention services, or other activities that bridge their family's resources with society's broader offerings. Many children in his age group will not have these experiences unless a reason exists for specialized interventions.

Between age 3 and 5 is the preschool period, when children are becoming still more independent in their self-care and becoming increasingly involved with other services (e.g., Head Start and daycare) and peers. At this age we see high rates of child abuse reports that do not result in ongoing services or placement into foster care (Wulczyn et al., 2005), perhaps because more universal service mechanisms yield reports but also yield more resources to protect the children in their own homes.

Between the years of 6 and 10, children's primary new developmental task is to engage successfully with school and to balance the expectations and responsibilities of family, school, and peers. By age 11 or somewhat older, children are transitioning to a second stage of independence, reaching beyond parent and school supervision and facing exposure to choices that may result in antisocial or high-risk behaviors.

Although we adopt a developmental perspective for our current study, we do not adhere closely to any particular developmental theory for the selection of variables or the interpretation of models. The developmental perspective serves instead to generate hypotheses about what may be occurring within an age group. Developmentalists from different theoretical perspectives will likely explain results in their own terms. For example, Dozier and Fisher come from different theoretical perspectives—social learning theory and attachment theory, respectively—but have collaborated to explain and change the parenting of young children in foster care (Dozier, Albus, Fisher, & Sepulveda, 2002).

Because our analyses are of case outcomes, which are determined by many factors other than child development or even family characteristics, most determining factors are unmeasured here, including, among others, local interpretations of policies; availability of quality services; organizational capacity and resources; child welfare services traditions and customs; child welfare worker training and practice; extended family support; and caregiver–child interactions. Although some developmental and contextual models are almost sufficiently complex to conceptualize the impact of these factors on child development (e.g., Sameroff & McKenzie, 2003; Zielinski & Bradshaw, 2006), previous work on which to build our modeling of the influences of these factors on case outcomes is limited.

Our data come from the National Survey of Child and Adolescent Well-Being (NSCAW), the first longitudinal national probability study of the well-being of children reported to child protective services because of alleged child maltreatment. The size of the NSCAW out-of-home care sample used here does not match the size reported previously (e.g. Wildfire, Barth, & Green, 2007), because a special definition of *out-of-home care* was developed for the current analysis. Children included were those whom child welfare workers reported as being placed out of home within 6 months of initial contact with child welfare services. Those children who returned home within 14 days of out-of-home placement or who were in out-of-home placement for fewer than 30 days and in emergency shelters were not included in the reunification denominator. Children who were reported as living with kin but who were not reported as being in child welfare custody were not considered to be in an out-of-home placement. The number of children meeting our out-of-home placement definition was 1,166.

Children were *reunified* if they experienced a placement out of home and then a placement defined as *in home*. Children reportedly living in a parent's home were considered to be in home, as were children who reportedly were living with kin but were not in child welfare custody. *Time in out-of-home care* was defined as the time between the beginning of the out-of-home placement and the time of the first subsequent in-home placement, regardless of any other, intervening types of placement. All 1,166 child maltreatment cases were used for the reunification analysis, missing data having been imputed with the use of MPlus. For the reentry analysis only 526 of the total of 710 cases of children found to have reentered care were used, because missing data were not imputed for this analysis.

The NSCAW data collected in four waves spanning 36 months indicate that about 10% of children who come into contact with child welfare services enter out-of-home care immediately after the child maltreatment investigation. Prior reunification analyses of children entering out-of-home care have helped clarify the likelihood of reunification 18 months after investigation, raising new hypotheses about age-based differences. Children 6 to 10 years of age are more likely to experience reunification than other age groups. During the first 18 months after the close of the investigation, children initially placed in nonkinship foster care were found to be almost five times as likely to reunify with parents as children initially placed with kin, whereas children with a borderline or clinical Child Behavior Checklist (CBCL; Achenbach, 1991b) or whose caregivers were active substance users were significantly less likely to return home (Wildfire et al., 2007). The relationship between reunification and gender, mental health problems (as reflected by the CBCL), and the cumulative risk score differs by race for this age group. Children of other races and white male children are more likely to return to their own homes than white female children. Similarly, children of other races, regardless of CBCL and cumulative risk score, are more likely to be reunified than white females, whereas black or African American children with borderline or clinical CBCL scores are significantly less likely to return home. Testing interactions between these key predictors of reunification will offer additional precision in generating hypotheses that may explain reunification outcomes and inform future policy, program, and practice responses.

Methods

Measures

CHILDREN'S BACKGROUND CHARACTERISTICS Predictor variables included children's ages in months, race/ethnicity, gender, urbanicity, and primary type of abuse—all as reported by the investigative child welfare worker at Wave 1 and by the administrative child welfare worker at Wave 2 (12 months), Wave 3 (18 months), and Wave 4 (36 months).

CHILDREN'S EMOTIONAL AND BEHAVIORAL PROBLEMS The *proportion of clinical scores* was the ratio of the number of instruments with scores in a clinical range to total number of relevant instruments. The clinical assessments used in NSCAW were the Social Skills Rating System (Gresham & Elliott, 1990), the Bayley Infant Neurodevelopmental Screener (Aylward, 1995), the Kaufman Brief Intelligence Test (K-BIT; Kaufman & Kaufman, 1990), the CBCL (Achenbach, 1991b, 1992), the Children's Depression Inventory (CDI; Kovacs, 1992), the Vineland Adaptive Behavior Scales Screener (Sparrow, Carter, & Cicchetti, 1993), the Preschool Language Scale–3 (Zimmerman, Steiner, & Pond, 1992), the Mini Battery of Achievement (Woodcock, McGrew, & Werder, 1994), the Battelle Developmental Inventory (Newborg, Stock, Wnek, Guildubaldi, & Svinicki, 1984), the Youth Self-Report (Achenbach, 1991a), and the Teacher's Report Form (Achenbach, 1991c).

FAMILY RISK FACTORS Risk factors for the family from which the child was removed were captured in indicators for prior child welfare involvement; parental depression as measured by the self-reported Composite International Diagnostic Interview (CDI; World Health Organization, 1990); substance abuse by the primary or secondary caregiver; recent arrest; current domestic violence; harsh, neglectful, and severely violent parenting as measured by the Conflict Tactics Scales Parent to Child (CTS-PC; Straus, 2001); and a cumulative risk score of risk that characterized the family as *low risk* or *medium to high risk*. Additional family risk measures included an indicator for parental monitoring of the child, as reported by children aged 10 or older, as well as an indicator for alcohol or drug abuse by primary or secondary caregivers, as identified by the child welfare worker at baseline. Initial placement type and reentry information were reported by the child welfare worker.

PLACEMENT AND REENTRY The child welfare worker reported the child's initial placement type and any reentry to out-of-home care.

Analyses

The reunification analysis involved factors affecting the hazard rate or likelihood of the first reunification, after children's first out-of-home placement, within a 36-month period. We report hazards ratios (HRs), which can be interpreted as likelihood of reunification as compared with the reference group. We follow the convention of reporting the 95% confidence interval (CI), which provides a conservative test of the significance of the HR by checking whether the 95% CI covers the value of one (i.e., the threshold for inferring no difference from the reference group).

A sizable number of observations had some missing data on model covariates. Observations with missing information are included in the Cox proportional hazards models, with use of maximum likelihood for missing data (Arbuckle, 1996). This method results in consistent estimates, on the assumption that information is missing at random as conditioned on the variables in the model. Retaining all observations maximizes the observed information used in the analysis and requires less assumption than case-wise deletion, which assumes information is missing completely at random. Clustering effects and sampling weights were controlled for.

In the reentry analysis the dependent variable was defined as reentry to out-of-home care after reunification with the family of origin. Placement type was controlled for. The analyses began with examination of bivariate descriptive information on the characteristics of all children who entered out-of-home care and were reunified for two age groups of children: preschool children aged 5 or younger and school-aged children 6 or older. In preparation for multivariate analyses, Cox proportional hazard models were used for each age group to estimate the bivariate relationship between risk of reentry into out-of-home care and each child or family risk factor and placement. A significant relationship indicated the need to include a specific risk factor or agency/parental postreferral action in multivariate models that assessed the relationship between background factors and reentry. Multivariate Cox proportional HRs were modeled separately for the two age groups, estimating the relative risk of reentry at any time within the 36 months for children with different characteristics and risk factors while controlling for time to reunification. Factors included in the multivariate model were identified through significance tests of the bivariate analyses; critical theoretical factors identified by previous research were included. Because the sample is the result of a complex, multilevel sampling design, all analyses were with the use of SUDAAN software (RTI International, 2007).

Results

Reunification for Children Aged Birth to 2 Years

We report the sample characteristics and estimated Cox HRs and 95% CI model for children aged birth to 2 years old at baseline (Table 8.1). Cox regression models test the relationship between the child, family, and placement characteristics and the probability of reunification. These models calculate an HR estimate for each covariate entered into the model. The HR expresses the relative rate of reunification for children with different characteristics as compared to a reference group. For example, the HR estimate of 0.37 for the 57% of children aged birth to 2 years old with high family cumulative risk means that the relative rate of reunification is 63% $(100 - [HR^*100])$ lower than the rate for the 34% of children with medium family risk (the reference group). The inclusion of covariates in the multivariate model

Table 8.1   Sample Characteristics and a Cox Proportional Hazards Model Showing the Main Effect of Predictor Variables on the Hazard Rate of Reunification, Children Aged Zero to 2 Years at Baseline

Variable	Weighted % (SE)	Hazard Ratio (95% CI)	
Age at baseline (0–6 months)	40.85% (3.76)		
7 months to 2 years	59.15% (3.76)	1.39	(0.88, 2.19)
Gender (female)	50.46% (3.30)		
Male	49.54% (3.30)	1.29	(0.79, 2.10)
Race (white)	31.28% (5.38)		
African American	35.11% (5.05)	0.97	(0.48, 1.95)
Hispanic	23.72% (5.03)	1.20	(0.56, 2.56)
Other	9.88% (2.66)	1.42	(0.59, 3.39)
Urbanicity (nonurban)	12.24% (4.60)		
Urban	87.76% (4.60)	1.15	(0.57, 2.30)
Initial placement type (foster care)	28.52% (4.18)		
In home[†]	33.6% (4.27)	0.59	(0.33, 1.08)
Kinship care ***	12.47% (2.77)	0.21	(0.10, 0.45)
Group care/other *	25.40% (2.93)	0.61	(0.38, 0.96)
Prior CWS involvement (No)	51.01% (5.56)		
Yes	48.99% (5.56)	0.74	(0.45, 1.22)
Family cumulative risk (medium)	33.73% (4.26)		
Low	9.51% (2.87)	1.69	(0.78, 3.67)
High**	56.76% (4.67)	0.37	(0.21, 0.67)
Primary maltreatment type (physical abuse)	16.61% (3.99)		
Failure to provide	33.13% (3.16)	0.70	(0.40, 1.21)
Failure to supervise	25.18% (3.53)	0.63	(0.34, 1.14)
Sexual abuse and other[†]	25.08% (3.82)	0.52	(0.27, 1.01)
Domestic violence at time of investigation (No)	70.27% (4.81)		
Yes	29.73% (4.81)	1.46	(0.81, 2.61)
Substance abuse of primary or secondary caregiver (No)	40.49% (4.81)		
Yes	59.51% (4.81)	1.48	(0.91, 2.43)
Primary caregiver's recent history of arrests (No)	55.41% (5.17)		
Yes	44.59% (5.17)	1.43	(0.92, 2.22)
Family having trouble paying for basic necessities (No)	45.91% (5.17)		
Yes	54.09% (5.17)	0.87	(0.58, 1.32)
Sample unweighted N	415–511	511	
Weighted % of reunification	49.13%		

Note: Reference groups are shown in parentheses.
*p < .05, [†]p < .1, **p < .01. ***p < .001.
CI, confidence interval; CWS, child welfare service.

calculates the HR while controlling for the relationship of other child and family characteristics to reunification.

The statistically significant HR estimates for other covariates in the model are as follows: Among children younger than 3 years old, the 12% who were initially placed in kinship care and the 25% initially placed in group care and other settings had a significantly lower rate of reunification than the 29% of children initially placed in nonkinship foster care ($p < .001$ and $p < .05$, respectively). The 25% of children who had experienced sexual abuse or other forms of maltreatment had significantly lower rates of reunification than the 17% of children who had experienced physical abuse ($p < .10$).

Reunification for Children Aged 3 to 5 Years

We report the sample characteristics and estimated Cox HRs and 95% CI for the model of reunification for children aged 3 to 5 years old at baseline (Table 8.2). Again, children with high cumulative family risk were much less likely, with a 68% lower rate, to be reunified than children with low to medium cumulative family risk

Table 8.2   Sample Characteristics and a Cox Proportional Hazards Model Showing the Main Effect of Predictor Variables on the Hazard Rate of Reunification, Children Aged 3–5 Years at Baseline

Variable	Weighted % (SE)	Hazard Ratio (95% CI)	
Gender (female)	79.84% (7.85)		
Male	20.16% (7.85)	1.18	(0.45, 3.07)
Race (white)	49.66% (6.37)		
African American	12.45% (4.90)	1.35	(0.39, 4.65)
Hispanic	22.56% (9.80)	1.78	(0.59, 5.36)
Other	15.33% (8.68)	0.69	(0.09, 5.45)
Urbanicity (nonurban)	10.81% (5.16)		
Urban	89.19% (5.16)	0.51	(0.14, 1.88)
Initial placement type (foster care)	17.19% (7.45)		
In home	34.3% (7.12)	0.48	(0.11, 2.11)
Kinship care	36.35% (6.56)	1.06	(0.31, 3.60)
Group care/other	12.16% (6.92)	1.03	(0.11, 9.52)
Prior CWS involvement (No)	47.77% (4.54)		
Yes	52.23% (4.54)	1.00	(0.31, 3.18)
Family cumulative risk (low or medium)	53.34% (6.55)		
High[†]	46.66% (6.55)	0.32	(0.09, 1.15)
Primary maltreatment type (physical abuse)	16.33% (8.76)		
Failure to provide	12.04% (6.84)	0.12	(0.01, 1.57)
Failure to supervise**	55.32% (16.92)	0.10	(0.02, 0.47)
Sexual abuse and others	16.31% (7.85)	1.06	(0.27, 4.16)
Domestic violence at time of investigation (No)	59.38% (14.76)		
Yes	40.62% (14.76)	0.47	(0.13, 1.66)
CBCL Total borderline/clinical (No)[†]	56.98% (6.63)		
Yes	43.02% (6.63)	0.41	(0.15, 1.15)
Substance abuse of primary or secondary caregiver (No)	59.98% (6.63)		
Yes**	40.02% (6.63)	6.64	(1.71, 25.82)

(continued)

Table 8.2 (continued)

Variable	Weighted % (SE)	Hazard Ratio (95% CI)	
Primary caregiver's recent history of arrests (No)	61.51% (12.99)		
Yes	38.49% (12.99)	1.38	(0.30, 6.41)
Family having trouble to pay basic necessities (No)	69.89% (10.17)		
Yes	30.11% (10.17)	1.10	(0.46, 2.61)
Sample unweighted N	102–119	119	
Weighted % of reunification	32.14%		

Note: Reference groups are shown in parentheses.
***$p < .001$, **$p < .01$, *$p < .05$, †$p < .1$.
CBCL, Child Behavior Checklist; CI, confidence interval; CWS, child welfare service.

($p < .05$). Children whose most serious type of maltreatment was supervisory neglect had a 90% lower rate of reunification than children whose primary maltreatment was physical abuse ($p < .01$). The 43% of children with a clinical or borderline score on the CBCL had a 59% lower reunification rate than the reference group ($p < .10$). A somewhat unexpected finding was that children removed from substance-abusing caregivers were almost seven times as likely to be reunified than children of caregivers without substance abuse problems ($p < .01$).

Reunification for Children Aged 6 to 10 Years

Among children aged 6 to10 years old, those with a clinical or borderline score on the CBCL had a 57% lower reunification rate than the reference group ($p < .01$) (Table 8.3). Maltreatment type was also associated with reunification in this age group, with victims of sexual abuse and failure to supervise being significantly less likely to be reunited with their birth families than physical abuse victims. No other HRs surpassed the 95% threshold of statistical significance.

Reunification for Children Aged 11 Years or Older

Demographic factors emerged as significant predictors of reunification rates among older foster children. Male children had a significantly lower reunification rate than female children ($p < .05$) (Table 8.4). Black, or African American, youth and other youth from non-white, non-Hispanic backgrounds were less likely to be reunified than white and Hispanic youth 11 years old or older ($p < .05$). Both prior child welfare involvement and high cumulative family risk were associated with lower likelihood of reunification ($p < .05$ and $p < .10$, respectively). Primary maltreatment type *failure to supervise* and *other* were also associated with a statistically

Table 8.3 Sample Characteristics and a Cox Proportional Hazards Model Showing the Main Effect of Predictor Variables on the Hazard Rate of Reunification, Children Aged 6–10 Years at Baseline

Variable	Weighted % (SE)	Hazard Ratio (95% CI)	
Gender (female)	50.56% (7.58)		
Male	49.44% (7.58)	0.70	(0.34, 1.47)
Race (white)	44.99% (7.92)		
African American	31.2% (7.24)	0.57	(0.23, 1.43)
Hispanic	18.63% (7.46)	1.80	(0.70, 4.61)
Other	5.18% (1.82)	1.29	(0.45, 3.74)
Urbanicity (nonurban)	12.56% (5.81)		
Urban	87.44% (5.81)	1.11	(0.48, 2.57)
Initial placement type (foster care)	19.26% (4.75)		
In-home	48.65% (7.56)	1.66	(0.82, 3.37)
Kin care	16.77% (5.11)	1.15	(0.65, 2.05)
Group care/other	15.33% (4.72)	0.54	(0.17, 1.67)
Prior CWS involvement (No)	45.26% (7.91)		
Yes	54.74% (7.91)	0.90	(0.53, 1.53)
Family cumulative risk (low or medium)	44.82% (8.13)		
High	55.18% (8.13)	1.26	(0.70, 2.28)
Primary maltreatment type (physical abuse)	36.82% (8.43)		
Sexual abuse[†]	11.29% (3.20)	0.37	(0.13, 1.06)
Failure to provide	17.96% (3.83)	0.74	(0.39, 1.42)
Failure to supervise*	23.92% (6.10)	0.34	(0.13, 0.91)
Others	10.02% (3.15)	0.99	(0.34, 2.86)
Domestic violence at time of investigation (No)	74.38% (6.25)		
Yes	25.62% (6.25)	0.55	(0.15, 1.93)
CBCL total borderline/clinical (No)	44.03% (7.31)		
Yes[**]	55.97% (7.31)	0.43	(0.26, 0.72)
Substance abuse of primary or secondary caregiver (No)	57.49% (6.81)		
Yes	42.51% (6.81)	1.33	(0.71, 2.50)
Primary caregiver's recent history of arrests (No)	75.47% (5.37)		
Yes	24.53% (5.37)	0.49	(0.19, 1.26)
Family having trouble to pay basic necessities (No)	51.89% (7.40)		
Yes	48.11% (7.40)	1.52	(0.79, 2.92)
Sample unweighted N	217–266	266	
Weighted % of reunification	55.36%		

Note: Reference groups are shown in parentheses.

***$p < .001$, **$p < .01$, *$p < .05$, [†]$p < .1$.

CBCL, Child Behavior Checklist; CI, confidence interval; CWS, child welfare service.

significant reduction in reunification rates ($p < .05$). Children who visited with their mothers less often than once a month had reunification rates much lower than children who visited with their mothers one or more times per month ($p < .05$ for both).

Table 8.4 Sample Characteristics and a Cox Proportional Hazards Model Showing the Main Effect of Predictor Variables on the Hazard Rate of Reunification, Children Aged 11+ Years at Baseline

Variable	Weighted % (SE)	Hazard Ratio (95% CI)	
Gender (female)	55.10% (6.44)		
Male*	44.9% (6.44)	0.50	(0.25, 1.00)
Race (white)	39.54% (7.97)		
African American**	42.02% (8.43)	0.36	(0.17, 0.75)
Hispanic	13.39% (5.29)	0.57	(0.20, 1.59)
Other†	5.04% (1.53)	0.57	(0.32, 1.02)
Urbanicity (nonurban)	14.74% (5.09)		
Urban	85.26% (5.09)	1.36	(0.63, 2.95)
Initial placement type (foster care)	21.55% (6.70)		
In home	48.08% (7.43)	1.24	(0.45, 3.43)
Kinship care	6.26% (1.92)	0.90	(0.20, 4.00)
Group care/other	24.12% (5.38)	0.62	(0.25, 1.53)
Prior CWS involvement (No)	38.55% (7.07)		
Yes*	61.45% (7.07)	0.48	(0.26, 0.89)
Cumulative family risk (low or medium)	42.47% (7.14)		
High†	57.53% (7.14)	2.12	(0.96, 4.68)
Primary maltreatment type (physical abuse)	27.88% (6.91)		
Sexual abuse	14.10% (3.66)	0.51	(0.20, 1.34)
Failure to provide	14.87% (6.20)	0.42	(0.13, 1.38)
Failure to supervise*	29.76% (5.36)	0.46	(0.22, 0.96)
Others*	13.40% (3.77)	0.27	(0.09, 0.85)
Domestic violence at time of investigation (No)	82.95% (3.74)		
Yes	17.05% (3.74)	1.14	(0.50, 2.64)
CBCL total borderline/clinical (No)	48.98% (7.09)		
Yes	51.02% (7.09)	1.04	(0.47, 2.28)
Substance abuse of primary or secondary caregiver (No)	71.37% (4.57)		
Yes	28.63% (4.57)	0.66	(0.35, 1.25)
Primary caregiver's recent history of arrests (No)	81.74% (3.78)		
Yes	18.26% (3.78)	1.66	(0.58, 4.78)
Family having trouble to pay basic necessities (No)	68.73% (4.98)		
Yes	31.27% (4.98)	1.00	(0.47, 2.12)
Child placed in new neighborhood (No)	12.56% (2.89)		
Yes	87.44% (2.89)	0.68	(0.30, 1.53)
Child's frequency to see mother (1+ times per month)	59.24% (9.31)		
Never or once a month**	40.76% (9.31)	0.20	(0.07, 0.62)
Self-reported delinquent behavior (1–9 counts)	15.99% (2.79)		
None	52.06% (7.18)	0.71	(0.34, 1.49)
10 counts or more	31.96% (7.59)	0.80	(0.34, 1.89)
Sample unweighted N	204–270	270	
Weighted % of reunification	44.34%		

Note: Reference groups are shown in parentheses.

*p < .05, †p < .1, **p < .01, ***p < .001.

CBCL, Child Behavior Checklist; CI, confidence interval; CWS, child welfare service.

Statistically Significant Main Effects on Reunification Across Age Groups

Although significant contributors to reunification varied across age groups, the effect of maltreatment retained its significance across all age groups (Table 8.5). Family cumulative risk was also significant in three of the four age groups, but the direction of the effect changed with increasing age: Higher cumulative risk was associated with lower reunification rates for children younger than 6 years old but was associated with higher reunification rates in the oldest group. A clinical or borderline CBCL score had a significant negative influence on reunification among the 3–5 year olds and 6–10 year olds. Substance abuse by caregivers was associated with reunification only for the 3–5 years olds: Children in this age group with a parent substance abuser were, unexpectedly, much more likely to reunify than those without a parent substance abuser. Prior child welfare services involvement mattered only in the oldest age group, and initial placement type mattered only in the youngest age group. Apparently, previous findings on the lower rates of reunification after kinship care (Wildfire et al., 2007) apply largely to infants under the care of grandparents, aunts, uncles, and other kin. The demographic characteristics of gender and race emerged as significant predictors only in the oldest age group.

Table 8.5 Summary of Significant Factors Affecting Reunification (Main Effects)

	Age 0–2 Years	Age 3–5 Years	Age 6–10 Years	Age 11+ Years
Age at baseline		NA	NA	NA
Gender				*
Race				**
Urbanicity				
Initial placement type	***			
Prior CWS involvement				*
Cumulative family risk	**	†		†
Primary maltreatment type	†	**	*	*
Domestic violence at time of investigation				
CBCL total borderline/clinical	NA	†	**	
Substance abuse of primary or secondary caregiver		**		
Primary caregiver's recent history of arrests				
Family having trouble paying for basic necessities				
Child placed in new neighborhood	NA	NA	NA	
Child's frequency to see mother	NA	NA	NA	**
Self-reported delinquent behavior	NA	NA	NA	

***$p < .001$, **$p < .01$, *$p < .05$, +$p < .1$, based on the p value of adjusted Wald F.

CBCL, Child Behavior Checklist; CI, confidence interval; CWS, child welfare service; NA, not applicable.

Reentry Risk Factors for Children Aged Zero to 5 Years

Among the reunified children aged 5 or younger, well more than half (59.5%) were male (Table Table 8.6). White, non-Hispanic children made up the largest racial/ethnic group among young children, with 38.4% of the sample, while 29.6% of children were black, non-Hispanic; 23.6% were Hispanic; and 8.4% were identified as "other." Among children aged 5 or younger, the average age was 34.9 months (2.9 years). The majority (87.0%) of younger children lived in an urban setting. The majority (68.6%) who were reunified by the 36-month mark had neglect as their most serious maltreatment type, while 24.9% were physically abused, 0.7% were sexually abused, and 5.8% had another type of abuse reported as the primary type

Table 8.6 Descriptive Statistics of All Children in NSCAW Study Sample Who Reunified With Parents Within 36 Months

Variable	Study Sample of All Reunified (OOH-IH) Children		Reunified Children in Study Sample Ages 0 Through 5		Reunified Children in Study Sample Ages 6 Through 15	
	Unweighted n	Weighted %	Unweighted n	Weighted %	Unweighted n	Weighted %
Sample	710	100%	369	100.00%	341	100.00%
Age (in months) [Mean (SE)]	88.29 (4.13)		34.85 (3.58)		125.79 (3.54)	
0–6 years old	416	49.17%	369	100.00%	0	0%
7–15 years old	294	50.83%	0	0%	341	100.00%
Race						
White/non-Hispanic	262	40.05%	114	38.37%	148	41.22%
Black/non-Hispanic	265	33.91%	155	29.64%	110	36.90%
Hispanic	124	19.25%	66	23.62%	58	16.19%
Other	58	6.79%	33	8.36%	25	5.69%
Gender						
Male	380	57.30%	211	59.46%	169	55.79%
Female	330	42.70%	158	40.54%	172	44.21%
Urbanicity						
Urban	606	84.59%	323	86.95%	283	82.93%
Nonurban	104	15.41%	46	13.05%	58	17.07%
Primary type of abuse						
Physical abuse	143	31.33%	60	24.90%	83	35.56%
Sexual abuse	62	4.85%	7	0.66%	55	7.60%
Neglect	382	52.89%	231	68.60%	151	42.54%
Other	53	10.94%	24	5.84%	29	14.31%
CBCL total score						
Normal	223	53.37%	78	51.73%	145	54.06%
Borderline/clinical	238	46.63%	47	48.27%	191	45.94%
Proportion of clinical scores [Mean (SE)]	0.29 (0.02)		0.29 (0.04)		0.29 (0.04)	
Prior child welfare involvement						

Table 8.6 (continued)

Prior involvement	316	54.90%	139	45.81%	177	61.17%
No prior involvement	306	45.10%	181	54.19%	125	38.38%
Caregiver substance abuse at baseline						
Substance abuse	320	30.92%	183	39.70%	137	24.76%
No substance abuse/ don't know	390	69.08%	186	60.30%	204	74.24%
Parent arrested						
Parent arrested	107	21.57%	63	22.74%	44	20.96%
Parent not arrested/ don't know	603	78.43%	306	77.26%	297	79.04%
Domestic violence at baseline						
Domestic violence reported at baseline	203	24.41%	107	29.33%	96	20.96%
No domestic violence	507	75.59%	262	70.67%	245	79.04%
High monitoring	89	39.24%	0	0.00%	89	39.24%
Family risk						
Low/medium risk	314	59.22%	180	67.69%	134	53.47%
High risk	353	40.78%	160	32.31%	193	46.53%
Child's initial setting						
In-home	290	60.14%	155	55.62%	135	63.34%
Foster care	229	23.43%	134	30.47%	95	18.44%
Kinship care	142	12.11%	72	13.20%	70	11.34%
Group/residential	38	4.32%	6	0.71%	32	6.88%
Time in OOH care prior to initial reunification (in months) [Mean (SE)]	11.93 (2.00)		10.51 (0.84)		12.93 (3.41)	
Reentry						
Reentry in OOH care	157	18.04%	76	15.85%	81	19.57%
No reentry into OOH care	553	81.96%	293	84.15%	260	80.43%
Time to reentry (in months) [Mean (SE)]	8.89 (1.37)		10.14 (2.88)		7.92 (1.53)	
Time to reentry (in months) (Median)	4.56		4.61		4.52	
Time to reentry (in months)						
0–2	40	28.38%	22	35.45%	18	24.36%
3–5	49	23.25%	23	16.48%	26	27.10%
6–11	29	21.91%	17	20.16%	12	22.90%
12–17	19	10.09%	3	3.19%	16	14.02%
18–23	10	6.29%	5	8.15%	5	5.24%
24–29	5	1.20%	3	1.45%	2	1.06%
30–35	5	8.88%	3	15.14%	2	5.33%

CBCL, Child Behavior Checklist; NSCAW, National Survey of Child and Adolescent Well-Being; OOH, out-of-home care.

of abuse. The Total Problems CBCL score indicated that behavior problems were at a borderline or clinical level at baseline for about half (48.3%) of the children aged 2 to 5 years.[2] The average proportion of clinical scores was 0.29 ($SE = 0.04$) for children aged 5 or younger. At baseline, 45.8% of the families of the reunified children aged zero to 5 years had previous child welfare involvement. Caregivers experienced a substantial number of family risk factors as well. The overall cumulative risk for the family was considered high for about one in three (32.3%) of the families of the younger children, while 67.7% of the children had low or medium family risk.

Although all the children in the sample were in out-of-home care and reunified at some point during the 36-month study period, they differed with regard to their initial placement types. For children between birth and 5 years old, more than half (55.6%) were initially left in home, while almost a third (30.5%) were placed in nonkinship foster care, more than one tenth (13.2%) were placed in kinship care, and 0.7% were placed in group or residential homes. For children aged 5 or younger, the average time spent in out-of-home care before reunification was 10.5 ($SE = 0.84$) months. Almost one fifth (15.8%) of the reunified children aged 5 or younger reentered out-of-home care within 36 months. When reentry did occur, it was often soon after reunification—more than one third (35.4%) of the reentries occurring in the first 2 months. The average time for young children to reenter out-of-home care was 10.1 ($SE = 2.9$) months after reunification, with a median time to reentry of 4.6 months.

Reentry Factors for Children Aged 6 Years or Older

Among children aged 6 years or older, well more than half (55.8%) of those reunified were male (see Table 8.6). The largest racial/ethnic group was white, non-Hispanic (41.2%), whereas 36.9% were black, non-Hispanic; 16.2% were Hispanic; and 5.7% were identified as "other." Among older children whose ages ranged from 6 to 15 years, the average age was 125.8 ($SE = 3.4$) months, or about 9 years of age, on entering the study. The majority (82.9%) of these older reunified children lived in an urban setting. The most common primary maltreatment type was neglect (42.5%), while 35.6% were physically abused, 14.3% suffered an abuse type other than physical or sexual, and 7.6% were sexually abused. The Total Problems CBCL score indicated that behavior problems were at a borderline or clinical level at baseline for almost half (45.9%) of these children. The proportion of clinical scores was 0.4 for children aged 6 years or older, meaning that they had a score in the clinical range on about one of every three assessments; most had at least one score in the clinical range. According to a baseline risk assessment, the majority (61.2%) of the families of the reunified children aged 6 or older had previous child welfare involvement. The overall cumulative risk for the family was considered high for almost half (46.5%). Almost one quarter (24.8%) had a primary or secondary caregiver with a substance abuse problem at baseline; 21% had caregivers with a recent history of arrest.

Among older children who were reunified, almost three fourths (63.3%) were initially left in home, while 18.4% were placed in nonkinship foster care, 11.3% were placed in kinship care, and 6.9% were placed in group or residential homes. The average spent in out-of-home care before reunification was 12.9 ($SE = 3.4$) months. Approximately one fifth (19.6%) of the reunified children aged 6 or older reentered out-of-home care within 36 months. The average time for older children to reenter out-of-home care was 7.9 ($SE = 1.5$) months, with a median time to reentry of 4.5 months.

Statistically Significant Main Effects on Reentry Across Age Groups

Of the 710 children who were reunified with a parent or relative after an out-of-home placement, 22.1% subsequently reentered out-of-home care within the 36-month study period. Among preschool children, 15.9% reentered out-of-home care; among children aged 6 years or older, 19.6% reentered (see Table 8.6).

Although most of the bivariate relationships between each child-specific, familial, and agency/parent postreferral factor and the time to reentry to out-of-home care were not statistically significant, several factors emerged as potentially important predictors for inclusion in the multivariate analyses. Among the preschoolers, primary type of maltreatment was significant ($p < .05$): Younger children with a report of sexual abuse had a HR of 2.54, indicating that they who were sexually abused had a hazard for reentry into out-of-home care that was between two and three times the risk for children who were physically abused. Additionally, children removed for protective reasons other than abuse or neglect had an HR of 2.59, meaning that they also had a hazard of reentry into out-of-home care that was between two and three times the risk for physically abused children. No other bivariate relationships were statistically significant for this age group.

For children aged 6 to 15, most of the child-specific, familial, and agency/parent postreferral factors again were not significantly related to the hazard of reentry; however, children with a higher proportion of clinical scores were more likely to reenter care ($p = .05$). Both borderline or clinical CBCL scores and prior involvement with child welfare were statistically significant at the .10 level. Older children with borderline or clinical CBCL scores had an HR of 2.57, indicating a risk of reentry between two and three times the reentry rate for children with CBCL scores in the normal range. Similarly, children without prior child welfare involvement had an HR of 2.24, indicating that children not previously known to child welfare services had a risk of reentry into out-of-home care that was more than two times that for children with previous involvement with child welfare services, perhaps because child welfare agencies are willing to take greater chances on reunification with children previously unknown to child welfare services.

We report the results of the multivariate Cox proportional hazard model for children aged 5 or younger (Table 8.7). Factors in the multivariate model included the significant factor from the bivariate analysis (primary type of maltreatment) and demographic factors, such as age, gender, race/ethnicity, and urbanicity. The theoretically based factors of proportion of clinical scores, prior child welfare involvement, caregiver substance abuse, parent arrest, domestic violence, initial placement type, and time in out-of-home care before reunification were also included. Total Problems CBCL score was dropped from the analysis because the scores were available for only the narrow age band of 3–5 year olds. When we controlled for all other variables, child maltreatment type and time in out-of-home care before reunification were the only statistically significant factors predicting reentry. Children aged 5 years or younger who were removed primarily for reasons of neglect had an HR of 2.39, indicating that the hazard for reentry into out-of-home care after reunification was for these children more than twice that for children whose primary maltreatment type was physical abuse. Additionally, younger children whose most serious type of maltreatment was other than abuse or neglect were much less likely to reenter than children who had been physically

Table 8.7   Hazard Ratio and Significance of Cox Regression Model for Time to Reentry for Children Ages Birth Through 5 Years

Variable: Reference Category	Hazard Ratio	p value
Unweighted n's	302	
Age (in months)	0.99	.61
Race: white/non-Hispanic	1	.09
Black/non-Hispanic	0.56	
Hispanic	1.01	
Other	2.47	
Gender: male	0.89	.84
Urbanicity: nonurban	1.45	.67
Primary type of abuse: physical abuse	1	.00***
Sexual abuse	0.00	
Neglect	9.48	
Other	7.60	
Proportion of clinical scores	1.29	.78
Prior child welfare involvement: no involvement	1.31	.64
Caregiver substance abuse: no/don't know	0.74	.23
Parent arrest: no/ don't know	0.77	.74
Domestic violence at baseline: no/don't know	1.02	.97
Family risk: high risk	1.11	.89
Initial placement: in-home	1	.50
Foster home	2.66	
Kinship care	1.55	
Group/residential	1.17	
Time in OOH care prior to reunification	0.91	.02*

Note: The model becomes overspecified with the inclusion of severe parenting variables, parental monitoring, and CIDI depression variables, so these were excluded from the model.
***$p < .001$, *$p < .05$.
OOH, out-of-home.

abused. The finding that a longer time in care before reunification was significantly related to reduction of reentry rates is consistent with prior research.

Factors in the multivariate model for children 5 or older included the significant and marginally significant factors from the bivariate analysis (proportion of clinical scores, CBCL score, prior child welfare involvement), as well as demographic and theoretically based factors, such as age, gender, race/ethnicity, urbanicity, primary type of maltreatment, caregiver substance abuse, parent arrest, domestic violence, overall family risk, initial placement type, and time in out-of-home care before reunification. When we controlled for all other variables, initial placement type was the only significant ($p < .01$) factor predicting reentry into out-of-home care for children aged 6 years or older (Table 8.8).

Children aged 6 or older with an initial placement in foster homes had an HR of 3.53, indicating that the hazard for reentry into out-of-home care after reunification for children initially placed in foster homes was between three and four times the hazard rate for children whose initial "placement" was in their original home. Older children initially placed in kinship care had an HR of 0.44, meaning

Table 8.8   Hazard Ratio and Significance of Cox Regression Model for Time to Reentry for Children Ages 6 Years and Older

Variable: Reference Category	Hazard Ratio	p Value
Unweighted *n*'s	282	
Age (in months)	1.01	.11
Race: white/non-Hispanic	1	.17
Black/non-Hispanic	0.30	
Hispanic	0.48	
Other	0.83	
Gender: male	0.68	.52
Urbanicity: nonurban	0.42	.18
Primary type of abuse: physical abuse	1	.32
Sexual abuse	0.99	
Neglect	0.69	
Other	2.57	
CBCL score: borderline/clinical	1.36	.67
Proportion of clinical scores	1.33	.82
No prior child welfare involvement: involvement	2.00	.14
Caregiver substance abuse: no/don't know	1.61	.31
Parent arrest: no/don't know	0.80	.77
Domestic violence at baseline: no/don't know	0.80	.64
Family risk: high risk	0.58	.26
Initial placement: In-home	1	.01**
Foster home	3.53	
Kinship care	0.44	
Group/residential	0.72	
Time in OOH care prior to reunification	0.98	.25

Note: The model becomes overspecified with the inclusion of severe parenting variables, parental monitoring, and CIDI depression variables, so these were excluded from the model.
**$p < .01$.

OOH, out-of-home.

children aged 6 or older with an initial placement in kinship care had a hazard of reentry into out-of-home care after reunification that was significantly lower than the hazard for children initially left in home. Finally, older children initially placed in a group or residential setting had an HR of 0.72, indicating that these children had a hazard of reentry into out-of-home care that was 28% less than the hazard for those children initially placed in home. The finding on the significantly lower rate of reentry for children discharged home from kinship foster care is consistent with past research.

Discussion

Our findings on reunification underscore the limitations of much child welfare policy and practice, which assumes meaningful discussions about child welfare problems can be based on the problems involved (i.e., poverty, substance abuse, or problem behavior) without addressing the development status of the child. For the youngest and oldest children, problem behavior is not related to reunification, but for the middle age groups it is significantly related. A child aged 3 to 10 years old with behavior problems has a significantly lower likelihood of reunification than children without behavior problems. The findings suggest that the relationship between high family risk and reunification is negative for infants, nonsignificant for the middle age groups, and positive for the oldest age group. Perhaps these differences reflect different assessments of child vulnerability at different developmental stages. Although some slight model differences reduce the precision of these comparisons, the design of reunification services should be responsive to the possibility of these age-specific differences.

As with reunification, reentry correlates depend on age. Although our analysis was limited to two age groups, predictors of reentry had little in common across them. For the younger children, risk of reentry to out-of-home placement was associated with maltreatment type (neglected children being at higher risk) and time in care (longer time in care before reunification translating into lower risk). These findings are consistent with a developmental perspective on children who reenter foster care because of high levels of family problems and poverty: These problems of parental incapacity would be particularly expected in the face of very young children's high levels of health, nutritional, and developmental need. Apparently, and consistent with much prior research, children reunified after a shorter time in foster care confront a much larger quality range of home environments than children with lengthier stays. Consequently, some of these home environments are less able to support their safe development after reunification.

Among older children who are reunified and reenter care, initial placement in foster care, as opposed to initial retention in the parental home, is associated with eventual reentry to foster care. Consistent with prior research, initial placement in kinship care appears to be protective against reunified children's return to foster care.

This effect may be partially explained by the selection of less problematic children into kinship care, because children who enter kinship care have distinct characteristics, including fewer developmental and behavioral problems (Barth, Guo, & Green, 2007), when compared with children who enter nonkinship foster care.

A selection effect also may operate on the types of children discharged to parental care. If the selection effect were for less-troubled children to enter kinship care, then one would probably expect to observe a protective effect of kinship care for younger children similar to the one for older children. Because this cross-age effect was not observed in the current study, other explanations are required. Perhaps the kinship care selection process allows for the retention of relatively challenging older children in kin custody. That is, less pressure exists to send children home if they are living with kin; fewer troubled children going home, with probably fewer troubled caregiver–child relationships for those who do return home, yield fewer reentries. That the pattern differs for children in nonkinship foster care suggests that child welfare workers may face more flexible expectations for timely reunification when children are in kinship care than when they are in nonkinship foster care.

Conclusion

These findings expand on the emerging evidence that the implementation of child welfare services varies by age group (Berrick, 1998; Wulczyn et al., 2005) and types of care (Grogan-Kaylor, 2001). Although some commonalities among age groups persist (e.g., maltreatment types), some of the current findings strengthen the argument that analyses failing to recognize or test for the influence of developmental stage or age on case outcomes are unlikely to yield results with precision sufficient for an understanding of any age group.

The child welfare system has made substantial progress in establishing methods to prevent placements into foster care, to adopt children who would otherwise remain in foster care for a lengthy time, and to help older youth make a better transition to adulthood. Reunification is the single slowest area of child welfare services to develop. Indeed, reasonable evidence exists that, while other forms of exit from care increased at the beginning of the twenty-first century, reunification rates have declined (Barth, Wulczyn, & Crea, 2005). Little effort has been made to create a funding mechanism for reunification services or to develop services rooted in the realities of family life. Berrick's (2008) *Take Me Home* does offer important observations about the conditions that families and caseworkers encounter when they try to reintegrate children into the children's parental homes. Moreover, the Oregon Social Learning Center is mapping some of the family dynamics among families with substance abuse problems who are attempting reunification and family-treatment approaches (Miller et al., 2006). Although these efforts to acknowledge and understand the conditions surrounding attempted reunification are promising, they will not prove as useful as they could be—and as they must be to have a safe and fair child welfare program—until financing reform provides as much funding and support for achieving adoption and supporting youth who emancipate as it does for children and families seeking to be safe and together.

NOTES

1. We thank Mark Testa for substantial editorial and analytic work on this chapter.
2. The CBCL was administered only for children aged 2 or older who were placed in out-of-home care and reunified.

REFERENCES

Achenbach, T. M. (1991a). *Integrative guide for the 1991 CBCL/4-18, YSR, and TRF profiles.* Burlington, VT: University of Vermont, Department of Psychiatry.

Achenbach, T. M. (1991b). *Manual for the Child Behavior Checklist/4-18 and 1991 profile.* Burlington, VT: University of Vermont, Department of Psychiatry.

Achenbach, T. M. (1991c). *Manual of the Teacher's Report Form and 1991 Profile.* Burlington, VT: University of Vermont, Department of Psychiatry.

Achenbach, T. M. (1992). *Manual for the Child Behavior Checklist/2-3 and 1992 profile.* Burlington, VT: University of Vermont, Department of Psychiatry.

Arbuckle, J. L. (1996). Full information estimation in the presence of incomplete data. In G. A. Marcoulides & R. E. Schumacker (Eds.), *Advanced structural equation modeling: Issues and techniques* (pp. 243–277). Hillsdale, NJ: Erlbaum.

Aylward, G. P. (1995). *Bayley Infant Neurodevelopmental Screener.* San Antonio, TX: Psychological Corporation.

Barth, R. P., Courtney, M. E., Berrick, J. D., & Albert, V. (1994). *From child abuse to permanency planning: Child welfare services pathways and placements.* New York: Adeline De Gruyter.

Barth, R. P., Guo, S., & Green, R. L. (2007). Developmental outcomes for children in kinship and nonkinship care: Findings from the National Survey of Child and Adolescent Well-Being. In R. Haskins, F. Wulczyn, & M. B. Webb (Eds.), *Child protection research from the National Survey of Child and Adolescent Well-Being* (pp. 187–206). Washington, DC: Brookings Institution.

Barth, R. P., Wulczyn, F. H., & Crea, T. (2005). From anticipation to evidence: Research on the Adoption and Safe Families Act. *Journal of Law and Social Policy, 12,*371–399.

Berrick, J. D. (1998). When children cannot remain home: Foster family care and kinship care. *Future of Children, 8*(1), 72–87.

Berrick, J. D. (2008). *Take me home: Protecting America's vulnerable children and families.* New York: Oxford University Press.

Berrick, J. D., Needell, B., Barth, R. P., & Jonson-Reid, M. (1998). *The tender years: Toward developmentally sensitive child welfare services.* New York: Oxford University Press.

Connell, C. M., Katz, K. H., Saunders, L., & Tebes, J. K. (2006). Leaving foster care—the influence of child and case characteristics on foster care exit rates. *Children and Youth Services Review, 28,* 780–798.

Courtney, M. E. (1994). Factors associated with the reunification of foster children with their families. *Social Service Review, 69*, 226–241.

Courtney, M. E., McMurtry, S. L., & Zinn, A. (2004). Housing problems experienced by recipients of child welfare services. *Child Welfare, 83*(5), 393–422.

Davis, I., Landsverk, J., Newton, R., & Ganger, W. (1996). Parental visiting and foster care reunification. *Children and Youth Services Review, 18*(4/5), 363–382.

Dozier, M., Albus, K., Fisher, P. A., & Sepulveda, S. (2002). Interventions for foster parents: Implications for developmental theory. *Development and Psychopathology, 14*(4), 843–860.

Eamon, M. K. (2002). *The effect of economic resources on reunification of Illinois children in substitute care.* Urbana, IL: Children and Family Research Center.

Fanshel, D., & Shinn, E. (1978). *Children in foster care: A longitudinal study.* New York: Columbia University Press.

Festinger, T. (1996). Going home and returning to foster care. *Children and Youth Services Review, 18*(4-5), 383–402.

Frame, L., Berrick, J. D., & Brodowski, M. L. (2000). Understanding reentry to out-of-home care for reunified infants. *Child Welfare, 79*(4), 339–369.

Fraser, M., Walton, E., Lewis, R. E., Pecora, P. J., & Walton, W. K. (1996). An experiment in family reunification: Correlates of outcomes at one-year follow-up. *Children & Youth Services Review, 18*(4/5), 335–361.

Goerge, R. M. (1990). The reunification process in substitute care. *Social Service Review, 64*(3), 422–457.

Goerge, R. M., & Lee, B. J. (1998). *Reunification of children in substitute care in Illinois: 1987–1996.* Urbana, IL: Children and Family Research Center.

Gresham, F. M., & Elliott, S. N. (1990). *Social Skills Rating System manual.* Circle Pines, MN: American Guidance Service.

Grogan-Kaylor, A. (2001). The effect of initial placement into kinship foster care on reunification from foster care: A bivariate probit analysis. *Journal of Social Service Research, 27*(4), 1–31.

Harris, M. S., & Courtney, M. E. (2003). The interaction of race, ethnicity, and family structure with respect to the timing of family reunification. *Children and Youth Services Review, 25*(5/6), 409–429.

Hayward, R. A., & DePanfilis, D. (2007). Foster children with an incarcerated parent: Predictors of reunification. *Children and Youth Services Review, 29*(10), 1320–1334.

Hess, P. M., & Folaron, G. (1991). Ambivalences: A challenge to permanency for children. *Child Welfare, 70*(4), 403–424.

Kaufman, A., & Kaufman, N. (1990). *Kaufman Brief Intelligence Test (K-BIT).* Circle Pines, MN: American Guidance Service.

Kohl, P., & Barth, R. P. (2007). Child maltreatment recurrence among children remaining in-home: Predictors of re-reports. In R. Haskins, F. Wulczyn, & M. B. Webb (Eds.), *Child protection: Using research to improve policy and practice* (pp. 207–225). Washington, DC: Brookings Institution.

Kortenkamp, K., Green, R. L., & Stagner, M. (2004). The role of welfare and work in predicting foster care reunification rates for children of welfare recipients. *Children & Youth Services Review, 26*, 577–590.

Kovacs, M. (1992). *Children's Depression Inventory.* North Tonawanda, NY: Multi-Health Systems.

Landsverk, J., Davis, J., Ganger, W., Newton, R., & Johnson, I. (1996). Impact of children psychosocial functioning on reunification from out-of-home placement. *Children and Youth Services Review, 18*(4/5), 447–462.

Leathers, S. (2002). Parental visiting and family reunification: Could inclusive practice make a difference? *Child Welfare, 81*(4), 595–616.

Lu, E. Y., Landsverk, J., Ellis-Macleod, E., Newton, R., Ganger, W., & Johnson, I. (2004). Race, ethnicity, and case outcomes in child protective services. *Children and Youth Services Review, 26*, 447–461.

Marsh, J. C., Ryan, J. P., Choi, S., & Testa, M. (2006). Integrated services for families with multiple problems: Obstacles to family reunification. *Children & Youth Services Review, 28*, 1074–1087.

McDonald, T., Bryson, S., & Poertner, J. (2006). Balancing reunification and reentry goals. *Children and Youth Services Review, 28*(1), 47–58.

Miller, K. A., Fisher, P. A., Fetrow, B., & Jordan, K. (2006). Trouble on the journey home: Reunification failures in foster care. *Children and Youth Services Review, 28*(3), 260–274.

Needell, B., Brookhart, M. A., & Lee, S. (2003). Black children and foster care placement in California. *Children and Youth Services Review, 25*(5/6), 393–408.

Newborg, J., Stock, J. R., Wnek, L., Guildubaldi, J., & Svinicki, J. (1984). *Battelle Developmental Inventory: With recalibrated technical data and norms: Examiner's manual.* Itasca, IL: Riverside.

Risley-Curtiss, C., Stromwall, L. K., Truett Hunt, D., & Teska, J. (2004). Identifying and reducing barriers to reunification for seriously mentally ill parents involved in child welfare cases. *Families in Society, 85*(1), 107–118.

RTI International. (2007). *SUDAAN user's manual, release 9.0.1.* Research Triangle Park, NC: Author.

Sameroff, A. J., & Mackenzie, M. J. (2003). Research strategies for capturing transactional models of development: The limits of the possible. *Development and Psychopathology, 15*(3), 613–640.

Sparrow, S. S., Carter, A. S., & Cicchetti, D. V. (1993). *Vineland Screener: Overview, reliability, validity, administration, and scoring.* New Haven, CT: Yale University Child Study Center.

Stein, T. J., Gambrill, E. D., & Wiltse, K. T. (1978). *Children in foster homes—achieving continuity of care.* New York: Prager Publishers.

Straus, M. A. (2001). *Handbook for the Conflict Tactics Scales (CTS): Including revised versions CTS2 and CTSPC.* Durham, NH: Family Research Laboratory, University of New Hampshire.

Terling, T. (1999). The efficacy of family reunification practices: Reentry rates and correlates of reentry for abused and neglected children reunited with their families. *Child Abuse & Neglect, 23*(12), 1359–1370.

Webster, D., Shlonsky, A., Shaw, T., & Brookhart, M. A. (2005). The ties that bind II: Reunification for siblings in out-of-home care using a statistical technique for examining non-independent observations. *Children & Youth Services Review, 27*, 765–782.

Wells, K., & Guo, S. Y. (1999). Reunification and reentry of foster children. *Children and Youth Services Review, 21*(4), 273–294.

Wildfire, J., Barth, R. P., & Green, R. L. (2007). Predictors of reunification. In R. Haskins, F. Wulczyn, & M. B. Webb (Eds.), *Child protection: Using research to improve policy and practice* (pp. 155–170). Washington, DC: Brookings Institution.

Woodcock, R. W., McGrew, K. S., & Werder, J. K. (1994). *Woodcock-McGrew-Werder Mini-Battery of Achievement*. Itasca, IL: Riverside.

World Health Organization. (1990). *Composite International Diagnostic Interview (CIDI), Version 1.0*. Geneva, Switzerland: World Health Organization.

Wulczyn, F. (2004). Family reunification. *Future of Children, 14*(1), 95–113.

Wulczyn, F., Barth, R. P., Yuan, Y. T., Jones Harden, B., & Landsverk, J. (2005). *Beyond common sense: Child welfare, child well-being, and the evidence for policy reform.* New Brunswick, NJ: Aldine Transaction.

Wulczyn, F., Brunner, K., & Goerge, R. (1999). *An update from the multistate foster care data archive foster care dynamics 1983–1997*: Chapin Hall Center for Children at the University of Chicago.

Zielinski, D. S., & Bradshaw, C. P. (2006). Ecological influences on the sequelae of child maltreatment: A review of the literature. *Child Maltreatment, 11*, 49–62.

Zimmerman, I. L., Steiner, V. G., & Pond, R. E. (1992). *PLS-3: Preschool Language Scale-3* San Antonio, TX: The Psychological Corporation.

9

Racial and Ethnic Diversity in the Initial Child Welfare Experience

Exploring Areas of Convergence and Divergence

ROBERT M. ORTEGA, ANDREW GROGAN-KAYLOR, MARY
RUFFOLO, JENELL CLARKE, AND REBECCA KARB

The child welfare system has weathered controversy about the overwhelming number of children of color entering its services. More than half of maltreated children in out-of-home care are non-white, which represents a sizeable change in the composition of children placed in foster care during the late twentieth century and early twenty-first century (Administration for Children and Families, 2006b; Administration on Children, 2005; Smith & Devore, 2004). The steady wave of immigrant families seeking refuge in the United States adds significantly to the U.S. minority population, especially to those living in poverty (Annie E. Casey Foundation, 2006). Cataclysmic events such Hurricane Katrina on the U.S. Gulf Coast and the terrorist attacks of September 11, 2001, have displaced or disrupted minority families, through loss or separation of parents and other family members, overwhelming human services, including the child welfare system (Administration for Children and Families, 2002; U.S. Government Accountability Office, 2006).

Concepts like *overrepresentation, disproportionality,* and *disparities* have emerged to characterize these families' reliance on such services (Derezotes, Poertner, & Testa, 2005; Hill, 2006). *Overrepresentation* denotes that a particular group of children constitutes a larger proportion in the child welfare system than it does in the general population (Table 9.1). *Disproportionality* characterizes a situation in which a particular racial or ethnic group of children constitutes a higher percentage of those in foster care than other racial or ethnic groups (Hill, 2006). The terms *disproportionate treatment* and *disparities* refer to disparate or inequitable treatment or patterns of service utilization (e.g., in terms of types, quality, availability, and accessibility of services at various decision points).

Table 9.1 Overrepresentation and Disproportionality in Foster Care for the U.S. Child Population

Ethnic Group	No. and Percent of Youth under 18 Years in the U.S. Population*	No. of Youth Placed in Foster Care by Race/ Ethnic Group**	Percent of Child Welfare Population Compared to Their Proportion in the General Population	Percent of Youth Placed Respective to Their Ethnic Population (Disproportionality)	Ratio Comparing Percentages Across Ethnic Groups Provides the Ratio
White	181,732,083 (75%)	208,537	43% (Underrepresented)	.6%	
African American	26,564,524 (11%)	166,482	34% (Overrepresented)	3.1%	Af. Am. over three times more likely than white children to be in foster care
Latino	28,226,834 (12%)	93,996	19% (Overrepresented)	1.6%	Hisp/Lat. slightly more than 1½ times more likely than white children to be in foster care
American Indian	2,007,107 (1%)	10,617	2% (Overrepresented)	1%	NA / AN slightly more than 1½ times more likely than white children to be in foster care
Asian Pacific Islander	2,863,390 (1%)	4,406	1% (No difference)	—	No difference when compared to white children
Total children	241,393,938 (100%)	484,038	100%	—	

* U.S. Census population released Wednesday May 10, 2006; Table 3; Selected age groups for the population by race and Hispanic origin for the United States, July 1, 2005.

** The AFCARS Report: Preliminary FY 2005 estimates as of September 2006 (13). Adoption and Foster Care Analysis and Reporting System (AFCARS) data submitted for the FY 2005, 10/1/04 through 9/30/05. Note: Table omits both Unknown/Unable to Determine and Two or More Non-Hispanic categories

Disparity comparisons are usually made between children of color and similarly situated white children (Courtney et al., 1996).[1]

We want to qualify upfront our position that viewing children of color as monolithic groups is problematic because doing so fails to recognize the variation among these different groups—variation based on a host of differences. Generic race or ethnicity categories fail to differentiate these children, for example, according to ancestry, language, geographic region, economic and immigrant status, generation, and other important sociodemographic characteristics. In many states, as well as national reports, categorizing racial and ethnic minority children further ignores the growing biracial and multiracial ancestry that is a more accurate representation of these children. This lack of clarity and relative diffusion poses a serious challenge to the child welfare system's ability to accurately count and account for the growing number of racial and ethnic minority children in its care (Ortega, Gutierrez-Najera, & Guillean, 1996).

To begin, we summarize the current literature on racial discrepancies in the child welfare population, using the race or ethnicity categories *African American, Latino, American Indian,* and *Asian Pacific Islander American* (APIA). We acknowledge the considerable variation in terminology for race and ethnicity categories; even in this volume, for example, most authors have used terms that correspond to those used in the National Survey on Child and Adolescent Well-Being (NSCAW) data collection. More important, we admittedly proceed at the risk of overgeneralizing membership in racial or ethnic categories and believe strongly in the need to move toward research that is more sensitive to within-group differences.

The literature offers four organizing perspectives for understanding child welfare representation discrepancies between children of color and white children: *(1)* as a matter of social (in)justice, *(2)* in connection with traditional culture, *(3)* as a consequence of child welfare systemic and larger policy decisions, and *(4)* as a consequence of research limitations. Each perspective contributes to an understanding not only of the phenomenon but also of potential consequences and implications for child welfare. Importantly, these perspectives overlap; they are not in reality mutually exclusive—a fact that the field of child welfare will need to confront if it is to fulfill its responsibilities to the increasing number of children of color committed to its care.

A Social (In)justice Perspective

The social (in)justice perspective focuses on ecological, environmental, structural, social, and individual experiences that connect meaning, context, power, and history to overall experience (Finn & Jacobson, 2003). For child maltreatment, relevant discussions focus on disproportionate vulnerability and exposure to risk factors nested along the personal, interpersonal, and social continuum of the human experience. Child maltreatment from a social justice perspective is associated with major personal, interpersonal, and social disadvantages that impair, or result in barriers and obstacles to, effective parenting. High-need children (e.g., those with a complex array of special needs); parents with mental health problems; poor parenting role models; problematic involvement in illegal substances, alcohol, and crime; home instability or homelessness; income instability; exposure to domestic violence; separation or risk of separation from family; parent's incarceration; and the like are all highly correlated both with social inequalities and with child maltreatment. Relevant literature focuses on ecological, environmental, structural, social, and individual experiences that connect meaning, context, power, and history to experience, and similar topics that emphasize the wide range of factors associated with child maltreatment, including living in areas with high concentrations of poverty, high rates of crime and substance abuse, high levels of child maltreatment and displacement, pervasive joblessness, weak informal social networks, inadequate formal support, experience with discrimination, and other community factors that prescribe disadvantage to families and communities in which an overwhelming number of racial and ethnic minority families reside (Hay & Jones, 1994). Conversely, the "visibility hypothesis" suggests that a higher probability exists for racial minority children to be placed in foster care when they live in geographic locations where their proportions in the population are low in comparison with their proportions in other areas (Garland, Ellis-MacLeod, Landsverk, Ganger, & Johnson, 1998; Harris & Courtney, 2003; Jones, 1997).

A power dimension embodies notions that bias, prejudice, discrimination, and racism make the poorest of the poor and particular groups among the poor— single parents, young caregivers, and those with young children—most susceptible to physical violence, poor health care, and other social disadvantages (Hay & Jones, 1994; Jones & McCurdy, 1992; Wrong, 1995). Attention is drawn to decisions made about children and families of color by persons from the majority culture, assumptions made about risks to safety and security, and treatment of children and families of color once their cases are opened to child welfare services (Roberts, 2002).

Historical references to the consequences of power differentials speak to the seemingly inescapable legacy of past experiences that are ideologically organized to place racial and ethnic minority individuals and groups in particular vulnerable contexts and conditions. The American Indian experience, for example, is often recounted in U.S. dominant society as part of past European explorers' heroic discoveries. Educational textbook reconstructions, stereotypes, mascots, and modern dramatizations in the media continue to locate American Indians in roles subservient to the majority culture. Lost in translation is the deeply felt perspective among American Indians of a legacy of genocide and loss of language and culture to the original explorers and colonists of the U.S. continent. The majority culture's traditional version of U.S. history continues to shape the experiences and actions of both majority and racial/ethnic minority members of society.

A Traditional Cultural Parenting Practices Perspective

Another lens on race and ethnic discrepancies in child welfare is the traditional cultural parenting practices perspective. A growing literature is profiling the cultural experiences of different racial and ethnic groups to enhance understanding of child maltreatment and issues involved in addressing it (Caughy & Franzini, 2005; Collier, McClure, Collier, Otto, & Polloi, 1999; Coohey, 2001; Derezotes et al., 2005; Elliot & Urquiza, 2006; Fluke, Yuan, Hedderson, & Curtis, 2003; Futa, Hsu, & Hansen, 2001; Korbin & Spilsbury, 1999; Locke, 1998; Lynch & Hanson, 1998; Meston, Heiman, Trapnell, & Carlin, 1999; Terao, Borrego, & Urquiza, 2001). Korbin (2002) rightly calls for "unpacking" the relationship between cultural practices and maltreatment to account for intra- and intercultural variability. Doing so likely promotes a better understanding of the cultural context for maltreatment and improves on research engaging the relationship between race, ethnicity, culture, and child maltreatment (Roberts, Rule, & Innocenti, 1998).

Studies using this perspective have carefully examined cultural factors and racial and ethnic differences that provide important contexts for considering child rearing and, by extension, child maltreatment. Elliot and Urquiza (2006) emphasize Africentric values and beliefs about family unity (*Umoja*), self-determination (*Kujichagulia*), and collectivism and responsibility (*Ujima*) as essentials upheld by African American families in raising and socializing their children. *Familismo, personalismo,* mutualism, folk beliefs, and fatalism are suggested as most salient among persons of Latino ancestry. References to Latino culture highlight ways families rely on each other more than on nonfamily, which translates into older children's caring for younger siblings, norms of privacy, and low social visibility, especially among immigrant families who remain strongly connected with their country of origin (Hutchins, Ortega, & Quintanilla, in press; Ortega, 2000, 2006). Persons of Asian ancestry are presented as firmly emphasizing filial piety, family representation through achievement, emotional self-control, conformity, collectivism, harmony, and humility (Coalition for Asian American Children and Families, 2001; Futa et al., 2001). Hunt, Gooden, and Barkdull (1999) assert that a true cultural understanding of American Indians involves an acceptance of American Indian values of autonomy, solidarity, competence, spirituality, balance, and wisdom.

A Child Welfare System and Policy Perspective

The child welfare "system," other systems, larger policy enactment, and caseworker decision making have probably garnered the greatest attention in discussions of racial or ethnic discrepancies in child welfare. A wealth of literature focusing on a broad range of explanations, from preentry into foster care, through permanency-planning decisions, to exiting from foster care, and, more recently, to reentry into foster care. Hill (2006) offers an excellent review of issues relevant to caseworker decision making: child maltreatment reporting, investigating, substantiating, placing, and exiting.[2]

System-response concerns include differential criteria for maltreatment substantiation, placement of children of color outside the home and into less desirable environments, differential duration of out-of-home placement, differential referral to the juvenile justice system for behavioral problems, referral to inadequate public-sector social services rather than to private-sector agencies, and lack of in-home or other support services (Barth, Green, & Miller, 2001; Hogan & Sui, 1988; McMurtry & Lie, 1992; Morton, 1999). In terms of service delivery, concerns have been raised about the range and quality of services, service availability and accessibility, and ongoing support for families to prevent further child maltreatment (Brown & Bailey-Etta, 1997). Additional challenges include the low number of adoptive homes and other permanency options, older youth, high rates of need for special services, and other barriers and obstacles that maintain many children of color in temporary substitute care (Courtney et al., 1996).

Child welfare work itself has been associated with discrepancies involving children of color: Large caseload size and inefficiency in caseload management, high caseworker turnover, caseworker bias, insufficient professional training, systemic assumptions governing caseworker–family matches, lack of bilingual or linguistically proficient staff, poor or nonexistent interpreter services, and inaccessibility of other health and human services (e.g., substance abuse treatment) have been identified as key factors (Hill, 2006). Priority of social policies favoring placement rather than family preservation, promoting termination of parental rights over reunification, and sanctioning financial incentives for nonkinship rather than kinship connections reflect larger, institutional forces that should be considered.

A Research Quality Perspective

Research quality offers yet another reason for the discrepant number of children of color in child welfare. Criticisms of research raise concerns about the legitimacy of a focus on "color." Low quality or nonexistence of data, limited geographical scope of studies, scarcity of comprehensive nationwide studies, uneven findings, methodological differences (e.g., differences in the unit of analysis—child, parent, caseworker, foster parents), combination of different source of data (i.e., mixing findings from administrative or cross-sectional data with longitudinal data), inadequate analytic strategies, failure to separate race from socioeconomic status, lack of common definitions, failure to distinguish within-group differences of racial and ethnic groups, lack of acknowledgement of variation of family contextual functioning, failure to account for race or ethnic-specific dynamics (e.g., recentness of migration and geographic location), culturally and linguistically biased data collection instruments, and other problems have been leveled to either discredit or deem suspect causal explanations and implicit assumptions about race. Concern has also been raised about the intersystem relationships such as between child welfare and juvenile justice or mental health that further complicate, and perhaps compromise, a reasonable, more evidence-based understanding since it argues that the matter is not just a "child welfare system" challenge (Barth, Courtney, & Berry, 1994).

Research Agenda for a New, Integrated Perspective

Despite the usefulness of each of these four perspectives, viewing children of color as several homogeneous groups is in itself problematic because generic race or ethnicity categories fail to differentiate these children according to ancestry, language, geographic region, economic and immigrant status, generation, and other important sociodemographic characteristics. Moreover, in many state and national reports, categorizing racial and ethnic minority children ignores the increasingly biracial and multiracial ancestry of these groups of children. This lack of clarity and relative diffusion pose a serious challenge to the child welfare system's ability to accurately count and account for the growing number of racial and ethnic minority children in its care (Ortega et al., 1996).

The field of child welfare needs an alignment of these multiple, intersecting perspectives, one that offers a more reasonable understanding. Rather than searching for ways to disentangle and isolate each strand in the complexity, we suggest a more integrative approach: Does "color" matter? The literature supports a resounding "yes," but the discussion must extend beyond color (Derezotes et al., 2005). Figure 9.1 models the four traditional perspectives, although the dynamic interplay between and among these dimensions, in terms of frequency, duration, intensity, influence, historical impact, and the like, are only implicit.

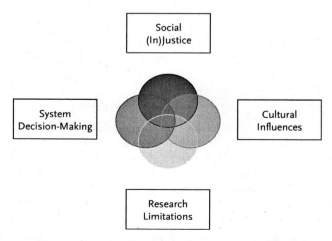

Figure 9.1   Synthesis model of "causes" of overrepresentation and disproportionality.

To address this need for an integrative perspective, we use baseline (Wave 1) data from NSCAW, the first longitudinal U.S. probability study on children referred to the child welfare system because of alleged child maltreatment. Analyzing and synthesizing these data, we offer a high-level perspective on the following questions: What are the sociodemographic characteristics of children of color on entry into the child welfare system? What are these children's primary baseline case characteristics (e.g., substantiation of maltreatment allegations, maltreatment type, placement)? Are individual, interpersonal, and environmental risk factors observed that further distinguish these children from those in different racial and ethnic subgroups? To what extent do these children diverge from and converge with each other in their child welfare profiles, and how do these comparisons help researchers, clinicians, caseworkers, other service providers, and policy makers better understand issues of overrepresentation and disparity? Our aim is to distinguish these children, with respect to sociodemographic or other relevant factors, within their own racial or ethnic subgroups. Engaging those in child welfare policy, research, and planning, we use our findings to enrich important discussions about racial and Latino ethnic differences in this population.

Methods

Measures

In addition to reporting on background characteristics, including racial and ethnic identities, children participated in a Wave 1 assessment for risk factors. Literature supports each of the NSCAW measures as indicating a particular risk affecting children's outcomes: low engagement with school, trauma (Bernard, 2002), childhood depression, poor physical health, community disadvantages, problematic relationship with the caregiver, inadequate monitoring by the caregiver, and caregiver's drug dependence or alcohol dependence (Ammerman & Hersen, 1990; Widom & Hiller-Sturmhofel, 2001; Wooley & Grogan-Kaylor, 2006).

RACIAL AND ETHNIC IDENTITIES Three NSCAW data collection questions asked respondents about their racial and ethnic identities, the first asking whether they considered themselves to be white, black or African American, Asian American, or "other" and allowing multiple categories to be selected. According to NSCAW documentation, "When more than one race was reported by a respondent, the rarest race (of five categories) was assigned, based on 1990 U.S. Census data." Rather than accounting for respondents' full self-identifications, in other words, NSCAW's measure of race included only the *rarest* race group of all that the respondent selected. From rarest to most common, the U.S. Census racial group rankings were American Indian or Alaskan Native; Asian, Native Hawaiian, or other Pacific Islander; black or African American; white; and Other. To capture Latino or Hispanic ethnicity, the child or his or her caregiver was asked whether the child could be considered Hispanic. Those self-identified as Hispanic were then asked the particular region of Latin America from which they derived this ethnic identity.

SCHOOL ENGAGEMENT   The school engagement measure was composed of 11 child-reported items whose options spanned a Likert scale (1 = *never* to 4 = *almost always*). Some of these items asked children whether they enjoyed being in school, whether they completed their homework, and whether they "got along with" teachers and other students. Reliability was .82.

TRAUMA   Children reported their symptoms of anxiety, depression, posttraumatic stress, sexual concerns, dissociation, and anger on the Trauma Symptom Checklist for Children (Briere & Runtz, 1989). The total scale score was the measure of a child's trauma. Reliability was .84. A single item was used to measure children's health: Children reported on their overall health status, using a Likert scale (i.e., excellent, very good, good, fair, poor).

COMMUNITY RISK   On the nine-item Community Environment Scale (Abt Associates, 1996), primary caregivers reported neighborhood risk factors (e.g., presence of gangs, drug involvement, assaults) and neighborhood protective factors (e.g., parent involvement with children, helpfulness of neighbors, feelings of safety). A sum score of the mean of the nine items was developed to measure the overall neighborhood environment. Reliability was .88.

CAREGIVER–CHILD RELATIONSHIP   The caregiver–child relationship was assessed with an eight-item shortened version of the Relatedness Scale from the Rochester Assessment Package for Schools (Connell, 1991; Lynch & Cicchetti, 1991). Children responded to questions that focused on their emotions when they were around their caregiver and on their sense of being loved, trusted, and treated fairly. All eight items were averaged, creating a single score. Reliability was .82.

CAREGIVER'S SUPERVISION   Caregivers' monitoring of their child was assessed on a Likert scale developed by Dishion, Patterson, Stollmiller, & Skinner (1991). Questions addressed how often the child informed his or her caregiver that he or she was leaving, how often the child informed the caregiver where he or she was going and with whom, and how often the caregiver told the child what time to be home or the child told the caregiver what time he or she would be home. Reliability was .65.

CAREGIVER'S DRUG AND ALCOHOL DEPENDENCE   With the World Health Organization's Composite International Diagnostic Interview Short Form (CIDI-SF; Kessler, Andrews, Mroczek, Ustun & Wittchen, 1998), caregivers' alcohol and drug dependence was assessed. Research on the CIDI-SF has supported the test-retest reliability and validity of these scales (Kessler et al., 1998).

Analyses

Analysis of the NSCAW sample requires an array of analytic strategies to capture its complex sampling design and rich data set. Because we are describing these children at baseline, with a focus on race and ethnicity, we often employ simple univariate descriptive statistic, such as tables of means and proportions that use estimators appropriate for the complex survey context. Often we are interested in how an indicator differs for children in different racial or ethnic groups and will employ bivariate statistics, such as comparison means across groups or cross-tabulations. When using these bivariate statistics, we also use estimators that account for the complex survey nature of the sample. Notably, bivariate analyses cannot directly answer complex causal questions like whether racial or ethnic disparities exist in the operation of the child welfare system. Such questions will be answered only by multivariate work that not only accounts for the race and ethnicity of children involved with the child welfare system but also controls for the differences in risk factors and family background.

Results

Our analyses ordinarily included all children in the NSCAW sample—that is, both unsubstantiated and substantiated cases; however, one variable required our focus on not only the entire sample but also the subpopulation of children whose child maltreatment allegations were eventually substantiated. This variable was the setting in which children were placed at Wave 1 (baseline interview). Although entire-sample intergroup comparisons are interesting, placement decisions are more appropriately studied with the subsample of maltreatment cases that were substantiated.

Children's Background Characteristics

For gender, the data indicate an equal distribution for the entire sample, with an increase in female children (53%) among substantiated maltreatment cases (Table 9.2). In our analyses of race, 55.8% of the children were white, 28.9% were African American, 6.2% were American Indian, 2.4% were APIA, and 6.7% were "Other." In the measure specifically pertaining to children's Latino ethnic identity, 18.2% of the children at baseline were identified as Latino, while 81.8% identified as non-Latino. We isolated Latino ethnicity to portray baseline information possibly unique to this rapidly increasing ethnic population, many members of which live in poverty and are exposed to risk factors highly correlated with child maltreatment. Interestingly, approximately 96% of the children identifying with the "other" race group identified themselves as Latino, which indicates that many of these children did not perceive themselves as members of any one of the designated racial groups.

In terms of age, 36.1% of the entire sample was in the age range 6 to 10 years, followed by 24.6% of children aged 11 or older, meaning 60.7% of the population

Table 9.2 Children's Background Characteristics at Wave 1

	Entire Sample			Substantiated Cases		
	Obs	Estimated Percentage	SE	Obs	Estimated Percentage	SE
Gender						
Male	2,727	50.0%	1.8%	1,308	46.4%	2.5%
Female	2,774	50.0%	1.8%	1,422	53.6%	2.5%
Race						
Black or African American	1,862	28.9%	2.8%	955	27.9%	3.8%
White	2,815	55.8%	3.4%	1,365	58.1%	4.0%
American Indian	341	6.2%	0.8%	150	4.6%	0.7%
Asian / Pacific Islander	142	2.4%	0.6%	65	2.8%	1.0%
Other	336	6.7%	1.9%	192	6.5%	1.7%
Latino						
Latino	956	18.2%	2.4%	518	20.7%	3.3%
Not Latino	4,528	81.8%	2.4%	2,200	79.3%	3.3%
Age (years)						
0–2	1,996	18.9%	0.9%	1,066	22.5%	1.8%
3–5	833	20.4%	1.2%	383	17.2%	2.4%
6–10	1,492	36.1%	1.5%	709	36.7%	3.0%
11+	1,179	24.6%	1.1%	571	23.5%	1.8%
Income						
Total household	$21,828		$553	$23,629		$877
Per person	$5,622		$117	$6,170		$213

were at least 6 years old. Children aged 0 to 2 years (18.9%) and those aged 3 to 5 years (20.4%) were in almost equal proportions.

Primary Case Characteristics

Substantiation rates were similar for white, African American, Asian and Pacific Islander American (APIA), and Latino children (between 33.2% and 34.1%) but were lower for American Indian children (21.8%; Table 9.3).

Table 9.3 Rates of Substantiation, by Race and Latino Ethnicity

Race/Ethnicity	Rate	SE
African American	33.2%	3.6%
White	34.1%	3.1%
American Indian	21.8%	4.6%
APIA	34.3%	8.0%
Other	28.7%	5.7%
Adjusted Wald Test: $F = 1.88$, $p = .124$		
Latino	33.9%	3.1%
Non-Latino	32.3%	2.8%

Adjusted Wald Test: $F = 0.18$, $p = .673$.

No statistically significant differences among race/ethnicity groups emerged for type of child maltreatment that the caseworker judged to be the most serious alleged (Table 9.4). Across all groups, physical abuse (27.2%) and supervisory neglect (failure to supervise the child; 27.1%) accounted for more than half the primary reasons for case investigation, followed by physical neglect (failure to provide for the child; 19.4%), sexual abuse (11.0%), and emotional abuse (7.4%).

For substantiated cases, however, significant differences emerged among race categories ($p < .01$). For all races, supervisory neglect (28.2%) remained a relatively

Table 9.4   Most Serious Type of Child Maltreatment Alleged, by Race

| | Type of Abuse by Race | | | | | |
| | Entire Sample | | | | | |
Type of Maltreatment	Black/African American	White	American Indian	APIA	Other	Total
Physical abuse	23.4%	29.0%	20.0%	30.2%	33.2%	27.2%
Sexual abuse	8.5%	11.0%	18.8%	12.6%	14.0%	11.0%
Emotional abuse	4.4%	8.6%	6.1%	5.3%	12.5%	7.4%
Physical neglect	20.4%	19.2%	17.4%	23.7%	16.8%	19.4%
Neglect	31.5%	26.0%	24.9%	21.1%	22.1%	27.1%
Abandonment	2.7%	0.7%	5.0%	1.0%	0.6%	1.5%
Moral/legal abuse	1.0%	0.6%	0.0%	0.0%	0.0%	0.5%
Educational abuse	2.9%	1.0%	3.0%	0.0%	0.0%	1.6%
Exploitation	0.2%	0.1%	0.0%	0.0%	0.0%	0.1%
Other	5.5%	3.7%	4.3%	6.5%	0.6%	4.1%
Total	100%	100%	100%	100%	100%	100%

Pearson chi-squared $= 214.34$, $p = .144$.

| | Substantiated Cases | | | | | |
Type of Maltreatment	Black / African American	White	American Indian	Asian/ PI	Other	Total
Physical abuse	28.6%	22.1%	21.6%	14.3%	14.2%	23.1%
Sexual abuse	4.3%	12.4%	29.9%	7.9%	9.1%	10.7%
Emotional abuse	4.5%	14.7%	9.9%	5.1%	41.6%	13.1%
Physical neglect	17.5%	14.4%	13.8%	34.7%	4.1%	15.2%
Neglect	32.1%	27.7%	10.8%	36.1%	26.7%	28.2%
Abandonment	3.0%	1.5%	1.8%	0.0%	1.6%	1.9%
Moral/legal abuse	1.0%	1.3%	0.0%	0.0%	0.0%	1.0%
Educational abuse	2.5%	1.5%	10.5%	0.0%	0.1%	2.1%
Exploitation	0.2%	0.2%	0.0%	0.0%	0.0%	0.1%
Other	6.4%	4.4%	1.7%	2.0%	2.6%	4.6%
Total	100%	100%	100%	100%	100%	100%

Pearson chi-squared $= 551.0$, $p = .0003$.

common "most serious" type of maltreatment, followed by physical abuse
(23.1%), physical neglect (15.2%), emotional abuse (13.1%), and sexual abuse
(10.7%). Together, approximately 90% of initial referrals were attributed to
these maltreatment types. For African American children, physical abuse appeared
prominent, while sexual abuse was notably lower. For American Indian children
with substantiated cases, supervisory neglect was lower while sexual abuse and
educational abuse were notably high. Physical neglect and supervisory neglect were
also notably high among APIA children with substantiated cases; physical abuse
and emotional maltreatment were low.

As with the results for race, physical abuse (32.4%) and supervisory neglect
(25.3%) accounted for more than half the reportedly "most serious" type of
maltreatment allegation for Latino children (Table 9.5). Physical neglect, emotional abuse, and sexual abuse collectively accounted for 38.7%. Results from

Table 9.5 Most Serious Type of Child Maltreatment Alleged, by Latino Ethnicity

Type of Maltreatment	Entire Sample		
	Latino	Non-Latino	Total
Physical abuse	32.4%	26.0%	27.2%
Sexual abuse	11.6%	10.9%	11.0%
Emotional abuse	12.6%	6.3%	7.4%
Physical neglect	14.5%	20.5%	19.4%
Supervisory neglect	25.3%	5.4%	27.1%
Abandonment	1.8%	1.5%	1.5%
Moral/legal abuse	0.0%	0.6%	0.5%
Educational abuse	0.5%	1.8%	1.6%
Exploitation	0.0%	1.4%	0.1%
Other	1.1%	4.8%	4.1%
Total	100%	100%	100%

Pearson chi-squared = 105.38, p = .014.

Type of Maltreatment	Substantiated Cases		
	Latino	Non-Latino	Total
Physical abuse	26.4%	22.2%	23.1%
Sexual abuse	10.0%	10.9%	10.7%
Emotional abuse	26.3%	9.6%	13.1%
Physical neglect	7.5%	17.2%	15.2%
Supervisory neglect	24.4%	29.3%	28.2%
Abandonment	1.6%	1.9%	1.9%
Moral/legal abuse	0.3%	1.2%	1.0%
Educational abuse	1.3%	2.3%	2.1%
Exploitation	0.0%	0.2%	0.1%
Other	2.3%	5.2%	4.6%
Total	100%	100%	100%

Pearson chi-squared = 214.56, p = .049.

substantiated cases were significant. For the Latino child sample, emotional abuse emerged as far more prominent, while physical neglect was particularly low.

For both unsubstantiated and substantiated cases, we report on whether children remained in their homes or were placed out of home at baseline (Table 9.6). No statistically significant differences by race emerged for placement; initially, most children remained in their homes (88.7%). About two thirds (64.6%) remained in home without services, meaning also without in-home services (e.g., mental health counseling) beyond standard child welfare case management. Among the four racial groups (excluding "other"), initial in-home placements ranged from 86.5% for black or African American children to 89.3% for white children. In-home placements with no services ranged from a low of 59.8% for black children to 66.8% for white children.

Significant differences ($p < .01$) in baseline living arrangements emerged across the substantiated subpopulations of children. Most notably, white children were less likely to be placed out of the home than African American children or APIA children. Furthermore, African American children were much more likely than other children

Table 9.6 Children's Placement at Wave 1, by Race

Children's Placement/ Services	Entire Sample					
	African American	White	American Indian	APIA	Other	Total
Total in home	86.5%	89.3%	88.5%	87.0%	94.6%	88.7%
No services	59.8%	66.8%	62.2%	53.7%	72.8%	64.6%
Services	26.7%	22.4%	26.3%	33.3%	21.7%	24.1%
Nonkinship foster care	5.9%	3.9%	3.7%	7.1%	1.6%	4.4%
Kinship foster care	5.9%	5.0%	4.4%	5.3%	3.2%	5.1%
Group home	0.7%	1.1%	2.0%	0.5%	0.6%	1.0%
Other out of home	1.1%	0.8%	1.5%	0.0%	0.0%	0.9%
Total	100%	100%	100%	100%	100%	100%

Pearson chi-squared $= 66.73$, $p = .189$.

Children's Placement/ Services	Substantiated Cases					
	African American	White	American Indian	APIA	Other	Total
Total in home	71.6%	81.5%	76.7%	78.4%	91.0%	79.0%
No services	32.5%	46.3%	22.0%	45.9%	67.7%	42.7%
Services	39.1%	35.2%	54.7%	32.5%	23.3%	36.3%
Nonkinship foster care	13.6%	8.6%	7.2%	18.0%	4.1%	9.9%
Kinship care	12.4%	7.6%	6.7%	2.5%	3.9%	8.5%
Group home	1.2%	1.5%	4.8%	1.1%	0.8%	1.5%
Other out of home	1.2%	0.8%	4.8%	0.0%	0.0%	1.0%
Total	100%	100%	100%	100%	100%	100%

Pearson chi-squared $= 259.3$, $p = .0028$.

APIA, Asian Pacific Islander American.

Table 9.7   Children's Placement at Wave 1, by Latino Ethnicity

| | Entire Sample | | |
Children's Placement/Services	Latino	Non-Latino	Total
Total in home	90.4%	88.2%	88.7%
No services	69.2%	63.6%	64.6%
Services	21.2%	24.6%	24.1%
Nonkinship foster care	3.5%	4.5%	4.4%
Kinship foster care	3.8%	5.3%	5.1%
Group home	0.7%	1.1%	1.0%
Other out of home	0.8%	1.0%	0.9%
Total	100%	100%	100%

Pearson chi-squared = 13.21, $p = .505$.

| | Substantiated Cases | | |
Children's Placement/Services	Latino	Non-Latino	Total
Total in home	87.0%	77.1%	79.0%
No services	59.0%	38.5%	42.7%
Services	28.0%	38.6%	36.3%
Nonkinship foster care	6.9%	10.7%	9.9%
Kinship foster care	4.7%	9.5%	8.5%
Group home	0.9%	1.7%	1.5%
Other out of home	0.5%	1.1%	1.0%
Total	100%	100%	100%

Pearson chi-squared = 125.9, $p = .0028$.

to be placed into kinship care. American Indian children were more likely than other groups to remain in their homes with services; they were also more likely, when placed out of home, to live in group care or other types of placements.

For Latino children, results indicate no significant differences from non-Latino children; however, for substantiated cases differences were statistically significant ($p < .01$; Table 9.7). Latino children were less likely to be removed from the home than non-Latino children and more likely to remain in home with no services. Additionally, Latino children were less likely than non-Latino children to be placed in kinship foster care.

Individual, Interpersonal, and Environmental Risk and Promotive Factors

At Wave 1 (baseline), children's risk factors for the primary racial groups and Latino ethnicity did not differ on measures of school engagement, trauma, and health (Table 9.8). Among racial groups significant differences ($p < .05$) emerged for depression, with American Indian children evidencing the highest rates of depression and African American children showing the lowest. Depression was not associated with whether children were Latino. American Indian, African American, and Latino

Table 9.8 Children's Risk Factors at Wave 1, by Race

Children's Risk Factor	Af Am	White	American Indian	APIA	Other
School engagement	0.032	−0.02	0.036	0.002	0.179
	(.032)	(.031)	(.094)	(.087)	(.12)
Trauma	49.66	50.03	49.13	46.27	48.39
	(.74)	(.87)	(1.74)	(2.15)	(3.12)
Depression*	48.55	50.38	52.53	50.39	51.86
	(.68)	(.79)	(1.16)	(2.5)	(2.09)
Health	1.91	1.85	1.83	1.84	1.85
	(.05)	(.04)	(.15)	(.18)	(.12)
Community risk*	.18	−.06	.22	0	.02
	(.05)	(.04)	(.10)	(.12)	(.06)
Caregiver's relationship*	.11	−.01	−.35	.35	.21
	(.08)	(.06)	(.17)	(.20)	(.10)
Caregiver's monitoring*	−.09	−.09	−.20	−.08	.39
	(.06)	(0.5)	(.13)	(.17)	(.11)
Caregiver's drug	.034	.03	.012	.025	.003
Dependence*	(.011)	(.007)	(.006)	(.014)	(.001)
Caregiver's alcohol	.035	.018	.017	.006	.001
dependence*	(.01)	(.005)	(.008)	(.005)	(0)

*Adjusted Wald Test significant at $p < .05$.
Af Am, African American; APIA, Asian Pacific Islander American.

Table 9.9 Children's Risk Factors at Wave 1, by Latino Ethnicity

Children's Risk Factor	Latino	Non-Latino
School engagement	0.091	−0.003
	(.07)	(.021)
Trauma	49.78	49.64
	(1.3)	(.68)
Depression	51.78	49.75
	(1.32)	(.63)
Health	1.90	1.86
	(.08)	(.03)
Community risk*	.13	.01
	(.05)	(.03)
Caregiver relationship	−.23	.07
	(.14)	(.06)
Caregiver monitoring	.04	−.09
	(.07)	(.04)
Caregiver drug	.019	.03
dependence	(.009)	(.006)
Caregiver alcohol	.004	.025
dependence*	(.001)	(.005)

*Adjusted Wald Test significant at $p < .05$.

children reported high levels of community risk at baseline, whereas white children tended to come from neighborhoods with lower risk levels ($p < .05$).

Both the quality of the child's relationship with the caregiver and the caregiver's level of child monitoring produced significant differences by race. American Indians had the overall lowest scores. AAPI children presented with the highest score on child–caregiver relationship and the lowest score on the caregiver's monitoring. Neither the child's relationship with the caregiver nor the caregiver's monitoring of the child was associated with ethnicity.

Caregivers' drug dependence and alcohol dependence produced significant differences by race (Table 9.9). African American children presented with the highest scores on both measures. No significant ethnicity differences were found for caregiver's drug dependence but were found for caregiver's alcohol dependence, with Latino children having lower scores than non-Latinos.

Discussion

In terms of convergence and divergence, and drawing from both our current analyses and the extant literature, we offer here a profile for the racial groups and Latino ethnicity.

Black or African American Children

Consistent with the literature, NSCAW data suggest that African American children are the most overrepresented and disproportionate racial group in foster care (both kinship and nonkinship). This difference arises from both its higher proportion in the child population investigated for maltreatment and its higher proportion of substantiated cases resulting in removal from the home. Moreover, because of a history of exclusion in the early child welfare system, African American children have been placed in out-of-home care at alarmingly high rates. The Administration for Children, Youth, and Families (2005) has reported preliminary estimates that signal the persistent overrepresentation of African American children in foster care, although national foster care data indicate that the higher percentage varies greatly by geographic location (Derezotes et al., 2005). Even after controlling for contributing factors such as age, neighborhood poverty, and reason for maltreatment, studies indicate that African American children are more likely to enter foster care than both white and Latino children (Needell, Brookhart, & Lee, 2003).

Taking into account both reported and unreported cases, the frequently cited data from the National Incidence Study of Child Abuse and Neglect (NIS-1, NIS-2, NIS-3) show for maltreatment incidence no significant difference between African American children and white children (Administration for Children and Families, 2008). In our study the most notable differences for African American children related to the most serious type of maltreatment alleged (e.g., high physical abuse and low sexual abuse). Despite the disadvantaging characteristics associated with a higher risk of maltreatment for black or African American children (e.g., low household income, single-parent families, unemployment), compared with white children these children actually have a direct risk of maltreatment that is lower, meaning that they are, without apparent explanation, disproportionately represented in the child welfare system and particularly in foster care.

Gryzlak, Wells, and Johnson (2005), in their study of the role of race in the child welfare system's decision to open an investigation for child maltreatment, found that the child welfare system site, allegation, type of injury, source of report, completeness of the data-recording form, gender of the child, age of the youngest child in sibling groups, and type of parental problems, were significant predictors of the decision to investigate. The race of the child, however, had no overall effect on the decision. Findings showed that white children were more likely to be screened in than black or African American children when the allegation involved sexual abuse; for all other allegations of maltreatment, however, African American children were more likely to be screened in for investigation. Sedlak and Schultz's (2005) findings, based on the NIS data, revealed a significant interaction between race and maltreatment type: African American children who were physically neglected were three times as likely to be investigated as their white counterparts in similar condition (35%, as opposed to 11%).

When they examined the association of caseworker's and child's race/ethnicity with screening decisions, Gryzlak and colleagues found that non-white caseworkers screened in 65% of their cases for investigation, while white workers screened in 49% of their cases. When caseworker and child were of the same race/ethnicity, nearly half of the cases were screened in for investigation. When the child's race and caseworker's race did not match, non-white caseworkers were much more likely to screen in for investigation (76.6%) than white caseworkers (40.4%), which perhaps indicates the non-white caseworkers' willingness to protect and the white caseworkers' reluctance to intrude into the lives of families.

Even though some studies suggest race has no initial influence in child welfare system decision making, race does seem to matter as children progress deeper into the system. Needell, Brookhart, and Lee (2003) have found that black or African American children in California were more likely than white or Latino children to be removed from their caregiver and placed in foster care, even when other factors (e.g., age, reason for maltreatment, neighborhood poverty) are taken into account. Harris, Tittle, and Poertner (2005), though their own study suggests no significant effect of race on placement decisions, cite national child welfare statistics showing that race/ethnicity exerted a significant influence over placement decisions: The majority of white (72%) and Latino (60%) children received in-home services, whereas most African American children (56%) were removed from their homes.

In the NSCAW data, we find that, among substantiated maltreatment cases, African American children are more likely than children of other races to be placed into kinship foster care. This finding, which coincides with others (Goerge & Lee, 2005), may reflect the tradition of kinship care in African American cultures.

Alternatively, it may reflect the child welfare system's failure to address this population's needs, because research indicates that kinship caregivers receive less support than other foster caregivers and that family reunification is not as successfully achieved in kinship families (Scannapieco, 1999).[3]

Although our results indicate a significantly lower risk of depression among African American children, they also indicate a higher risk of living with a caregiver's drug dependence and alcohol dependence. Bernard (2002) argues that recovery for African American children who have been maltreated within their families requires an understanding of how they interpret and name their experiences as abusive. It is difficult to understand, however, what the naming and speaking of trauma may entail for these children when their lived realities are embedded in a broader context of oppression, disenfranchisement, and racism that has already stigmatized them. When African American children's lived experiences encompass familial disarray amid societal racism as contradictory yet somehow mutually reinforcing realities, their capacity to name maltreatment as such will be particularly problematic. Although this racial group may have relatively low rates of depression, essentially, as Bernard argues, the parents' issues silence these children and can encourage them to block painful emotions, ultimately putting their emotional and psychological well-being at risk.

Once in care, children of color receive differential treatment (Brown & Bailey-Etta, 1997; Courtney et al., 1996; Lawrence-Webb, 1997; Wulczyn, 2003). In particular, research findings have persistently shown that African American children have longer stays in out-of-home care than their white counterparts. Wulczyn (2003), using data from the Multi-State Data Archive, asserts that being African American resulted in a 21% longer stay in out-of-home care than being white did, after accounting for factors such as calendar year of entry, age at entry, urbanicity, state, gender, and type of care. Not only are African American children more likely to enter placement, but they are less likely to leave it (Wulczyn, 2003). This exit dynamic, related to the length of stay in care, also contributes to the disproportional representation of African American children in out-of-home care (Barth, Miller, Green, & Baumgartner, 2000, 2001).

Understanding the causes of the overrepresentation of African American children in out-of-home care constitutes a major challenge to the child welfare system because it raises questions about the equity of the system and may even evince unequal treatment. Better data are needed to address this complex, multifaceted issue.

Hispanic or Latino Children

Latino children of all ages are victims of child maltreatment, accounting in 2005 for approximately 14% of the national child maltreatment population (Administration for Children and Families, 2006b).[4] Our analysis indicates that Latino children comprised roughly 18% of children with investigated maltreatment cases and comprised 29% of those with substantiated cases, consistent with national studies.

The substantiated cases revealed Wave 1 (baseline) rates of emotional abuse significantly higher for Latino children, with rates of physical neglect lower than rates for non-Latino children.

The literature focusing on child welfare and Latinos reveals consistent themes distinguishing Latino families: firm commitment to family interaction, maintenance of values consistent with interdependence, and flexibility in responding to familial and extrafamilial stressors (Church, 2006; Figueroa, 1996; Hutchins et al., in press; Ortega, 2006; Williams, 1990). Shortcomings with regard to these qualities have long been associated in this population with child behavior problems and a range of childrearing challenges (Adler, Ovando, & Hocevar, 1984; Church, 2006; Rio, Santisteban, & Szapocznik, 1991). Tension between acculturation and maintenance of traditional culture, including language, has also been implicated in Latino family conflicts, although exposure to drugs, alcohol, and domestic violence is a growing concern (Buriel, Calzado, & Vasquez, 1982; Rio et al., 1991). Latino family composition and family functioning are being stressed by shifts in social stratification, shifts in mores concerning fertility, changing gender roles, intermarriage, and cultural diffusion (Jiobu, 1988; Ortiz, 1995; Vega, 1995; Williams, 1990; Zambrana & Dorrington, 1998). Consequently, discussions about the relatively high levels of emotional abuse among Latino families must extend beyond parent–child interactions and recognize the broader threats stemming from changing family structure and functioning, tensions surrounding the drive for economic well-being, and value conflicts associated with acculturation (Ortega, 2006).

Zambrana and Dorrington (1998) described the social, economic, and family structure variables that place specific Latino subgroups at risk for child maltreatment. Current data reconfirm that Latino persons tend to have larger families than non-Hispanic groups, are less likely to complete high school, are more likely to be dispersed throughout the United States yet live in Latino-concentrated areas, are more likely to live in poverty, and are more likely to rely on family for child care (Pew Hispanic Foundation, 2005). When these stressors result in child maltreatment, particularly in geographic areas where Latino people are concentrated, a growing number of these children are removed from their homes (Church, 2006). Current research raises concerns about placing Latino children in nonkinship foster homes without assessing their cultural needs—needs that, insufficiently resolved in the dominant culture, may have contributed to a situation fostering their maltreatment in the first place; also of concern are their longer durations of placement, especially for older Latino youth (Church, 2006).

Among their major stressors, Latino families are facing increasing rates of poverty, with increasing needs for public assistance, mobility assistance, health insurance, adoptive homes, and child protection. Especially among the growing immigrant population, Latino children continue to be identified as among the poorest of the poor (National Center for Children in Poverty, 2008). Their parents are more likely than other parents to seek work yet remain in low-skill, low-paying jobs (Pew Hispanic Foundation, 2005).

Perpetuating low pay and poverty are challenges associated with education. Parents of Latino children remain under- and uneducated: Grouped with non-Latino persons, proportionately they showed only slightly better high school completion rates in 2000 than they showed in the 1970s (Chapa & de la Rosa, 2004; U.S. Department of Education, 2000). Latino children and youth themselves are more likely than non-Latino white children to be two or more grades behind in school, with poor English skills and a lack of academic support increasing the likelihood of grade repetition. In some areas of the country, the high school dropout rate for Latino youth may exceed 80%, and this figure captures only those who have graduated from middle school and have attended high school.

Like their parents, Latino adolescents also face issues associated with segregation, migration or immigration, and acculturation (Pew Hispanic Foundation, 2005). Increasingly, their struggles are complicated by an environment of pervasive mortality (particularly among males), school dropout, substance abuse, sexually transmitted diseases, gang violence, and teen pregnancy (Rothe, 2004). Depression and suicide attempts due to the accumulated effects of family burden, school problems, psychiatric and acculturation problems, and value conflicts further complicate the Latino adolescent experience (Queralt, 1993; Rothe, 2004; Zambrana & Dorrington, 1998).

One may expect the concern for the welfare of Latino children and adolescents to be rapidly increasing, especially because the Latino population has increased at a faster rate than non-Latino populations (Enchautegui, 1995). Because little research has focused on Latino families, however, whether child welfare services can meet their needs remains unknown. Only recently has a concerted effort been made to assess the role child welfare services play in the lives of Latino children (Ortega et al., 1996). The dramatic increase in the Latino child population, the large and growing number of Latino children in poverty, the increasing concern about child maltreatment among Latino families, and evidence that Latino children are more likely to enter the child welfare system without receiving services argue for urgency in closely examining the child welfare status and service needs of Latino children (Church, 2006; Church, Gross, & Baldwin, 2005). Understanding issues unique to growing up Latino—segregation and marginalization, language differences, mobility, cultural barriers to services, increasing numbers of immigrant youth entering care, and acculturative stress—will lead to better care for Latino children and youth (Rothe, 2004; Zambrana & Dorrington, 1998). Because of the particularly wide range of contextual stressors these children face, an ecological developmental approach may best reveal Latino children's and adolescents' vulnerability to maltreatment, the reasons their needs remain underserved, and perhaps solutions to these problems.

American Indian Children

In the United States in 2000, 32.9% of the American Indian population was younger than age 18 although the percentage according to tribal groupings ranged from 26.5% to 38.9% (U.S. Census Bureau, 2002, p.5). Moreover, the percent of American Indian men participating in the labor force was 66.7% compared to 70.7% of the general population. American Indian women reflected comparable percent labor force participation to the general population (57.6% vs. 57.5%). When compared to the general population, American Indians were less likely to be employed in management, professional and related occupations (24.3% vs. 33.6%), substantially more likely to earn less in terms of full-time, year-round wages ($28,890 vs. $37,057), and more likely to live in poverty (25.7% vs. 12.4%) (U.S. Census Bureau, 2002, pp.10–12).

Cross, Earle, and Simmons (2000) offer sobering data about the American Indian condition: 45% of American Indian mothers have their first child before the age of 20, 38% of American Indian children aged 6 to 11 years live below the federal poverty level, and 27% of all American Indian households are maintained by a female single parent.

Over the past four centuries, American Indians have struggled to maintain their culture and tribal governments as U.S. federal policies have attempted to eradicate, relocate, or assimilate them. The U.S. government's relationship with American Indians has shifted back and forth from one of taking control away from the tribes to permitting greater tribal control over American Indian communities. Despite the great diversity among American Indian tribes, their shared commitment to sovereignty has ensured their survival into the twenty-first century (Cross et al., 2000).

According to Cross and colleagues (Cross et al., 2000; Fox, 2004; Hand, 2006), the imposition of a Euro-American child welfare paradigm on American Indian communities has significantly impeded American Indian tribes' ability to exercise their traditional forms of childrearing. From the 1800s until the mid-1950s, American Indian children experienced large-scale forced removal to boarding schools (Burchard, 1970). By 1900, more than 17,000 American Indian children were enrolled in boarding schools funded by the U.S. federal government (Cross, 2000; Davis, 2001), with effects on American Indian families that were devastating. American Indian children learned during this period about physical and sexual abuse (Cross, 2000; Johansen, 2000; Macqueen, 2000): In the boarding schools, children were frequently beaten with whips, chained or shackled, and locked in closets, basements, or bathrooms (Johansen, 2000). These children remained isolated from their families and tribal communities; these boarding schools raised several generations of American Indian parents (Davis, 2001).

In the subsequent 1960s and 1970s, American Indian children were about six times more likely than other children to be placed in foster care; many were placed in homes or institutions that were not American Indian (U.S. Government Accountability Office, 2006). Placement was often because of child neglect deriving from impoverished conditions and differences from mainstream society's childrearing practices (Bigfoot, 2000). Attempts to reestablish the power to exercise traditional American Indian forms of childrearing began with the passage of the Indian Child Welfare Act of 1978 (ICWA; 25 U.S.C. § 1901–63). Congress enacted

ICWA in 1978 to protect the rights of American Indian children and families and to restore to tribal governments a central decision-making role in protecting the children's safety and well-being. The major goals of ICWA were and are "to protect the best interests of Indian children" and "to promote the stability of Indian tribes and families" (25 U.S.C. § 1902). ICWA offered two important distinctions: *(1)* active efforts to provide remedial services and programs in order to prevent a tribal child's separation from his or her family and *(2)* the use of a qualified expert witness, such as a recognized tribal cultural authority or lay expert, to make a decision regarding best interests of the child in cases of suspected child maltreatment. Recent evidence suggests a reasonable degree of compliance with ICWA, although more work must be done to train caseworkers on ICWA mandates and to institute "best practices" (Limb, Chance, & Brown, 2004, p. 1288).

Unfortunately, since these earlier times, national statistics on maltreatment of American Indian and Alaska Native children generally have been problematic (Earle, 2000; Earle & Cross, 2001; Fox, 2003). Current reporting mechanisms result in underreporting of maltreatment (Earle, 2000). National, up-to-date data on children subject to ICWA are also difficult to obtain (U.S. Department of Education, 2005). According to available national data, American Indian children in 2001 constituted 0.9% of the U.S. population younger than 18 years of age but represented 2% of the U.S. population in foster care, and 2% of those waiting to be adopted (Administration on Children, 2001). Our analysis is based on 6.2% of the NSCAW baseline sample, or 341 American Indian children, and 4.6%, or 150, of substantiated cases. The proportion of American Indian children in both NSCAW samples is disproportionate to their representation in the U.S. general population.

American Indian children are disproportionately represented in the foster and adoptive care populations, as well, despite the passage of the Indian Child Welfare Act of 1978. Researchers have asserted that the disproportion of American Indian children in the child welfare system can be traced to U.S. federal policies on the American Indian tribes and the imposition of the Euro-American child welfare paradigm on an indigenous people (Bigfoot, 2000; Hand, 2006; Limb & Perry, 2003; Roberts, 1998). Consequently, tribal communities have lost much from their traditional lifestyles, cultural values and teachings, social norms and sanctions, and parental guidance and instruction (Bigfoot, 2000). The long history of boarding schools, foster care with non-Native families, and inappropriate child placement practices have contributed to the rise in child maltreatment itself (Cross et al., 2000). The mechanisms of this rise include increased stress, with limited coping strategies; unemployment, with limited marketing skills; limited resources; harsh, inappropriate disciplining of children; excessive drug and alcohol usage by adolescents and adults; unchanneled anger and aggression in response to cultural oppression, gang violence, hate crimes, racism, and high rates of incarceration; and undesirably channeled anger and aggression in the form of domestic violence, suicide, and homicide.

Our results among substantiated cases suggest that American Indian children experience significantly high incidence of sexual abuse and educational maltreatment, with significantly lower rates of substantiated cases of neglect. The children in the NSCAW sample also had a higher probability of being left in their original homes with services; moreover, they were significantly more likely than other racial groups to be removed from their homes and placed in group care or other residential care. Although detailed information is urgently needed to assess maltreatment perpetration (especially sexual abuse), appropriateness of placement, service needs, and adequacy of services provided, out-of-home placement into group homes and other residential care appears to predominate research concerns. It is important, however, that the field of child welfare recognize and acknowledge that current placement decisions for American Indian children are uniquely influenced by the time required to determine whether the Indian Child Welfare Act applies, the availability of American Indian foster and adoptive homes, and the level of cooperation between states and tribes (U.S. Department of Education, 2005).

With regard to baseline child risk factors, the NSCAW data indicate that American Indian children, of all groups, evidence the highest levels of depression, the lowest quality of relationship with caregivers, and the lowest level of caregiver monitoring. As Hand (2006) emphasizes, from the Ojibwe tribal perspective and consistent with other American Indian tribal communities, children are seen as embedded in extended family networks, where relatives and community members watch over their well-being and physical disciplining of children is extremely rare. Childrearing practices involve parental affection and inclusion in daily work, availability of extended family as caregivers, grandparents and elders as teachers and role models, and community involvement in child care and protection (Hand, 2006). American Indian tribes in the United States value children as "gifts from the Creator" and have some of the oldest, most positive traditions regarding the protection of children (Cross et al., 2000).

Our appropriately contextualized NSCAW results suggest that growing up as an American Indian child remains, for some, compromised by tensions between the broad experience of being an American and state citizen and that of being a tribal member (Weaver, 1998). Although several culturally responsive tribal child welfare prevention programs have emerged in recent years to build on the strengths of American Indian communities, a lack of stable and adequate funding for these programs is one of the most serious barriers to tribes' ability to protect their children in a new era (Cross et al., 2000).

Asian American and Pacific Islander Children

Little is known about the experiences of APIA children in the child welfare system. In the NSCAW baseline sample, 2.4%, or 142 children, were APIA; 2.8%, or 65 children, were APIA. Arguably, APIA children and families have not been considered a population of primary concern in child welfare (Coalition for Asian American Children and Families, 2001).

APIA children are identified and treated as one homogenous group in the child welfare system, even though this population is characterized by great diversity. The APIA population in the United States comprises about 4.4% of the total population and relatively younger than the general population with roughly 26% younger than age 18 compared to 23% for the general population (U.S. Census Bureau, 2002). This population comes from the Far East, Southeast Asia, and the Indian Subcontinent, representing seven different ethnicities (Chinese, Filipino, Japanese, Asian Indian, Korean, Vietnamese, and Hawaiian; Schwartz, 2002). Almost half of the APIA persons live in California, Hawaii, and Texas (Ro, 2002), with New York and New Jersey also having a significant APIA population. The different peoples within the APIA population have distinct political, cultural, language, socioeconomic, and religious characteristics. Many APIA immigrants arrive in the United States with limited education, little experience living in large urban areas, and few marketable job skills (Coalition for Asian American Children and Families, 2001). The poverty rate for different APIA groups varies widely, with the Hmong Americans (60%) and the Cambodian Americans (40%) having the highest poverty rates (Schwartz, 2002). The diversity of the APIA population is often overlooked; consequently, unique needs of APIA children often remain unaddressed by the child welfare system.

In general, traditional APIA families are hierarchical, with the parents fulfilling a role that is authoritarian. In some Asian countries corporal punishment is common, and parents may not be affectionate with their children (Coalition for Asian American Children and Families, 2001). In Asian cultures harmony with the environment; respecting the interests and wishes of parents and elders, without question; and avoiding "loss of face" or shame in society are central components of the APIA families' worldview (Futa et al., 2001). Newly immigrant APIA families experience conflicts with mainstream parenting methods and are reluctant to seek services (Coalition for Asian American Children and Families, 2001). APIA youth often report their own parents to the child protective service system when they encounter cultural conflicts or parent–child power struggles (Lu et al., 2004).

Communication in mainstream culture can for these families be particularly problematic. In many APIA immigrant families, few members older than age 14 speak English well, which means these households are "linguistically isolated" (Reeves & Bennett, 2003). Language barriers can exacerbate discrimination against APIA families; the use of children as interpreters is often problematic (Chand, 2005). Certain health care practices used in APIA families, such as "coining" or "spooning," differ from mainstream medical treatments and may leave red marks on the child's skin that can be misinterpreted as evidence of abuse (Coalition for Asian American Children and Families, 2001). Most reports alleging child "neglect," moreover, are actually due to the families' financial situation and lack of resources (Coalition for Asian American Children and Families, 2001).

Our analysis of baseline NSCAW data revealed significant differences for this group of children. Among substantiated cases for this group, particularly high were the incidences of physical and supervisory neglect. Conversely, physical abuse and emotional abuse were notably low. A significantly high score on caregiver relationship and low score on caregiver monitoring were notable among substantiated cases. Placement of APIA children at Wave 1 indicates that APIA children in general remain in their home, but when they are placed out of home they are significantly more likely than other children to be placed in nonkinship foster care and significantly less likely to be placed with kin. Chan, Dang, and Fan (2000) raise concern that when APIA children are placed in the foster care system, many are placed in non-Asian household, where conflicting language, diet, religious practices, and childrearing values make it difficult for the child to adjust and then difficult for the child to reunify with his or her birth family.

White Children

In 2002 more than one half of all child maltreatment victims were white (54%) (National Clearinghouse on Child Abuse and Neglect, 2005). Nevertheless, the child maltreatment rate for white children is 11 per 1,000 children, which is much lower than the rate for children of color (National Clearinghouse on Child Abuse and Neglect, 2005). Although white children younger than 18 years of age account for 75% of the U.S. child population, these children account for only 43% of the children in out-of-home care. Moreover, white youth in out-of-home care are significantly more likely than African American or Latino youth to receive referrals for counseling and psychotherapy services (Garland, Landsverk, & Lau, 2003). These children also spend less time than those from other racial and ethnic groups in out-of-home placement (Wulczyn, 2003). White children are more likely than other racial groups to be sexually abused (Cappelleri, Eckenrode, & Powers, 1993), although our data support this finding only slightly. Child neglect investigations in white families are linked to poverty (Slack, Holl, McDaniel, Yoo, & Bolger, 2004). In these families perceived material hardship, infrequent employment, low parental warmth, use of physical discipline, and children's frequent television viewing predict child neglect (Slack et al., 2004).

Reviewing literature on the experiences of white children and families in the child welfare system, we had difficulty finding any information about different European-American ethnic groups and immigration status as it relates to child maltreatment rates and types. Most studies reported child maltreatment information that assumed a "colorblind" experience for youth in the system or discussed white children and families only in relation to other racial groups.

Multiracial Children

By providing U.S. citizens an opportunity to indicate whether they represented more than one race, the year 2000 U.S. Census revealed that 6.8 million persons, or 2.4% of the U.S. population, identify as biracial or multiracial. Within this subpopulation, approximately half were younger than 18 years old, although regional variations were clear. The increase in interracial dating and marriage, the growing number of persons of color in the United States, federal policies designed to increase racial integration in schools and the workforce, and similar trends have been cited as reasons for this finding. Challenges for multiracial children and families focus on discrimination, pressures to ally with one race or ethnicity over the other (e.g., school or job applications that allow an applicant to indicate one race), racial devaluation, and peer pressure and sanctions against associating with persons whose racial or ethnic identification eschews traditional stereotypes. For these individuals, negotiating cultures and sometimes different languages can require a delicate balancing of different attitudes, beliefs, practices, and worldviews (Dalmage, 2004).

In the child welfare system, approximately 2% of the more than one-half million children are identified with more than one race. Results from general studies of biracial youth suggest they are particularly vulnerable to delinquency, school problems, internalized symptoms of psychological distress, and low self-regard (Milan & Keiley, 2000). To date, there is a dearth of studies in the child welfare literature that explicitly and systematically examine the needs of biracial and multiracial children and youth. That the number of these children is increasing and that differential needs exist have brought these children to the attention of child welfare experts (Derezotes et al., 2005; Miller & Garan, 2008; Miranda, 2003). As the number of children who identify as multiracial increases, so too should preparation to meet their needs in ways that accommodate the additional challenges associated with their racial and ethnic identities.

Conclusion

We have brought together here our initial analysis of NSCAW Wave 1 (baseline) data with a wide range of discussions on the topic of racial and ethnic overrepresentation and disproportion; we suggest a multidimensional approach toward understanding this pervasive and complex concern.

A social justice perspective centers on a social concern relevant to the disproportionate number of children of color vulnerable to harm, instability, and insecurity as a consequence of cultural misunderstanding, displacement, and disadvantage. Linked to this discussion are durable inequalities exclusive to populations of color, inequalities that prevent social and economic mobility. These social consequences, accompanied by poverty, inadequate access to resources, and the like have strong correlates to child maltreatment.

Often couched in this discussion is the confounding relationship between class and race (Bernard, 2002; Hampton & Newberger, 1985). A social justice perspective, with its inclusion of power (and privilege), draws attention to an ongoing societal racialization that advantages some and disadvantages others in ways separate from but intersecting with class and other social identities (Miller & Garan, 2008). A social justice perspective argues that the overrepresentation of children of color may reflect the racialized social barriers and obstacles that can impair parents' ability to raise their children in home and neighborhood environments without the imposition of stresses and strains that interfere with efforts to develop and maintain a nurturing environment. Certainly, as the need for public assistance increases, so too does the likelihood that such families incur the scrutiny and intrusion that come with asking for help (Miller & Garan, 2008; Roberts, 2002).

A cultural perspective challenges the field of child welfare to consider the parenting practices of our families of color not as pathological child caring, but as some combination of best cultural intentions and culturally specific safeguards. As suggested in previous discussions, parenting practices that do not conform to mainstream childrearing practices are often consistent with values, beliefs, and attitudes unique to culturally different families. These families may further implement disciplinary practices targeted at safeguarding their children from cultural assimilation or from engagement in behaviors that are inconsistent with their cultural upbringing and for which even harsher social consequences would otherwise ensue. For cultures impassioned about their family bonding, it is hard to imagine a worse consequence than to lose a member to forces outside their control. In a qualitative study sponsored by the Administration for Children and Families, Children's Bureau (Administration for Children and Families, 2006a), *Perspectives from the Child Welfare Community*, an overall concern was whether cultural differences are appreciated by caseworkers:

> In many cases, participants felt that their colleagues, across racial and ethnic groups and job categories, brought preconceived ideas or biases against minority groups, most often African Americans, to their position within the agency. Participants, most often African American participants, identified racial bias as a common problem that frequently interfered with good decision making. They felt that many staff, but Caucasian staff in particular, lacked exposure to cultures other than their own and had no context for understanding the cultural norms and practices of minority populations. (p. iii)

Evidence in our study raises questions about differential abuse or neglect types as reasons for child maltreatment investigations. We advocate for more open discussions about differential parenting responses that may be embedded in cultural beliefs. Perhaps more open dialogue with families about their cultural views on discipline may challenge strict adherence to the more ambiguous definitions of *maltreatment*. Cultural humility supports the notion that families must have an essential role in raising their children and in educating caseworkers about the values and beliefs parents hold regarding child raising. This perspective has its roots in the medical field and certainly has merit in child welfare practice (Tervalon & Murray-Garcia, 1998).

Child welfare system responses themselves warrant attention (Hill, 2006). Although we did not undertake an in-depth comparison of caseworkers' decisions with caseworkers' race and children's race, a concern raised in the literature begs for research about differences based on race in assessment, maltreatment substantiation, and decision making. Berger, McDaniel, and Paxson (2005), for example, found racial bias in judgments made by racially or ethnically different professionals in actual case decisions: "Race matters when people are assessing the parenting behavior of others. There are systematic racial differences in how black and white interviewers rate parenting techniques, mothers' characteristics, and the behavior and appearance of children. These differences call into serious question the idea that reports of child maltreatment are colorblind" (Berger, McDaniel, & Paxson, 2005, p. 29).

Answering questions about the overrepresentation of children of color begins with the judgments made about whether to report child maltreatment; it continues in exploring the question of disparities, which asks, "Are children of color treated, on contact with the child protective system, differently in ways that account for their overrepresentation?" Several other discussions in this book reflect on this question with implications for further study.

That an overwhelming number of children of color are in the child welfare system is supported by NSCAW data. With the rapidly increasing populations of color; the influx of children, youth, and families because of immigration; continued educational and economic disadvantages that epitomize institutional and historical injustices among families and children of color; anticipated and unanticipated social events; and the burgeoning human services system, much work must be anticipated in child welfare policy and practice to accommodate the unique cultural socialization experiences, language, and service needs of our diverse population. Necessity calls for the continued study of the children of color population in the child welfare system. With improvements in data—improvements such as those offered by NSCAW—better integration of cultural perspectives for understanding and serving this population, identification of possible remedies to ensure equitable treatment of all children who come into contact with the child welfare system, and the remediation of social injustices as part of our child welfare mission, we can progress toward a future that ensures for all children a safe, secure environment at home and in our communities.

NOTES

1. We write with full awareness of the major sources of disagreement about whether "race" or ethnicity is a spurious predictor of the observed racial and ethnic discrepancies in the child welfare population (e.g., Barth et al., 2001; Brown & Bailey-Etta, 1997; Courtney et al., 1996; Fluke et al., 2003; Lu et al., 2004; Needell et al., 2003; Lawrence-Webb, 1997).
2. *Substantiation* is the child welfare system's official case decision that allegations of child maltreatment are valid.
3. Barth and colleagues (Chapter 8) draw attention to informal kinship care among African Americans in order to better account for lower reunification rates for this population.
4. Most of the victim reports in 2004 were from either California or Texas, but administrative data have limitations related to differing definitions of abuse and neglect, errors and lags in reporting, poor quality assurance of recordkeeping, and variation in what states report,

including race and ethnicity (Goerge, Wulczyn, & Harden, 1994). Determining the true number of Hispanic or Latino children who are maltreated is problematic.

REFERENCES

Abt Associates. (1996). *Design report: National evaluation of family support programs.* Bethesda, MD: Author.

Adler, P., Ovando, C., & Hocevar, D. (1984). Familiar correlates of gang membership: An exploratory study of Mexican-American youth. *Hispanic Journal of Behavioral Sciences,* 6(1), 65–67.

Administration for Children and Families. (2002). Program improvement plans: An agenda for change. *National child welfare resource center for family-centered practice: Best practice, next practice.* Retrieved January 5, 2009, from http://www.hunter.cuny.edu/socwork/nrcfcpp/downloads/newsletter/BPNPSpecial02.pdf

Administration for Children and Families. (2006a). Adoption and foster care analysis and reporting system (AFCARS) interim 2003 estimates as of June 2006. *The AFCARS report.* Retrieved August 15, 2008, from http://www.acf.hhs.gov/programs/cb/stats_research/afcars/tar/report10.htm

Administration for Children and Families. (2006b). *Child maltreatment 2004.* Retrieved December 23, 2008, from http://www.acf.hhs.gov/programs/cb

Administration for Children and Families. (2008). Child Welfare Information Gateway. *The National Incidence Study of Child Abuse and Neglect.* Retrieved December 15, 2008, from http://www.childwelfare.gov/systemwide/statistics/nis.cfm

Administration on Children, Youth and Families. (2001). *National Survey of Child and Adolescent Well-Being: Local child welfare agency survey: Report.* Washington, DC: Author.

Administration on Children, Youth and Families. (2005). *The AFCARS report* (No. 10). Washington DC: Author.

Ammerman, R. T., & Hersen, M. (1990). *Children at risk: An evaluation of factors contributing to child abuse and neglect.* New York: Springer.

Annie E. Casey Foundation. (2006). *Undercounted and underserved: Immigrants and refugee families in the child welfare system.* Baltimore MD: Author.

Barth, R. P., Courtney, M. E., & Berry, M. (1994). Timing is everything: An analysis of the time to adoption and legalization. *Social Work Research, 18*(3), 139–148.

Barth, R. P., Green, R. L., & Miller, J. M. (2001). *Toward understanding racial disproportionality in child welfare services receipt.* Paper presented at the Race Matters Forum: Examining the Overrepresentation of African Americans in the Child Welfare System, Chevy Chase, MD.

Barth, R. P., Miller, J. M., Green, R. L., & Baumgartner, J. N. (2000). *Children of color in the child welfare system: Toward explaining their disproportionate involvement in comparison to their numbers in the general population.* Chapel Hill: Unpublished manuscript, University of North Carolina at Chapel Hill, School of Social Work, Jordan Institute for Families.

Barth, R. P., Miller, J. M., Green, R. L., & Baumgartner, J. N. (2001, January). *Toward understanding racial disproportionality in child welfare service recipients.* Paper presented at the Race Matters Forum, University of Illinois, Urbana-Champaign.

Berger, L., McDaniel, M., & Paxson, C. (2005). Assessing parenting behaviors across racial groups: Implications for the child welfare system. *Social Service Review, 79*(4), 653–688.

Bernard, C. (2002). Giving voice to experiences: Parental maltreatment of Black children in the context of societal racism. *Child and Family Social Work, 7*(4), 239–251.

Bigfoot, D. S. (2000). History of victimization in Native communities. In D. Bigfoot (Ed.), *Native American topic-specific monograph series.* Washington, DC: Office for Victims of Crime.

Briere, J., & Runtz, M. (1989). The Trauma Symptom Checklist (TSC-33): Early data on a new scale. *Journal of Interpersonal Violence, 4,* 151–163.

Brown, A. W., & Bailey-Etta, B. (1997). An out-of-home care system in crisis: Implications for African American children in the child welfare system. *Child Welfare, 76*(1), 65–83.

Burchard, B. (1970). *Education of American Indians: Boarding schools for American Indian youth.* National Study of American Indian Education, U.S. DHEW: Washington, DC: Bureau of Research, Series IV, No. 2, Final Report.

Buriel, R., Calzado, S., & Vasquez, R. (1982). The relationship of traditional Mexican-American culture to the adjustment and delinquency among three generations of Mexican-American male adolescents. *Hispanic Journal of Behavioral Sciences, 1,* 45–55.

Cappelleri, J. C., Eckenrode, J., & Powers, J. L. (1993). The epidemiology of child abuse: Findings from the Second National Incidence and Prevalence Study of Child Abuse and Neglect. *American Journal of Public Health, 83,* 1622–1624.

Caughy, M. O., & Franzini, L. (2005). Neighborhood correlates of cultural differences in perceived effectiveness of parental disciplinary tactics. *Parenting, Science and Practice, 5*(2), 119–151.

Chan, S., Dang, S., & Fan, L. (2000). *Child abuse and neglect services. A seat at the table: Toward a national agenda for Asian Pacific American children.* New York: Coalition for Asian American Children and Families.

Chand, A. (2005). Do you speak English? Language barriers in child protections social work with minority ethnic families. *British Journal of Social Work, 35,* 807–821.

Chapa, J., & de la Rosa, B. (2004). Latino population growth, socioeconomic and demographic characteristics, and implications for educational attainment. *Education and Urban Society, 36*(2), 130–149.

Church, I., W. T. (2006). From start to finish: The duration of Hispanic children in out-of-home placements. *Children and Youth Services Review, 28,* 1007–1023.

Church, I., W. T., Gross, E. R., & Baldwin, J. (2005). Maybe ignorance is not always bliss: The disparate treatment of Hispanics within the child welfare system. *Children and Youth Services Review, 27,* 1279–1292.

Coalition for Asian American Children and Families. (2001). *Crossing the divide: Asian American families and the child welfare system.* New York: Author.

Collier, A. F., McClure, F. H., Collier, J., Otto, C., & Polloi, A. (1999). Culture-specific views of child maltreatment and parenting styles in a Pacific-Island community. *Child Abuse & Neglect, 23*(3), 229–244.

Connell, J. (1991). Competency, autonomy, and relatedness: A motivational analysis of self-system processes. In M. Gunnar & L. Sroufe (Eds.), *Self-processes and development* (Vol. 23, pp. 43–77). Hillsdale, NJ: Erlbaum.

Coohey, C. (2001). The relationship between familism and child maltreatment in Latino and Anglo families. *Child Maltreatment, 6*(2), 130–142.

Courtney, M. E., Barth, R. P., Berrick, J. D., Brooks, D., Needell, B., & Park, L. (1996). Race and child welfare services: Past research and future directions. *Child Welfare, 75*(2), 99–137.

Cross, T. (2000). Tribal perspectives on over-representation of Indian children in out-of-home care. *Permanency Planning Today, 1*(1), 7–11.

Cross, T., Earle, K. A., & Simmons, D. (2000). Child abuse and neglect in Indian country: Policy issues. *Families in Society, 81*(1), 49–58.

Dalmage, H. (2004). *The politics of multiracialism: Challenging racial thinking.* New York: State University of New York Press.

Davis, J. (2001). American Indian boarding school experiences: Recent studies from Native perspectives. *Organization of American Historians Magazine of History, 15*, 20–22

Derezotes, D., Poertner, J., & Testa, M. (2005). *Race matters in child welfare: The overrepresentation of African American children in the system.* Washington, DC: Child Welfare League of America.

Dishion, T. J., Patterson, G. R., Stoolmiller, M., & Skinner, M. L. (1991). Family, school, and behavioral antecedents to early adolescent involvement with antisocial peers. *Developmental Psychology, 27*(1), 172–180.

Earle, K. A. (2000). *Child abuse and neglect: An examination of American Indian data.* Seattle, WA: Casey Family Programs.

Earle, K. A., & Cross, A. (2001). *Child abuse and neglect among American Indian / Alaska Native children: An analysis of existing data.* Seattle, WA: Casey Family Programs.

Elliot, K., & Urquiza, A. (2006). Ethnicity, culture and child maltreatment. *Journal of Social issues, 62*(4), 787–809.

Enchautegui, M. E. (1995). *Policy implications of Latino poverty.* Population Studies Center. Washington DC: The Urban Institute.

Figueroa, L. (1996). *Cultural competence and Latino adoption: Cultural factors that influence the adoption process. Report of findings from a parent survey.* Washington, DC: Technical Report, Administration on Children, Youth and Families (DHHS), National Adoption Information Clearinghouse.

Finn, J. L., & Jacobson, M. (2003). *Just practice: A social justice approach to social work.* Peosta, IA: Eddie Bowers.

Fluke, J. D., Yuan, Y. T., Hedderson, J., & Curtis, P. (2003). Disproportionate representation of race and ethnicity in child maltreatment investigation and victimization. *Children and Youth Services Review, 25*(5/6), 359–373.

Fox, K. A. (2003). Collecting data on the abuse and neglect of American Indian children. *Child Welfare, 82*(6), 707–726.

Fox, K. E. (2004). Are they really neglected? A look at worker perceptions of neglect through the eyes of a national data set. *First Peoples Child and Family Review, 1*(1), 73–82.

Futa, K. T., Hsu, E., & Hansen, D. J. (2001). Child sexual abuse in Asian American families: An examination of cultural factors that influence prevalence, identification and treatment. *Clinical Psychology: Science and Practice, 8*, 189–209.

Garland, A. F., Ellis-MacLeod, E., Landsverk, J. A., Ganger, W., & Johnson, I. (1998). Minority populations in the child welfare system: The visibility hypothesis reexamined. *American Journal of Orthopsychiatry, 68*(1), 142–146.

Garland, A. F., Landsverk, J. A., & Lau, A. S. (2003). Racial/ethnic disparities in mental health service use among children in foster care. *Children and Youth Services Review, 25*(5–6), 491–507.

Goerge, R., & Lee, B. (2005). The entry of children from the welfare system into foster care: Differences by race. In D. M. Derezotes, J. Poertner, & M. F. Testa (Eds.), *The overrepresentation of African American children in the system: Race matters in child welfare*. Washington, DC: Child Welfare League of America Press.

Goerge, R., Wulczyn, F. H., & Harden, A. W. (1994). *Foster care dynamics 1983–1992. A report from the multistate foster care data archive*. Chicago: Chapin Hall Center for Children at University of Chicago.

Gryzlak, B., Wells, S., & Johnson, M. (2005). The role of race in child protective services screening decisions. In D. M. Derezotes, J. Poertner & M. F. Testa (Eds.), *The overrepresentation of African American children in the system: Race matters in child welfare*. Washington, DC: Child Welfare League of America Press.

Hampton, R. L., & Newberger, E. H. (1985). Child abuse reporting: Significance of severity, class, and race. *American Journal of Public Health, 75*(1), 56–60.

Hand, C. (2006). An Ojibwe perspective on the welfare of children; Lessons of the past and visions of the future. *Children and Youth Services Review, 28*, 20–46.

Harris, G., Tittle, G., & Poertner, J. (2005). Factors that predict the decision to place a child in substitute care. In D. Derezotes (Ed.), *Race matters in child welfare: The overrepresentation of African American children in the system* (pp. 163–172). Washington, DC: Child Welfare League of America.

Harris, M. S., & Courtney, M. E. (2003). The interaction of race, ethnicity, and family structure with respect to the timing of family reunification. *Children and Youth Services Review, 25*(5/6), 409–429.

Hay, T., & Jones, L. (1994). Societal interventions to prevent child abuse and neglect. *Child Welfare, 73*(5), 379–403.

Hill, R. (2006). Synthesis of research on disproportionality in child welfare: An update. *Casey CSSP Alliance for Racial Equity in the Child Welfare System Report*. Retrieved December 23, 2008, from http://www.cssp.org/major_initiatives/racialEquity.html

Hogan, P., & Sui, S. (1988). Minority children and the child welfare system: An historical perspective. *Social Work, 33*, 493–498.

Hunt, D. E., Gooden, M., & Barkdull, C. (1999). *Walking in moccasins: Indian child welfare in the 21st century*. Dubuque, IA: Eddie Bowers.

Hutchins, C., Ortega, R. M., & Quintanilla, M. (in press). Promoting adoption and foster care with Latino families: AdoptUSKids Program, Department of Health and Human Services, Administration for Children and Families.

Jiobu, R. (1988). *Ethnicity and assimilation*. Albany: State University of New York Press.

Johansen, B. E. (2000). Education—The nightmare and the dream: A shared national tragedy, a shared national disgrace. *Native Americas, 17*(4), 10–19.

Jones, E., & McCurdy, K. (1992). The links between types of maltreatment and demographic characteristics. *Child Abuse & Neglect, 16*(2), 201–215.

Jones, L. P. (1997). Social class, ethnicity, and child welfare. *Journal of Multicultural Social Work, 6*(3/4), 123–138.

Kessler, R. C., Andrews, G., Mroczek, D., Ustun, T. B., & Wittchen, H.-U. (1998). The World Health Organization Composite International Diagnostic Interview Short Form (CIDI-SF). *International Journal of Methods in Psychiatric Research, 7*, 171–185.

Korbin, J. E. (2002). Culture and child maltreatment: Cultural competence and beyond. *Child Abuse & Neglect, 26*(6–7), 637–644.

Korbin, J. E., & Spilsbury, J. C. (1999). Cultural competence and child neglect. In
H. Dubowitz (Ed.), *Neglected children: Research, practice, and policy* (Vol. 69–88).
Thousand Oaks, CA: Sage Publications.

Lawrence-Webb, C. (1997). African American children in the modern child welfare system:
A legacy of the Flemming Rule. *Child Welfare, 76*(1), 9–30.

Limb, G. E., Chance, T., & Brown, E. F. (2004). An empirical examination of the Indian Child
Welfare Act and its impact on cultural and familial preservation for American Indian
children. *Child Abuse & Neglect, 28*(12), 1279–1289.

Limb, G. E., & Perry, R. (2003). Public child welfare and the American Indian: A California
profile. *Children and Youth Services Review, 25*(10), 823–841.

Locke, D. C. (1998). *Increasing multicultural understanding: A comprehensive model*
(2nd ed.). Thousand Oaks, CA: Sage Publications.

Lu, E. Y., Landsverk, J., Ellis-Macleod, E., Newton, R., Ganger, W., & Johnson, I. (2004).
Race, ethnicity, and case outcomes in child protective services. *Children and Youth
Services Review, 26*, 447–461.

Lynch, E. W., & Hanson, M. J. (Eds.). (1998). *Developing cross-cultural competence: A guide
for working with children and their families* (2nd ed.). Baltimore, MD: Brookes.

Lynch, M., & Cicchetti, D. (1991). An ecological-transactional analysis of children and
contexts: The longitudinal interplay among child maltreatment, community
violence and children's symptomatology. *Development and Psychopathology, 10*(2),
235–257.

Macqueen, A. (2000). Four generations of abuse: Canada's unfinished business of
compensation. *Native Americas, 17(4),* 20–23.

McMurtry, S. L., & Lie, G. (1992). Differential exits of minority children in foster care. *Social
Work Research and Abstracts, 28*, 42.

Meston, C. M., Heiman, J. R., Trapnell, P. D., & Carlin, A. S. (1999). Ethnicity, desirable
responding, and self-reports of abuse: A comparison of European- and Asian-ancestry
undergraduates. *Journal of Consulting and Clinical Psychology, 67*(1), 139–144.

Milan, S., & Keiley, M. K. (2000). Biracial youth and families in therapy: Issues and
interventions. *Journal of Marital and Family Therapy, 26*(3), 305–315.

Miller, J., & Garan, A. (2008). *Racism in the United States.* Belmont, CA: Thompson Brooks/
Cole.

Miranda, G. E. (2003). Domestic transracial adoption and multiraciality. In M. P. P. Root &
M. Kelley (Eds.), *Multiracial child resource book: Living complex identities.* Seattle, WA:
MAVIN Foundation.

Morton, T. D. (1999). The increasing colorization of America's child welfare system. *Policy
and Practice, 23*, 23–30.

National Center for Children in Poverty. (2008). Retrieved January 12, 2009, from http://
www.nccp.org

National Clearinghouse on Child Abuse and Neglect. (2005). *Child maltreatment 2003:
Summary of findings.* Retrieved November 12, 2007, from http://nccanch.acf.hhs.gov/
pubs/factsheets/canstats.cfm

Needell, B., Brookhart, M. A., & Lee, S. (2003). Black children and foster care placement in
California. *Children and Youth Services Review, 25*(5/6), 393–408.

Ortega, R. M. (2000). Child welfare and Latino adolescents. In M. Montero-Sieburth &
F. A. Villarruel (Eds.), *Making invisible Latino adolescents visible.* New York: Farmer
Press.

Ortega, R. M. (2006). Latinos, domestic violence and child abuse. In R. Fong, R. McRoy, & C. O. Hendricks (Eds.), *Culture and interpersonal violence*. Alexandria, VA: Council on Social Work Education.

Ortega, R. M., Gutierrez-Najera, L., & Guillean, C. (1996). *Latinos and child welfare / Latinos y el bienestar del nino: Voces de la comunidad*. Unpublished manuscript, University of Michigan School of Social Work.

Ortiz, V. (1995). The diversity of Latino families. In R. Zambrana (Ed.), *Understanding Latino families*. Thousand Oaks, CA: Sage.

Pew Hispanic Foundation. (2005). Hispanics: A people in motion. Retrieved January 10, 2009, from http://www.pewhispanic.org

Queralt, M. (1993). Psychosocial risk factors associated with suicide in a small community sample of Latino adolescent attempters. *Social Work in Education, 15*(2), 91–103.

Reeves, T., & Bennett, C. (2003). *The Asian and Pacific Islander population in the United States, March 2002*. Washington, DC: U.S. Census Bureau.

Rio, A. T., Santisteban, D. A., & Szapocznik, J. (1991). Juvenile delinquency among Hispanics: The role of family in prevention and treatment. In M. Sotomayor (Ed.), *Empowering Latino families: A critical issue for the 90's* (pp. 191–214). Milwaukee, WI: Family Services America.

Ro, M. (2002). *Overview of Asian and Pacific Islanders in the United States and California*. Washington, DC: Center for Policy Alternatives.

Roberts, D. (2002). *Shattered bonds: The color of child welfare*. New York: Basic Books/ Civitas.

Roberts, M. (1998). The Indian Child Welfare Act: Implications for culturally competent service providers. *Michigan Child Welfare Law Journal, 2*(2), 7–11.

Roberts, R. N., Rule, S., & Innocenti, M. S. (1998). *Strengthening the family-professional partnership in services for young children*. Baltimore, MD: Brookes.

Rothe, E. (2004). Hispanic adolescents and their family: Sociocultural factors and treatment considerations. *Adolescent Psychiatry, 28*, 251–278.

Scannapieco, M. (1999). Kinship care in the public child welfare system: A systematic review of the research. In R. L. Hegar & M. Scannapieco (Eds.), *Kinship foster care: Policy, practice, and research*. New York: Oxford University Press.

Schwartz, W. (2002). *The Asian Pacific Islander population in the U.S.* (ERIC Digest 181, EDO-UD-02-00). New York: ERIC Clearinghouse on Urban Education, Institute for Urban and Minority Education.

Sedlak, A., & Schultz, D. (2005). Race differences in child protective services investigations of abuse and neglected children. In D. M. Derezotes, J. Poertner & M. F. Testa (Eds.), *The overrepresentation of African American children in the system* (pp. 97–118). Washington DC: Child Welfare League of America.

Slack, K. S., Holl, J. L., McDaniel, M., Yoo, J., & Bolger, K. (2004). Understanding the risks of child neglect: An exploration of poverty and parenting characteristics. *Child Maltreatment, 9*(4), 395–408.

Smith, C., & Devore, W. (2004). African American children in the child welfare and kinship system: From exclusion to overinclusion. *Children and Youth Services Review, 26*, 427–466.

Terao, S. Y., Borrego, J., J., & Urquiza, A. J. (2001). A reporting and response model of culture and child maltreatment. *Child Maltreatment, 6*(2), 158–168.

Tervalon, M., & Murray-Garcia, J. (1998). Cultural humility versus cultural competence: A critical distinction in defining physician training outcomes in multicultural education. *Journal of Health Care for the Poor and Underserved, 9*(2), 117–125.

U.S. Census Bureau. (2002). The Asian and Pacific Islander population of the United States, March 2002. Retrieved December 22, 2008, from http://www.census.gov/prod/ 2003pubs/p20-540.pdf

U.S. Department of Education. (2000). *Dropout rates in the United States: 2000.* Washington, DC: National Center for Educational Statistics.

U.S. Department of Education. (2005). *25th annual (2003) report to Congress on the implementation of the Individuals with Disabilities Act* (Vol. 1): Author.

U.S. Government Accountability Office. (2006). *Child welfare: Federal action needed to ensure states have plans to safeguard children in the child welfare system displaced by disaster.* Washington, DC: Author.

Vega, W. (1995). The study of Latino families; A point of departure. In R. Zambrana (Ed.), *Understanding Latino families.* Thousand Oaks, CA: Sage Publications.

Weaver, H. N. (1998). Indigenous people in a multicultural society: Unique issues for human services. *Social Work, 43*(3), 203–211.

Widom, C. S., & Hiller-Sturmhofel, S. (2001). Alcohol abuse as a risk factor for and consequence of child abuse. *Alcohol Research and Health, 25,* 52–57.

Williams, N. (1990). *The Mexican American family: Tradition and change.* Dix Hill, NY: General Hall.

Wooley, M., & Grogan-Kaylor, A. (2006). Protective family factors in the context of neighborhood: Promoting positive school outcomes. *Family Relations, 55,* 93–104.

Wrong, D. (1995). *Power: Its forms, bases and uses.* New Brunswick, NJ: Transaction.

Wulczyn, F. (2003). Closing the gap: Are changing exit patterns reducing the time African American children spend in foster care relative to Caucasian children? *Children and Youth Services Review, 25*(5/6), 431–462.

Zambrana, R. E., & Dorrington, C. (1998). Economic and social vulnerability of Latino children and families by subgroup: Implications for child welfare. *Child Welfare, 77*(1), 5–27.

PART III

The Survey Study Design and Mental Health Services Research

Since the mid-1980s a significant change has taken place in researchers' understanding of mental health services for children and youth in the United States. This understanding emphasizes the empirical finding now well established that substantial proportions of children involved with service systems other than mental health either experience the debilitating symptoms and consequences of mental disorders and conditions, or are at high risk of developing these disorders and conditions. Empirical research suggests that more mental health services are delivered to youth in non–specialty mental health sector services than to those in the specialty mental health sector (Burns et al., 1995).

Part 3 adds five new chapters that apply the National Survey of Child and Adolescent Well-Being (NSCAW) data to the rapidly expanding body of knowledge about children and adolescents in the child welfare system, their need for and use of mental health service, and the impact of contextual variables (child welfare agency attributes) on child mental health outcomes. Each chapter demonstrates some of the unique strengths of the NSCAW study design and presents major findings extending the robust empirical research literature that has been rapidly developing since the early 1990s.

Research on mental health service delivery, at a minimum, requires methods for estimating two critical domains: the need for mental health care and the use of such care. In addition, these estimates for need and use must be for defined populations. Methods in NSCAW for measuring mental health care need and use were based largely on methods used in prior work, ensuring that the measures selected were standardized and had considerable use in multiple field studies, including local studies of mental health care for this population. A strong emphasis on meeting these two criteria was a hallmark of the measurement selection process for the full NSCAW study.

What is unique about the NSCAW design as it relates to the examination of mental health care is not the measures selected but the defined population, as shown in two different limitations to prior studies. First, prior research on need for and use of mental health care had focused almost exclusively on the out-of-home portion of the children involved in child welfare, the single exception being papers based on the Great Smoky Mountains Study of Youth (Burns, Angold, & Costello, 1992; Burns et al., 1995). In contrast, NSCAW allows estimates to be made for all children initially identified through investigation, including children who are placed in out-of-home care after investigation, children who remain with their biological families and have cases opened to receive additional child welfare services, and children who remain with their biological families and for whom no case is opened to link the family to child welfare services after the index maltreatment investigation. In this regard, a noteworthy major finding from NSCAW was the high level of mental health need among the large proportion of children in families where investigation was the only service provided by child welfare.

Second, prior studies of need for and use of mental health care for even the out-of-home child welfare population were confined to U.S. city, county, or state locales. In contrast, the NSCAW multistage sampling design allows investigators to generate national estimates for the child welfare population in the United States, as measured by number of investigations. These estimates critically inform policy development at the federal level, which is the locus of control in so many areas of child welfare policy because of federal funding streams such as Title IV-E. However, the NSCAW sampling design, which usually specifies the county as the basis for the primary sampling unit, accrues an additional benefit.[1] For the first time, estimates for need and use of mental health care can be compared among approximately 90 diverse local areas at the county level, because most child welfare practice in the United States is administratively bounded by county government. Variations in child welfare practice therefore can be linked to variations in estimates for the domains of need and use of services. These design features make NSCAW a landmark study and promote it to the forefront of research in U.S. child service systems. No other child-serving system (mental health, juvenile justice, education) boasts the research capacity to examine policy and practice patterns both from a national perspective and across diverse local areas. Glisson's Chapter 13 and Foster and Wells' Chapter 14 take full advantage of this multilevel data.

Another critical element of NSCAW is the longitudinal cohort design, which was enhanced by strategies for estimating monthly indicators of living arrangements (in home with no child welfare services, in home with child welfare services, and out of home), as well as use of mental health care (receiving or not receiving care). Although longitudinal cohort designs have been used in prior local studies, the 36-month timeframe for NSCAW exceeds that for almost all other studies; moreover, prior local studies have not included both the in-home and out-of-home populations.

An additional design feature of NSCAW is measurement of mental health care need and use for both the child and the child's caregiver. This feature is congruent with the mission focus of child welfare on both children and parents within family systems that show substantial risks in the areas of safety, permanence, and child well-being. Information on both caregiver and child permits examination of how mental health service delivery for the caregiver may affect service delivery and outcomes for the child.

In addition to the benefits of the NSCAW longitudinal cohort sampling and measurement design features, the NSCAW design has revealed several methodological issues that complicate the use of NSCAW data. In the area of measurement, need for mental health care was typically assessed with the Achenbach Child Behavior Checklist, a standardized dimensional and psychometric approach in the tradition of child psychology. In Chapter 10, Horwitz and colleagues used the Vineland Adaptive Behavior Scales in addition to the Child Behavior Checklist when analyzing service use among the youngest children in the study. Child welfare has large proportions of very young children; most behavior scales and mental health diagnostic measures that have been used in mental health services research are either inappropriate or insensitive as indicators of the need for mental health care in such young children.

In contrast, as the reader will note in the study of caregivers by Burns and her colleagues (Chapter 12), measurement of need for mental health care for parent caregivers (but not substitute caregivers such as foster or kinship parents) was based on the diagnostic approach of psychiatry, with simulated *Diagnostic and Statistical Manual of Mental Disorders* (American Psychiatric Association, 1994) diagnostic modules for depression and substance use but not the whole range of *DSM-IV* diagnoses. This chapter shows the power gained in analysis of specific diagnostic conditions when the measure of need is also diagnostic. Because most mental health treatment decisions are best driven by identification of specific needs for treatment, this study can offer extremely detailed analyses of services provided and their outcomes. The dimensional approach used for measurement of children's mental health care need in the NSCAW study, as demonstrated in the chapter by Horwitz and colleagues, affords less specificity in the analyses of diagnoses and conditions.

For child mental health service use, the measurement instrument of choice was the Child and Adolescent Services Assessment (Burns, Angold, Magruder-Habib, Costello, & Patrick, 1994), which had been used in prior studies, such as the Great Smoky Mountains Study. However, because of the time constraints of the omnibus survey used in NSCAW, the specification of volume of services was truncated generally to include only type of service, as well as the month of onset and the month of offset for use of the type of service. This truncation means that assumptions have to be made about whether the service use was continuous (i.e., monthly) in the time between onset and offset. Chapter 11, by Landsverk and colleagues, illustrates how these assumptions can be made for an effective analysis of whether involvement in child welfare services is linked first to onset and then to offset in mental health service receipt.

It is noteworthy that the NSCAW design does not include a feature found in a number of important local studies—namely, capitalizing on the availability of administrative data to record actual service use (Halfon, Berkowitz, & Klee, 1992; Harman, Childs, & Kelleher, 2000; Leslie, Landsverk, Horton, Ganger, & Newton, 2000; Takayama, Bergman, & Connell, 1994). This recording of actual use has usually been done with Medicaid data because Medicaid is the major funder for mental health care, especially for children residing in out-of-home care. The use of administrative data has the immense advantage of allowing precise dating for unit of mental health service use, in addition to providing an excellent estimate of volume of use. Studies based on administrative data alone do not, however, enjoy the advantages of NSCAW and several local studies, for which good standardized measurement mental health need is available through survey methods. Although NSCAW survey data could be linked to administrative data on service use, no study has yet done so.

Investigators are just beginning to exploit the NSCAW study data to examine the influence of contextual variables on individual outcomes. The approaches introduced here in Part 3 are only beginning to show the potential to yield exciting new findings and innovative methods in future work derived from this landmark study.

NOTES

1. For further details, see Chapter 1 (this volume), which addresses NSCAW study design.

REFERENCES

American Psychiatric Association. (1994). *Diagnostic and statistical manual of mental disorders* (4th ed.). Washington, DC: Author.

Burns, B. J., Angold, A., & Costello, E. J. (1992). Measuring child, adolescent, and family service use. In L. Bickman & D. J. Rog (Eds.), *Evaluating mental health services for children*. San Francisco: Jossey-Bass.

Burns, B. J., Angold, A., Magruder-Habib, K., Costello, E. J., & Patrick, M. K. S. (1994). *The Child and Adolescent Services Assessment (CASA), parent interview and child interview*. Durham, NC: Developmental Epidemiology Program, Department of Psychiatry, Duke University Medical Center.

Burns, B. J., Costello, E. J., Angold, A., Tweed, D., Stangl, D., Farmer, E. M. Z., et al. (1995). Children's mental health service use across service sectors. *Health Affairs, 14*(3), 147–159.

Halfon, N., Berkowitz, G., & Klee, L. (1992). Children in foster care in California: An examination of Medicaid reimbursed health services utilization. *Pediatrics, 89*(6), 1230–1237.

Harman, J. S., Childs, G. E., & Kelleher, K. J. (2000). Mental health care utilization and expenditures by children in foster care. *Archives of Pediatrics & Adolescent Medicine, 154*, 1114–1117.

Leslie, L. K., Landsverk, J., Horton, M. B., Ganger, W., & Newton, R. R. (2000). The heterogeneity of children and their experiences in kinship care. *Child Welfare, 79*(3), 315–334.

Takayama, J. I., Bergman, A. B., & Connell, F. A. (1994). Children in foster care in the state of Washington: Health care utilization and expenditures. *Journal of the American Medical Association, 271*(23), 1850–1855.

Patterns and Predictors of Mental Health Services Use by Children in Contact With the Child Welfare System

SARAH McCUE HORWITZ, MICHAEL S. HURLBURT, AND JINJIN ZHANG

With 3.3 million referrals to child welfare system agencies, involving 6 million children in 2005 and 523,000 children in out-of-home care as of September 30, 2003, the health and well-being of children in the child welfare system is of considerable public health importance (Administration for Children and Families, 2005, 2007). These children, particularly those in out-of-home care, have been identified with high levels of physical and mental health problems, as well as developmental and educational challenges (Chernoff, Combs-Orme, Risley-Curtiss, & Heisler, 1994; Clausen, Landsverk, Ganger, Chadwick, & Litrownik, 1998; Combs-Orme, Chernoff, & Kager, 1991; Halfon, Mendonca, & Berkowitz, 1995; Hochstadt, Jaudes, Zimo, & Schachter, 1987; Klee & Halfon, 1987; McIntyre & Keesler, 1986; Pilowsky, 1995; Schor, 1982, 1989; Simms, 1989; Stein, Evans, Mazumdar, & Rae-Grant, 1996; Swire & Kavaler, 1977; Szilagyi, 1998; U.S. General Accounting Office, 1995). Estimates of mental health problems range from 23% to 80%, with 35% to 80% of these children experiencing chronic health problems, up to 43% experiencing growth abnormalities, about one third having untreated health conditions, and between 31% and 67% experiencing educational difficulties (Chernoff et al., 1994; Clausen et al., 1998; Pilowsky, 1995; Schor, 1989; Simms, 1989; Stein et al., 1996; Szilagyi, 1998).

For almost 30 years as evidence has accumulated regarding the potential magnitude of these problems, numerous professional organizations have issued guidelines for the assessment and treatment of children involved with the child welfare system, particularly those in out-of-home care. In 1987 the American Academy of Pediatrics issued recommendations for the assessment of children entering substitute care (American Academy of Pediatrics, 1987). These recommendations were followed by a 1988 Child Welfare League of America publication, "Standards for Health Care Services for Children in Out-of-Home Care" (Child Welfare League of America, 1988). Both documents, with more recent recommendations by the American Academy of Pediatrics (American Academy of Pediatrics, 1994, 2002), urge comprehensive assessments by experienced professionals, with consistent, continual follow-up care; however, as the extant literature emphasizes, few existing standards are met, and children's physical and mental health needs remain unaddressed (American Academy of Pediatrics, 2002; Simms, Dubowitz, & Szilagyi, 2000; Simms & Halfon, 1994).

Many explanations for these unmet health and mental health needs have been offered, including absence of clear state policies, little access to prereferral health histories, lack of consistent systems of service, effects of managed care, and lack of service use information, particularly for children in the child welfare system but not foster care (Klee & Halfon, 1987; Simms et al., 2000). This lack of information is particularly important for mental health services because research has documented that children who remain in home incur high levels of mental health needs—nearly as high as those of children in foster care—and children placed in foster care use Medicaid-reimbursed mental health services at many times the rate that other Medicaid-covered youth do (Burns et al., 2004; Clausen et al., 1998; Halfon, Berkowitz, & Klee, 1992; McIntyre & Keesler, 1986; Pilowsky, 1995; Stein et al., 1996).

Studies on health services use in general and mental health services use in particular have lagged behind studies documenting need. In fact, studies of patterns and predictors of mental health services for children in the child welfare system were scarce until the early 1990s (for one exception, see Moffatt, Peddie, Stulginshas, Pless, & Steinmetz, 1985). This fledgling literature on mental health services falls into four categories: large administrative database studies of Medicaid-insured children, including children in foster care; single-site studies of children in foster care, including a rich set of studies from San Diego; small, often treatment, studies involving children in the child welfare system but not out-of-home care; and the National Survey of Child and Adolescent Well-Being (NSCAW), the first nationally representative study of children referred to the child welfare system because of alleged child maltreatment. Because these four types of studies differ from one another in terms of focus, variables, and results, reviewing them categorically permits insight into patterns and predictors of services for mental health problems.

Large Database Studies

Beginning with the seminal work of Halfon and colleagues (1992), six studies have examined Medicaid databases to (1) determine amount of service use for mental health conditions, (2) compare mental health services use by children in foster care with use by Medicaid-insured children not in foster care, *(3)* determine costs of mental health services, *(4)* identify types of services used for mental health problems, *(5)* track changes in services over time, and, most recently, *(6)* link placement stability with mental health services use (Table 10.1; dos Reis, Zito, Safer, & Soeken, 2001; Halfon et al., 1992; Harman, Childs, & Kelleher, 2000; Rubin et al., 2005; Snowden, Cuellar, & Libby, 2003; Takayama, Bergman, & Connell, 1994); Halfon and colleagues (1992), using medical claims data, found that children in foster care, although representing only 4% of Medicaid-eligible users, accounted for 41% of all mental health services users, with 10 to 20 times the rate of utilization for some services. Interestingly, only mental health problems and psychiatric services showed large differences in use (Halfon et al., 1992). In examining health care utilization expenditures for Medicaid-insured children in Washington State, Takayama and colleagues (1994) also found large differences in use of specific services, including mental health services, by children in foster care; moreover, they documented large differences in expenditures between children in foster care and those receiving assistance from the then-available Aid to Families with Dependent Children (AFDC).

In 2000 Harman et al. examined type of services and expenditures for mental health problems of children eligible for Medicaid because they were in foster care, qualified for Supplemental Security Income (SSI) because of disabilities, or were supported by AFDC. Using Medicaid claims and eligibility files for children aged 5 to 17 years and living in seven counties in southwestern Pennsylvania, Harman and colleagues found that children in foster care were 3 to 10 times more likely than the other children to receive a mental health diagnosis and had diagnostic, utilization, and expenditure patterns resembling those of children on AFDC because of disabilities. Dos Reis and colleagues (2001) likewise examined use of mental health services for children with different medical aid categories. Using Medicaid claims data for one mid-Atlantic suburban county, they found that the prevalence of mental health disorders and the use of mental health services were considerably higher for children in foster care than for those on SSI or AFDC.

Snowden, Cuellar, and Libby (2003) used Medicaid claims for two managed-care sites and one fee-for-service site to examine differences in use of mental health services for minority and nonminority children in foster care and pre- and post-capitated managed care. They found that inpatient days were reduced for white youth, but no increase in outpatient services use offsets this reduction. After the introduction of capitated managed care, Hispanic and African American children were more likely to receive care in residential treatment facilities than they were before the introduction of capitated managed care. Even more recently, Rubin and colleagues (2005), linking Medicaid claims data with child welfare data, examined the effect of placement stability and health status on use and costs of mental health services. As hypothesized, multiple placements and episodic foster care, as well as physical health care costs, age, and gender, predicted use of mental health services.

These studies establish that children in foster care have higher mental health services use rates and costs than other children supported by public insurance;

Table 10.1A Characteristics Related to Mental Health Services Use

Study Type	Age	Gen	Ethnicity					Ins	Placement					Placements	P H Prob	Epi FC	Med FC	Maltreatment			PSYC DX	Impaired FP ED (Low)	CW visits	Care Time (High)	STAT Area
		M	C	AA	H	As	O		H	H/S	FC	Rel	Grp					PHY	SEX	NEG					
Large Database Studies																									
Halfon et al., 1992	+																								
Takayama et al., 1994																									
Harman et al., 2000																									
dos Reis et al., 2001	+	NS	+	+			−																		
Snowden et al., 2003				+	+																				
In, Out Res, Claims																									
Rubin et al., 2005	+	+	−	−	−	−	−							+	+	+	−								
Individual Sites																									
McMillan et al., 2004; *Life inpt, INT*	−	+	−	+	+	+	−											+	+	−	+				
McMillan et al., 2004; *Life res, INT*	−	+	−	+	+	+	+											NS	NS	NS	+				
McMillan et al., 2004; *Life outpt, INT*	−	NS	−	−	−	−	−											+	+	−	NS				
McMillan et al., 2004; *Cur res, INT*	NS	NS	NS	+	+	+	+			NS								+	NS	NS	+				
McMillan et al., 2004; *Cur outpt, INT*	NS	NS	NS	−	−	−	−					+						NS	NS	NS	+				
Farmer et al., 2001; *INT, MH*	NS	NS		−				NS			+C	+									+				
Zima et al., 2000; *ADHD, INT*	+	NS	+					NS						NS	NS							NS	NS	NS	NS

Zima et al., 2000 ethnicity: ←versus others→

Table 10.1A (continued)

Zima et al., 2000; *Other diag, INT*	NS	NS	NS	NS	NS	NS	NS		NS	NS				NS		NS	+	+	NS
San Diego Studies																			
Blumberg et al., 1996; *mult vs. sgl*	+	−	NS	NS	NS	NS		+					+						NS
Garland et al., 1996; *INT*	+	NS									+	+	−	CBCL (+)					
Leslie et al., 2000; *INT*	+	+	No diff	−	−		Ref	−			NS	NS	NS	CBCL (+)					
Garland & Besinger, 1997; *Recs*	Controlled−	−				←Controlled→				←Controlled→	+			CBCL (+)					
Garland et al., 2000; *ANY/INT*	+		−	−		+					+	−		CBCL (+)					
CPS (Not Just FC)																			
Trupin et al., 1993; *quest*	+					+													
Ezzell et al., 1997; *INT*	NS	NS	NS	NS	NS	NS	NS												
Horowitz et al., 1997; *vsts/questions*	NS	+	+	+	+	NS	NS		Un	NS	All sex abused			CBCL/ CDI (+)					
Kolko et al., 2003; *INT/ ANY*	NS	NS	NS	NS	NS	NS					All phys abused			NS	NS	NS	NS		
NSCAW Studies (All INT)																			

(continued)

Table 10.1A (continued)

Study Type	Age	Gen	Ethnicity					Ins	Placement					P H	Epi FC	Med FC	Maltreatment			PSYC	Impaired	FP	CW	Care	STAT
		M	C	AA	H	As	O		H	H/S	FC	Rel	Grp	Prob	FC		PHY	SEX	NEG	DX		ED visits Low	visits	Time High	Area
Burns et al., 2–5; ANY	NS	NS		NS	NS	NS	NS		NS	NS	NS	NS	NS							+					
Burns et al., 6–10; ANY	NS	NS		–	NS	NS	–		–								NS	NS	NS	+					
Burns et al., 11+; ANY	NS		NS	NS	NS	NS	NS		–								NS	NS	–	+					
Leslie et al., 2004; ANY/OUT	+	NS	NS	NS	NS	NS	NS				Ref	–	+				NS	+	–	+					
Hurlburt et al., 2004; ANY/OUT	+	NS		–			NS	NS		+	+	+	+				+	NS	NS	NS					
Farmer et al., 2005; Any service	+	+		–			NS	Un(–)			+	+					NS	NS	–	CBCL (+)					
Farmer et al., 2005; MH	–	NS	NS	NS	NS	NS	NS	NS			+						+	NS	NS	CBCL (+)					
Farmer et al., 2005; School	NS	NS	NS	NS	NS	NS	NS	NS	NS	NS	NS	NS	NS				NS	NS	NS	NS					
Farmer et al., 2005; Justice	+	NS	NS	NS	NS	NS	NS	NS	NS	NS	NS	NS	NS				NS	NS	NS	NS					
Farmer et al., 2005; Medical	+	NS	NS	NS	–	NS	NS	NS	NS	NS	NS	NS	NS				NS	NS	NS	NS					
Stahmer et al., 2005; Any	+	NS		–			NS			–	←R→						NS	NS	+	BEH/ DEV +					
Leslie et al., 2005; OUT	+	NS		–	NS	–	NS	+		–	←R→						+	NS	NS	CBCL (+)					

Table 10.1B (continued)

Study Type	Family Stress/ Risk	Maltreat Home	Family Structure	Admit Abuse	Maltreat Got Service	Age of abuse onset	No. of Abuse Incidents	Family Function	Prior Maltreat	Abuse Severity	Subs Elig for Agency/Serv	Links	MH Provider Supply	County-Level Poverty	County Child Popul.
Large Database Studies															
Halfon et al., 1992															
Takayama et al., 1994															
Harman et al., 2000															
dos Reis et al., 2001															
Snowden et al., 2003															
In, Out Res, Claims															
Rubin et al., 2005															
Individual Sites															
McMillan et al., 2004; Life inpt, INT															
McMillan et al., 2004; Life res, INT															
McMillan et al., 2004; Life outpt, INT															
McMillan et al., 2004; Cur res, INT															
McMillan et al., 2004; Cur outpt, INT															
Farmer et al., 2001; INT, MH															
Zima et al., 2000; ADHD, INT															
Zima et al., 2000; Other diag, INT															

(continued)

Table 10.1B (continued)

Study Type	Family Stress/ Risk	Maltreat Home	Family Structure	Admit Abuse	Maltreat Got Service	Age of abuse onset	No. of Abuse Incidents	Family Function	Prior Maltreat	Abuse Severity	Subs Elig for Agency/Serv	Links	MH Provider Supply	County-Level Poverty	County Child Popul.
San Diego Studies															
Blumberg et al., 1996; *mult vs. sgl*															
Garland et al., 1996; *INT*															
Leslie et al., 2000; *INT*															
Garland & Besinger, 1997; *Recs*															
Garland et al., 2000; *ANY/INT*															
CPS (Not Just FC)															
Trupin et al., 1993; *quest*	+														
Ezzell et al., 1997; *INT*		NS	NS	NS	NS										
Horowitz et al., 1997; *vsts/ questions*						+	+	NS							
Kolko et al., 2003; *INT/ANY*					NS				NS	NS	NS				
NSCAW Studies (All INT)															
Burns et al., 2–5; ANY	NS														
Burns et al., 6–10; ANY	NS														
Burns et al., 11+; ANY	Parent MH+														
Leslie et al., 2004; *ANY/OUT*															
Hurlburt et al., 2004; *ANY/ OUT*	NS											-	NS	NS	NS
Farmer et al., 2005; *Any service*	+														
Farmer et al., 2005; *MH*	NS														
Farmer et al., 2005; *School*	-														
Farmer et al., 2005; *Justice*	NS														
Farmer et al., 2005; *Medical*	NS														
Stahmer et al., 2005; *Any*															
Leslie et al., 2005; *OUT*															

Table 10.1C (continued)

Study Type	Family Stress/Risk	Maltreat Home	Family Structure	Admit Abuse	Maltreat Got Service	Age of Abuse Onset	No. of Abuse Incidents	FAM FUNC	Prior Maltreat	Abuse Severity	Subs Elig for Agency/Serv
Large Database Studies											
Halfon et al., 1992											
Takayama et al., 1994											
Harman et al., 2000											
dos Reis et al., 2001											
Snowden et al., 2003											
In, Out Res, Claims											
Rubin et al., 2005											
Individual Sites											
McMillan et al., 2004; *Lifetime inpatient, INT*											
McMillan et al., 2004; *Lifetime residential, INT*											
McMillan et al., 2004; *Lifetime outpatient, INT*											
McMillan et al., 2004; *Current residential, INT*											
McMillan et al., 2004; *Current outpatient, INT*											
Farmer et al., 2001; *INT, MH*											
Zima et al., 2000; *ADHD, INT*											
Zima et al., 2000; *Other diagnosis, INT*											
San Diego Studies											
Blumberg et al., 1996; *mult vs. single*											

(continued)

Table 10.1C (continued)

Study Type	Family Stress/Risk	Maltreat Home	Family Structure	Admit Abuse	Maltreat Got Service	Age of Abuse Onset	No. of Abuse Incidents	FAM FUNC	Prior Maltreat	Abuse Severity	Subs Elig for Agency/Serv
Garland et al., 1996; *INT*											
Leslie et al., 2000; *INT*											
Garland & Besinger, 1997; *Records*											
Garland et al., 2000; *ANY/INT*											
CPS (Not Just FC)											
Trupin et al., 1993; *quest*				NS							
Ezzell et al., 1997; *INT*	+	NS	NS	NS							
Horowitz et al., 1997; *visits/ questions*					NS	+		NS			
Kolko et al., 2003; *INT/ANY*					NS		+		NS	NS	NS
NSCAW Studies (All INT)											
Burns et al., 2–5; *ANY*	NS										
Burns et al., 6–10; *ANY*											
Burns et al., 11+; *ANY*	Parent MH+										
Leslie et al., 2004; *ANY/OUT*											
Hurlburt et al., 2004; *ANY/ OUT*	NS										
Farmer et al., 2005; *Any service*	+										
Farmer et al., 2005; *MH*	NS										
Farmer et al., 2005; *School*	-										
Farmer et al., 2005; *Justice*	NS										
Farmer et al., 2005; *Medical*	NS										
Stahmer et al., 2005; *Any*											
Leslie et al., 2005; *OUT*											

Table 10.1D (continued)

Study Type	Links	MH Provider Supply	County-Level Poverty	County Child Population
Large Database Studies				
Halfon et al., 1992				
Takayama et al., 1994				
Harman et al., 2000				
dos Reis et al., 2001				
Snowden et al., 2003				
In, Out Res, Claims				
Rubin et al., 2005				
Individual Sites				
McMillan et al., 2004; *Lifetime inpatient, INT*				
McMillan et al., 2004; *Lifetime residential, INT*				
McMillan et al., 2004; *Lifetime outpatient, INT*				
McMillan et al., 2004; *Current residential, INT*				
McMillan et al., 2004; *Current outpatient, INT*				
Farmer et al., 2001; *INT, MH*				
Zima et al., 2000; *ADHD, INT*				
Zima et al., 2000; *Other diagnosis, INT*				
San Diego Studies				
Blumberg et al., 1996; *mult vs. single*				

(continued)

Table 10.1D (continued)

Study Type	Links	MH Provider Supply	County-Level Poverty	County Child Population
Garland et al., 1996; *INT*				
Leslie et al., 2000; *INT*				
Garland & Besinger, 1997; *Records*				
Garland et al., 2000; *ANY/INT*				
CPS (Not Just FC)				
Trupin et al., 1993; *quest*				
Ezzell et al., 1997; *INT*				
Horowitz et al., 1997; *visits/questions*				
Kolko et al., 2003; *INT/ANY*				
NSCAW Studies (All INT)				
Burns et al., 2–5; *ANY*				
Burns et al., 6–10; *ANY*				
Burns et al., 11+; *ANY*				
Leslie et al., 2004; *ANY/OUT*				
Hurlburt et al., 2004; *ANY/OUT*	—	NS	NS	NS
Farmer et al., 2005; *Any service*				
Farmer et al., 2005; *MH*				
Farmer et al., 2005; *School*				
Farmer et al., 2005; *Justice*				
Farmer et al., 2005; *Medical*				
Stahmer et al., 2005; *Any*				
Leslie et al., 2005; *OUT*				

Note: Possible respondents for each case may be reduced from four to two or three, depending on service receipt and school status.

however, until the studies by Snowden and colleagues (2003) and Rubin and colleagues (2005), few predictors of mental health services use other than foster care placement were investigated.

Single-Site Studies

The documentation of high need for and use of mental health services prompted investigations whose data on predictors, or correlates, were generated by cohorts developed in single-site studies and published beginning in the mid-1990s. Zima, Bussing, Yang, and Belin (2000) used the Los Angeles County Department of Children and Family Services (DCFS) Management Information System to identify 6- to 12-year-old children placed out of home in three of the eight county service areas. Data were gathered through DCFS records, home interviews with the foster parent and child, and telephone interviews with the child's teacher. A county clinician identified 80% of the children as having at least one mental health diagnosis, with services use among them in the previous 12 months common but not universal. The most common features related to services use were older age and white race/ethnicity for children diagnosed with attention-deficit/hyperactivity disorder. Number of caseworker visits and foster parent education were related to use for those with other diagnoses.

Farmer and colleagues (2001) examined mental health services use for 9- to 13-year-old children in the Great Smoky Mountains Study, a longitudinal study of mental health problems and service use in a rural area of the southeastern United States. Children studied were those with a history of foster care, those with social services involvement but no foster care placements, and those in poverty with no known contacts or placements. The authors found high rates of mental health problems in all three groups, but no differences in problems or lifetime rates of services use emerged between the foster care and social services contact groups, both showing very high mental health service use across all sectors. This high use rate differed significantly from that of the poverty group, indicating that social service contact was associated with use of services, particularly specialty services. For specialty mental health, education, and medical care sectors, use was related to need; in addition, for education and medical care sectors public health insurance was an important predictor.

Another single-site study of services use examined older youth in the foster care system in Missouri (McMillen et al., 2004). The authors interviewed 90% of 17-year-old youth in eight counties and found that 94% had used mental health services over their lifetimes, 83% had used services in the past year, and 66% were current users. Twenty-five percent reported service use predating foster care. The authors found that children of color were less likely to receive psychotropic medications, residential or group care, and outpatient therapy than white children. Other important correlates of psychotropic medication use and outpatient therapy included younger age at entry into foster care, current disorder, and living situation; correlates of residential care included physical abuse and current disorder.

One site, San Diego, has produced a considerable research portfolio on mental health services use and predictors for children in out-of-home care. Investigators at the Child and Adolescent Services Research Center in San Diego developed the Foster Care Mental Health Study, a cohort of children aged 16 or younger and referred to the primary receiving facility for maltreated children in San Diego County between May 1990 and October 1991. Blumberg, Landsverk, Ellis-Macleod, Ganger, and Culver (1996), with data derived from this longitudinal cohort of 1,352 children, noted considerable overlap between social services and mental health services (17.4%); additionally, multisystem youth were older, were more likely to have been removed for physical abuse, were more likely to have been placed in a group home, and had lower functioning scores. Overall, public mental health services use was related to older age; few children in the multisystem strata had received treatment before placement (16.2%).

Using a subset of the original cohort, 662 children aged 2 to 17 years who were in foster care for at least 5 months, Garland, Landsverk, Hough, and Ellis-MacLeod (1996) investigated whether the most serious type of maltreatment alleged was related to use of mental health services. Overall, 56% of the sample received some mental health service while in care, with children placed because of sexual or physical abuse, those in the clinical range on the Child Behavior Checklist (CBCL; Achenbach, 1991), and those who were older having higher likelihood of service use; children placed because of neglect or caretaker absence were less likely than those removed for physical or sexual abuse to receive services. Furthermore, the authors found that the frequency of outpatient visits for these children was high—an average of 15.4 visits in 6 months, indicating ongoing treatment.

Garland and Besinger (1997) subsequently examined racial and ethnic differences in court referrals for mental health services for children in foster care. Examining court records for 142 children aged 2 to 16 and enrolled in the Foster Care Mental Health Study, Garland and Besinger found that mental health service use in the year before placement was rare: Children were more often ordered into counseling or psychotherapy (59.2%). Examining use both before the child's removal and in the 6 months after disposition, they found that African American and Hispanic children were less likely than white children to receive psychotherapy—even after controlling for potentially confounding factors such as age, type of maltreatment, and prior service use. Although differences by ethnicity in caseworkers' recommendations for services were few, they did exist in court orders for services.

Garland and colleagues (2000) next investigated racial differences in mental health services use in the San Diego cohort, while controlling for the effects of other potential confounders such as severity of need, gender, age, and type of maltreatment. Within the first 6 months of placement, 65.3% of white children received care, whereas 50.0% of African American and 46.6% of Hispanic children received care. Logistic regression results indicated that older age, higher CBCL scores, and sexual or physical abuse as the reason for placement, were all related positively to use; neglect, African American race, and Latino ethnicity were negatively related to use. An interaction between race and need meant that African American children with high need were as likely to receive services as white children with similar need.

Leslie and colleagues (2000) examined the role of placement type and the use of mental health services in 480 of the San Diego cohort who were at least 2 years old and still in kinship foster care 4 months after placement. At the 18-month follow-up, 41.5% of the children had at least one mental health visit documented, with age, male gender, and elevated CBCL scores being positively associated; placement pattern (kinship at some point in the out-of-home placement), an absent caregiver, and Latino or Asian race/ethnicity were negatively associated.

Disconcertingly, results from single-site studies, though confirming service use as determined by need, also evince service use as determined by sociodemographic and placement characteristics such as race/ethnicity, age, and living situation.

Non–Foster Care Child Welfare System Studies

Among the studies examining mental health services use are a few on children with protective services involvement but not out-of-home care. These studies involve children and families referred for treatment, usually have small samples, and always investigate an array of variables more properly "clinical" than those of the larger studies of mental health services use among children in foster care. Trupin, Tarico, Low, Jemelka, and McClellan (1993) examined 191 randomly selected children, aged 3 to 18 years, from Washington's child welfare system. Time elapsed between onset of emotional problems and date of first service receipt revealed considerable delay. When barriers to service receipt were examined, 19% were child focused (e.g., poor cooperation), 21% were systems focused (e.g., lack of coordination among providers), and 58% were family focused (e.g., lack of compliance with recommendations or inability to afford services).

Ezzell, Swenson, and Faldowski (1999) investigated the relationship between child, family, and case characteristics and mental health services utilization for 37 Medicaid-eligible children monitored by the child welfare system after substantiation of physical abuse. Forty-three percent received mental health services; 43% received medical services. The factor related to mental health services utilization was family stressors. When the maltreating caregiver did not live at home, the child was more likely to receive services.

Horowitz, Putnam, Noll, and Trickett (1997) examined a sample of 6- to 16-year-old girls referred for treatment after sexual abuse; most received individual treatment as well as group or family treatment. Total number of treatment sessions was predicted by ethnicity (with minorities receiving fewer sessions), severity of abuse, early age of onset of abuse, and childhood psychopathology.

More recently, Kolko, Baumann, and Caldwell (2003) examined the correlates of treatment in 68 children referred to Allegheny County Children and Youth

Services. After 6 months, 19.1% of children had received a treatment (individual or group therapy, partial hospitalization, probation). Correlates of treatment receipt at the 6-month follow-up included type of maltreatment (sexual abuse) and a tendency for children who received services to have families or parents who received services. Record reviews of service use in the 2 years after the 6-month follow-up showed 55% of children receiving treatment and 50.8% placed outside the home at least once. Services at the first follow-up were related to receipt of services at the second follow-up. In general, child treatment was not associated with a lower rate of child placement or reabuse.

The National Survey of Child and Adolescent Well-Being

The NSCAW data address many of the other studies' shortcomings, including the lack of national samples and the heavy focus on children placed in nonkinship foster care. The initial article on mental health services use in the NSCAW sample (Burns et al., 2004) found that 47.9% of children, as identified by the CBCL, needed these services. Only 15.8% of children had received any mental health services in the 12 months preceding the baseline interview; only 24.4% of those with need had received any. For 2–5 year olds, CBCL scores in the clinical range and sexual abuse as a reason for referral correlated with service use. For 6–10 year olds, CBCL scores in the clinical range and out-of-home placement were associated with increased service use, while black children had lower use. For those 11–14 years old, CBCL scores in the clinical range, out-of-home placement, and parental severe mental illness were associated with higher rates of service use.

Leslie et al. (2005) examined the relationship between mental health service use and entry into child welfare among the 3,592 children aged 2 to 14 years at baseline. They found that the likelihood of mental health services use increased immediately after child welfare system contact, decreased about 3 months after contact, and differed by level of child welfare system involvement. Children who remained in their homes with no child welfare services were one third as likely to use mental health services as those who were placed in out-of-home care. Those who remained in their homes with child welfare services were half as likely to use services as children placed in out-of-home care. Other important predictors of service use included older age, white race/ethnicity, physical abuse, neglect or abandonment, insurance, and need as measured by the CBCL.

Leslie and colleagues (2003), in a companion study to NSCAW, investigated child welfare agencies' policies for inclusive and comprehensive (i.e., physical, mental, and developmental) evaluations for children entering care. They found that 42.6% of the agencies reported having comprehensive policies across domains, 14% specified physical and developmental assessments, and 18.3% specified only physical health assessments. Agencies with inclusive policies reported increased numbers of children receiving assessments.

Hurlburt and colleagues (2004) expanded on the county-level contextual data in NSCAW by examining the ways child welfare and mental health services systems integration and supply of mental health providers related to use of mental health services by the 2,823 children who were either placed out of home or remained in home with child welfare services. This first longitudinal analysis of NSCAW data, examining service use between the time of contact with protective services and the Wave 2 (12-month follow-up) interviews, found that, with the key county variables in the model, age was negatively related to service use, as was black or African American race; physical, emotional, or sexual abuse and any type of foster care were positively related to use. Most important, counties with stronger services integration showed less discrepancy in service use between black and white children.

Stahmer and colleagues (2005) examined developmental and behavioral needs against service use in the youngest children in the NSCAW sample, 2,813 children younger than 6 years old. They found that both toddlers and preschoolers had high rates of mental health and developmental need, regardless of postinvestigation placement. Use of any service was related to need, as well as to older age, race/ethnicity, abandonment, and out-of-home placement.

Farmer and colleagues (Farmer et al., in press) examined current mental health services use at the Wave 3 (18-month follow-up) interview: 32.7% of children were in the clinical range on the CBCL, and 23.8% were receiving some type of service, with specialty mental health providers (16.2%) and schools (15.2%) being the most common. Predictors of any service use were older age, male gender, nonkinship foster care, high parental risk scores, and clinical-range CBCL scores; negatively related to use were black or African American race, neglect, and lack of insurance.

Data Set Characteristics, Test Variables, and Goals

Research on service use by children in contact with the child welfare system, much of it focusing on children in out-of-home care, provides considerable information on the need for and use of services for different segments of the child welfare population. Studies across geographic areas indicate that children in out-of-home care have very high rates of service use. Consistently, these studies show that rates of service use increase with age and that black or African American race/ethnicity may have an important inverse relationship with service use over time. A large increase in use of mental health services in the months following contact with child welfare is common, with much lower rates of service use in the months before contact, although increases in use may be greater for children in out-of-home care.

Despite the helpfulness of this information, our understanding of patterns of and predictors of mental health service use could be improved. First, we must understand differences in service use patterns among children whose families have different levels of involvement with child welfare, from referral and investigation only to placement in out-of-home care. Second, to understand patterns of increase and decrease in service use over time, as well as how these patterns relate specifically to contact with the child welfare system, we must extend analysis over a longer period of time and examine total use of services rather than point-in-time estimates. Third, examination of patterns of service use in developmental age groups can illuminate pathways into and drivers of services that may shape children's experience with mental health services over longer periods of time. Finally, a national perspective would help bridge local findings with broader patterns and predictors of service use.

The NSCAW study is the first nationally representative study of its kind. One of its unique features is its focus not only on children placed out of home but also on children who remain in their homes after the child welfare system's investigation of child maltreatment. Here we focus on the 3,120 children who were aged 2 years or older at Wave 1 and for whom a caregiver's interview was available at both the Wave 1 and Wave 4 interviews. This sample included 759 children (9.6% weighted) in out-of-home care at Wave 1; 1,340 children (24.2% weighted) living at home, with child welfare services delivered to the family; and 1,021 children (66.2% weighted) remaining at home without child welfare services. Child welfare services could range from minimal (e.g., information and/or referral to community services delivered by peripheral organizations) to intense (e.g., regular contact with a child welfare caseworker).

Our analyses support the following goals: (1) to describe services received for mental health problems over the entire 36 months of NSCAW, including type and duration of receipt in months; (2) to investigate possible service use predictors suggested in the extant literature for two time periods, study entry to 18 months and 18 to 36 months; and (3) to assess the mental health services use in the two main service settings, specialty mental health services and school-based services, as it affects future service use in these sectors.

Methods

Information about children, their families, and their use of specialty and school-based mental health services was drawn from sections of the NSCAW surveys completed at each wave: Wave 1 (baseline), Wave 2 (12-month follow-up), Wave 3 (18-month follow-up), and Wave 4 (36-month follow-up). Data come from interviews with caseworkers at Wave 1and from interviews with current caregivers at each subsequent wave. For children remaining in their homes, caregiver respondents were usually biological parents; for those removed from their homes, respondents were kinship or nonkinship foster caregivers or group-care staff.

Measures

CHILD BACKGROUND CHARACTERISTICS   Children's age, gender, and race/ethnicity were collected as part of the initial case identification procedure and were confirmed through caregiver and caseworker interviews.

CHILD PLACEMENT   For descriptive purposes, the child's placement at baseline was classified into one of six categories (Table 10.2). In subsequent analyses, the various out-of-home placements (formal placement in kinship or nonkinship foster care, group care, or other out-of-home setting) were combined into one category. Most analyses used three primary placement categories: *(1)* at home, no child welfare services; *(2)* at home, with child welfare services; and *(3)* out of home.

MALTREATMENT HISTORY   Caseworkers identified the types of suspected maltreatment leading to the child welfare investigation, including what they viewed as the most serious type, using a modified Maltreatment Classification Scale (Achenbach, 1991). The most serious type of maltreatment reported, originally 10 categories, was reduced to 5 categories: *(1)* physical abuse, *(2)* sexual abuse, *(3)* physical neglect (failure to provide for the child), *(4)* supervisory neglect (failure to supervise the child), and *(5)* other types of maltreatment (abandonment, educational maltreatment, moral or legal maltreatment, exploitation, etc.). Caseworkers' reports were based on their own knowledge, as well as case records.

FAMILY RISK FACTORS   Caseworkers also answered a short family risk assessment comprising single questions about whether the following risk factors characterized the family at the time of investigation: *(1)* primary or secondary caregiver's active alcohol or drug abuse; *(2)* primary caregiver's serious mental health or emotional problems; *(3)* primary caregiver's intellectual or cognitive impairments; *(4)* primary caregiver's physical impairments; *(5)* primary caregiver's impaired parenting (e.g., failure to supervise, unrealistic expectations of child, inappropriate discipline); *(6)* monetary problems (including inability to provide basic necessities); and *(7)* active domestic violence.[1]

INSURANCE STATUS   At each wave, each child's insurance status was classified as *(1)* Medicaid, *(2)* private or Civilian Health and Medical Program of the Uniformed Services (CHAMPUS), or *(3)* no insurance.

CHRONIC HEALTH PROBLEMS   At each wave, caregivers answered a question about whether the child had any health problem that "lasted a long time or came back again and again."

BEHAVIORAL PROBLEMS   The CBCL, a widely used and psychometrically established measure (Cicchetti, Sparrow, & Carter, 1991), was used to estimate each child's emotional and behavioral problems and need for mental health treatment. Two caregiver-report forms were used, one for children 2 to 3 years old and another for children 4 to 18 years old. Children having a CBCL Total Problems score at or above the clinical cutoff ($T = 64$) were identified as having clinically significant levels of need.

DAILY-LIVING SKILLS   The Vineland Adaptive Behavior Scales (VABS) Screener assesses daily functional skills in children. Screener scores correlate highly with the Vineland Full Scale score. The daily-living skills section of the VABS screener was

Table 10.2 Characteristics at Wave 1 (Baseline), Wave 3 (18 Months), and Wave 4 (36 Months) of Children Referred to Child Welfare for Maltreatment

Characteristic	Wave 1 % (SE)	Wave 3 % (SE)	Wave 4 % (SE)
Age[a]	30.1 (1.6)		
2–5	42.0 (2.0)	—	—
6–10	27.9 (1.5)		
11+			
Gender			
Male	49.7 (1.9)	—	—
Female	50.3 (1.9)		
Race/ethnicity			
Black	27.8 (2.9)		
White	48.2 (3.5)		
Hispanic	17.5 (2.1)	—	—
Other	6.5 (0.8)		
Current placement			
Home, no child welfare services	66.2 (2.0)	90.0 (0.9)	
Home, with child welfare services[b]	24.2 (1.7)		
Non-relative foster care	3.3 (0.4)	4.0 (0.7)	—
Relative foster care	4.5 (0.6)	4.4 (0.6)	
Group home/residential treatment	1.0 (0.3)	1.0 (0.2)	
Other	0.8 (0.2)	0.6 (0.2)	
Primary maltreatment type at baseline[c]			
Physical abuse	28.9 (1.8)		
Sexual abuse	12.8 (1.7)		
Physical neglect/failure to provide	18.6 (1.7)	—	—
Supervision neglect	29.0 (1.7)		
Other	10.7 (1.5)		
Report of maltreatment prior to CD[d]	53.9 (2.1)	—	—
Parental risk factors			
Drug/alcohol abuse	18.8 (1.6)		
Severe mental illness	13.9 (1.6)		
Cognitive impairment	6.1 (0.8)		
Physical impairment	5.3 (0.7)		
Impaired parenting skills	34.5 (2.2)	—	—
Monetary problems	22.8 (1.6)		
Domestic violence	12.8 (1.2)		
Any risk factor	56.4 (2.3)		
Mean risk factors (SE)	1.04 (0.05)		
Insurance type			
Medicaid	59.8 (2.1)	61.9 (1.7)	66.2 (1.9)
Private and CHAMPUS	27.5 (1.5)	29.5 (1.6)	27.3 (1.6)
None	12.7 (1.5)	8.6 (1.2)	6.5 (1.1)
Chronic health problems	28.4 (1.5)	23.9 (1.8)	25.1 (1.9)
CBCL			
2-5, Total ≥ 64	23.8 (2.8)	26.5 (3.2)	25.7 (2.8)
6–10, Total ≥ 64	33.8 (2.9)	27.9 (3.1)	23.5 (2.6)
≥11, Total ≥ 64	42.3 (3.4)	40.1 (3.5)	31.1(3.3)
CBCL (wtd mean, unwtd SD)			
2–5, Total	55.2 (11.2)	56.1 (11.3)	55.4 (11.8)

Table 10.2 (continued)

6–10, Total	56.6 (12.5)	54.6 (13.0)	53.8 (12.8)
≥11, Total	60.1 (12.4)	58.9 (11.8)	57.5 (12.6)
Vineland (wtd mean, unwtd SD)			
2–5	88.7 (18.2)	91.1 (19.0)	91.4 (19.9)
6–10	96.8 (23.0)	101.1 (22.1)	98.6 (23.1)

[a]Sample includes children ages 2 years old or older for whom an interview was present at both Waves 1 and 4.

[b]At Wave 1, a distinction was made between children at home in families in which some kind of child welfare services were initiated and in which no child welfare services were initiated. At Wave 3, this same distinction was not available for analyses.

[c]More than one type of maltreatment was reported for some children. This variable represents the most serious type of maltreatment, as judged by the caseworker.

[d]CD, contact date. The contact date is the date at which the child was referred to child welfare, prompting an investigation. As a result of prior referrals to child welfare, many children had previous contact with child welfare. Thus, the contact date represents the date for this specific referral and does not necessarily represent a child's first ever contact with child welfare.

CBCL, Child Behavior Checklist.

administered at each wave to current caregivers of children aged 10 years or younger (Ascher, Farmer, Burns, & Angold, 1996): The data therefore covered a portion of the study sample, not the full sample; furthermore, some children aged out of the VABS screener at the follow-up waves. The VABS screener was used mainly descriptively and to model service use among the youngest children.

USE OF MENTAL HEALTH SERVICES Current caregivers responded to questions about children's mental health services in an adapted version of the Child and Adolescent Services Assessment (Federal Interagency Forum on Child and Family Statistics, 2005). Focus was directed toward three primary classes of services. *Specialty mental health services* (outpatient and inpatient) meant use of a mental health center; a private psychiatrist, psychologist, social worker, or psychiatric nurse for emotional, behavioral, learning, or attentional issues; in-home counseling (not including visits by case workers or isolated home visits by a case manager or other mental health clinician); day treatment; psychiatric hospitalization in a dedicated psychiatric hospital unit or in an inpatient unit of a medical hospital; or residential treatment. *School-based services* meant use of a therapeutic nursery; school guidance counselor, psychologist, or social worker; or special education classes or services for an emotional disturbance. *Medical mental health services* meant visiting a medical doctor for emotional or behavioral, learning, or attention problems.

Children were characterized with regard to whether they had received each type of service between the time of the child maltreatment investigation and the Wave 3 interview (approximately 18 months), and between the Wave 3 and Wave 4 interviews (approximately 19 to 36 months). Use of specialty mental health and school-based services before the child welfare investigation was also characterized, although, because of the structure of the NSCAW interviews, some differences in variable definitions before the protective service contact dates exist.

Analyses

Analyses focus on patterns of mental health services use across the 36-month study period, dividing service use into the timeframe after the child welfare investigation of maltreatment allegations (Waves 1, 2, and 3) and 18 months later (Wave 4). Descriptive analyses characterize the entire target sample and in some cases provide further detail by three broad developmental groups at Wave 1: 2- to 5-year-old children, 6- to 10-year-old children, and 11- to 14-year-old children. Subsequent analyses of patterns of service use, both descriptive and predictive, were stratified by these groupings.

Models of mental health service utilization relied on a series of logistic regression models. Initial models examined use of any type of mental health service between the contact date and the Wave 3 interview, and then between the Wave 3 and 4 interviews. More fine-grained follow-up models then focused on use of specialty and school-based mental health services separately in each timeframe, again by age group. Models examined predictors of service utilization in each time period. Extensions of those models were examined, taking into account prior use of mental health services. Models including prior service use provided information about continuity of services across timeframes and about those variables most related to change in service use across timeframes.

All analyses used sampling weights that account for the NSCAW sampling plan, and all analyses were conducted with SUDAAN software to account for the sampling design (RTI International, 2007).

Results

Among children aged 2 to 14 years and involved with the child welfare system, more were 6 to 10 years old (42.0%) or 2 to 5 years old (30.1%) than 11 to 14 years old (27.9%); males and females were almost equally represented; and black or African American children (27.8%) were more heavily represented in this sample than in the general population (16%; Table 10.2; Farmer et al., in press). Most children for whom an investigation occurred remained in their homes, with 66.2% remaining at home with no child welfare services initiated, as was the case 18 months after the child welfare investigation (90%). Placement in nonkin foster care occurred for 3.3% of children, a rate that remained relatively constant at Wave 3, though some children may have returned home while others were removed. Few children (4.5%) were placed in kinship foster care. Eighteen months later this percentage declined to less than 4.4%. Group homes and residential treatment remained constant at around 1%.

An estimated 28.9% of the children came into contact with child protective services because of a physical abuse report; 12.8%, because of a sexual abuse report; 18.6%, because of a report of physical neglect; and 29.0% because of a report of supervisory neglect. Repeat maltreatment reports were common—53.9% of children had had a report before baseline. Prior abuse was not related to the most serious type of maltreatment at initial contact.

Caseworkers reported many different risk factors to be present in families at the time of the child welfare investigation. Impaired parenting skills (34.5%), monetary problems (22.8%), and drug or alcohol problems (18.8%) were the most frequent. Caseworkers identified more than one half of families as having at least one parental risk factor (56.4%). Families from which the child was removed or for which child welfare services were initiated were much more likely to have risk factors than families in which the child remained at home and no child welfare services were initiated (data not shown).

Medicaid was the most common insurer for families in the study and the percentage of children covered increased at each wave, beginning at 59.8% at baseline and increasing to 66.2% by Wave 4. Although private insurance coverage and CHAMPUS remained steady at 27% to 29%, the proportion of children who were uninsured declined from 12.7% to 6.5% by Wave 4. Reported chronic health problems remained fairly steady, ranging from 28.4% to 23.9%.

Clinical Assessments and Mental Health Services Use at Waves 1 Through 4

Total CBCL scores in the clinical range, indicating problems warranting mental health services, were common and increasingly present across age groups. At Wave 1, 23.8% of 2–5 year olds, 33.8% of 6–10 year olds, and 42.3% of children aged 11 years or older had clinical-level CBCL scores. The percentage of children with clinical-level CBCL scores remained steady at about 25% for 2–5 year olds, decreased from 33.8% to 23.5% for 6–10 year olds, and decreased from 42.3% to 31.1% for children aged 11 years or older. Adaptive functioning as assessed by VABS was available for 2–5 and 6–10 year olds. The 2–5 year old group demonstrated low normal levels of adaptive functioning throughout the 36-month follow-up period. Among 6–10 year olds, average functioning scores were in the normal range at all waves.

Use of all mental health services increased as children aged (Table 10.3), but for all age ranges the percentage of children using services was greater between entry to the child welfare system and Wave 3 than between Waves 3 and 4. Similar overall increases in service use as children aged were observed for school-based and specialty mental health services. The increase in use of medical services for mental health problems, however, showed considerably less of an age gradient. Overall, 28.9% of 2–5 year olds used services from the contact date to Wave 3 (18 months later), whereas 49.5% of 6–10 year olds and 64.1% of children aged 11 years or older used mental health services.

Among 6–10 year olds, school-based mental health services were the most common type of service received, both before the contact date and in the 18 months afterward, although specialty services also remained common. Nearly half of all 6–10 year olds used some type of mental health service between the contact date

Table 10.3 Proportion of Children Receiving Different Types of Mental Health Services in Three Separate Timeframes: Prior to Contact Date, Between the Contact Date and the Wave 3 Interview, and Between the Wave 3 and Wave 4 Interviews, Stratified by Age Group

	Aged 2–5 Years				Aged 6–10 Years				Age 11+ Years			
	CD % (SE)	CD–W3 % (SE)	W3–W4 % (SE)	CD–W4	<CD % (SE)	CD–W3 % (SE)	W3–W4 % (SE)	CD–W4	<CD % (SE)	CD–W3 % (SE)	W3–W4 % (SE)	CD–W4
MH outpatient[a]	7.0 (1.5)	21.5 (2.7)	16.1 (2.3)	28.1 (2.7)	16.2 (2.2)	31.9 (3.1)	21.8 (2.7)	38.1 (3.6)	32.5 (3.4)	49.1 (3.7)	23.8 (2.6)	52.0 (3.7)
MH inpatient[b]	0.8 (0.3)		1.0 (0.7)		5.4 (1.0)		4.5 (1.0)		15.2 (2.1)		9.0 (1.5)	
School[c]	7.0 (1.8)	11.6 (2.3)	15.4 (2.1)	21.5 (3.2)	28.0 (2.6)	37.0 (2.8)	29.3 (2.7)	46.9 (2.7)	40.3 (3.2)	47.1 (3.8)	24.1 (2.6)	52.8 (4.0)
Medical[d]		11.5 (2.2)	9.1 (1.8)			17.0 (1.8)	10.9 (2.0)			20.1 (2.2)	10.5 (2.0)	
Summaries												
Any service use from:												
Single category		17.3 (2.2)	16.5 (2.4)			22.8 (2.6)	21.2 (2.3)			23.1 (2.2)	20.0 (2.6)	
Multiple categories		11.6 (1.8)	10.5 (1.8)			26.7 (2.7)	17.9 (2.5)			41.0 (3.5)	17.3 (2.3)	
No services use		71.1 (2.8)	73.0 (2.8)			50.5 (3.0)	60.9 (3.2)			35.9 (3.7)	62.7 (3.7)	
Any MH service		28.9 (2.8)	27.0 (2.8)	40.3 (3.4)		49.5 (3.0)	39.1 (3.2)	58.1 (2.6)		64.1 (3.7)	37.3 (3.7)	67.9 (3.6)

[a]Mental health outpatient services include the following: (1) mental health or community health center; (2) private psychiatrist, psychologist, social worker, or psychiatric nurse for emotion, behavior, learning, or attention issues; (3) in-home counseling (not including visits by case workers or isolated home visits by case manager or other mental health clinician) for these issues; and (4) day treatment.

[b]Inpatient mental health services include the following: (1) psychiatric hospital or psychiatric unit; (2) hospital medical inpatient unit; and (3) residential treatment.

[c]School-based services include the following: (1) therapeutic nursery; (2) school guidance counselor, school psychologist, school social worker; and (3) special education classes or services (emotional disturbance).

[d]Medical services for mental health defined as: medical doctor for emotion, behavior, learning, or attention problems.

CD, contact date; MH, mental health.

and Wave 3; almost 40%, between Wave 3 and Wave 4. Children aged 11 years or older had the highest rates of service utilization between the contact date and Wave 3, with 64.1% receiving some kind of mental health service, these being almost equally divided between school-based and specialty mental health providers. Between Waves 3 and 4, rates of service use declined substantially, to an overall rate lower than that among children aged 6 to 10 years in the same timeframe.

Approximately 20% of each age group used services from a single sector, with increasingly larger percentages of children using services from multiple sectors in the older age groups. Looking at use of any mental health service from contact date to Wave 4, we find that 40.3% of 2–5 year olds, 58.1% of 6–10 year olds, and 67.9% of children aged 11 years or older received some service.

Factors Related to Service Use

Mental health services use also varied by other key features identified in the literature review (Table 10.4). For children 2 to 5 years of age at study entry, we found that between contact date and Wave 3, school services were related to race/ethnicity (black or African American children received fewer services), being in kinship foster care or a group home, and having CBCL scores in the clinical range. Likewise, specialty mental health services were related to race/ethnicity, any type of out-of-home placement, primary maltreatment type, and high CBCL scores. In Waves 3 to 4, outpatient mental health services continued to be less common for black children than for other race/ethnicity groups and was now less common for those in kinship care and those without insurance.

For 6–10 year olds, school services, which were received by three times as many children in this age group as in the groups of 2–5 year olds, now strongly favored males, no longer showed any race/ethnicity differences, were related to being in a group home or residential treatment center, were more common for physically abused children than for children with other forms of primary maltreatment, and were strongly related to CBCL scores in the clinical range. Outpatient mental health services also increased, though only by 50%, no longer showed race/ethnicity differences, strongly favored children in nonkinship foster care and group settings, and continued to be driven by CBCL scores indicating clinical need. Between Waves 3 and 4, correlates of school services remained unchanged, with two exceptions: *(1)* children in kinship foster care were more likely to receive services than children in other living arrangements, and *(2)* those who were physically abused were less likely to receive services than those with other forms of primary maltreatment. Wave 3 and 4 correlates of outpatient mental health services remained unchanged.

For the oldest children (aged 11 years or older), "other" race/ethnicity, placement in a group home, physical abuse as primary maltreatment, and high CBCL scores were related to more school-based service use from contact date to the Wave 3 interview; for outpatient mental health services these characteristics and lack of insurance were important. In the Wave 3 to Wave 4 interval, "other" race/ethnicity

Table 10.4 Percentages of Children Using Mental Health Services (School-Based, Specialty, and Total) as a Function of Select Child Characteristics, Stratified by Age Group and Timeframe (Contact Date to Wave 3 and Wave 3 to Wave 4)

	2–5 Year Olds						6–10 Year Olds					
	CD–Wave 3			Wave 3–Wave 4			CD–Wave 3			Wave 3–Wave 4		
	School (%)	OP (%)	Total (%)	School (%)	OP (%)	Total (%)	School (%)	OP (%)	Total (%)	School (%)	OP (%)	Total (%)
Total	11.6	21.5	28.9	15.4	16.1	27.0	37.0	31.9	49.5	29.3	21.8	39.1
Gender												
Male	11.7	22.4	29.6	16.2	17.4	26.3	46.5	34.9	55.6	37.0	27.4	50.0
Female	11.5	20.6	28.0	14.5	14.7	27.7	26.9	28.7	43.1	21.1	15.8	27.6
Race/ethnicity												
Black	7.1	11.3	18.2	5.7	7.6	14.2	33.3	26.3	43.7	28.0	17.2	36.1
White	11.4	26.2	33.3	19.0	20.5	34.2	43.7	39.4	57.3	34.0	27.1	45.3
Hispanic	18.6	25.0	33.7	22.6	18.6	30.7	32.9	23.1	45.1	14.7	18.9	24.8
Other	13.3	20.2	27.4	5.8	11.2	13.7	19.4	26.0	33.7	37.8	12.3	43.7
Current placement (W1)												
In home, no services	12.8	19.0	28.2				31.2	24.0	42.8			
In home, services	8.6	22.1	24.6				49.3	42.4	60.2			
Non-relative foster care	22.2	49.8	67.4				49.5	76.3	78.9			
Relative foster care	5.1	41.7	45.9				59.4	58.8	72.3			
Group home/RTC	35.0	97.2	97.2				38.6	99.7	99.7			
Other	8.6	11.2	13.2				44.3	20.4	54.9			

Table 10.4 (continued)

Current placement (W3)												
Home				14.8	13.4	23.9				28.6	18.7	36.1
Non-relative foster care				15.8	65.9	71.6				34.7	81.2	85.4
Relative foster care				18.4	19.6	28.0				46.2	19.9	57.6
Group home/RTC				0.0	0.0	0.0				78.4	81.7	87.4
Other				0.0	0.0	0.0				47.5	81.9	95.4
Primary maltreatment type												
Physical abuse	12.3	18.6	25.5	16.0	11.1	26.5	47.0	34.2	57.3	34.2	28.5	43.8
Sexual abuse	12.4	28.7	29.2	31.0	19.9	36.4	30.5	32.1	45.1	33.4	21.5	40.8
Physical neglect/FTP	8.4	10.3	18.9	6.4	15.0	17.8	37.5	31.4	46.0	28.0	16.6	35.1
Lack of supervision	15.3	28.5	38.5	10.0	17.9	27.5	30.7	28.6	48.2	27.4	18.3	37.0
Other	3.7	16.9	27.8	34.1	21.1	37.2	27.9	38.7	44.0	21.6	20.4	33.8
Insurance type (Wave 1)												
Medicaid	13.0	19.3	30.0				41.1	37.2	54.8			
Private and CHAMPUS	10.3	24.1	25.4				31.0	26.0	41.6			
None	7.3	29.3	29.6				28.6	19.1	39.5			
Insurance type (Wave 3)												
Medicaid				16.4	19.6	28.8				28.2	23.4	38.8
Private and CHAMPUS				12.4	10.6	22.3				28.5	17.8	36.5
None				11.0	5.7	17.0				37.8	15.6	45.2
CBCL baseline												
Total ≥ 64	26.9	45.2	49.7	33.2	29.8	42.5	62.2	58.9	76.5	43.4	36.1	57.8
Total < 64	6.8	14.1	22.3	9.8	11.8	22.1	24.2	18.1	35.8	22.1	14.4	29.6
CBCL Wave 3												
Total ≥ 64	27.9	39.3	51.1	29.3	30.4	41.8	63.1	60.9	81.5	48.6	44.7	64.2
Total < 64	4.4	16.5	20.4	9.7	10.8	20.3	28.1	20.4	38.3	21.6	11.9	28.8

(continued)

Table 10.4 (continued)

| | >=11 years old | | | | | |
| | CD – Wave 3 | | | Wave 3 – Wave 4 | | |
	School %	OP %	Total %	School %	OP %	Total %
Total	47.1	49.1	64.1	24.1	23.8	37.3
Gender						
Male	55.0	46.5	67.2	26.6	24.3	41.7
Female	40.9	51.2	61.6	22.2	23.4	33.8
Race/Ethnicity						
Black	43.1	39.3	61.2	26.7	25.6	37.5
White	47.3	49.9	63.3	19.8	24.0	38.3
Hispanic	45.1	52.1	64.3	21.4	17.6	24.1
Other	70.3	80.7	83.5	54.4	29.7	64.2
Current Placement (W1)						
In home, no services	46.7	44.9	61.8			
In home, services	43.2	45.2	57.9			
Non-Relative Foster Care	46.0	89.0	92.5			
Relative Foster Care	45.9	62.8	74.6			
Group Home/RTC	72.3	94.4	99.8			
Other	91.2	65.2	94.2			
Current Placement (W3)						
Home				23.8	21.1	35.9
Non-Relative Foster Care				28.8	62.1	71.2
Relative Foster Care				19.5	31.9	39.4
Group Home/RTC[3]				68.3	88.6	91.6
Other				26.0	50.8	51.2

Table 10.4 (continued)

Primary Maltreatment Type						
Physical Abuse	61.1	57.0	75.8	22.4	28.3	39.9
Sexual Abuse	25.6	33.8	50.4	22.9	17.1	29.2
Physical Neglect/FTP[4]	46.8	49.0	58.1	26.3	21.7	37.0
Lack of Supervision	50.0	48.3	65.4	29.6	23.1	39.6
Other	33.3	49.7	60.4	23.8	21.7	35.6
Insurance Type (Wave 1)						
Medicaid	51.1	59.0	72.9			
Private & CHAMPUS	47.6	41.9	60.9			
None	31.0	28.8	37.9			
Insurance Type (Wave 3)						
Medicaid				28.0	30.7	44.8
Private & CHAMPUS				20.3	18.1	28.0
None				17.3	13.9	36.1
CBCL Baseline						
Total>=64	60.4	70.4	20.6	34.9	34.7	52.1
Total<64	37.4	33.5	47.2	16.2	15.7	26.5
CBCL Wave 3						
Total>=64	62.7	71.0	83.6	39.0	42.3	60.1
Total<64	40.1	39.7	56.6	15.0	13.7	24.3

[1] CD = contact date
[2] OP = Outpatient
[3] RTC = Residential Treatment Center
[4] FTP = Failure to Provide

Table 10.5   Months of Outpatient Specialty Mental Health Service Use in Each Timeframe, Stratified by Age Group

Age Group	2–5 Years		6–10 Years		11+ Years		Total	
	CD–W3	W3–W4	CD–W3	W3–W4	CD–W3	W3–W4	CD–W3	W3–W4
Months	(%)	(%)	(%)	(%)	(%)	(%)	(%)	(%)
0	76.4	81.2	65.7	75.2	47.2	74.6	63.8	74.6
1–2	7.2	5.3	6.2	7.4	6.9	8.6	6.7	8.6
3–6	4.6	2.7	6.2	3.3	9.4	3.7	6.6	3.7
7+	11.8	10.7	21.9	14.1	36.5	13.1	22.9	13.1

CD, contact date.

continued to be important for school services, as did "other" placement with high CBCL scores. Outpatient mental health services were associated with all out-of-home placements except kinship care, were driven by Medicaid as the insurer, and were strongly associated with high CBCL scores.

In addition to examining key features of mental health services use, we examined duration of such use (in months), to glean whether services were largely evaluations or ongoing therapy. As shown in Table 10.5, among children receiving outpatient specialty services in each timeframe, most had services in 3 or more months in the timeframe. With increasing age, those having service use for only 1 to 2 months—likely amounting to an evaluation or early termination of service—declined as a proportion of all children receiving services. We compared the percentage of children having three or more visits with the percentage of children with CBCL clinical-range scores at the beginning of the time interval for service use (e.g., CBCL score at baseline for service use from baseline to Wave 3). Except for the oldest age group in the first follow-up interval, all age groups showed more need than service use, with the largest discrepancies between need and use occurring from Wave 3 to Wave 4.

Predictors of Service Use Among Children Aged 2 to 5 Years

Staged multivariate analyses, conducted by age group, were used to examine predictors of any mental health service use between the child welfare contact date and Wave 3 (approximately 18 months later), and then between Wave 3 and Wave 4 (approximately 18 to 36 months after the contact date). Subsequent analyses were to examine predictors of the two most common classes of mental health services: school based and specialty (for changes in overall rates of service use as they inform these findings, see Table 10.3).

For 2- to 5-year-old children, service use rates increased most between the child welfare contact date and Wave 3 for specialty mental health services, with a smaller increase in school-based services. Positive predictors at Waves 1 to 3 of any mental health services use for 2–5 year olds at study entry were kindergarten age, out-of-home placement, supervisory neglect's occasioning protective services contact, and CBCL scores of at least 64; whereas African American, or black, race (and higher VABS scores) were negatively related to services use. Positive predictors from Wave 3 to 4 of any mental health services use for 2–5 year olds were kindergarten age, sexual abuse as a reason for placement, and a relatively greater number of family risk factors. Again, being black and higher VABS scores were negatively related to mental health services use (Table 10.6).

We found that, between contact with child welfare and Wave 3, 2- to 5-year-old children in out-of-home care and with lower VABS scores compared to those who remained in their homes or those with higher VABS scores were more likely to receive school-based services (Table 10.7). Adding to our model school-based service use that preceded the contact date revealed strong continuity in service use among those already receiving services. Furthermore, results from adding this variable indicated that older children were more likely to begin receiving services, consistent with their entry to elementary school (OR = 4.61; CI: 1.25, 17.05).

A somewhat different pattern of predictors appeared for specialty mental health services. Children in out-of-home care, with higher numbers of family risk factors, clinical-level CBCL scores, and one of a set of different types of primary maltreatment, including sexual abuse and supervisory neglect, were more likely than their counterparts to receive specialty mental health services. Including prior use of school and specialty services in the model once again revealed strong continuity in service use among previous users of services, changing little the overall pattern of service use predictors. However, after adjusting for use of mental health services in the 12 months preceding study entry, Medicaid as a payer was negatively related to use of mental health services (OR = 0.34; CI: 0.11, 1.03).

Between Waves 3 and 4, rates of school-based mental health service use continued to increase, rivaling rates of specialty mental health service use. During this period, predictors of school-based service use changed somewhat. School-aged children were substantially more likely to receive services than the small proportion of children not yet of school age. The CBCL, which had a positive but nonsignificant relationship with school-based service use between the contact date and Wave 3, positively predicted use of school-based mental health services, as did referral to child welfare for sexual abuse. Negative predictors of service use included VABS scores and, now, being black or African American. Addition of specialty and school-based services use between the contact date and Wave 3 again revealed high continuity in school-based service use from one period to the next (OR = 9.25; CI: 3.92, 21.82 for school services) and some (though not significant) prediction of school-based service use by prior specialty service use (OR = 2.43; CI: 0.83, 7.14 for specialty services).

For specialty mental health services between Waves 3 and 4, the use of which declined from the 18 months immediately after the contact date, the pattern of predictors of service use changed substantially. Some of the few significant predictors of service use included older age, black or African American race/ethnicity (lower likelihood of using services) and VABS scores (more likely to receive services

Table 10.6 Logistic Regression Predictors of Any Mental Health Service Use in Two Time Periods (Contact Date to Wave 3 and Wave 3 to Wave 4) Among 2- to 5-Year-Old Children

	CD–Wave 3			Wave 3–Wave 4		
	β	OR [CI]	p	β	OR [CI]	p
Age						
Younger than kindergarten	0.00	—	*	0.00	—	
Kindergarten	0.84	2.31 [1.02, 5.22]		1.68	5.39 [2.43, 11.98]	***
Gender						
Male	0.18	1.2 [0.66, 2.18]		−0.02	0.98 [0.49, 1.96]	
Female	0.00	—		0.00		
Race/Ethnicity						
Black/non-Hispanic	−0.97	0.38 [0.15, 0.98]	*	−1.01	0.37 [0.17, 0.79]	*
White/non-Hispanic	0.00			0.00		
Hispanic	0.02	1.02 [0.53, 1.95]		−0.02	0.98 [0.51, 1.89]	
Other	−0.27	0.77 [0.26, 2.25]		−1.24	0.29 [0.08, 1.09]	
Level of CW involvement						
In home, no CW services	0.00	—		0.00		
In home, with CW services	−0.54	0.58 [0.32, 1.06]		—	—	
Out of home	0.86	2.36 [0.89, 6.23]		0.91	2.49 [0.8, 7.79]	
Primary abuse type						
Physical	0.69	1.99 [0.92, 4.29]		0.92	2.52 [0.92, 6.94]	
Sexual	0.57	1.78 [0.43, 7.39]		1.30	3.65 [1.13, 11.76]	*
Physical neglect	0.00	—		0.00	—	
Supervisory neglect	1.19	3.28 [1.21, 8.88]	*	0.52	1.68 [0.59, 4.81]	
Other	0.87	2.38 [0.78, 7.24]		0.47	1.6 [0.43, 5.99]	
Prior report of maltreatment	−0.43	0.65 [0.34, 1.22]		0.10	1.1 [0.54, 2.25]	
No. of family risk factors	0.28	1.33 [1.05, 1.69]	*	0.22	1.25 [1.03, 1.52]	*
Vineland	−0.03	0.97 [0.95, 0.99]	*	−0.02	0.98 [0.96, 0.99]	**
Child insurance status						
Medicaid	0.04	1.04 [0.49, 2.2]		0.45	1.56 [0.48, 5.09]	
Private and CHAMPUS	−0.22	0.81 [0.32, 2.01]		0.21	1.23 [0.34, 4.44]	
None	0.00	—		0.00	—	
CBCL						
≥64	1.16	3.18 [1.47, 6.88]	**	0.49	1.63 [0.62, 4.29]	
≤63	0.00	—		0.00	—	
Chronic health problem	0.05	1.05 [0.47, 2.35]		−0.09	0.91 [0.37, 2.23]	

Notes: Children were selected into this analysis because they were 2–5 years old at the time of the Wave 1 interview. For analysis of service use between Waves 3 and 4, children would have been approximately 18 months older.

Wave 1 value used in the contact date to Wave 3 model; Wave 3 value used in the Wave 3 to Wave 4 model.

At the Wave 1 interview, level of child welfare involvement was categorized into: (a) in home, no child welfare services, (b) in home, with child welfare services, and (c) out of home. At the Wave 3 interview, the level of child welfare involvement was categorized into (a) in home, and (b) out of home.

*p = .05 , **p=.01

CBCL, Child Behavior Checklist; CD, contact date; CW, child welfare.

Table 10.7 Logistic Regression Predictors of School-Based and Outpatient Specialty Mental Health Service Use in Two Time Periods Among 2- to 5-Year-Old Children (Contact Date to Wave 3 and Wave 3 to Wave 4)

	CD–W3 (School)			CD–W3 (Specialty)			W3–W4 (School)			W3–W4 (Specialty)		
	β	OR [CI]	P	β	OR [CI]	P	β	OR [CI]	P	B	OR [CI]	P
Age²												
Younger than kindergarten	0.00	—		0.00	—		0.00			0.00		
Kindergarten	1.27	3.58 [1, 12.81]	*	0.54	1.72 [0.83, 3.56]		3.69	40.02 [14.57, 109.9]	***	1.46	4.32 [1.87, 9.95]	***
Gender												
Male	−0.01	0.99 [0.36, 2.71]		0.21	1.23 [0.59, 2.58]		0.50	1.64 [0.8, 3.37]		0.36	1.44 [0.66, 3.13]	
Female	0.00			0.00			0.00			0.00		
Race/ethnicity												
Black/non-Hispanic	−0.49	0.61 [0.13, 2.8]		−1.01	0.36 [0.12, 1.09]		−1.17	0.31 [0.11, 0.88]	*	−1.12	0.32 [0.12, 0.89]	*
White/non-Hispanic	0.00			0.00			0.00			0.00		
Hispanic	0.45	1.57 [0.45, 5.46]		0.05	1.05 [0.44, 2.53]		0.35	1.42 [0.6, 3.34]		−0.09	0.91 [0.28, 2.94]	
Other	0.32	1.38 [0.34, 5.55]		−0.10	0.91 [0.2, 4.18]		−1.22	0.29 [0.08, 1.11]		−0.72	0.48 [0.12, 2.03]	
Level of CW involvement												
In home, no CW services	0.00			0.00			0.00			0.00		
In home, with CW services	−0.53	0.59 [0.24, 1.43]		−0.25	0.78 [0.39, 1.55]							
Out of home	0.28	1.33 [0.44, 4.01]		0.87	2.38 [0.78, 7.25]		0.04	1.04 [0.28, 3.87]		1.52	4.55 [1.21, 17.06]	*
Primary abuse type												
Physical	0.50	1.65 [0.56, 4.89]		1.06	2.89 [0.99, 8.45]		1.13	3.08 [1.01, 9.46]	*	−0.08	0.92 [0.33, 2.62]	

(continued)

Table 10.7 (continued)

	CD–W3 (School)			CD–W3 (Specialty)			W3–W4 (School)			W3–W4 (Specialty)		
	β	OR [CI]	P	β	OR [CI]	P	β	OR [CI]	P	B	OR [CI]	P
Sexual	−0.08	0.93 [0.1, 8.69]		1.52	4.58 [1.26, 16.63]	*	2.12	8.3 [2.31, 29.84]	**	0.58	1.79 [0.59, 5.5]	
Physical neglect	0.00			0.00			0.00			0.00		
Supervisory neglect	0.72	2.06 [0.37, 11.52]		1.65	5.21 [1.54, 17.59]	**	0.36	1.43 [0.55, 3.71]		−0.01	0.99 [0.31, 3.22]	
Other	−0.84	0.43 [0.03, 6]		1.01	2.74 [0.67, 11.15]		0.93	2.54 [0.64, 10.04]		0.61	1.84 [0.43, 7.79]	
Prior report of maltreatment	−0.26	0.77 [0.32, 1.85]		−0.15	0.86 [0.4, 1.86]		−0.17	0.84 [0.35, 2.02]		0.02	1.02 [0.52, 2.01]	
No. of family risk factors	−0.10	0.9 [0.67, 1.22]		0.40	1.5 [1.16, 1.94]	**	0.19	1.21 [0.94, 1.57]		0.22	1.25 [0.96, 1.63]	
Vineland	−0.05	0.96 [0.93, 0.99]	**	−0.01	0.99 [0.96, 1.01]		−0.03	0.97 [0.95, 0.99]	**	−0.03	0.97 [0.95, 0.99]	**
Child insurance status												
Medicaid	0.72	2.05 [0.44, 9.54]		−0.65	0.52 [0.22, 1.25]		0.35	1.41 [0.31, 6.41]		1.36	3.88 [0.7, 21.39]	
Private and CHAMPUS	0.57	1.76 [0.31, 9.9]		−0.21	0.81 [0.3, 2.17]		−0.04	0.96 [0.21, 4.38]		0.98	2.66 [0.5, 14.27]	
None	0.00			0.00			0.00			0.00		
CBCL												
≥64	1.20	3.33 [1.01, 10.97]	*	1.77	5.89 [2.57, 13.48]	***	0.83	2.29 [0.92, 5.68]		0.64	1.9 [0.84, 4.26]	
≤63	0.00			0.00			0.00			0.00		
Chronic health problem	−0.28	0.76 [0.22, 2.58]		0.03	1.03 [0.46, 2.35]		−0.22	0.81 [0.31, 2.07]		−0.46	0.63 [0.26, 1.54]	

Notes: Wave 1 value used in the contact date to Wave 3 model. Wave 3 value used in the Wave 3 to Wave 4 model.

At the Wave 1 interview, level of child welfare involvement was categorized into the following: (a) in home, no child welfare services, (b) in home, with child welfare services, and (c) out of home. At the Wave 3 interview, level of child welfare involvement was categorized into (a) in home and (b) out of home.

*p=.05, **p=.01

CBCL, Child Behavior Checklist; CD, contact date; CW, child welfare.

with lower scores). Type of maltreatment and family risk factors no longer predicted use; out-of-home placement was no longer a statistically significant predictor. Addition to the model of specialty sector services use from the contact date to Wave 3 revealed strong continuity in service use from one timeframe to the next (OR = 4.13; CI: 1.70, 10.04) but did not change other variables in the model.

Predictors of Service Use Among Children Aged 6 to 10 Years

Predictors of any type of mental health service use for 6- to 10-year-old children were somewhat different from those of 2- to 5-year-old children (Table 10.8). Age, family risk factors, and clinical-level CBCL scores predicted increases in service utilization between the contact date and Wave 3, with CBCL having a much stronger relationship with service use in this age group than among 2–5 year olds. Black children continued to have substantially lower rates of service use than white children, even after controlling for other variables. Between Waves 3 and 4, males, the small proportion of children remaining in out-of-home care, children in families with more risk factors at baseline, and children with high CBCL scores were more likely than counterparts to receive some kind of mental health service.

Subsequent analyses once again revealed somewhat different sets of predictors for school-based and specialty mental health services (Table 10.9). Between the contact date and Wave 3, older children in this age range, males, those residing at home and having child welfare services, and those with clinical-level CBCL scores were more likely to receive school-based services. The association of the CBCL with school-based mental health service use was notably stronger than it was for 2–5 year olds. Black children were much less likely to use school-based services than white children. Inclusion of variables representing prior history of service use revealed strong continuity of service use among those previously receiving school-based services (OR = 17.71; CI: 7.95, 39.45). In addition, children seemed to be crossing over from use of specialty mental health services to use of school-based mental health services, as evidenced by the strong prediction of school-based service use from prior history of specialty mental health services (OR = 6.18; CI: 2.17, 17.65).

Many predictors of specialty mental health service use by 6–10 year olds from contact to Wave 3 resembled those for 2–5 year olds. Children in out-of-home care, with greater family risk factors, and with higher CBCL scores were more likely to use specialty mental health services. Black children were much less likely to use specialty mental health services than white children. As with school-based services, strong continuity in service use existed from before contact to after contact (OR = 11.45; CI: 4.74, 27.71), with a notable relationship also existing between use of school-based services before contact date and specialty mental health service use between the contact date and Wave 3 (OR = 3.08; CI: 1.70, 5.60).

Between Waves 3 and 4, predictors of school-based mental health service use for 6–10 year olds changed somewhat. Males continued to have increased likelihood of service use, as did children with clinical-level CBCL scores. The small

Table 10.8 Logistic Regression Predictors of Any Mental Health Service Use in Two Time Periods (Contact Date to Wave 3 and Wave 3 to Wave 4) Among 6- to 10-Year-Old Children

	CD–Wave 3			Wave 3–Wave 4		
	β	OR [CI]	p	B	OR [CI]	p
Age						
6–7	0.00	—		0.00	—	
8–10	0.61	. 1.84 [1, 3.38]	*	−0.86	0.42 [0.17, 1.03]	
11–12				−0.51	0.60 [0.25, 1.46]	
Gender						
Male	0.43	1.54 [0.94, 2.52]		1.02	2.79 [1.56, 4.98]	***
Female	0.00			0.00		
Race/ethnicity						
Black/non-Hispanic	−0.82	0.44 [0.23, 0.85]	*	−0.19	0.83 [0.44, 1.57]	
White/non-Hispanic	0.00			0.00		
Hispanic	−0.19	0.83 [0.41, 1.66]		−0.36	0.70 [0.26, 1.86]	
Other	−0.97	0.38 [0.14, 1.01]		0.18	1.20 [0.47, 3.07]	
Level of CW involvement						
In home, no CW services	0.00					
In home, with CW services	0.25	1.28 [0.7, 2.33]		0.00		
Out of home	0.59	1.81 [0.81, 4.02]		1.76	5.80 [1.90, 17.64]	**
Primary abuse type						
Physical	0.61	1.84 [0.81, 4.16]		0.61	1.84 [0.72, 4.66]	
Sexual	0.06	1.06 [0.45, 2.48]		0.21	1.23 [0.43, 3.52]	
Physical neglect	0.00			0.00		
Supervisory neglect	0.12	1.13 [0.51, 2.5]		−0.11	0.90 [0.35, 2.30]	
Other	−0.18	0.84 [0.35, 1.98]		−0.12	0.89 [0.32, 2.45]	
Prior report of maltreatment	−0.05	0.95 [0.51, 1.78]		0.22	1.24 [0.68, 2.26]	
No. of family risk factors	0.26	1.3 [1.03, 1.65]	*	0.20	1.22 [1.03, 1.45]	*
Child insurance status						
Medicaid	0.72	2.06 [0.91, 4.69]		−0.93	0.40 [0.12, 1.34]	
Private and CHAMPUS	0.38	1.47 [0.61, 3.49]		−0.81	0.45 [0.12, 1.68]	
None	0.00			0.00		
CBCL						
≥64	1.59	4.9 [2.9, 8.26]	***	1.77	5.84 [3.04, 11.22]	***
≤63	0.00			0.00	1.00 [1.00, 1.00]	
Chronic health problem	−0.01	0.99 [0.52, 1.85]		0.41	1.50 [0.77, 2.91]	

Notes: Wave 1 value used in the contact date to Wave 3 model. Wave 3 value used in the Wave 3 to Wave 4 model.

At the Wave 1 interview, level of child welfare involvement was categorized into the following: (a) in home, no child welfare services, (b) in home, with child welfare services, and (c) out of home. At the Wave 3 interview, level of child welfare involvement was categorized into the following: (a) in home, and (b) out of home.

*p=.05, **p=.01, ***p=.001

CBCL, Child Behavior Checklist; CD, contact date; CW, child welfare.

Table 10.9 Logistic Regression Predictors of School-Based and Outpatient Specialty Mental Health Service Use in Two Time Periods Among 6- to 10-Year-Old Children Between Contact Date and Wave 3 and Wave 3 and Wave 4

	CD–W3 (School)			CD–W3 (Specialty)			W3–W4 (School)			W3–W4 (Specialty)		
	β	OR [CI]	p	β	OR [CI]	p	β	OR [CI]	p	β	OR [CI]	p
Age												
6–7	0.00			0.00			0.00	—		0.00	—	
8–10	0.74	2.09 [1.13, 3.86]	*	0.24	1.27 [0.67, 2.41]		−0.34	0.71 [0.32, 1.59]		−0.92	0.4 [0.13, 1.19]	
11–12							−0.28	0.76 [0.32, 1.82]		−0.22	0.8 [0.33, 1.92]	
Gender												
Male	0.98	2.67 [1.57, 4.53]	***	0.08	1.08 [0.63, 1.85]		0.95	2.58 [1.48, 4.5]	***	0.32		
Female	0.00			0.00			0.00			0.00		
Race/ethnicity												
Black/non-Hispanic	−0.70	0.5 [0.27, 0.92]	*	−0.94	0.39 [0.19, 0.79]	**	−0.03	0.97 [0.54, 1.76]		−1.14	0.32 [0.14, 0.76]	*
White/non-Hispanic	0.00			0.00			0.00			0.00		
Hispanic	−0.14	0.87 [0.47, 1.62]		−0.73	0.48 [0.15, 1.55]		−0.71	0.49 [0.18, 1.34]		0.10	1.1 [0.38, 3.21]	
Other	−1.37	0.25 [0.1, 0.68]	**	−0.52	0.59 [0.22, 1.58]		0.14	1.15 [0.45, 2.94]		−0.93	0.39 [0.15, 1.04]	
Level of CW involvement												
In home, no CW services	0.00			0.00								
In home, with CW services	0.68	1.97 [1.13, 3.43]	*	0.45	1.57 [0.83, 3.00]		0.00			0.00		
Out of home	0.39	1.48 [0.64, 3.43]		1.06	2.88 [1.35, 6.15]	**	0.85	2.35 [0.81, 6.81]	*	1.63	5.12 [2.34, 11.2]	***

(continued)

Table 10.9 (continued)

	CD–W3 (School)			CD–W3 (Specialty)			W3–W4 (School)			W3–W4 (Specialty)		
	β	OR [CI]	p	β	OR [CI]	p	β	OR [CI]	p	β	OR [CI]	p
Primary abuse type												
Physical	0.37	1.45 [0.66, 3.18]		0.26	1.3 [0.58, 2.93]		0.49	1.63 [0.64, 4.14]		0.88	2.41 [1.03, 5.64]	*
Sexual	−0.34	0.71 [0.31, 1.67]		0.02	1.02 [0.48, 2.18]		0.07	1.07 [0.38, 3]		0.42	1.52 [0.51, 4.55]	
Physical neglect	0.00			0.00			0.00			0.00		
Supervisory neglect	−0.54	0.58 [0.31, 1.09]		−0.12	0.88 [0.42, 1.85]		−0.12	0.89 [0.37, 2.14]		0.03	1.03 [0.38, 2.77]	
Other	−0.70	0.5 [0.17, 1.48]		0.29	1.33 [0.52, 3.42]		−0.07	0.93 [0.35, 2.5]		−0.09	0.91 [0.29, 2.91]	
Prior report of maltreatment	0.15	1.17 [0.67, 2.04]		−0.31	0.73 [0.42, 1.28]		0.41	1.51 [0.8, 2.86]		−0.24	0.79 [0.4, 1.55]	
No. of family risk factors	0.15	1.16 [0.93, 1.44]		0.24	1.27 [1.02, 1.6]	*	0.11	1.11 [0.94, 1.32]		0.17	1.18 [0.96, 1.46]	
Child insurance status												
Medicaid	0.58	1.78 [0.72, 4.43]		0.64	1.9 [0.87, 4.12]		−1.16	0.31 [0.1, 1]	*	0.12	1.13 [0.39, 3.29]	
Private and CHAMPUS	0.49	1.63 [0.63, 4.23]		0.51	1.66 [0.76, 3.62]		−0.78	0.46 [0.13, 1.69]		−0.38	0.68 [0.2, 2.31]	
None	0.00			0.00			0.00			0.00		
CBCL												
≥64	1.55	4.7 [2.54, 8.7]	***	1.59	4.89 [2.93, 8.17]	***	1.34	3.8 [2.1, 6.88]	***	2.11	8.28 [4.53, 15.14]	***
≤63	0.00			0.00			0.00			0.00		
Chronic health problem	0.10	1.1 [0.57, 2.12]		0.15	1.16 [0.6, 2.27]		0.49	1.64 [0.87, 3.07]		−0.12	0.88 [0.5, 1.56]	

Note: Wave 1 value used in the to Wave 3 model. Wave 3 value used in the Wave 3 to Wave 4 model.

At the Wave 1 interview, level of child welfare involvement was categorized into the following: (a) in home, no child welfare services, (b) in home, with child welfare services, and (c) out of home. At the Wave 3 interview, level of child welfare involvement was categorized into the following: (a) in home and (b) out of home.

*p=.05, **p=.01, ***p=.001

CBCL, Child Behavior Checklist; CD, contact date; CW, child welfare.

percentage of children remaining in out-of-home care during this period also had higher rates of school-based mental health service use. Inclusion of service use between the contact date and Wave 3 in the multivariate model again revealed substantial continuity in service use, and it suggested that children with Medicaid were less likely to begin receiving services than uninsured children (OR = 0.22; CI: 0.06, 0.74). Predictors of specialty mental health service use remained relatively consistent in the Wave 3 and 4 period. Children in out-of-home care and with clinical-level CBCL scores continued to have much higher rates of service use. Black children once again had markedly lower levels of specialty mental health service use than white children. During this period, children reported to child welfare because of physical abuse allegations also had higher rates of specialty mental health service use. Continuity of service use from contact date to Wave 3 remained relatively high (OR = 5.31; CI: 2.34, 12.07), with further evidence of crossover in types of service use from school-based to specialty mental health services in the time between contact date and Wave 3, and between Wave 3 and Wave 4 (OR = 2.67; CI: 1.05, 6.80).

Predictors of Service Use Among Children Aged 11 Years or Older

For those children aged 11 years or older at study entry, predictors of any mental health services use between baseline and Wave 3 were out-of-home placement, physical abuse, Medicaid or private/CHAMPUS insurance, and clinical-range CBCL scores (Table 10.10). Examining services use from Wave 3 to 4, we found that Hispanic children were much less likely to receive services than other race/ ethnicity groups, while children placed out of their homes and those with elevated CBCL scores continued to be more likely to receive services than their counterparts.

Between the contact date and Wave 3, some consistency with and some differences from 6–10 year olds appeared in predictors of mental health service use for this age group. Older children already showed evidence of lower rates of school-based mental health service use in this period, consistent with the lower service utilization rates observed in Table 10.3 for this age group between Waves 3 and 4. Males again had higher rates of school-based service use, as did children with clinical range CBCL scores (Table 10.11). For the first time, insurance coverage was positively associated with receiving school-based mental health services. Incorporating prior history of service use into the model showed consistency over time in service use and suggested that those children in out-of-home care and those whose primary maltreatment was physical abuse were more likely than others to begin receiving services.

Positive predictors of specialty mental health service use were out-of-home placement, clinical-level CBCL scores, and, again, insurance. Consistent with analyses for younger age groups, black, or African American, children continued to have much lower levels of specialty mental health service utilization. Adding prior history of service use revealed continuity over time in service use and suggested that those children reported for physical abuse were more likely than

Table 10.10 Logistic Regression Predictors of Any Mental Health Service Use in Two Time Periods (Contact Date to Wave 3 and Wave 3 to Wave 4) Among Children ≥11 Years Old

	CD–Wave 3			Wave 3–Wave 4		
	β	OR [CI]	p	β	OR [CI]	p
Age						
11–12	0.00	—		0.00	—	
13–14	−0.53	0.59 [0.32, 1.07]		−0.50	0.61 [0.29, 1.26]	
15+				−0.39	0.67 [0.28, 1.6]	
Gender						
Male	0.49	1.63 [0.94, 2.82]		0.50	1.65 [0.92, 2.96]	
Female	0.00	1 [1, 1]		0.00		
Race/Ethnicity						
Black/non-Hispanic	−0.30	0.74 [0.41, 1.34]		−0.10	0.91 [0.46, 1.8]	
White/non-Hispanic	0.00			0.00		
Hispanic	−0.40	0.67 [0.28, 1.6]		−1.04	0.35 [0.13, 0.97]	*
Other	0.70	2.01 [0.48, 8.34]		0.73	2.08 [0.58, 7.45]	
Level of CW involvement						
In home, no CW services	0.00					
In home, with CW services	−0.03	0.97 [0.43, 2.2]		0.00		
Out of home	1.70	5.47 [1.85, 16.23]	**	0.81	2.24 [0.97, 5.17]	
Primary abuse type						
Physical	1.52	4.56 [1.7, 12.24]	**	0.72	2.05 [0.84, 5]	
Sexual	0.93	2.52 [0.88, 7.22]		0.88	2.41 [0.82, 7.06]	
Physical neglect	0.00			0.00		
Supervisory neglect	0.53	1.7 [0.74, 3.88]		0.21	1.24 [0.56, 2.76]	
Other	0.64	1.9 [0.68, 5.36]		0.42	1.52 [0.52, 4.5]	
Prior report of maltreatment	0.18	1.2 [0.7, 2.07]		0.28	1.33 [0.66, 2.66]	
No. of family risk factors	−0.07	0.93 [0.77, 1.14]		0.05	1.05 [0.89, 1.25]	
Child insurance status						
Medicaid	2.26	9.56 [2.75, 33.32]	***	1.11	3.04 [0.98, 9.43]	
Private and CHAMPUS	1.46	4.29 [1.31, 14.08]	*	0.43	1.53 [0.38, 6.15]	
None	0.00			0.00		
CBCL						
≥64	1.39	4.01 [2.16, 7.47]	***	1.59	4.91 [2.81, 8.58]	***
≤63	0.00			0.00		
Chronic health problem	0.06	1.06 [0.57, 1.97]		0.21	1.24 [0.63, 2.43]	

Notes: Wave 1 value used in the contact date to Wave 3 model. Wave 3 value used in the Wave 3 to Wave 4 model.

At the Wave 1 interview, level of child welfare involvement was categorized into the following: (a) in home, no child welfare services, (b) in home, with child welfare services, and (c) out of home. At the Wave 3 interview, level of child welfare involvement was categorized into the following: (a) in home and (b) out of home.

*p=.05, **p=.01, ***p=.001

CBCL, Child Behavior Checklist; CD, contact date; CW, child welfare.

Table 10.11 Logistic Regression Predictors of School-Based and Outpatient Specialty Mental Health Services in Two Time Periods Among Children ≥11 Years Old Between Contact Date and Wave 3 and Wave 3 and Wave 4

	CD–W3 (School)			CD–W3 (Specialty)			W3–W4 (School)			W3–W4 (Specialty)		
	β	OR [CI]	p	β	OR [CI]	p	β	OR [CI]	p	β	OR [CI]	p
Age												
11–12	0.00	—		0.00	—		0.00	—		0.00		
13+ (13–14 for W34)	−0.83	0.44 [0.28, 0.68]	***	−0.13	0.88 [0.45, 1.72]		−0.57	0.57 [0.26, 1.23]		−0.24	0.78 [0.38, 1.63]	
15–16							−0.71	0.49 [0.22, 1.11]	[,]	−0.05	0.95 [0.42, 2.18]	[,]
Gender												
Male	0.74	2.09 [1.18, 3.68]	*	−0.17	0.84 [0.46, 1.55]		0.44	1.55 [0.83, 2.9]		0.24	1.27 [0.63, 2.57]	
Female	0.00			0.00			0.00	1 [1, 1]		0.00	1 [1, 1]	
Race/ethnicity												
Black/non-Hispanic	−0.34	0.71 [0.34, 1.48]		−0.76	0.47 [0.23, 0.93]	*	0.42	1.53 [0.77, 3.04]		0.12	1.13 [0.57, 2.23]	
White/non-Hispanic	0.00			0.00			0.00			0.00		
Hispanic	−0.37	0.69 [0.31, 1.55]		0.11	1.11 [0.45, 2.78]		−0.09	0.91 [0.31, 2.63]		−0.58	0.56 [0.18, 1.7]	
Other	0.58	1.79 [0.6, 5.32]		1.19	3.3 [0.75, 14.46]		1.29	3.62 [1.04, 12.68]	*	−0.20	0.82 [0.27, 2.5]	
Level of CW involvement												
In home, no CW services	0.00			0.00								
In home, with CW services	0.15	1.16 [0.58, 2.33]		0.06	1.06 [0.56, 2.01]		0.00	1 [1, 1]		0.00	1 [1, 1]	
Out of home	0.45	1.57 [0.69, 3.56]		1.98	7.22 [2.98, 17.51]	***	0.21	1.23 [0.58, 2.63]		1.35	3.87 [1.72, 8.71]	**

(continued)

Table 10.11 (continued)

	CD–W3 (School)			CD–W3 (Specialty)			W3–W4 (School)			W3–W4 (Specialty)		
	β	OR [CI]	p	β	OR [CI]	p	β	OR [CI]	p	β	OR [CI]	p
Primary abuse type												
Physical	0.88	2.41 [0.95, 6.15]		0.87	2.39 [0.96, 5.95]		0.19	1.21 [0.43, 3.39]		0.88	2.42 [1.1, 5.32]	*
Sexual	0.00	1 [0.35, 2.86]		0.00	1 [0.33, 3.06]		0.96	2.61 [0.75, 9.04]		0.61	1.84 [0.58, 5.84]	
Physical neglect	0.00			0.00			0.00			0.00		
Supervisory neglect	0.26	1.3 [0.56, 3.02]		0.03	1.04 [0.48, 2.24]		0.34	1.4 [0.53, 3.73]		0.15	1.16 [0.52, 2.61]	
Other	−0.33	0.72 [0.32, 1.6]		0.25	1.29 [0.5, 3.34]		0.14	1.15 [0.37, 3.59]		0.50	1.65 [0.51, 5.33]	
Prior report of maltreatment	0.20	1.22 [0.67, 2.22]		0.36	1.44 [0.81, 2.55]		0.14	1.15 [0.58, 2.29]		0.21	1.24 [0.59, 2.6]	
No. of family risk factors	−0.00	1 [0.82, 1.21]		0.02	1.02 [0.85, 1.23]		−0.01	0.99 [0.8, 1.22]		0.14	1.15 [0.92, 1.44]	
Child insurance status												
Medicaid	1.39	4.02 [1.19, 13.51]	*	1.92	6.8 [2.03, 22.77]	**	0.70	2.01 [0.62, 6.49]		1.42	4.16 [1.31, 13.18]	*
Private and CHAMPUS	1.27	3.56 [1.05, 12.1]	*	1.20	3.32 [1.12, 9.81]	*	0.51	1.66 [0.44, 6.26]		0.99	2.68 [0.64, 11.2]	
None	0.00			0.00			0.00			0.00		
CBCL												
≥64	0.91	2.48 [1.48, 4.16]	***	1.66	5.24 [2.81, 9.76]	***	1.34	3.8 [2.21, 6.55]	***	1.53	4.61 [2.49, 8.51]	***
≤63	0.00			0.00			0.00			0.00		
Chronic health problem	0.37	1.44 [0.77, 2.7]		0.22	1.25 [0.72, 2.15]		0.25	1.29 [0.7, 2.36]		0.08	1.08 [0.45, 2.59]	

Notes: Wave 1 value used in the contact date to Wave 3 model. Wave 3 value used in the Wave 3 to Wave 4 model.

At the Wave 1 interview, level of child welfare involvement was categorized into the following: (a) in home, no child welfare services, (b) in home, with child welfare services, and (c) out of home. At the Wave 3 interview, level of child welfare involvement was categorized into the following: (a) in home and (b) out of home.

*p=.05, **p=.01, ***p=.001

CBCL, Child Behavior Checklist; CD, contact date; CW, child welfare.

those reported for other kinds of maltreatment to begin receiving specialty mental health services.

Between Wave 3 and 4, during which time a large proportion of children in this age group stopped receiving services, predictors of service use once again changed somewhat. The one consistent predictor of service use, clinical-level CBCL score, continued to predict school-based mental health service use. Children from "other" racial/ethnic backgrounds, for the first time, were substantially more likely to receive services than white children, and the parameter estimate for black children was positive, if not significant. For specialty mental health services, out-of-home care, report of physical abuse, clinical-level CBCL scores, and insurance predicted increased use rates. As with school-based services, the parameter estimate for black children was positive for the first time, though not significant.

Discussion

Our results broadly illustrate—across ages groups, over an extended period of time—mental health service use by children referred to the child welfare system for maltreatment. One of the most important considerations enjoined by these results is the timing of mental health service initiation against indicators of need among children in different age groups.

Patterns of Service Use Among the Youngest Children

As pointed out by Burns and colleagues (2004), although a considerable proportion of children do receive services for their mental health problems, a sizable portion, particularly those who are young, do not (Burns et al., 2004). By 18 months after contact with child welfare, 28.9% of children aged 2 to 5 years received some type of service for a mental health problem, compared with 49.5% of 6–10 year olds and 64.1% of those aged 11 years or older. These figures are tempered by the knowledge that only 16.4% of those aged 2 to 5 years, 28.1% of those aged 6 to 11 years, and 45.9% of those 11 years or older receive services that are likely more than an evaluation. Although the difference between need for and use of services for younger children may not seem particularly large compared with that for older children, our analyses show that adaptive behavior is another major factor in need for and use of services among younger children. When this factor, as well as delays in other developmental domains, is accounted for in need assessment, the gap between need and use is considerable for younger children (Farmer et al., in press).

Our analyses suggest that this large gap between need and use among young children occurs for several reasons. First, in the absence of contact with child welfare, young children in this vulnerable population have low rates of service use overall, as indicated by the low rates of specialty and school-based services before contact with child welfare among 2- to 5-year-old children. Second, a clear driver in the delivery of services to young children—and to children across all the age groups—is the educational system. The Great Smoky Mountains Study results first emphasized the importance of the educational system as a provider of mental health services (Leslie et al., 2005). Until children age into the educational system, however, rates of service use in that sector are quite low, so children predominantly begin to receive services through specialty and medical care sectors. Our data show that, for young children, the medical care system is as prominent as the educational system. Most do not interact with the educational system, after all, until they are at least 5 years old, whereas they interact with the medical care system beginning at birth. It takes time for these sectors, in conjunction with child welfare, to identify and begin to respond to need, which necessarily widens the gap between need and service use among younger children in particular. The very young's persistent underreceipt of services apparently spans different problem types. Stahmer and colleagues (2005) noted the same pattern when they examined developmental services for the youngest: children 0–2 years old, regardless of need, received fewer services than children 3–5 years old.

Other variables play substantial roles in patterns of early service use. One notable such factor is race/ethnicity. Black or African American children, especially, are substantially less likely to receive mental health services in all age groups, but this pattern begins at the earliest of ages, despite our controlling for other variables. Lower rates of service use for black children occur in both school and specialty services, but especially in the specialty services through middle childhood and into early adolescence. That racial/ethnic group can impede receipt of services even in the presence of need has been noted in many previous studies (Ascher et al., 1996; Blumberg et al., 1996; Burns et al., 1995; Burns et al., 2004; Ezzell et al., 1999; Farmer et al., 2001; Farmer et al., in press; Federal Interagency Forum on Child and Family Statistics, 2005; Garland & Besinger, 1997; Garland et al., 1996, 2000; Horowitz et al., 1997; Kolko et al., 2003; Leslie et al., 2000, 2003, 2005; McMillen et al., 2004; Rubin et al., 2005; Snowden et al., 2003; Stahmer et al., 2005; Staudt, 2003; Zima et al., 2000) and has been explored by Garland and colleagues (Garland et al., 2000; Garland, Landsverk, & Lau, 2003). Our data suggest a reason that the data on race/ethnicity in the site-specific studies varies. In this national study, racial/ethnic variations in services use differed by age, with younger black children and older Hispanic youth being less likely than white non-Hispanic counterparts to use services.

Continuity of Services and Service-Sector Crossover

Our current data argue the importance of examining the predictors of services developmentally. For each age group, the constellation of statistically significant predictors is different. For preschool children (aged 2 to 5 years), increases in any mental health services are associated with age, out-of-home placement, supervisory neglect, CBCL scores in the clinical range, and lower functioning on VABS. Notably, VABS is a reasonably strong predictor of service use, whereas the CBCL is not as strong a predictor of service use in this particular age group; this pattern suggests that service use in this youngest age group is prompted by older age, interactions with the educational system, level of child welfare system involvement, and adaptive functioning. For children in middle childhood (6 to 10 years of age), out-of-home care, family risk factors, and clinically high CBCL scores are positively related to service use; age is marginal and black race/ethnicity is related, once again, to lower use. Here we again see level of child welfare system involvement and need as drivers, though without the influence of functioning (VABS), suggesting that mental health need is a major driver. For the oldest age group, gender, out-of-home placement, physical abuse as a reason for placement, Medicaid as the insurer, and clinically high CBCL scores are positively related to use; Hispanic ethnicity is negatively related. For this group need, level of child welfare system involvement and insurance combine as the predictors of mental health service use. Although the form of need changes over time (from an emphasis on functioning to more "traditional" emotional and behavioral symptoms), across ages children's needs generally do determine who receives services.

Our current data indicate that predictors of services use differ by sector, although they remain reasonably constant over the two follow-up intervals. School services are driven by age and functioning among the younger children, being male for the older children, out-of-home care, need as measured by the CBCL, prior school services, and, for some ages, primary reason for placement. Except for gender, school service use is based mainly on need. Mental health specialty-sector services show a pattern differing from that of school-based services. Out-of-home placement, most serious type of maltreatment alleged, physical or sexual abuse, elevated CBCL scores, and prior mental health services use consistently relate to use. Prior school services predict specialty use for the two older age groups; non-white race/ethnicity is associated with lower use rates; and, in the oldest age group, Medicaid as the insurer is an important predictor of specialty services.

That out-of-home placement is related to specialty-sector use was expected and confirms previous work. Whether children whose situations warrant removal from their homes have more problems because of their maladaptive family-of-origin environments, because of the trauma of removal, or because of some combination of reasons, they have clearly indicated needs (Chernoff et al., 1994; Clausen et al., 1998; Combs-Orme et al., 1991; Halfon et al., 1995; Hochstadt et al., 1987; Klee & Halfon, 1987; McIntyre & Keesler, 1986; Pilowsky, 1995; Schor, 1982, 1989; Simms, 1989; Stein et al., 1996; Swire & Kavaler, 1977; Szilagyi, 1998; U.S. General Accounting Office, 1995). Similarly, those placed because of physical or sexual abuse have been identified as having considerable mental health needs (Garland et al., 1996). Despite these well-documented origins of need, however, that placement and most serious type of maltreatment alleged are so strongly related to specialty-sector use, even after adjusting for need according to the CBCL, suggests either that professionals involved with these children harbor presumptions about which children need services, or that our measurement of need for service in this population fails to capture some important components of need (Staudt, 2003).

One other important observation here has received little prior attention: continuity of service for children and, for some age groups, the increased likelihood of service use in one sector after service use in another. With regard to continuity, throughout all multivariate analyses it was strongly evident that children who had received services previously were much more likely to continue receiving the same kind of service than children without such a history were to receive initial service. This pattern persists, whether we refer to services use before contact with the child welfare system and in the 18 months after contact, or whether we consider the interval between the first 18 months after contact and the second 18 months. This result implies that the threshold of initial service receipt is a critical one for children in need to pass in order to receive services later. This implication is supported, indirectly, by the regular CBCL odds ratio declines that occurred in models that controlled for prior service use, as compared with those that did not. Except for the earliest timeframe for the youngest children receiving specialty mental health services, at which point few children were already receiving specialty mental health services, this decline occurs for every age group at every wave and for each type of service. The lower CBCL odds ratios when controlling for prior history of service use suggests that CBCL scores do not so much predict who enters into services as they predict who continues to receive services already initiated.

In addition to continuity within each type of service use, some points showed strong evidence of crossover from using services in one sector to using services in another. For example, school-aged children receiving specialty mental health services seem particularly likely to begin receiving school-based services if they are already receiving specialty services, and vice versa, even after controlling for level of need. The reasons for these crossover patterns are not entirely clear, but they suggest that entering services through at least one sector may be a critical threshold for some children to pass on their way to eventual services in another sector.

Conclusion

Together, the low rates of service use among the youngest children, the findings about the importance of continuity of service use, and the crossover between sectors suggest that finding ways to connect young children and their families with services as early as possible is critical to bringing an appropriate response to bear on children's mental health needs before intervention becomes much more difficult to accomplish.

Although gaps between need for and use of services persist, our data do show that being reported to child welfare for suspected maltreatment dramatically increases the proportion of children receiving some type of mental health services. In each age group the proportion receiving school-based or specialty mental health services during the 18 months after referral to child welfare is uniformly and markedly higher than lifetime rates before referral. This finding is consistent with results of event-history analyses showing notable increases in rates of specialty mental health service use in the months after contact with child welfare as compared with rates in the months before contact (Leslie et al., 2005). This increase is likely due to the actions of both individuals in the child welfare system (child welfare investigators, caseworkers, foster caregivers) and those alleging the child maltreatment. The results of Leslie et al. suggest that much of the increase for specialty mental health services, in particular, is because of the actions of individuals in the child welfare system. Children in families for whom no child welfare services were initiated showed much smaller changes in rates of entry to mental health care before and after the contact date than children in families with more intensive child welfare involvement. That child welfare system contact appears to act as a major pathway for effecting connections between children and the mental health services they need is encouraging.

The results, although encouraging with respect to the number of older children receiving some service for their mental health problems, suggest areas for improvement. Younger children, those with child welfare system contacts because of neglect, and those from some racial/ethnic backgrounds continue to receive fewer services, even though they have considerable need. Because children with these sociodemographic and risk characteristics are well represented in the child welfare population, these findings about the level of unmet need in this vulnerable group of children are sobering. Professionals responsible for the welfare of these children must be mindful of these deficiencies and must put in place assessment and treatment procedures to ensure that every child with mental health needs receives appropriate care.

NOTE

1. We give the frequency of each risk factor and use a composite number of risk factors to analyze patterns of mental health service use.

REFERENCES

Achenbach, T. M. (1991). *Manual for the Child Behavior Checklist/4-18 and 1991 profile.* Burlington, VT: University of Vermont, Department of Psychiatry.

Administration for Children and Families. (2005). *Child welfare outcomes 2003: Annual report to Congress.* Washington, DC: U.S. Government Printing Office.

Administration for Children and Families. (2007). *Child maltreatment 2005.* Washington, DC: Author.

American Academy of Pediatrics, Committee on Early Childhood Adoption and Dependent Care. (1987). Health care of foster children. *Pediatrics, 79,* 644–646.

American Academy of Pediatrics, Committee on Early Childhood Adoption and Dependent Care. (1994). Health care of children in foster care. *Pediatrics, 93,* 335–338.

American Academy of Pediatrics, Committee on Early Childhood Adoption and Dependent Care. (2002). Health care of young children in foster care. *Pediatrics, 109,* 536–541.

Ascher, B. H., Farmer, E. M. Z., Burns, B. J., & Angold, A. (1996). The Child and Adolescent Services Assessment (CASA): Description and psychometrics. *Journal of Emotional and Behavioral Disorders, 4*(1), 12–20.

Blumberg, E., Landsverk, J., Ellis-Macleod, E., Ganger, W., & Culver, S. C. (1996). Use of public mental health system by children in foster care: Client characteristics and service use patterns. *Journal of Mental Health Administration, 23*(4), 389–405.

Burns, B. J., Costello, E. J., Angold, A., Tweed, D., Stangl, D., Farmer, E. M. Z., et al. (1995). Children's mental health service use across service sectors. *Health Affairs, 14*(3), 147–159.

Burns, B. J., Phillips, S. D., Wagner, H. R., Barth, R. P., Kolko, D. J., Campbell, Y., et al. (2004). Mental health need and access to mental health services by youth involved with child welfare: A national survey. *Journal of the American Academy of Child and Adolescent Psychiatry, 43*(8), 960–970.

Chernoff, R., Combs-Orme, T., Risley-Curtiss, C., & Heisler, A. (1994). Assessing the health status of children entering foster care. *Pediatrics, 93*(4), 594–601.

Child Welfare League of America. (1988). *Standards for health care. Services for children in out-of-home care.* Washington, DC: Author.

Clausen, J. M., Landsverk, J., Ganger, W., Chadwick, D., & Litrownik, A. (1998). Mental health problems of children in foster care. *Journal of Child and Family Studies, 7,* 283–296.

Combs-Orme, T., Chernoff, R. G., & Kager, V. A. (1991). Utilization of health care by foster children: Application of a theoretical model. *Children and Youth Services Review, 3,* 113–129.

dos Reis, S., Zito, J. M., Safer, D. J., & Soeken, K. L. (2001). Mental health services for youths in foster care and disabled youths. *American Journal of Public Health, 91,* 1094–1099.

Dowd, K., Kinsey, S., Wheeless, S., Thissen, R., Richardson, J., Suresh, R., et al. (2006). *National Survey of Child and Adolescent Well-Being combined Waves 1-4 data file users' manual, restricted release version.* Ithaca, NY: National Data Archive on Child Abuse and Neglect, Cornell University.

Ezzell, C. E., Swenson, C. C., & Faldowski, R. A. (1999). Child, family and case characteristics: Links with service utilization in physically abused children. *Journal of Child and Family Studies, 8,* 271–284.

Farmer, E. M. Z., Burns, B. J., Chapman, M. V., Phillips, S. D., Angold, A., & Costello, E. J. (2001). Use of mental health services by youth in contact with social services. *Social Service Review, 75*(4), 605–624.

Farmer, E. M. Z., Mustillo, S. A., Wagner, H. R., Burns, B. J., Kolko, D. J., Barth, R. P., et al. (in press). Service use and multisector use by youth in contact with child welfare. *Children and Youth Services Review.*

Federal Interagency Forum on Child and Family Statistics. (2005). *America's children: Key national indicators of well-being, 2005.* Washington, DC: U.S. Government Printing Office.

Garland, A. F., & Besinger, B. A. (1997). Racial/ethnic differences in court referred pathways to mental health services for children in foster care. *Children and Youth Services Review, 19*(8), 651–666.

Garland, A. F., Hough, R. L., Landsverk, J. A., McCabe, K. M., Yeh, M., Ganger, W. C., et al. (2000). Racial and ethnic variations in mental health case utilization among children in foster care. *Children's Services: Social Policy, Research and Practice, 3,* 133–146.

Garland, A. F., Landsverk, J. A., & Lau, A. S. (2003). Racial/ethnic disparities in mental health service use among children in foster care. *Children and Youth Services Review, 25*(5–6), 491–507.

Garland, A. F., Landsverk, J. L., Hough, R. L., & Ellis-MacLeod, E. (1996). Type of maltreatment as a predictor of mental health service use for children in foster care. *Child Abuse & Neglect, 20*(8), 675–688.

Halfon, N., Berkowitz, G., & Klee, L. (1992). Children in foster care in California: An examination of Medicaid reimbursed health services utilization. *Pediatrics, 89*(6), 1230–1237.

Halfon, N., Mendonca, A., & Berkowitz, G. (1995). Health status of children in foster care. *Archives of Pediatrics & Adolescent Medicine, 149,* 386–392.

Harman, J. S., Childs, G. E., & Kelleher, K. J. (2000). Mental health care utilization and expenditures by children in foster care. *Archives of Pediatrics & Adolescent Medicine, 154,* 1114–1117.

Hochstadt, N. J., Jaudes, P. K., Zimo, D. A., & Schachter, J. (1987). The medical and psychosocial needs of children entering foster care. *Child Abuse & Neglect, 2,* 53–62.

Horowitz, L. A., Putnam, F. W., Noll, J. G., & Trickett, P. K. (1997). Factors affecting utilization of treatment services by sexually abused girls. *Child Abuse & Neglect, 21*(1), 35–48.

Hurlburt, M. S., Leslie, L. K., Landsverk, J., Barth, R. P., Burns, B. J., Gibbons, R. D., et al. (2004). Contextual predictors of mental health service use among children open to child welfare. *Archives of General Psychiatry, 61*(12), 1217–1224.

Klee, L., & Halfon, N. (1987). Mental health care for foster children in California. *Child Abuse & Neglect, 11,* 63–74.

Kolko, D. J., Baumann, B. L., & Caldwell, N. (2003). Child abuse victims' involvement in community agency treatment: Service correlates short-term outcomes and relationship to reabuse. *Child Maltreatment, 8*(4), 273–287.

Leslie, L. K., Hurlburt, M. S., James, S., Landsverk, J., Slymen, D. J., & Zhang, J. J. (2005). Relationship between entry into child welfare and mental health service use. *Psychiatric Services, 56*(8), 981–987.

Leslie, L. K., Hurlburt, M. S., Landverk, J., Rolls, J., Wood, P. A., & Kelleher, K. J. (2003). Comprehensive assessments for children entering foster care. *Pediatrics, 112*(1), 134–142.

Leslie, L. K., Landsverk, J., Ezzet-Lofstrom, R., Tschann, J. M., Slymen, D. J., & Garland, A. F. (2000). Children in foster care: Factors influencing outpatient mental health service use. *Child Abuse & Neglect, 24*(4), 465–476.

McIntyre, A., & Keesler, T. Y. (1986). Psychological disorders among foster children. *Journal of Clinical and Child Psychology, 15,* 297–303.

McMillen, J. C., Scott, L. D., Zima, B. T., Ollie, M. T., Munson, M. R., & Spitznagel, E. (2004). Use of mental health services among older youths in foster care. *Psychiatric Services, 55*(7), 811–817.

Moffatt, M. Z. E. K., Peddie, M., Stulginshas, J., Pless, I. B., & Steinmetz, N. (1985). Health care delivery to foster children: A study. *Health and Social Work, 9,* 71–96.

Pilowsky, D. (1995). Psychopathology among children placed in family foster care. *Psychiatric Services, 46,* 906–910.

RTI International. (2007). *SUDAAN user's manual, release 9.0.1.* Research Triangle Park, NC: Author.

Rubin, D. M., Alessandrini, E. A., Feudtner, C., Mandell, D. S., Localio, A. R., & Hadley, T. (2005). Placement stability and mental health costs for children in foster care. *Pediatrics, 113*(5), 1336–1341.

Schor, E. L. (1982). The foster care system and health status of foster children. *Pediatrics, 69,* 521–528.

Schor, E. L. (1989). Foster care. *Pediatrics in Review, 10,* 209–216.

Simms, M. D. (1989). The foster care clinic: A community program to identify treatment needs of children in foster care. *Journal of Developmental and Behavioural Pediatrics, 10*(3), 121–128.

Simms, M. D., Dubowitz, H., & Szilagyi, M. A. (2000). Health care needs of children in the foster care system. *Pediatrics, 106,* 909–918.

Simms, M. D., & Halfon, N. (1994). The health care needs of children in foster care: A research agenda. *Child Welfare, 73,* 505–523.

Snowden, L. R., Cuellar, A. E., & Libby, A. M. (2003). Minority youth in foster care: Managed care and access to mental health treatment. *Medical Care, 42*(2), 264–274.

Stahmer, A. C., Leslie, L. K., Hurlburt, M., Barth, R. P., Webb, M. B., Landsverk, J., et al. (2005). Developmental and behavioral needs and service use for young children in child welfare. *Pediatrics, 116*(4), 891–900.

Staudt, M. M. (2003). Mental health services utilization by maltreated children: Research findings and recommendations. *Child Maltreatment, 8*(3), 195–203.

Stein, E., Evans, B., Mazumdar, R., & Rae-Grant, N. (1996). The mental health of children in foster care: A comparison with community and clinical samples. *Canadian Journal of Psychology, 41,* 385–391.

Swire, M. R., & Kavaler, F. (1977). The health status of foster children. *Child Welfare, 56,* 635–653.

Szilagyi, M. (1998). The pediatrician and the child in foster care. *Pediatrics in Review, 19,* 39–50.

Takayama, J. I., Bergman, A. B., & Connell, F. A. (1994). Children in foster care in the state of Washington: Health care utilization and expenditures. *Journal of the American Medical Association, 271*(23), 1850–1855.

Trupin, E. W., Tarico, V. S., Low, B. P., Jemelka, R., & McClellan, J. (1993). Children on child protective service caseloads: Prevalence and nature of serious emotional disturbance. *Child Abuse & Neglect, 17,* 345–355.

U.S. General Accounting Office. (1995). *Foster care: Health needs of many young children are unknown and unmet.* Washington, DC: U.S. Government Printing Office.

Zima, B. T., Bussing, R., Yang, X., & Belin, T. R. (2000). Help-seeking steps and service use for children in foster care. *Journal of Behavioral Health Services & Research, 27*(3), 271–285.

11

Exits From Out-of-Home Care and Continuity of Mental Health Service Use

JOHN LANDSVERK, MICHAEL S. HURLBURT, LAUREL LESLIE, JENNIFER ROLLS, AND JINJIN ZHANG

A robust empirical literature exists on the use of mental health services by children referred to the child welfare system because of alleged child maltreatment. Horwitz, Hurlburt, and Zhang (see Chapter 10, this volume) systematically and substantially update prior reviews of this literature (e.g., Landsverk, Garland, & Leslie, 2002), including publications based on the National Survey of Child and Adolescent Well-Being (NSCAW). With the single exception of continuity of care, topics reviewed in that chapter as meaningfully informing the empirical literature have addressed referred children's patterns of access to and use of mental health care. As Horwitz and colleagues document, most of these studies have focused, moreover, on children and adolescents whom the child welfare system has removed from the home of origin and placed in foster care.

No empirical studies have systematically and directly examined patterns of mental health service use when children exit foster care or the child welfare system. Entry and access can be characterized as a problem of *onset*. In other words, the question governing the literature is whether entry into the child welfare system is associated with an increased propensity for onset of mental health care. The relationship between exit from child welfare settings, especially out-of-home care, and use of mental health care may be considered a problem of *offset* or continuity of care. From the perspective of continuity or discontinuity of care, the question becomes, do children who need and are receiving mental health services when they are in child welfare settings continue to receive such care after they exit those settings?

In a broader sense, both the onset and the offset questions are about relationships between two child service systems, the child welfare system and the mental health system. From an organizational perspective, these two systems are independently structured, with separate legal authority and mandates, separate funding mechanisms, and altogether different functions in the United States. Onset and offset questions concern the possible flow of clients between these two service systems or, from another perspective, the overlap in the populations being served by the two service systems. Especially important in a framework of access to care and continuity of care is consideration of the relationships between these two systems in the context of time.

Garland and colleagues have provided a conceptual understanding of how these two systems—together with other child-serving systems, such as juvenile justice, special education in schools, and alcohol and drug services—differ in their population gender and age distributions and how entry into these systems is related to mental health need (Garland, Hough, Landsverk, & Brown, 2001). They offer insights into client flow or exchange between the two systems over time. From the perspective of need for mental health care, the mental health system is a tertiary care system, or one in which clients have already identified need for mental health services.[1] Children's entry into the mental health service system occurs, therefore, because of their identified need for such care.

The child welfare system, by contrast, is a service system that is secondary in relation to mental health need. Children enter this system not through the direct identification of need for mental health care, but instead because of identified parental behaviors considered to place children's safety at risk. In simple terms, children enter the child welfare system because of their caregivers' child abuse and neglect, not usually because of their own identified emotional or behavioral problems. Nevertheless, children involved with the child welfare system do incur great risk for development of mental health problems deriving from the abusive and neglectful behaviors of their caregivers; these caregivers' behaviors have been observed to be sufficiently risky, in fact, to warrant report of these children to the child protective system, the child's usual entry point to the child welfare system.[2]

Garland and colleagues characterize the child welfare system as involving children at a much earlier age, on average, than the other secondary or tertiary service systems. Their conceptual framework for understanding child welfare and mental health service systems suggests that the flow from secondary to tertiary systems is crucial, and it is essentially a question of access to mental health care for those involved with child welfare. Nonetheless, it also implies that continuity of care in the tertiary mental health system may be critical for children exiting the child welfare system if these children continue to need such care. No studies have shown that children exiting the child welfare system are at less risk for emotional and behavioral problems than when they entered. The absence of this issue from the literature enjoins our research on continuity of care, as well as initial access to care, in order that the long-term well-being of this population of vulnerable children may be appropriately supported.

Systems of Care and the Functions
of the Child Welfare System

The questions of mental health service system onset and offset related to entry to and exit from the child welfare system are informed by two disparate policy arenas. The systems-of-care policy literature arose from observations about the enormous challenges involved in providing mental health care for children and adolescents, especially those who emerge as clients in non–mental health service systems (e.g., child welfare and juvenile justice). The system-of-care initiative in the United States proposed a specific approach to addressing these challenges, an approach that included the integration of care from child mental health and non–mental health systems. The second wave of policy literature delineated the basic functions of the U.S. child welfare system as providing children safety, permanence, and well-being. The third function, the well-being of children, increasingly has become linked with the need for and use of mental health services. These two perspectives, followed by literature on the onset question, are reviewed here.[3]

Since the mid-1980s, the characterization and understanding of mental health services for children and youth in the United States have evolved significantly. This evolution began with Knitzer's (1982) resounding critique of the lack of integration in mental health service provision for children and adolescents, especially for in-need children who were involved with other service systems, such as child welfare and juvenile justice. The response to Knitzer's call for significant reform in the way mental health services were delivered to children came swiftly, and with a value-based model of mental health care, by the original proponents of system-of-care principles (Stroul & Friedman, 1986). Underlying this response was the recognition that children and adolescents with significant mental health needs are found and cared for in multiple sectors of care beyond the specialty mental health sector, including child welfare, juvenile justice, education, general health or primary care, and alcohol and drug services. In fact, empirical research has suggested that more mental health services are delivered to youth in non–specialty mental health sector services than in the specialty mental health sector (Burns et al., 1995). This reality has driven policy efforts to better integrate child and youth services across service sectors, as is reflected by the national Child and Adolescent Service System Program (CASSP) principles (Day & Roberts, 1991) that have been so influential in shaping service delivery policies and funding demonstration models.

We would note that the positive impact of this integration effort on client-level outcomes was assumed in the system-of-care model; however, Bickman's well-designed Fort Bragg and Stark County, Ohio, studies found no evidence for positive mental health clinical outcomes after implementations of the system-of-care model, despite observed service delivery changes that the model predicted (Bickman, 1996; Bickman, Summerfelt, & Bryant, 1996). These disappointing results suggest that the system-of-care model has not solved the problems attending provision of mental health care to children in service systems such as child welfare; instead, these results have urged incorporation of more evidence-based interventions into these services systems.

The second perspective in which the onset and offset questions are framed concerns the child welfare system functions. Although the two functions of protecting children (safety) and preserving families (permanence) are considered critical, the third mission element of child well-being has increasingly commanded attention (see Wulczyn, Barth, Yuan, Jones Harden, & Landsverk, 2005, pp. 7–20). Despite this increased attention to well-being, safety and permanence are often characterized as the primary responsibility of the child welfare system, whereas the well-being of children is usually considered more complex in terms of locus of primary responsibility because it requires services often delivered by agencies outside child welfare—agencies such as physical and mental health, developmental services, and education. Consequently, children's and adolescents' referral to and use of these other service delivery systems is critical to the fulfillment of the child welfare system's child well-being mission.

Onset and Access to Mental Health Care

Research has unequivocally documented the high rates of mental health need and service use in child welfare populations.[4] We note, in particular, the systematic analysis of the onset issue by Leslie et al. (2005). This study used NSCAW Wave 3 (18-month follow-up) cohort data on children aged 2 to 14 years at study enrollment; it tested the onset hypothesis in a more comprehensive way than any prior study by examining onset at entry into the child protective services investigation, at the time of case opening by the child welfare system, and at entry into out-of-home care. The onset of mental health services increased significantly immediately after initial contact with the child welfare system, varied by level of child welfare involvement, and then leveled off by 3 months after initial contact. The statistical model tested in the study indicated that all three groups of children were more likely to receive mental health services after involvement with the child welfare system was initiated by an investigation; however, the proportion receiving mental health care was directly related to the level of involvement: Those children remaining in their homes without child welfare services after investigation were about one-third as likely as those in out-of-home care to use mental health services; those remaining in their homes and receiving additional child welfare services after investigation were approximately one-half as likely as those in out-of-home care to use mental health services. From these findings, the authors concluded that child welfare functions as a "gateway" to the mental health service system, with the gateway widening as the child proceeds deeper into the system.

Horwitz, Hurlburt, and Zhang (Chapter 10, this volume) have conducted additional analyses of the NSCAW mental health services data for the full

36-month duration (Waves 1 through 4) and also have found support for the onset hypothesis: Being reported to child welfare was associated with what they have termed a "dramatic" rate increase in children receiving some form of mental health services, a finding consistent with Leslie and her colleagues (2005). The finding of an onset effect in both of these studies is especially robust because they used quite different methods and timeframes to address the onset question. Horwitz and her colleagues have suggested an interesting mechanism for this effect: child welfare system actions at the level of individual roles, such as those of investigators, caseworkers, foster parents, and possibly even the initial reporters of suspected abuse and neglect. Exactly how these individual-level activities produce the onset effect is not explained by the authors. Whatever the mechanisms, however, strong evidence now exists that child welfare serves as a gateway to the mental health service system, with greater use of mental health care corresponding with more intensive system involvement.

Offset and Continuity of Mental Health Care

In contrast with the onset question, the offset question has received little examination. Because the child welfare system serves as a gateway to the mental health service system, one would expect exits from the child welfare system to correspond with exits from the mental health service system—or what we term *offset*. In essence, this problem is one of continuity of care, especially when the child's need for mental health services remains high even after exit from child welfare services.

Only the study by Horwitz and colleagues has examined this issue of continuity (see Chapter 10). The authors approach the problem by comparing the rates of mental health service use in the first 18 months of NSCAW to the rates in the second 18 months and by examining the size of the odds ratios for the predictor, Child Behavior Checklist (CBCL; Achenbach, 1991) scores, as a measure of mental health need. Their analyses suggest a high level of service continuity from one 18-month period into the next, with children much more likely to receive services in the later period if they received specialty mental health services in the first period. They found this pattern to hold for two different groups of children receiving prior services: one receiving service both before investigation and in the 18 months after investigation, and another without a history of service use before investigation but with service use in the first 18 months after investigation. The authors interpret this finding as supporting a threshold mechanism, one whereby the passage from not receiving to receiving mental health care is critical to receipt of services in a later time period.

The threshold interpretation was further supported, though indirectly, by the size of the effect of need (as measured by CBCL scores) on use of mental health services. When prior service use was controlled in the model, the CBCL odds ratio decreased. This finding was especially robust because it was observed for every age group (except for the very earliest timeframe for the youngest children receiving specialty mental health services at each time point and for each type of service). Nonetheless, though these analyses suggest a greater continuity than expected, the evidence marshaled for the test is primarily indirect (odds ratio changes when controlling for prior service use) or somewhat crude (comparison of use rates between two broad timeframes).

Data Set Characteristics, Test Variables, and Goals

We focus on the issue of continuity and offset by examining use of mental health services for youth when they exit out-of-home care. The prospective longitudinal design of NSCAW is foundational for our analytic design, which takes advantage of a natural experiment that occurred with the NSCAW child population over the course of the 36 months of observation—namely, the return home by either Wave 3 or Wave 4 children who were in out-of-home care at Wave 1 and for whom use of mental health services was reported at Wave 1. Use of mental health services was measured at all Waves in NSCAW; moreover, each child's placement and mental health service onset and offset were able to be coded at each of the 36 months of the study timeframe, which allowed us to examine continuity and discontinuity in use of mental health services directly after children's reunification with biological parents. In addition to the child's living arrangements and mental health service use, level of need for such services was measured at each NSCAW wave, together with other likely predictors of service use, which allowed us to examine the continuity and discontinuity patterns of such use while controlling for critical, potentially confounding factors.

Two phases for each of two methods were employed to test the *offset* hypothesis. Both phases used a sample of children who reportedly used mental health services during their time in out-of-home care. Under Method 1, children in out-of-home care at Wave 1 and simultaneously receiving specialty mental health services were selected for a Wave 3 service use comparison between those children who had reunified with those who had not. A similar approach was adopted for children who remained in out-of-home care at Wave 3 and simultaneously received specialty mental health services: We compared Wave 4 service use rates of those children who had reunified by Wave 4 with the rates of those who had not.

The samples were limited to children aged 2 years or older at the Wave 1 (baseline) interview, because the CBCL was not used for children younger than 2 years. A total of 324 children were identified for Phase 1 of Method 1, which examined use of mental health services at Wave 3. In this sample of children, 33.4% had been reunified by Wave 3, and 66.6% remained in out-of-home care. For the second phase of Method 1, 310 children were identified because they were in out-of-home care and receiving mental health services at Wave 3. Among these children, 14.2% had been reunified by Wave 4, and 85.8% remained in out-of-home care.

We devised a second method of testing in order to benefit from the capability NSCAW's longitudinal (36-month) design affords to code mental health service use and reunification status by month. Method 2 allowed a more detailed comparison of children's cessation of service use with their concurrent placement status. We had concluded after Method 1 testing that more cases could be drawn into the analysis by identifying any case in which mental health services were received at the same time that a child was in out-of-home care, not only when this conjunction occurred at the time of the Wave 1 interview, as was done in Method 1. Consequently, we decided to examine whether the likelihood of discontinuation of mental health service use is greater in the months after reunification than in months in which children remain in out-of-home care. To simplify this approach somewhat, Method 2 analysis was limited to cases in which mental health service use started concurrently with or after a child had entered out-of-home care. Using this approach, we identified 453 children who, between Wave 1 and Wave 3, began using specialty mental health services while in out-of-home care. For these children, 15.2% were reunified by Wave 3 and 84.8% continued in out-of-home care.

Because the movement into out-of-home care has shown by far the largest gateway to the mental health system, our examination of continuity and discontinuity of mental health services after exits from out-of-home care offers the most rigorous test of our offset hypothesis. This hypothesis is that child welfare has a gate that "swings both ways," meaning that exits from child welfare are expected to be associated with decreases in use of mental health services, even when we control for need, precisely as entry into child welfare has been shown to be associated with service use increases.

Methods

Measures

All variables used in our analyses were chosen to be comparable to those used in Leslie et al.'s test (2005) of the onset hypothesis.

BASELINE LEVEL OF CHILD WELFARE INVOLVEMENT   Three levels of children's involvement with the child welfare system were obtained from case records and from NSCAW interviews with the caseworker: *(1)* residence in-home with biological parent, with no child welfare services received; *(2)* residence in-home with biological parent, with child welfare services received; and *(3)* removal from the home and placement in out-of-home care.

CHILD BACKGROUND CHARACTERISTICS   Sociodemographic information (child's age, gender, and race/ethnicity) was obtained from caregivers. Ages at entry into the study were collapsed into three groups: aged 2 to 5 years, 6 to 10 years, and 11 years or older.

MALTREATMENT HISTORY   Caseworkers identified alleged types of maltreatment for the current episode of child welfare involvement, using a modified Maltreatment Classification Scale (Manly, Cicchetty, & Barnett, 1994). Children could receive codes for more than one type of maltreatment. Five indicator variables for maltreatment were created. *(1)* physical abuse, *(2)* sexual abuse, *(3)* physical neglect (failure to provide for the child), *(4)* supervisory neglect (failure to supervise the child), and *(5)* other (a residual category).

CHILD MENTAL HEALTH NEEDS   Caregivers reported on their child's mental health needs, responding to the CBCL (Achenbach, 1991). The CBCL is a widely used measure of behavioral problems, with established reliability and validity that has been standardized by age and gender on large populations of children from different socioeconomic backgrounds (Achenbach, 1991) and has previously been used in research with child welfare populations (Garland, Landsverk, Hough, & Ellis-MacLeod, 1996; Landsverk et al., 2002; Simms, 1989). Two forms of the CBCL were used, one for children aged 2 to 3 years and another for children aged 4 to 18 years. Three standardized scores, normed by age and gender, were obtained: an Internalizing Problems score, an Externalizing Problems score, and a Total Problems score. Youth were considered in need of mental health services if they scored in the clinical range (64 or higher) on any one of the three scales. To avoid inflating the estimate of need, in the multivariate model we used the clinical cut-point (63/64) instead of the borderline range. Multivariate models were run with the CBCL configured as either a continuous variable or a dichotomized variable with the 63/64 cut-point. The dichotomized variable can be interpreted as testing a higher threshold of behavioral problems, one that is more properly congruent with a clinical interpretation of need for mental health services.

CHILD MENTAL HEALTH SERVICE USE   Children' use of mental health services was measured with an adapted version of the Child and Adolescent Services Assessment (Burns, Angold, & Costello, 1992). Caregivers were asked at baseline, Wave 2 (12 months), Wave 3 (18 months), and Wave 4 (36 months) about service use from the following specialty mental health care settings: clinic-based specialty mental health services (e.g., community mental health clinics); therapeutic nursery; day treatment; private professionals, such as psychiatrists, psychologists, social workers, and psychiatric nurses; and family doctors or other medical doctors. For each of the 36 months of the study, a variable was created for evidence of mental health service use.

Analyses

Because our analyses are not based on random assignment but on a naturally occurring shift in children's living environments, the control for potential confounding variables in these analyses is especially important. The design and samples for testing the overall offset hypothesis were constructed as multiple tests, with the understanding that similar findings across somewhat different approaches would be particularly robust. This approach can be problematic, of course, if findings strongly vary among the multiple tests, because interpreting whether the variation in findings is due to differences in test designs or samples is difficult. Nevertheless, we sided with multiple approaches with multiple tests to most rigorously examine an overall hypothesis in this nonexperimental cohort design.

Our analyses focused separately on children who had reported use of mental health services sometime during the 36-month period. Continuity of mental health service use for youth exiting out-of-home care was compared with that for youth not exiting out-of-home care for both groups under Method 1. For Method 2, a data set was constructed that created a continuous monthly history of mental health service use for each child in the months after the child welfare system contact date. In this data set having one record per month for each child, mental health service use was noted as present in the month of each interview in which the caregiver reported that the child was receiving mental health services. Data about month and year of service use were then used to indicate the months in which services started and stopped. Whenever ambiguity arose about whether services continued during all months between two interviews, all intervening months between the onset month and the offset month were also considered as months in which services were received if current service use was reported in both longitudinal interviews.

The authors used logistic regression, event history analysis, and multivariate Cox proportional-hazards modeling (Singer & Willett, 2003). All analyses were conducted first without controls for need for mental health care; because of the importance of need for mental health care as a predictor in models of service use, they were then conducted while controlling for need as measured by the CBCL. CBCL scores as an indicator of need for mental health care were entered into analyses in two ways: as a continuous variable and as a dichotomous variable using the cut-point of 63/64. Age, gender, and race/ethnicity were also entered into the analyses as covariates.

We used event history analysis to examine the relationship between level of child welfare involvement and the likelihood of mental health service offset, controlling for key covariates identified in prior research. This statistical approach has been used to describe changes in the likelihood of an event across time for different groups (Singer & Willett, 2003).

Univariate analyses were initially conducted to assess the reliability of these associations. Afterward, to test the proportionality assumption, we tested for an interaction between each of the covariates and time (Allison, 1995). No statistically significant interactions were found, and a proportional-hazards model was employed to simultaneously estimate the relationships of multiple predictors with the likelihood of mental health service use initiation. The proportional-hazards model provides relative risk ratios for each variable included in the model, controlling for the other variables in the model. Because data were collected from respondents across multiple waves, early censoring (i.e., before Wave 3, or 18 months after contact with child welfare) did occur for some observations; however, such censoring was addressed naturally as part of the multivariate Cox proportional-hazards model. We accounted for sample weights and the two-stage cluster sample design in all analyses with use of the statistical software SUDAAN (RTI International, 2007).

Results

Distributions on background variables are reported for all three samples used in testing the offset hypothesis (Table 11.1). They are shown as separate samples, without significance testing for differences between the samples.[5] The distributions on age, gender, race/ethnicity, most serious type of maltreatment alleged (according to caseworker's judgment), CBCL score dichotomized into *high* and *low*, and reunification status are shown in Table 11.1 for Method 1, Wave 3; Method 1, Wave 4; and Method 2.

Method 1 Comparisons of Reunified and Out-of-Home Children

Method 1 selected children in out-of-home care at Wave 1 who also were receiving specialty mental health services at the same time. As noted, this sample may have included a small number of children who were receiving mental health care prior to

Table 11.1 Background Variables for Methods to Test Offset Hypothesis

	Method 1, Wave 1 to Wave 3 (n = 324) n (%)	Method 1, Wave 3 to Wave 4 (n = 310) n (%)	Method 2 (n = 453) n (%)
Child age			
2–5	36 (11.9)	53 (18.8)	92 (27.0)
6–10	125 (32.4)	115 (37.5)	177 (35.8)
11+	163 (55.8)	142 (43.7)	184 (37.2)
Child gender			
Male	162 (58.6)	152 (53.5)	206 (45.6)
Female	162 (41.4)	158 (46.5)	247 (54.4)
Child race/ethnicity			
Black	101 (31.0)	102 (29.4)	150 (31.4)
White	161 (49.2)	139 (48.7)	192 (46.8)
Hispanic	38 (14.8)	46 (16.6)	71 (15.8)
Other	24 (5.0)	20 (5.4)	38 (6.1)
Primary abuse			
Physical abuse	68 (31.1)	64 (27.1)	86 (24.4)
Sexual abuse	72 (15.2)	58 (11.2)	81 (9.4)
Fail to provide	41 (19.3)	51 (20.3)	76 (18.1)
Fail to supervise	86 (26.0)	85 (36.3)	127 (41.3)
Other	31 (8.4)	21 (5.0)	39 (6.8)
CBCL			
≥64	204 (59.4)	181 (58.6)	235 (49.5)
<64	120 (40.6)	118 (41.4)	204 (50.5)
Reunified			
Yes	80 (33.4)	33 (14.2)	92 (15.2)
No	244 (66.6)	277 (85.8)	354 (84.8)

CBCL, Child Behavior Checklist.

investigation by child protective services, estimated as less than 3% by Leslie and colleagues (2005). Rates of specialty mental health service use reported for the child at the Wave 3 interview (18 months) were compared for those children who had reunified and those who remained in out-of-home care. The analysis under Method 1 was then extended to children remaining in out-of-home care at Wave 3 and receiving specialty mental health services at the same time, using the identical approach for Wave 4 comparison of rates of specialty mental health service use between those children who had reunified and those who remained in out-of-home care.

Contrary to expectations under the offset hypothesis, using data from Wave 1 to Wave 3 and from Wave 3 to Wave 4 produced no indication that children reunifying with their parents were less likely than children remaining out of home to continue receiving specialty mental health services at later time points. Specifically, the analyses indicated that 75% of the 64 children reunified by Wave 3 continued to receive specialty mental health services, compared with 64% of the 244 children who remained in out-of-home care. Examining the 310 children reportedly in out-of-home care at Wave 3 and receiving specialty mental health services at the same time, we found that 58% of the 33 children reunified by Wave 4 continued to receive specialty mental health services, compared with 61% of the children who remained in out-of-home care by the same endpoint. When these differences were tested for statistical significance at the .05 level, neither was significant. We also note that the rate of continuity for specialty mental health service use was quite high, ranging between 64% and 75% for the Wave 1 to Wave 3 comparison and between 56% and 61% for the Wave 3 to Wave 4 comparison.

These comparisons were then submitted to a multivariate test to control for a number of predictor variables, including need for mental health care as measured by scores on the CBCL, using logistic regression to test for differences between reunified and nonreunified children at Wave 3 and then at Wave 4. These logistic regressions are presented in Tables 11.2 and 11.3, with separate regressions shown in each table for the two different ways of coding CBCL scores as the indicator of need for mental health services: namely, as a continuous variable and then as a categorical, dichotomous variable.

The findings in Table 11.2 indicate that children reunified by Wave 3 were as likely to continue use of specialty mental health services as children who remained in out-of-home care. In fact, in the logistic regression whose equation used the continuous form of the CBCL score, the rate of use for the reunified children was significantly higher than the rate of use for the children remaining in out-of-home care. The differences observed between the reunified and nonreunified children when the CBCL score was entered as a categorical, dichotomous variable, however, were not statistically significant, even though the differences were in the same direction as those in the prior test. Few of the other control variables were shown to predict specialty mental health services use, with the exceptions being the measure of need (in both ways of coding the CBCL scores) and Hispanic background. The

Table 11.2   Logistic Regression on Specialty Mental Health Service Use at Wave 3, Method 1, Wave 1 to Wave 3 ($n = 324$)

	CBCL as Continuous Variable			CBCL as Categorical Variable (≥ 64 vs. < 64; < 64 as Reference Group)		
	β	OR [CI]	p	β	OR [CI]	p
Age	0.03	1.04 (0.90, 1.19)		0.06	1.06 (0.93, 1.21)	
Gender						
Male	−0.20	0.82 (0.26, 2.52)		−0.19	0.83 (0.26, 2.67)	
Female	—	—		—	—	
Race/ethnicity						
Black/non-Hispanic	0.74	2.10 (0.87, 5.08)		0.64	1.89 (0.75, 4.80)	
White/non-Hispanic	—	—		—	—	
Hispanic	1.66	5.25 (1.07, 25.80)	*	1.40	4.04 (0.89, 18.38)	
Other	0.14	1.15 (0.39, 3.37)		−0.01	0.99 (0.30, 3.31)	
Primary abuse type						
Physical	0.25	1.29 (0.22, 7.44)		0.03	1.03 (0.18, 5.80)	
Sexual	−0.57	0.56 (0.12, 2.56)		−0.72	0.48 (0.12, 2.01)	
Physical neglect	—	—		—	—	
Supervisory neglect	−0.33	0.72 (0.14, 3.75)		−0.63	0.53 (0.11, 2.58)	
Other	−1.23	0.29 (0.04, 2.15)		−1.47	0.23 (0.04, 1.37)	
CBCL total	0.06	1.07 (1.02, 1.12)	**	1.61	5.01 (1.62, 15.54)	**
Reunification						
Yes	1.01	2.75 (1.04, 7.25)	*	0.97	2.64 (0.95, 7.36)	
No	—	—		—	—	

$^*p \leq .05$, $^{**}p \leq .01$, $^{***}p \leq .001$.
CBCL, Child Behavior Checklist.

race/ethnicity finding was statistically significant only when the CBCL score was entered as a continuous variable in the logistic regression.

The findings in Table 11.3 indicate no statistically significant differences between reunified and nonreunified in their use of specialty mental health services at Wave 4. Few other predictors were consistently related to Wave 4 use of specialty mental health care, except for the two different codings of CBCL scores as indicators of need.

Method 2 Comparisons of Reunified and Out-of-Home Children

Method 2 exceeded the relatively rough comparisons of reunified and out-of-home children, the information for which came from Wave 1, 3, and 4 data collection alone. For Method 2 a month-by-month data file was constructed that showed onset and offset of specialty mental health care, as well as any reunification date. This data set allowed a more refined analysis, one that showed exactly when children stopped use of specialty mental health services, comparing placement status (out-of-home or reunified) each month. Essentially, this method provided

Table 11.3   Logistic Regression on Specialty Mental Health Service Use at Wave 4, Method 1, Wave 3 to Wave 4 ($n = 310$)

	CBCL as Continuous Variable			CBCL as Categorical Variable (≥64 vs.<64)		
	β	OR [CI]	p	β	OR [CI]	p
Age	0.11	1.12 (0.97, 1.28)		0.12	1.13 (0.98, 1.31)	
Gender						
Male	−0.15	0.86 (0.26, 2.80)		0.10	1.11 (0.35, 3.50)	
Female	—	—		—	—	
Race/ethnicity						
Black/non-Hispanic	1.76	5.80 (1.60, 21.00)	**	1.55	4.70 (1.40, 15.75)	*
White/non-Hispanic	—	—		—	—	
Hispanic	0.83	2.29 (0.44, 11.81)		0.63	1.87 (0.43, 8.25)	
Other	−0.27	0.76 (0.14, 4.16)		−0.27	0.77 (0.13, 4.44)	
Primary abuse type						
Physical	0.68	1.97 (0.38, 10.26)		0.69	2.00 (0.39, 10.16)	
Sexual	0.09	1.10 (0.31, 3.88)		0.06	1.06 (0.35, 3.21)	
Physical neglect	—	—		—	—	
Supervisory neglect	0.08	1.08 (0.29, 4.07)		−0.08	0.93 (0.24, 3.56)	
Other	1.67	5.33 (0.98, 29.12)		1.13	3.11 (0.58, 16.63)	
CBCL total	0.07	1.08 (1.03, 1.12)	**	1.18	3.25 (0.98, 10.80)	
Reunification						
Yes	−0.88	0.41 (0.10, 1.75)		−0.47	0.63 (0.15, 2.59)	
No	—	—		—	—	

$*p \leq .05$, $**p \leq .01$, $***p \leq .001$.
CBCL, Child Behavior Checklist.

a continuous history of mental health service use (or nonuse) for each child in the months after the initial child welfare system contact date. Analyses for Method 2 were limited to cases in which specialty mental health service use began with or after a child's entry to out-of-home care.

A survival analysis approach was first adopted for assessing the likelihood that children would stop receiving specialty mental health services (the event), controlling for several variables and including a time-varying variable for placement dichotomized as out-of-home or in-home (reunified). With this approach, the month in which specialty mental health services started while the child was out of home was considered to be the first month, even if these services began a few or many months after the child welfare contact date. Figure 11.1 displays the survival curves for the two groups of children: those who reunified and those who remained in out-of-home care. The graph shows that throughout the 15 months after onset of mental health services, more than 70% of children in either group continued to receive such services, with the reunified group actually demonstrating higher levels of continuity of mental health care. Beyond the 15-month point, estimates likely become fairly unstable because the Wave 3 interview was scheduled to occur 18 months after the initial child welfare contact date. The

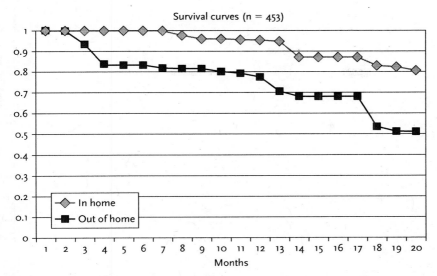

Figure 11.1 Proportion of continuing use of specialty mental health services after first month of starting use, by reunification status (Method 2, *n* = 453).

survival proportions are based on a weighted number of cases, using the NSCAW Wave 4 weight.

Fundamentally, the survival curves presented for Method 2 in Figure 11.1 are reasonably consistent with results from Method 1, even though cases selected in the two analyses are somewhat different. Method 1 includes some children whose specialty mental health services started before placement in out-of-home care, whereas Method 2 includes some children placed out of home or starting specialty mental health service use after Wave 1. Both find that substantial percentages of children continue to use specialty mental health services 15 to 18 months later. Neither approach suggests that children returning home are more likely to have poor continuity of care with respect to specialty mental health services. In fact, as a group, many children beginning to receive specialty mental health services while in out-of-home care seem likely to continue to receive such services 12 to 15 months later.

Models for predicting use of specialty mental health services were tested with Cox proportional-hazards methods to examine the likelihood that discontinuation of service use was a function of any of several covariates, including age, gender, race/ethnicity, most serious type of abuse alleged, CBCL score, and the time-varying placement variable. The first two models shown in Table 11.4 use the CBCL score in continuous form. In the first model, the time-varying placement variable is treated as a main effect in order to assess whether the likelihood of service use discontinuation is greater for all months that a child is at home than for out-of-home time, assuming that the differential hazard of discontinuation is the same for out-of-home and in-home placement at all

Table 11.4   Cox Proportional-Hazards Models Predicting Likelihood of
Discontinuing Specialty Mental Health Service Use (Method 2, $n = 453$),
Child Behavior Checklist Score as Continuous Variable

	Model 1 (Without Interaction)			Model 2 (With Interaction)		
	Hazard Ratio	95% [CI]	p	Hazard Ratio	95% [CI]	p
Age	0.80	0.71, 0.92	***	0.80	0.71, 0.92	***
Gender						
Male	0.58	0.25, 1.35		0.58	0.25, 1.36	
Female	—	—		—	—	
Race/ethnicity						
Black/non-Hispanic	1.79	0.53, 5.99		1.78	0.53, 6.00	
White/non-Hispanic	—	—		—	—	
Hispanic	0.87	0.21, 3.57		0.87	0.21, 3.58	
Other	1.26	0.47, 3.26		1.27	0.50, 3.23	
Primary abuse type						
Physical	0.86	0.26, 2.81		0.86	0.26, 2.82	
Sexual	0.74	0.29, 1.86		0.75	0.28, 1.97	
Physical neglect	—	—		—	—	
Supervisory neglect	1.51	0.64, 3.56		1.51	0.64, 3.58	
Other	0.09	0.02, 0.43	**	0.09	0.02, 0.43	**
CBCL total (continuous)	0.97	0.94, 0.99	*	0.97	0.94, 1.00	*
Out of home status						
Out of home	1.16	0.49, 2.75		1.41	0.10, 19.96	
In home (RU)	—	—		—	—	
Time *Out-of-home status				0.99	0.84, 1.16	

$*p \leq .05, **p \leq .01, ***p \leq .001.$
CBCL, Child Behavior Checklist. RU, Reunified

months. The second model includes a time-by-placement interaction term to
assess whether the likelihood of service use discontinuation, relative to the rate
associated with remaining in out-of-home care, is greater in the first few months
that a child returns home than it is in later months. Neither model revealed a
relationship between the placement variable and the likelihood of service use
discontinuation, whether discontinuation was treated as a main effect or as an
interaction with time (Table 11.4).

The same two models are presented again, except the CBCL score is entered
as a categorical, dichotomized variable (Table 11.5). Consistent with the findings in Table 11.4, neither model revealed a relationship between the placement
variable and the likelihood of service use discontinuation, whether discontinuation was treated as a main effect or as an interaction with time. Notably,
across all the Cox proportional-hazards models, older age, "other" as the most
serious type of maltreatment alleged, and nonclinical CBCL scores were significantly associated with the likelihood of discontinuing specialty mental
health service use.

Table 11.5   Cox Proportional-Hazards Models Predicting Likelihood of Discontinuing Specialty Mental Health Service Use (Method 2, $n = 453$), Child Behavior Checklist Score as Dichotomized Variable

	Model 1 (Without Interaction)			Model 2 (With Interaction)		
	Hazard Ratio	95% [CI]	p	Hazard Ratio	95% [CI]	p
Age	0.82	0.72, 0.93	***	0.82	0.72, 0.93	**
Gender						
Male	0.60	0.29, 1.25		0.60	0.29, 1.27	
Female	—	—		—	—	
Race/ethnicity						
Black/non-Hispanic	1.88	0.58, 6.14		1.87	0.57, 6.13	
White/non-Hispanic	—	—		—	—	
Hispanic	0.92	0.24, 3.50		0.92	0.24, 3.52	
Other	1.35	0.51, 3.61		1.37	0.52, 3.60	
Primary abuse type						
Physical	0.94	0.29, 3.00		0.94	0.29, 3.01	
Sexual	0.86	0.34, 2.20		0.87	0.33, 2.32	
Physical neglect	—			—		
Supervisory neglect	1.45	0.63, 3.31		1.45	0.63, 3.34	
Other	0.11	0.02, 0.50	**	0.11	0.02, 0.51	**
CBCL total						
≥64	0.36	0.18, 0.73	**	0.36	0.18, 0.72	**
<64	—	—		—	—	
Out-of-home status						
Out of home	1.22	0.51, 2.92		1.69	0.10, 29.18	
In home (RU)	—	—		—	—	
Time* out-of-home status				0.98	0.83, 1.16	

$*p \le .05$, $**p \le .01$, $***p \le .001$.
CBCL, Child Behavior Checklist.

Discussion

We initiated this study with the argument that, for children involved in the child welfare system, examination of continuity of mental health care may be as important as examination of access to that care. No empirical evidence in the literature showed, after all, that children exiting out-of-home care have significantly fewer emotional and behavioral problems than when they entered. Furthermore, from a child welfare policy perspective, entry into and exit from child welfare services should be based on the child's risk of harm from parents' maltreatment behaviors rather than on the child's own behavioral and emotional functioning.

Our results are based on multiple tests using different longitudinal cohorts and varying statistical techniques for analyzing longitudinal specialty mental health service use data over time. Consistently, we found no empirical support for the expectation that children reunified with their parents would show less use of specialty mental health services than children remaining in out-of-home care.

One comparison even showed statistically significant greater use of such care by children reunified with their parents. The robustness of our rejection of the offset hypothesis is assured by this consistency of findings across our multiple tests. Beyond comparisons, the results showed a high continuity of specialty mental health service use for both groups of children. Notably, this finding is consistent with the high level of continuity of care reported by Horwitz, Hurlburt, and Zhang (see Chapter 10).

Conclusion

Good news is apparent in the lack of empirical support for the offset hypothesis. Our current analyses indicate much more continuity of mental health care for the NSCAW sample of children experiencing out-of-home care than had been antici- pated. With the strong empirical evidence for the onset hypothesis, our findings strongly suggest that the involvement of children with the child welfare system is positively associated with this vulnerable population's increased access to specialty mental health services and that their exit from this system triggers no diminish- ment of this service receipt. The child welfare system as gateway to mental health care does not, in other words, "swing both ways."

The support for the onset hypothesis and lack of support for the offset hypothesis together support a positive conceptualization of the child welfare system, from a public health perspective, as a gateway system.[6] If one thinks of the child protection system as a kind of surveillance system for unsafe parenting and the associated increased risk of emotional and behavioral problems in children, then one can by logical extension think of the child welfare system as a gateway to other service systems that can address the increased emotional and behavioral problems in children. Evidence that child welfare potentiates greater access to mental health care and that continuity of such care is not contingent on a child's remaining in out-of-home care bodes well for a child welfare system whose mission is in part to place children who are at risk for mental health problems into trajectories of care that address these problems.

Caveats to the positive view of this broader role for child welfare do exist. First, despite evidence of greater access to mental health care for children involved with child welfare, clear evidence exists that many more children need mental health care than are identified and referred for such care (Burns et al., 2004). Furthermore, it appears that the greatest access to mental health care requires the higher levels of child welfare involvement, such as removal from biological parents to out-of-home care—even when mental health need is accounted for. Findings in Part 2 of this volume suggest that this level of need is quite high in children who receive investigative services for maltreatment but receive no further child welfare services, as well as in investigated children who receive further child welfare services while remaining with their biological families. A far better way to use the child welfare system as a mental health surveillance and referral system related to child well-being would entail identification and referral of children for ameliorative care on the basis of need, instead of on the basis of relative penetration into the child welfare system.

We close by cautioning against examination of service access and continuity apart from questions of service appropriateness and quality. Access to ineffective or inappropriate mental health care provides no better benefit to children than no access at all. Improving access to care and continuity of care does not guarantee the care received will meet need and improve child well-being. In fact, the research studies by Bickman on the impact of the systems-of-care model (Bickman, 1996; Bickman et al., 1996) exemplify access improvements not associated with better outcomes for youth receiving care from public mental health systems. Weisz and colleagues have presented meta-analyses on outcomes from usual public mental health care, showing a lack of effectiveness (Weisz, Doss, & Hawley, 2006). Mental health care also may be inappropriate. For example, despite strong evidence of high rates of externalizing behavior problems in children involved with the child welfare system, public service systems provide much mental health care directly to the child when research evidence supports, instead, the use of parent-training models to address problematic behaviors in children.[7] Although the research of Bickman and Weisz does not address effectiveness of mental health care specifically for children involved with child welfare, most of the care received by the child welfare population is provided by public mental health systems under Medicaid funding, a fact that compounds our caution against equating improved access with improved benefit.

NOTES

1. For a discussion of primary, secondary, and tertiary kinds of prevention or the equivalent universal, targeted, and clinical kinds of intervention, see Offord, Kraemer, Kazdin, Jensen, and Harrington (1998).
2. This high risk for mental health problems among maltreated children is well documented in Part 2 of this volume and reviewed by Horwitz, Hurlburt, and Zhang in Chapter 10.
3. Our review of the systems-of-care and child welfare–function perspectives has been greatly informed by Landsverk, Hurlburt, and Leslie (2007).
4. Horwitz, Hurlburt, and Zhang (Chapter 10, this volume) provide an extensive review; see also more generally Part 1 (this volume), which addresses the psychosocial functioning of children involved with child welfare.
5. Significance testing would have been inappropriate in this instance because we are submitting the hypothesis to three slightly different tests, not comparing the three samples as three groups.
6. For an excellent discussion of child welfare from a public health perspective, see Garrison (2005).
7. Regarding appropriate services for behavioral problems, we can relay a promising direction that does address the effectiveness of care—namely, rethinking the provision of mental health care by service systems outside the child welfare system. The most promising

treatments for these externalizing behavior problems use intensive forms of parent training to change the parental response to the child's behaviors rather than work directly with the child in typical therapy sessions. Chamberlain and Fisher from the Oregon Social Learning Center have shown promising outcomes from the use of multidimensional treatment foster care (MTFC; Chamberlain, 2003; Chamberlain & Reid, 1991; Fisher, Burraston, & Pears, 2006; Fisher, Gunnar, Dozier, Bruce, & Pears, 2006; Fisher & Kim, in press), while Chamberlain and colleagues, with a modified version of MTFC, have shown promising outcomes with kin and nonkin foster parents (Fisher et al., 2006; Price et al., 2008). In related work, Chaffin has shown the effectiveness of parent–child interaction therapy with biological parents whose children had been in foster care (Chaffin et al., 2004). This research direction is taking evidence-based mental health interventions directly into child welfare settings and shows great promise for child well-being by strengthening the substitute and biological parent responses to behavior problems by children and adolescents.

REFERENCES

Achenbach, T. M. (1991). *Manual for the Child Behavior Checklist/4–18 and 1991 profile.* Burlington, VT: University of Vermont, Department of Psychiatry.

Allison, P. D. (1995). *Survival analysis using the SAS system: A practical guide.* Cary, NC: SAS Institute.

Bickman, L. (1996). Reinterpreting the Fort Bragg Evaluation findings: The message does not change. *Journal of the Mental Health Administration, 23*(1), 137–145.

Bickman, L., Summerfelt, W. T., & Bryant, D. (1996). The quality of services in a children's mental health managed care demonstration. *Journal of the Mental Health Administration, 23*(1), 30–39.

Burns, B. J., Angold, A., & Costello, E. J. (1992). Measuring child, adolescent, and family service use. In L. Bickman & D. J. Rog (Eds.), *Evaluating mental health services for children.* San Francisco: Jossey-Bass.

Burns, B. J., Costello, E. J., Angold, A., Tweed, D., Stangl, D., Farmer, E. M. Z., et al. (1995). Children's mental health service use across service sectors. *Health Affairs, 14*(3), 147–159.

Burns, B. J., Phillips, S. D., Wagner, H. R., Barth, R. P., Kolko, D. J., Campbell, Y., et al. (2004). Mental health need and access to mental health services by youth involved with child welfare: A national survey. *Journal of the American Academy of Child and Adolescent Psychiatry, 43*(8), 960–970.

Chaffin, M., Silovsky, J. F., Funderburk, B., Valle, L. A., Brestan, E. V., Balachova, T., et al. (2004). Parent–child interaction therapy with physically abusive parents: Efficacy for reducing future abuse reports. *Journal of Consulting and Clinical Psychology, 72*(3), 500–510.

Chamberlain, P. (Ed.). (2003). *Treating chronic juvenile offenders: Advances made through the Oregon Multidimensional Treatment Foster Care model.* Washington, DC: American Psychological Association.

Chamberlain, P., & Reid, J. B. (1991). Using a specialized foster care community treatment model for children and adolescents leaving the state mental hospital. *Journal of Community Psychology, 19,* 266–276.

Day, C., & Roberts, M. C. (1991). Activities of the child and adolescent service system program for improving mental health services for children and families. *Journal of Clinical Child Psychology, 20,* 340–350.

Fisher, P. A., Burraston, B., & Pears, K. (2006). Permanency in foster care: Conceptual and methodological issues. *Child Maltreatment, 11,* 92–94.

Fisher, P. A., Gunnar, M. R., Dozier, M., Bruce, J., & Pears, K. C. (2006). Effects of therapeutic interventions for foster children on behavioral problems, caregiver attachment, and stress regulatory neural systems. *Annals of the New York Academy of Sciences, 1094,* 215–225.

Fisher, P. A., & Kim, H. K. (2007). Intervention effects on foster preschoolers' attachment-related behaviors from a randomized trial. *Prevention Science, 8,* 161–170.

Garland, A. F., Hough, R. L., Landsverk, J. A., & Brown, S. A. (2001). Multi-sector complexity of systems of care for youth with mental health needs. *Children's Services: Social Policy, Research and Practice, 4,* 123–140.

Garland, A. F., Landsverk, J. L., Hough, R. L., & Ellis-MacLeod, E. (1996). Type of maltreatment as a predictor of mental health service use for children in foster care. *Child Abuse & Neglect, 20*(8), 675–688.

Garrison, M. (2005). Reforming Child Protection: A Public Health Perspective. *Virginia Journal of Social Policy and the Law, 12,* 590–634.

Knitzer, J. (1982). *Unclaimed children: The failure of public responsibility to children and adolescents in need of mental health services.* Washington, DC: Children's Defense Fund.

Landsverk, J., Garland, A. F., & Leslie, L. K. (2002). Mental health services for children reported to child protective services. In J. E. B. Myers & J. Briere (Eds.), *The APSAC handbook on child maltreatment* (2nd ed.). Thousand Oaks, CA: Sage Publications.

Landsverk, J., Hurlburt, M. S., & Leslie, L. K. (2007). Systems integration and access to mental health care. In R. Haskins, F. Wulczyn & M. B. Webb (Eds.), *Child protection: Using research to improve policy and practice.* Washington, DC: Brookings Institution Press.

Leslie, L. K., Hurlburt, M. S., James, S., Landsverk, J., Slymen, D. J., & Zhang, J. J. (2005). Relationship between entry into child welfare and mental health service use. *Psychiatric Services, 56*(8), 981–987.

Manly, J. T., Cicchetty, D., & Barnett, D. (1994). The impact of subtype, frequency, chronicity, and severity of child maltreatment on social competence and behavior problems *Development and Psychopathology, 6,* 121–143.

Offord, D. R., Kraemer, H. C., Kazdin, A. E., Jensen, P. S., & Harrington, R. (1998). Lowering the burden of suffering from child psychiatric disorder: Trade-offs among clinical, targeted, and universal interventions. *Journal of the American Academy of Child and Adolescent Psychiatry, 37*(7), 686–694.

Price, J. M., Chamberlain, P., Landsverk, J., Reid, J. B., Leve, L. D., & Laurent, H. (2008). Effects of a foster parent training intervention on placement changes of children in foster care. *Child Maltreatment, 13*(1), 64–75.

RTI International. (2007). *SUDAAN user's manual, release 9.0.1.* Research Triangle Park, NC: Author.

Simms, M. D. (1989). The foster care clinic: A community program to identify treatment needs of children in foster care. *Journal of Developmental and Behavioural Pediatrics, 10*(3), 121–128.

Singer, J. D., & Willett, J. B. (2003). *Applied longitudinal data analysis: Modeling change and event occurrence.* New York: Oxford University Press.

Stroul, B., & Friedman, R. (1986). *A system of care for children and youth with severe emotional disturbances* (rev. ed.). Washington, DC: Georgetown University Child Development Center, CASSP Technical Assistance Center.

Weisz, J. R., Doss, A. J., & Hawley, K. M. (2006). Evidence-based youth psychotherapies versus usual clinical care: A meta-analysis of direct comparisons. *American Psychologist, 61,* 671–689.

Wulczyn, F., Barth, R. P., Yuan, Y. T., Jones Harden, B., & Landsverk, J. (2005). *Beyond common sense: Child welfare, child well-being, and the evidence for policy reform.* New Brunswick, NJ: Aldine Transaction.

12

Caregiver Depression, Mental Health Service Use, and Child Outcomes

BARBARA J. BURNS, SARAH A. MUSTILLO, ELIZABETH
M.Z. FARMER, DAVID J. KOLKO, JULIE McCRAE, ANNE
M. LIBBY, AND MARY BRUCE WEBB

Parents suffering from depression can be overwhelmed by the otherwise everyday challenges of raising a child, and these feelings likely affect their parenting skills. Conversely, when children of these caregivers suffer maltreatment and face a preponderance of risk factors in their lives, the resulting problem behaviors may easily exacerbate their parent's depression and sense of being overwhelmed. Existing literature documents effects in both directions: Maternal depression can affect child mental health, and child emotional or behavioral difficulties may have an impact on maternal depression (Walker, 2008). Even if the precise causal relationships cannot be theoretically confirmed, they can and should be considered from the perspective of when and how the child welfare system should intervene clinically with the primary caregiver, usually the mother, and with the child. The implications here apply to clinicians, researchers, and policy makers.

Depression occurs at high rates in the general population and can persist and recur (American Psychiatric Association, 1994). According to the National Comorbidity Survey Replication (NCS-R), a large ($n = 9,282$) national household survey, the lifetime prevalence of major depression is 16.6% (20.8% for any mood disorder). The presence of major depression reported or observed in the 12 months preceding the NCS-R was 6.7% (9.5% for any mood disorder; Wang et al., 2005). Women are at a significantly higher risk for it than men (Kessler et al., 2005). The World Health Organization (2002) has projected that depression will become the second leading cause of disability worldwide by 2020.

Because no published estimates of depression exist specifically for caregivers involved with the child welfare system, rates among low-income women may provide a reasonably accurate gauge of risk of depression in the child welfare system population—more accurate than rates in the general population provide. For example, Rosen, Tolman, and Warner (2004), with a sizable sample ($n = 753$) of welfare recipients, reported that one fourth met criteria for depression at baseline (though only 16.5% did a year later). The baseline rate in this study was twice the NCS-R rate for women 18 to 59 years of age, suggesting the possibility of even higher rates for caregivers in contact with the child welfare system than for those in the NCS-R. Our current study relies on data from the National Survey of Child and Adolescent Well-Being (NSCAW), the first longitudinal, national probability study of the well-being of children reported to the child welfare system because of allegations of child maltreatment. Inclusion of the same research diagnostic measure in NSCAW as in the Rosen et al. welfare recipient study creates an opportunity to compare findings and assess the prevalence, course, and outcomes of depression among caregivers involved with the child welfare system.

Contributing greatly to the practical implications of our work is the fact that depression is treatable. Antidepressant medications and psychosocial interventions, particularly cognitive-behavioral therapy and interpersonal therapy, have demonstrated clinical benefit across many studies. According to Insel, "For each of these interventions, one can say with some confidence that at least 40% of a cohort with depression will show statistically significant reductions in unbiased ratings of depression" (2006, p. 5). Such findings apply to ethnically diverse women and women living in poverty (Miranda et al., 2003). Equally encouraging, adults with depression are seeking treatment at rates higher than in the past (although the extent to which treatment meets clinical guidelines is not fully known). Among depressed adults nationwide, one third sought services from a mental health specialist (psychiatrist or other mental health professional) in the year preceding assessment (Wang et al., 2005). Higher estimates of treatment sought (70.1% for depressed women and 55.2% for depressed men) were reported in another national survey (Office of Applied Studies, 2005). By contrast, a somewhat lower 12-month rate of about a quarter (26.3%) was reported for welfare recipients (Rosen et al., 2004). The first published NSCAW caregiver service use estimate was 23% for those with alcohol, drug, and mental health problems (as reported by the child welfare system caseworker), but this population is more broadly defined than the population suffering from depression (Libby et al., 2006). The NSCAW findings contribute a greater perspective to our work—a span of 3 years—on mental health service use in this population, as well as an array of predictors of caregivers' and children's mental health service use.

Recognition of the extensiveness of depression in the NSCAW caregiver population and provision of services to alleviate this suffering are consistent with both a humanitarian perspective and a specifically child welfare perspective. Many parents with severe mental illness were themselves poorly parented and maltreated (Brunette & Drake, 1997), which means they likely acquired ineffective parenting knowledge and skills by example (Nicholson, Sweeney, & Geller, 1998; Tajima, 2000). Parenting is a major social role and often a key to one's sense of self. Reducing parental stress and distress is a critical first step toward more effective parenting and, consequently, an improved sense of self-worth.

The literature is replete with studies that document the consequences of caregiver depression for children (for a review, see Nicholson, Biebel, Hinden, Henry, & Stier, 2001; Oyserman, Mowbray, Meares, & Firminger, 2000; Silverstein, Augustyn, Cabral, & Zuckerman, 2006). For example, parenting style may affect learning environment and attachment for infants; it may affect the parent's ability to sustain social interaction or use a positive tone with their preschoolers and school-aged children; and it may make parents critical and negative toward their adolescents. The severity and chronicity of depression may exacerbate such strain in the mother–child relationship, although the findings are mixed. For children who show significant behavioral disturbances, mothers with depression are less likely to attach with them. The consequences of caregiver depression are many and are mutually reinforcing.

The relationships among parental depression, parenting style, and child development and behavior enjoin our better understanding of whether mental health services can favorably affect caregiver depression and child outcomes. Some literature indicates that treating depressed parents can favorably influence child outcomes (e.g., Beardslee, Gladstone, Wright, & Cooper, 2003; Gunlicks & Weissman, 2008; Weissman et al., 2006). These studies do not target children with depressed parents in contact with the child welfare system, but NSCAW affords an opportunity to examine this population. Benefitting from the rich longitudinal NSCAW data set, we therefore address three major research aims here: to explore the prevalence and correlates of major depression in caregivers of children in contact with child welfare; to identify the rates, predictors, and outcomes of mental health service use for caregivers with major depression; and to examine the impact of mental health service receipt by depressed caregivers on their children.

We expected that caregivers' receipt of mental health services would relieve depression, facilitate better parenting, and result in better outcomes for their children. Anticipated better child outcomes included improved clinical status, fewer out-of-home placements, and decreased rates of alleged maltreatment. Alternatively, in the context of caregiver depression, poverty, uncertainty about quality of treatment, and high rates of problems among these caregivers' children, their receipt of mental health services may be an indicator of severity or chronicity of these troubles rather than a harbinger of better outcomes: Mental health treatment alone may not suffice to fully treat caregivers in these circumstances or to match the level of their children's problems, even when the children also receive treatment.

Methods

Analyses included data from NSCAW Wave 1 (baseline), Wave 3 (18-month follow-up), and Wave 4 (36-month follow-up) interviews with caregivers and caseworkers. Only families whose child lived in the primary caregiver's home after a report of child maltreatment were included ($n = 4,285$). Of these families, all with children younger than 2 years old were excluded because reliable mental health data for these children were not available ($n = 3,063$). Of these, 104 cases were missing information on parental depression, so they were excluded to yield the analytical sample ($n = 2,959$). All analyses were weighted to account for the complex sample design.

Measures

BASELINE RISK ASSESSMENT A project-developed risk assessment was used to assess the presence of 21 family risk factors. Caseworkers indicated whether each risk factor was present during the investigation. Six individual items were used in the current study: poor parenting skills, excessive discipline, financial strain, low social support, domestic violence, and prior report of maltreatment. In addition to these individual items, a cumulative risk variable was created to count the number of family risks present (1 if present, 0 if not present) as a proportion of the total risk. The frequency distribution of the proportions was then divided into tertiles, creating a risk score of *low* (less than 21% of risks), *moderate* (21% to 40% of risks), or *high* (more than 40% of risks) for each family.

BACKGROUND CHARACTERISTICS Biological parents constituted 87% of the caregivers. Marital status was assessed at each wave, the instrument asking caregivers whether they were married, separated, divorced, widowed, or never married. A dichotomous variable was created to indicate *currently married*. At baseline and at Wave 4 caregivers were asked about their current employment situation: full time, part time, sometimes employed, unemployed and looking for work, not working for family reasons, not working because of illness, retired, not working because did not want to work, student, and other. We collapsed these categories into three groups: *full time, part time,* and *unemployed.* Poverty status for the NSCAW families at baseline was calculated in accordance with U.S. Census Bureau guidelines (Administration for Children and Families, 2008), including both the family's income level and the number of adults and children in the household. A dichotomous variable was created to indicate families living at or below the federal poverty level (equal to or less than 99% of the poverty level) or above the poverty level (equal to or more than 100% of the poverty level).

URBANICITY Urbanicity of the primary sampling unit, usually a county, was according to U.S. Census definitions. *Urban* was defined as greater than 50% of the population living in the urban area; *nonurban* was defined as all other areas that did not meet this description (NSCAW Research Group, 2002).

CAREGIVER DEPRESSION AND SUBSTANCE DEPENDENCE Caregivers reported their level of depression and substance dependence with the CIDI-SF (Kessler, Andrews, Mroczek, Ustun, & Wittchen, 1998). The CIDI-SF is a set of screening scales developed from the full-length CIDI, a structured diagnostic measure of adult psychiatric disorders; it was designed to correspond with the *Diagnostic and Statistical Manual of Mental Disorders* (American Psychiatric Association, 1980, 1994). Caregivers in the NSCAW study were administered the CIDI-SF scales for major depressive episode, drug dependence, and alcohol dependence at each wave, which covered the 12 months preceding the interview. Compared with psychiatric standards, classification accuracy of the CIDI-SF, together with the CIDI, on these scales ranges from 93% to 98% (Kessler et al., 1998). Two dichotomous variables were created to indicate any major depressive episode and any substance dependence between baseline and Wave 4.

TYPE OF MALTREATMENT A modification of the Maltreatment Classification System (Barnett, Manly, & Cicchetti, 1993) was used to capture information about the index maltreatment report to the child welfare system. Caseworkers, equipped with case records, responded to a series of questions about the index maltreatment report, indicating each type of maltreatment present in the report and, in cases of multiple types of maltreatment, the type they judged to be the most serious.

CAREGIVER MENTAL HEALTH AND SUBSTANCE ABUSE SERVICE RECEIPT Caregivers and caseworkers reported caregivers' receipt of mental health and substance abuse services, using a project-developed measure. Caregivers reported on the following services: clinic or doctor visits, day treatment, emergency room visits, and hospitalization. Caseworkers reported whether caregivers received services "for an emotional or psychological problem." Caregiver and caseworker reports were combined to create two dichotomous variables indicating service receipt between baseline and Wave 4: any mental health services and any substance abuse services.

CHILD MENTAL HEALTH SERVICE RECEIPT Caregivers reported on children's receipt of mental health services from baseline to the Wave 4 (36-month) follow-up, using a modified version of the Child and Adolescent Services Assessment (Burns, Angold, Magruder-Habib, Costello, & Patrick, 1994). Services were specialty outpatient (mental health or community health center, therapeutic nursery, day treatment, or visit with a psychiatrist, psychologist, social worker, or psychiatric nurse), nonspecialty outpatient (in-home counseling or visits with a school guidance counselor, school psychologist, or social worker), and inpatient (psychiatric hospitalization, residential treatment, or emergency shelter). Categories were collapsed to create a dichotomous indicator for any mental health services received at any time between baseline and Wave 4.

CHILD PLACEMENT Children's placement in out-of-home care over the study period was measured with a combination of placement status at the time of the Wave 4 interview (in home or out of home) and the proportion of time the child spent in out-of-home care between baseline and the Wave 3 interview at 18 months (0% to 100% of the time). A dichotomous variable was created to indicate whether the child spent any time in out-of-home care from baseline to Wave 4.

SUBSEQUENT REPORTS OF CHILD MALTREATMENT   For each child, caseworkers indicated whether additional maltreatment reports were received over the 36 months since the initial investigation. An adjustment was made to fully capture the proportion of children with new reports. Because caseworkers were interviewed only when a case was open at baseline or had been opened anytime after baseline (as prompted by a new report or a caregiver's report of services), cases without a caseworker interview for a particular wave were treated as not having a new report.

CHILD EMOTIONAL AND BEHAVIORAL PROBLEMS   Children's mental health was assessed with the Total Problems scale and the Internalizing and Externalizing broad-band scales of the Child Behavior Checklist (CBCL), a well-validated measure indicating a child's emotional and behavioral problems (Achenbach, 1991). *T* scores equal to or greater than 64 are considered clinical, indicating a need for treatment; scores of 60 to 63 are considered borderline. Our current study used caregivers' reports, with different versions for younger (aged 2 to 3 years) and older (aged 4 to 18 years) children. Internal consistency of the CBCL Internalizing, Externalizing, and Total Problems scales in the NSCAW study at baseline ranges from .80 to .95 for 2–3 year olds and from .90 to .96 for 4–15 year olds, as measured by Cronbach's alpha (Administration for Children and Families, 2008).

Missing Data

Missing data were minimal for most baseline variables; however, 9% to 12% of data were missing for most of the included parental risk factors. For parental risk factors in the regression analyses, therefore, we used a cumulative risk variable; it was set to *missing* only if all parental risk factor variables were missing. The percentage missing on the cumulative variable was 7%, and these cases were excluded from analysis. Missing data on the longitudinal variables (caregiver depression, service use, child CBCL) were more common and largely a result of wave nonresponse rather than item nonresponse. Weights were adjusted for wave nonresponse. The children who lived in their homes at baseline and the children aged 2 years or older were less likely overall to have wave nonresponse than those who were placed out of home or were younger than 2 years old.

Analyses

Because of a complex survey design involving stratification, selection of children into the study by primary sampling unit (usually county child welfare agency), and probability weighting, all analyses were conducted with Stata 9.0 survey commands (StataCorp, 2005). With sampling weights analyses were adjusted for children's unequal probabilities of selection into the study; all reported percentages and means were weighted. Bivariate analyses were based on a Pearson χ^2 statistic converted to an F statistic with noninteger degrees of freedom, using a second-order Rao and Scott (1981, 1984) correction. Multivariate analyses were conducted with the use of logistic regression for survey data.

Three sets of analyses were conducted. First, descriptive and demographic characteristics of the sample were examined. Second, using bivariate analyses, we examined study variables by receipt of service among caregivers with depression. Finally, we used survey logistic regression to examine four different dependent variables. Model 1 examined the predictors of mental health service among caregivers with depression. Model 2 showed the regression of caregiver depression predicting the child's CBCL score in the clinical range, and Model 3 tested for the mediating effects of caregiver mental health services. Because caregiver mental health service use and child CBCL score were measured at each wave, we pooled information across individuals. Consequently, each measurement of the dependent variable is included in the model, while controlling for time with baseline as the comparison. Pooling information this way introduces correlated observations across time. Because we could not adjust for both the complex survey design and the within-subject correlation, we ran the models by using both logistic regression for complex survey data and generalized estimating equations with the binary family, logit link, and unstructured correlation matrix. Because results differed little, we report only the models that adjusted for the complex survey design.

Models 4 to 7 examine the effects of caregiver depression on child placement (Model 4) and subsequent maltreatment (Model 6), while also testing for the mediating effects of mental health services (Models 5 and 7). Because child placement and subsequent reports of maltreatment were measured retrospectively across the entire study period for only some participants, we modeled child placement and subsequent reports of maltreatment as positive if they were reported anytime during the 36-month follow-up period. These models do not control for time as the models for caregiver service receipt and child's CBCL do, because the pooling is being done at the variable level rather than at the model level.

Mediation was considered significant if the following conditions were met: *(1)* The independent variable significantly predicted the mediator, *(2)* the independent variable significantly predicted the dependent variable, *(3)* the mediator significantly predicted the dependent variable, and *(4)* the effect of the independent variable on the dependent variable was reduced in the presence of the mediator. We also ran the Sobel and Goodman tests of significance (MacKinnon & Dwyer, 1993; MacKinnon, Warsi, & Dwyer, 1995).

Results

Caregiver and Child Characteristics

Descriptive statistics are reported here for the entire sample ($n = 2,959$) and include caregiver and child demographic characteristics, service use, child outcomes by Wave 4, and the proportion of caregivers with baseline depression or substance dependence over 36 months. Most caregivers were female (88.7%) and aged 25 to 34 years (44.6%) or 35 to 44 years (30.6%) at baseline. Fourteen percent were younger than 25, and about 10% were 45 or older. At baseline more than one half of caregivers were white (52.2%), one quarter were black or African American, 15.9% were Hispanic, and 6.9% belonged to another racial/ethnic group.

More than a quarter of caregivers (30%) lacked a high school diploma, compared with 43.5% who were high school graduates. Approximately one fifth (20%) had some college, but only 5.2% had at least a college degree. Nearly one third reported being married, and nearly 60% were employed full or part time. More than three quarters of families lived in an urban setting at baseline. More than half of families (51.6%) were living below the federal poverty level at baseline, but caseworkers reported that only 21.6% families were experiencing financial strain.

For caregiver risk factors, caseworkers reported that 12% of caregivers had a history of domestic violence at baseline, one third were judged to have poor parenting skills, and 16% used excessive discipline. Low social support was a problem for 29.6% of caregivers, and a prior report of maltreatment existed for more than half of the children. Many caregivers (40%) met criteria for major depression at some point during the study, and 8.7% met criteria for substance dependence. Only about a fifth (20.9%) of caregivers received mental health services by Wave 4, while a higher proportion (8.1%), relative to reported prevalence, received substance abuse treatment.

For child characteristics, 30% were aged 2 to 5 years, 42.4% were aged 6 to 10 years, and 27.6% were aged 11 years or older. Half were female. More than a quarter (27%) were black or African American, while almost half were white. Hispanic children accounted for 17.8% of the sample, and 7.1% were classified as "other." The most prevalent type of maltreatment was neglect (47.2%), followed by physical abuse (29.4%). More than a tenth (12%) had sexual abuse as their most serious type of maltreatment. Between a quarter and a third (30%) of children had a new report of maltreatment by Wave 4.

In terms of mental health, nearly one half (46.2%) of children had a CBCL score in the clinical range at some point during the study. Thirty-one percent experienced clinical-level internalizing behavior problems, and 44.4% experienced clinical-level behavior problems, as reported by caregivers. Mental health services were delivered to 44.3% of children, and 16.2% of children experienced at least one out-of-home placement by Wave 4.

Turning from these descriptive statistics for the overall sample (not tabulated) to focus on depressed- and nondepressed-caregiver service use, we note that among all caregivers more than a third received a diagnosis of depression; one third of these caregivers received mental health services over time. Although nondepressed caregivers may have experienced other psychiatric conditions requiring care, their expected use of mental health services remained low (Fig. 12.1). By contrast, caregivers with depression started high at baseline (24%) and increased to one third (almost 35%) by Wave 4, compared with 11.6% among nondepressed caregivers ($p < .001$). The type of service used was largely outpatient, with much less use of other types of care (2.4% hospital, 2.5% emergency room, and 4.3% day treatment).

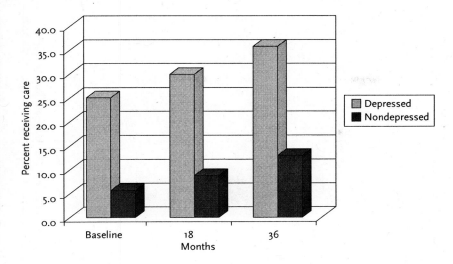

Figure 12.1. Cumulative mental health service use by depressed and nondepressed caregivers.

Outside of service use, variables distinguishing caregivers with depression from those without depression included only two: caregiver poverty (56.9% of those with depression, as opposed to 48.1% of those without) and three times the rate of diagnosed substance dependence (14.5% of those with depression, as opposed to 4.8% of those without). Child characteristics that differed for depressed caregivers were percentage in the clinical range on the CBCL. This result was significant for Internalizing, Externalizing, and Total Problems scale scores, the rates across scales indicating that 40.3% to 58.0% or more of the children needed treatment. For the outcome variables analyzed in subsequent regressions, children with a depressed caregiver were much more likely to receive mental health services (52.5%) and to be the subject of a subsequent report of maltreatment (38.4%, as opposed to 23.6%) by Wave 4 (Table 12.1).

Caregivers With Depression Who Receive Mental Health Services

Tables 12.2 and 12.3 show the distribution of mental health services received by caregivers with depression at baseline, Wave 3 (18 months), and Wave 4 (36 months), according to child and caregiver characteristics. These analyses address the question, among caregivers with depression, who receives services? Results show that caregiver gender and educational level were significantly associated with the caregiver service receipt, as were the child's gender and sexual abuse as the most serious child maltreatment type reported at baseline. Caregivers with less than a high school education and those with a college degree or more were more likely than those with a high school diploma or some college to receive

Table 12.1 Descriptive Statistics for Nondepressed, Depressed, and Depressed Caregivers Who Received Mental Health Services and Their Children ($n = 2,959$)

Characteristic	Nondepressed Caregivers $n = 1,816$ (59.7%)	Depressed Caregivers $n = 1,143$ (40.3%)	Depressed Caregivers Who Received Mental Health Services by Wave 4[a] $n = 388$ (33.9%)
Caregiver age			
<25	14.5	13.4	16.4
25–34	42.0	49.2	44.2
35–44	33.0	27.3	31.3
45–54	7.6	8.0	7.4
55+	3.0	2.1	0.6
Female	88.4	88.9	92.2
Race			
Black	28.0	20.5	21.0
White	48.2	57.9	60.5
Hispanic	17.6	13.7	11.9
Other	6.9	8.0	6.5
Highest degree			
<HS	29.9	30.9	33.1
HS	42.9	44.6	44.5
Some college	21.3	20.4	15.2
BA/BS and above	5.9	4.1	5.2
Married	30.1	31.8	27.7
Parental employment			
Full-time	46.7	41.3	37.2
Part-time	16.2	12.1	12.9
Unemployed	37.2	46.6	50.0
Poverty	48.1*	56.9	56.5
Urban residence	78.9	72.0	74.5
Risk factors			
Poor parenting skills	29.9	27.2	30.2
Financial strain	20.1	23.3	22.2
Low social support	28.4	31.5	29.5
Excessive discipline	15.4	17.1	16.6
Domestic violence	12.9	10.4	10.7
Prior report of abuse	52.3	57.1	59.5
Diagnosis and service use			
Substance dependence (any wave)	4.8*	14.5	14.4
Both depression and substance dependence	—	46.1	41.7
Mental health services by Wave 4	11.6*	33.9	100.0
Substance abuse services by Wave 4	9.0	9.1	4.6
Child age			
2–5	28.8	32.1	37.5
6–10	45.3	38.4	32.7
11+	26.0	29.5	29.9

Table 12.1 (continued)

Characteristic	Nondepressed Caregivers	Depressed Caregivers	Depressed Caregivers Who Received Mental Health Services by Wave 4[a]
	$n = 1,816$ (59.7%)	$n = 1,143$ (40.3%)	$n = 388$ (33.9%)
Female	49.9	49.4	44.4
Race			
Black	29.5	23.6	25.9
White	44.6	52.8	52.2
Hispanic	19.1	16.1	16.4
Other	6.8	7.5	5.6
Type of abuse			
Physical	31.2	26.4	19.6
Sexual	10.6	14.6	17.2
Neglect	46.4	46.4	49.6
Other	11.8	12.7	13.7
Child outcomes			
CBCL (clinical range any wave)			
Internalizing	24.6*	40.3	58.7
Externalizing	35.1*	57.9	75.7
Total	38.0*	58.0	74.0
Placement by Wave 4	16.2	15.1	17.5
Mental health services by Wave 4	38.2*	52.5	65.2
New report of abuse by Wave 4	23.6*	38.4	50.8

Note: Percentage at baseline unless otherwise noted.
[a]A subset of depressed caregivers.
*$p < .05$, testing differences between nondepressed and depressed caregivers.

services. At Wave 3, caregivers with female children and caregivers of alleged sexual abuse victims were more likely to receive mental health services.

Table 12.3 presents the results of bivariate analyses of depressed caregiver mental health service receipt over 36 months, according to baseline risk factors, children's clinical scores, out-of-home placement, mental health services, and re-reports. For each time interval, for caregivers with depression, Table Table 12.3 shows the percentage with and the percentage without each caregiver and child characteristic who received mental health services. For example, among caregivers with depression, 25.5% of those not living in poverty received mental health services, compared with 22.3% of those living in poverty at baseline. Services for caregiver substance use, child CBCL in clinical range, child mental health services, and subsequent report of maltreatment were significantly associated with receipt of mental health services among caregivers with depression. Specifically, caregivers receiving services for substance use were more likely to receive mental health services. Caregivers of children with Internalizing, Externalizing, and Total Problems CBCL scores in the clinical range were more likely to receive services

Table 12.2 Characteristics Associated With Mental Health Service Use Among Caregivers With Depression ($n = 1,143$)

Characteristic	Percent of Caregivers Receiving Mental Health Services		
	Baseline	Wave 3	Wave 4
Caregiver age			
<25	28.0	51.7	48.2
25–34	21.5	21.7	31.3
35–44	27.2	35.4	37.7
45–54	19.0	37.7	49.3
Sex			14.5
Male	17.3	26.3	5.0**
Female	24.8	30.7	40.1
Race			
Black	16.7	26.7	37.1
White	27.1	32.1	38.5
Hispanic	26.5	23.7	25.7
Other	18.6	42.0	31.8
Highest degree			
<HS	42.2	30.9	33.1
HS	16.8	27.0	38.5
Some college	12.2	34.6	35.6
BA/BS and above	66.2**	35.1	46.3
Married	14.9	30.1	24.2
Parental employment			
Full-time	22.6	NA	37.6
Part-time	13.5	NA	38.2
Unemployed	56.2	NA	73.1
Child age			
2–5	37.3	29.8	47.5
6–10	18.3	29.3	25.0
11+	19.9	32.0	41.4
Sex			
Male	23.9	20.3	30.3
Female	24.4	39.2*	43.8
Race			
Black	15.5	28.3	41.3
White	26.9	33.4	37.9
Hispanic	31.7	24.4	25.7
Other	19.5	28.6	28.8
Type of abuse			
Physical	14.6	24.1	34.8
Sexual	36.6	70.5*	33.8
Neglect	26.8	30.2	36.6
Other	21.7	19.2	45.1

*$p < .05$, **$p < .01$.
NA, not applicable.

Table 12.3 Characteristics Associated With Mental Health Service Use Among Caregivers with Depression ($n = 1,143$)

	Baseline		Wave 3		Wave 4	
	Percent Receiving Mental Health Services					
Characteristic	*Without Characteristic*	*With Characteristic*	*Without Characteristic*	*With Characteristic*	*Without Characteristic*	*With Characteristic*
Caregiver Characteristics						
Poverty	25.50	22.30	34.50	26.60	33.60	37.60
Urban	26.30	23.30	35.10	28.20	30.40	37.90
Risk factors						
Poor parenting skills	23.80	31.50	28.40	39.70	34.30	39.70
Financial strain	25.50	21.40	32.20	25.70	36.20	34.10
Low social support	27.10	20.00	33.80	25.00	37.10	32.20
Excessive discipline	24.90	27.10	31.20	39.10	35.10	47.70
Domestic violence	25.30	20.60	30.60	38.48	34.40	51.60
Prior report of abuse	25.80	24.70	28.80	35.00	32.20	38.80
Diagnosis and service use						
Depression	21.20	34.50	29.30	39.20	37.10	31.30
Substance dependence	22.57	36.46	29.20	42.60	36.30	28.60
Substance use services	19.50	60.57**	29.90	32.70	33.70	60.30
Child Characteristics						
CBCL (clinical range wave)						
Internalizing	22.40	28.20	23.70	45.70*	26.50	59.50**
Externalizing	18.00	30.30	19.20	43.80**	22.30	53.30**
Total	18.20	29.80	18.00	44.50**	24.50	49.70**
Placement by Wave 4	24.50	25.50	31.90	18.90	35.50	28.50
MH services by Wave 4	19.70	27.70	21.20	38.50*	27.80	42.70
New report of abuse by Wave 4	15.40	36.30	29.30	32.10	29.90	44.80*

*$p < .05$, **$p < .01$.

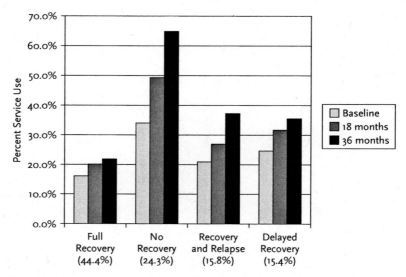

Figure 12.2.   Cumulative mental health service use and recovery for depressed caregivers.

by Wave 3 and by Wave 4, as were caregivers of children receiving mental health services at Wave 3. Finally, caregivers with a child who had a subsequent report of maltreatment were more likely to receive services by Wave 4.

Figure 12.2 presents four patterns of recovery from depression: depressed at baseline and fully recovered at Wave 3; depressed at baseline and never recovered during the study; depressed at baseline, recovered by Wave 3, and relapsed by Wave 4; and depressed at baseline, with delayed recovery by Wave 4. A significant proportion of caregivers with depression recovered from depression (44.4%) early, with only 18% to 21% of this group receiving any mental health services over time. The one fourth of caregivers who had not recovered by Wave 4 had received mental health services at an increasing rate, from 32% at baseline to 50% at Wave 3, and 65% by Wave 4, which indicates a delayed recognition of the greater severity of the disorder and consequent need. For the caregivers who recovered early and relapsed (15.8%), mental health service provision increased moderately from 20% to nearly 30% by Wave 4. The delayed-recovery group (15.4% who met criteria for recovery by Wave 4) experienced an incremental increase in mental health service use from one fourth to more than one third.

Relationships Among Caregiver Depression, Mental Health Service Use, and Child Outcomes

The first model shows the results of a logistic regression model for complex survey data of the predictors of mental health service use among caregivers with depression (Table 12.4). Although the category *caregiver having a college degree or*

Table 12.4   Survey Logistic Regression Model on Characteristics Predicting Mental Health Service Use Among Caregivers With Depression

	Mental Health Service Use	
	Model 1	
Characteristic	OR	SE
Age	1.00	0.02
Female	2.17	1.19
Highest degree		
HS	0.70	0.26
Some college	0.91	0.38
Poverty	0.72	0.30
Urban	1.24	0.31
Risk factors		
Medium	1.36	0.55
High	1.97	0.90
Child CBCL (clinical range any wave)		
Internalizing	1.03	0.01*
Externalizing	1.03	0.01*
Child placement by Wave 4	0.62	0.32
Child mental health services by Wave 4	1.17	0.33
Time (baseline)		
Wave 3	1.52	0.45
Wave 4	1.84	0.50*
Observations	1,123	1,123

*$p < .05$, **$p < .01$.
CBCL, Child Behavior Checklist.

more was highly associated with service use in the bivariate statistics, the cell size was too small for regression analyses when limited to caregivers with depression. Consequently, for this model we had to combine this category with that of *caregiver with some college*. Combining the categories masks the elevated rate of service use among the highly educated. Beyond education, children's high Internalizing and Externalizing CBCL scale scores meant their caregivers were more likely to receive services. The dummy variable for time (36 months) was also significant, indicating that caregivers were more likely to receive services later rather than earlier.

We included a logistic model in which the child clinical-range CBCL score was regressed on caregiver depression, while controlling for various caregiver and child characteristics (Table 12.5). Caregiver depression significantly predicted child's clinical-range CBCL score, as did child's mental health services (Model 2). Model 3 tested for the mediating effects of caregiver mental health service use. Caregiver mental health services significantly predicted child CBCL but reduced the effects of caregiver depression only slightly. The effect of caregiver mental health services was positive, indicating an association with clinical-range CBCL scores.

Table 12.5   Survey Logistic Regression of Caregiver Depression Predicting Child
CBCL Score in the Clinical Range, Testing for Mediating Effects of
Caregiver Mental Health Services

| Characteristic | Child CBCL Score | | | |
| | Model 2 | | Model 3 | |
	OR	SE	OR	SE
Caregiver Characteristics				
Age	1.00	0.02	1.01	0.02
Female	1.18	0.33	1.13	0.30
Highest degree				
High school	0.92	0.19	0.93	0.19
Some college	0.87	0.26	0.87	0.26
Poverty	1.07	0.19	1.08	0.18
Urban	0.67	0.11*	0.67	0.11*
Risk factors				
Medium	1.15	0.20	1.13	0.20
High	1.26	0.27	1.22	0.26
Diagnosis and service use				
Depression	2.78	0.47**	2.51	0.40**
Substance dependence	1.03	0.31	1.02	0.31
Mental health services to caregiver			1.72	0.32**
Child Characteristics				
Age	1.01	0.03	1.01	0.03
Female	1.03	0.17	0.98	0.16
Mental health services by Wave 4	4.92	0.93**	4.69	0.88**
New report of abuse by Wave 4	1.36	0.21	1.27	0.20
Time				
Wave 3	0.79	0.11	0.77	0.11
Wave 4	0.65	0.11*	0.62	0.11*
Observations	4,658		4,658	

$*p < .05, **p < .01.$
CBCL, Child Behavior Checklist.

The next set of models (Table 12.6) permitted examination of effects of
caregiver depression on child placement, with separate testing of caregiver
mental health services, which possibly mediated these effects. For placement
(Model 4), caregiver older age and parental risk factors were significantly and
positively associated with out-of-home placement, whereas caregiver depression
was not. Because depression had no effect, no mediation was tested; caregiver
mental health service receipt in itself did not significantly predict child placement
(Model 5). With caregiver mental health service receipt in the model, caregiver age
lost significance while subsequent child maltreatment became significant for out-
of-home placement. An interaction revealed that depressed parents who received
mental health services were significantly less likely to have their children placed

Table 12.6 Survey Logistic Regression Results of the Effects of Caregiver Depression on Child Placement, Testing for Mediating Effects of Caregiver Mental Health Services

Characteristic	Placement			
	Model 4		Model 5	
	OR	SE	OR	SE
Caregiver Characteristics				
Age	1.01	0.01**	1.00	0.02
Female	0.95	0.36	0.70	0.33
Highest degree				
High school	0.62	0.20	0.68	0.24
Some college	0.72	0.29	0.59	0.31
BA/BS and above	0.58	0.33	0.83	0.60
Poverty	1.46	0.34	1.20	0.37
Urban	1.23	0.33	1.59	0.40
Risk factors				
Medium	1.83	0.59	2.35	1.10
High	3.19	1.11**	4.05	1.96**
Diagnosis and service use				
Depression (any wave)	0.79	0.20	1.65	0.79
Substance dependence (any wave)	0.95	0.40	0.70	0.41
Mental health services by Wave 4			4.20	1.75**
Depression and mental health services			0.22	0.07**
Child Characteristics				
Age	0.98	0.03	1.01	0.05
Female	1.08	0.25	0.99	0.28
CBCL (clinical range any wave)				
Internalizing	0.73	0.21	0.72	0.22
Externalizing	1.32	0.45	1.33	0.57
Mental health services by Wave 4	1.36	0.42	1.53	0.53
Report of subsequent maltreatment	1.66	0.49	2.33	0.84*
Observations	1,667		1,667	

*$p < .05$, **$p < .01$.
CBCL, Child Behavior Checklist.

than depressed caregivers without services and nondepressed caregivers with and without services.

Subsequent reports of child maltreatment were predicted by poverty, urban residence, parental risk, caregiver depression, child's externalizing behavior, and mental health services for the child (Table 12.7, Model 6). Those living in poverty or an urban setting were significantly more likely to experience a new report of maltreatment. Medium and high parental risk, as compared with low, and caregiver depression significantly increased the risk of subsequent maltreatment, as did child's externalizing behavior and mental health services for child. When caregiver

Table 12.7   Survey Logistic Regression Results of the Effects of Caregiver Depression on Subsequent Report of Child Maltreatment, Testing for Mediating Effects of Caregiver Mental Health Services

| | Subsequent Maltreatment | | | |
| | Model 6 | | Model 7 | |
Characteristic	OR	SE	OR	SE
Caregiver Characteristics				
Age	1.00	0.01	1.00	0.02
Female	0.67	0.19	0.64	0.21
Highest degree				
High school	0.83	0.16	0.77	0.14
Some college	0.92	0.25	0.85	0.24
BA/BS and above	1.97	1.22	1.64	1.08
Poverty	1.72	0.37*	1.77	0.41*
Urban	1.98	0.49**	2.04	0.51**
Risk factors				
Medium	1.79	0.43*	1.78	0.41*
High	2.21	0.58**	2.24	0.67**
Diagnosis and service use				
Depression (any wave)	1.60	0.33*	1.39	0.31
Substance dependence (any wave)	1.19	0.47	1.33	0.57
Mental health services by Wave 4			1.82	0.42**
Child Characteristics				
Age	0.95	0.04	0.95	0.04
Female	0.75	0.16	0.72	0.16
CBCL (clinical range any wave)				
Internalizing	1.00	0.20	0.88	0.18
Externalizing	1.90	0.48*	1.73	0.47*
Mental health services by Wave 4	1.61	0.34*	1.58	0.33*
Observations	1,984		1,984	

$*p < .05, **p < .01.$
CBCL, Child Behavior Checklist.

mental health service receipt was added to Model 7, the effect of caregiver depression was reduced to insignificance. This model met all four conditions for mediation (results not shown); both the Sobel and the Goodman tests were significant. The effect of caregiver service receipt was positive, however, indicating that the children of caregivers who received mental health services were more likely to be re-reported for child maltreatment.

Discussion

Sparse information exists in the literature about the extent of depression (based on standardized diagnostic criteria) among these caregivers, the likelihood of their receiving mental health services, and subsequent child outcomes. Prior studies with smaller samples and shorter follow-up periods have alluded to possible relationships between children in contact with the child welfare system, the characteristics of their caregivers, and mental health service use for caregiver and child. Our current findings, based as they are on a longitudinal, national probability study of families involved with the child welfare system are new, though not necessarily unexpected.

Caregiver Depression, Family Characteristics, and Mental Health Service Use

Forty percent of caregivers received a diagnosis of depression based on research diagnostic criteria. This rate exceeds the rate for female recipients of Temporary Assistance for Needy Families (Rosen et al., 2004) and greatly exceeds the general-population 12-month prevalence rate of 6.7% (Kessler et al., 2005). The caregiver rate for exposure over 36 months dramatically exceeds even the general-population lifetime rate (16.6%). Age, gender, race, educational level attained, urbanicity, and risk factors were essentially comparable between caregivers with and those without depression. Two exceptions were a higher proportion in poverty and three times the rate of substance dependence. Clinical need among children of depressed caregivers was exceptionally elevated and encompassed emotional disorders for 40.3% and behavioral disorders for 58.0%.

One third of caregivers with depression and two thirds of their children used mental health services by Wave 4 (36 months)—rates significantly higher than those for nondepressed caregivers (caregivers, 11.6%; children, 38.2%). Caregivers with depression were much more likely to receive mental health services than caregivers without depression at all three wave assessments, increasing from 25% at baseline to 34% by Wave 4. Nonetheless, mental health service use rates for these depressed caregivers were considerably lower than national rates (i.e., 41% in a year) for depressed adults (Wang et al., 2005).

Predictors of Mental Health Service Use Over Time

At Wave 3, daughters of caregivers with depression were much more likely than sons to use mental health services. Children who were victims of sexual abuse showed a significant increase in mental health service use at Wave 3 (70.5%, as opposed to 36.7% at baseline). Caregivers with depression who used substance abuse services were more likely (60.6%) to also receive mental health services at baseline than caregivers with depression who did not use substance abuse services. Caregivers with depression whose children were in the clinical range on the CBCL were more likely to receive mental health services by Waves 3 and 4.

The full-recovery group, the largest of the groups, managed to recover with only a small proportion receiving any mental health services. The relapse and delayed-recovery groups received services at a much higher rate, and service use by the caregivers whose depression persisted exceeded the other three groups by a factor of two or more, indicating slightly greater recognition of need, willingness to accept professional help, or better access to mental health services.

Children of caregivers who had major depression and who received mental health services were much more likely than other children to have clinical-range CBCL scores and more likely to receive mental health services themselves. Children of caregivers with depression were significantly less likely to be placed when their caregivers received mental health services by Wave 4; instead, the presence of high risk factors and subsequent maltreatment predicted placement. Children were more likely to be reported for subsequent maltreatment if their caregivers had depression, their caregivers received mental health services, they lived in an urban area, they lived in poverty, they had high family risk factors, they had a clinical-range Externalizing CBCL score, or they had received mental health services, which suggests that multiple factors are associated with re-reports of maltreatment.

These findings raise concerns about the future of caregivers and their children. Among concerns, for caregivers, are the high prevalence of depressive disorder, the persistence of illness, limited and delayed access to mental health services, and the uncertain effectiveness of such services when received. Data from the NSCAW study do not indicate whether treatment received was necessarily evidence based or whether it was of intensity and duration sufficient to result in therapeutic benefit. Whether the quality of mental health services is more of an issue for depressed caregivers in contact with child welfare than it is for other caregivers receiving public-sector mental health services is not known.

For children the concerns relate to extraordinarily high rates of emotional and behavioral disorders when their caregiver is depressed, minimal shifts in their clinical status (even when caregiver, child, or both receive mental health services), and exposure to subsequent maltreatment at rates higher than those for children whose caregivers are not depressed. When caregivers use mental health services, these more numerous subsequent maltreatment reports may be due to increased surveillance and other related factors (see Barth, Gibbons, & Guo, 2006). Caregivers in the child welfare system, depressed or not, are at risk in their homes and communities, which further challenges them and their children; moreover, even when mental health treatment is received, it is insufficient to buffer environmental risks.

These findings also offer limited but encouraging news. Caregivers may obtain mental health services by 36 months after contact with the child welfare system at a rate comparable to the 1-year rate for depressed adults in the United States. Depressed caregivers' children obtain mental health services at an increasingly higher rate over time, which indicates greater system responsiveness to the child's needs than to the caregiver. A critical finding was that mental health service use by depressed caregivers did not predict out-of-home placement (despite increased re-reports of maltreatment). Losing their children because of the stigma associated with treatment, a fear often voiced by caregivers, was not found here (Hearle, Plant, Jenner, Barkla, & McGrath, 1999).

Questions of Effective Clinical Care for Children and Their Caregivers

Caregivers with depression face immense challenges, not the least of which is parenting a child who has been maltreated and exhibits serious emotional or behavioral problems in an environment that is less than supportive. Our findings and consequent concerns raise serious questions about how more effectively to address such a complex array of needs. They suggest a need for an increased understanding of barriers to caregivers' prompt access to clinical care and a need for more effective treatment and meaningful coordination between caregiver treatment and child treatment, especially because the level of need for both caregivers and children is so high. The Working Group on Overcoming Barriers to Reducing the Burden of Affective Disorders (Kataoka, Zhang, & Wells, 2002) has underscored the research gap concerning "the access, quality or outcomes of care for socially disadvantaged women with affective disorders or their dependents" (p. 665). These matters necessarily address themselves to three levels of considera-tion: the child welfare system, the mental health system, and the caregivers and children themselves.

To what extent do the barriers reside in the child welfare system? Many obstacles may impede the caseworker's facilitation of mental health service use (i.e., knowledge about depression, assessment, and referral skills; availability of quality mental health services and linkages to them; time to address these tasks and to follow up with caregivers once treatment begins). Response to these barriers calls for clear child welfare policy on the training of caseworkers, a prioritization of caregiver mental health, related adjustments in caseload, and establishment of liaisons with mental health service systems. In NSCAW, linkages between child welfare and local mental health services increased rates of children's mental health service receipt (Hurlburt et al., 2004); similar linkages may promote caregivers' mental health service access, although for caregivers this kind of linkage may also require a close relationship with the adult service system.

Alternatively, questions about the responsiveness of the mental health system are pertinent:

- Are effective treatments for depression available in the community?
- Are services geographically accessible? If not, is transportation provided?
- Are services provided at times when caregivers can use them, particularly if they are working?
- Is the mental health system able to provide outreach or home-based services for caregivers who cannot travel to a clinic appointment?

- Do mental health systems serve caregivers with clinical conditions, and to what extent are services for the caregiver and child coordinated?
- Do mental health systems coordinate with child welfare agencies to provide family-based care?

Caregivers' anxieties about treatment and its costs are the two primary reasons that they do not seek treatment (Rosen et al., 2004). The depressed caregiver's perception may be that seeking mental health services poses a threat rather than a support in a situation already under surveillance: Caregivers may be concerned about the general stigma associated with mental illness and—although not confirmed by NSCAW data—the accompanying risk of losing custody of a maltreated child (Jacobsen, Miller, & Kirkwood, 1997; Mowbray, Oyserman, & Ross, 1995). Doubts about the benefits of treatment or negative prior experience with mental health services for them or their child may also deter service use. Most caregivers receiving mental health services have children also receiving treatment. Lacking time and resources to manage both types of services, usually delivered in separate child and adult service systems, may lead caregivers to obtain services for the child only. Anxiety about cost, as well, driven by lack of public or private insurance, is a significant barrier.

Models for Better Provision of Clinical Care to Children and Their Caregivers

Understandably, answers to these questions do not come from the NSCAW data. Among the many aims of NSCAW, an in-depth analysis of factors associated with caregivers' successful or unsuccessful help-seeking was not feasible. We therefore turn to the literature to identify opportunities for addressing some of these issues. Cook and Steigman (2000), for example, offer some principles for working with parents with a mental illness and their children:

- Ongoing availability of services;
- Family as the focus of service delivery;
- A service mix of treatment, rehabilitation, and support;
- Sensitivity to stigma associated with mental illness and prejudices faced by caregivers with mental illness;
- Sensitivity to caregivers' custody concerns;
- Improved parenting as the foundation for caregiver recovery; and
- Interagency collaboration.

Additionally, Cook and Steigman (2000) list a comprehensive set of recommended services. Although these apply to mental illnesses other than depression, they clearly apply to depressed caregivers:

- Assessment of caregiver strengths and needs;
- Case management;
- Peer support, self-help, and caregiver mentoring;
- Medication management;
- Birth control counseling and pregnancy decision making and support;
- Crisis and respite care;
- Foster care support and linkage;
- Trauma and abuse counseling;
- Substance abuse treatment;
- Marital and family counseling;
- Housing and supports for independent living;
- Child development and parenting skills training;
- Assistance with school issues;
- Advance-directive planning and support; and
- Benefits and public-entitlement counseling.

Whether for the majority of depressed caregivers this full array of services is warranted instead of more targeted services answering to individual assessments remains a topic for future investigation.

The Massachusetts group (Hinden, Biebel, Nicholson, & Mehnert, 2005), which has done the most systematic research and thinking about approaches to

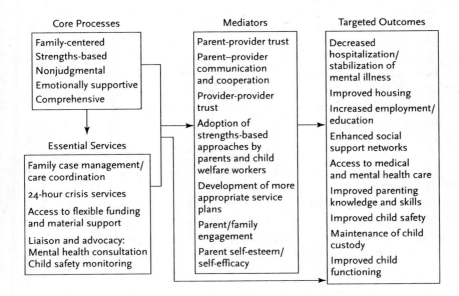

Figure 12.3. Hypothesized intervention model. (From Hinden, B. R., Biebel, K., Nicholson, J., & Mehnert, L. (2005). The Invisible Children's Project: Key ingredients of an intervention for parents with mental illness. *Journal of Behavioral Health Services and Research, 32,* 393–408.)

meeting the needs of parents with mental illness, have proposed a conceptual model to guide the provision of mental health services to parents (caregivers) and children (Fig. 12.3). This model is consistent with Cook and Steigman's principles and services array but adds the option of considering the services, processes, and mediators that would most likely lead to desirable outcomes for caregivers and their children. Before this model can be followed, of course, critical steps toward entry into mental health services must first be undertaken—namely, screening and engagement.

For screening, two identified measures have been tested in Colorado and Florida sites: the Child Abuse Potential and the Brief Symptom Inventory. These brief, easily administered inventories bring together caregiver symptoms of mental illness and the potential to abuse a child (Rinehart et al., 2005). Although exploration of the usefulness of these two measures in larger samples is warranted, they and possibly other measures may provide a method for identifying caregivers for referral to mental health specialists.

After screening, the critical next step is to engage caregivers and children in treatment. Research has shown high rates of failure to arrive for initial treatment or return visits (i.e., 50% to 70% of children who need services never have contact, or they quit prematurely; Kazdin, Mazurick, & Bass, 1993). To address the problem of caregiver and child engagement in treatment, investigators McKay, Stoewe, McCadam, and Gonzales (1998) tested ways to increase participation in services. Adding a combined engagement intervention (as opposed to a telephone intervention alone or the usual intake procedures), resulted in 89% coming in for initial care. In order to increase the treatment participation of depressed caregivers, the telephone interview can clarify the need for mental health care, increase the caregiver's investment and efficacy in relation to seeking help, identify attitudes about and previous experiences with mental health care, and overcome concrete obstacles to service access. The initial treatment session can then clarify the role of the caseworker, the role of the agency, the intake process, and possible service options; can establish foundations for a collaborative working relationship; can identify concrete, practical concerns that can be immediately addressed; and can overcome barriers to ongoing involvement with the agency.

In a study focused on engagement, Podorefsky, McDonald-Dowdell, and Beardslee (2001) documented the importance of such strategies. They adapted their interventions, which had been developed and tested with white, middle-class families with parental depression, to a low-income, culturally diverse community. A sequence of alliance-building events promoted engagement at the levels of community, family, and caregiver. Among the lessons learned were the importance of intensive engagement efforts by the clinician and the family and a focus on immediate daily concerns.

Screening and engagement strategies are initial steps toward case identification and treatment involvement. The next critical question is whether clinical interventions are available that can effectively address the caregiver's depression and the child's emotional or behavioral problems. Several candidate approaches addressing the needs of depressed caregivers and at-risk children emerge from the existing scientific literature: home visitation, an enhanced home visitation with cognitive-behavioral therapy, and an integrated family approach to treat depressed caregivers with children who have disruptive behavior disorders.

Research on interventions for depressed caregivers has focused largely on parenting skills in home visitation services. Mixed findings across studies may be due to methodological problems in the research or in the design of the particular intervention (see Brunette & Dean, 2002). One consistent finding has been that long-term interventions (delivered for a year or longer) improve mother–child relationships, but short-term interventions are ineffective.

One group of investigators subsequently evaluated the role of depression and trauma in the use of home visits. They found that recent violent trauma was related to disruption of service delivery, but increased telephone contact between mothers and home visitors improved results (Stevens, Ammerman, Putnam, & Van Ginkel, 2002). Sensing an opportunity for a more targeted intervention for depression, these authors added cognitive-behavioral therapy to home visits for mothers with depression. A substantial reduction in depression was observed (i.e., 84.6% of mothers were fully or partially remitted from major depression, and functional impairment was reduced; Ammerman et al., 2005). Despite the small sample ($n = 26$) and a pre-post study design, that home-based provision of an evidence-based clinical intervention was successfully provided as an alternative to clinic-based care begs for controlled replication.

An even more targeted intervention addresses both caregiver depression and children's behavioral problems. The Cognitive-Behavioral Family Intervention (CBFI), which integrates cognitive strategies to treat depression with the teaching of parenting skills, was compared with Behavioral Family Intervention (BFI) for treatment of oppositional and disruptive behavior in children (Sanders & McFarland, 2006). Both interventions reduced caregiver depression and children's problem behavior at the end of treatment; however, at the 6-month follow-up the findings for both caregiver depression and child behavior favored CBFI (53%) over BFI (13%). This carefully conducted, though small, randomized clinical trial of CBFI offers a model of integrated parent and child treatment and warrants replication studies. Moreover, because in NSCAW the prevalence of internalizing problems in children with depressed caregivers was high, consideration of a family intervention that addresses both maternal and childhood depression is warranted.

Limitations

Despite the extraordinarily ambitious scope of NSCAW, we acknowledge several study limitations concerning primarily a need for additional information. Although difficult to obtain in a national study already burdening respondents with lengthy interviews, this information may improve understanding of caregiver depression and service use. Additional information about depression onset, chronicity, severity, and prior treatment, for example, would be helpful because the impact of caregiver depression on the child varies with the child's developmental stage (see Oyserman et al., 2000). Conversely, diagnosis-specific information and intensity of mental health service provision for the children could help identify the impact of effective child treatment on caregiver depression. Information about depressed caregivers' trauma history would likely influence the type of treatment intervention, response to treatment (Gladstone et al., 2004), and other co-occurring conditions requiring treatment. Also helpful would be information on whether treatment was focused on depression and, if so, the type, quality, and dose of treatment, as well as whether the interventions were evidence based (e.g., antidepressant medication, cognitive-behavioral therapy, interpersonal therapy) and completed: Guideline-driven treatment is not likely to be highly available across the country (e.g., medication compliance; Olfson, Marcus, Tedeschi, & Wan, 2006). Information about insurance benefits for caregivers, instead of only their children, would help reveal the role insurance fulfills as a barrier to or facilitator of treatment for caregivers. Sensitivity to change on the major child outcome measure, the CBCL, is questionable. Questions remain about whether the CBCL reliably measures change, including the child's benefit from treatment and the child's long-term response to parental depression or treatment.

Conclusion

Surprisingly, for the families in NSCAW caregiver rates of major depression were extremely high—even rampant—while, compared with service use by depressed adults in the general U.S. population, service use was delayed. Because caregivers involved in child welfare are at risk and under enhanced surveillance, one might expect their enhanced access to treatment. Fortunately, the children's high rates of pathology and need for treatment corresponded more closely with increased access to mental health services over time, even though this correspondence was not as likely for their depressed caregivers.

That risk factors were generally no greater for depressed caregivers than for nondepressed caregivers was expected, but, intuitively, the combination of depression and family risk factors exacerbates challenges to effective parenting. Although efficacious interventions for children with emotional and behavioral problems exist (Burns, Hoagwood, & Mrazek, 1999; Farmer, Dorsey, & Mustillo, 2004), child/caregiver-combined interventions are currently limited and not fully tested. Nevertheless, the clear link between caregiver depression and child psychopathology urges joint treatment for both caregiver depression and the child's emotional or behavioral disorders. Although several interventions in the literature integrate treatment this way, further evaluation of such approaches is indicated, as is further research on parenting style among depressed caregivers, including those from ethnically diverse populations. Our current findings enjoin not only this further treatment-development research, but also concomitant policy for both the child welfare and the mental health service systems.

REFERENCES

Achenbach, T. M. (1991). *Manual for the Child Behavior Checklist/4-18 and 1991 profile.* Burlington, VT: University of Vermont, Department of Psychiatry.

Administration for Children and Families. (2008). *National Survey of Child and Adolescent Well-Being: Conditions of children and families at intake into child welfare services.* Washington, DC: Author.

American Psychiatric Association. (1980). *Diagnostic and statistical manual of mental disorders* (3rd ed.). Washington, DC: Author.

American Psychiatric Association. (1994). *Diagnostic and statistical manual of mental disorders* (4th ed.). Washington, DC: Author.

Ammerman, R. T., Putnam, F. W., Stevens, J., Holleb, L. J., Novak, A. L., & Van Ginkel, J. B. (2005). In-home cognitive-behavior therapy for depression: An adapted treatment for first-time mothers in home visitation. *Best Practices in Mental Health, 1,* 1–14.

Barnett, D., Manly, J. T., & Cicchetti, D. (1993). Defining child maltreatment: The interface between policy and child research. In D. Cicchetti & S. L. Toth (Eds.), *Defining child maltreatment: The interface between policy and child research* (Vol. 8, pp. 7–73). Norwood, NJ: Ablex.

Barth, R. P., Gibbons, C., & Guo, S. (2006). Substance abuse treatment and the recurrence of maltreatment among caregivers with children living at home: A propensity score analysis. *Journal of Substance Abuse Treatment, 30*(2), 93–104.

Beardslee, W. R., Gladstone, T. R., Wright, E. J., & Cooper, A. B. (2003). A family-based approach to the prevention of depressive symptoms in children at risk: Evidence of parental and child change. *Pediatrics, 112*(2), 119–131.

Brunette, M. F., & Dean, W. (2002). Community mental health care for women with severe mental illness who are parents. *Community Mental Health Journal, 38*(2), 153–165.

Brunette, M. F., & Drake, R. E. (1997). Gender differences in patients with schizophrenia and substance abuse. *Comprehensive Psychiatry, 38*(2), 109–116.

Burns, B. J., Angold, A., Magruder-Habib, K., Costello, E. J., & Patrick, M. K. S. (1994). *The Child and Adolescent Services Assessment (CASA), parent interview and child interview.* Durham, NC: Developmental Epidemiology Program, Department of Psychiatry, Duke University Medical Center.

Burns, B. J., Hoagwood, K., & Mrazek, P. J. (1999). Effective treatment for mental disorders in children and adolescents. *Clinical Child and Family Psychology Review, 2*(4), 199–254.

Cook, J., & Steigman, P. (2000). Experiences of parents with mental illnesses and their service needs. *Journal of NAMI California, 11,* 21–23.

Farmer, E. M., Dorsey, S., & Mustillo, S. A. (2004). Intensive home and community interventions. *Child and Adolescent Psychiatric Clinics of North America, 13*(4), 857–884.

Gladstone, G. L., Parker, G. B., Mitchell, P. B., Malhi, G. S., Wilhelm, K., & Austin, M. P. (2004). Implications of childhood trauma for depressed women: An analysis of pathways from childhood sexual abuse to deliberate self-harm and revictimization. *American Journal of Psychiatry, 161*(8), 1417–1425.

Gunlicks, M. L., & Weissman, M. M. (2008). Change in child psychopathology with improvement in parental depression: A systematic review. *Journal of the American Academy of Child and Adolescent Psychiatry, 47*(4), 379–389.

Hearle, J., Plant, K., Jenner, L., Barkla, J., & McGrath, J. (1999). A survey of contact with offspring and assistance with child care among parents with psychotic disorders. *Psychiatric Services, 50*(10), 1354–1356.

Hinden, B. R., Biebel, K., Nicholson, J., & Mehnert, L. (2005). The Invisible Children's Project: Key ingredients of an intervention for parents with mental illness. *Journal of Behavioral Health Services & Research, 32*(4), 393–408.

Hurlburt, M. S., Leslie, L. K., Landsverk, J., Barth, R. P., Burns, B. J., Gibbons, R. D., et al. (2004). Contextual predictors of mental health service use among children open to child welfare. *Archives of General Psychiatry, 61,* 1217–1224.

Insel, T. R. (2006). Beyond efficacy: The STAR*D trial. *American Journal of Psychiatry, 163*(1), 5–7.

Jacobsen, T., Miller, L. J., & Kirkwood, K. P. (1997). Assessing parenting competency in individuals with severe mental illness: A comprehensive service. *Journal of Mental Health Administration, 24*(2), 189–199.

Kataoka, S. H., Zhang, L., & Wells, K. B. (2002). Unmet need for mental health care among U.S. children: Variation by ethnicity and insurance status. *American Journal of Psychiatry, 159*(9), 1548–1555.

Kazdin, A. E., Mazurick, J. L., & Bass, D. (1993). Risk for attrition in treatment of antisocial children and families. *Journal of Clinical Child Psychology, 22,* 2–16.

Kessler, R. C., Andrews, G., Mroczek, D., Ustun, T. B., & Wittchen, H.-U. (1998). The World Health Organization Composite International Diagnostic Interview Short Form (CIDI-SF). *International Journal of Methods in Psychiatric Research, 7,* 171–185.

Kessler, R. C., Berglund, P., Demler, O., Jin, R., Merikangas, K. R., & Walters, E. E. (2005). Lifetime prevalence and age-of-onset distributions of *DSM-IV* disorders in the National Comorbidity Survey Replication. *Archives of General Psychiatry, 62*(6), 593–768.

Libby, A. M., Orton, H. D., Barth, R. P., Webb, M. B., Burns, B. J., Wood, P., et al. (2006). Alcohol, drug, and mental health specialty treatment services and race/ethnicity: A national study of children and families involved with child welfare. *American Journal of Public Health, 96*(4), 628–631.

MacKinnon, D. P., & Dwyer, J. H. (1993). Estimating mediated effects in prevention studies. *Evaluation Review, 17,* 144–158.

MacKinnon, D. P., Warsi, G., & Dwyer, J. H. (1995). A simulation study of mediated effect measures. *Multivariate Behavioral Research, 30,* 41–62.

McKay, M. M., Stoewe, J., McCadam, K., & Gonzales, J. (1998). Increasing access to child mental health services for urban children and their caregivers. *Health and Social Work, 23*(1), 9–15.

Miranda, J., Chung, J. Y., Green, B. L., Krupnick, J., Siddique, J., Revicki, D. A., et al. (2003). Treating depression in predominantly low-income young minority women: A randomized controlled trial. *Journal of the American Medical Association, 290*(1), 57–65.

Mowbray, C. T., Oyserman, D., & Ross, S. R. (1995). Parenting and the significance of children for women with a serious mental illness. *Journal of Mental Health Administration, 22,* 189–200.

Nicholson, J., Biebel, K., Hinden, B., Henry, A., & Stier, L. (2001). *Critical issues for parents with mental illness and their families.* Rockville, MD: Center for Mental Health Services, Substance Abuse and Mental Health Services Administration.

Nicholson, J., Sweeney, E. M., & Geller, J. L. (1998). Mothers with mental illness: Part I. The competing demands of parenting and living with mental illness. *Psychiatric Services, 49*(5), 635–642.

NSCAW Research Group. (2002). Methodological lessons from the National Survey of Child and Adolescent Well-Being: The first three years of the USA's first national probability study of children and families investigated for abuse and neglect. *Children and Youth Services Review, 24*(6/7), 513–541.

Office of Applied Studies. (2005). *Results from the 2004 National Survey on Drug Use and Health: National findings.* DHHS Publication SMA 05-4062, NSDUH Series H-28. Rockville, MD.

Olfson, M., Marcus, S. C., Tedeschi, M., & Wan, G. J. (2006). Continuity of antidepressant treatment for adults with depression in the United States. *American Journal of Psychiatry, 163*(1), 101–108.

Oyserman, D., Mowbray, C. T., Meares, P. A., & Firminger, K. B. (2000). Parenting among mothers with a serious mental illness. *American Journal of Orthopsychiatry, 70*(3), 296–315.

Podorefsky, D. L., McDonald-Dowdell, M., & Beardslee, W. R. (2001). Adaptation of preventive interventions for a low-income, culturally diverse community. *Journal of the American Academy of Child and Adolescent Psychiatry, 40*(8), 879–886.

Rao, J. N. K., & Scott, A. J. (1981). The analysis of categorical data from complex sample surveys: Chi-squared tests for goodness of fit and independence in two-way tables. *Journal of the American Statistical Association, 76*, 221–230.

Rao, J. N. K., & Scott, A. J. (1984). On chi-squared tests for multiway contingency tables with cell proportions estimated from survey data. *Annals of Statistics, 12*, 46–60.

Rinehart, D. J., Becker, M. A., Buckley, P. R., Dailey, K., Reichardt, C. S., Graeber, C., et al. (2005). The relationship between mothers' child abuse potential and current mental health symptoms: Implications for screening and referral. *Journal of Behavioral Health Services & Research, 32*(2), 155–166.

Rosen, D., Tolman, R. M., & Warner, L. A. (2004). Low-income women's use of substance abuse and mental health services. *Journal of Health Care for the Poor and Underserved, 15*(2), 206–219.

Sanders, M. R., & McFarland, M. (2006). Treatment of depressed mothers with disruptive children: A controlled evaluation of cognitive behavioral family intervention. *Behavior Therapy, 31*, 89–112.

Silverstein, M., Augustyn, M., Cabral, H., & Zuckerman, B. (2006). Maternal depression and violence exposure: Double jeopardy for child school functioning. *Pediatrics, 118*(3), 792–800.

StataCorp. (2005). *Stata statistical software, release 9.* College Station, TX: Author.

Stevens, J., Ammerman, R. T., Putnam, F. G., & Van Ginkel, J. B. (2002). Depression and trauma history in first-time mothers receiving home visitation. *Journal of Community Psychology, 30*, 551–564.

Tajima, E. A. (2000). The relative importance of wife abuse as a risk factor for violence against children. *Child Abuse & Neglect, 24*(11), 1383–1398.

Walker, J. (2008). Cargiver-child: Mutual influences on mental health. *Focal Point, 22*(2), 2–3.

Wang, P. S., Lane, M., Olfson, M., Pincus, H. A., Wells, K. B., & Kessler, R. C. (2005). Twelve-month use of mental health services in the United States: Results from the National Comorbidity Survey Replication. *Archives of General Psychiatry, 62*(6), 629–640.

Weissman, M. M., Pilowsky, D. J., Wickramaratne, P. J., Talati, A., Wisniewski, S. R., Fava, M., et al. (2006). Remissions in maternal depression and child psychopathology: A STAR*D-child report. *Journal of the American Medical Association, 295*(12), 1389–1398.

World Health Organization. (2002). *The world health report 2002: Reducing risks, promoting healthy life.* Geneva: World Health Organization.

13

Organizational Climate and Service Outcomes in Child Welfare Systems

CHARLES GLISSON

Child welfare systems nationwide investigate 3 million child maltreatment cases each year. These investigations identify approximately 900,000 children annually who have been abused or neglected (Administration for Children and Families, 2006a, 2006b). Although the children are referred to child welfare systems because of neglect or abuse, many have serious emotional and behavioral problems that can follow them into adulthood (Administration for Children and Families, 2004; Burns et al., 2004; Hazen, Hough, Landsverk, & Wood, 2004).[1] The high risk of chronic emotional and behavioral problems among these children underscores the need for timely, appropriate care that reduces the risk; however, a significant portion of these children never receive the care they need (Administration for Children and Families, 2004; Burns et al., 2004).

Timely, appropriate care requires that an individual caseworker assume responsibility for each maltreated child's well-being and establish a relationship with the child and the family that helps the caseworker identify the child's unique needs, determine whether the child would benefit from out-of-home residential care, select an appropriate residential setting if needed, and ensure that the child and family receive needed services. Although several factors affect the caseworker's performance, studies indicate that the caseworker's success is in part a function of the work environment of the child welfare agency in which the caseworker is employed (Glisson & Green, 2006; Glisson & Hemmelgarn, 1998; Glisson & James, 2002; U.S. General Accounting Office, 2003). Caseworkers in more positive child welfare work environments have better work attitudes (e.g., higher job satisfaction and commitment), are less likely to quit their jobs, deliver higher-quality services, and are more effective (Glisson, 2002, 2008; Glisson & Green, 2006;

Glisson & Hemmelgarn, 1998; Glisson & James, 2002). A report by the U.S. General Accounting Office (2003) has identified poor work environments as a major factor in determining the high rates of caseworker turnover and the poor quality of services provided to children in many child welfare systems nationwide. Others have argued that a social service or mental health organization's work environment is important to service quality and outcomes because it affects the service provider's relationship with the client, the service provider's level of effort, whether the most appropriate intervention and service protocols are adopted, how they are implemented, and whether they are sustained (Glisson, 2002; Glisson & Green, 2006; Glisson, Landsverk et al., 2008; Glisson, Schoenwald, Kelleher et al., 2002; Hoagwood, Burns, Kiser, Ringeisen, & Schoenwald, 2001; Hohmann & Shear, 2002; Jensen, 2003; Schoenwald & Hoagwood, 2001). As with other kinds of complex, high-stress work, a positive and supportive work environment is a necessary, if not sufficient, condition for optimal caseworker performance in child welfare systems (Edmondson, Bohmer, & Pisano, 2001; Huy, 2002).

The Organizational Climate of Child Welfare Systems

The influence of organizational climate on the performance of various types of work organizations has been the focus of extensive research over the past half century. The research suggests that organizational climate is an important determinant of the organization's effectiveness in many different kinds of settings (for early reviews, see Hellreigel & Slocum, 1974; James & Jones, 1980; Payne & Pugh, 1975; Schneider, 1975). Although most of this research has been conducted in business and industrial organizations, attention increasingly has been given to nonprofit, public, and human service organizations (Ostroff & Schmitt, 1993; Soloman, 1986). Although few studies address child welfare systems specifically, the limited results on human service organizations indicate that climate affects human service organizations as profoundly as it affects business and industrial organizations (Glisson & Green, 2006; Glisson & Hemmelgarn, 1998; Glisson & James, 2002; Ostroff & Schmitt, 1993).

Successful child welfare services require caseworkers to be responsive to unexpected problems, attentive to the individual, unique needs of each child, tenacious in navigating the complex bureaucratic maze of state and federal regulations, and adept at winning the trust and confidence of a diverse group of children and families. Moreover, caseworkers must perform their jobs in highly stressful situations that can involve, for example, angry family members or seriously emotionally disturbed children.

As with relationships formed between teachers and their students, successful relationships between caseworkers and children referred to child welfare agencies enable caseworkers to identify, understand, and address each child's individual strengths and needs. Caseworkers form and sustain each relationship in the face of heavy caseloads and the challenges inherent in working with children who have been mistreated; and they must meet these children's needs despite the barriers presented by courts, bureaucratic service systems, and extremely limited resources.

For their work to be successful, caseworkers must be viewed by the children and families they serve as available, responsive (Dozier, Cue, & Barnett, 1994), and characterized by what Wahler (1994) has described as *social continuity*. That is, the caseworkers' actions must be predictable, appropriate, and welcomed by their clients over an extended period of time in order to establish a pattern of interaction on which the children and families can rely. For these reasons, effective casework relationships are more likely to occur in child welfare agencies with positive, supportive organizational climates that enable caseworkers to be fully engaged in their efforts to serve individual children.

The nature of caseworkers' responsibilities in child welfare systems, the seriousness of the behavioral and emotional problems experienced by the children and families they serve, and the demands of judges, attorneys, advocates, and others explain why previous studies of child welfare case management teams found that organizational climate affects case managers' work attitudes and the quality and outcomes of the services they provide (Glisson & Durick, 1988; Glisson & Hemmelgarn, 1998; Glisson & James, 2002). Poor work environments in child welfare systems compound the challenges faced by caseworkers in serving maltreated children by contributing to job-related stress, high turnover, and services that are depersonalized (Cyphers, 2001; Glisson, Dukes, & Green, 2006; Glisson & James, 2002; U.S. General Accounting Office, 2003).

Climate as an Organizational Concept

The definition of *climate* used here includes a distinction between *psychological climate* and *organizational climate* (James & James, 1989; James, James, & Ashe, 1990; James & Jones, 1974). *Psychological climate* is the individual employee's perception of the impact of his or her work on his or her own well-being (James & James, 1989). When individuals who work in the same organizational system, service region, or work unit have the same perceptions, these shared perceptions can be aggregated to describe their *organizational climate* (Glisson & James, 2002; James, 1982; Jones & James, 1979; Joyce & Slocum, 1984).

Although organizational climate is measured with multiple dimensions (e.g., personal accomplishment, depersonalization, emotional exhaustion, role conflict, role overload), the individual's perception of the overall positive or negative psychological impact of his or her work environment has been defined as a single, second-order, general climate factor (James & James, 1989; James et al., 1990). This single, second-order factor has been described as representing the workers' overall sense of psychological safety and meaningfulness of their work (Brown & Leigh, 1996; Glisson & Hemmelgarn, 1998; Glisson & James, 2002). Unfortunately, the studies that have identified a single, second-order factor have relied on samples from a single organization or, at best, a small sample of two or three organizations. The literature offers no studies of organizational climate that use a large, nationwide sample of organizations; therefore, the current study of 88 child welfare agencies participating in the National Survey on Child and Adolescent Well-Being (NSCAW) provides an ideal opportunity to examine the second-order-factor structure of climate in a large, nationwide sample of child welfare caseworkers.

Cross-Level Relationships With Climate

Studies of a variety of types of organizations, including human services, have linked *psychological* climate to individual work attitudes and behavior (Glisson & Durick, 1988; Hackman & Oldham, 1975; Herman, Dunham, & Hulin, 1975; Herman & Hulin, 1972; Morris & Sherman, 1981), but only a few studies have examined the cross-level association of *organizational* climate with individual-level outcomes (Glisson & Green, 2006; Glisson & Hemmelgarn, 1998; Glisson & James, 2002). Moreover, these few studies were conducted on multiple units or service regions within a single organization or on a small number of organizations. The focus here is on the cross-level association of organizational climate with individual child-level service outcomes in a large, nationwide sample of child welfare agencies.

The estimation of the cross-level relationships with organizational climate must reflect the multilevel nature of the relationship (Klein & Kozlowski, 2000a, 2000b). Problems occur when variables such as organizational climate are defined at higher levels (e.g., service system) and then measured at the individual level without aggregating the individual-level responses to the higher levels. Problems also occur when the relationships among variables are examined at a single level (e.g., organizational), although some variables are defined at an organizational level and others are defined at an individual level. The potential for these problems necessitates clarity in specifying the levels at which the variables operate, the explicit models used to create measures of higher-level variables, and the links between lower- and higher-level variables.

Links between individual-level variables, such as service outcomes, and organizational-level variables that characterize the service systems in which those individuals are clustered require statistical models that provide estimates of relationships between variables operationalized at different levels (Hedeker & Gibbons, 2006; James & Williams, 2000; Raudenbush & Bryk, 2002; Rousseau, 1985). Although cross-level inferences can be made using various approaches, models described collectively in various literatures as *mixed effects, random effects, random coefficient,* and *hierarchical linear models* are most appropriate for making cross-level inferences that link the characteristics of individuals to the characteristics of the higher-level collectives in which they are nested (Hedeker & Gibbons, 2006; Raudenbush & Bryk, 2002).

When such models are applied to organizational research, questions about cross-level relationships in multilevel studies can be formulated as two- or three-level random intercepts and random slopes models. The random intercepts and random slopes models can be applied when, as in the current study, key predictors include variables measured at both the individual and organizational levels and when the outcome variable is measured at the individual level. If such data were analyzed only at the individual level and if the clustering of individuals were ignored, then standard errors possibly would be misestimated. If such data were aggregated and analyzed only at the organizational level (e.g., using unit means as outcomes), individual-level predictors would be excluded, possibly resulting in inefficient, biased estimates of organizational effects. Random intercepts and slopes models avoid these problems; individual-level outcomes can be assessed as a function of the characteristics of both the individuals and the organizational systems in which those individuals are nested.

Composition Model for Climate

Composition models are used to guide the aggregation of individual data to describe collectives (e.g., families, service systems, regions, communities). Here, composition models specify the functional relationships between climate constructs that reference the same content but describe phenomena at the individual level (i.e., psychological climate) that differ qualitatively from phenomena described at the service system level (i.e., organizational climate; Chan, 1998; Rousseau, 1985). Composition models used to aggregate data to form the higher-level construct therefore fulfill an important role in cross-level inferences that link organizational climate to individual-level outcome variables (Glisson & James, 2002).

The *direct consensus* model of *elemental composition* provides a useful framework for understanding the composition of climate (Chan, 1998). This model specifies consensus among the individuals in an organizational service system, unit, or region, as a precondition for operationalizing the higher-level construct (e.g., organizational climate) as an aggregate of the individual-level responses (e.g., psychological climate). In the present example, a shared psychological climate in a child welfare service system—represented by a value of .70 or higher on the r_{wg} index of within-group consensus at the caseworker level—is a prerequisite for calculating organizational climate as a mean of the caseworker responses to the psychological climate measure (Glisson & James, 2002; James, Demaree, & Wolf, 1984). The use of composition models to measure service system characteristics (e.g., organizational climate) requires not only that perceptions of the psychological impact of their work be shared by the caseworkers who provide services within the same child welfare agency service system but also that the perceptions between child welfare agency service systems vary (Glisson & James, 2002; Klein & Kozlowski, 2000a, 2000b). These between-agency differences are assessed with the ANOVA-based eta-squared and random effects–based intraclass correlation coefficient (ICC; Bliese, 2000; Glisson & James, 2002)

Data Set Characteristics, Test Variables, and Goals

The NSCAW sample of child welfare agencies and children used in the current analyses was selected according to a stratified two-stage sample design.[2] At the first stage, the United States was divided into nine sampling strata. Eight of the strata corresponded to the eight states with the largest child welfare caseloads, and the ninth stratum consisted of the remaining states. Within these strata, 92 primary sampling units (PSUs) in 97 counties were defined as child welfare service areas. In most cases, the PSUs corresponded to counties, but in rural areas two or more contiguous counties formed a PSU, while in urban counties more than one PSU comprised a single county. In some instances agency service areas were combined to form a PSU, and in others a single agency served more than one PSU. The complete NSCAW sample contained 97 child welfare agencies; the current study includes 88 of these agencies, 76% of which are located in metropolitan statistical areas and classified as urban agencies.[3] A total of 1,696 caseworkers associated with the 88 child welfare agencies, an average of 19 caseworkers per agency (ranging from 4 to 70), were interviewed in NSCAW and were included in the current study.

The current study also includes a subsample of the NSCAW total sample of 5,501 children who were referred to the sampled agencies for maltreatment investigations from October 1999 to December 2000. The subsample was those children between the ages of 4 and 16 years (3,212) for whom abuse or neglect allegations were either *substantiated* or *indicated* (1,678).[4] The number of children in the current sample was then reduced by 38 children because of exclusion of 9 of the agencies. The final sample comprised 1,640 children, in 88 child welfare agencies, who were school aged and had substantiated or indicated cases of maltreatment.

This current study builds on previous studies by examining the cross-level association of child welfare agency organizational climate with service outcomes measured as improvements in the sampled children's overall psychosocial functioning. The study is similar to previous studies that linked the work environments of child welfare systems to service quality and outcomes (Glisson & Green, 2006; Glisson & Hemmelgarn, 1998; Glisson & James, 2002). Unlike previous studies, however, which focused on child welfare systems in one state or geographical location, this one examines the association between organizational climate and service outcomes in a nationwide sample of child welfare agencies. The goals here are three-fold: to describe and confirm the second-order factor structure of the selected climate measures in a nationwide sample of child welfare caseworkers, to determine whether service-region aggregation of caseworker perceptions of psychological climate is justified, and to assess the cross-level relationship of organizational climate with individual child-level service outcomes.

Methods

The caseworker sample from the 88 agencies that were interviewed in NSCAW was 82% female, 66% white, 23% black or African American, and 11% Hispanic, with a mean and mode age between 30 and 39 years. Most of the caseworkers (65%) held bachelor's degrees, and almost a third (32%) held master's degrees, with most in the sample (62%) having majored in disciplines other than social work.

The children in the subsample used for the current analyses ranged in age from 4 to 16 years and had a mean age of 9 years (Table 13.1). About half of the children

Table 13.1   Sample Characteristics of Children Aged 4 to 16 Years With Substantiated or Indicated Cases ($n = 1,678$)

	Nominal Variables		Continuous Variables			
	Value	Percent	Mean	SD	Min.	Max.
Age			9.19	3.25	4	16
Baseline raw CBCL (total)			43.28	28.82	0	179
Family income (annual)	1 (<5,000)	4.6	5.53	3.01	1	11
	2 (5,000–9,999)	12.6				
	3 (10,000–14,999)	13.2				
	4 (15,000–19,999)	11.9				
	5 (20,000–24,999)	19.8				
	6 (25,000–29,999)	7.0				
	7 (30,000–34,999)	5.8				
	8 (35,000–39,999)	4.6				
	9 (40,000–44,999)	4.3				
	10 (45,000–49,999)	3.8				
	11 (50,000–54,999)	12.3				
Gender	Female	54.8				
	Male	45.2				
Race/ethnicity	African American	30.2				
	American Indian/Alaska Native	1.9				
	Asian	1.0				
	Hawaiian/Pacific Islander	1.0				
	Hispanic	15.4				
	White	58.3				
Level of harm	1 (none)	7.1	2.84	.86	1	4
	2 (mild)	25.3				
	3 (moderate)	43.6				
	4 (severe)	24.0				

CBCL, Child Behavior Checklist.

were female (55%), and about half represented minority groups, including black or African American (30%), Hispanic (15%), Native American (2%), Asian (1%), and Native Hawaiian or other Pacific Islander (1%). Family income levels were positively skewed, with about half of the families having incomes between $20,000 and $25,000 annually, the mean income being between $25,000 and $30,000.

Measures

CHILD EMOTIONAL AND BEHAVIORAL PROBLEMS   Child emotional and behavioral problems were measured with the Child Behavior Checklist (CBCL) at Waves 1 (baseline), 3 (18-month follow-up), and 4 (36-month follow-up). The CBCL is a well-known, validated, standardized measure of a child's overall problems in psychosocial functioning (Achenbach, 1991). Children express problems in psychosocial functioning as internalizing and externalizing behaviors; changes in their psychosocial functioning can be assessed by monitoring these behavioral problems (McMahon, 1994; Oilendick & King, 1994). The current study uses the CBCL Total Problems scale score, a sum of Internalizing and Externalizing subscale scores, to monitor changes in the children's overall functioning across Waves 1, 3, and 4. The CBCL was completed by the child's current primary caregiver.

CHILD LEVEL OF HARM   Child harm level was measured as the investigative case-worker's initial assessment of the level of harm to the child that resulted from the abuse or neglect that occasioned the investigation. The investigative caseworkers are not the same caseworkers who provide child welfare services to the children after abuse or neglect is substantiated. This distinction is important because organizational climate was measured from the responses of caseworkers who provide child welfare services to children. The investigative caseworker assessed harm to the child on a scale from 1 (*none*) to 4 (*severe*), with a median and mode of 3 (*moderate*), a mean of 2.84, and a standard deviation of 0.86 (Table 13.2).

ORGANIZATIONAL CLIMATE   Organizational climate was assessed with scales selected from the Organizational Social Context (OSC) measurement system (Glisson, Landsverk et al., 2008; Glisson, Schoenwald, Kelleher et al., 2008). The scales were linked in previous research to caseworkers' attitudes toward their jobs and organizations and to the quality and outcomes of services in child welfare organizations (Glisson & Durick, 1988; Glisson & Hemmelgarn, 1998; Glisson & James, 2002). Five OSC scales selected for NSCAW were administered at Wave 2 (12 months after baseline) to 1,689 caseworkers who provided child welfare services through the identified agencies: Personal Accomplishment (e.g., "I have accomplished many worthwhile things in this job"), Depersonalization (e.g., "I've become more callous toward people since I took this job"), Emotional Exhaustion (e.g., "I feel emotionally drained from my work"), Role Conflict (e.g., "I have to do things on the job that are against my better judgment"), and Role Overload (e.g., "The amount of work I have to do keeps me from doing a good job"). NSCAW used the intact OSC scales with

Table 13.2   Exploratory Factor Analysis With First Subsample of Caseworkers ($n_1 = 836$)

Scale	Reliability	Stressful Climate	Engaged Climate
Emotional exhaustion	.89	.774	−.193
Role conflict	.84	.872	−.065
Role overload	.81	.971	−.180
Personal accomplishment	.73	−.109	.948
Depersonalization (reversed)	.69	−.361	.645
Eigenvalues		2.908	1.032
Percent variance		58.162	20.639
Component correlation		−.330	

some minor rewording (e.g., the word "clients" was replaced with "children") and excluded one item from the Depersonalization scale ("It's hard to feel close to the clients I serve"). The alpha reliabilities for these scales with this sample were .72 (Personal Accomplishment), .69 (Depersonalization), .89 (Emotional Exhaustion), .83 (Role Conflict), and .81 (Role Overload).

Analyses

NSCAW's large, nationwide sample of caseworkers provides an ideal opportunity to examine the factor structure of the selected OSC measures of organizational climate. The sample was divided randomly into two subsamples of 44 agencies each. One subsample of 44 agencies includes 836 caseworkers and the other sample of 44 agencies includes 860 caseworkers. An exploratory factor analysis (EFA) of the five scales was conducted with the first subsample to identify the second-order factors; a second-order confirmatory factor analysis (CFA) was then conducted with the second subsample to confirm the second-order factors identified in the first subsample.

A within-agency consistency analysis using r_{wg} was conducted to provide evidence that caseworkers' responses to climate scales agreed with the responses of the other caseworkers in the same agency (James, Demaree, & Wolf, 1993). This analysis is a prerequisite for composing the individual-level responses to higher-level (i.e., organizational) constructs. In addition to within-agency consistency analysis, between-agency analyses using eta-squared by way of ANOVA and using ICC by way of random effects were conducted to test whether between-group differences existed among the agencies. This step is important because, if consistency in responses spans the entire sample of organizations, then consistent responses can occur within organizations but without between-group differences: Within-group consistency and between-group differences confirm that a meaningful collective (e.g., the agency) has been selected for aggregation and study (Rentsch, 1990).

Two three-level hierarchal linear modeling (HLM) analyses, one incorporating differential sampling weights at each level and one incorporating no sampling weights, were used to estimate the cross-level relationship between organizational climate and child-level psychosocial functioning outcomes (Hedeker, Gibbons, & Flay, 1994; Raudenbush & Bryk, 2002; Raudenbush, Bryk, Cheong, & Congdon, 2000). A three-level HLM analysis of a random intercepts and random slopes model describes the contribution of organizational climate to predicting the change in each child's psychosocial functioning across Waves 1, 3, and 4, controlling for each child's initial harm level, age, gender, race, family income, and location (urban or nonurban). The weighted analysis incorporates differential probability sampling weights at the three levels (i.e., time, child, and agency) to provide improved population estimates of the trend or growth in child functioning as a function of child characteristics and organizational climate.

Results

Factor Structure of Climate

As a first step in the analysis of the factor structure of climate, the 88 child welfare agencies were randomly divided into two groups of 44 agencies each. Caseworkers from each group of agencies formed two samples of caseworkers for the following factor analyses ($n_1 = 836$, $n_2 = 860$). An EFA of the total scores from each of the five climate scales was conducted with the first subsample ($n_1 = 836$), using principal components analysis. The first two components extracted in the analysis had Eigenvalues greater than 1 and were included in an oblique (oblimin) rotation procedure (Table 13.2).

Table 13.2 shows the component pattern matrix for the first subsample ($n_1 = 836$) after the oblique rotation. The two factors are labeled *stressful climate* and *engaged climate* to reflect the scales that most highly correlate with them. The *stressful climate* factor is defined by Role Overload ("The amount of work I have to do keeps me from doing a good job"), Role Conflict ("I have to do things on the job that are against my better judgment"), and Emotional Exhaustion ("I feel emotionally drained from my work"). The *engaged climate* factor is defined by Personal Accomplishment ("I have accomplished many worthwhile things in this job") and by the *inverse* of Depersonalization ("I've become more callous toward people since I took this job").

A CFA was conducted with the second subsample of respondents ($n_2 = 860$) to confirm the two second-order factors. A CFA of the proposed measurement model shown in Figure 13.1 was conducted with LISREL 8, using maximum likelihood estimation procedures (Jöreskog & Sörbom, 2005). The measurement model included the individual items of the five scales as indicators of the first-order factors: the scales measuring personal accomplishment, depersonalization, emotional exhaustion, role overload, and role conflict. The two second-order factors were specified as *(1)* engaged climate (formed by personal accomplishment and the inverse of depersonalization); and *(2)* stressful climate (formed by role overload, role conflict, and emotional exhaustion). The two second-order factors were allowed to correlate, and correlations among the error terms for the indicators (i.e., scale items) were constrained to zero. With strategies described by Bollen (1989), Byrne (1998), and others, the objective was to confirm the five first-order latent constructs as measured by their respective scale items (using responses to items for each scale as manifest indicators of the first-order factors) and the two second-order factors (engaged climate and stressful climate) that were identified in the EFA.

The coefficients associated with the paths represented in Figure 13.1 and the scale reliabilities in the second half of the sample are reported (Table 13.3). All item coefficients were between .40 and .89, scale reliabilities were between .69 and .90, and second-order coefficients were between .56 and 1.00. The coefficients and reliabilities in Table 13.3, together with the fit indices (Table 13.4), support the two second-order and five first-order factors. Fit indices in Table 13.4 include the

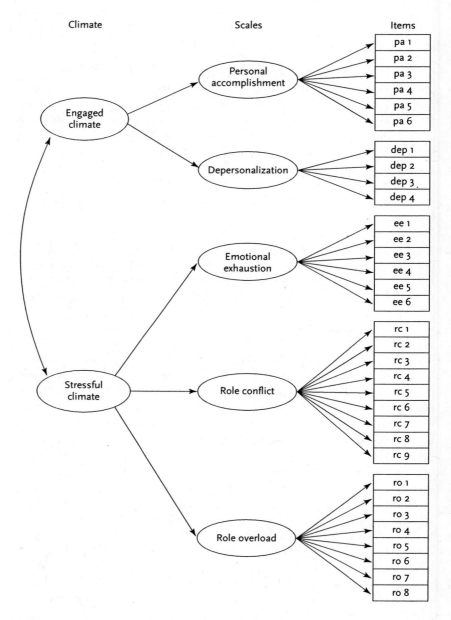

Figure 13.1 Second-order confirmatory factor analysis with second subsample of caseworkers ($n_2 = 860$).

Table 13.3   CFA Measurement Model With Second Subsample ($n_2 = 860$)

Second-Order Factors	First-Order Factors—Scales		Scale Items
Engaged climate		Reliabilities	
1.000	Personal accomplishment	.72	
	.598		pa 1
	.792		pa 2
	.531		pa 3
	.427		pa 4
	.776		pa 5
	.403		pa 6
.556	Depersonalization (reversed)	.69	
	.544		dep 1
	.839		dep 2
	.816		dep 3
	.486		dep 4
Stressful climate			
.816	Emotional exhaustion	.90	
	.873		ee 1
	.817		ee 2
	.830		ee 3
	.893		ee 4
	.721		ee 5
	.805		ee 6
.975	Role conflict	.83	
	.634		rc 1
	.551		rc 2
	.730		rc 3
	.629		rc 4
	.491		rc 5
	.622		rc 6
	.732		rc 7
	.642		rc 8
	.659		rc 9
.931	Role overload	.82	
	.651		ro 1
	.510		ro 2
	.612		ro 3
	.762		ro 4
	.610		ro 5
	.752		ro 6
	.720		ro 7
	.759		ro 8

CFA, confirmatory factor analysis.

standardized root mean squared residual (SRMR), root mean square error of approximation (RMSEA), comparative fit index (CFI), and other fit indices. These indices include absolute indices (SRMR, RMSEA), as well as an incremental fit index (CFI) in which the hypothesized model is assessed in comparison with a

Table 13.4   CFA Fit Indices for Second Subsample ($n_2 = 860$)

Index	Value
Root mean square error of approximation (RMSEA)	.070
Normed fit index (NFI)	.955
Non-normed fit index (NNFI)	.960
Comparative fit index (CFI)	.963
Incremental fit index (IFI)	.963
Relative fit index (RFI)	.951
Standardized root mean square residual (SRMR)	.078

CFA, confirmatory factor analysis.

null model. Because different indices can provide different information and are sensitive to different aspects of model fit, multiple indices were examined. For example, SRMR is more sensitive to the specified factor covariance structure, and RMSEA is more sensitive to the specified factor loadings (Hu & Bentler, 1999).

Guidelines for evaluating models with fit indices specify CFI > .90 for acceptable model fit in applied social science research (Byrne, 1998). Applied guidelines specify acceptable fit for RMSEA < .10, moderate fit for RMSEA < .08, and close fit for RMSEA < .05 (Browne & Cudeck, 1993; MacCallum, Browne, & Sugawara, 1996). Hu & Bentler (1999) recommend a cutoff value for SRMR of .08 or less to be used with either a cutoff value of close to .95 for CFI or a cutoff value close to .06 for RMSEA. Using these guidelines, the fit indices in Table 13.4 provide support for the proposed measurement model that specifies climate as composed of two second-order factors which are labeled here as *engaged climate* and *stressful climate*. This factor structure for the scales selected for NSCAW replicates the OSC factor structure confirmed in a previous nationwide study of mental health clinics (Glisson, Landsverk et al., 2008).

Within-Group Consistency

To describe the level of agreement among the caseworkers associated with each of the 88 child welfare agency service systems, an index of within-group consistency of responses, r_{wg}, was computed for each of the five climate scales (Glisson & James, 2002; James et al., 1993). The range of indices and averages across the child welfare agencies are reported for each construct (Table 13.5). The r_{wg} values for five scales range between .68 and .98 across the individual agencies, with agency averages for each scale ranging between .83 and .93. These values indicate an acceptable level of within-group consistency of responses in this sample of child welfare agencies. That is, child welfare caseworkers associated with specific agency service systems agree in their perceptions of the psychological impact of their work. These values and the CFA results already described, together with the between-group differences described next, justify aggregation of caseworker-level responses to measure agency-level organizational climate.

Table 13.5   Within-Agency Consistency Analysis for Caseworkers in 88 Agencies ($n = 1,696$)

Construct	r_{wg}		
	Min.	*Max.*	*Average*
Personal accomplishment	.75	.98	.93
Depersonalization	.68	.96	.84
Emotional exhaustion	.68	.97	.83
Role conflict	.71	.96	.90
Role overload	.78	.96	.89

Between-Group Differences

Caseworker perceptions of the impact of their work must differ by agency service system if agency-level climate is to explain criterion variance at the level of the individual. Between-agency differences in caseworkers' responses to the climate scales were calculated using the ICC and eta-squared. The ICC (type 1) computed by way of a random effects model indicates the proportion of total *variance* that can be attributed to the child welfare agency; ANOVA-based eta-squared indicates the proportion of total *variation* that can be attributed to the agency (see Bliese, 2000; Cohen & Cohen, 1983; Raudenbush & Bryk, 2002). Typically, type 1 ICC values are much smaller than eta-squared values (Bliese, 2000). In this analysis, the ICC values were indeed small, but statistically significant, indicating that a proportion of the variance in responses to the climate scales is attributable to the child welfare agency in which the caseworkers were employed (.02 to .07; Table 13.6). The eta-squared values indicate that the proportion of total variation in responses that is attributable to agency is somewhat larger (.06 to .12) and also statistically significant. The square roots of these values are equivalent to correlations of .24 to .35 between the agency and its caseworkers' responses to the climate scales.

The total scores of the scales that composed each of the two second-order factors were summed to yield values for each: *Stressful climate* was computed by

Table 13.6   Between-Agency Analysis for Caseworkers in 88 Agencies ($n = 1,696$)

Construct	Agency Variance	Agency Variance	ICC	MS_{BG}	MS_{WG}	Eta Squared
Personal accomplishment	.14	9.28	.02*	1007.77	14714.89	.06*
Depersonalization	.12	7.14	.02*	841.47	11447.27	.07*
Emotional exhaustion	.72	25.91	.03**	3467.65	41633.42	.08***
Role conflict	1.46	34.84	.04***	5612.77	55861.11	.09***
Role overload	2.17	27.94	.07***	5992.60	44720.62	.12***

$^*p < .05, ^{**}p < .01, ^{***}p < .001.$

summing the caseworkers' responses to the Role Overload, Role Conflict, and Emotional Exhaustion scales; *engaged climate* was computed by summing the caseworkers' responses to the Personal Accomplishment scale and the inverse of the Depersonalization scale. Organizational climate measures operationalized as *stressful climate* and *engaged climate* were then composed for each agency by aggregating by agency the caseworkers' scores on the specified scales. These agency compositions were used in the analyses of relationships between the agency-level climate measures (*engaged climate* and *stressful climate*) and the individual-level criterion (children's psychosocial functioning).

Hierarchical Linear Models

In accordance with strategies outlined in Hedeker and Gibbons (2006) and Raudenbush and Bryk (2002), two three-level HLM analyses (an unweighted analysis and an analysis incorporating probability sampling weights at all three levels) were conducted to test the hypothesized relationships between organizational climate (i.e., stress, engagement) and the individual-level outcomes of child-level psychosocial functioning. The multilevel analyses were conducted with the use of maximum likelihood estimation (Hofmann, Griffin, & Gavin, 2000; Raudenbush & Bryk, 2002). Among other information, the mixed-effects hierarchical analyses provides *(1)* estimates of the association between child-level characteristics and child-level outcome criteria, *(2)* estimates of the incremental proportions of variance in child-level outcomes explained by agency-level characteristics and child-level characteristics, and *(3)* estimates of the cross-level association of the dimensions of organizational climate with child outcomes.

In Level 1 of the three-level analysis, the time that the CBCL was administered (measured as months from the initial investigation) was the predictor of the raw CBCL Total Problems score for each child. In Level 2, child-level covariates (e.g., initial harm level, age, gender, racial or ethnic group, family income) were added to control for the association of these variables with the child's psychosocial functioning at baseline and with the trend or growth in the child's psychosocial functioning over time. In Level 3, agency-level covariates (stressful climate, engaged climate, urban location) were added to estimate the relationships that link each agency-level variable with the child-level trend in functioning over Waves 1, 3, and 4, after controlling for the effects of the child-level covariates.

The first of the two three-level analyses did not incorporate probability sampling weights. At Level 1, the "time level," raw CBCL Total Problems scores were examined as a function of the number of months since the initial investigation. Wave 1 CBCL scores were obtained an average of 4 months after the initial child maltreatment investigation, Wave 3 CBCL scores were obtained at 18 months, and Wave 4 CBCL scores were obtained at 36 months. The average raw CBCL Total Problems scores decreased (i.e., improved) slightly ($-.143$) each month, with an overall average decrease of 5 points [$-.143 \times 36 = -5.148$] over 36 months (Table 13.7). However, this trend varied significantly by agency, and

Table 13.7 Unweighted Three-Level HLM Random Intercepts and Slopes Analysis of Children's Psychosocial Functioning (Unconditional Model at Levels 2 and 3)

Fixed Effect	Coefficient	SE	t Ratio	p Value
Average initial psychosocial functioning (CBCL) level	43.527***	.941	46.278	.000
Average change per month in psychosocial functioning (CBCL) level	−.143	.030	−4.741	.000

Random Effect	Variance Component	df	x^2	p Value
Level 2 (children)				
Initial functioning	520.732***	1398	3666.489	.000
Change per month	.194***	1398	1942.228	.000
Level 3 (agency)				
Mean agency initial functioning level	26.645**	86	134.505	.001
Mean agency change in functioning	.027**	86	134.805	.001

Level 1 Coefficient	Percentage of Variance Between Agencies
Initial functioning level	4.87
Change in functioning	12.22

$*p < .05, **p < .01, ***p < .001.$
CBCL, Child Behavior Checklist; HLM, hierarchal linear modeling.

both child- and organizational-level variables explained variance in the trends or growth curves for each child. As shown in Table 13.7, the proportion of between-agency variance in the children's change in functioning was almost three times the proportion of between-agency variance in the children's baseline functioning. In other words, more variability was found from agency to agency in the children's rate of change than in their initial functioning, which is evidence that child outcomes varied by child welfare agency.

The trend or growth in the children's psychosocial functioning varied as a function of agency location and agency climate, after controlling for harm level and child demographics (Table 13.8). Children served by agencies in urban locations experienced less improvement over time; children served by agencies with more engaged climates experienced more improvement (lower CBCL scores) over time. Controlling for initial differences, harm level, and child demographics, over a 36-month period after the investigation, children served by agencies in urban areas are predicted to have CBCL Total Problem scores that increase 5 points (.152 × 36 = 5.472) more (i.e., worse) than children served by agencies in nonurban areas.

Controlling for baseline differences, harm level, and child demographics, the difference between the estimated raw CBCL score at 36 months in the least engaged climate (engagement score of 29.42) and most engaged climate (engagement score of 39.67) is 15.87 points [(39.67 − 29.42)(−.043)(36 months) = 15.867]. The change in child functioning over the 36-month period that is associated with organizational climate can be illustrated with specific children's profiles. As shown in Table 13.9,

Table 13.8 Unweighted Three-Level HLM Random Intercepts and Slopes Analysis of Children's Psychosocial Functioning

Fixed Effect	Coefficient	SE	t Ratio	p Value
Child's functioning at initial investigation (intercept at month = 0)				
Intercept	28.938***	2.847	10.166	.000
Urban agency	−1.996	1.986	−1.005	.318
Child age	1.289***	.197	6.543	.000
Female	−5.644***	1.440	−3.920	.000
Income	.225	.199	1.130	.259
Hispanic	−4.323*	1.982	−2.181	.029
American Indian/Alaska Native	−7.209	4.558	−1.582	.114
Asian	−8.819	7.124	−1.238	.216
African American	−3.361	1.809	−1.859	.063
Hawaiian/Pacific Islander	−12.014	6.897	−1.742	.081
Harm level	2.880***	.770	3.741	.000
Change in child's functioning per month (slope for month)				
Intercept	1.759*	.796	2.209	.030
Urban agency	.152*	.062	2.437	.017
Engaged climate	−.043**	.016	−2.678	.009
Stressful climate	−.004	.005	−.685	.495
Child age	−.021**	.008	−2.757	.006
Female	−.003	.048	−.059	.954
Income	−.004	.007	−.597	.550
Hispanic	−.088	.076	−1.159	.247
American Indian/Alaska Native	.013	.151	.086	.932
Asian	.003	.312	.010	.992
African American	−.001	.059	−.024	.981
Hawaiian/Pacific Islander	.414	.332	1.248	.212
Harm level	−.002	.029	−.061	.952

Random Effect	Variance Component	df	x^2	p Value
Level 2 (children)				
Initial functioning	488.147***	1389	3582.632	.000
Change per month	.187***	1389	1934.375	.000
Level 3 (agency)				
Mean agency initial functioning level	17.819*	85	116.877	.012
Mean agency change in functioning	.021**	83	125.128	.002

Level 1 Coefficient	Percentage of Variance Explained at Child Level	Percentage of Variance Explained at Agency Level
Initial functioning level	6.25	33.12
Change in functioning	3.61	22.22

*p < .05, **p < .01, ***p < .001.
HLM, hierarchal linear modeling.

Table 13.9   Estimated CBCL T Scores 36 Months After Initial Investigation as a
Function of Organizational Climate

Children's Profiles	HLM Model	Least Engaged Climate	Most Engaged Climate
White male in urban location with average baseline	Weighted	70*	56
values on family income, harm level, and age	Unweighted	67*	58
African American female in urban location with	Weighted	65*	51
average baseline values on family income, harm	Unweighted	63*	55
level, and age			

*CBCL T score above clinical borderline of 60–63.
CBCL, Child Behavior Checklist; HLM, hierarchal linear modeling.

among children with average values on age, baseline CBCL, family income, and
initial harm level, a white, non-Hispanic male served by an urban agency with the
least engaged organizational climate (i.e., the lowest *engaged climate* score in the
sample of 29.42) is predicted to have a CBCL raw score at 36 months of 52.65 and a *T*
score of 67, well above the clinical borderline of 60 to 63. If served by an urban agency
with the most engaged organizational climate (i.e., the highest engaged climate score
in the sample of 39.67), the same boy is predicted to have a raw score at 36 months of
36.77 and a *T* score of 58, which is below the clinical range of the CBCL.

Referring to the second example shown in Table 13.9, an African American
female who is in the unweighted analysis with average values on age, baseline CBCL,
family income, and harm level and who is served by an urban agency with the least
engaged organizational climate, is expected to have a CBCL raw score at 36 months
of 43.50 and *T* score of 63, which is at the top of the clinical cut-score of 60 to 63. For
comparison, the same girl served by an urban agency with the most engaged
organizational climate would have an expected CBCL total raw score at 36 months
of 27.62 and *T* score of 55, which is below the clinical range on the CBCL.

To estimate population coefficients linking child and agency characteristics to
outcomes among children served by child welfare systems nationwide, a three-level
HLM analysis of the same model was conducted with probability sampling weights at
all three levels. The weighted analysis assessed the same model used in the
unweighted analysis. For the weighted analysis, three sets of sampling weights were
generated from the population sampling units for the three levels of the analysis,
represented by measurement occasion or time at the first level, the child at the second
level, and the child welfare agency at the third level. The agency was defined as the
child welfare region within which the services were delivered. Nationwide, child
welfare services are provided within formally defined regions that, as illustrated by
the caseworkers' responses shown in Tables 13.5 and Table 13.6, create organizational climates that distinguish one agency service region from another. Child welfare
agency service regions are structured most frequently by county, but highly populated counties encompass more than one service region, and, in areas of sparsely
populated counties, more than one county is included in a service region.

Table 13.10   Weighted Three-Level HLM Random Intercepts and Slopes Analysis of Children's Psychosocial Functioning (Unconditional Model at Levels 2 and 3)

Fixed Effect	Coefficient	SE	t Ratio	p Value
Average initial psychosocial functioning (CBCL) level	42.998***	1.749	24.586	.000
Average change per month in psychosocial functioning (CBCL) level	−.146	.057	−2.567	.012

Random Effect	Variance Component	df	x^2	p Value
Level 2 (children)				
Initial functioning	118.195***	1323	1018434.395	.000
Change per month	.102***	1323	525644.541	.000
Level 3 (agency)				
Mean agency initial functioning level	63.997***	85	2104.666	.000
Mean agency change in functioning	.065***	85	1393.749	.000

Level 1 Coefficient	Percentage of Variance Between Agencies
Initial functioning level	35.13
Change in functioning	38.92

*p < .05, **p < .01, ***p < .001.
CBCL, Child Behavior Checklist; HLM, hierarchal linear modeling.

The weighted findings replicate the findings for organizational climate reported for the unweighted analysis (Tables 13.10 and 13.11). These results indicate, again, that the between-agency variance in the change in children's functioning after the initial investigation is greater than the between-agency variance in the functioning of the children at the time of the initial investigation. This is to say that the children served by different agencies are more similar in functioning when they are first referred for services than they are after receiving services. This provides support for the assertion that child welfare agencies are not equally successful in improving the well-being of the children they serve; moreover, the weighted results estimate that an even larger portion of the variance in children's change in total problem behavior is a function of the particular agency (39%).

As shown in Table 13.10, the findings in the weighted analysis replicate the finding in the unweighted analysis that children who were served by agencies with the most engaged climates experienced better outcomes than those who were served by the least engaged climates. In the weighted analysis, after controlling for child demographics and agency location, the difference between the estimated raw CBCL Total Problems score at 36 months among children served in the least engaged climate (engagement score of 29.42) and those served in the most engaged climate (engagement score of 39.67) is 28.04 points [(39.67 − 29.42) (.076) (36 months) = 28.04], more than 12 points greater than the difference estimated

Table 13.11 Weighted Three-Level HLM Random Intercepts and Slopes Analysis of Children's Psychosocial Functioning

Fixed Effect	Coefficient	SE	t Ratio	p Value
Child's functioning at initial investigation (intercept at month = 0)				
Intercept	36.376***	8.092	4.495	.000
Urban agency	−2.790	3.203	−.871	.386
Child age	1.702***	.333	5.111	.000
Female	−8.498***	2.266	−3.751	.000
Income	.007	.432	.016	.987
Hispanic	−4.406	4.745	−.927	.354
American Indian/Alaska Native	.702	11.635	.060	.952
Asian	−1.642	6.506	−.252	.801
African American	−4.575	3.261	−1.403	.161
Hawaiian/Pacific Islander	−21.285	11.148	−1.909	.056
Harm level	−.383	2.097	−.183	.855
Change in child's functioning per month (slope for month)				
Intercept	3.250*	1.627	1.997	.049
Urban agency	.218*	.097	2.256	.027
Engaged climate	−.076*	.038	−2.006	.048
Stressful climate	−.010	.008	−1.300	.198
Child age	−.031**	.010	−3.153	.002
Female	.063	.077	.810	.418
Income	.008	.011	.706	.480
Hispanic	−.080	.064	−1.248	.213
American Indian/Alaska Native	.050	.420	.118	.906
Asian	−.015	.164	−.090	.929
African American	−.011	.095	−.112	.912
Hawaiian/Pacific Islander	.644*	.274	2.348	.019
Harm level	.036	.035	1.019	.309

Random Effect	Variance Component	df	x^2	p Value
Level 2 (children)				
Initial functioning	109.831*	1314	983976.552	.000
Change per month	.100***	1314	522115.772	.000
Level 3 (agency)				
Mean agency initial functioning level	53.138***	84	2062.362	.000
Mean agency change in functioning	.051***	82	1721.674	.000

Level 1 Coefficient	Percentage of Variance Explained at Child Level	Percentage of Variance Explained at Agency Level
Initial functioning level	7.08	16.97
Change in functioning	1.96	21.54

*p < .05, **p < .01, ***p < .001.
HLM, hierarchal linear modeling.

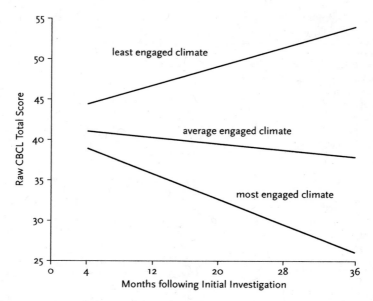

Figure 13.2   Graph from weighted three-level HLM analysis of raw CBCL total problems scores as a function of time × engaged climate. CBCL, Child Behavior Checklist; HLM, hierarchal linear modeling.

in the unweighted analysis. This difference is illustrated with the HLM graphing feature for the three-level weighted model (Fig. 13.2).

Figure 13.2 illustrates the change in psychosocial functioning for children served by agency systems with the least engagement, the average level of engagement, and the most engagement. The gap between the extremes of the graphs at 36 months equals a difference of 28 points on the raw CBCL Total Problems score adjusted for the child's age, gender, race, level of harm, and family income. The weighted analysis provides a larger estimate of the clinical significance of the association between climate and children's outcomes than the unweighted analysis, and additional evidence that the relationship between climate and outcomes can be generalized to the population of children served by child welfare agencies nationwide.

A second graph, also generated by the HLM analysis of the weighted three-level model, illustrates the association between organizational climate and children's outcomes (Fig. 13.3). In this graph, the trends or growth curves for children served by child welfare systems in the lowest and highest quartiles of engagement show a difference in children's functioning at 36 months of approximately 13 points as measured by raw CBCL Total Problems scores. The graph shows that the children served by 25% of the child welfare systems that had the least engaged climates in the sample had losses in functioning (i.e., increased problem scores) over a 3-year period. Moreover, the graph shows that the children served by the 25% of the child welfare systems that had the most engaged climates in the sample made significant gains in functioning (i.e., decreased problem scores).

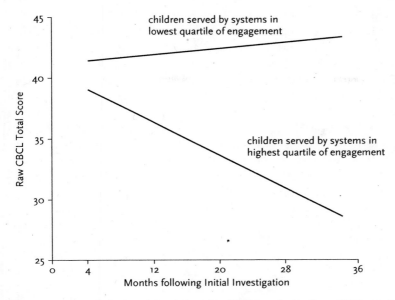

Figure 13.3 Graph from weighted three-level HLM analysis of raw CBCL total problems scores as a function of time × engaged climate. CBCL, Child Behavior Checklist; HLM, hierarchal linear modeling.

Discussion

The study's most important finding is that improvements in psychosocial functioning are significantly greater for maltreated children served by child welfare systems with more positive organizational climates (e.g., engaged climates that caseworkers describe as high in personal accomplishment and low in depersonalization), after controlling for the initial harm to the child as assessed by the investigative caseworker, the child's baseline functioning, age, gender, family income, race, and the agency's location (urban versus nonurban). The differences in outcomes between the agencies with the best and worst climates are both clinically and statistically significant, as illustrated with the statistical significance of the coefficients for engaged climate in the two analyses, differences in CBCL *T* scores for selected children's profiles shown in Table 13.9, and the graphs of raw CBCL scores in Figures 13.2 and 13.3.

The association documented between organizational climate at the agency level and service outcomes at the children's level is particularly important because the measures of these two constructs, climate on the one hand and service outcomes on the other, as well as the assessment of initial harm, relied on independent measurement methods and ratings by three independent sources. Harm was assessed by the investigative caseworker, outcomes were assessed by the child's primary caregiver at the time of each assessment, and organizational climate was measured as an aggregation of the perceptions of caseworkers who provided child welfares services in the system that served the child. The common method error variance that plagues much of the research using related techniques does not account for any portion of the covariance between the constructs assessed here.

Caseworkers' success in providing child welfare services depends heavily on their consideration of each child's and family's unique needs, their availability and responsiveness, their attention to unexpected problems and crises, and their tenacity in navigating bureaucratic and judicial hurdles to provide the most needed services or most appropriate residential placement for each child. Meeting these challenges requires individualized casework, personalized relationships between the caseworker and child, and a sustained focus on achieving the best results for each child (Glisson, 1992; Glisson et al., 2006; Glisson & Hemmelgarn, 1998). The current findings suggest that caseworkers who provide services in child welfare systems that have more engaged climates (i.e., in which caseworkers describe high levels of personal accomplishment and low levels of depersonalization) are more likely to meet these challenges. This study replicates with national data previous findings linking climate and outcomes in a regional study of child welfare offices (Glisson & Hemmelgarn, 1998).

This study also contributes to knowledge about organizational climate in several areas. First, the NSCAW sample of child welfare agencies provided a rare opportunity to examine the factor structure of organizational climate across a large, nationwide sample of caseworkers, with use of a well-established instrument (OSC; Glisson, Landsverk et al., 2008). This finding is important because previous factor analyses with smaller samples and fewer organizations found that climate scales defined a single second-order dimension. After randomly dividing the present sample of 88 agencies into two groups of 44 agencies each, an exploratory factor analysis of the scale scores of 836 caseworkers in the first group identified two second-order factors; these factors were confirmed in a second-order CFA of the responses of 860 caseworkers in the second group.

Previous studies of smaller samples found that the organizational climate of child welfare case management teams predicted work attitudes, service quality, and service outcomes (Glisson & Green, 2006; Glisson & Hemmelgarn, 1998; Glisson & James, 2002). The current study is the first, however, to examine the cross-level effects of organizational climate with a national sample of child welfare agencies, and it adds significantly to previous studies that describe the effects of work environment on child welfare services.

Some limitations warrant mention, among them the limited number of climate scales included in the study and the nonexperimental nature of the research design. The study included five climate scales, but the findings cannot be generalized to climate indicators that were not included in NSCAW. The climate scales selected for the study predicted service quality, service outcomes, and work attitudes in previous studies (Glisson & Durick, 1988; Glisson & Hemmelgarn, 1998; Glisson & James, 2002); however, other scales could provide different findings on the effect of climate on individual-level criteria.

Although the HLM approach provides an ideal model for assessing the nested data used to examine the cross-level association of organizational characteristics with individual outcome criteria, the research design does not support true causal inferences. Two of the three criteria for causal inference were met for the association between organizational climate and improvements in the children's psychosocial functioning. Organizational climate was assessed at Wave 2 before the children's psychosocial outcomes were assessed at Waves 3 and 4, so the hypothesized cause preceded the effect, and a significant cross-level association between climate and service outcomes was found in both three-level HLM analyses; however, without the benefit of random assignment and the experimental manipulation of climate, unmeasured variables that could explain the association between organizational climate and service outcomes remain uncontrolled.

Conclusion

The findings of this study emphasize the need for more information about the links between organizational climate and service outcomes. Although the evidence is growing that social and mental health service organizational characteristics, such as organizational climate, affect service outcomes, much remains to be learned about the mechanisms that explain this effect. The findings also point to the need for more information about how the organizational climates of child welfare agencies can be improved. A randomized controlled study of an organizational intervention designed to improve the climates of mental health and social service organizations—labeled ARC for Availability, Responsiveness, and Continuity—found that the planned organizational intervention lowered caseworker turnover by two thirds and significantly improved organizational climate in child welfare case management teams (Glisson et al., 2006). A second randomized controlled study of ARC found that the organizational intervention improved both system and clinical outcomes of an evidence-based, youth mental health treatment program implemented in 14 counties (Glisson, Schoenwald, Hemmelgarn et al., 2009). However, much more work remains before researchers understand how such effects can be sustained and translated into better service outcomes across a variety of mental health and social service agencies.

With this study based on national NSCAW data, it is increasingly apparent that the organizational characteristics of child welfare systems are associated with service quality and outcomes. Understanding the mechanisms of this effect, however, and identifying the ways positive organizational climates can be created and sustained in the work environments of child welfare agencies belong to the future of child welfare research. Although work has begun on designing and testing organizational intervention strategies for creating positive organizational climates, and though the results of the first true experiments are promising, additional experimental studies of organizational interventions are required to fully explore the potential benefits of such interventions for improving the work environments and, consequently, the service outcomes of child welfare systems.

NOTES

1. *Substantiation* is the child welfare system's official case decision that allegations of child maltreatment are valid.
2. The NSCAW study design that guided the selection of the child welfare agencies, case-workers, and children in the current study, as well as the interview protocols used in NSCAW, has been fully described elsewhere (Burns et al., 2004; Dowd et al., 2006; NSCAW Research Group, 2002). See, especially, Chapter 1 of this volume.
3. The current study excludes one of the original 97 agencies because the children sampled in that agency did not meet the criteria of being aged 4 to 15 years and having substantiated cases of maltreatment. Also excluded were five agencies because the small number of caseworkers (i.e., one or two) surveyed from those agencies was inadequate to assess organizational climate. Three additional agencies were excluded because the sampled caseworkers provided markedly inconsistent responses in their perceptions of organizational climate, resulting in an unacceptable *rwg* statistic (Glisson & James, 2002).
4. The age of the children selected at baseline was restricted to a minimum of 4 years because of the difficulty in obtaining valid, sensitive assessments of the psychosocial functioning of children younger than 4 years in field studies of this type and because different instruments were used to assess the psychosocial functioning of children younger than 4 years. Some states have a third case disposition, *indicated,* which means evidence of child maltreatment exists but is insufficient to substantiate the allegations.

REFERENCES

Achenbach, T. M. (1991). *Manual for the Child Behavior Checklist/4-18 and 1991 profile.* Burlington, VT: University of Vermont, Department of Psychiatry.

Administration for Children and Families. (2004). *Summary of the results of the 2001–2004 child and family service reviews.* Retrieved August 15, 2008, from http://www.acf.hhs.gov/programs/cb/cwmonitoring/results/index.htm.

Administration for Children and Families. (2006a). Adoption and foster care analysis and reporting system (AFCARS) interim 2003 estimates as of June 2006. *The AFCARS report.* Retrieved August 15, 2008, from http://www.acf.hhs.gov/programs/cb/stats_research/afcars/tar/report10.htm

Administration for Children and Families. (2006b). *Child maltreatment 2004.* Retrieved December 23, 2008, from http://www.acf.hhs.gov/programs/cb

Bliese, P. (2000). Within-group agreement, non-independence, and reliability. In K. Klein & S. Kozlowski (Eds.), *Multi-level theory, research, and methods in organizations* (pp. 349–381). San Francisco: Jossey-Bass.

Bollen, K. A. (1989). *Structural equations with latent variables.* New York: Wiley.

Brown, S. P., & Leigh, T. W. (1996). A new look at psychological climate and its relationship to job involvement, effort, and performance. *Journal of Applied Psychology, 81*(4), 358–368.

Browne, M. W., & Cudeck, R. (1993). Alternative ways of assessing model fit. In K. A. Bollen & J. S. Long (Eds.), *Testing structural equation models* (pp. 136–162). Newbury Park, CA: Sage Publications.

Burns, B. J., Phillips, S. D., Wagner, H. R., Barth, R. P., Kolko, D. J., Campbell, Y., et al. (2004). Mental health need and access to mental health services by youth involved with child welfare: A national survey. *Journal of the American Academy of Child and Adolescent Psychiatry, 43*(8), 960–970.

Byrne, B. M. (1998). *Structural equation modeling with LISREL, PRELIS, and SIMPLIS: Basic concepts, applications, and programming.* Mahwah, NJ: Erlbaum.

Chan, D. (1998). Functional relations among constructs in the same content domain at different levels of analysis: A typology of composition models. *Journal of Applied Psychology, 83,* 234–246.

Cohen, J., & Cohen, P. (1983). *Applied multiple regression/correlation analysis for the behavioral sciences* (2nd ed.). Hillsdale, NJ: Erlbaum.

Cyphers, G. (2001). *Report from the Child Welfare Workforce Survey: State and county data and findings.* Washington, DC: American Public Human Services Association.

Dowd, K., Kinsey, S., Wheeless, S., Thissen, R., Richardson, J., Suresh, R., et al. (2006). *National Survey of Child and Adolescent Well-Being combined Waves 1–4 data file users' manual, restricted release version.* Ithaca, NY: National Data Archive on Child Abuse and Neglect, Cornell University.

Dozier, M., Cue, K. L., & Barnett, L. (1994). Clinicians as caregivers: Role of attachment organization in treatment. *Journal of Consulting and Clinical Psychology, 62,* 793–800.

Edmondson, A. C., Bohmer, R. M., & Pisano, G. P. (2001). Disrupted routines: Team learning and new technology implementation in hospitals. *Administrative Science Quarterly, 46,* 685–716.

Glisson, C. (1992). Structure and technology in human service organizations. In Y. Hasenfeld (Ed.), *Human services as complex organizations.* Beverly Hills, CA: Sage Publications.

Glisson, C. (2002). The organizational context of children's mental health services. *Clinical Child and Family Psychology Review, 5*(4), 233–253.

Glisson, C. (2008). Organizational climate, job satisfaction, and service outcomes in child welfare agencies. In R. Patti (Ed.), *Handbook of human services management* (pp. 119–141). Thousand Oaks, CA: Sage Publications.

Glisson, C., Dukes, D., & Green, P. (2006). The effects of the ARC organizational intervention on caseworker turnover, climate, and culture in children's service systems. *Child Abuse & Neglect, 30*(8), 855–880.

Glisson, C., & Durick, M. (1988). Predictors of job satisfaction and organizational commitment in human service organizations. *Administrative Science Quarterly, 33,* 61–81.

Glisson, C., & Green, P. (2006). The effects of organizational culture and climate on the access to mental health care in child welfare and juvenile justice systems. *Administration and Policy in Mental Health and Mental Health Services Research, 33*(4), 433–448.

Glisson, C., & Hemmelgarn, A. (1998). The effects of organizational climate and interorganizational coordination on the quality and outcomes of children's service systems. *Child Abuse & Neglect, 22*(5), 401–421.

Glisson, C., & James, L. R. (2002). The cross-level effects of culture and climate in human service teams. *Journal of Organizational Behavior, 23,* 767–794.

Glisson, C., Landsverk, J. A., Schoenwald, S. K., Kelleher, K. J., Hoagwood, K. E., Mayberg, S., et al. (2008). Assessing the organizational social context (OSC) of mental health services: Implications for research and practice. *Administration and Policy in Mental Health and Mental Health Services Research, 35,* 98–113.

Glisson, C., Schoenwald, S. K., Hemmelgarn, A., Green, P., Dukes, D., Chapman, J. E., et al. (2009). The effectiveness of MST and ARC in a two level strategy for implementing EBT based mental health services for delinquent youth. Manuscript submitted for publication.

Glisson, C., Schoenwald, S., Kelleher, K., Landsverk, J. A., Hoagwood, K. E., Mayberg, S., et al. (2008). Therapist turnover and new program sustainability in mental health clinics as a function of organizational culture, climate, and service structure. Administration and Policy in Mental Health and Mental Health Services Research, 35, 124–133.

Hackman, J. R., & Oldham, G. R. (1975). Development of the Job Diagnostic Survey. Journal of Applied Psychology, 60, 159–170.

Hazen, A. L., Hough, R. L., Landsverk, J. A., & Wood, P. A. (2004). Use of mental health services by youths in public sectors of care. Mental Health Services Research, 6(4), 213–226.

Hedeker, D., & Gibbons, R. D. (2006). Longitudinal data analysis. Hoboken, NJ: Wiley.

Hedeker, D., Gibbons, R. D., & Flay, B. R. (1994). Random-effects regression models for clustered data with an example from smoking prevention research. Journal of Consulting and Clinical Psychology, 62, 757–765.

Hellreigel, D., & Slocum, J., Jr. (1974). Organizational climate: Measures, research, and contingencies. Academy of Management Journal, 17, 255–280.

Herman, J. B., Dunham, R. B., & Hulin, C. L. (1975). Organizational structure, demographic characteristics, and employee responses. Organizational Behavior and Human Performance, 13(2), 206–232.

Herman, J. B., & Hulin, C. L. (1972). Studying organizational attitudes from individual and organizational frames of reference. Organizational Behavior and Human Performance, 8, 84–108.

Hoagwood, K., Burns, B. J., Kiser, L., Ringeisen, H., & Schoenwald, S. (2001). Evidence-based practice in child and adolescent mental health services. Psychiatric Services, 52, 1179–1189.

Hofmann, D. A., Griffin, M. H., & Gavin, M. B. (2000). The application of hierarchical linear modeling to organizational research. In K. J. Klein & S. W. J. Kozlowski (Eds.), Multilevel theory, research and methods in organizations (pp. 467–511). San Francisco: Jossey-Bass.

Hohmann, A. A., & Shear, M. K. (2002). Community-based intervention research: Coping with the "noise" of real life in study design. American Journal of Psychiatry, 159(2), 201–207.

Hu, L., & Bentler, P. M. (1999). Cutoff criteria for fit indexes in covariance structure analysis: Conventional criteria versus new alternatives. Structural Equation Modeling, 6, 1–55.

Huy, Q. N. (2002). Emotional balancing of organizational continuity and radical change: The contribution of middle managers. Administrative Science Quarterly, 47, 31–69.

James, L. A., & James, L. R. (1989). Integrating work environment perceptions: Explorations into the measurement of meaning. Journal of Applied Psychology, 74, 739–751.

James, L. R. (1982). Aggregation bias in estimates of perceptual agreement. Journal of Applied Psychology, 67, 219–229.

James, L. R., Demaree, R. G., & Wolf, G. (1984). Estimating within-group interrater reliability with and without response bias. Journal of Applied Psychology, 69, 85–98.

James, L. R., Demaree, R. G., & Wolf, G. (1993). RWG: An assessment of within-group interrater agreement. Journal of Applied Psychology, 75, 306–309.

James, L. R., James, L. A., & Ashe, D. K. (1990). The meaning of organizations: An essay. In B. Schneider (Ed.), Organizational climate and culture (pp. 40–84). San Francisco: Jossey-Bass.

James, L. R., & Jones, A. P. (1974). Organizational climate: A review of theory and research. *Psychological Bulletin, 81,* 1096–1112.

James, L. R., & Jones, A. P. (1980). Perceived job characteristics and job satisfaction: An examination of reciprocal causation. *Personnel Psychology, 33,* 97–135.

James, L. R., & Williams, L. J. (2000). The cross-level operator in regression, ANCOVA, and contextual analysis. In K. J. Klein & S. W. J. Kozlowski (Eds.), *Multilevel theory, research, and methods in organizations.* San Francisco: Jossey-Bass.

Jensen, P. S. (2003). Commentary: The next generation is overdue. *Journal of the American Academy of Child and Adolescent Psychiatry, 42*(5), 527–530.

Jones, A. P., & James, L. R. (1979). Psychological climate: Dimensions and relationships of individual and aggregated work environment perceptions. *Organizational Behavior and Human Performance, 23,* 201–250.

Jöreskog, K. G., & Sörbom, D. (2005). *LISREL 8 for Windows.* Lincoln, IL: Scientific Software International.

Joyce, W. F., & Slocum, J. W. (1984). Collective climate: Agreement as a basis for defining aggregate climates in organizations. *Academy of Management Journal, 24,* 721–742.

Klein, K. J., & Kozlowski, S. W. J. (2000a). From micro to meso: Critical steps in conceptualizing and conducting multilevel research. *Organizational Research Methods, 3,* 211–236.

Klein, K. J., & Kozlowski, S. W. J. (2000b). *Multilevel theory, research, and methods in organizations.* San Francisco: Jossey-Bass.

MacCallum, R. C., Browne, M., W., & Sugawara, H. M. (1996). Power analysis and deterimination of sample size for covariance structure modeling. *Psychological Methods, 1,* 130–149.

McMahon, R. J. (1994). Diagnosis, assessment, and treatment of externalizing problems in children: The role of longitudinal data. Special section: Childhood psychopathology. *Journal of Consulting and Clinical Psychology, 62*(5), 901–917.

Morris, J. H., & Sherman, J. D. (1981). Generalizability of an organizational commitment model. *Academy of Management Journal, 24,* 512–526.

NSCAW Research Group. (2002). Methodological lessons from the National Survey of Child and Adolescent Well-Being: The first three years of the USA's first national probability study of children and families investigated for abuse and neglect. *Children and Youth Services Review, 24*(6/7), 513–541.

Oilendick, T. H., & King, N. J. (1994). Diagnosis, assessment, and treatment of internalizing problems in children: The role of longitudinal data. *Journal of Consulting and Clinical Psychology, 62,* 918–927.

Ostroff, C., & Schmitt, N. (1993). Configurations of organizational effectiveness and efficiency. *Academy of Management Journal, 36,* 1345–1361.

Payne, R., & Pugh, D. (1975). Organization structure and organization climate. In M. D. Dunnette (Ed.), *Handbook of industrial-organizational psychology* (pp. 1125–1174). Chicago: Rand McNally.

Raudenbush, S. W., & Bryk, A. S. (2002). *Hierarchical linear models: Applications and data analysis methods.* Thousand Oaks, CA: Sage Publications.

Raudenbush, S. W., Bryk, A. S., Cheong, Y., & Congdon, R. T. (2000). *HLM 5: Hierarchical linear and nonlinear modeling.* Chicago: Scientific Software International.

Rentsch, J. R. (1990). Climate and culture: Interaction and qualitative differences in organizational meanings. *Journal of Applied Psychology, 75,* 661–668.

Rousseau, D. M. (1985). Issues of level in organizational research: Multi-level and cross-level perspectives. In B. M. Stow & L. L. Cummings (Eds.), *Research in organizational behavior* (pp. 1–37). Greenwich, CT: JAI Press.

Schneider, B. (1975). Organizational climates: An essay. *Personnel Psychology, 28*, 447–479.

Schoenwald, S. K., & Hoagwood, K. (2001). Effectiveness, transportability, and dissemination of interventions: What matters when? *Psychiatric Services, 52*(9), 1190–1197.

Soloman, E. E. (1986). Private and public sector managers: An empirical investigation of job characteristics and organizational climate. *Journal of Applied Psychology, 71*, 247–259.

U.S. General Accounting Office. (2003). *Child Welfare: HHS could play a greater role in helping child welfare agencies recruit and retain staff* (GAO-03-357). Washington, DC: Author.

Wahler, R. G. (1994). Child conduct problems: Disorders in conduct or social continuity? *Journal of Child & Family Studies, 3*, 14.

14

Information Management, Interagency Collaboration, and Outcomes in Child Welfare Agencies

E. MICHAEL FOSTER, REBECCA WELLS, AND YU BAI

When parents are unable to ensure their children's safety, child welfare agencies have a mandate to intervene. These agencies may be part of the public health and human service bureaucracy or may be private nonprofit organizations that contract with the state or county. In either instance they rely on public funds and are required to pursue their mission in ways specified by legislation (Child Welfare League of America, 1989). Their shared mandates include investigating allegations of abuse or neglect; deciding whether children need to be removed from their homes and, if so, where they will live; and facilitating children's and parents' access to health and human services (Darlington, Feeney, & Rixon, 2004).

Agency services may include counseling, health care, parenting classes, out-of-home placement, and referrals to other health and social service agencies. Regardless of which service or combination of services is provided, however, successful outcomes depend on case management. In effecting case management, child welfare agencies' fundamental challenge is processing information to inform decisions about appropriate placement and service use. Child welfare agencies strive to assess risk accurately, to follow consistent case management procedures, and to track child and family progress. In addition, child welfare agencies coordinate with local health and human service providers to provide services that the agencies do not themselves provide. Such coordination is both essential, in that vulnerable families often have pressing needs for services, and challenging for caseworkers to achieve, given resource scarcities and, frequently, parental ambivalence.

The Need to Balance Competing Values

Because of the many demands child welfare agencies face, a particularly germane conceptualization of their management is the *competing values* framework, whose central premise is that organizations must balance simultaneous emphases on internal factors and on environmental factors, as well as on predictability and on flexibility (Quinn, 1988; Quinn, Faerman, Thompson, & McGrath, 1996; Quinn, Spreitzer, & Hart, 1992). For instance, according to the notion of competing values, child welfare agencies must monitor and coordinate internal processes predictably and efficiently. Ideally, case management decisions will reflect particular child and family situations, not differences in experience or values across caseworkers. At the same time, child welfare agencies frequently do not provide all the services that vulnerable families need. Instead, they must rely on the police and courts to make appropriate referrals, on schools to help children stay academically engaged and frequently to provide mental health services, and on mental health care providers and substance abuse treatment agencies to provide behavioral services to children or caregivers. Child welfare agencies must adjust case management to the availability of local services, as well as develop ties to other child-serving agencies, in hopes of collectively addressing complex needs.

One way child welfare agencies may balance simultaneous needs for internal stability and external adaptation is to develop strong capacities in both internal information processing and interagency collaboration. Structured risk assessment, for example, may help agencies make appropriately consistent decisions about placements and services, while ties with other agencies may help caseworkers attain the services that families need. Conceptually, information processing and interagency collaboration may be viewed in a competing values framework as representing complementary domains of management: the *internal process* model and the *open systems* model. As the name suggests, the internal process model of management emphasizes predictability of internal operations. Within this domain fall tools to support evidence-based decisions about placement and services, formalized procedures for case management, and information systems to track case progress. The internal process model is relevant to child welfare agencies because typically caseworkers must make difficult decisions based on ambiguous information and then track large numbers of families with complex challenges. Systematic information processing tools may overcome the inherent limitations of overworked individual caseworkers.[1]

The internal process model emphasizes control of operations within organizations, whereas the open systems model focuses on adaptation to changing external environments. The open systems model is relevant to child welfare agencies for several reasons. One is that child welfare agencies typically lack sufficient resources to provide children and their families with needed health and social services (U.S. General Accounting Office, 2003). Consequently, collaboration with other child- and parent-serving organizations is critical to supporting children's safety and well-being. Unfortunately, change among local providers may coincide with frequent restructuring of payment systems, as well as high turnover within those external agencies. This combination greatly complicates efforts to provide families with adequate, integrated services (indeed, it often dooms efforts entirely; Steib & Blome, 2004). Child welfare agencies therefore must continually renew and extend relationships with health and social service providers, as well as schools, to address the interrelated obstacles to children's well-being.

Initiatives in the United States have begun to build on the premise that information systems and interagency collaboration are critical to improved child outcomes. Child and Family Services Reviews now required of all states by the U.S. federal government heavily emphasize the use of data for accountability, as well as collaboration with other child-serving agencies. In part because of such extensive external audits, states have made major efforts to improve their automated information systems (Administration for Children and Families, 2007). In addition, one of the most influential movements in the late twentieth century and early twenty-first century child advocacy community has been *systems of care*. Reacting to a perception that vulnerable children were poorly served by fragmented services, these initiatives have sought to improve accountability and facilitate coordination among agencies serving children with serious mental health and related risk factors (Dosser, Handron, McCammon, & Powell, 2001).

One important challenge facing child welfare agencies involves customizing services to the needs of individual children and caregivers. Such tailoring entails both internal information processing and interagency collaboration (with the boundaries between the two depending on how many services the child welfare agency provides; Fig. 14.1). Internally, structured tools for risk assessment, use of

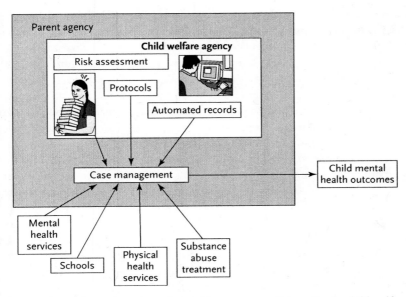

Figure 14.1   Information processing and interagency collaboration in child welfare.

written protocols to guide case-related decisions, and automated records may improve consistency of decisions across similar situations, creating an institutional memory that reduces the impact of caseworker turnover on service continuity. Externally, coordination with other agencies is often vital to procure the services needed for an individual caregiver or child.

Systematic Information Processing

On the basis of complex, ambiguous information, caseworkers must make quick decisions about vulnerable children. Structured risk assessment tools are intended to help overcome individual decision makers' inherent cognitive limitations; they can enhance consistency across caseworkers and the predictive validity of their judgments (Baird & Wagner, 2000). Evidence suggests that structured risk assessments help caseworkers make better decisions about placements (Grove & Meehl, 1996; Shlonsky & Wagner, 2005). Moreover, research has begun to attribute to these practices improved placement outcomes. When a 3-year study, for example, involved examination of nine child welfare agencies implementing a pilot structured decision-making case management system, the intervention agencies experienced improved reunification rates, while similar agencies without the intervention did not. Furthermore, children served by the pilot agencies had no increased risk of subsequent returns to foster care (Johnson & Wagner, 2005).[2]

Other written protocols, such as those addressing placements of siblings and services after reunification, also may enhance consistency. Evidence from mental and physical health care settings indicates that such consistency, again, may improve outcomes. Aarons (2004) found that the presence of written policies regarding treatment of any of four common mental disorders was associated with providers' openness to evidence-based practices, although this study did not trace such practices to child outcomes. In a separate study, therapist adherence to evidence-based practices was associated with improved posttreatment child outcomes (Schoenwald, Sheidow, Letourneau, & Liao, 2003). The literature on hospitals that support excellent nursing practices (called *magnet* hospitals for their ability to attract and retain nurses) also suggests that evidence-based practices are part of a bundle of processes that improve patient outcomes (Scott, Sochalski, & Aiken, 1999).

Case records automation is also often part of broader efforts to improve information processing (e.g., Johnson & Wagner, 2005). Potential benefits of automated records include timelier prompts for case reviews, more complete data to inform decisions, and better continuity when the individuals supervising any given case change. Social workers are often ambivalent about computerized records management, however, especially when they believe such systems slow their work (Moses, Weaver, Furman, & Lindsey, 2003). For this reason, as well as that of inadequate administrative support and lack of end-users' participation in systems development, information systems initiatives may fail to achieve their potential (Savaya, Spiro, Waysman, & Golan, 2004). Overall, evidence suggests that such systematic approaches to internal information processing may enhance agency capacity to tailor services appropriately to children's needs. The effectiveness of such informational capacity, however, arguably hinges on a number of conditions that are frequently not present, including user-friendly interfaces, computer support, adequate training, and customization to agency and case manager needs.

Interagency Collaboration

Interorganizational relationships are "the relatively enduring transactions, flows, and linkages that occur among or between an organization and one or more organizations in its environment" (Oliver, 1990, p. 241). Frequent partners of child welfare agencies include mental health treatment providers, schools (which often provide mental health care), and health and social service agencies (Administration on Children, 2001).

Research sometimes has found interagency collaboration to lead to improved service coordination; such collaboration has yet to be linked, however, to better outcomes for children. One study found that children in foster care who were enrolled in a designated primary care network were more likely to receive all types of health services except inpatient hospitalizations (Jaudes, Bilaver, Goerge, Masterson, & Catania, 2004). Previous analyses on data from the National Survey of Child and Adolescent Well-Being (NSCAW) found that greater levels of coordination between child welfare agencies and mental health treatment providers were associated with stronger correspondence of mental health service need with service receipt and decreased differences in service receipt between non-Hispanic white children and black or African American children (Hurlburt et al., 2004). This study fulfilled a limited focus, however, one that yielded evidence on only one preliminary effect of interorganizational relationships: child welfare agencies' ties to mental health agencies. Moreover, it stopped short of tracing this one effect to child outcomes.

The only study attempting to trace interorganizational relationships to outcomes for youth had a mix of null and negative results: Comparing 12 counties with care coordination teams to 12 comparison counties, all in Tennessee, Glisson and Hemmelgarn (1998) found that interorganizational service coordination in public service systems for children was negatively related to service quality and unrelated to children's psychosocial outcomes. The literature provides no empirical foundation for predicting better child outcomes on the basis of agencies' interorganizational relationships. Nevertheless, intuitively and logically a strong argument persists in the field of child welfare that better coordination leads to better outcomes. Interagency collaboration continues to be the focus of numerous public and private reform efforts. Moreover, linkages to appropriate services are a major focus of Child and Family Services Reviews that are the primary vehicle for federal accountability efforts.

Data Set Characteristics, Test Variables, and Goals

Despite advancements in the child welfare community, the empirical literature linking both internal and interagency management practices to child outcomes is sparse (Glisson & Hemmelgarn, 1998). Little is known about the types of agencies that embrace both an internal process model and an open systems model. Moreover, many other agency processes and external factors (such as service availability) shape what services families receive and how, in turn influencing child outcomes. Our current analyses focus on internal information processing and interagency collaboration as two domains of agency activity necessary to broker between vulnerable families and human services. Our goals are as follows: to determine whether a type of child welfare agency exists that employs both systematic information processing and active interagency collaboration (an *information-collaboration* type); to identify, if this type does exist, the ways it differs from others in terms of structural factors that may affect individual children (e.g., needs of the specific populations served, resource levels, local social service infrastructure); and to assess whether "information-collaboration" agencies achieve more improvement in children's well-being than other agencies.

To fulfill these goals, we use data from NSCAW, the first longitudinal U.S. probability survey on the well-being of children reported to the child welfare system because of allegations of child maltreatment. Data come from Wave 1 (baseline), Wave 2 (12-month follow-up), Wave 3 (18-month follow-up), and Wave 4 (36-month follow-up). We perform agency-level analysis and then multilevel modeling using agency attributes to predict children's mental health status.

Of the 92 agency directors contacted as part of NSCAW, 84 completed the Local Agency Director Interview (LADI), and 70% completed an additional self-administered questionnaire (SAQ) either personally or through other staff. The analyses here eliminated six agencies with extensive data missing resulting in response rates that ranged from 31 (37%) for annual turnover to 84 (100%) for protocol use, with 17.8% being the overall rate for data missing from directors' set of responses. Sequential multiple regressions were used to impute these missing values (Raghunathan, Lepkowski, Hoewyk, & Solenberger, 2001) on the basis of all model data for each agency. The type of each imputation regression depended on the nature of the variable (e.g., binary versus continuous). Ten imputed agency-level data files were in this way generated by 10 iterations.

The initial sample for the multilevel analyses included 3,802 children 2 years or older who had been referred and investigated for maltreatment between October 1999 and December 2000.[3] Data about agency characteristics existed for 3,206. Further restricting the sample to children who received child welfare agency services and for whom agency data were available resulted in a final analytic sample of 2,337 children in 79 agencies. The sample was then split by gender because of previous evidence that factors affecting boys' development differ from those affecting girls' development (e.g., Reinherz, Giaconia, Hauf, Wasserman, & Silverman, 1999).

Methods

Measures

SYSTEMATIC INFORMATION PROCESSING   Three measures from the LADI or SAQ indicated systematic information processing: *(1)* the number of decision junctures at which the agency director indicated caseworkers used structured risk assessments (ranging from decisions about whether to investigate to those concerning whether to reunify a child with a family after an out-of-home placement), *(2)* the number of processes for which written protocols were required (ranging from placement decisions to aftercare services), and *(3)* a yes/no question about whether the agency's case records were automated.[4]

INTERAGENCY COLLABORATION   Two measures were used to indicate the level of interagency collaboration: *(1)* as reported by the director, the number of ways that the agency worked with mental health providers, substance abuse treatment providers, police, juvenile justice, and schools; and *(2)* a yes/no question about whether the agency automatically referred children to health or public health services in cases involving drug-affected infants.[5] Although only a small percentage of child welfare cases involve drug-affected infants, we took this practice to indicate an ongoing case-level connection between child welfare and local health care.

SERVICE DEMAND   The number of reports (including those that were not subsequently investigated) was included in the cluster analysis as a measure of the level of demand for agency services.

POPULATION SERVED   Urban status was reflected through a dummy variable indicating that more than 50% of children were from counties classified as urban by the U.S. Census Bureau in 1990 (Dowd et al., 2006). The percentages of children with clinical-range (scores higher than 63) emotional or behavioral problems according to the Child Behavior Checklist and the percentages of children with chronic health problems as reported by the current caregiver were used to indicate the levels of demands on agency resources.

RESOURCES   A funds-per-child measure was calculated as total agency expenditures in the previous year divided by the number of reports. Funds per child, number of full-time staff equivalents, and staff turnover were included as indications of agencies' financial and human resources; turnover is often high in child welfare (Alliance for Children and Families, 2001), impeding agencies' capacity to help children. Controlling for agency embeddedness in the local health and social services infrastructure isolated the effects of management strategies such as formation of ties with schools and physical and mental health providers: Freestanding entities were assigned a value of 1; units embedded in a larger agency, zero.

EMOTIONAL AND BEHAVIORAL PROBLEMS   Children who have been abused or neglected suffer from disproportionately high levels of such internalizing problems as depression and anxiety (Burns et al., 2004; Dubowitz, Pitts, & Black, 2004). Abuse and neglect also greatly increase risks that children will behave aggressively and have difficulty developing and sustaining interpersonal relationships (Greenberg, 1999; Kolko, 1992). Children's mental health is a critical outcome for the child welfare system because of its immediate effects on the children themselves, their families, and other children and because of implications for the ways these children function in society as they mature. The current study measured children's externalizing and internalizing symptoms according to the current caregiver's responses on the CBCL (Achenbach, 1991). Each scale (Internalizing, Externalizing, and Total Problems) ranges from zero to 100; scores higher than 63 are considered to be in the clinical range warranting treatment. Advantages of the CBCL include extensive empirical validation; standardized scores that allow comparisons across ages and between genders, although these comparisons are prone to floor effects for nonclinical samples (Achenbach, 1991); a functional approach more informative to child welfare professionals than diagnostic measures; and less vulnerability to cultural bias than diagnostic measures may have (Cheung & Snowden, 1990; Heflinger, Simpkins, & Combs-Orme, 2000; Woodward, Dwinell, & Arons, 1992).

CONTROL VARIABLES   Child-level covariates were included in the multilevel models to control for potential confounders of associations between agency attributes and children's mental health outcomes. Dummy variables were used to indicate in-home placement; age between 2 and 5 years; male gender; the most serious type of maltreatment alleged, as reported by the caseworker (physical maltreatment; sexual maltreatment; and neglect), with the referent group being any other form of abuse or neglect; white racial identity; Medicaid-insured status, and having low or medium risk (as opposed to high risk) for reabuse (according to the caseworker's assessment).[6]

Analyses

Cluster-by-case analyses categorized child welfare agencies according to systematized information processing tools and interagency collaboration. Two reasons existed for this stage of analysis: The conceptual intent was to reveal whether a cluster of agencies existed that had high levels of both sets of management approaches hypothesized to support improved child outcomes (information-collaboration agencies). Second, the limited number of agencies available in even NSCAW's nationwide sample restricted statistical power—a constraint expected to affect future studies as well. The identification of clusters of agency management was intended, therefore, to provide an empirically validated basis for using a parsimonious measure of management in both current and subsequent analyses. Agency measures compared across clusters were not weighted by agency size. The result is a depiction of patterns at the agency level rather than the relative frequency of different agency attributes among children.

Cluster analyses were run on the 10 imputed files, and results were averaged across the 10 sets of output. An agglomerative hierarchical clustering algorithm yielded clusters based on the average dissimilarity between the two groups of agencies in their values for use of structured risk assessment; use of written protocols; automated records; total number of ties with other agencies; and whether the child welfare agency made automatic referrals to public health agencies in cases involving drug-affected infants. The number of clusters was based on the Calinski and Harabasz (1974) pseudo-F index and the Duda and Hart (1973) Je(2)/Je(1) index, which uses a pseudo-T-squared (Rabe-Hesketh & Everitt, 2003). Both stopping rules assume larger values as clusters become more distinct.

The next stage of modeling tested the predictive validity of the agency typology, using multilevel (mixed effects) models that explicitly accounted for the nesting of multiple observations within children, as well as children within agencies (Jöreskog & Sörbom, 2004). Because the outcomes can change over time, this model also may be referred to as a *growth curve*, although in this case decreasing scores over time indicate progress (i.e., reduction in symptoms). Mathematically, each model predicted a dimension of the CBCL (i.e., internalizing or externalizing), measured for each child in each agency at each data collection wave. Weights were employed at the time, child, and agency levels. Our approach to modeling child mental health outcomes was to start with single-gender samples and to pool the samples if a shared pattern of associations emerged with outcomes for variables of interest.

Results

Cluster Characterizations

Results from the two cluster analysis stopping rules differed slightly: The Calinski and Harabasz pseudo-F index value peaked when the agencies fell into five clusters, whereas the Duda and Hart index was highest for a four-cluster solution. On the basis of this exploratory stage of research, the more granular, five-cluster outcome was chosen as potentially revealing more relevant variation. No one cluster fit the theorized information-collaboration maximer profile expected to best facilitate improved child outcomes. One cluster, however, had uniformly higher systematic information processing than other clusters; another cluster had an extremely high number of interagency ties. Other differences in context and in resource levels emerged among agency clusters: the populations they served, their resource levels, and their embeddedness within the local social service infrastructure (Table 14.1).

The largest by far, the cluster labeled *underresourced majority* in Table 14.1 was comprised of 50 agencies. Its numerical predominance was reflected in descriptive statistics close to average in most respects, including levels of interagency collaboration; however, these agencies also had consistently above-average use of systematic information processing. The mean number of decision junctures for which directors reported use of structured risk assessment procedures was 22% higher than the mean

Table 14.1 Child Welfare Agency Clusters, Descriptive Statistics

	Mean % Across All Agencies	Under-resourced Majority (n = 50)	Percent Above/ Below Overall Mean	Medium-Small, Well Resourced (n = 13)	Percent Above/ Below Overall Mean	Small Rich (n = 15)	Percent Above/ Below Overall Mean	Very Small Urban (n = 3)	Percent Above/ Below Overall Mean	Very Large, Poor Urban (n = 5)	Percent Above/ Below Overall Mean
Management Practices Used to Create Clusters											
Information processing											
Mean no. of risk assess procedures	3.93	4.78	22%	3.38	–14%	2.60	–34%	4.67	19%	0.40	–90%
Mean no. of ways protocols used	3.00	3.49	17%	3.31	11%	1.07	–64%	3.00	0%	3.00	0%
Percentage using automated records	73%	99%	36%	2%	–97%	53%	–27%	0%	–100%	100%	37%
Interagency ties											
Mean no. of interagency ties	20.11	20.79	3%	16.54	–18%	15.93	–21%	35.00	74%	26.20	30%
Percentage that automatically refer cases involving drug-affected infants to health or public health agency	52%	54%	4%	82%	58%	19%	–63%	33%	–36%	60%	16%

Table 14.1 (continued)

Additional Descriptive Information

Population served											
Mean no. of reports per year	14,004	13,898	−1%	11,533	−18%	9,850	−30%	2,490	−82%	40,848	192%
Percentage children urban	72%	68%	−5%	72%	0%	69%	−4%	100%	39%	100%	39%
Percentage clinical CBCL	33%	33%	1%	32%	−2%	30%	−8%	25%	−23%	43%	32%
Percentage children chronic	24%	25%	−2%	25%	2%	26%	6%	20%	−18%	25%	2%
Resources											
Mean funds per report	463.20	346.27	−25%	600.02	30%	806.95	74%	607.71	31%	158.79	−66%
Mean FTE staff	545.17	553.50	2%	461.95	−15%	365.58	−33%	73.45	−87%	1,500.02	175%
Mean reports per FTE staff per year	25.84	25.11	−3%	24.97	−3%	26.94	4%	33.90	24%	27.23	5%
Annual turnover as percentage of FTE staff	26%	23%	−11%	26%	1%	27%	4%	27%	4%	50%	93%
Embeddedness											
Percentage of agencies in larger agencies	79%	90%	14%	69%	−13%	53%	−33%	67%	−15%	80%	1%
Mean no. of contracts	1.72	1.69	−2%	2.03	18%	2.09	21%	0.67	−61%	0.80	−54%

CBCL, Child Behavior Checklist; FTE, full-time equivalent staff.

for the sample, mean use of protocols was 17% higher than the mean rate for the sample, and these agencies were 36% more likely to use automated case records than the sample as a whole. Funding per child was 25% less than mean funding per child for the overall sample. Slightly (14%) more than the overall sample mean number were embedded in larger agencies rather than self-standing.

The 13 agencies in the cluster labeled *medium-small, resource abundant* had a mean of 462 full-time staff, 15% less than the overall mean of 545. Similarly, they averaged 18% fewer reports per year than did the full sample. Structurally, what most distinguished this cluster was resource levels, with funds spent per report being a full 30% more than average. Slightly (13%) fewer than the overall sample mean number were embedded in larger agencies rather than self-standing. This cluster had a pattern of internal information processing that was mixed: Structured risk assessment was used at 14% fewer decision points than average, protocols were used 11% more than average, and automated record use was extremely rare (only 2% of this cluster, as opposed to 73% overall). Attributing this low use of auto-mated records to these agencies' smaller size may seem reasonable; however, more than half of another cluster, the *small, rich* agencies, which averaged fewer reports per year, did use an automated system. Because both these types of agency enjoy relative resource abundance, our current data suggest no reason for the dramatic difference between the two in use of information systems. Also mixed for *medium-small, resource-abundant* agencies was interorganizational connection. Members of this cluster reported having somewhat fewer (18%) ties with other agencies than average, but they were 58% more likely than average to automatically refer drug-affected infants to health or public health agencies.

The most notable contrast for the cluster of 15 agencies labeled *small rich* was their funding per report, which was 74% higher than average. Other distinctions included being relatively small, with full-time-equivalent staff numbering 33% fewer than the mean for the overall sample (366, as opposed to 545). Similarly, the mean annual number of reports received by these agencies was 9,850, a full 30% fewer than the sample mean of 14,004. Only slightly more than half of these agencies (53%) were embedded in larger agencies, as opposed to 79% of the overall sample. They contracted out 21% more services than average but engaged in less voluntary collaboration, with 21% fewer interagency ties than the overall sample and a 63% lower frequency of automatically referring drug-affected infants to health or public health agencies. Agencies in this cluster also showed far less use of standardized tools for internal information processing, using structured risk assessment tools 34% less often than average for the overall sample, using written protocols 64% less often, and using automated records 27% less often.

The cluster labeled *very small urban* in Table 14.1 represented a rare type of child welfare agency; its membership of three agencies constituted fewer than 5% of the sample of 86 agencies. They averaged only 73 full-time staff, receiving 2,490 reports per year. Compared with the management domains used to form these clusters, this cluster was distinguished by having 74% more interagency ties than average. Overall this cluster was the most collaborative, although only one of the three members automatically referred drug-affected infants to a health or public health agency. Members of this rare type also enjoyed unusually high levels of funding (31% higher than the overall mean per child) and served entirely urban and unusually healthy populations. These agencies provided one of only two notable contrasts with overall sample means for children's clinical statistics, with 23% fewer children reported to be in clinical CBCL ranges. Perhaps because of these agencies' very small sizes, none reported use of automated records.

Except for the urbanicity of the children served, the cluster labeled *very large, poor, urban* contrasts sharply with the one labeled *very small urban*. Comprised of only five agencies, this cluster was small. Nevertheless, together they received more than half of all annual reports for the entire sample, averaging 40,848 each. On average, members of this cluster had almost three times the average number of staff members and number of reports. Their funding per child was 66% lower than the mean of $463, at only $159. Interestingly, these agencies were characterized by notably high turnover—twice the average levels; however, this high turnover was not attributable to high caseloads. In fact, agencies in the *very small urban* cluster had higher average caseloads than this monetarily underresourced cluster. Paradoxically, these agencies served children who were 31% more likely than average to be in the clinical range of the CBCL, yet the use of structured risk assessment was 90% lower than the average use rate. Use of automated records was higher than average, probably because of large agency size.

Not a single information-collaboration cluster of agencies emerged; instead, one cluster, the *underresourced majority,* emphasized systematic information processing, and another, the *very small urban* cluster, was distinguished by very high levels of one indicator of interagency collaboration.

Correlations of Attributes Across Clusters

Table 14.2 lists correlations between some of the most salient attributes emerging from the descriptive statistics in Table 14.1. Overall, children's levels of need (operationalized as proportion with clinical CBCL scores and proportion with chronic health conditions) varied far less than the organization of the agencies addressing them. A large negative correlation between the percentage of children with clinical CBCL levels and funding per child ($\rho = -.79$) prompted examination of correlations between children's needs and management practices and between management practices and funding (Table 14.2). The percentage of children with chronic conditions was virtually uncorrelated with funding, but this finding may reflect the lack of variation in severity. No consistent pattern of association between children's needs and management strategies emerged: Of the 10 correlations, half were positive and half were negative. What did emerge as relatively consistent was the associations between the two types of child need and each management strategy: In four of five instances, both the percentages of children with clinical CBCL scores and the percentages of those with chronic

Table 14.2　Correlations Between Cluster Attributes ($n = 5$)

Children's needs and agency resources	
Percentage children with clinical CBCL levels and per-child funding	−0.79
Percentage children with chronic health problems and per-child funding	−0.02
Children's needs and agency resources	
Percentage children with clinical CBCL levels and use of risk assessments	−0.81
Percentage children with chronic health problems and use of risk assessments	−0.58
Percentage children with clinical CBCL levels and use of protocols	0.20
Percentage children with chronic health problems and use of protocols	−0.39
Percentage children with clinical CBCL levels and automated records	0.73
Percentage children with chronic health problems and automated records	0.45
Percentage children with clinical CBCL levels and interagency collaboration	−0.18
Percentage children with chronic health problems and interagency collaboration	−0.88
Percentage children with clinical CBCL levels and referrals to public health	0.46
Percentage children with chronic health problems and referrals to public health	0.21
Management practices and agency resources	
Use of risk assessments and funding	0.39
Use of protocols and funding	−0.64
Use of automated records and funding	−0.68
Collaboration and funding	−0.28
Referrals to public health and funding	−0.49

CBCL, Child Behavior Checklist.

health problems had the same direction of association with a given management strategy (with the exception of protocol use). In two of these instances, automated records and referrals to public health, the associations were consistently positive and moderate to high (ρ ranging from .21 to .73). This finding suggests that these management strategies may be used in response to especially high levels of need.

The second pattern to emerge from the correlational analyses at the cluster level was that most management strategies (with the exception of structured risk assessments) were negatively associated with funds per report. This somewhat surprising finding suggests the possibility that agency directors are using these management strategies to compensate for resource deficiencies. Because of the small number of cluster attributes (only five) and the fact that potential confounders are not controlled for, these conclusions are highly speculative.

The Child Population

Although all the children in this sample were subjects of completed child maltreatment investigations and were receiving some child welfare agency services, at Wave 1 four of every five (83% of boys and 79% of girls) were still in their homes. About a third of the sampled children were between 2 and 5 years old. For more than one quarter of these children physical abuse was the most serious type of maltreatment

Table 14.3   Child Measure Descriptive Statistics

Variable	Boys Weighted mean/percent (SD)	Girls Weighted mean/percent (SD)
Child Behavior Checklist scores		
Internalizing at Wave 1	55.88 (0.82)	53.62 (0.68)
Externalizing at Wave 1	57.34 (0.79)	56.32 (0.64)
Placement		
In-home placement (1 = yes)	83%	79%
Age		
Between 2 and 5 years old (1 = yes)	33%	31%
Maltreatment type		
Physical maltreatment (1 = yes)	27%	21%
Sexual maltreatment (1 = yes)	6%	14%
Neglect (1 = yes)	42%	42%
Race		
White (1 = yes)	45%	41%
Insurance		
Medicaid (1 = yes)	65%	66%
Child risk level, summary measure		
Low risk (1 = yes)	34%	28%
Medium risk (1 = yes)	29%	35%
High risk (1 = yes)	29% (0.03)	28% (0.03)

alleged (27% of boys and 21% of girls). Girls were more than twice as likely as boys to have had sexual abuse cited as the most serious type of maltreatment (14%, as opposed to 6%). The most frequent type of maltreatment for both boys and girls was neglect (42% for both boys and girls). Almost half of these children were white (45% of boys and 41% of girls). The majority (65% of boys and 66% of girls) were insured through Medicaid. Caseworkers had assessed about a third (34% of boys and 28% of girls) as low risk; another third (29% of boys and 35% of girls) were medium risk, and a comparable proportion (29% of boys and 28% of girls) were high risk; the remainder (8% of boys and 9% of girls) had not been evaluated for risk (See Table 14.3).

Multilevel Modeling

Figure 14.2 depicts variation in the change in children's internalizing and externalizing CBCL levels over time and across the different agency clusters for pooled samples of both boys and girls. The differences in intercept values and slopes indicate variation across clusters, both in the characteristics of children when they entered the agency and in their change over time. On average, children served by agencies in all five clusters improved, at least slightly. (Reductions in the CBCL measures represent reduced symptoms.) The trends over time were generally linear, suggesting that the linear specification used in the full multilevel modeling fits the data reasonably well.

The multilevel models include agency and child-level predictors for Wave 1 CBCL levels and changes in individual children's CBCL scores over time. In general,

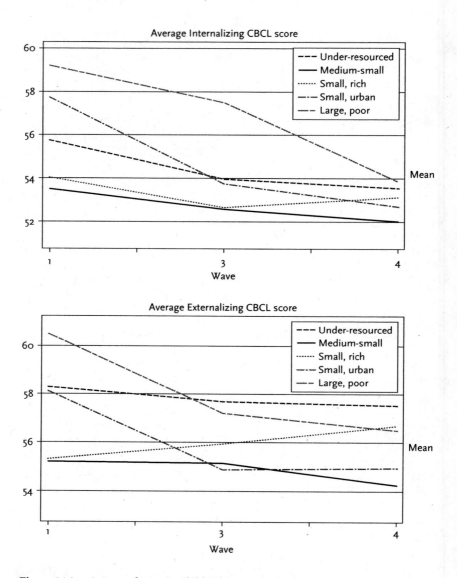

Figure 14.2. Average change in Child Behavior Checklist levels across agency clusters, weighted pooled samples of boys and girls ($n = 2,337$).

controlling for potentially relevant child-level demographics and risk factors, no Wave 1 variation across agency clusters emerged for CBCL scores. The only association was that between being in the *large, poor, urban* cluster of child welfare agencies and much higher (worse) Wave 1 Internalizing scores for girls than for girls in the referent *underresourced majority* cluster.

Table 14.4 Multilevel Models Predicting Internalizing Levels With Agency Clusters

	Boys			Girls		
	COEFF	SE	p	COEFF	SE	p
Random effects						
Intercept	57.947	1.838	.000	55.502	3.001	.000
Wave	−0.324	0.465	.485	−2.081	0.300	.000
Child level						
In home	1.334	1.338	.319	−2.413	2.336	.302
Age ≤ 5	−5.941	1.329	.000	−0.610	1.465	.677
White	1.558	0.720	.031	0.749	0.922	.417
Medicaid	−0.139	1.844	.940	−0.487	1.283	.704
Physical abuse	−1.874	1.362	.169	1.596	3.500	.648
Sexual abuse	1.577	1.542	.307	1.664	3.796	.661
Neglect	−1.637	1.770	.355	1.152	3.174	.717
Low risk	2.037	1.983	.304	−1.653	2.442	.498
Medium risk	−1.101	2.025	.587	1.430	1.361	.293
Agency level						
"Medium-small" cluster	−5.920	3.233	.067	−7.153	4.160	.086
"Small, rich" cluster	3.053	1.741	.080	0.845	1.991	.671
"Very small urban" cluster	2.594	2.278	.255	−3.209	1.750	.067
"Large urban" cluster	2.237	2.357	.343	6.872	1.876	.000
Medium-small* wave	0.716	1.226	.560	3.338	1.356	.014
Small, rich* wave	−1.259	0.781	.107	0.938	0.489	.055
Very small urban* wave	−0.888	1.554	.568	2.104	0.937	.025
Large urban* wave	−1.825	1.106	.099	−0.660	0.605	.276

Some associations were found between agency cluster and girls' changes in Internalizing scores and boys' changes in Externalizing scores (Tables 14.4 and 14.5). Girls in the *medium-small, resource-abundant* cluster and the *very small urban* cluster tended to improve *less* than girls in the *underresourced majority* cluster, all else being

Table 14.5 Multilevel Models Predicting Externalizing Levels With Agency Clusters

	Boys			Girls		
	COEFF	SE	p	COEFF	SE	p
Random effects						
Intercept	60.728	3.171	.000	57.061	2.518	.000
Wave	0.484	0.323	.134	−1.103	0.348	.002
Child level						
In home	−2.497	2.128	.241	−0.153	2.402	.949
Age ≤ 5	−4.731	1.716	.006	−1.616	1.798	.369
White	4.077	1.252	.001	0.358	0.948	.706
Medicaid	1.218	1.574	.439	1.718	0.833	.039
Physical abuse	−1.051	1.951	.590	2.732	2.464	.267
Sexual abuse	3.041	3.611	.400	2.590	3.491	.458

(continued)

Table 14.5 (continued)

	Boys			Girls		
	COEFF	SE	p	COEFF	SE	p
Neglect	−2.424	1.819	.183	−0.820	2.803	.770
Low risk	0.765	2.249	.734	−1.949	2.210	.378
Medium risk	−0.063	1.566	.968	0.583	1.468	.691
Agency level						
"Medium-small" cluster	0.328	2.372	.890	−5.053	3.083	.101
"Small, rich" cluster	1.443	1.698	.396	−1.257	1.820	.490
"Very small urban" cluster	−0.857	2.343	.714	−1.951	3.433	.570
"Large urban" cluster	1.011	2.581	.695	0.948	2.010	.637
Medium-small* wave	−2.412	0.651	.000	2.992	1.822	.101
Small, rich* wave	−1.438	0.399	.000	0.536	0.741	.469
Very small urban* wave	−0.836	1.036	.419	0.685	1.071	.522
Large urban* wave	−2.612	1.154	.024	−0.607	0.768	.429

equal. Boys in the *medium-small, small rich,* and *large, poor, urban* clusters tended to improve *more* than boys in the *underresourced majority* cluster.

The absence of a clear pattern of results when we used agency clusters as predictors prompted us to undertake additional, post hoc analyses. In these models agency cluster was replaced with the five management attributes that had been used to form clusters; this model provided a more granular exploration of the roles of systematic information processing and interagency collaboration in supporting children's improvement over time. As in Glisson's analyses (Chapter 13, this volume), an additional covariate was included at the agency level to indicate whether the agency was in an urban location.

Results of these post hoc models indicate a number of cross-sectional associations between agency management practices and children's Wave 1 (baseline) CBCL scores (Tables 14.6 and 14.7). Girls served by agencies using more automated

Table 14.6 Multilevel Models Predicting Internalizing Levels With Specific Agency Attributes

	Boys			Girls		
	COEFF	SE	p	COEFF	SE	p
Random effects						
Intercept	62.694	3.151	.000	57.934	4.137	.000
Wave	−3.955	1.776	.026	1.196	0.958	.212
Child level						
In home	0.757	1.419	.594	−2.449	2.509	.329
Age ≤ 5	−6.688	1.088	.000	0.100	1.380	.942
White	0.845	0.832	.310	−0.983	1.175	.403
Medicaid	0.191	2.129	.929	−0.394	1.497	.792
Physical abuse	−1.675	1.263	.185	1.943	3.444	.573

Table 14.6 (continued)

Sexual abuse	1.268	1.411	.369	2.588	3.782	.494
Neglect	−2.445	1.747	.162	1.784	3.184	.575
Low risk	1.682	1.750	.337	−1.312	2.288	.566
Medium risk	−0.527	1.898	.781	1.302	1.474	.377
Agency level						
Urban	−2.751	1.395	.049	−2.418	1.760	.169
Assessments	−0.152	0.461	.741	−0.368	0.468	.432
Protocol use	0.371	0.902	.681	0.466	0.493	.345
Automated records	0.869	1.501	.563	3.989	1.039	.000
Interagency ties	−0.173	0.105	.099	−0.233	0.098	.018
Health referral	0.096	1.110	.931	0.762	1.427	.593
Urban* wave	1.208	0.998	.226	−0.178	0.808	.825
Assessment* wave	−0.088	0.250	.723	−0.355	0.320	.267
Protocol * wave	0.375	0.476	.431	0.233	0.331	.481
Automated* wave	0.155	0.791	.845	−2.700	0.659	.000
Interagency* wave	0.075	0.082	.359	0.037	0.057	.516
Referral* wave	0.835	1.014	.410	−0.288	0.935	.758

Table 14.7 Multilevel Models Predicting Externalizing Levels With Specific Agency Attributes—Part 2

	Boys			Girls		
	COEFF	SE	p	COEFF	SE	p
Random effects						
Intercept	62.813	3.380	.000	57.001	3.283	.000
Wave	−2.666	0.920	.004	−0.593	1.150	.606
Child level						
In home	−3.571	2.135	.094	−0.418	2.514	.868
Age ≤5	−5.467	1.513	.000	−1.052	1.602	.511
White	3.524	1.392	.011	−0.230	1.431	.872
Medicaid	0.410	1.568	.794	1.820	0.846	.031
Physical abuse	0.099	1.780	.956	2.791	2.341	.233
Sexual abuse	3.568	3.274	.276	2.676	3.237	.408
Neglect	−1.387	1.907	.467	−0.509	2.738	.852
Low risk	1.156	1.886	.540	−1.670	2.147	.437
Medium risk	0.235	1.382	.865	0.063	1.447	.965
Agency level						
Urban	−0.882	1.211	.466	−3.118	1.292	.016
Assessments	−0.268	0.362	.458	0.397	0.363	.274
Protocol use	0.687	0.769	.371	0.769	0.411	.061
Automated records	3.500	1.939	.071	2.486	0.967	.010
Interagency ties	−0.272	0.115	.018	−0.286	0.101	.005
Health referral	0.620	0.810	.444	2.735	0.953	.004
Urban*wave	0.171	0.562	.760	0.213	0.836	.799
Assessment* wave	−0.065	0.110	.556	−0.462	0.413	.264
Protocol * wave	0.136	0.249	.586	0.315	0.362	.385
Automated* wave	0.608	0.526	.248	−1.323	0.724	.067
Interagency* wave	0.125	0.040	.002	0.093	0.062	.135
Referral* wave	−0.870	0.411	.034	0.208	1.106	.851

records tended to have higher (worse) initial Internalizing and Externalizing CBCL scores. Conversely, girls served by agencies with more interagency ties tended to have lower initial Internalizing and Externalizing CBCL scores. Boys served by agencies with more interagency ties also tended to have lower initial Externalizing CBCL scores; no significant association emerged involving boys' Internalizing scores. Girls in agencies that automatically referred child welfare cases involving drug-affected infants to public health agencies or other health providers tended to have higher initial Externalizing CBCL scores.

As in the models using agency clusters as predictors, the associations with changes over time in CBCL scores were limited to Internalizing scores for girls and Externalizing scores for boys. Girls tended to improve *more* in internalizing symptoms in agencies with automated case records. Boys tended to improve *less* in externalizing symptoms in agencies with more interagency ties, but they also improved *more* in agencies that automatically referred drug-affected infant cases to health agencies.

Discussion

Our purpose in this study has been to contribute to the child welfare literature by testing how sets of child welfare agency management practices might affect child outcomes. Although cluster analyses indicated distinct patterns of management across child welfare agencies, no one cluster fitted the ideal type of information-collaboration agency; however, a different cluster was especially high in each respective management domain: the "underresourced majority" cluster was highest in systematic information processing; and the "very small urban" cluster was highest in overall interagency collaboration (i.e., total number of ties with other agencies). In addition to these differences in management practices, across the five clusters substantial variation in resource levels and structures of the local social service infrastructure were observed. Less cross-cluster variation was found in indicators of children's needs. In a preliminary test of whether agency management affects child outcomes, even a measure as crude as a single indicator of management practices predicted variation in some elements of mental health change over time. Further analyses, however, failed to reveal a clear pattern of associations between agency management and children's improvement over 36 months.

Readers familiar with the U.S. child welfare system may not be surprised to learn that in this national sample the variation in management practices across child welfare agency clusters bore no apparent relation to children's needs. Even more sobering, the clusters of agencies with higher proportions of children needing mental health services had below-average funds per case. Such agencies apparently seek to compensate for a scarcity of internal resources through interagency collaboration, which one previously cited study found can improve the fit between mental health needs and service receipt (Hurlburt et al., 2004). Most of child welfare agencies' funding derives from states. One way to make child welfare services more equitable across agencies may be to base funding allocations on a combination of child and parent acuity, case volume, and the level of related services available locally from other agencies.

We found more cross-cluster variation in child welfare agency management practices than in the characteristics of children served by different clusters. The multilevel models shown in Tables 14.4 and 14.5 support this inference, with cross-sectional associations between clusters and children's CBCL levels showing that, once potentially relevant child attributes were controlled for, virtually no significant cross-cluster difference emerged in children's initial mental health needs. The more granular post hoc analyses shown in Tables 14.6 and 14.7 do reveal, however, a number of associations between agency management practices (such as use of interagency connections) and children's initial mental health needs. These results support the inference that agency management practices may to some extent reflect the differential need profiles of children being served. The directions of associations are not, however, consistently intuitive: On the one hand, agencies serving girls with more initial mental health needs appear to be using more automated records; this association fits the speculation that agencies use more systematic information processing when they serve children with more complex and severe needs. On the other hand, models controlling for child risk and enabling factors, as well as for agencies' urbanicity, showed that agencies serving children with *lower* initial mental health needs had *more* interagency ties. Additional research should explore the reasons for these seemingly inconsistent associations between the various agency management practices and children's need levels.

Three clusters of agencies were associated with greater reduction in boys' externalizing behaviors over time than was found in the largest cluster, which was used as a referent (Tables 14.4 and 14.5): the medium-small resource-abundant cluster, the small rich cluster, and the large, poor, urban cluster. These clusters span an extremely broad range, from those with the most funds per report to those with the least, with no associated pattern in management attributes among them. Results were similarly mixed for associations between specific management attributes and changes over time in children's CBCL scores (Tables 14.6 and 14.7).

Perhaps the most notable pattern across the models was that the only significant associations between agency attributes (for either cluster membership or specific management practices) and changes over time in girls' CBCL scores were in internalizing symptoms, whereas for boys the only significant associations with changes in CBCL scores were in externalizing symptoms. It is possible that agencies are attending more to internalizing problems in girls and more to externalizing in boys. Certainly, the contrasting patterns of results indicate that future analyses would do well to begin with single-gender analyses and then pool only if the patterns are similar.

The two most significant limitations of this study were the potential for omitted-variable bias and a reliance on high-level administrators' perceptions of practices that occurred largely at operational levels. Some important sources of variation in agency practice were not measured. For example, evidence-based actuarial risk assessments tend to perform better than those based on expert consensus (Baird & Wagner, 2000; Shlonsky & Wagner, 2005); however, the NSCAW interview with local agency directors did not prompt for which basis each agency employed. Other factors not incorporated in the current analyses, such as work climate (Glisson & Hemmelgarn, 1998), supervisory support (Gregoire, 1994; Latting et al., 2004; Yoo & Brooks, 2005), and caseworkers' professional discretion (Littell & Tajima, 2000) also likely affect agency performance. In addition, this model did not include factors beyond agency management that likely affect child outcomes, most notably the local availability of health and social services.

Even though directors have overall responsibility for agency operations, reliance on a single, high-level informant at each agency may have undermined the validity of agency management measures. Agency directors may have believed, for instance, that caseworkers were using structured risk assessment processes and computers at more junctures in case management than they actually were. Evidence exists that in practice these tools may be either underutilized or appropriated for unplanned uses, such as garnering increased services by overstating case severity (Schwalbe, 2004). Agency directors also may have reported interagency ties that existed at policy levels but were not active at operational levels. Conversely, directors may not have been fully aware of the informal relationships caseworkers had effected with individuals at other agencies to secure services. Moreover, because NSCAW interviewed agency directors only once, we could not test agency management attributes for stability over time; therefore, model results may reflect changes in internal information processing or in interagency collaboration. It is unlikely, however, that agencies' practices in either dimension changed sufficiently to move an agency from one cluster to another between waves.

Conclusion

Every year 3 million U.S. children are referred to the child welfare system on allegations of child maltreatment (Administration for Children and Families, 2006). The safety and well-being of endangered children depend on accurate identification of their needs and competent implementation of plans to address those needs; the solvency of the system depends on valid determinations of when services are *not* essential. Society owes abused and neglected children empirically validated approaches to their welfare. To this end, we have sought with these analyses to advance the evidential basis for child welfare agency management.

One strength of the current study, as well as of Glisson's study (Chapter 13, this volume), is the inclusion of both causes and consequences of agency practices. While structure and process operate at the agency level, they are not exogenous to the processes of interest. Presumably, agencies adopt practices in response to how children in their care are faring. An agency, for example, may cooperate with other agencies to compensate for access problems experienced by uninsured families. A naïve analysis linking such practices to key outcomes might suggest that interorganizational collaboration makes uninsured children worse off. Indeed, the literature in this area already contains examples of better practices supposedly producing worse outcomes. As is true for processes operating at a single individual level (the individual or the family), identifying cause and effect relationships is difficult.

It is hardly incredible that the management practices examined here failed to yield improved child outcomes in besieged child welfare agencies employing frequently inexperienced, overwhelmed caseworkers. Indeed, it is easy to imagine how any management strategy could fail under such conditions (U.S. General Accounting Office, 2003). Nevertheless, the potential for both internal information processing and interagency coordination to support better decisions and service access argues for more investigation into how and when such benefits could be realized. One logical next step in such research would be to examine best practices, perhaps using qualitative techniques to understand when caseworkers are able to use systematic information tools and external ties to support better case management.

Future investigations may build on the one presented here in several valuable ways. First, researchers may examine how factors both within and beyond agencies moderate associations between child welfare agency management and child outcomes. Perhaps agency-level strategies help children, for example, only when caseworkers have the experience, training, and time to actualize intended benefits. Organizational climate, as Glisson (2007) examines it, may interact with actions taken by managers; consequently, the success of agency strategies may depend on how "engaged" the climate is for caseworkers, as well as how buffered caseworkers feel from stressors. The success of agency strategies also may depend heavily on local resource availability. To provide realistic guidance to child welfare agency directors and policy makers, such interactions must be explored.

Future research should also probe how service experiences mediate between agency management and child outcomes. In theory, when agencies are better managed, children and parents receive more appropriate services and follow-up, experiencing in turn better outcomes (e.g., less reabuse, swifter achievements of permanent placements after removal from home, better mental health and academic and social functioning). Do they? These are some of the next compelling questions for NSCAW researchers to address.

NOTES

1. That caseworkers are so frequently overwhelmed relates to a third management domain of central importance to child welfare agencies: the human relations model, which addresses how organizations support their staff (Quinn, 1988). In "Organizational Climate and Service Outcomes in Child Welfare Systems" (Chapter 13, this volume), Charles Glisson focuses entirely on this domain, examining how child welfare caseworkers' organizational climate affects children's mental health over time. In this respect, these two chapters, which employ the same modeling approaches, provide complementary perspectives on child welfare agency management.

2. This study was not, however, a randomized control trial, so some or all of the differences may be attributable to self-selection bias.

3. The exclusion of children younger than 2 years was due to the unavailability of the outcome measure, the Child Behavior Checklist (CBCL) for younger children.

4. The reported points at which any form of structured risk assessment could have been used were as follows: when deciding to investigate, when deciding whether allegations of mal-treatment were substantiated, when deciding what services to provide, when deciding whether to close an in-home services case, and when deciding whether to reunify a child. The reported processes for which written protocols could have been required were as follows: situations in which family reunification services were not required, situations in which an out-of-home child's siblings were being entered into foster care, investigation of families when drug-affected infants were involved, and situations in which aftercare services were being provided after reunification.

5. The reported ways that child welfare agencies could have collaborated with other agencies were as follows: discussion and information sharing; development of interagency agreements and memoranda of understanding; cross-training of staff; joint planning or policy formula-tion for service delivery; working with the other agency on child welfare cases; or joint budgeting or resource allocation.

6. Composite Wave 1 measure based on 25 items in the risk assessment section of the caseworker instrument, including caregiver's substance abuse, history of excessive discipline of the child by the caregiver, family stressors, and low social support. Categorized by the NSCAW research group (Richard Barth) as *low risk* 1, *medium risk* 1. *High risk* was used as the referent group.

REFERENCES

Aarons, G. A. (2004). Mental health provider attitudes toward adoption of evidence-based practice: The Evidence-Based Practice Attitude Scale (EBPAS). *Mental Health Services Research*, 6(2), 61–74.

Achenbach, T. M. (1991). *Manual for the Child Behavior Checklist/4-18 and 1991 profile.* Burlington, VT: University of Vermont, Department of Psychiatry.

Administration for Children and Families. (2006). *Child maltreatment 2004.* Retrieved December 23, 2008, from http://www.acf.hhs.gov/programs/cb

Administration for Children and Families. (2007). States' statewide automated child welfare information system (SACWIS) status. Retrieved August 2, 2007, from http://www.acf.hhs.gov/

Administration on Children, Youth and Families. (2001). *National Survey of Child and Adolescent Well-Being: Local child welfare agency survey: Report.* Washington, DC: Author.

Alliance for Children and Families. (2001). *The child welfare workforce challenge: Results from a preliminary study.* Washington, DC: Alliance for Children and Families, American Public Human Services Association & Child Welfare League of America.

Baird, C., & Wagner, D. (2000). The relative validity of actuarial- and consensus-based risk assessment systems. *Children and Youth Services Review*, 22(11–12), 839–871.

Burns, B. J., Phillips, S. D., Wagner, H. R., Barth, R. P., Kolko, D. J., Campbell, Y., et al. (2004). Mental health need and access to mental health services by youth involved with child welfare: A national survey. *Journal of the American Academy of Child and Adolescent Psychiatry, 43*(8), 960–970.

Calinski, T., & Harabasz, J. (1974). A dendrite method for cluster analysis. *Communications in Statistics, 3,* 1–27.

Cheung, F. K., & Snowden, L. R. (1990). Community mental health and ethnic minority populations. *Community Mental Health Journal, 26*(3), 277–291.

Child Welfare League of America. (1989). *Child Welfare League of America standards for service for abused or neglected children and their families.* Washington, DC: Child Welfare League of America.

Darlington, Y., Feeney, J. A., & Rixon, K. (2004). Complexity, conflict and uncertainty: Issues in collaboration between child protection and mental health services. *Children and Youth Services Review, 26,* 1175–1192.

Dosser, D. A., Jr., Handron, D., McCammon, S., & Powell, J. Y. (2001). *Children's mental health: Exploring systems of care in the new millennium.* New York: Haworth Social Work Practice Press.

Dowd, K., Kinsey, S., Wheeless, S., Thissen, R., Richardson, J., Suresh, R., et al. (2006). *National Survey of Child and Adolescent Well-Being combined Waves 1-4 data file users' manual, restricted release version.* Ithaca, NY: National Data Archive on Child Abuse and Neglect, Cornell University.

Dubowitz, H., Pitts, S. C., & Black, M. M. (2004). Measurement of three major subtypes of child neglect. *Child Maltreatment, 9*(4), 344–356.

Duda, R. O., & Hart, P. E. (1973). *Pattern classification and scene analysis.* New York: Wiley.

Glisson, C. (2007). Assessing and changing organizational culture and climate for effective services. *Research on Social Work Practice, 17,* 736–747.

Glisson, C., & Hemmelgarn, A. (1998). The effects of organizational climate and interorganizational coordination on the quality and outcomes of children's service systems. *Child Abuse & Neglect, 22*(5), 401–421.

Greenberg, M. T. (1999). Attachment and psychopsychology in childhood. In J. Cassidy & P. R. Shaver (Eds.), *Handbook of attachment theory and research.* New York: Guildford Press.

Gregoire, T. K. (1994). Assessing the benefits and increasing the utility of addiction training for public child welfare workers: A pilot study. *Child Welfare, 73*(1), 69–81.

Grove, W. M., & Meehl, P. E. (1996). Comparative efficiency of informal (subjective, impressionistic) and formal (mechanical, algorithmic) prediction procedures: The clinical-statistical controversy. *Psychology, Public Policy, & Law, 2*(2), 293–323.

Heflinger, C. A., Simpkins, C. G., & Combs-Orme, T. (2000). Using the CBCL to determine the clinical status of children in state custody. *Children and Youth Services Review, 22*(1), 55–73.

Hurlburt, M. S., Leslie, L. K., Landsverk, J., Barth, R. P., Burns, B. J., Gibbons, R. D., et al. (2004). Contextual predictors of mental health service use among children open to child welfare. *Archives of General Psychiatry, 61,* 1217–1224.

Jaudes, P. K., Bilaver, L. A., Goerge, R. M., Masterson, J., & Catania, C. (2004). Improving access to health care for foster children: The Illinois model. *Child Welfare, 83*(3), 215–238.

Johnson, K., & Wagner, D. (2005). Evaluation of Michigan's foster care case management system. *Research on Social Work Practice, 15*(5), 372–380.

Jöreskog, K. G., & Sörbom, D. (2004). *LISREL 8.7 for Windows.* Lincolnwood, IL: Scientific Software International.

Kolko, D. J. (1992). Characteristics of child victims of physical violence: Research findings and clinical implications. *Journal of Interpersonal Violence, 7,* 244–276.

Latting, J. K., Beck, M. H., Slack, K. J., Tetrick, L. E., Jones, A. P., Etchegaray, J. M., et al. (2004). Promoting service quality and client adherence to the service plan: The role of top management's support for innovation and learning. *Administration in Social Work, 28*(2), 29–48.

Littell, J. H., & Tajima, E. A. (2000). A multilevel model of client participation in intensive family preservation services. *Social Service Review, 74*(3), 405–435.

Moses, T., Weaver, D., Furman, W., & Lindsey, D. (2003). Computerization and job attitudes in child welfare. *Administration in Social Work, 27*(1), 47–67.

Oliver, C. (1990). Determinants of interorganizational relationships: Integration and future directions. *Academy of Management Review, 15*(2), 241–265.

Quinn, R. E. (1988). *Beyond rational management: Mastering the paradoxes and competing demands of high performance.* San Francisco: Jossey-Bass.

Quinn, R. E., Faerman, S. R., Thompson, M. P., & McGrath, M. R. (1996). *Becoming a master manager: A competency framework.* (2nd ed.). New York: Wiley.

Quinn, R. E., Spreitzer, G. M., & Hart, S. L. (1992). Integrating the extremes: Crucial skills for managerial effectiveness. In S. Srivastva & R. E. Fry (Eds.), *Executive and organizational continuity* (pp. 222–252). San Francisco: Jossey-Bass.

Rabe-Hesketh, S., & Everitt, B. (2003). *Handbook of statistical analyses using Stata.* Boca-Raton, FL: Chapman & Hall/CRC Press.

Raghunathan, T. E., Lepkowski, J. M., Hoewyk, J. V., & Solenberger, P. (2001). A multivariate technique for multiply imputing missing values using a sequence of regression models. *Survey Methodology, 27*(1), 85–95.

Reinherz, H. Z., Giaconia, R. M., Hauf, A. M., Wasserman, M. S., & Silverman, A. B. (1999). Major depression in the transition to adulthood: Risks and impairments. *Journal of Abnormal Psychology, 108*(3), 500–510.

Savaya, R., Spiro, S. E., Waysman, M., & Golan, M. (2004). Issues in the development of a computerized clinical information system for a network of juvenile homes. *Administration in Social Work, 28*(2), 63–79.

Schoenwald, S. K., Sheidow, A. J., Letourneau, E. J., & Liao, J. G. (2003). Transportability of multisystemic therapy: Evidence for multilevel influences. *Mental Health Services Research, 5*(4), 223–239.

Schwalbe, C. (2004). Re-visioning risk assessment for human service decision making. *Children and Youth Services Review, 26*(6), 561–576.

Scott, J. G., Sochalski, J., & Aiken, L. (1999). Review of magnet hospital research: Findings and implications for professional nursing practice. *Journal of Nursing Administration, 29*(1), 9–19.

Shlonsky, A., & Wagner, D. (2005). The next step: Integrating actuarial risk assessment and clinical judgment into an evidence-based practice framework in CPS case management. *Children and Youth Services Review, 27*(4), 409–427.

Steib, S. D., & Blome, W. W. (2004). Like musical chairs? Become a child welfare worker. *Child Welfare, 83*(4), 381–384.

U.S. General Accounting Office. (2003). *Child Welfare: HHS could play a greater role in helping child welfare agencies recruit and retain staff* (GAO-03-357). Washington, DC: Author.

Woodward, A. M., Dwinell, A. D., & Arons, B. S. (1992). Barriers to mental health care for Hispanic Americans: A literature review and discussion. *Journal of the Mental Health Administration, 19*(3), 224–236.

Yoo, J., & Brooks, D. (2005). The role of organizational variables in predicting service effectiveness: An analysis of a multilevel model. *Research on Social Work Practice, 15*(4), 267–277.

NAME INDEX

SUBJECT INDEX